A map of the world

ame Dependent territories of Commonwealth states (in brackets) SCALE 1 : 88,000,000

Textquellennachweis

S. 32–33: TUC 1997, 2001, 2003, 2006 © http://excellence.qia.org.uk/media/doc/YoungApprentice.doc
S. 54–55: adapted from Larry Fondation „Deportation at Breakfast" © 1991 Larry Fondation, Leaping Dog Press/Asylum Arts
S. 59: www.direct.gov.uk/EducationAndLearning/14to19/OptionsAt16/index.htm © Crown Copyright
S. 62–64: Before I Die: Jenny Downham © Random House Group Company (ISBN 978-0-552-77462-8)
S. 88: Slumdog Millionär © www.kinocritics.com/film_review

Orange **Line**

Grundkurs 6

Herausgeber: Frank Haß

Ernst Klett Verlag
Stuttgart • Leipzig

Orange Line 6 Grundkurs

für Klasse 10 an allen differenzierenden Schulen

Im Auftrag des Verlags herausgegeben von:
Frank Haß, Kirchberg

Unter besonderer Mitwirkung von:
Harald Weisshaar, Bisingen

Erarbeitet von:
Holly De Marco, Cambridge; Elizabeth Rutledge, München

Unter besonderer Mitwirkung von:
Hamida Aziz, Tübingen; Sheila McBride, Stuttgart

Beratung:
Anette Christiani, Dortmund; Ulf Degen, Braunschweig; Ingrid Hartmann-Scheer, Kaarst; Margitta Kuty, Greifswald; Monika Teichmann, Wuppertal; Annegret Preker-Franke, Bielefeld

1. Auflage ISBN 978-547560-1 (fester Einband) 1 6 5 4 3 2 1 | 2014 2013 2012 2011 2010

1. Auflage ISBN 978-547660-8 (flexibler Einband) 1 6 5 4 3 2 1 | 2014 2013 2012 2011 2010

Alle Drucke dieser Auflage sind unverändert und können im Unterricht nebeneinander verwendet werden. Die letzte Zahl bezeichnet das Jahr des Druckes.

Redaktion: Susanne Vetter; Cornelia Schaller, Lektorat editoria, Fellbach

Gestaltung: Marion Köster; Ulrike Wursthorn, Stuttgart
Illustrationen: Sylvia Wolf, Wiesbaden; Scivos/Klett Perthes (Karte Vorsatz vorne); Perthes World Atlas, 2nd Printing 2009, Revised, p. 78–79, Gotha 2006 (Karte Vorsatz hinten)
Umschlaggestaltung: Koma Amok, Stuttgart
Umschlagfoto: Getty Images (fotonika/Berg), München
Reproduktion: Meyle + Müller, Medien-Management, Pforzheim
Druck: Stürtz, Würzburg

Printed in Germany
ISBN 978-3-12-547560-1 (fester Einband)
ISBN 978-3-12-547660-8 (flexibler Einband)

9 783125 475601 9 783125 476608

Welcome back to Orange **Line**!

Hier ein kurzer Überblick über Band 6:

Die vier **Topics** (Kapitel) können in beliebiger Reihenfolge bearbeitet werden. Innerhalb jedes Topics gibt es obligatorische Teile und 2 **Options** (Themen zur Auswahl). Zu jeder Option gibt es **Tasks** (Aufgaben). Diese werden in einer Gruppe bearbeitet und schließen immer mit einer **Presentation** in der Klasse ab.
Ein Topic besteht aus:

Check-in	Einstimmung auf das Hauptthema anhand von Fotos
Aspects	Kurze Texte und Verständnisübungen
Options (x2)	Texte, Übungen und Aufgaben
Words in action	Wortschatzarbeit
Check-out	Selbstüberprüfung
Test yourself!	Vorbereitung auf Abschlusstests

In den Teilen **A project** findest du jeweils nach den Topics 1 und 3 einen Lesetext. Diese Texte sind nicht obligatorisch und sind thematisch von den Topics unabhängig. Sie bieten dir die Möglichkeit, dich mit literarischen Texten zu beschäftigen. Nach Topic 4 findest du zwei weitere **Projects**: *People, pictures and images* sowie *The European Union.*

Nach den Topics findest du folgende Teile:
Skills (Arbeitstechniken und Fertigkeiten) und **Grammar** (Grammatik). Bei manchen Übungen und Aufgaben innerhalb der Topics findest du Verweise auf diese Teile.
Der **Skills**-Teil beinhaltet Tipps zu Lern- und Arbeitstechniken und nützliche Ausdrücke.
Im **Grammar**-Teil kannst du nachschlagen, wenn du dir unsicher bist, z. B. beim Verfassen von eigenen Texten. Dort findest du auch neue Grammatikthemen. In dem Teil **Overview** (Übersicht) kannst du z. B. Aktiv und Passiv in einer Tabelle zusammengefasst anschauen.
Der Teil **Grammar practice** bietet darüber hinaus Übungen zu jedem neuen Thema an.

Weitere Übungen findest du in dem Teil **Mediation and communication**.
Am Ende des Buches befindet sich der Teil **Vocabulary** (Vokabelliste). Hier findest du nicht nur alle neuen Vokabeln, sondern auch Wortfeld- und Wortbildungsübungen sowie Kästen zu *Everyday English*. Das **Dictionary** (Wörterbuch) listet die Vokabeln alphabetisch auf. Es ist zum Nachschlagen gedacht.

Erläuterungen:

Let's talk	Lasst uns reden
Let's listen	Lasst uns zuhören
Work with a picture	Vorbereitung auf mündliche Prüfung
Task	Hauptaufgabe bei einer Option
Presentation	Arbeitsergebnisse in der Klasse präsentieren
Online-Link	⇨ 547560-0001
Skills	2, 18
Skills aus Band 5	5

◎	Übung auf CD
1 Person	Einzelarbeit
2 Personen	Partnerarbeit
3 Personen	Gruppenarbeit
✲	Diese Übungen/Punkte sind besonders knifflig.
Grammar	G 5, 7
Overview	Ov 3

4 Topics
Maybe these photos and comments can help you to choose.

Topic 1 – A 'global' language

Is English the same all over the world? What exactly is Hinglish? How important is English, for example, in sports?

▶ If you choose Topic 1, you'll learn all about English.

Topic 2 – Living democracy – human rights

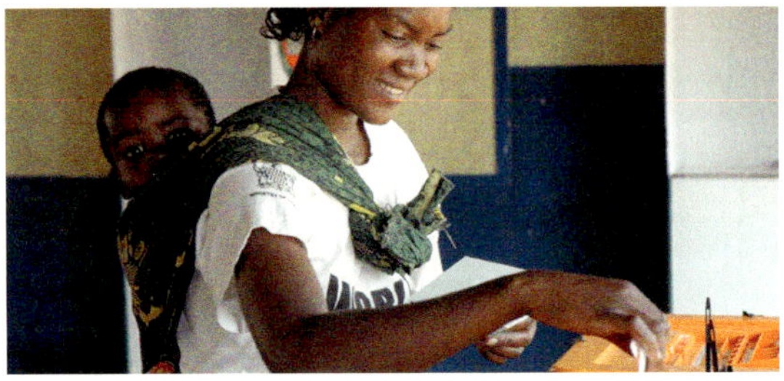

We all have rights, but where did they come from and how are they protected?

▶ In Topic 2 you can find out more about democracy in the past and today.

Topic 3 – Our world in our hands

There are lots of problems in the world, but we can't expect others to solve them for us.

▶ Read more about these problems and how we can all help in Topic 3.

Topic 4 – Choices and decisions

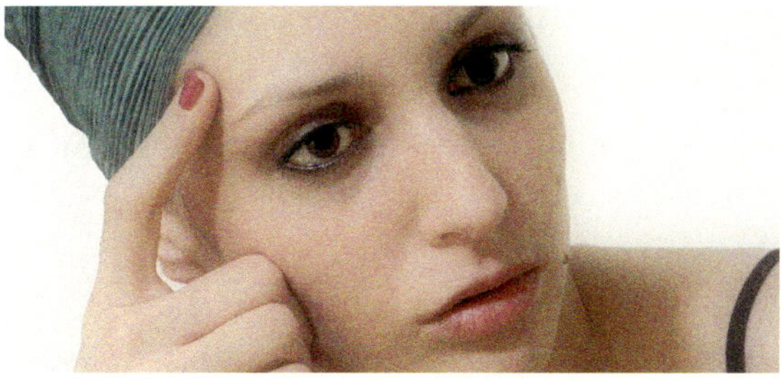

At 16 everyone has more rights but also more responsibilities.

▶ Topic 4 tells you more about 'life' decisions and how to make them.

Topic 1 A 'global' language

1

International backpackers in the Canadian Rockies

1. Work with a picture: (→ p. 2/ex. 1)
   a) Look at photo 1 and read the caption. What are the people doing and saying? What do you think?
   b) Did your partner have the same idea? If not, what was different?

too wide/difficult • be scared • give me your hand • be careful • slowly/carefully • good boots • fun/dangerous/exciting/… • don't look down • …

2. a) Look at photos 2–5. Describe the setting. Start like this: The people in picture … are in / near / on / … .
   b) Which language(s) are the people speaking? What do you think and why?

1,1
3. a) Listen to five short dialogues. Match each dialogue with a photo.
   b) Listen again. Choose the most interesting dialogue. Tell a partner why you think it's interesting.

4. a) Look at the map at the front of your book and find the countries mentioned on pages 8–9. What is (are) the official language(s) there?
   b) Choose one of the countries and in 1–2 sentences say what you know about it.

2

Angela Merkel and China's Prime Minister, Zeng Peiyan, in China

3

Philipp Lahm joins a football game at an international school in South Africa

4

Shark alarm in Australia

5

A meeting of two media stars, 50 Cent and Thomas Gottschalk, in Germany

⇨ 547560-0001

A Ever-changing English

You may know that English is still the most important language in business, on the Internet and in technology. And perhaps you've heard that Japanese pilots speak to the tower at Tokyo airport in English. But did you know that some words and phrases have come into English from other languages, like the word 'pukka' (= real), in the subtitle of a new book by **B. K. Mahal**? This mixture of English and Indian languages is known as 'Hinglish' (Hindi + English) – and it is spreading fast, not only because of Bollywood! It is spoken by many people with an Asian background in Britain and also by people on the Indian sub-continent. Want to know more? Well, then do read the book **The Queen's Hinglish**!

INFO Deutsch + Englisch = Denglisch
Examples: gemailt, gechillt, downloaden, scrollen …
Other mixtures include Spanglish, Chinglish …

B The common language

➔ Option 1

Eurofoot Summer Camps for girls and boys
in the UK, Canada, Germany, Asia & South Africa

One of our sponsors is offering three free places to promising young people who aren't able to pay the fees!

Do you love playing football and want to improve your skills? Then come to our Eurofoot camp!
We give professional coaching to young football players (8–18) from all parts of the world.
Our world famous coaches are all former international players They can speak several different languages, but training sessions are in English. Each coach has a group of up to twelve players and the groups are moved around. While you are here, the coaches will assess you: We may invite promising young players to do trials for a place in an international football academy!
For more information or to apply for a place at one of our camps, please e-mail Bobby Brown: ➔ CAMP INFO

1 New trends in English 5 5

a) *Before you read the review (text A), look at the book cover. What do you think the book is about?*

b) *Now read the text and check your answer.*

c) *Read the text again. Finish the sentences.*
1. The word 'pukka' means … .
2. Hinglish is a mixture of … .
3. Hinglish is spoken by … .
4. The mixture of German and English is called … .

2 The language of sports 5 (→ p. 3/ex. 2)

a) *Read the ad (text B). Eurofoot is a …*
1. football boot.
2. football camp.
3. hiking trip.

b) *Read the ad (text B) again carefully. Who are they?*
1. Who is offering three free places at Eurofoot?
2. Who may get a free place?
3. Who can take part in the camp?
4. Who are the coaches?
5. Who may go to an international academy?
6. Who can you write to for more information?

C Where do they speak Inuktitut?

FACT BOX
- Canada is in North America, north of the United States.
- Canada has two official languages, English and French.
- 67.5% of Canadians speak only English.
- 85% of French speakers live in Quebec.
- In the Northwest Territories 9 Native Canadian (Aboriginal) languages are official, too.
- The majority (and official) language in the north Canadian region of Nunavut is Inuktitut.
- Chinese, Italian, German and some languages from India are non-official languages there.

1 *At Vancouver airport*
2 *In Winnipeg, Manitoba*
3 *In Nunavut*

1

2

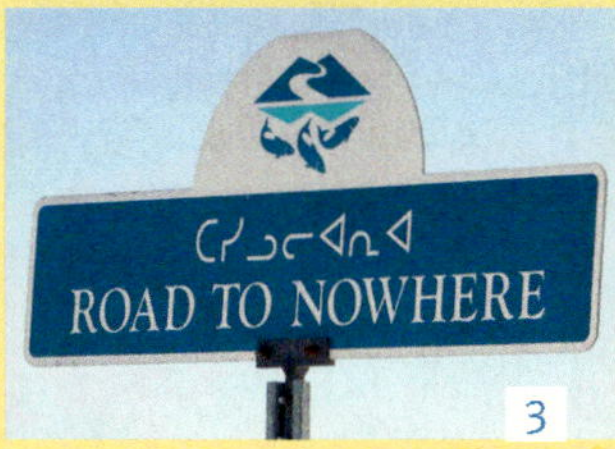

3

[rue] [striːt]

D Spot on careers

➔ Option 2

Info on next week's careers talk

Many companies have parts of their business abroad. But why? Well, to cut costs: They may pay workers less in that country - or running costs may be lower.

For example, some international banks and public transport services now have call centres in India!

David MacDonald was worried when his company in Britain decided to do the same. Would he soon be out of a job?

To hear what David's employer, Vince Hall, said about his situation, listen to our podcast report: ➔ PODCAST

WE'RE GOING TO HAVE TO LET YOU GO...WE'VE FOUND SOMEONE IN CHINA WHO IS 45% BETTER AT BEING YOU FOR 24% LESS

⇨ 547560-0002

3 Let's talk: Languages in Canada

a) *What do you know about Canada? (3 facts)*

b) *Read the fact box. List the official and non-official languages in Canada. What do the facts tell you about Inuktitut?*

c) *Look at the map at the back of your book. Find all the places in the fact box.*

d) *Look at the Canadian signs. Match them with a fact from the fact box.*

4 Let's listen: *E* for *E*nglish and ... 13 7, 15 (→ p. 3/ex. 3, 4)

1, 2

a) *Before you listen: Look at the cartoon. Then read text D. What was David worried about? Why?*

b) *Look at these words and then listen. Which three words does his boss use to describe David?*

electric • excited • energetic • embarrassing • empty • enterprising • exact • experienced

c) *David's great extra skill, according to his boss, is*

computers • explaining in English • writing English • learning English

A world language

EUROFOOT WEBZINE

HOW USEFUL IS ENGLISH IN THE WORLD OF SPORT?

A report from our teenager football camp in Germany by Coach Sven Paldowsky

In the past parents would worry about their kids' English. They used to think that talking to the other footballers and the coaches would be difficult. But now they needn't worry – those days are gone. Coaching is in English because kids these days are all able to understand the language. So English really does help to bring us all together. To give you and your parents an idea of how this works, we talked to some kids from this year's camp and asked them about their English:

Hi, there. I'm Andrea Ziebarth from Vancouver, Canada. English and French are official languages there. I'm sort of bilingual because at school we mostly speak French. So it's easier for me here! German?! No, I'm hopeless at German – although my grandparents were from Hamburg! In fact, that's where my cousin Ina is from. She's here at the camp, too. Her English is OK, but her football is amazing! She'll be on the German women's team one day, I'm sure!

Hi, my name is John Dhlomo and I'm from Cape Town, South Africa. My mother tongue is Zulu but I also speak English. I was really lucky: I got a scholarship to come here! At first I was worried because I couldn't speak German. But everyone at camp speaks English! Now my new mate, Jakob, is teaching me some German: That's 'megastark'!

Hi, my name is Jakob Veit. I'm German. I was surprised when our coaches spoke English to us. I know this is an international camp, but we're in Germany! English is my worst subject. But, well, words like 'foul', 'offside' or a 'header' are no problem: They're international, I guess. It was hard in the first week – till I made some friends. Now I can practise my English as well as my football!

Hello, I'm Faye Jiayi from Hong Kong. Chinese (Cantonese) and English are our official languages. Both are important everywhere now, especially if you work for a big company. My friend Andrea, for example, is from Vancouver. She says that signs at the airport there aren't only in French and English – they're in Chinese, too! I just can't believe it! Well, no one here speaks Chinese, so I'm glad I can speak English!

Task: To learn about the role of English in different countries

1 Where is English useful? 5 (→ p. 4/ex. 5)

a) *In which situations could English be useful to you in your country? Make a list each. Compare your ideas.*

b) *Read up to line 5. Where is the camp? What language do the coaches use there? Why?*

c) *What countries are the flags from?*
If you're not sure, check on the Internet.

1

2

3

4

d) *Read the reports by Andrea, John, Jakob and Faye. Match each one with a flag/country.*

e) *Read the reports again. Who's who?*

1. This person has a cousin from Hamburg.
2. This person is not good at English.
3. This person got a football scholarship.
4. This person thinks 'foul' is international.
5. This person says English is important in companies.
6. This person is sort of bilingual.
7. This person has a mate who can speak German.
8. This person has a friend who speaks French.

1,3 2 Let's listen: More about John Dhlomo 13 15 (→ p. 4/ex. 6)

a) *Before you listen: Find the country where John comes from on the map at the front of your book. What continent is it in?*

b) *Listen to John's report. Has John ever been to a Eurofoot camp before?*

c) *Listen again and look at the box. Which information do you hear?*

1. John plays in a school league. • 2. His school had a party. • 3. He had extra training sessions. • 4. He lost his homework. • 5. He got extra homework. • 6. His coach applied to Eurofoot last spring.

3 Some facts about English (→ p. 5/ex. 7, 8)

a) *Read the info on the right. Find the most interesting fact.*

b) *Compare and decide on one fact between you. Write it on a card. Change something about the fact so that it is wrong. Write this on a card, too.*

c) *Put all the true and false statements face down and play memory. When you get a pair, say which fact is correct.*

English is …
… the most widely (spoken and written) language in the world. It was spread by traders and by settlers.
… still an official language in former British colonies like Australia, the US, Canada and India.
… the official language in more than 55 countries including the UK and Ireland.
… an official language in many African countries.
… one of South Africa's 11 official languages.
… spoken as a foreign language by over 700 million people.
… used by pilots internationally.

4 Presentation: A quiz 9 (→ p. 5/ex. 9)

a) *Make a poster about 'English in the world'. Use the information from the 'Webzine', your Aspects page and the facts from Ex. 3.*

b) *Let the class look at it for ten minutes and think of 3–4 questions.*

c) *The class forms two teams. Your group reads out a fact and a wrong version of it. The teams choose the correct version and write it down. You check the answers. Which team had the most correct?*

Widen your horizons

David MacDonald and his colleagues visit their old school to give a talk on how they developed their career.

Here are their profiles.

Mia Wang

Education: 5 GCSEs (Maths, English, Music, Geography, Computers); IT training course (Database Administrator)

Job experience: Trainee + 2 years in insurance company as personal assistant

Skills: Computers, bilingual (Chinese/English), organizing

Strengths: I'm a good organizer (I stay calm!), I'm mobile; also outgoing, helpful, creative

Weaknesses: No teaching diploma, chocolate ice-cream

My dream: To be the first woman on Mars

In the next 12 months: A change in career

Interesting info: I like driving fast cars

The sky's the limit!

Ali Hassan

Education: 6 GCSEs (English, Maths, Science, Computers, French, Art) apprenticeship

Job experience: 4 years in customer services department of insurance company; group leader

Skills: Selling, computers, English, Hindi

Strengths: I can sell things (even my ideas), computer skills, I'm mobile, get on with people; also reliable & independent

Weaknesses: Don't get on with spiders! I can't speak Chinese (but you can learn, right?!).

My dream: To spend a few years in Asia

In the next 12 months: I really do want my own business

Interesting info: I teach disabled kids to swim

A career in advertising – or in Bollywood?

David MacDonald

Education: 5 GCSEs (English, Maths, Computers, French, Geography); BTec diploma (basic course)

Job experience: 6 years in customer services department in an insurance company; insurance salesman

Skills: Computers & English, communicating, selling

Strengths: Hard working, mobile, helpful, have new ideas

Weaknesses: I have no teaching qualification, I can't speak Chinese (yet!), I'm a bit chaotic

My dream: To have my own office with a leather sofa

In the next 12 months: I would like to find a really exciting job

Interesting info: I love Chinese opera and mountain climbing!

Guess why they called me 'Curly'!

Task: To learn to make the most of your skills

1 Strengths and weaknesses 6 4

a) *Think: Look at the list of strengths and weaknesses. What about you? Which strengths and weaknesses do you have? Write a short list for each. You can add your own ideas.*

reliable • outgoing • helpful • creative • get upset/angry • active • independent • bit clumsy • good at listening • calm • enterprising • bit chaotic (paper work!) • adaptable • sometimes uncertain • ...

b) *Pair: What does your partner think of you? Check your lists.*

c) *Share: Does someone in your group have a special strength or talent which no one else has? What is it?*

4–6 2 Let's listen: En route to the leather sofa! 13 15 (→ p. 6/ex. 10)

a) *Listen to the introduction of David's talk (part A).*
What (one) problem did he have as a boy?
What two things was he good at? Choose from the box.

computers • taking photos • hairdressing • maths • singing • sports • talking • burgers

In my office on the thirty-seventh floor

b) *Read the sentences. Then listen to David as he talks about steps along his career path (part B). Put the sentences in the right order.*

1. We decided to write our profiles.
2. My friends and I had to think and act fast!
3. The job at the insurance company was great.
4. I was tired of schools so I took a temporary job.
5. One day we had some awful news.

Listen again and check the order.

c) *Listen to part C about their plans. What was David's idea? What qualification do they need for this? Who is the man in the picture? Where is he? What's his job now?*

3 Who am I? 6 (→ p. 6/ex. 11,12)

a) *Look at the profiles on page 14. Use them to write your own profile on the computer and then print it.*

b) *Exchange profiles. Maybe your partner sees other strengths/weaknesses in you which you can add.*

c) *Discuss in which job your strengths could be useful. (Think of leader, creative and team qualities.) But remember to be polite!*

4 Presentation: A gallery walk 8 (→ p. 7/ex. 13,14)

a) *Use your answers from Ex. 2 and prepare a report about David's careers path.*

b) *Tell your class about David's career in your own words.*

c) *Some of you set up a job market in your classroom. The others display all your profiles from Ex. 3. The class reads them in a gallery walk and tries to say what job from the market each person should do.*

1 Explanations and definitions

Find the right word or phrase.

1. It's a mixture of English and some Indian languages.
2. You are this if you can speak two languages equally well.
3. If you go to a foreign country, you go … .
4. This is a company which has offices worldwide.
5. It's a part of a continent.
6. If you have a positive future, your future is … .
7. This is more than half of a group of people/the population.
8. You're this when you're active and full of ideas and strength.
9. This is a person who does sports training sessions.

majority
international business
energetic
Hinglish
coach
promising
abroad
sub-continent
bilingual

2 International sports

a) *Read this text. Look at the tip box below and write down the sentences with the correct English words.*

One of our (1) is offering three free places to (2) young people who aren't able to pay the fees! Do you love playing (3) and want to improve your skills? Then come to our Eurofoot (4) this summer!
We give (5) (6) to young football players from all parts of the world.
Our world famous coaches are all former international players. They can speak several different languages, but (7) are in English. Each coach has a group of up to twelve players and the groups are moved around. While you are here, the coaches will assess you: We may invite promising young players to do trials for a place in an international football (8)!

Menschen/Firmen, die finanzielle Unterstützung bieten • viel versprechend • eine Sportart • bedeutet auch Zeltplatz • von Profis/Experten • Sportunterricht • Sportübungs-Einheit • eine Art Schule

b) *Look back at the text on page 10. Did you remember all the words?*

3 Job words

a) *What could Ali, Mia and David say about each other? Choose three words/phrases from the box for each and write down a sentence for each speech bubble.*

good at selling • a bit chaotic • well organized • reliable • creative • hard working • independent • full of new ideas • outgoing

b) *Did you have the same words as your partner? Look back at Option 2 and check your answers.*

OPTION 1

✔ … talk about the role of English in the world.

a) *Choose the correct meaning for these words from the box on the right:*

mother tongue • official language • bilingual person • foreign language • world language	speaker of two languages • international language • language of a different country • a person's main language • language of a country (for example used by government)

b) *Name three situations in your country in which you could have to use English.* Ov6

✔ … present facts and figures about the English language.

a) *Correct these statements about English.*

1. Over 700 people speak English as a foreign language.
2. It was spread by traders and pilots.
3. It's the official language in 50 countries.
4. It's an official language in Germany, Canada and India.
5. South America has 11 official languages.
6. English is used by farmers internationally.

b) *Name four countries where English is* ***the*** *or* ***an*** *official language.*

OPTION 2

✔ … talk about strengths and weaknesses. Ov6, 7

a) *Look at these people, who are doing different jobs. Think of how each person should be.*

1

2

3

4

b) *Think of one weakness which could cause problems or be dangerous in each of the above jobs.*

c) *Which of these jobs could/couldn't you do? Say why.*

✔ … decide why English could be important in some jobs.

In which of these jobs is English an important skill? Why? Where is it not so important but useful?

emergency helper • mechanic • person at a tourist info desk • secretary in a big company • train driver • international coach • newsagent • hairdresser • diving instructor • bank manager • milkman • film director • policeman • travel agent

✔ … prepare yourself for a job interview. Ov1, 2, 5

a) *Imagine you are in an interview for your dream job. Use your profile to answer these questions.*

1. When did you leave school?
2. What was/were your favourite subject(s)?
3. Have you had any on-the-job experience?
4. What holiday jobs have you done?

b) *Give the interviewer two reasons (special skills or strengths) why you think you should get the job.*

(→ p. 8/ex. 15; p. 9/ex. 16)

Young people in the Canadian North (→ pp. 10–12)

In an interesting project a school in Iqaluit presented their region – Nunavut, Canada – to young people worldwide. One class put their views online. This is the class's introductory[1] page:

Iqaluit High School

Back to Iqaluit High School homepage

- **INTRODUCTION** Who we are/our goals
- **GEOGRAPHY/MAP** Iqaluit, Nunavut is here
- **NUNAVUT HISTORY** We're ancient & young!
- **CULTURE & LANGUAGE** Wanna speak Inuktitut?
- **TEENAGERS OF IQALUIT** Worries and interests

INTRODUCTION

So you've found us, way up in the north of Canada: We guess that means you want to know more about us!

If you click on the map, you'll see Nunavut. Our school is in the regional[2] capital, Iqaluit. Iqaluit (ee-kah-loo-eet) means 'place of many fish'! Nunavut has over 2 million km² of wide open spaces. It's cold (January –30°C on average) in the winter – and it's only light from 9:30 a.m. to 2:00 p.m. In summer (July average 15° C) it's never night! Do you also have 'Northern Lights'? That's when the sky lights up[3] in fantastic colours – a real attraction for tourists!

Nunavut is very young: It officially became a region in Canada in 1999. But of course the history of Nunavut – the land and the Inuit people – is very old ... thousands of years old ...

At school we have Math and Science and lots of other subjects. We also have lessons on our Inuit culture[4] and language (Inuktitut) and learn things like how to prepare animal skins[5] and build a 'kamatik', a wooden sled[6] that is pulled behind a snowmobile. Sleds are very important here: They're used to carry tools[7] on hunting trips.

Outside school, too, we keep up our traditions (like our big spring festival). And music – traditional, modern or mixed – is an important part of our culture. Maybe you'd like to know more about throat[8] singing, for example ...

Without our youth club we, teenagers of Iqaluit, would be lost! Here are a few of our interests and worries:

Valerie, 15

I can't wait for the winter because I've got a new skidoo (snowmobile)! There's enough snow for skidooing. But my grandad says he notices global warming: The ice is not so thick these days so hunting on sea ice is getting dangerous.

Mike & Tom, 15 & 16

We meet at the club or hang out at the café at Astro Hill (mall[9]). In winter we take part in an igloo[10] building competition. In summer we go biking. But lots of kids have real alcohol problems, some don't survive! What is there for us in the future? Will we get jobs after school?

Amber, 14

I play computer games and go hunting[11] – for seals for example – with my family. It's a good thing we can hunt because most food gets here by plane or ship. So it's too expensive – e.g. a family box of chicken pieces costs $44 here (about $20 in Toronto)!

For more, visit the youth club site or link up with us by e-mail

[1]introductory [ˌɪntrəˈdʌktri] – *Einführungs-*, [2]regional [ˈriːdʒnl] – *regional,* [3]to light up [laɪt‿ˈʌp] – *aufleuchten,* [4]culture [ˈkʌltʃə] – *Kultur,* [5]skin [skɪn] – *Haut,* [6]wooden sled [ˌwʊdn ˈsled] – *Holzschlitten,* [7]tool [tuːl] – *Werkzeug,* [8]throat [θrəʊt] – *Kehle,* [9]mall [mɔːl] – *Einkaufszentrum,* [10]igloo [ˈɪgluː] – *Iglu,* [11]to hunt [hʌnt] – *jagen*

A Reading

1 Skim[1] the text and find out the name of the capital of Nunavut and how big the region is.

2 Read the web page carefully, complete the sentences and write them down.

a. Nunavut is in	1 western Canada.	2 the north of Canada.	3 Toronto.
b. The school is in	1 Iqaluit.	2 Toronto.	3 Astro Hill.
c. The city's name means	1 'Northern Lights'.	2 'wide open spaces'.	3 'place of many fish'.
d. The region was founded	1 in 1999.	2 a thousand years ago.	3 by hunters[2].
e. At school there kids learn	1 to drive skidoos.	2 German and Science.	3 Inuktitut.
f. Sleds are important for	1 snowmobiles.	2 carrying tools.	3 throat singing.
g. Iqaluit kids would be lost	1 without a youth club.	2 without tourists.	3 without winter.

3 Read what some young people say about their lives. Match Mike/Tom, Valerie and Amber to one interest and one worry. Choose from the box.
You can start like this: One of Mike and Tom's interests is … . They are worried about … .

throat singing • skidooing • colourful skies • the big alcohol problem • computer games • global warming • igloo building • how expensive food is • making wooden sleds • long dark winters

B Language

Look at the words from the text and find the correct meaning.

a. views (line 2)	1 picture	2 opinions	3 sights
b. spaces (line 7)	1 areas of land	2 places to sit	3 pieces of sky
c. survive (line 41)	1 enjoy life	2 keep friends	3 stay alive

1,7 ◎ **C Listening: Beatboxing: traditional, modern or mixed?**

1 Tapisa, an Inuit teenager, is talking about her hobby. Listen. Which picture goes best with the report?

A

B

C

2 The report is called 'Beatboxing – traditional, modern or mixed'. Find the correct reason for this title.

a. Tapisa loves traditional Inuit sports and more modern sports where people fight.
b. Tapisa is a throat singer who likes different styles – old Inuit, modern and the two mixed together.
c. Tapisa is an artist who makes traditional drums and plays old, modern and a mix of the two on them.

3 Listen to the report again. Are the sentences right or wrong?

a. In Canada this is a hobby for boys only.
b. The sounds may be like phones or bells ringing.
c. It's a competition to see who can last longest.
d. It goes on for three minutes.
e. The performers only use traditional music.
f. Lucie Idlout won an expensive CD in 2003.

[1]to skim [skɪm] – *überfliegen*, [2]hunter ['hʌntə] – *Jäger/in*

D Speaking

Dog sled racing[1]

Skidooing

Hanging out

Building an igloo

1 Describing

What are the people doing in the photos? Which activity would you prefer[2] to do? Why?

2 Discussing

Would you like to live in the Arctic region? One of you thinks of three pros of living there (and examples of how modern technology could make your life easier). The other collects three cons. Tell each other your ideas.

3 Role play

You find a link to the website of a youth club in Iqaluit, Nunavut. You'd like to find out about young people's activities there. You call the number on the website via the Internet.

You: *(Sage deinen Namen, wo du lebst und dass du auch Zeit im Jugendhaus verbringst. Erzähle, warum du anrufst.)*
Doug: Hi there! I'm Doug. Well, we have lots of activities, like our Halloween Dance. And we play table-tennis, soccer or do our computer projects here. What about your club?
You: *(Erkläre, dass du ins Jugendhaus gehst, um Freunde zu treffen. Sage, dass du dort auch gerne zur Kinonacht gehst.)*
Doug: Oh, yes, we show films, too – but not in the summer because there's summer camp then.
You: *(Sage, dass es bei euch kein Sommercamp gibt. Erwähne eine sonstige Sommerveranstaltung – zum Beispiel Musikfestivals oder Workshops.)*
Doug: Well, our big community festival is in spring … .
You: *(Frage, was für ein Event das ist und wie lang es geht.)*
Doug: We celebrate[3] the start of spring for a whole week with igloo building competitions, snowmobile or dog team races and Inuit games.
You: *(Sage, dass das sehr interessant klingt. Frage, ob es schwer ist, ein Iglu zu bauen.)*
Doug: Well, it's not my strong point! The snowmobile race is more my thing!
You: *(Drücke dein Erstaunen aus und frage, ob es Fotos vom Rennen gibt.)*
Doug: Yes. Lots! I can send you some great ones. What's your e-mail address? …

[1]racing ['reɪsɪŋ] – *Rennen*, [2]to prefer [prɪ'fɜː] – *bevorzugen*, [3]to celebrate ['seləbreɪt] – *feiern*

E Mediation and communication

A friend is visiting you from abroad. She sees the page on an Inuit competition which you've just printed out. She says it looks interesting, but her English isn't very good. Answer her questions.

SPONSORED BY THE RSPE (REGIONAL SOCIETY OF PROFESSIONAL ENGINEERS)
So you think you're good at igloo building? Then take part in our this year's

'BUILD THE BEST IGLOO' COMPETITION
on the weekend of 12th February

The goal of our competition goes further than building igloos: We wish to show people how engineering[1] is important in our everyday lives and how it helps to solve practical problems. If young kids understand this, they might become more interested in science … well, and maybe even in engineering!

We invite you to come and build your own house of ice. Your team can be your family, your friends, people at school or work – or a happy mix of any of these! You may take the whole weekend to finish your igloo.

But we have one very important rule:
You may only use traditional and environmentally friendly tools like snow spades[2] and saws[3].
Our judges are all professional engineers & expert igloo builders, too! They'll look at your work and decide:

- ➜ how well it's built (design & size[4]),
- ➜ if it's strong enough to carry at least one big truck tyre[5] &
- ➜ if it's safe to live in! (Teams get bonus points if they spend a night in their igloo.)

The teams will get good, hot meals during the competition.
Each member of the winning team will get one of our glamorous glass igloo awards with their names on it.

This year visitors may also vote on the best igloo, so you can also win a special, surprise 'public[6] favourite' prize! Tell all your friends and family to come along and support the event!

There's a limit of 10 teams, so don't miss our deadline[7] of 10th January!
For info & advice about suitable igloo dimensions[8], e-mail us!

a. Was ist das für ein Event?
b. Was will der Veranstalter damit erreichen?
c. Gibt es besondere Regeln? Welche?
d. Was passiert mit dem Reifen?
e. Ich verstehe „bonus points", aber wofür erhält man sie?
f. Was bekommen die Gewinner?

F Writing

1 Skills

Imagine you are in a youth club and you'd like to organize a Spring or Winter Festival. Decide on three typical events (activities, competitions …). Who could you ask to be sponsors or to give money for it? Who could you ask locally for help? Think of two activities you could do to make the money which you'll need for the festival.

2 Writing

Think of a good name for your festival. Write a short report (50–80 words) which you could send to possible sponsors. Say why you think the festival is a good idea to have. Describe the events which you wish to organize.

[1]engineering [ˌendʒɪ'nɪərɪŋ] – *Ingenieurswesen,* [2]spade [speɪd] – *Schaufel,* [3]saw [sɔː] – *Säge,* [4]size [saɪz] – *Größe,* [5]tyre ['taɪə] – *Reifen,* [6]public ['pʌblɪk] – *Öffentlichkeit,* [7]deadline ['dedlaɪn] – *hier: Einsendeschluss,* [8]dimension [daɪ'menʃn] – *hier: Größe*

A geocaching adventure

1,8–12

▶ You can use a dictionary if you don't understand some of the words.

GEOCACHING

Geocaching ist eine moderne Art der Schatzsuche. Der Schatz (*Geocache*) ist in der Natur versteckt. Meist befindet er sich in einer wasserdichten Verpackung (von sehr kleinen Behältern (*micro*) bis hin zu richtigen Kisten (*large*). Die Schatzsucher orientieren sich mithilfe eines GPS Geräts (*GPS device*) und Koordinaten (*bearings*) und gelangen so zu der Stelle, an der der Cache versteckt ist.
Der Cache enthält neben einem Logbuch, in das man sich eintragen sollte, auch Tauschgegenstände (*trading objects*). Der Finder kann sich – bevor er den Cache zurücklegt – einen Gegenstand aussuchen und einen im Wert etwa gleichen neuen Gegenstand hineinlegen.

Auf speziellen Geocaching-Internetseiten ist jeder Cache registriert.
Neben Koordinaten und Informationen zur Größe des Caches kann hier jeder Schatzsucher auch seine Kommentare zum Cache vermerken.
Es gibt einfache Caches, bei denen die Koordinaten direkt zum Cache führen, und mehrstufige Caches, bei denen verschiedene Caches nacheinander gefunden werden müssen, um ans Ziel zu kommen. Einen besonderen Reiz haben die FTFs (*first to find*) – neue Caches, die noch keiner zuvor gefunden hat.

Simon and Helen are going on a geocaching trip with their friend Avril and her new boyfriend, Logan. In this extract they are getting ready to leave for Yosemite National Park.

A Simon suddenly saw white flashes of light. They flew across his eyes and seemed to burn into them as they went. He closed his eyes. But the flashes became even stronger. He fought hard against the panic that was rising in him.
But there was nothing he could do to stop the awful feeling creeping[1] up from his shoulders. It felt like hundreds of spiders running all over his head. He heard the sound of wings and of thunder[2] in the distance. Then it was over.

He wiped[3] the sweat[4] from his face and looked across at Helen, who had just got into the car.

As her eyes caught his, she said, worried, "Hey, Sy, you OK? You look like you've just seen a ghost!"

"Er – no, I'm OK," Simon said. Then, to change the subject, he asked, "Did you hear that thunder, Helen?"

She looked at him and thought: Thunder? There wasn't a cloud in the Californian midsummer sky!

"No," she said slowly. "Listen, Sy. I know how you feel about Avril's new 'football superhero'. But we don't know him. I mean maybe Logan isn't really such a bigmouth[5]."

"Well," he said, "I guess we'll find out pretty soon!"

They drove across town to get Avril and Logan. Simon shuddered[6] suddenly as he

[1]to creep [kri:p] – *kriechen,* [2]thunder ['θʌndə] – *Donner,* [3]to wipe [waɪp] – *wischen,* [4]sweat [swet] – *Schweiß,* [5]bigmouth ['bɪgmaʊθ] – *Großmaul,* [6]to shudder ['ʃʌdə] – *schaudern*

thought of the flashes and the creeping. The last time was four years ago. Why had they come back? OK, OK, he said to himself. It's over, at least for now, so relax! It's a great day, I got my dad's SUV and I'm on a geocaching trip with Helen!

***

B In Yosemite the group left the SUV[1] at Curry Village and used the shuttle service to get to their starting point as marked out by their GPS device.

On the trail[2], Avril said, "Everyone is going for the same cache! There'll be traffic lights[3] at the next trail crossing[4]!"

"Yeah," agreed Logan, "I thought we wanted a nice remote spot, all to ourselves!" He winked at[5] Avril.

"No, you guys," said Simon, who had a detailed trail map in his hand. "They're all going to the waterfall near here, I bet. Our route is much longer and it'll be quite a climb!"

"Aw, but I love waterfalls," said Avril, disappointed.

"Yosemite's full of them," said Logan. "Hey, Simon, put that map away. Not heard of GPS? Come on, folks, follow me. Waterfalls, here we come!"

Simon looked at Helen and rolled[6] his eyes. Logan checked his GPS and turned left. Soon the teenagers found themselves alone in the woods[7]. But then the trail suddenly opened out. Ah, sweetgrass[8], thought Simon. But sweetgrass didn't grow in these parts. So what was happening here? He shuddered although the sun burned down on him.

"It's sweetgrass," he said to the others. "We had lots of the stuff back in Oregon, where I lived as a kid. It's a sacred plant that Native Americans use."

"Wow!" said Helen as she took a deep breath[9]. "It really smells sweet and sort of strange."

"Yeah," agreed Avril. "It makes you feel funny."

"Na," said Logan, "it's real cool here. Let's lie down for a bit and rest."

sweetgrass

"It's too hot to lie out here," said Simon. "Somewhere with shade would be better."

"You're right, Sy," said Avril. "I'm beginning to feel real dizzy."

***

C They walked uphill along a stream. Still climbing, the trail took them deeper into the woods, till suddenly they arrived at a waterfall. Simon couldn't believe his eyes. He rubbed[10] them and looked again. He had stood right on this rock on last year's trip. But everything about the place was different now. And the waterfall – It was … perfect.

But why was it so silent? It was like paradise, but it sent a shudder down Simon's spine[11]. Something was warning him. But of what? And how could he explain this to the others? Simon then noticed that the others were looking at him strangely. He quickly pushed his weird[12] feelings away.

"Hey, Sy," said Helen. "Logo's found us a fantastic spot! Let's picnic here."

"Yeah, Logo," added Avril and smiled sweetly at her hero. "It's ultra magic!"

"It's just GPS," said Simon, looking at his device. They ate and talked about the cache they'd find.

"I bet it's an FTF," said Logan. "And the finder will be me, of course!"

"You mean us," said Simon with a laugh, "or are you going up there alone?"

"I hope it's something good," said Avril. "I've got this heart-shaped[13] stone to trade."

"Hey, I'm hot," said Logan, without looking. "What do you bet that I can jump off that boulder[14] – headfirst into the water?"

"I'd bet you, one pretty damaged skull[15]!"

[1]SUV [ˌesju:ˈvi:] – *Geländewagen,* [2]trail [treɪl] – *Wanderweg,* [3]traffic lights (*pl*) [ˈtræfɪk ˌlaɪts] – *Ampel,* [4]crossing [ˈkrɒsɪŋ] – *Kreuzung,* [5]to wink at sb [wɪŋk] – *jmdm. zuzwinkern,* [6]to roll [rəʊl] – *rollen,* [7]woods (*pl*) [wʊdz] – *Wald,* [8]sweetgrass [ˈswi:tgrɑ:s] – *Mariengras, duftendes Gras,* [9]to take a deep breath [breθ] – *tief Luft holen,* [10]to rub [rʌb] – *reiben,* [11]spine [spaɪn] – *Wirbelsäule,* [12]weird [wɪəd] – *seltsam,* [13]heart-shaped [ˈhɑ:tʃeɪpt] – *herzförmig,* [14]boulder [ˈbəʊldə] – *Felsbrocken,* [15]skull [skʌl] – *Schädel*

laughed Simon. "It looks deep but it isn't. I've swum here."

"Let's swim on our way back," said Avril, trying to get the picture of Logan's damaged skull out of her mind. "We should move on."

Logan almost ran up the rocky[1] trail near the waterfall. Simon heard the sound of thunder and looked up at the sky. Clear blue. He saw a path which led[2] towards the waterfall.

"Hey, Logan," said Simon, "we're not in a race, you know! We're doing this trip for fun!"

"Look who's talking about fun!" shouted Logan. "Our map reader with no sense of adventure!"

"Listen," said Simon. "I'm just saying slow down[3]. And maybe don't only think of yourself all the time!"

"Come on, stop it, you guys!" said Helen.

***

D The trail led between two huge, white boulders. Logan stopped in the space, which was just wide enough for him. With a hand on each boulder he acted as if he wanted to push them open. Simon checked his GPS device for bearings.

"Hey, Av!" said Logan, with a silly smile. "How about a snapshot of your big hero?"

Avril got out her cell phone, took a snap and said, "OK, Mr Hero, if it makes you happy!"

"Cool rocks," he said, "like guards[4] at a gate!"

Then before they could say anything, Logan took out a neon highlighter[5] and wrote: "Logo was here!"

"Logo," said Helen, "you can't do that! You know the park rules – and they're not there for nothing!"

At that moment there was a loud crackling[6] in the air. The hairs on their heads seemed to stand up.

"Quick," said Simon, "let's get the cache and go!"

He looked at his GPS device – dead! And their cell phones, too! He checked his map and said, "We're close. I checked the device a few minutes ago. The cache is near here, I'm sure."

The cache was registered as a micro, so it was small. They looked behind rocks and in little bushes.

"Hey, these stones could be markers – I bet it's here!" cried Logan as he began to dig. Soon he hit an object.

"I got it!" he shouted as he pulled out a – bone[7]! And there were more to follow.

"Hey, what a stupid cache! Not even a box. Just bones!" he added angrily.

"Maybe they're human!" exclaimed[8] Helen and put her hand to her mouth.

"Logan," cried Avril, "don't touch them!"

"Hey," said Simon, "what the hell are you doing! It's a grave, stupid!"

But his sentence was lost in terrible thunder.

***

E The sky was suddenly grey and heavy with rain. A handful of bones lay white against the earth. Red blood began to flow[9] from the grave. They turned and ran towards the two white boulders. The storm broke and rain came down in torrents[10]. They ran through the gap[11], one after the other. Lightning[12] zapped[13] to the ground behind them. The boulders shuddered and began to close.

[1]rocky ['rɒki] – *felsig,* [2]to lead, led, led [li:d, led, led] – *führen,* [3]to slow down [sləʊ͜'daʊn] – *langsamer gehen,* [4]guard [gɑ:d] – *Wache,* [5]neon highlighter [ˌni:ɒn 'haɪlaɪtə] – *neonfarbener Leuchtstift,* [6]crackling ['kræklɪŋ] – *Geknister,* [7]bone [bəʊn] – *Knochen,* [8]to exclaim [ɪks'kleɪm] – *ausrufen,* [9]to flow [fləʊ] – *fließen,* [10]in torrents [ɪn 'tɒrnts] – *wasserfallartig,* [11]gap [gæp] – *Lücke,* [12]lightning ['laɪtnɪŋ] – *Blitze,* [13]to zap [zæp] – *schießen*

Logan was last. He dived through just in time! But the boulders had his backpack. And a bit of his shirt was caught between the rocks. He was trapped!

"Wait! They've got me!" he cried out. "Help!"

They all ran back. Helen cut him free with her penknife. Then they half ran, half slid[1] down the trail, which was now more like a fast stream between the rocks. The sky was nearly black, although it was only early afternoon. The earth itself seemed to vibrate[2] with the thunder. Lightning crashed in zigzags[3] through the dark.

"We have to get away quick, or the lightning will hit us!" shouted Simon. He waved to them all urgently.

Their GPS equipment and cell phones were still not working. And worse – the trail was now very difficult to follow. They were in the middle of a nightmare with no chance to wake up from it!

Simon grabbed Logan and pulled him along. Logan was whispering crazily 'They nearly got me!' – again and again. Simon stopped to get his bearings. Suddenly the sky above them flashed white with hundreds of lightning explosions. They crashed down dangerously like spears[4] of fire.

Then, one of the spears landed directly behind them – and gave them a terrible shock. The earth sizzled[5] where the lightning had hit the ground …

[adapted from ***Red earth, white bone*** by Hamida Aziz]

1 The setting 2

Describe the time and place where the story happens. There are several strange things about it. Write them down. Find pictures in a magazine and make a poster.

2 The storyline 2

Make a list of important things that happen.

3 The characters 2

a) *Collect information about the characters in a grid (names, sort of person, …).*
b) *What picture do you have of the characters? Describe them.*
c) *Imagine you are going to make a film. Which famous actors could play the characters? Say why.*

4 What will happen next? 8, 11

a) *Collect ideas on how the story could go on.*
b) *Compare your ideas in class. Choose the best ending for the story.*

5 Your opinion 11

Get together in groups of 3–4 and talk about the story.

- What do you like about it?
- What don't you like so much?
- Would you like to read the book? Why/Why not?
- Which of the characters do you like best and why?

[1]to slide, slid, slid [slaɪd, slɪd, slɪd] – *schlittern,* [2]to vibrate [vaɪ'breɪt] – *vibrieren,* [3]zigzag ['zɪgzæg] – *Zickzack,* [4]spear [spɪə] – *Speer,* [5]to sizzle ['sɪzl] – *zischen*

Topic 2 Living democracy – human rights

1

Child with gun in Texas

1. Work with a picture: (→ p. 13/ex. 1, 2)
   a) Look at photo 1. Describe it to your partner.
   b) Work with a picture: Look at the caption and talk to your partner about photo 1. The ideas in the box can help you.

> What a(n) crazy/interesting/stupid/terrible/surprising/ … photo!
> I really (don't) like it because the picture makes me/us …
> … angry about carrying guns.
> … want/never want to carry a gun.
> … think about age limits (society/reasons for violence).
> … laugh because small kids don't carry guns!
> I can't believe you can buy …

2. a) Look at all the photos. Choose one phrase from below which matches each picture best. (→ p. 13/ex. 3)
   Say which right they're using: In picture … the person is/the people are using the right to … .

> freedom of the press • carry guns • have friends • take part in elections • drive a car • a fair court trial • spend money as you like • say what you think in public • an education

2 TV journalists on the Israel-Lebanon border

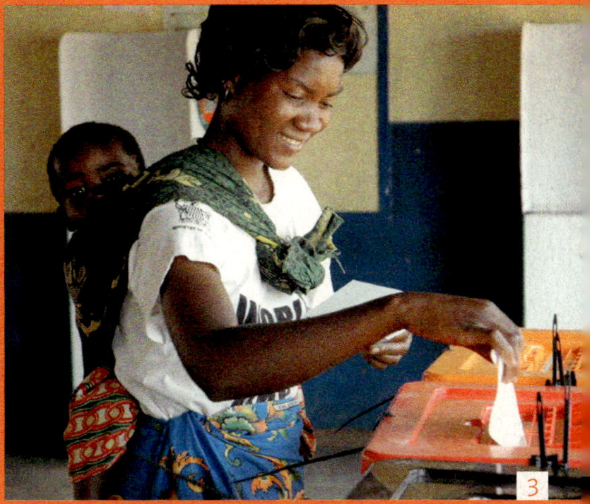

3 South Africa: One woman, one vote

4 Speaker at Speaker's Corner in London

5 Inside a US court of law

b) Listen to some people's comments on the speaker at 'Speaker's Corner'. What do they say?

1,13

1 The tourists think the speaker is …
   a. not much fun. b. disturbing people. c. very funny.
2 The woman thinks he's …
   a. interesting. b. too loud. c. laughing at the tourists.
3 The man thinks they should …
   a. ban speakers. b. arrest speakers. c. take photos of speakers.

⇨ 547560-0003

A The Middle Ages in England (1066–1485)

The Middle Ages probably mean knights on horses and beautiful ladies in castles to many of you. But most people at this time weren't either of these. They were probably serfs – the lowest class in the feudal system. As a serf you lived in a hut and didn't have much to eat. You certainly didn't have your own horse! Even servants had a higher social position. Just above them came soldiers and freemen. Then came knights, who were below barons and bishops. At the top was the king, who owned most of the land in England. He gave some to loyal barons or knights. Serfs belonged with the land. They had to work on it and give their land owner everything they produced. They were given a small field so that they could feed themselves and their family. The only right they had was to be protected by their owner. However, with a charter called 'Magna Carta' (which was first drawn up in 1215), things began to look better for serfs ...

Time for an update?

Laws are often made to protect us and our rights. Some of these laws (like the ones in Magna Carta) are very old but still important today. Others are just old – and surely need an update: Did you know, for example, that women in Vermont must ask their husband's permission to wear false teeth? Or that you're breaking British law if you die in the Houses of Parliament? There's even a law which says Englishmen older than 14 must do two hours of bow and arrow practice a day. But have you ever heard of anyone who actually does this? So why do laws like these still exist? Well, because it would cost a lot of time and money if you wanted to get rid of them!

If you drive blindfolded in Alabama, you're breaking the law!

→ Option 1

1 Let's talk: The lowest class 5

a) *What do you think of when you hear 'The Middle Ages'? Start a mind map.*

b) *Read text A. Add all the information from it to your mind map.*

c) *Make a pyramid to show society in the Middle Ages. What was a serf's life like? Write notes.*

d) *Think about some rights which you have but which you wouldn't have as a serf in a feudal system. Make a list.*

e) *If you were a serf in such a system, what would you miss most?*

2 Old laws for old rights 7 18 (→ p. 14/ex. 4)

a) *Read the info box about old laws and decide which you find the strangest.*

b) *Look at the cartoon and invent a situation like this for the law you chose in a). Draw a scene for the situation and put key words into it.*

c) *Now write 3–5 sentences about your scene under your drawing.*

d) *Do a gallery walk with all the drawings and let your group/class vote on the best idea.*

 Für Topic 2 brauchst du: Bedingungssätze (Typ I + II) → Ov 7 • das Passiv → Ov 5

B Freedom of the press

British reporter kidnapped in Gaza City street attack

BBC not able to contact journalist and "concerned for his safety"

Yesterday masked men took a British journalist from his car in the Gaza Strip. The Palestinian police say gunmen followed Alan Johnston from his office and kidnapped him just outside his apartment. Police found his car and business cards at the scene. The BBC report that they aren't able to contact him and are "concerned for his safety". Mr Johnston (44) is the only foreign reporter still in Gaza.

He has been there for three years, knows a lot about the local situation and can provide important information for future reporters. Kidnappings of this kind are now common in Gaza, that's why most of the staff of international organisations have been flown out of the region. The kidnappings are not usually a protest against foreigners or their countries; most often they are used in the violent battle of power between different rival groups.

The last foreign hostage was a South American photographer, who was kidnapped on 1st January and set free a week later.

Alan Johnston, BBC journalist

➔ Option 2

C Rights at work

A

B

⇨ 547560-0004

3 A dangerous job! 5 (→ p. 14/ex. 5)

a) *Look at the headline (part B) and the photo with its caption. Say who the article is about, what his job is and what happened to him.*

b) *Read the text. Correct these sentences.*
1. They met Alan in his apartment.
2. The BBC is able to contact him.
3. Alan has been in Gaza for five years.
4. So he can provide future reporters.
5. Kidnappings are not common in Gaza.
6. They are always a protest against foreigners.
7. The last hostage was from South Africa.
8. He was set free on 1st January.

c) *Find pros and cons (two each) for being a reporter like Alan. Compare with your partner.*

d) *Would you like to be a reporter like Alan? Write a short text. Use your list from c).*

1,14 ◎

4 Let's listen: Employees' rights 13 (→ p. 14/ex. 6)

a) *Look at part C. Match each caption with a cartoon:*
1. "Well done! You are our 'Employee of the Week'. That means your work load will increase, but your pay will stay the same."
2. "We are looking for people who can quickly adapt to changes in the workplace."

b) *Three managers talk about their workers. Listen and find a talk to go with each cartoon.*

c) *Listen again. Which four sentences did they say?*

It gives them a good feeling. • We pay more now. • You need to keep moving. • They must check out. • They arrive when they want. • They think that we have millions.

d) *Would you like to work for the first, second or third manager? Give a reason.*

Head of State

A Duties

Every November the Queen opens Parliament at Westminster. In the 'Queen's Speech' from the House of Lords she tells people about the government's future plans. But why does the Queen do this, and not the Prime Minister?

Britain is a democracy with a parliament elected by the people. Its government sits in the House of Commons. But it also still has a Royal Family.

But did you know that the Queen isn't allowed to enter the House of Commons? Or that the Queen's Speech was actually written by the Government and not by the Queen?

The Queen opens Parliament because she is Head of State. She also signs new laws. These duties are important: If, for example, the Queen refused to open Parliament, then there wouldn't be a UK Government! And if she refused to pass a bill or a law, she could stop the Government's plans!

Treaties with other nations are signed by the Queen, but she isn't allowed to make them. And she has to remain neutral in political matters: For example, she can't support one political party or their policies.

Yet Queen Elizabeth still plays a formal role in British politics – she receives ambassadors and visits hospitals etc. And she is also patron of many organisations and charities, is present at big social events and, in summer, she holds garden parties.

The Queen does have some power: She can still refuse to appoint a Prime Minister even if he or she was chosen by the party. And every Tuesday at 6.30 p.m. she meets the Prime Minister to discuss state matters. She studies confidential, official papers which are brought to her every day, no matter where in the world she is, in traditional red boxes.

B A public attraction

Jane took her American friend Yolanda to see the Crown Jewels at the Tower of London. When they arrived, they had to wait in a long queue. They began to talk about what is similar and different in their countries.

"So why do you still have a queen?" Yolanda asked her English friend.

"Well," Jane answered, "I don't know – It's just history!"

"But it's an old system," said Yolanda, "– one person ruling a country!"

"The Queen doesn't rule now," laughed Jane.

"Look, this leaflet says 'She has to stay neutral in all political matters'. The government has got the power." Then she added, "It sits in Westminster, in the Houses of Parliament – and Big Ben – which we passed on the bus."

"Ah!" said Yolanda. "But why 'Houses'? It's only one building, right?

"Well," explained Jane, "British parliament has two parts: the *House* of Lords and the *House* of Commons.

"Oh, OK. That's sort of like in the US," said Yolanda.

"Only our government has three parts. But I wish we had a king or queen. Then we'd have our own Royal Family and all that juicy gossip ..."

They both laughed. Some kids in front of them turned to look at them.

"I don't know about that!" said Jane. "I thought Americans find monarchy outdated! And maybe they're right!"

"Outdated!" Yolanda cried. "I bet half of the people here are from the US!"

"Well, that's just because it's all so romantic: queens, crowns and jewels," said Jane. "But, you know, the Queen isn't there just to keep you tourists happy all day! She has got a lot of duties ..."

Task: To learn about some of the duties of a head of state

1 State matters

Think about your Head of State. When did you last see him/her on TV? What was the reason? Start a mind map (with your Head of State/government, duties, where parliament is …). Not sure? Check on the Internet.

2 A quiz: The Queen's duties 4 (→ p. 15/ex. 7, 8)

a) ***Think:*** *Look at the pictures (part A). Choose the right answer. Try and guess if you are not sure.*

1. The Queen has to …
   a. go to social events. b. decide which films are good. c. give James Bond a job.
2. She signs all …
   a. UK passports. b. CDs of the group 'Queen'. c. treaties with other nations.
3. She also …
   a. holds big garden parties. b. visits Buckingham Palace. c. grows flowers.
4. This box is for the Queen's …
   a. private letters. b. favourite stories. c. confidential and official papers.
5. It's the Queen's job to …
   a. go to court. b. open parliament. c. sit in parliament every day.

b) ***Pair:*** *Now read about the Queen's duties (text A). Compare your answers to a) with your partner.*

c) ***Pair:*** *Make a list of all the Queen's duties. Are any of them the same as those of your Head of State? Which of the Queen's duties is most/least interesting? Say why.*

d) ***Share:*** *Discuss your opinions from c) in your group and vote on it.*

3 Queen or President? 13 5 (→ p. 16/ex. 9)

a) *Read text B. Find one thing that is the same in the UK and the US. Find one thing which is different.*

b) *Yolanda thinks Americans are interested in the Royal Family because …*

1. the US is a democracy.
2. they don't have their own Royal Family.
3. monarchy is outdated.

c) *Write 2–3 sentences about monarchy. Say why you think this. Compare with your partner.*

is very glamorous • is outdated • many countries don't have a monarchy • country gets money through tourists • have too much power • it's not fair • may cost a lot • …

15 d) *Write two lists, one for 'Queen' and one for 'US President'. Listen to the end of the conversation in text B. Put the phrases from the box in the right list. Some can go in both.*

(not) elected • born royal • White House • head of government • meets ambassadors • head of state • Buckingham Palace • suggests policies • wears a crown

4 Presentation: A poster 1 18 (→ p. 16/ex. 10)

a) *Make a poster about the Queen as Head of State. Write useful words on your poster with translations (e.g. monarch – König/in, Monarch/in; royal – …).*

b) *Now use your poster to tell your class about the Queen's duties. Use your info from Ex. 1 and your list from Ex. 2c) and say what is different from/the same as the duties of your Head of State.*

Democracy on the job

Young apprentices (YAs) in tricky situations

CARD A

Someone often makes nasty comments about your religion/family background. When you ask them to stop, they say that you can't take a joke.

CARD E

A colleague of the opposite sex shows interest in you and asks you to go for a drink after work.

CARD B

The rules say that you mustn't use office phones or e-mail for private matters. But sometimes colleagues call friends, play 'Solitaire' or surf the Net and say that you can do the same.

CARD F

A colleague often puts their face very close to yours when they are talking to you. They also come up behind you and rest their hand on your shoulders when they start a conversation.

CARD C

In school you had a lesson on health & safety at work, but you missed it. At work you had a session on health & safety but it was hard to follow and you felt too nervous to ask questions.

CARD G

Another YA seems to get more opportunities. You ask why: Your boss says that they've developed better skills and so can try more ambitious projects.

CARD D

In a health & safety session you learn that wearing protective clothing is very important for some tasks. But some colleagues take these off when the supervisor goes away.

CARD H

Your colleagues use a lot of bad language at work and they often read out articles from magazines or tell jokes which you find very rude or even sexist.

Task: To find out about rights and duties at work

1 Work experience 14 4

a) *Think: Start a mind map about a 'work experience' which you have done. Include info like:*

where you did it • what kind of tasks they gave you • what the atmosphere at work was like • how long the experience was • what rights/duties you had • what you liked best/least

If they offered you a job there in the future, would you take it? Why/why not?

b) *Pair: Tell your partner about your work experience. Think of a problem someone had/could have there. How did/could they solve it? Discuss.*

c) *Share: Act a dialogue about your work experience for the others in your group. Your partner asks questions from 1a) and you give answers. Your group votes on the most interesting one.*

2 Problems at work 2 (→ p. 17/ex. 11, 12)

a) *Look at the pictures and read the cards. Make a list of key words. Choose a key word as heading for each card.*

b) *What advice would you give the YA in each of the situations? Add notes to your list.*

3 Advice for YAs 3 (→ p. 17/ex. 13; p. 18/ex. 14)

a) *Skim the eight tips on the right. Match each one to a problem from the cards on page 32.*

b) *Look at your list (Ex. 2). Add any tips which you don't have on your list.*

c) *Now, in your group, collect all the rights and duties which you have as a YA.*

4 Presentation: A panel of experts

(→ p. 18/ex. 15)

a) *Write each of the texts from page 32 on a card. Hang up large copies of the cartoons. Distribute the cards among the 'audience'. Give them time to check new words.*

b) *The others in your class try to match their cards with the cartoons. Your group is the 'panel of experts' and chooses a chairperson. He/she checks the audience's results from 4a).*

c) *The audience reads out each card and an 'expert' uses his/her notes from Ex. 2 and 3 and gives advice.*

ADVICE SHEET

1. The school should inform those YAs who missed an important lesson. YAs must ask if they do not understand something.
2. If you aren't interested, tell the person firmly: Never agree to meet someone who you don't know alone. Follow the law on drinking alcohol.
3. You have the right to be treated with respect. If someone bullies or harasses you, you should inform your supervisor and your teacher.
4. You must wear personal protective clothing. YAs should speak to their supervisor or teacher about this.
5. In male-dominated workplaces you may experience sexism or hear bad language – a situation which is difficult to stop. However, the firm should offer work experiences suitable for 14 – 16 year-olds.
6. All YAs should be given equal opportunities to learn and develop their skills. YAs should discuss problems with their supervisor and their teacher.
7. You must tell the person not to stand too close or touch you from behind. If he/she doesn't stop, you should inform your supervisor and/or teacher.
8. YAs should ask their supervisor about rules on private use of the Internet and phone and should follow those rules.

1 The odd one out

Find the word or phrase that doesn't fit in the group.

1. cars – citizens – laws – society
2. rights – freedom – duties – movies
3. policy – jewellery – government – system
4. serfs – farms – knights – barons
5. empty – court – judge – evidence
6. elections – political party – balloons – vote
7. journalist – sign – newspaper – information
8. corner – president – prime minister – queen
9. bills – House of Lords – parliament – station
10. boss – letter – colleagues – apprentice

2 Opposites

Match the opposites.

private • polite • outdated • legal • war • false • kidnap • in danger • check in • to agree • friendly

rude • check out • public • illegal • true • peace • set free • modern • nasty • to refuse • safe

3 Famous people and places

a) *Choose the right caption for each picture. Which person goes with which building?*

1

2

3

4

5

6

the Prime Minister
Buckingham Palace
the President
the Houses of Parliament
the Queen
the White House

b) *Which pictures are from the UK and which are from the US?*

c) *Write one sentence for each photo. The words in the box can help you.*

Head of State • Parliament • opens Parliament • head of government • is/isn't elected • is born royal • House of Commons/Lords • …

4 Rights and duties on the job

Find the correct word and complete the definitions.

1. The person you work with is your … a. employer. b. colleague. c. employee.
2. YA is short for … a. young awards. b. youth actor. c. young apprentice.
3. A male-dominated workplace has … a. more men. b. more letters. c. no women.
4. When someone harasses you, they … a. talk to you. b. bother you. c. lie to you.
5. The person who looks after YAs is a … a. employee. b. secretary. c. supervisor.
6. A more ambitious project is usually … a. more regular. b. more difficult. c. more hurtful.
7. You wear protective clothing to … a. not get hurt. b. look good. c. be popular.

OPTION 1

✔ … recognise important people/groups of people in politics in the US/UK. Ov3

a) *US or UK – or both? Sort the words and make two lists.*

Prime Minister | president | king/queen (monarch) | monarchy | government | citizens | political parties

b) *Explain three of the words from a).*
Example: A president can be the head of a state and/or a government.

c) *Say which people from the box above are elected.*

d) *How can citizens take part in these democratic systems?*

✔ … describe the Queen's role as Head of State.

Find five of the Queen's duties:

signs treaties • meets foreign ambassadors • supports a political party • makes government policies • sends red boxes to government • reads the Queen's Speech • meets the Prime Minister once a week • sits in the House of Commons • goes to important social events

✔ … talk about the Queen's power/activities and what she isn't allowed to do.

Which of these statements are false? Look back at Option 1 to see if you were right.

1. The queen must never suggest new bills.
2. She can write new laws.
3. She is allowed to enter the House of Commons.
4. She must never open Parliament.
5. She isn't allowed to make treaties.
6. The government writes the Queen's Speech.
7. She must always appoint a Prime Minister.
8. She can refuse to appoint a Prime Minister.

✔ … explain who your Head of State and head of government are. What do they do in their positions?

Find a photo for each person which shows him/her carrying out one of their duties. Write two sentences for each situation: Say where they are and what they are doing.

OPTION 2

✔ … give advice on problems at work. Ov7

Use full sentences and say what you would do in these situations:

1. A colleague gets too close and puts his hand on my shoulders. – If a colleague got …, I'd … .
2. Some colleagues take off their protective clothing when the supervisor is away.
3. Someone makes nasty comments about my religion.
4. Our supervisor gives another young apprentice more interesting projects than me.
5. A lot of my colleagues tell rude and sexist jokes.
6. A colleague says I should watch a video clip on the Internet with him during work.
7. I don't understand how to use a piece of equipment.

✔ … talk about rights and duties at work.

a) *Name five rights which you have as a YA.*

b) *Name three duties.*

(→ p. 19/ex. 16; p. 20/ex. 17)

What is the Commonwealth?

(→ pp. 21–23)

The British monarch is the Head of the Commonwealth and now Head of State in 16 of its 53 independent states (almost a third of the world's population!). But what is the Commonwealth and how did it start?

1 EARLY DAYS

The idea of the Commonwealth goes back to the 19th century – when Britain had colonies all over the world. This 'British Empire[1]' took natural[2] resources (like sugar and chocolate for example) from these countries and also used some of their people as slaves.
Canada was the first colony (1867) to become a separate nation: Independent of and equal to Britain, it pledged allegiance to the British Crown. Then other countries followed: e.g. Australia (1899), New Zealand (1907) and South Africa (1910). And so the idea of a free and equal British 'Commonwealth of Nations' began. At first this was only for colonies which were 'white' and the official language was English.

2 CHANGES

The British Commonwealth didn't become multiracial until after India had become independent (1947). The new nation wished to stay with the Commonwealth, but they didn't want to pledge allegiance to the Crown. Many other colonies which got their independence from Britain after the Second World War felt the same. This was the starting point for a new idea of Commonwealth. The word 'British' was dropped and countries no longer had to pledge allegiance to the Crown. In 1957 Ghana, the first African-ruled state, became a member and many others followed.

3 GOALS TODAY

The Commonwealth is a mixed group of nations which undertakes a number of activities together. It now stands for democracy and human rights and has common goals such as fighting poverty and intolerance – and things like HIV and AIDS.

4 YOUNG COMMONWEALTH

What do young people think about the Commonwealth? Here is an interview with Vasanti Sharma – a 17-year-old from Chandigarh, India.

Q: At school you learnt about the British Empire and the Commonwealth, right?
A: Yes, we learnt all about how hard life was with the British as rulers. My grandma also told me about the Empire and the awful fight for independence.
Q: So for you the Commonwealth is negative?
A: Well, no. Today it's different. Today the member states try to build bridges between countries. The idea is to give people a better quality of life and to look after our planet …
Q: What exactly do they do?
A: They've got the CYP. That's the Commonwealth Youth Programme, for example. I hope to take part next year. The CYP offers training in all kinds of areas, like youth development …

For more information about Vasanti Sharma and the CYP listen to the rest of the interview on the CD.

[1]empire ['empaɪə] – *Reich,* [2]natural ['nætʃrl] – *natürlich*

A Reading

1 Before you read: match these words with their correct meanings.

a. resources (l. 14) b. nation (l. 21) c. Crown (l. 23) d. multiracial (l. 35)
e. independence (l. 43) f. African-ruled (l. 52) g. to undertake (l. 57) h. intolerance (l. 62)

1 Unduldsamkeit, Intoleranz
2 Unabhängigkeit
3 Nation, Land
4 von Afrikanern (selbst) regiert/bestimmt
5 Monarchie, Königshaus
6 Rohstoffe, Bodenschätze, Ressourcen
7 unternehmen, durchführen
8 durch viele Rassen (Ethnien) gemischt

2 Read the text. Put the info under the right heading – Early days, Changes, or Goals today.

a. Democracy and human rights are now important for the Commonwealth countries.
b. The Commonwealth's first African-ruled state was Ghana.
c. Now the Commonwealth is a lot of different countries that organize activities together.
d. The British Empire got richer and used slavery.
e. The British Commonwealth then became just the 'Commonwealth'.
f. Today they want to fight poverty and intolerance.
g. The first colonies to be independent were 'white'.
h. The idea started in the 19th century.
i. The Commonwealth was only multiracial after India joined.

B Language

1 Find the words/phrases in the texts 1–3 which mean the opposite of

a. different b. in the end c. added d. alone

2 Find the words in the texts 1–3 which have a similar meaning to these words/phrases:

a. free b. country c. the total number of people in a country d. poor living conditions

1, 16

C Listening: Young Commonwealth

1 Before you listen: Read text 4 about the Young Commonwealth Programme. Answer the questions.

a. Where is Vasanti from?
b. What was life like when the British were rulers there?
c. What do member states now try to build?
d. What is the idea of the Commonwealth today? (2 things)
e. What is the CYP and what does it offer to young people?

2 Listen to the rest of the interview with Vasanti. Correct the underlined words or phrases.

a. The people on the Commonwealth Youth Programme are between <u>16 and 30</u>.
b. There are courses at all levels: You can train to become a <u>mechanic</u>.
c. Vasanti wants to do a course in <u>New</u> Development.
d. Volunteers in Chandigarh do street plays or <u>dances</u> in villages.

3 Listen again. Choose an ending to complete each sentence.

a. For the CYP development means more than …
b. In the CYP young people must …
c. Vasanti got interested in the CYP …
d. The goal of their voluntary work is …

1 to inform young people about HIV and AIDS.
2 actively take part in changing society.
3 sending food or doctors to poor countries.
4 when she saw a play which they performed.

D Speaking

1

2

1 Describing

a. Say where you think the volunteers in the photos are. What do you think they're doing? What skills do you think they need?

b. Imagine you'd like to work as a volunteer abroad. Say where you would like to work, what you would like to do and what skills you could offer. Think of one problem which you might have there. Ask about two things you would like to know.

2 Role play

You're interested in working as a volunteer abroad. You call the Emergency Volunteer Service. What do you say?

EVS: Hello, Emergency Volunteer Service. This is Sandy Law speaking. How can I help you?
You: *(Sage deinen Namen. Erzähle, dass du an einem Projekt im Ausland interessiert bist.)*
Sandy: Is there a special country or kind of project which you're interested in?
You: *(Sage, dass du gerne an einem Bauprojekt mitarbeiten möchtest. Erkläre, dass du nicht sicher bist, wohin du gehen sollst.)*
Sandy: Well, we urgently need helpers in Thailand. What skills do you have?
You: *(Erkläre, dass du schon einmal bei einem Bauprojekt geholfen hast und dass du gut mit Holz arbeiten kannst.)*
Sandy: Great! The volunteers in Thailand are needed to rebuild a whole village.
You: *(Drücke dein Entsetzen aus und frage, was passiert ist.)*
Sandy: There was a terrible storm there. They need people to clean up, transport building materials, cook for the workers and build new houses …
You: *(Sage, dass du helfen wirst, da wo die Organisatoren dich brauchen.)*
Sandy: That's good. So, when could you come into the office and fill in the form?
You: *(Frage, ob sie dir die Formulare und Infos per E-Mail schicken könnte.)*
Sandy: Well, you'll find the form and further info on our website. Just fill in the form and send it to us … Oh, and I nearly forgot: A doctor must check you, too.
You: *(Sage, dass du sofort zum Arzt gehen wirst. Sage auch, dass du versuchen wirst, alles so schnell wie möglich zu erledigen. Vergiss nicht, dich höflich zu verabschieden.)*

E Mediation and communication

You are in England, at the Commonwealth Museum, with your parents. They see a brochure on the Commonwealth Games and are interested, but their English isn't very good. Try to answer their questions in German.

The Commonwealth of Nations presents:

The "Green Games"
3 – 14th October

Opening ceremony at the Jawaharlal Nehru Stadium, Delhi

DELHI 2010
XIX COMMONWEALTH GAMES
COME OUT AND PLAY

INDIA PLAYS HOST

For the first time ever India is playing host to the Games and we plan to make this an event you'll never forget!

OUR GUESTS

85 Commonwealth members across the world are registered to take part in the Games – England, Scotland, Wales, N. Ireland, Canada, Australia and many African states like Kenya and Zambia, to name just a few.

SPORTS OF ALL KINDS

There are all kinds of sports events (17 in all) like athletics[1], boxing, badminton, cycling[2], gymnastics, hockey, table tennis, weightlifting[3] and shooting. But there are also special sports such as bowls[4], rugby 7s and netball, which are mainly[5] played in countries that are Commonwealth member states.

PAST GAMES

The 1st Commonwealth Games were held in Hamilton, Canada, in 1930 (then[6] called the British Empire Games). The Games take place every 4 years. The last event was held in Melbourne, Australia in 2006. The next proud host will be Scotland in 2014.

WHY THE "GREEN GAMES"?

We want to make sure that the environment is not damaged through the Games. So we are partners of the United Nations Environment Programme (UNEP). For example, we've pledged to

- make Delhi's public transport system better (e.g. solar panels & rainwater collectors at each bus station),
- start a tree-growing campaign,
- build our Games Village in an environmentally friendly way,
- make sure the Games Village uses renewable[7] energy.

a. Was ist das für eine Sportveranstaltung?
b. Wer kann daran teilnehmen?
c. Was für Sportarten sind vertreten?
d. Wann gab es die erste Veranstaltung dieser Art?
e. Wo war das letzte Event?
f. Warum spricht man von „Green Games"?

F Writing

1 Skills

Collect important ideas about the Commonwealth in a mind map (how it grew, who belongs to it, what it stands for, programmes and events which they have …).

2 A magazine article

Use your mind map and write a short report (60–80 words) about the Commonwealth for an international youth magazine.

[1]athletics [əθ'letɪks] – *Leichtathletik*, [2]cycling ['saɪklɪŋ] – *Radfahren*, [3]to lift [lɪft] – *heben*, [4]bowls [bəʊlz] – *Bowling*, [5]mainly ['meɪnli] – *hauptsächlich*, [6]then [ðen] – *damals*, [7]renewable [rɪ'nju:əbl] – *erneuerbar*

Topic 3 Our world in our hands

1

Food flown into the UK from abroad

2

Local, organic products in England

1. Work with a picture: Choose one photo (1–6). Say why you think the photographer took the photo. (article/leaflet/newspaper report/advert/…).
2. Compare your photo from Ex. 1 with the photo beside it. Say something about where they were taken and what they show. Explain the contrast between the two pictures.
3. Look at all the photos and link each of them to the title of this topic. Think about buildings, natural resources, food production, … . (→ p. 24/ex. 1, 2)

3 *Young men using water in New York City*
4 *Women carrying water in Ethiopia, East Africa*
5 *Lots of lights at Christmas time in Seattle*
6 *Building eco houses in Wales*

A Changing our life style

How big is *your* footprint?

When you walk you produce a footprint. But did you know that you also have a '*carbon* footprint'? The 'carbon' has to do with carbon dioxide (one of the main greenhouse gases). What exactly is this footprint and how is it produced? It's the total amount of greenhouse gases that you make yourself. Things that affect your carbon footprint are e.g. where and how you travel, the things that you buy, your daily activities and the way you live. Reports say that each year the UK has a carbon footprint of around 7 tons of carbon dioxide (CO_2) per person! So it's time for us all to teach ourselves a new way of life. Here are some ideas to start with:

Electricity & heating: How much hot water do you use to wash yourself or your clothes? Heating water raises your footprint. Try to use less hot water. Turn down your heating thermostat, change to low energy light bulbs and turn off equipment left on standby. You'll also save a lot of money!

Food and drink: It may seem strange, but even food and drinks increase our carbon footprint: Imagine the greenhouse gases made by transporting food and bottles of water. Then add the emissions from producing packaging and the plastic bottles and later recycling them! So think before you shop!

Air travel: A good way to reduce your footprint is not to travel by air.

Car: How far you drive, how much fuel your car uses per mile and the number of passengers per trip affects your carbon footprint.

➜ Option 1

B A cartoon: Ways to reduce your carbon footprint

Mrs M.: He told me that he wanted to walk to school …

Mrs B.: Well, that's one way he won't leave a carbon footprint!

⇨ 547560-0006

1 Our environment 5 (→ p. 25/ex. 3)

a) *Before you read: Choose the right answers.*

1. Greenhouse … are bad for our world.

trees • gases • houses • farmers

2. A carbon footprint is … .

a foot mark on black sand • a text which you print out • the effect that you have on the environment • a kind of passport

b) *Read text A. Were you right?*

c) *Make a grid with all the things that increase emissions and ways to reduce them.*

increase	reduce
…	…

1,17

2 Let's listen: Don't be so lazy! 13 15 (→ p. 25/ex. 5)

a) *Ben wants his brother's help. Listen and find out where Ben is in each dialogue.*

1. In part A Ben is at …
   a. school b. home c. a party.
2. In part B he's in a …
   a. shop b. lesson c. car.

b) *Listen again and match the sentence parts.*

	+	
1. Terry said that the shops were 2. Katie said that they still had to get 3. Ben asked if the packets were 4. Katie said that they didn't want	+	a. OK. b. all that packaging. c. just down the road. d. the apples.

 Für Topic 3 brauchst du: Pronomen → Ov 8, G 3 • Indirekte Rede → G 1–2

C What's new on the job market?

GLOBAL WARMING BRINGS NEW JOBS

By now most of us have heard about environmental changes that are caused by global warming. People who want to stop these changes are 'going eco' or 'going green'. This means for example that their homes are low energy and their cars are environmentally friendly so that they can reduce CO_2 emissions.

'Safe' progress means big business!
But global warming has its sunny side: There are more jobs because of it. Eco technology is trying to make 'safe' progress. And it's now big business!

Job centres worldwide report
We e-mailed job centres around the world to get a better idea. They all reported that they needed people who worked directly for the environment – like rangers, zookeepers and technical assistants.

More traditional jobs turn eco
Eco products mean jobs for millions of people, too: designers, food experts, shop assistants, engineers and many others. At the same time most people in more traditional jobs now feel they need training to keep up with eco trends: textile workers, heating engineers, farmers and builders, to name just a few ...

→ Option 2

3 A cartoon: No footprint? 9,12,14 7

a) *Look at the cartoon and its caption (part B). Why do you think the boy is walking on the cars?*
1. He doesn't like riding to school.
2. He can't get through the traffic jam.
3. He thinks it's a good trick.
4. His teacher told him that he had to reduce his carbon footprint.

b) *Do a class survey: Find out how most of you get to school (by car/bus/train/bike, on foot?)*

c) *Discuss which way causes the most/least carbon emissions.*
I think going on/by ... causes ... because ... .

4 Let's talk: Jobs to help the planet – and yourself 5

(→ p. 25/ex. 4)

a) *Before you read part C: Look at the title. Think of one job that global warming brings and describe it.*

b) *Read the text. Correct the underlined words in the sentences below. Take turns and tell your partner.*
1. People are 'going <u>crazy</u>'.
   No, it says that they're 'going eco' or ... .
2. 'Green' and 'eco' describe people who try to <u>increase</u> their CO_2 emissions.
3. There are more jobs because of <u>good heating</u>.
4. Eco technology is trying to make <u>quick</u> progress.
5. Job centres have jobs for people like <u>actors</u>.
6. Eco products mean <u>more food</u> for lots of people.
7. People in traditional jobs feel they need <u>more money</u>.

So what's your excuse?

ALIVE Magazine Special

Healthy for yourself and for the environment

by Jude Keenan

We often find excuses, for example, for eating what we shouldn't eat. There are thousands of diets on the Internet and masses of books about how we can train ourselves not to overeat.

Fruit and vegetables are good for us. Even *young* people know this. But many admit that they eat too much sugar and fat although they know that these things can cause heart disease and diabetes. And any kid can tell you that it's not enough to *watch* sport on TV (or even out in the fresh air): It's far better for you to *do* sport yourself!

Japanese seaweed salad

But what if you are eating the 'right' kind of food – is that healthy food really healthy for the environment? Well, if it's not good for the environment then, in the long run, it can't be good for us either.

Let's look at an example: Henry Healthiman trained himself always to eat an apple instead of a chocolate bar in his break. One day someone asked him where the apple came from. What did he answer? He said that it came from the supermarket! Of course, he had no idea of its country of origin. But then, do you know where the fruit that *you* eat comes from?

Our food can come from anywhere on Earth – from the next farm or from countries that are thousands of miles away. You may say that apples from New Zealand, for example, taste better. But they travel a long way to get to you. That adds to global warming and increases your carbon footprint. Will your next New Zealand apple taste as good, now that you know this?

Of course, you need to get the balance right: In huge cities like London or big industrial areas pollution is very high and poisons get into the soil, into our food and even into our water. This could be a good reason for buying food or drinks that come from further away. But how far do you need to go? Well, maybe not as far as the pop star 'Birdie Seed' in the following poem:

Exotic is nice

Pretty Birdie Seed
Only loved to feed
On Japanese seaweed!

To stay healthy and cute
She ordered her fruit
From near and from far.
It came to the star
At the cocktail bar
By ship, plane and car,
Which made the air stink
But she wanted her drink!
Well, all that dirt
Made her lungs hurt
And made her eyes sore.
Now, will she have more?

Exotic is nice,
But it has its price!

Exotic fruit cocktail

Task: To find ways to help yourself and the environment

1 What's healthy? 5 2 (→ p. 26/ex. 6)

a) *Before you read: What's healthy/not so healthy to eat? Talk to your partner. Check if you were right on the Net (search under "healthy eating").*

b) *Read the text. What does Jude Keenan say about diets, fruit and vegetables, sugar and fat? Start like this:* He says that there are … . / He says that … is/are … .

c) *Why does the writer say that healthy food may not really be healthy?*
1. Fat is bad for you. 2. You eat too much of it. 3. Food from far away increases your footprint.

1,18 ### 2 Let's listen: How far do you need to go? 4, 13 2

a) *Read the poem from the article. Check all the new words. Shut your book and listen.*

b) *What does Birdie love to eat? What's in her cocktail drink? What made her lungs hurt?*

c) *Listen again. Then one of you reads the poem aloud but leaves out some of the underlined words. The other keeps his/her book shut and tries to guess the words.*

d) *Do you like Birdie? Why/Why not? Write a short text.*

3 And what about the water you drink? 14 2 (→ p. 26/ex. 7, 8)

a) *Read the brochure about bottled/tap water. What does it want you to do?*

WHY BOTTLED WATER?
- It's cool, modern and more refreshing.
- It's handy: Just drink and throw away the bottle.
- It's healthier than drinks like coke.
- It's a huge industry that gives people jobs.
- It tastes better than tap water.
- One billion people round the world don't have safe tap water. Bottled water could help them.

WHY TAP WATER?
- Tap water is safe – it's tested daily.
- It's up to 500 times cheaper than bottled water.
- Plastic bottles cause mountains of garbage: 60 million a day are thrown away in the US alone.
- A filter (about $9) makes tap water taste better.
- Hundreds of times more greenhouse gases are emitted in producing 1 litre of bottled water.

b) *Which do you think is better – bottled water or tap water? Why? Discuss with your partner.*

It's clear that … • But tap/bottled water is cheaper/more expensive. • It's better/worse for your health/the environment/ … • I don't agree! It's just as safe/tasty/modern as … • But in some places … • Yes, but … • …

c) *Agree on the most convincing argument for tap water/bottled water. Use the phrases in b) and write down the reasons for your choice.*

4 Presentation: A survey 9, 12 (→ p. 27/ex. 9, 10)

a) *Split the group into two. Each half writes a questionnaire (4–5 questions) on water or on food.*

b) *Do your survey in class and present your results.*

c) *Talk about your results in class. Decide on three things that you could change to help the environment.*

Interested in eco building?

A Jobs on the building site

BUILDING

3.5 Careers in eco building

So you're thinking of a job in eco building? Any building project will involve lots of workers in different jobs: from architects, construction managers and insulation engineers to bricklayers, roofers, carpenters, electricians and plumbers, heating installers and even gardeners.
So what's different in eco building? And what about the workers on an eco building site? Well, they build in a way which is 'kind' to the environment! You need tools and the same kind of jobs are done – but they have to know about eco technologies in their field. Here are examples of workers on an eco building site:

1 Glaziers put in special double-glazed windows to insulate the building.

2 Installers ('Green' heating engineers) install solar heating systems.

3 Carpenters lay floors made of wood from local forests.

4 Plumbers install water-saving appliances.

5 Electricians install solar cell systems for electricity.

6 Gardeners plan an eco-friendly garden.

B An eco house

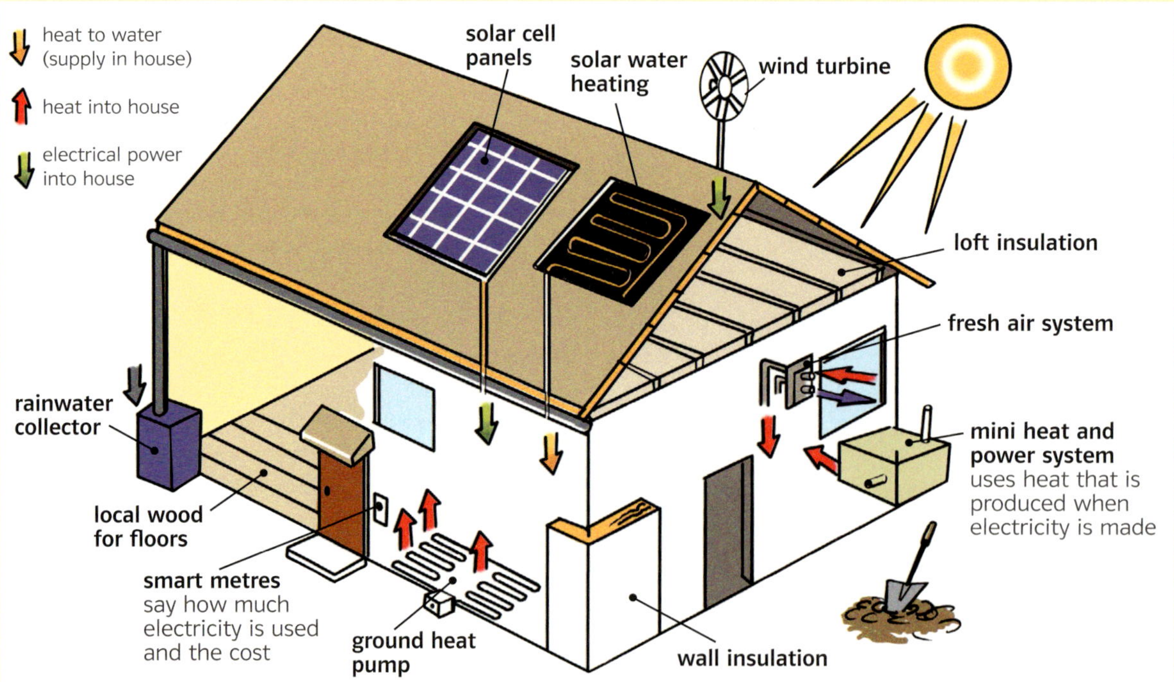

Task: To choose an eco career

1 Careers for the environment 1 2

a) *Before you read: Look at the list of careers in the box. Look up the ones that you don't know.*

b) *Which of the jobs could be jobs for people who actively want to protect the environment? Make a list and add to it if you can. Compare your lists.*

park ranger • shop assistant • hairdresser • receptionist • builder • computer technician • town planner • diver • pilot • painter • digger • musician • engineer • astronaut • lorry driver • advertising agent • farmer • caretaker • politician • mechanic • cook • architect • …

2 Jobs in building 5 5 (→ p. 28/ex. 11, 12)

a) *Scan text A and pick out the jobs. Add new ones to your list from Ex. 1.*

b) *Now read the text again and find out what makes an eco house different from other houses.*
An eco house … 1. is more interesting. 2. has fewer workers. 3. is friendlier to the environment.

1,19 3 Let's listen: Guess the job 13 15 (→ p. 28/ex. 13)

a) *Five people are talking about their work. Listen and find out what each one's job is.*

b) *Listen again. Write a sentence to explain why you think this. Use the phrases in the box.*
I think he/she's a … because he/she says that … .

works outside/inside • loves wood • installs water-saving appliances • plants trees • walls are the most important product • can soon install solar heating systems • makes homes look nice outside • some systems use rainwater for toilets

c) *Which job is most interesting? Why?*
Example: … is interesting because you can …/I love working … .

4 An energy saving home

a) *Look at the workers in A and match each job with a part of the eco house (part B).*

b) *Read the eco rules on the right. Which one is important for which worker on the job in the house?*

c) *Look at the house and the rules again. What haven't the workers done yet?*
The (glaziers/installers/…) haven't … yet.

- Use **insulation** to control heat loss (doors, double-glazed windows, walls, roof).
- Use as little **water** as possible (rainwater in the garden; special plumbing).
- Use renewable (e.g. solar) **energy systems** for heating/hot water.
- Use natural light & low energy bulbs for **lighting**.
- Cut down on **electrical appliances** where possible (e.g. instead of dryer – space to dry clothes).
- Use natural **materials** (e.g. local wood, not PVC etc.).
- Make sure the **atmosphere is** healthy: The air is fresh & it's not too dry or damp.
- Use waste again (recycling).
- Plant an eco garden.

5 Presentation: A job market 14 3 (→ p. 29/ex. 14, 15)

a) *Write job names from Ex. 2a) onto cards. On larger cards, write your job descriptions.*

b) *One half of the class gets the job description cards. The other half gets the job name cards. Someone from the 'job name' group chooses a name card. One of this group acts it out. The other half of the class looks for the card with the correct job description and reads it out.*

c) *The class says what they like/don't like about each job and then votes on the best performance.*

1 Transport and electricity

a) *Put words from the box under the correct heading and make two lists. Some words or phrases can go under both.*

low energy bulbs • greenhouse gases • cars • fuel • carbon dioxide • distances • passengers • hot water • thermostat • equipment • standby • lorries • air travel • goods • carbon footprint • …

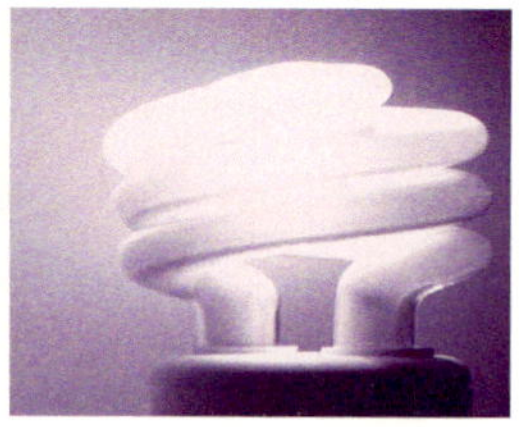

Transport & travel	Heating & electricity
cars …	low energy bulbs …

b) *Add more words to the lists.*

2 Climate changes bring other changes

Choose the right adjective and complete the sentences.

1. Environmental changes are caused by (*goblin/global/gold*) warming.
2. People are building (*low/saving/sunny*) energy homes because of this problem.
3. But climate changes have their (*funny/sunny/famous*) side, too.
4. Eco technology, for example, is trying to make (*quick/slow/safe*) progress.
5. And now there are many (*new/temporary/boring*) jobs in this field.
6. So it has become a (*big/natural/digital*) business.
7. Lots of teachers are now needed by (*tourist/language/job*) centres.
8. And many people feel they need training to keep up with (*fashion/eco/political*) trends.

3 Rhyming words

Read the lines about the environment. Complete each one with a rhyming word from the box.

try • lane • fair • fourteen • air • buy • rain • lie • train • stink • seaweed • bread • plane • seed • cry • pain • pear • die • drink

Do you really need
Japanese …?

Ask what – and why
Before you go & …!

THINK
about what
YOU …!

Hey, why not
Take the train –
Instead of
Taking a …?

DON'T YOU EVEN CARE
ABOUT POISONS IN
THE …?

4 An eco home

a) *Pick out the phrases in the box which go with the word eco home and start a mind map.*

double-glazed windows • no/bad insulation • low energy bulbs • natural materials • PVC • air fresh • air very dump • solar energy • renewable energy systems • traditional heating systems • uses lots of water • collects rainwater • recycling of waste • good use of natural lighting

b) *Add to your mind map.*

c) *Draw your 'dream' eco home and use your list to label it.*

OPTION 1

✔ … discuss healthy living.

a) *Name three things you can do to stay healthy.*

b) *Think of two excuses that you use when you eat or do things which are unhealthy.*

✔ … talk about yourself, your friends and the environment. G3

Choose the correct reflexive pronouns to complete the text.

My mum always makes (1) sandwiches to take to work and she tells me I should at least eat some fruit. But I never make (2) breakfast. I often buy (3) a bagel on the way to school. I think it's OK for you to buy (4) chocolate – my friends and I do that sometimes. But we keep (5) fit with sport and enjoy (6) at the same time! One of my friends, Tom, doesn't do much to keep (7) fit. He and his mate get (8) computer games and they play them all weekend. But at least he rides his bike to school like us. It's important for us all to teach (9) about what's healthy for the *environment*, too.

myself (2 x)
yourself
himself
herself
ourselves (3 x)
themselves

OPTION 2

✔ … report on eco jobs.

a) *What are the people's jobs?*

1

2

3

4

b) *Match the jobs with a statement about what could be eco about each one.*

1. All the kitchen appliances run on solar cells and we recycle waste, of course!
2. I think people still need cars. So we need to design low energy cars that don't cause pollution.
3. People don't think! They disturb plants and animals even in protected areas like this one.
4. We only sell healthy products which come from local farms.

c) *Report what the workers said to a friend.* The … said that all the kitchen … . Ov1–2

✔ … describe your 'dream' job.

What things are important for you in a job? Choose three things. The ideas in the box can help you.

work inside/outside • (not) high up • be your own boss • teamwork • friendly boss • good pay • work with your hands • permanent contract • (no) travel • work with tools • …

(→ p. 30/ex. 16; p. 31/ex. 17)

Making water safe to drink (→ pp. 32–34)

A straw that kills bacteria as you drink

Have you ever been thirsty[1] – and *really* needed something to drink? What did you do? You probably turned on a tap or opened a bottle. Well, imagine living somewhere where there are no taps or bottles – and very little water to drink. And the water that exists is full of highly dangerous bacteria. So if you drink it, you'll probably become very sick and even die! Sadly, this is what it's like for millions of people in the world today.

There are several effective ways to make water safe for drinking (e.g. filters) but they are often expensive. Scientists, voluntary organisations, some companies and governments are trying to develop cheaper alternatives. Here are two more recent[2] technologies for water purification[3]:

The first method is simple to use. It's a kind of 'personal water filter' – a big, fat straw[4] which you can wear on a string around your neck[5]. Just sip the water up through the straw! As you drink, the filters inside remove[6] or kill 99% of the bacteria, viruses etc. in the water. Then, to keep the straw clean, you blow air back through it after use. One personal filter lasts for about 700 litres, which is enough for an adult for a year (and up to two years for a child). And it costs about $3.00 – which is one disadvantage[7]: Three dollars may sound cheap (about the price of a coffee in Europe), but in countries where people only earn a dollar a day, it's very expensive!

Another invention for water purification is SODIS (**so**lar water **dis**infection). This is a cheap way of getting larger amounts of clean household[8] water supplies. UV light from the sun kills off bacteria. So by leaving water in transparent plastic or glass bottles in the sun dangerous bacteria in the water gets destroyed. The use of *transparent* bottles and the length[9] of time the bottles are kept in the sun are important factors in this method – the[10] cloudier and cooler the weather is, the[10] longer it takes! Six hours of sunlight are the minimum needed for safe results. WHO (World Health Organisation) suggests SODIS as a safe method for household water purification. Organisations used this technology successfully in the 2004 tsunami disaster in Southeast Asia to make contaminated water supplies safe to drink.

A different kind of 'solar panel' – SODIS in Southeast Asia

[1]thirsty ['θɜ:sti] – *durstig,* [2]more recent [mɔ: 'ri:snt] – *neuer,* [3]purification [ˌpjʊərɪfɪ'keɪʃn] – *Reinigung,* [4]straw [strɔ:] – *Trinkhalm,* [5]neck [nek] – *Hals,* [6]to remove [rɪ'mu:v] – *beseitigen,* [7]disadvantage [ˌdɪsəd'vɑ:ntɪdʒ] – *Nachteil,* [8]household ['haʊshəʊld] – *Haushalts-,* [9]length [leŋθ] – *Länge,* [10]the … the [ðə ... ðə] – *je … desto*

A Reading

1 Before you read: Look at the words in the box which are new but similar to German words (or other English words) you know. Guess their meaning.

bacteria (l. 5) • filter (l. 10) • method (l. 14) • disinfection (l. 25) • transparent (l. 28) • plastic (l. 28) • factor (l. 31) • contaminated (l. 39)

2 Match the words with the correct meaning.

a. You put water through this to get it clean.
b. This is when something is dirty.
c. These are very tiny life forms.
d. This is one important point or aspect.
e. This is the way something is done.
f. If you can see through something, then it's this.
g. It's usually a softer material than glass.
h. This is a way of making something clean.

3 Skim the text and find the best ending for the sentence:

The flyer is about a campaign[1] …
a. … informing people about the importance of water and ways to make it safe to drink.
b. … to teach people traditional methods of getting water out of the ground in hot countries.
c. … against methods of water purification which cause environmental disasters.

4 Read the text carefully and correct the underlined words in the sentences.

a. A special straw is a recent technology in water <u>transport</u>.
b. But this method is too <u>difficult</u> to use in poorer countries.
c. An advantage[2] of SODIS is that it's a cheap way of getting clean household <u>straws</u>.
d. An important factor for this method is the type of <u>bacteria</u> used.

B Language

Find the word or phrase in the text with the same or a similar meaning.

a. other possible ways b. something which keeps you alive c. terrible event

1, 20 ## C Listenin: Wells[3] and rigs[4]

1 Tanya Danes, a volunteer, is talking about drilling[5] wells for water. Listen and find the right answers.

a. Tanya is from …	1 Canada.	2 Ghana.	3 a village.
b. She now works in …	1 Canada.	2 Ghana.	3 a village.
c. She has been there for …	1 three weeks.	2 a few days.	3 many years.
d. Tanya's organisation has already built …	1 800 wells.	2 many new villages.	3 88 wells.
e. The price for one well was …	1 $ 30.	2 $ 800.	3 $ 7,000.

2 Before you listen look at the box of problems that a volunteer may have abroad. Which three problems does Tanya talk about?

the weather is too hot • can't speak the language • has to drink bottled water • feels lonely • has to work with very old equipment • gets ill • doesn't like the food

3 Now listen again and check your answers.

[1]campaign [kæm'peɪn] – *Kampagne,* [2]advantage [əd'vɑːntɪdʒ] – *Vorteil,* [3]well [wel] – *Bohrloch, Brunnen,* [4]rig [rɪg] – *Bohrvorrichtung,* [5]to drill [drɪl] – *bohren*

D Speaking

1

"Bad water kills more children than war."

2

"The water with all the answers."

1 Describing

a. Look at the two posters. Make a few notes on what is similar and what is different about them. Decide what each poster is advertising[1] or campaigning[2] for/against.

b. Choose one the posters and look at these captions. Which one do you think matches your poster best? Discuss with a partner.

Die with or die without? • The art of smart drinking • A shot of contaminated water • Bad water kills • Cool & trendy art: A bottle of Smart • For a start – drink Smart

c. What is good about the poster that you chose? Would you support the campaign/buy the product/...? Use your notes from 1 a. and explain why/why not.

2 Role play

Someone stops you in the street and asks you to give some money to a charity.

You: *(Frage höflich, für welche Organisation er das Geld sammelt.)*
Man: The organisation is called 'WaterAid'. Here's one of our brochures for you ...
You: *(Bedanke dich. Sage, dass du den Namen schon irgendwo gehört hast und dass du gerne mehr darüber erfahren möchtest.)*
Man: Well, you know, it's 'World Water Day' today. And we're a big charity organisation. We help people in poorer countries to get access to clean drinking water.
You: *(Frage, ob sie Wasser in Flaschen dorthin schicken.)*
Man: Well, no, of course not. That's not the answer! We offer technical training so people there can improve the quality of their water themselves.
You: *(Frage, ob es nicht Gebiete gibt, in denen die Leute wenig Wasser haben. Frage, was WaterAid in solchen Gebieten macht.)*
Man: Some of the money pays for drilling wells. But you still have to get the well water clean.
You: *(Bedanke dich für die Informationen. Sage, dass du WaterAid etwas/kein Geld geben möchtest. Erkläre, warum du das (nicht) tust. Verabschiede dich.)*

[1]to advertise ['ædvətaɪz] – *werben*, [2]to campaign [kæm'peɪn] – *kämpfen*

E Mediation and communication

You find some information in German for a school project on SODIS. Your English exchange partner is interested in how the method works, but his/her German isn't very good. Answer his/her questions.

Was bedeutet „Solar-Desinfektion"?

Solare Trinkwasser Desinfektion (SODIS) ist ein Wasseraufbereitungsverfahren, das die UV-Strahlung der Sonne nutzt, um Keime bzw. gefährliche Bakterien im Wasser abzutöten. Eine sichere Wasserquelle durch SODIS kann Leben retten, Voraussetzung ist allerdings die korrekte Anwendung.

1. Nur saubere, nicht beschädigte (speziell hierfür geeignete) PET-Flaschen benutzen.
2. Flaschen mit dem kontaminierten Wasser füllen und fest verschließen.
3. Die Flaschen sollten mindestens 6 Stunden in der Sonne liegen. Bei sehr wolkigen Wetterbedingungen kann es bis zu 2 Tagen dauern, bis alle Keime abgetötet sind.
4. Das saubere Wasser sollte immer nur in PET- oder Glasflaschen gelagert werden.
5. Nur aus sauberen Gläsern bzw. direkt aus der Flasche trinken.

Der Vorteil an dieser Methode ist, dass sie relativ leicht durchzuführen ist: Man benötigt weder kostspielige Geräte noch teure Arbeitskräfte.
Vor allem in Ländern mit viel Sonne funktioniert SODIS hervorragend. In Gebieten, in denen ungünstige Wetterverhältnisse herrschen, ist dieses Verfahren jedoch nicht zu empfehlen. Die Methode ist nicht für die chemische Reinigung und auch nicht für **sehr** trübes Wasser geeignet. Nicht ganz durchsichtige Flaschen könnten für die UV-Strahlung der Sonne nicht durchlässig genug sein, was eine nicht ausreichende Desinfizierung zur Folge hätte. Darüber hinaus besteht bei nicht geeigneten Flaschen (z.B. PVC-Flaschen) die Gefahr, dass Plastik in winzigen Mengen ins Wasser gelangt, was für Menschen bedenklich sein könnte.

a. What does SODIS use for disinfection?
b. What do you have to be careful about?
c. How long does the disinfection take?
d. What are the bottles in the pictures made of?
e. Are there any bottles that you shouldn't use?

F Writing

1 Skills

Think about what we use water for, where it's wasted and how we can save water.
Think of problems we and other people could have. Collect your ideas in a mind map.

2 A flyer

You want to help with a campaign called 'Water means life' at your school/neighbourhood/town.
Use your ideas from part 1 and write a text (50 – 80 words) for a handout[1] to inform pupils/households about the campaign.

[1]handout ['hændaʊt] – *Informationsmaterial*

1,21–24 Deportation[1] at breakfast

▶ You can use a dictionary if you don't understand some of the words.

1 Before you read

a) *Look at the title and the pictures on the opposite page. What could the story be about? What do you think?*

The signs on the windows lured[2] me inside. For a dollar I could get eggs, toast, and potatoes. The place looked better than most – family-run[3] and clean. The signs were neat[4]. The paper had yellowed some, but the black letters were clear. A green-and-white awning[5] was over the door, where the name 'Clara's' was written. Inside, the place looked old but friendly. The air smelled fresh, not of burnt oil. The menu was written on a board. It was short and clear. It showed the kinds of toast you could choose from.

Because I was alone, I sat at the counter[6], leaving the empty tables free for other customers that might come in. At the time, business was quiet. Only two tables had customers at them, and I was alone at the counter. But it was still early – not yet seven-thirty.

Behind the counter was a short man with dark black hair, and a beard. He was dressed all in chef's white – but he had no hat. He had a strong accent. The name 'Javier' was written on his shirt.

I ordered coffee, and asked for a minute to choose between the breakfast special for a dollar and the cheese omelette for $1.59. I ordered the omelette. The coffee was hot, strong, and fresh. I opened my newspaper on the counter and sipped at the coffee as Javier went to cook my meal.

b) *Which is correct? Javier …*

1. is a customer.
2. works behind the counter.

The eggs were on the grill, the bread was inside the toaster, when the authorities[7] came in. They grabbed Javier quickly and without a word, pushing his hands behind his back. He, too, said nothing. He did not protest, and they pushed him out the door and into their waiting car.

c) *Why do you think Javier is taken away?*

1. He's a criminal.
2. He's an illegal immigrant.

On the grill, my eggs were cooking. I looked around for another employee – maybe out back somewhere, or in the bathroom. I leaned over the counter and called for someone. No one answered. I looked behind me toward the tables. Two old men sat at one; two old women at the other. The two women were talking. The men were reading the newspaper. They had not noticed Javier's exit.

I could smell my eggs starting to burn. I wasn't quite sure what to do about it. I thought about Javier and looked at my eggs. After a few minutes, I got up from where I was sitting and went behind the counter.

I grabbed an apron[8], then picked up a flat spoon and turned my eggs. My toast had popped up[9], but it was not browned, so I put it down again. While I was cooking, the two old women came to the counter and asked to pay. I asked what they had had. They seemed surprised that I didn't remember. I checked the prices on the board and added up their order[10].

They paid slowly and went out, leaving me a dollar tip. I took my eggs off the grill and put them onto a clean plate. My toast had come up. I buttered[11] it and put it on my plate beside my eggs. I put the plate at my place at the counter, right next to my newspaper.

[1]deportation [ˌdi:pɔ:'teɪʃn] – *Abschiebung, Abtransport,* [2]to lure [lʊə] – *locken,* [3]family-run ['fæmli ˌrʌn] – *familiengeführt,* [4]neat [ni:t] – *ordentlich,* [5]awning ['ɔ:nɪŋ] – *Markise,* [6]counter ['kaʊntə] – *Theke, Tresen,* [7]authorities [ɔ:'θɒrətiz] – *hier: Grenzpolizei,* [8]apron ['eɪprən] – *Schürze,* [9]to pop up [pɒp‿'ʌp] – *hochspringen,* [10]order ['ɔ:də] – *Bestellung,* [11]to butter ['bʌtə] – *mit Butter bestreichen*

d) *Which is correct? The customers …*
   1. ask where Javier is.
   2. think the narrator[1] works in this place.
   3. complain[2] about the coffee.

As I began to come back from behind the counter to my seat, six new customers came through the door. "Can we pull some tables together?" they asked. "We're all one group." I told them yes. Then they ordered six coffees. I thought of telling them I didn't work there.

But perhaps they were hungry. I gave them their coffee. Their order was simple: six breakfast specials, all with eggs and toast. I got busy. Then the old men came to pay. More new customers began arriving. By eight-thirty, I had my hands full. With this kind of business, I couldn't understand why Javier hadn't some help. Maybe I'd put a 'help-wanted' ad in the newspaper tomorrow. I had never been in the restaurant business. There was no way I could run[3] this place alone.

[adapted from ***Deportation at breakfast*** by Larry Fondation]

2 What do you think?

a) *Why is Javier taken away?*
b) *Why does the narrator go behind the counter?*

3 Two parts 3

a) *Find the turning point[4] in this story and give a title to the parts before and after it.*
b) *Make a flow chart[5] about each part and say what happens in it.*

Flow chart part 1:

Man goes into diner.
↓
He reads the menu.
↓ ↓
He sees … | He smells …

4 The setting 3

a) *Collect information about the diner in a grid. Then draw a simple picture of the place inside.*
b) *Say when and where you think the story happens and why.*

5 Short stories 3

Look at Skill 3 and find important things in 'Deportation at breakfast' which show that it is a short story.

6 Illegal immigration 14

In groups of 4–5 find as much information as you can on illegal immigration in the US (books, newspapers, the Internet …). Why do people immigrate illegally? Start a discussion about the positive and negative aspects of immigration.

[1]narrator [nə'reɪtə] – *Erzähler/in,* [2]to complain [kəm'pleɪn] – *sich beschweren,* [3]to run [rʌn] – *betreiben,* [4]turning point ['tɜ:nɪŋ ˌpɔɪnt] – *Wendepunkt,* [5]flow chart ['fləʊ tʃɑ:t] – *Flussdiagramm*

Topic 4 Choices and decisions

1. Work with a picture: Look at photo 1. Imagine you were in their situation. How would you feel? The words/phrases in the box can help you.

> really awful • very excited • pretty stupid • unhappy/happy • angry with myself • awfully scared • unsure/worried about the future • ...

2. Each of you think of at least two situations where you have to make a big decision about something. Who could give you advice in such situations?

3. a) Look at all the photos. Choose a caption to go with each one.

   b) Do you have the same choices in your country? At what age? Not sure? Look on the Net.

> Training or college? • A partner for life • Choosing a way of life • Getting the right car • Your first job

4. Try to imagine how the young people feel in the photos on the right. Tell your partner. Does he/she feel the same in each situation? What's different? (→ p. 35/ex. 1, 2)

2

3

4

5

⇨ 547560-0007

A When is it legal?

LEGAL AGES

As a teenager you are not quite an adult but you are nearly one. In fact in some countries you can do lots of things an adult can do. You may drive a car or drink. But if you do both, it's most probably illegal – and, of course pretty dangerous, too!

There are lots of other big decisions, e.g. how responsible you are about having sex, which can affect you for the rest of your life.

The table below is an example of the ages at which you can do different things legally in the US:

Legal ages in the US for:

Leaving school	16 – 18*
Employment	14
Having sex	14 – 18*
Marriage	18
Driving a car	14 – 17*
Buying alcohol	21
Smoking	18 – 19*
Voting	18
Responsibility for criminal actions	6 – 10*

* Different states have different laws

'YOU'LL BE STARTING NURSERY SCHOOL SOON DARLING, SO WE NEED TO HAVE THE SEX, DRUGS AND DRINK CHAT...'

⇨ 547560-0008

1 Teenagers and adults 5, 15 5 (→ p. 36/ex. 3)

a) *Read the introduction. What is a teenager according to the text?*
A teenager is …
1. already an adult.
2. quite an adult.
3. nearly an adult.

b) *What examples of decisions that can affect you for the rest of your life are given in the text?*

c) *Imagine you spent three weeks in an American host family last summer. Now you are doing a project on legal ages at school. Ring your guest family to ask about young people's rights. Find out what you can/can't do at your age.*

2 In the US 7

a) *Look at the table. What can you do legally in most states of the US when you're 16?*

b) *Compare legal ages in the US and in your country. (If you are not sure, check the laws for your country on the Internet.) Have you got more/less freedom at 16?*

c) *Say which legal age(s) you (don't) agree with and why.*
I think it's right that you … because … .
I (don't) agree with the age for … because … .

too limiting/liberal • I'd like more freedom • not fair • equal rights • too young/old enough • the age for legal sex should be …

d) *Look at the cartoon. Should parents talk to children about sex? What do you think? Why?*

 Für Topic 4 brauchst du: Adverbien → G 5 • Past perfect → G 4

B Decisions at 16

You have two main choices in the UK.

You can continue schooling:

- ➜ Stay on at your school/go to a different school.
- ➜ Get more GCSEs/other qualifications at a college.
- ➜ Choose a specialist college that offers courses in landscape gardening, art, music, agriculture. Some specialist colleges also have courses for students with special needs or with disabilities.
  Get information about financial support for such courses at www.direct.gov.uk/extrahelp.

You can go for training/work:

- ➜ Do an apprenticeship (on-the-job training) and classes to get qualifications for a specific job.
- ➜ Find a job with training, where the employer organizes the training.
- ➜ Choose a job with time off for further training to improve your employment prospects.
- ➜ Go on a training programme to prepare you for work.
- ➜ Self-employment (rare at the end of Year 11). If you really want to do this, get expert advice first!

www.direct.gov.uk/en/educationandlearning/14to19/options-at16/index.htm

➜ Option 1

C A book cover

Tessa is a pretty normal teenager. She sees the world around her and wants to experience it. That would be no problem if she had all the time in the world. But time is the one thing that she hasn't got. She could live in her own 'inner world' and ignore people who can enjoy life more. Then she'd become really bitter and let her illness control her. Or she could use the time left to make her own dreams come true. It's her choice …

➜ Option 2

3 Let's talk: Different directions 2 (→ p. 36/ex. 4)

a) *Before you read: What will you do when you leave school? Do an apprenticeship/training? In what field? Continue schooling? Ask about your partner's plans. What are your and your partner's hopes and fears? Write a short text.*

b) *Read text B and explain the choices which UK kids have.*

c) *What about the situation in Germany? Do UK kids have any choices which are different from the choices you can make?*

4 Let's listen: Dreams or tragic reality? 13

1, 25 (→ p. 36/ex. 5)

a) *Before you listen: Read text C on the book cover. Why do you think Tessa hasn't got a lot of time? What two things could she do in her situation?*

She could … 1. find more time for problems.
2. let her illness control her.
3. control her illness and get well.
4. make her dreams come true.

b) *If you were Tessa, what would or wouldn't you do?*

c) *Listen to a critic who is talking about 'Before I die'. Why does he want you to read the novel?*

d) *The story is about …*
1. tragic aliens.
2. dramatic scenes.
3. real life.
4. bloody drinks.

Jobs in the car industry

An American company in profile

Automotive companies

> The US > Detroit > GM Motors **> Longbow's**

PROFILE

LONGBOW's Motor Co.

Headquarters: 1599 Boulder Way, Michigan 48905, USA
Chief Executive Officer (CEO): Cavendish Homer Longbow Junior

- HOME
- NEWS
- **PROFILE**
- CAREERS
- INTERNSHIPS
- DEPARTMENTS
  - > Manufacturing
  - > Human Resources
  - > Product Development
  - > Marketing & Sales
  - > IT
  - > Environment & Safety
  - > Finance
  - > PR

Longbow's started in 1910 when James Cavendish Longbow designed one of the first electric vehicles. They were quite popular then but went out of fashion. They're now real vintage cars and we've restored some of them for our museum.
Fifty years later James's great-grandson started a small family business and produced one of the first modern electric-powered cars. The firm grew extremely fast in the 1990s and moved into truck production in 2004.
Now we're the largest US manufacturers of highly modern, electric-powered vehicles – from sports cars to trucks! And we have 12,000 employees in two main sectors:

1. The automotive sector:
We design, develop, manufacture and sell cars and trucks for a worldwide market. Our main car models are 'Swallow' and 'Eagle'. Our trucks are called 'Greenroad'.
We sell cars, trucks and vehicle parts on the US and Canada market as well as all around the world. Our customers include rental, leasing and other companies, and also governments.
We offer other services such as vehicle accessories. And we also repair cars.

2. The financial sector:
We offer help to finance products to special customers and rental companies. We also give loans to dealers who, for example, want to open a salesroom or buy vehicles. We have great insurance services for both dealers and customers.

Task: To choose an internship

1 Car companies 1

a) *Collect names of car models. Choose your favourite one. Say what you like about it.*

lots of different models • environmentally friendly • very fast/extremely comfortable • very little fuel • really cool design • vintage/super modern style • …

b) *Find out more about your favourite model on the Internet.*

1. Who is the CEO of the company?
2. When and where was it founded?
3. Where are the company's headquarters?
4. How many people work there?

2 Jobs in the automotive industry 1 5 (→ p. 37/ex. 6)

a) *Read the company profile and look at the vehicles. Find one piece of info about each one.*

b) *Look at the menu to the left of the profile. Look up the words which you are not sure about.*

3 A summer job 7 3, 13 (→ p. 37/ex. 7; p. 38/ex. 8)

a) *Read which internships Longbow's offers.*

b) *Split the group into three mini groups. Each group chooses one internship job.*

c) *Find out more about your 'job' on the Net. Decide why you would/wouldn't like to do it.*

d) *Write a cover letter and a CV on the computer to apply for an internship.*

Summer Internships at Longbow's
After school go out into the 'real' world!
Do a summer internship at Longbow's Motor Company.
We need young people in these areas:

LONGBOW's Motor Co. Jobs

- **Mechanics in Manufacturing** to help assess damage to accident vehicles, make body shells and vehicle frames or restore vintage cars. You must be reliable and flexible, enjoy team work and love machines!

- **Two Computer Assistants in our IT department** to help computer specialists design new systems and support the ones that already exist in all our departments. Apart from basic computer skills you must have a good grade in Math. And you should be good at communicating.

- **Office Assistants in HR (Human Resources)/Finance/PR (Public Relations) departments.** Good team skills are especially important. You must be able to use modern communication equipment. You'll need good English and skills in organizing.

26 4 Let's listen: Two internships 13 (→ p. 38/ex. 9)

a) *Mel and Abdur are talking about their internship. Listen and say who got which job from Ex. 3a).*

b) *Listen again. Who is happy at Longbow's – Mel or Abdur?*

5 Presentation: A job panel 10, 11 (→ p. 38/ex. 10)

a) *One half of the panel uses Longbow's profile to present the company to the class. The other half then tells the class about the internships in Ex. 3a). All the others each choose an internship.*

b) *Each applicant says why the panel should choose him/her (skills, qualifications, …). The panel chooses the best applicant for each of the three internships.*

An extract from a novel: 'Before I die' *by Jenny Downham (adapte*

1 Before you read: Look at the photos and the title. Say what you already know about the novel.

2 Look at the people in the photos and say what you think could be happening.

3 Look at the box on the right before you start to read.

1. The first time you read the story, you don't have to understand every word to get an idea of what's happening. Read it for fun!
2. Read the story again. This time try to work out new words from the context.
3. Use an English/German dictionary for the words which you can't guess from the context.

Introduction:

Tessa is 16 and has been fighting leukaemia for four years. Now the doctors can't help her any more. So she decides to write a list of things she wants to do before she dies. One of the things on her list was to fall in love for the first time, but it didn't work. Now she feels bitter about life …

A The boy looks surprised when I stick my head over the fence and call him. He's perhaps eighteen, with dark hair and the shadow of a beard.

"Yeah?"

"Can I burn some things on your fire?"

He walks up the path towards me lazily. His hands are dirty and he has bits of leaf in his hair. He doesn't smile.

I lift up the two shoeboxes so he can see them. My best friend Zoey's dress lies across my shoulder like a flag.

"What's in them?"

"Paper mostly. Can I bring them round?"

He shrugs as if he doesn't care, so I walk through our side gate and step over the low wall that stands between the two houses, across his front garden and down the side of his house. He's already there, holding the gate open for me. I hesitate.

"I'm Tessa."

"Adam."

We walk silently down his garden path. I bet he thinks my boyfriend has just chucked me, that these are love letters. I bet he thinks, 'No wonder he dumped her, with that skeleton face and bald head.'

The fire is disappointing when we get there, just a pile of leaves and twigs with a few hopeful flames.

"The leaves were damp," he says. "Paper will get it going again."

I open one of the boxes and tip it upside down.

4 Stop and think: What do you think is in Tessa' shoeboxes? Love letters? Old clothes? Name three more things. Now read on and check if you were right.

B I had been keeping a diary from the day I noticed the first bruise on my spine – till the day, two months ago, when the doctors officially gave up on me. Four years of pathetic optimism burns well. Look at it flare! All the get-well cards I ever received burn and flake to nothing. Over four long years you forget people's names.

There was a nurse who used to draw cartoons of the doctors and put them by the bed to make me laugh. I can't remember her name either. Was it Louise? The fire spits, embers spark away into the trees.

"I'm unburdening myself," I tell Adam.

But I don't think he's listening. He's pulling some bramble slowly across the grass towards the fire.

It's the next box I hate the most. Me and Dad had often gone through it together while I was in hospital. 'You will get well again,' he had said as he ran a finger over a photo of me in school uniform on my first day at school. 'Here's one of you in Spain,' he had also said. 'Do you remember?' In that picture I looked thin and brown and hopeful. It was when a boy had whistled at me on the beach. My dad took the photo just then and said I'd never want to forget my first whistle.

But I do.

I suddenly want to run home and get more stuff. My clothes, my books.

C I say, "Next time you have a fire, can I come over again?"

Adam stands on one end of the bramble with his boot and folds the other end into the fire.

He says, "Why do you want to throw it all away?"

I squash the dress into a small ball. I throw it at the fire. I think it looks light before it even reaches the flames. Now it's up in the air and then it begins to melt into plastic.

"Dangerous dress," Adam says, and he looks right at me, as if he knows something.

All matter is made of particles. The more solid something is, the closer the particles are held together. People are solid, but inside is liquid. I think perhaps if you stand too close to a fire, it can change the particles of your body because I feel strangely dizzy and like I had no weight.

I'm not exactly sure what's wrong with me – maybe it's because I haven't been eating well – but I seem to not be grounded inside my body. The garden turns suddenly bright.

Like the sparks from the fire, which fall down softly onto my hair and clothes, the law of gravity says that all falling bodies must fall to the ground.

5 What will happen next? What do you think? The phrases in the box can help you. Read on and find out if you were right.

I think Tessa/Adam/they/ … will … .

fall into fire • save her • give her something to eat/drink • become friends • be angry • go to hospital • kiss each other • hold hands • …

D I'm surprised to find myself lying on the grass and looking up at Adam's face with clouds all around his head. I can't work it out for a minute.

"Don't move," he says. "I think you fainted."

I try to speak, but my tongue feels slow and it's so much easier to lie here.

"Are you diabetic? Do you need sugar? I've got a can of Coke here if you want some."

He sits down next to me, waits for me to sit up and then hands me the drink. My head buzzes as the sugar hits my brain. How light I feel, more ghostly than before, but so much better. We both look at the fire. The stuff from my boxes has all burned away – even the boxes themselves. The dress has turned to air. The ashes are still hot though, bright enough to attract a stupid moth. It crackles as its wings turn to dust. We both watch the space where it was.

I say, "You do a lot of gardening, don't you?"

"I like it."

"I watch you. Through my window, when you're digging and stuff."

He looks startled. "Do you? Why?"

"I like watching you."

He frowns, as if he's trying to work that out, seems about to speak for a moment, but looks away instead, his eyes travelling the garden.

"I'm planning a vegetable patch in that corner," he says. "Peas, lettuce, runner beans. Everything really. It's for my mum more than me."

"Why?"

He shrugs, looks up at the house as if talking about her might bring her to the window. "She likes gardens."

"What about your dad?"

"No. It's just me and my mum."

I notice some blood on the back of his hand. He sees me looking and wipes it away on his jeans.

"I should probably get on," he says. "Will you be all right? You can keep the Coke if you want."

He walks next to me as I make my way slowly up the path. I'm very happy that my photos and diary are burned, that Zoey's dress has gone. It feels as if different things will happen. I turn to Adam at the gate.

I say, "Thank you for helping."

He says, "At any time."

He has his hands in his pockets. He smiles and then looks away, down at his boots. But I know he sees me.

Task: To analyse an extract from a novel

1 The setting 2 (→ p. 39/ex. 11)

Which photo best matches the place where Adam and Tessa meet for the first time? Why do you think so?

1

2

2 Characters

2 (→ p. 39/ex. 12)

a) *Scan the parts of the story and make a list of people Tessa and Adam talk or think about. Which sentence goes with which person/people?*

1. This person tried to make Tessa laugh when she was in hospital.
2. This person likes gardens.
3. Tessa throws this person's dress into the fire.
4. Adam says this person isn't in his family.
5. This person took a photo of Tessa on the beach.
6. This person was on the beach, too.
7. These people gave up on Tessa two months ago.

b) *Make a list of things you know about Tessa and Adam – the way they look, what they say and do, how they react to others, … .*

3 The storyline

2, 8

a) *Put the following sentences in the right order and get the storyline.*

1. Tessa thinks she'll fall like the sparks from the fire.
2. Tessa meets her neighbour Adam for the first time.
3. He helps Tessa and offers her a drink.
4. She wants to burn stuff on a fire in Adam's garden.
5. Tessa goes home again.
6. As they watch the fire, Tessa begins to feel dizzy.
7. As Tessa burns her things, she remembers a time when she was still optimistic.
8. She faints and Adam is worried about her.
9. Before Tessa leaves, she thanks Adam.

b) *Find lines in parts A and B which tell you that Tessa is not optimistic any more. Which lines tell you that she's worried about Adam's opinion of her?*

c) *Read parts C and D again. How does Tessa and Adam's relationship develop? Choose two answers.*

1. They're both glad when Tessa leaves.
2. Adam and Tessa start to feel comfortable with each other.
3. They slowly get interested in each other.
4. Tessa begins to hate Adam because he's not friendly to her.

d) *Each pair chooses one of the parts A, C or D and prepares it as a dialogue. Practise it with your partner before you act it out in your group. Why do you think there is no dialogue in part B?*

4 The point of view

2 (→ p. 40/ex. 13)

Who tells us the story? Who else could have told the story? Say why you think the author chose this perspective.

5 Presentation: A review

11, 12 (→ p. 40/ex. 14)

a) *Split the group into three. Each mini group informs the class about a different aspect – the background/ setting, the storyline or the characters. Use Ex. 1–3 to help you. Present your info in a suitable way, e.g.:*

- Give an introductory talk and show the class a large picture of the setting.
- Act your dialogues for the storyline.
- Design a 'characters' poster. Put the names close/far from each other to show their relationship.

b) *After the presentation find out how many in the class would like to know more about Tessa's story.*

c) *Would this book be good as a film? What does the class think? Take a vote on it.*

1 Odd one out

a) *Find the one word or phrase which doesn't fit in the group.*

1. drinking alcohol – voting – marriage – criminal responsibility – souvenirs
2. different schooling – college – village – training – employment – internship
3. dreams – experiences – problems – inner world – relationships – government – choices
4. art – landscape gardening – agriculture – smoking – music – computers – business
5. employment – volleyball – employee – employer – job prospects – qualifications

b) *Choose the correct heading from the box for each group.*

international sports • world of work • parents' opinions • personal life • legal age • equipment • college courses • fashion • choices after school • the media

2 Departments

Match the jobs with the departments. Some jobs can go in more than one department.

mechanic • product research assistant • financial adviser • PR manager • careers officer • secretary • marketing assistant • computer assistant • sales manager • caretaker • product designer • safety officer • legal adviser • advertising assistant • environmental scientist • nurse/doctor

Manufacturing • Finance • Human Resources • IT • Product Development • Marketing & Sales • PR • Environment & Safety • Legal Department

3 Story words

Find the right word to complete the sentences.

1. The different people in the story are the … .
2. The writer of a story is known as the … .
3. A book which has one long story is called a … .
4. The way a person in the story sees events is his/her … .
5. The events that happen in a story are called the … .
6. The place(s) in a story is/are part of the … .
7. What people say in the story (in direct speech) is a … .
8. What is written about a film or a story in a magazine is called a … .
9. The name of a story is its … .
10. The title of a book is on its … .
11. Someone who writes about a film or a story in a magazine is a … .

title • point of view • cover • critic • novel • author • review • dialogue • storyline • characters • setting

OPTION 1

✔ … talk about choices in the UK at 16.

a) *What are the two directions into which British pupils can go at 16?*

b) *Name two choices in each of the directions in a).*

✔ … decide about an internship. G5

a) *Choose the right adverb and complete the text on an advert for an internship.*

I think the company sounds (*pretty/always*) good. My dad says that they're (*usually/really*) modern. Also, they make cars that go (*happily/extremely*) fast. And as you know, (*so/really*) fast cars are my big hobby!
For this internship it's (*especially/well*) important to have (*quite/openly*) good marks in Math. So that's OK for me. The advert also says that they're looking for (*carefully/very*) reliable young people who are also (*really/never*) flexible. Well, maybe I should apply. What do you think?

b) *Would you do an internship in an automotive company? Give two reasons for your choice.*

OPTION 2

✔ … understand how some ill people feel.

a) *Think of someone you know who is very ill. What is your impression of them? Do they look/act the same as before they got ill? What is different?*

b) *What advice would you give to other people who know that person, too? The ideas in the box can help you. Start like this:* I'd advise other people (not) to … .

ask what's wrong • watch him/her • act normally • offer help •
disturb him/her • visit him/her • …

✔ … decide what is really important to you in life.

Write a list of three things that you want to do before you are 21. Which is most important to you? Which is least important? Who or what could help you to do these things?

✔ … analyse an extract from a novel. G4

a) *Which of the pictures is a scene from the extract? Who are the characters? Where are they? What had happened before?*

1

2

3

b) *What did/didn't you like about the story? Write a short e-mail (20–30 words) and send it to a friend.*

(→ p. 41/ex. 15; p. 42/ex. 16)

STYLE and colours – what do they say about you?

(→ pp. 43–45)

Styles can be very different: sporty, elegant, trendy, business-like, playful[1], romantic and even shocking! You can choose one or the other or mix styles to give the impression you want. One important aspect of your 'style' is the clothes you wear. But colours are important, too.

"I'm calm." Blue gets the opposite reaction to red. It seems suitable for interviews as it gives the impression of a good working atmosphere.

"I'm alive and well!" People in this colour like to make others smile. They're also enterprising. Orange is full of energy. It attracts attention[2] but doesn't 'shout out' as much as red!

"I'm friendly!" This is also a romantic colour as it's a sweeter, softer version of red. Some people think it is only a colour for women but it also goes in and out of fashion for men, too.

"I'm timeless[3]!" Black can be elegant as it makes people look less heavy. It can also give an impression of mystery or power. In many countries it is the colour of death.

"I feel strong!" This colour attracts attention and gives a feeling of energy. It's not a colour to wear at an interview, or when you want to discuss a problem calmly.

"I feel positive!" This colour gives others the impression that you have an open mind and care about detail[3].

"I feel fresh and clean!" People wear this colour to keep cool in hot weather. Or when they marry. But in some societies they wear white when someone dies.

"I'm balanced[4]." Green is a warm and a cool colour. It makes people feel less nervous. That's why walls in hospitals are often light green. Green is good for the eyes.

Matching or Contrasting[5] Colours?

Of course colours can be mixed and matched. Or you may even use shocking contrasts! In certain[6] situations, like an interview, you have no real choice. You have to dress suitably. And that's when the colour(s) which we choose may be most important …

… Jobs & Interviews:

In some jobs there is a dress code – rules about what to wear. But if there isn't one, you should still think about how to dress as[7] clothes and colours can say a lot about you and your personality. And for a job interview you should dress a bit better than you would as an employee. So find out before your interview if the company has a dress code, e.g. formal – suit and tie[8], or not quite so formal. It may help to watch employees as they arrive for work. And if you're not sure, cover[9] tattoos and take off body jewellery for your interview.

Dress code checklist

- The clothes you wear should match your job.
- Your clothes, hair and shoes should be clean, sensible and neat[10]. You may have to tie[11] long hair back (lab or technical assistant, catering, etc.)
- Make-up shouldn't be overdone.
- Hats, headscarves[12] or caps are not worn in most jobs (except for religious traditions).
- You may need safety clothes, helmets, gloves, or glasses.

Remember: You never get a second chance to make a first impression!

[1]playful ['pleɪfl] – *spielerisch,* [2]attention [ə'tenʃn] – *Aufmerksamkeit,* [3]timeless ['taɪmləs] – *zeitlos,* [4]balanced ['bælənst] – *ausgeglichen,* [5]contrasting [kən'trɑːstɪŋ] – *kontrastierend,* [6]certain ['sɜːtn] – *gewisse,* [7]as [æz] – *weil,* [8]tie [taɪ] – *Krawatte,* [9]to cover ['kʌvə] – *abdecken,* [10]neat [niːt] – *gepflegt,* [11]to tie [taɪ] – *zusammenbinden,* [12]headscarf ['hedskɑːf] – *Kopftuch*

A Reading

1 Before you read

a. Look at the text headings. The article is about …
1 … colours which artists use. 2 … your favourite clothes. 3 … the message which clothes give.

b. What is a 'dress code'?
1 a secret way of dressing 2 rules of how to dress 3 clothes sizes[1] in numbers

2 Give the German meaning of the words.

elegant (l. 1) • romantic (l. 1) • shocking (l. 1) • version (l. 12) • personality (l. 42)

3 Read the text and check your answers to a., b. and c.

4 Read the text again and match the sentence parts.

a. You can choose a style to give
b. But people may get a different impression
c. This is because the colour or clothes that you wear
d. Even in jobs without written dress codes you should
e. A good tip for a job interview is to dress

\+

think about what you wear.
the impression that you want to give.
better than you would as an employee.
from the impression that you intend[2].
may give their own message.

5 Which colour would you wear for an interview and why? Which colour wouldn't you wear and why?

B Language

Find the word in the box that matches the definitions (a.–d.).
a. a jacket and trousers
b. not matching, e.g. colours
c. a kind of safety hat
d. an opportunity

chance • dress code • headscarf • suit • style • helmet • contrasting • energy

27 C Listening: As long as the job is good!

1 Listen to three interviews in London. Match the people (1–3) with a place.
a. transport company b. hotel c. sales department d. bank e. TV company

2 What does the interviewer want to find out? Choose the right answer from the box.

how many people are in their company • how they get to work • if they have a dress code • what their favourite colour is • if they would like to change their job • how they like their job

3 Listen again carefully and find out each person's opinion on clothes rules at work.

a. The first person …
1 thinks jackets are fine. 2 loves ties in summer. 3 only loves dark suits.

b. The second person …
1 says clothes rules are OK. 2 gets clothes dirty at work. 3 loves outrageous clothes.

c. The third person …
1 loves his new job. 2 never wears a tie. 3 thinks a tie may be good at interviews.

[1]size [saɪz] – *Größe*, [2]to intend [ɪn'tend] – *beabsichtigen*

D Speaking

1

2

3

4

1 Describing

a. Describe the people in each picture to your partner (clothes, hair, the way they're standing/ looking into the camera). Write notes.

b. Each of them is looking for a job. What job do you think each one is looking for? You may choose from the box or use your own ideas.

> sales • carpenter • marketing • a secretary's office • eco gardening • technical assistant • installer • …

Start like this: I think he/she is at an interview for a job in …/for a job as a (an) … .

c. Imagine you and your partner are preparing for a job interview. Decide what the job is. You may choose a job from the box in b. or use your own ideas. Give two skills/qualities you need for the job that you chose. Say what you'd wear for the interview.

2 Role play

You are at a job interview in a big company. Answer the interviewer's questions.

Interviewer: I see. So please tell me: Why are you interested in this job?
You: *(Erkläre, warum),* I have always been interested in … . / I was good at … in school. / I did work experience in … .
Interviewer: That's great. Now please tell me a bit about your work placement[1], voluntary or holiday jobs and some of your tasks there.
You: *(Denke an ein Praktikum oder einen Ferienjob. Erzähle, was du gemacht hast … .)*
Interviewer: Our company may offer jobs in our other branches[2] in future. Would you be interested?
You: *(Sage, dass du gern / nicht gern reist. Wenn ja, erwähne weitere Sprachen, die du sprichst.)*
Interviewer: That's fine. So, let's look at the job itself: Some people think that clothes and what you look like aren't important in a job like this. What's your opinion on that?
You: *(Sage deine Meinung dazu.)* I think … is more / less important than … . / … are equally … .
Interviewer: OK, that's fair enough … If you work for us, you must follow our dress code, you know.
You: *(Sage, dass du natürlich mit der Kleiderordnung einverstanden bist.)*
Interviewer: Fine. Now, do you have any questions you would like to ask?
You: *(Frage, wann du anfangen würdest.)*
Interviewer: We would like you to start in four weeks. Would that be OK for you?
You: *(Sage, dass das kein Problem wäre. Bedanke dich und verabschiede dich formell.)*

[1]work placement ['wɜ:k ˌpleɪsmənt] – *Praktikum,* [2]branch ['brɑ:nʃ] – *Zweigstelle*

E Mediation and communication

Is what you look like always important? You find an online article about a singer with a video of her in a British TV talent show. While you're watching it, your cousin asks you about the singer. His/her English isn't very good. Answer his/her questions.

Does a woman need talent and looks to be a big star?

In April 2009 Susan Boyle walked onto a TV show called 'Britain's Got Talent'. A week later a YouTube video of her performance had reached an audience of about 50 million people. That's nothing strange, you may say. But the 47-year-old Scottish woman is not our usual[1] image of a TV, pop or musical star. She's tubby[2], plain[3] and, it seems, uninterested in fashion. But when she began to sing with her beautiful strong voice, people found her fantastic. Suddenly her looks were no longer important. Susan Boyle became a sensation overnight. What do you, our readers, think about this?

Dear Mr Editor[4],
The way Susan Boyle sings is really out of this world. But I don't agree with what you say in your article. Of course, looks are important in show business! We want to see people who are especially attractive. But with Susan Boyle it's worse because she's the complete opposite of attractive. And she's about as trendy as a wet dishcloth[5].
But I think it was brave of her to sing on TV. So I wish her lots of luck in the talent show. But just imagine her on stage in some big musical – ugh! No, I'm sure she'll never make it as a star!
Yours, Marc Hunter (Shanklin, Isle of Wight)

Dear Sir/Madam,
I think what you wrote about Ms Boyle is right. So, she's not good-looking. Does that say anything about her as a person? It's great that a 'normal' woman can show she's brilliant and can become famous – and not because she looks great or has an exciting private life! And, I mean, who cares! All I know is that she has got a voice that sends you to paradise! I see her as a role model[6] for all the rest of us 'normal' people who have never dared[7] to reach for the stars! Thank you, Susan Boyle.
Yours, Mary Evans (Glasgow, Scotland)

[1]usual ['ju:ʒl] – *üblich*, [2]tubby ['tʌbi] – *mollig*, [3]plain [pleɪn] – *unansehnlich*, [4]editor ['edɪtə] – *hier: Verfasser*, [5]dishcloth ['dɪʃklɒθ] – *Geschirrtuch*, [6]role model ['rəʊl ˌmɒdl] – *Vorbild*, [7]to dare [deə] – *sich trauen*

a. Wer ist überhaupt diese Frau im Video?
b. Wie alt ist sie und wo singt sie gerade?
c. Und wie haben die Zuschauer reagiert?
d. Das sind doch Leserbriefe. Was wurden die Leser gefragt?
e. Sind die zwei Verfasser der gleichen Meinung?
f. Welche Argumente bringen sie zu dem Thema?

F Writing

1 Skills

Imagine that you meet someone for the first time. What is important to you? Make a list with examples. Here are some ideas: face – smiling, … / way he or she acts – shyly, … / clothes – colours (message?) …

2 Giving advice

Write a checklist (dos and don'ts) for an interview for a job (50 – 80 words). Give each point a heading and use full sentences to explain each one. Think about the impression the person and his/her clothes (colours, style) can give. Find a suitable heading for your checklist.

How we see and are seen

1 Different images

a) *Say which European country/countries you think these people are from. Give reasons.*

*The answers are below

b) *We link each of these pictures to a country. Why do you think we do this? Think about films, TV, your family, … .*

c) *Think of 4–5 more images that you have of people from other countries. Test them on your partner. Can he/she say which country they belong to?*

2 What we expect

a) *Read what some 10th Graders[1] from a US high school wrote about what they expect to find on their first visit to Germany. Is this image of Germany correct? Say why/why not.*

People	All Germans speak English. They are very friendly but they are a bit old-fashioned[2]!
Language	Bad language is common. Kids swear[3] in school even when teachers are around. Parents don't seem to worry if their kids use bad language either.
Getting around	Germany is tiny. You can drive round it in a few days. You can't drive a car in Germany until you are 18, but there is no speed limit[4] on highways there.
Clothes	You needn't wear smart[5] clothes to go out. All Germans wear traditional clothes at town festivals: Dirndls for girls and leather trousers for boys.
Food	Fridges[6] in houses are small! In restaurants you pay for every extra cup of coffee. But you can get a beer here as soon as you're 16!!
Shopping	Germans don't really like shopping. They do have malls[7] but most shops are closed on Saturday afternoons and on Sundays.
Nudity[8]	Germany is full of adverts, even in the street, showing people with few or no clothes! The really surprising thing is that everybody just walks past them. Germans take all their clothes off in the sauna. Some people may dislike[9] this idea but for others it could be a reason to visit Germany in the first place[10]!

b) *What is your image of the US? Write a similar list.*

c) *Discuss your lists from b). Where do you think your image of the US comes from?*

[1]grader ['greɪdə] – *Klässler/in,* [2]old-fashioned [ˌəʊld'fæʃnd] – *altmodisch,* [3]to swear [sweə] – *fluchen,* [4]speed limit ['spi:d ˌlɪmɪt] – *Geschwindigkeitsbegrenzung,* [5]smart [smɑ:t] – *schick,* [6]fridge [frɪdʒ] – *Kühlschrank,* [7]mall [mɔ:l] – *Einkaufszentrum,* [8]nudity ['nju:dəti] – *Nacktheit,* [9]to dislike [dɪs'laɪk] – *nicht mögen,* [10]in the first place [ɪn ðə 'fɜ:st pleɪs] – *überhaupt erst*

*1 England; 2 Italy; 3 Germany; 4 The Netherlands

The EU today

1 Our European family

Read the text and write five facts about the EU.

TOGETHER®
SINCE 1957

On 25 March 1957 six countries signed the Treaty of Rome which created the European Economic[1] Community or EEC. In 2007 27 members celebrated[2] the 50th Anniversary[3] of that treaty. Today all the member states have different cultures, languages and traditions, but they have the same values[4]: freedom, democracy, the rule of law, respect for human rights and equality[5].

2 EU countries

a) *Find the names of ten countries in the EU today. You can get help on the Internet. Put the names in a grid like this and complete it.*

Country	Capital city	Language(s)	Money	Member since
Austria	Vienna	German	euro	1995
Belgium	Brussels	…	…	…

b) *Choose one EU country and find out more about it. Why did they become members? What happened or changed after they had become members?*

3 Britain and the EU

a) *Did you know that there have always been people in Britain who do not want to be in the EU? Here are some of the arguments they have used (and still use) against Britain's membership[6]. Do you agree with them? Why/Why not?*

Britain was not allowed to be one of the first six member states.

We have stronger links with Commonwealth countries than with the Continent.

We don't need a strong euro – we have a strong pound.

Britain can't open her borders as easily as other countries in Europe.

We don't want centimetres and kilometres. We have used inches and miles for hundreds of years.

b) *Use your ideas from a) and make a poster to persuade[7] the people of Britain to stay in the EU.*

[1]economic [ˌiːkəˈnɒmɪk] – *wirtschaftlich*, [2]to celebrate [ˈseləbreɪt] – *feiern*, [3]anniversary [ˌænɪˈvɜːsri] – *Jahrestag*, [4]value [ˈvæljuː]– *Wert*, [5]equality [ɪˈkwɒləti] – *Gleichheit*, [6]membership [ˈmembəʃɪp] – *Mitgliedschaft*, [7]to persuade [pəˈsweɪd] – *überreden*

Arbeitstechniken und Fertigkeiten

Inhaltsverzeichnis

Den *Skills*-Anhang aus Band 5 (Seiten 74–90) findest du online unter ⇨ 547550-0009. Folgende Techniken und Fertigkeiten trainierst du in Band 6 besonders:

1 Ein zweisprachiges Wörterbuch benutzen

Manchmal verstehst du beim Lesen ein unbekanntes Wort nicht oder du kannst ein bereits bekanntes Wort in einem neuen Zusammenhang nicht erraten. Das Wort *„branch"* z. B. (in dem Text über „political systems" hinten im Buch) hat unterschiedliche Bedeutungen. Drei Beispiele:

1. *That big* ***branch*** *looks dangerous. It could fall off the tree in a storm.*
2. *A lot of British shops have* ***branches*** *in Paris.*
3. *The road* ***branches*** *off at the church.*

Mit Hilfe eines zweisprachigen Wörterbuchs kannst du die richtige Bedeutung herausfinden. Folgende Checkliste kann dir beim Nachschlagen helfen:

	Checkliste	Beispiele*
1	Entscheide zuerst, zu welcher Wortart das Wort, das du suchst, gehört. Die Wörter sind nach Wortarten (*noun, verb, adjective,* …) geordnet.	*noun: branch* *verb: to branch off*
2	Suche die richtige Bedeutung. Viele englische Wörter haben mehrere deutsche Bedeutungen. Die, die am häufigsten verwendet werden, stehen am Anfang. Jede Bedeutung hat eine eigene Nummer.	❶ Zweig, Ast ❷ Nebenfluss, [Fluss]Arm ❸ Zweigstelle
3	Wenn du dich für eine Übersetzung entschieden hast, musst du im deutsch-englischen Teil prüfen, ob die Übersetzung richtig ist.	E → Dt. 1. *branch* = ❶ Zweig, Ast Dt. → E 2. *Zweig* = (auch übertragen) *branch*

**Alle Pons Wörterbücher findest du online unter http://pons.eu/dict/search*

2 Romanauszüge

Ein Roman (*novel*) ist meistens fiktiv (erfunden). Der Autor/die Autorin denkt sich eine Handlung und Figuren aus. Der Ort und die Zeit, an dem/in der der Roman spielt, kann echt oder erfunden sein. Als Beispiel nehmen wir den Text *Before I die* von Jenny Downham (Seiten 62–64).

	Checkliste	**Begriffe**	**Beispiele**
1	Was könnte das Thema sein? Es ist oft in der Überschrift oder in der Einleitung zu finden. Lies diese Teile zuerst.	*theme*	*young girl who has found out that she is dying*
2	Welche Unterthemen kannst du finden? Wer steht mit wem in Konflikt?	*secondary theme(s)*	*relationships with friends and family; communicating*
3	Konzentriere dich dann auf die Figuren. Am wichtigsten ist die Hauptfigur bzw. sind die Hauptfiguren. Oft gibt es einen Protagonisten und einen Gegenspieler, die miteinander in Konflikt stehen.	*main character(s)* *protagonist* *antagonist*	*main characters: Tessa, Adam* *other characters: nurse Louise, Dad, Zoey, Adam's mum*
4	Beantworte die Fragen *Wo?* und *Wann?*. In einem Auszug bleiben Handlungsort und -zeit oft gleich. Diese können sich im Verlauf der ganzen Geschichte aber ändern.	*setting*	*where: garden behind house where Adam lives* *when: on one afternoon*
5	Kläre, wie die Handlung verläuft. Sie enthält immer einen Konflikt. Oft gibt es einen Wendepunkt, nach dem sich vieles, aber nicht immer alles, aufklärt oder löst.	*storyline* *conflict* *turning point*	*storyline: Tessa decides to burn her things (a box, a dress, …) in a fire in Adam's garden.* *turning point: She faints and Adam offers her a coke to help her.* *conflict: with father and herself*
6	Suche den/die Erzähler/in. Er/Sie kann die Sichtweise einer oder mehrerer Figuren haben oder die eines Außenstehenden.	*narrator* *point of view*	*narrator = Tessa* *The story is told from Tessa's point of view.*
7	Notiere dir weitere Aspekte, die dir für die Handlung oder zur Beschreibung der Figuren wichtig erscheinen.	*further aspects*	*Adam doesn't smile at the beginning of the story but at the end he smiles.*

3 Kurzgeschichten

Kurzgeschichten (*short stories*) haben vieles mit Romanen gemeinsam. Sie sind fiktiv (erfunden), aber viel kürzer. Als Beispiel nehmen wir den Text *Deportation at breakfast* (Seiten 54–55).

	Checkliste	**Begriffe**	**Beispiele**
1	Finde das Thema der Geschichte. Dieses wird oft im Titel erwähnt bzw. erläutert.	*theme*	*An illegal immigrant is taken away.*
2	Meistens gibt es nur eine oder zwei Hauptfiguren. Durch Beschreibungen des Erzählers, Äußerungen der Figuren und ihr Handeln erhält der Leser Informationen darüber, wie sie aussehen und was für Menschen sie sind.	*main character(s)*	*main characters: the narrator, Javier and the customers*
3	Beantworte die Frage *Wo?*. Der Ort, an dem sich alles abspielt, kann sich ändern. Beantworte die Frage *Wann?*. Die Zeitspanne, in der sich alles abspielt, ist begrenzt, z. B. auf einen Vormittag, einen Tag oder eine Woche.	*setting*	*where: in a diner in the US* *when: in the morning*
4	Kläre, wie die Handlung verläuft. Sie konzentriert sich auf **einen** Vorfall. Sie enthält oft **einen** Konflikt zwischen den Figuren und einen Wendepunkt, der zu einer Änderung führt.	*storyline* *conflict* *turning point*	*storyline: The narrator orders breakfast in a diner. The waiter is taken away by the authorities. Then the narrator does the waiter's job.* *conflict: Javier with authorities* *turning point: Javier is taken away.*
5	Betrachte den/die Erzähler/in. Er/Sie kann die Sichtweise einer oder mehrerer Figuren haben oder die eines Außenstehenden.	*narrator* *point of view*	*The story is told from the point of view of the I-narrator.*
6	Notiere besondere Merkmale der Geschichte, z. B. eine fehlende Einführung. Der Leser wird ohne jegliche Vorbereitung in die Situation ‚hineingeworfen'. Jedes Wort ist wichtig für den Leser.	*special features*	*There is no introduction. We don't know who and where the narrator is.*

4 Gedichte

Weil Gedichte und Lieder einprägsam sein sollen, werden Stilmittel (Reime, Rhythmus, …) verwendet, die das Behalten erleichtern. Mit Stilmitteln kann der Autor die Aufmerksamkeit der Leser auch auf bestimmte Teile des Gedichts lenken und so eine Aussage betonen.
Hier ein Beispiel (*Exotic is nice* Seite 44).

<table>
<tr><th></th><th>Checkliste</th><th>Beispiele</th><th>Begriffe</th></tr>
<tr><td>1</td><td>Lies dir das Gedicht durch. Finde das Thema des Gedichts. Die Überschrift kann dir dabei zumeist helfen.</td><td rowspan="5">Exotic is nice

Pretty Birdie Seed
Only loved to feed
On Japanese seaweed!

To stay healthy and cute
She ordered her fruit
From near and from far.
It came to the star
At the cocktail bar
By ship, plane and car,
Which made the air stink
But she wanted her drink!
Well, all that dirt
Made her lungs hurt
And made her eyes sore.
Now, will she have more?

Exotic is nice</td><td rowspan="5">theme

rhyme scheme

word pair

alliteration

contrast

repetition</td></tr>
<tr><td>2</td><td>Betrachte das Reimschema. Wenn sich z. B. zwei aufeinanderfolgende Verse reimen, gehört ihr Inhalt meistens zusammen.</td></tr>
<tr><td>3</td><td>Eine Änderung im Reimschema kann einen neuen Aspekt andeuten.</td></tr>
<tr><td>4</td><td>Finde Stilmittel wie z. B. Alliteration (Wiederholung von Lauten), Wortpaare, Kontraste oder Wiederholungen. Der Dichter benutzt sie, um zu zeigen, dass ihm diese Stelle des Textes besonders wichtig ist.</td></tr>
<tr><td>5</td><td>Falls es keine Reime gibt, hat das letzte Wort eines jeden Verses eine besondere Bedeutung. Es enthält oft einen Hinweis auf die Aussage des Gedichts.</td></tr>
<tr><td>6</td><td>Lies das Gedicht laut vor. Ist der Rhythmus immer gleich? Wie klingt es: angenehm, aggressiv, aufregend, …?</td><td>Pretty Birdie Seed (2+2+1)
To stay healthy and cute (1+1+2+1+1)
Well all that dirt (1+1+1+1)
Now, she will have more (1+1+1+1+1)</td><td>rhythm</td></tr>
<tr><td>7</td><td>Denke nach. Was sind deine eigenen Gedanken und Gefühle zu dem Gedicht? Wie wirkt es auf dich?</td><td>It is a sort of story, but the end is not what I expected. I like the poem because it shows that some people who think they are really 'cool' are really very stupid. I think the poet is laughing at them.</td><td>feelings</td></tr>
</table>

5 Sachtexte

1 Argumentative Texte

In Sachtexten, z. B. in einer Zeitung oder Zeitschrift, wird zumeist ein Thema/ein Problem diskutiert. Eine Aussage (*statement*) oder Frage wird von mehreren Seiten betrachtet, um zu einer Schlussfolgerung (*conclusion*) zu kommen. Ziel ist üblicherweise, die Leser für eine bestimmte Meinung zu gewinnen. Als Beispiel nehmen wir den Text *Head of State* (Seite 30).

	Checkliste	Beispiele
1	Lies die Überschrift und die Einleitung. Um welches Thema könnte es gehen?	*Why do we have a Queen?*
2	Schau dir die begleitenden Bilder von Personen oder Orten an. Sie können dir helfen, den Text besser zu verstehen.	*Pictures of the Queen as Head of State and in other roles. They show us what she does in her job.*
3	Diagramme oder Tabellen helfen dir vor allem bei wissenschaftlichen Texten.	*At the back of OL6: A flow chart shows the British political system and the position of the Queen.*
4	Die Argumente für oder gegen eine Sachfrage können in unterschiedlichen Formen dargestellt sein: • in einer Kette, mit den schwächsten Argumenten am Anfang • 1–2 Argumente jeweils mit Gegenargumenten • alle Argumente aus einer Perspektive, dann alle Gegenargumente	*Treaties with other nations … .* *But it also still has … .* *The Queen has to sign … .* *But she isn't allowed to … .* *She has to remain … .* *For example, she can't support … .*
5	Die Schlussfolgerung (*conclusion*) steht meistens im letzten Absatz.	*The Queen does have some power.*

2 Werbetexte

Auch Werbung/Werbetexte sind argumentative Texte. Ziel ist, die Leser von einem bestimmten Produkt zu überzeugen. Solche Texte enthalten oft rhetorische Mittel. Als Beispiel nehmen wir den Text *The common language* (Seite 10).

	Checkliste	Beispiele
1	Suche den Namen des Produkts. Dieser sollte immer als Erstes auffallen. Er wird oft größer und in einer auffälligen Schrift präsentiert.	*Eurofoot*
2	Schau dir sämtliche Bilder an. Was sagen sie über das Produkt aus?	*It's for young people, boys and girls. It's international. It's fun.*
3	Suche rhetorische Mittel (Wiederholungen, Übertreibungen, Vergleiche, Kontraste, …). Diese verstärken die Aussage.	*promising* (Wiederholung) *world famous* (Übertreibung) *promising players* (Alliteration)
4	Sammle weitere Merkmale, z. B. Angebote und direkte Aufforderungen, Versprechungen, … .	*Do you love …?* *… free places …* *Come to …!*

6 Ein persönliches Profil verfassen

Bevor du dich für eine Ausbildung/einen Job entscheidest, ist es gut, wenn du darüber nachdenkst, wo deine Stärken und Schwächen liegen. Mit diesen und weiteren Informationen kannst du ein persönliches Profil erstellen. Unten findest du als Beispiel ein Profil aus *Topic 1* (Seite 14).

	Checkliste	Beispiele	Bemerkungen
1	**Name**	*Ali Hassan*	Schreibe deinen Vornamen und dann deinen Familiennamen.
2	**Education**	*6 GCSEs (English, Maths, Science, Computers, French, Art)*	Liste alle Abschlussprüfungen in sämtlichen Fächern auf.
3	**Job experience**	*4 years in customer services department of insurance company; group leader*	Sage, welche Erfahrungen du schon gemacht hast und wo/wodurch. Sage, was du im Moment machst (Beruf, Schule, Studium). Gib ggf. an, welche Schulart du besuchst und welchen Abschluss du voraussichtlich erreichen wirst.
4	**Skills**	*selling, computers, English, Hindi*	Nenne Fertigkeiten, die auch für andere Tätigkeiten wichtig sein könnten.
5	**Strengths**	*I can sell things (even my ideas), computer skills, I'm mobile, get on with people; reliable, independent*	Denke an Dinge, die du immer gut machst, und an die, die für bestimmte Jobs sehr wichtig sein könnten. Sei ehrlich! Frage deine Freunde und Familie, wie sie dich beschreiben würden.
6	**Weaknesses**	*Don't get on with spiders. I can't speak Chinese.*	Du solltest dir eine Schwäche zurechtlegen, die für den Beruf nicht von Nachteil ist.
7	**Family***	*parents in Manchester, three younger brothers and two ol der sisters*	Diese Information könnte für einen Arbeitgeber/eine Arbeitgeberin wichtig sein, vor allem, wenn du längere Zeit im Ausland arbeiten sollst.
8	**My dream**	*to spend a few years in Asia*	Der Traum muss nicht mit einem bestimmten Job verbunden sein, aber er kann wichtig sein, wenn du eine schwierige Entscheidung treffen musst.
9	**In the next 12 months**	*I really do want my own business*	Die Antwort soll etwas mit deinen Zukunftsplänen bzw. Berufszielen zu tun haben.
10	**Interesting info**	*I teach disabled kids to swim*	Hier solltest du etwas erwähnen, das anderen helfen könnte, dich besser zu verstehen.

*Informationen über deine Familie kannst du zusätzlich geben.

7 Einen Begleitbrief schreiben

Den Musterbrief unten kannst du als Vorlage verwenden. Die markierten Teile müssen immer enthalten sein, manche musst du aber anpassen.

Amy Tan ❶
239 Gordon Ave. ❷
Liverpool LI 56 7TU ❸

Mr Richard Rich ❷
Sunshine Film Studios
440 Brighton Rd.
London SW 6 9OP

23 July 2012 ❺

Dear Mr Rich, ❹
Ref: Job as studio assistant ❻
❼ With reference to your ad on the Internet on 20th July, I would like to apply for a job as a studio assistant at Sunshine Film Studios in London. … .
I finished school on June 26. At the moment I am working as an assistant for a photographer. It is a temporary position and I am looking for a permanent job. I would really like to work in London. … .
I have some experience of the film world. I had a holiday job in a TV studio last year. My special skills are organising and working with people. … .
As you will see from my CV, I was born in China but I speak and write good English and German. I have some knowledge of Chinese, too. This could be useful with visitors who do not speak English. … .
I look forward to hearing from you soon.
Yours sincerely, ❽
Amy Tan
encl. ❾

❶ Name	In englischsprachigen Ländern schreibt man zuerst den Vornamen und dann den Nachnamen.
❷ Address	Bei Adressen steht die Hausnummer vor dem Straßennamen. Abkürzungen wie *St.* (*Street*), *Ave.* (*Avenue*), *Cl.* (*Close*), *Rd.* (*Road*) sind üblich.
❸ Postal codes	… sind von Land zu Land verschieden. Falls du an eine Firma schreibst, ist es gut, die Adresse genau so zu übernehmen, wie sie in der Anzeige steht.
❹ Dear …,	Verwende *‚Sir or Madam'* wenn du den Namen der Person nicht kennst. Schreibe bei Männernamen *Mr*, bei Frauennamen *Ms*. Vergiss nicht das Komma nach der Anrede!
❺ Date	Im *BE* steht der Tag vor dem Monat. Im *AE* steht der Monat vor dem Tag.
❻ Ref:	… bedeutet *‚reference'* (Betreff) und steht zwischen *Dear …* und dem ersten Satz des Briefes.
❼ The first word	… schreibt man immer groß.
❽ Closing	Wenn du die Anrede *‚Sir or Madam'* verwendest, dann schreibst du *‚Yours faithfully'*. Ansonsten *‚Yours sincerely'*. Vergiss nicht das *‚s'* bei *‚Yours'*.
❾ encl.	= *‚enclosed'* verwendest du, wenn du weitere Unterlagen beilegst (= Anlagen).

8 Texte ausformulieren und umgestalten

1 Einen Text ergänzen

Diese Checkliste kannst du verwenden, wenn du einen Text ergänzen möchtest (z. B. ein neues Ende schreiben). Als Beispiel nehmen wir den Text *A geocaching adventure* (Seiten 22–25).

	Checkliste	**Beispiele**
1	Lies den Originaltext. Um welche Textsorte handelt es sich, z. B. Sachtext, Kurzgeschichte, Gedicht, …? Aus welcher Perspektive wird der Orginaltext erzählt? Welche Zeit wird verwendet (*present, future, …*)?	*kind of text: story* *point of view: third person:* ***Simon*** *suddenly saw … .* ***The group*** *left the SUV … .* *time: past*
2	Überlege, welche Form (Text, Gedicht, Dialog, …) und Länge (1 Strophe, 1 Seite) dein Text haben soll.	*form: text* *length: 1 page*
3	Verfasse eine Kurzfassung des Inhalts in Notizform, in einer Mindmap oder in einem Flussdiagramm.	*4 friends hide → rain stops → mobiles work again → …*
4	Überprüfe den Stil des Originaltextes. Was ist dabei besonders oder merkwürdig, z. B. kurze oder lange Sätze, viel Erzähltext (*narrative*), direkte Rede, … .	*narrative + direct speech + description of landscape*
5	Überprüfe die Sprache des Originaltextes. Was fällt auf, z. B. Jugendsprache, *AE*, Kurzformen, … ?	*short forms: Na, OK, …* *AE:* ***pretty*** *damaged …*
6	Schreibe deinen Text in ganzen Sätzen auf. Versuche dabei den Stil des Originaltextes zu imitieren.	*Suddenly the rain stopped and Simon shuddered. 'The red earth is everywhere,' he thought.*
7	Prüfe, ob du alle Ideen in deinem Text untergebracht hast. Kontrolliere auch Rechtschreibung, Grammatik und Wortwahl.	*thundor = Wrong! (thunder)* *answers Helen = Wrong! (answer**ed** Helen)*
8	Ein Partner sollte den Originaltext und das Ende deines Textes lesen. Passt dein Text dazu? Was solltest du ändern?	*Helen took Logan's GPS.* *Wrong! (Simon's)*

2 Einen Text umwandeln

Manchmal musst du die Form eines Textes ändern, z. B. eine Geschichte in einen Dialog bzw. einen Dialog in eine Geschichte umwandeln. Die Checklisten auf dieser Seite können dir dabei helfen. Als Beispiel nehmen wir den Text *A public attraction* (Seite 30).

Checkliste		**Beispiele**
1 Einen Erzähltext in einen Dialog umwandeln	Markiere direkte Rede im Text. Schreibe dann die Namen der Sprecher und deren Äußerungen in Dialogform auf.	*Jane: Well, I don't know …*
	Erfinde einen Dialog für den Erzähltext. Dabei musst du überlegen, was die Figuren gesagt haben könnten. Füge Dialogwörter (*Well, So, Hey, …*) hinzu.	*Jane: Hey, Yolanda, would you like to go and see …?*
2 Einen Dialog in einen Erzähltext umwandeln	Lies den Dialog und beantworte die Fragen: Wer redet? Worüber reden sie?	*Jane and Yolanda are talking about the Queen.*
	Verwende indirekte Rede. Vergiss nicht die Zeit, Pronomen und eventuell Adverbien anzupassen. Dialogwörter (*So, Well, …*) müssen entfernt werden.	*Yolanda asked her English friend, why they still had a queen.*

9 Fragen vorbereiten

In vielen Situationen musst du Fragen vorbereiten und stellen, z. B. für ein Quiz, ein Interview oder eine Umfrage. Dafür kannst du die folgende Checkliste verwenden.

	Checkliste	Beispiele
1	Stelle fest, für welchen Zweck du die Fragen formulieren sollst, z. B. für eine Umfrage (*survey*), ein Interview (*interview*) oder ein Quiz (*quiz*).	*survey in group* *interview with a school sports star* *quiz in class*
2	Entscheide, zu welchem Thema du die Fragen stellen willst, z. B. eine Umfrage zum Thema *„Transport"*, ein Interview zum Thema *„Sport"*, …	*Survey: Travelling to school* *Interview: Favourite sportsmen/women* *Quiz: Questions on UK jobs*
3	Schreibe in Notizform auf, zu welchen Aspekten des Themas du Fragen stellen willst.	*Survey: Usually get to school? How long? Other ways? Public transport? Traffic/transport problems? …?* *Interview: Which sports? Name/s of favourites? Why? …?* *Quiz: Names of jobs? What they do? Anybody? Special words?*
4	Verwende deine Notizen, um Fragen zu formulieren. Stelle nicht immer Fragen mit den selben Anfängen, sondern benutze *‚Do, Have, Was, …?'* und die Fragewörter *‚Who, When, How, …?'*. Biete Alternativen (*multiple-choice questions*) an. Diese findest du eher in einer Umfrage oder einem Quiz.	*Interview: Where do you live? How do you usually get to school? How long does your journey take? Do you use other ways to …? How often do you …? Have you ever …?* *Survey: How long does it take?* *– 10 – 20 minutes* *– less than an hour* *– more than an hour*
5	Prüfe, ob deine Fragen thematisch geeignet sind, z. B. allgemeine Fragen in einer Umfrage, Fragen über Vorlieben bei einem Interview, Wissensfragen bei einem Quiz.	*Survey on how kids get to school: How long does it take?* *Interview on sports: What is your favourite sport?* *Quiz: What do you call a person who cuts hair?*
6	Bitte einen Partner/eine Partnerin, die Fragen zu überprüfen. Sind die Fragewörter richtig? Brauchst du das Verb *‚Do/Does/Did'* oder ein anderes Hilfsverb, um die Frage korrekt zu bilden? Welche Form ist hier richtig?	*Who/Where do you …?* *How do you/does she …?*
7	Bereite eine Einleitung vor. Du kannst sie dir auch in Stichpunkten notieren.	*Survey: Good morning. We are doing a survey on … . May I ask you some questions, please?* *Interview: Hello, … . We'd like to ask you a few questions about … .* *Quiz: Now that you have learnt about …, we would like you to do a short quiz on it. Here are the questions.*

10 Sich auf ein Vorstellungsgespräch vorbereiten

Es ist sehr wichtig, sich auf das Gespräch gut vorzubereiten. So bist du während des Gesprächs nicht so angespannt. Diese Checkliste kann dir helfen.

	Checkliste	**Beispiele**
1	Informiere dich z. B. im Internet vorher über die Stelle/die Firma/das Land/ … .	*Find out:* • *What exactly your duties would be.* • *What other products the company makes.* • *What other languages are spoken in the country where the job is.*
2	Überlege dir 2–3 Fragen, die du am Telefon stellen kannst, falls die Firma dich anruft.	*What do I need to bring with me?* *How long will the interview take?*
3	Frage, wenn möglich, bei einer Jobagentur nach, was du zu dem Gespräch anziehen sollst: einen Anzug/Rock/eine Jeans? Deine Kleidung muss auf jeden Fall sauber und gepflegt sein. Trage nicht zu viel Schmuck/Make-up.	*I have an interview for a job as a/an … .* *Could you please give me some advice?* *How should I dress for the interview?* *Should I wear a suit and tie/skirt/ … ?* *Can I wear jeans and a sweater?*
4	Bereite dich darauf vor, Fragen des Interviewers zu beantworten. Überlege, welche Fragen gestellt werden könnten.	*Why are you interested in this job? – I have always wanted to be/work/… .* *Have you worked abroad before? – No, I haven't but … . / Yes, I have. / … .* *What are your best subjects? – Maths and … . English, Science and … .* *What would you do if you had a difficult customer? – I would ask … /tell … /explain that … .* *Do you have any questions? – Yes, I do.*
5	Bereite ein paar Fragen vor. Du solltest immer Fragen stellen. Das zeigt, dass du an dem Job interessiert bist.	*Does your company offer any in-company training?* *Are there any other special company rules?* *Are there any important laws (that) I need to know about?*
6	Versuche dich zu entspannen. Schau den Interviewer an und lächle! Gib ihm/ihr die Hand, wenn er/sie es möchte. Deine ersten Worte sind wichtig. Richte dich danach, wie der Interviewer mit dir redet: Formell? Freundlich?	*Formal:* *Good morning/afternoon/…, Mr/Ms … . – Good morning. Nice to meet you.* *Please take a seat/sit down, Mr/Ms … . – Thank you.* *Informal:* *Hi/Hello, Pete/Sue/ …! – Hello!* *Take a seat! – Thanks!*
7	Sei ehrlich! Mach dir keine Sorgen, wenn du nicht alles verstehst. Der Interviewer weiß, dass dein Englisch nicht perfekt ist.	*Could you repeat the question, please?* *Excuse me. Could you say that again, please?* *Excuse me. What does (the word) … mean?* *I'm sorry. Could you speak more slowly, please?*

11 Kommentieren

Hier geht es um eine sachliche Wertung, die nicht beleidigend, sondern klar begründet ist. Negative Kritik soll möglichst mit Verbesserungsvorschlägen verknüpft werden. Diese Checkliste kann dir helfen.

	Checkliste	Beispiele
1	Formuliere in der Einleitung (*introduction*), worüber du schreiben/reden willst.	*I would like to talk about the article/story/ … by … .* *I would like to comment on …'s presentation.*
2	Beschreibe in einer Kurzfassung (*summary*), worum es geht. Wenn du über einen Film schreibst, ist es wichtig zu sagen, wo er spielt.	*The article/… is called … and is about … .* *The presentation was about … .* *The film is about … . The story takes place in … .* *The film tells the story of/shows pictures of … .*
3	Beschreibe den Aufbau (*structure*) des Textes und sage, was du davon hältst.	*The article has two/three … paragraphs. The presentation had … parts. I liked the introduction/photos/…, but … .*
4	Schildere kurz den Inhalt (*content*) und bewerte ihn sachlich.	*The … is about/tells the story of/describes … .* *It is/was quite good/really clever/interesting/ … .* *It has/had a lot of good points/… . But I don't think that … .*
5	Bewerte die Sprache (*language*) und den Stil (*style*).	*The language is OK/is sometimes too informal/ … .* *The text should be in the present/past/ … .*
6	Schlage Verbesserungen (*improvements*) vor.	*I think that it would be good/better to explain/describe/… .* *It might be better if the author/director changed … .*
7	Beschreibe die Figuren (*characters*) in einer Geschichte/einem Film.	*The main character(s) is (are) … .* *… is a very sad/happy/ … person who tries to/wants to/… .*
8	Bewerte auch visuelle Aspekte und den Ton.	*The first/… picture/scene in … is very exciting/beautiful/ … .* *The drawings of/zoom-in/close-up shots of … were great/… .* *The music goes well/doesn't really go with the action/is too loud.*
9	Sage, ob du die Geschichte/den Film empfehlen (*recommend*) kannst.	*I would/wouldn't recommend that you read/go to see … .* *It was really scary/exciting/… especially when … .*

12 Ergebnisse präsentieren

Wenn du die Ergebnisse z. B. einer Umfrage präsentierst, solltest du die Hinweise in dieser Checkliste beachten.

	Checkliste	Beispiele
1	Erkläre, worum es bei der Umfrage geht.	*We did a survey on … / to find out/ … .*
2	Sage, wer und wie viele Personen daran teilgenommen haben.	*We asked all the girls/boys in our group/class/in class … .* *There were … girls/boys. The total number was … .*
3	Führe Zahlen in einer Tabelle, einem (Fluss-)Diagramm oder einer Liste auf und erkläre sie.	*We'd like to show you some figures and explain them.* *The grid/flow chart/… shows … . A key to the symbols is at the side/… . The red/… bar/the scale represents … .*
4	Fasse die Ergebnisse zusammen.	*You can see that most/more than half of/no pupils … .*
5	Kommentiere die Ergebnisse.	*We were surprised/disappointed/… to find that … .*
6	Bedanke dich und biete die Möglichkeit, Fragen zu stellen.	*Thank you for listening.* *Are there any questions? / Does anyone have a question?*

13 Hörtexte verstehen

Hörtexte können manchmal schwer sein. Folgende Checklisten können dir helfen.

1 Gespräche

	Checkliste
1	Bereite dich vor. Überlege, was für ein Gespräch auf dich zukommen könnte, wo es stattfinden und wer dabei sein könnte. Überlege, was du schon über die Personen weißt: Was haben sie gemacht, wo kommen sie her, welche Meinungen vertreten sie?
2	Schreibe die Namen der Gesprächspartner in einer Liste auf und lasse Platz für Notizen.
3	Schreibe beim Hören neben jeden Namen Stichwörter zu dem, was gesagt wird/was passiert.
4	Bitte einen Partner/eine Partnerin, deine Notizen zu lesen bzw. zu verbessern.
5	Fasse das Gespräch/das Interview für einen Partner/eine Partnerin zusammen: Wer dabei war, was sie gesagt haben, was passiert ist. Hast du etwas Wichtiges vergessen?

2 Werbespots

	Checkliste	Beispiele
1	Höre dir die Begleitmusik/die Jingles an. Die Musik unterstreicht oft die Aussage des Werbetextes.	*cars, fast food companies, drinks companies, …*
2	Der Produktname wird oft mehrmals wiederholt.	*at the beginning, in the middle, at the end*
3	Achte auf die Sprache (Superlative, Vergleiche mit anderen Produkten, …).	*the greatest, … just as good as famous name products and it's cheaper, …*
4	Hör genau zu. Wirst du direkt angesprochen? So setzen Werbeleute Kunden oft unter Druck oder locken mit Angeboten und Versprechungen.	*Do you know where to find …?* *Don't miss this great offer!* *Buy one and you'll … . If you buy two, we'll … .*

14 An einer Diskussion teilnehmen

Bei einer Diskussion ist es wichtig zuzuhören und auf das Gesagte zu reagieren. Die Checkliste kann dir helfen.

	Checkliste	Beispiele
1	Kläre, wer teilnehmen wird, worüber diskutiert und wie lange geredet werden soll. Frage, ob du die eigene Meinung äußern oder eine andere vertreten sollst.	*group: Paul, Ali; Miriam, …* *topic: Tap water or bottled water? time: …*
2	Schreibe deine Ideen stichwortartig und nach Wichtigkeit geordnet auf ein Blatt.	*tap water = cheaper* *tap water = …*
3	Schreibe die Namen aller Gesprächspartner auf ein Blatt und lasse Platz für Notizen.	*1. Paul* *2. …*
4	Notiere neben jedem Namen, wer deiner (✓) und wer anderer (X) Meinung ist. Schreibe Stichwörter dazu. Markiere eine andere Meinung, die du gern übernehmen möchtest (✓✓) oder die du ganz blöd findest (XX).	*1. Paul: (XX) tap water is bad* *2. Ali: (✓) tap water is cheaper* *3. …*

15 Umgangsformen beachten

1 Begrüßungen

Wenn du mit englischen Muttersprachlern redest, solltest du nicht versuchen, deren Akzent/Slang zu imitieren. Es könnte unhöflich erscheinen. Folgende Tipps können dir in solchen Situationen helfen:

Land	Du hörst	Tipps	Du kannst antworten
Alle	*Hi!/Hello!*	Die meisten Völker verstehen ‚Hi'/‚Hello', oder einen Händedruck. Achte darauf, wie die Menschen sich in dem anderen Land begrüßen: Was sagen Menschen, die sich zum ersten Mal sehen? Wie begrüßen sich Freunde?	*Hi, … .* *Hello, Mr/Mrs… .* *Hi! My name is/I'm … .* *I'm from … .*
US	*Hi, …!* *How are you doing?*	In den USA ist es üblich, sich beim Vornamen zu nennen – auch bei der Arbeit. Man fragt: ‚*How are you doing, Gina?*'	*Hi, … . Good, thanks. And you?*
UK	*Good morning* *Nice to meet you.*	Benutze immer Mr/Ms plus Nachnamen bei Erwachsenen. Wenn jemand ‚How are you?' sagt, solltest du die Floskel wiederholen oder ‚Pleased to meet you.' sagen.	*Good morning/afternoon/ evening Mr/Ms/Mrs … .* *Pleased to meet you.*
Australia	G'day, …!	Sei nie zu formell in Australien, das wird als hochnäsig betrachtet. Vornamen sind üblich, auch zwischen Jugendlichen und Erwachsenen.	*G'day!*

2 Telefonieren

In englischsprachigen Ländern melden sich die Menschen am Telefon sehr unterschiedlich. Manche sagen ihren Namen (mit oder ohne Telefonnummer), manche sagen nur ‚*Hello*'. Es ist besonders bei formellen Gesprächen wichtig, angemessen zu reagieren. Unten findest du Beispiele:

Wenn jemand sich meldet, hörst du z. B.:	So kannst du darauf antworten:
Good morning, Burnt Hill Secondary School. *Sandie Bradshaw speaking.* *How can I help you?*	*Good morning, Ms Bradshaw. I'm ringing from Germany.* *My name is … . I wonder if you could help me.* *I just wanted to ask about … . / I need to speak to someone about/find out about … .*
Dann hörst du vielleicht folgenden Satz:	**Dann kannst du folgende Antwort geben:**
Hang on! I'll see if I can find Mr/Ms … . *I'm putting you through now.*	*OK. I'll hang on.* *Thank you.*

16 Sich persönlich äußern

In manchen Aufgaben sollst du über dich selbst sprechen. Diese Wendungen können dafür nützlich sein.

Über deine Meinung sprechen	Absichten äußern
In my opinion … • *The way I see it, …* • *I (don't) think …* • *I have the feeling/impression that …* • *I find it hard to believe that …* • *I (don't) agree with …* • *I couldn't agree more.* • *To be honest, I can't/don't …* • *I share the view that …* • *I am of exactly the same opinion as …* • *I would support the view that …*	*I suggest that we/you …* • *I'm going to talk about …* • *Shall I/we …?* • *Let's …* • *Let me …* • *I'd like to begin with/end with/finish …* • *First of all … / Secondly …*

Über Gefühle sprechen	Hoffnungen und Wünsche äußern
I'm excited/bored/sad/happy/... about .../ because ... • *I'm sick of ...* • *I (don't) feel sorry for ...* • *I'm enjoying this.* • *I'm so pleased.* • *I'm looking foward to it.*	*I (really) hope ...* • *I wish ...* • *I'd like to ...* • *It would be great if ...*

17 Internetrecherche

1. Suche nach Themen oder Stichwörtern

- Durchsuche vorhandene Themenangebote, z.B. bei Yahoo oder Web, nach dem gewünschten Thema, wähle dann ein Teilthema usw., z.B. Reise > Reisetipps > Klimatabellen > Las Vegas
- Verwende eine Suchmaschine, z.B. Google, um mit Stichwörtern zum Thema Informationen zu finden, z.B. Sehenswürdigkeit London.
- Die meisten Suchmaschinen verwenden ODER bei der Suche mit Stichwörtern. Das bedeutet, dass du alle Seiten angezeigt bekommst, die auch nur eines deiner Stichwörter enthalten. Wenn du also z.B. *new south wales* eingibst, bekommst du Seiten für Wales und South Wales in Großbritannien und für New South Wales in Australien.

Bei den meisten Suchmaschinen kann man zusätzlich ein + oder ein - vor einem Stichwort eingeben, um es ein- oder auszuschließen, z.B. *+martin +luther -king*.

Wenn du nach einer zusammenhängenden Wortfolge, z.B. einem Buchtitel, suchst, verwende Anführungszeichen, z.B. „Herr der Ringe".

- Um bessere Ergebnisse zu bekommen, hilft es meist, das ungewöhnlichste oder wichtigste Wort zuerst einzugeben.
- Wenn du zu wenige Treffer erhältst, überprüfe die Rechtschreibung oder verwende andere oder weniger Stichwörter.
- Wenn du zu viele Treffer erhältst, verwende mehr oder genauere Stichwörter.

2. Favoriten *(bookmarks)*

- Um leichter zu einer Seite zurückzukehren, die dir gefällt, kannst du ein *bookmark* setzen, indem du auf Favoriten im Menü klickst, indem du Strg-D drückst oder mit einem Klick der rechten Maustaste.
- Wenn du vergessen hast, ein *bookmark* zu setzen, kannst du mit Pfeil vorwärts oder rückwärts oder mit Strg-H auf alle Seiten zurückkehren, auf denen du während deiner Internetsitzung warst.

3. Auswertung der Ergebnisse/Treffer

- Glaube nicht alles, was du im Internet liest. Bedenke, dass dort jeder alles veröffentlichen kann. Bilde dir ein Urteil über die Vetrauenswürdigkeit einer Webseite, bevor du daraus Informationen verwendest. Ähnelt die Seite etwa eher www.spiegel.de oder eher www.nullachtfuenfzehn-blog.de?
- Bist du auf einer kommerziellen Webseite gelandet? Dann ist diese wahrscheinlich eher daran interessiert, dir etwas zu verkaufen als dir objektive Informationen zu geben.
- Enthält die Seite Fakten oder nur persönliche Meinungen?
- Könnte sich der/die Autor/in wirklich mit dem Thema auskennen, ist er/sie z.B. ein/e Uniprofessor/in oder ein/e Journalist/in?
- Überprüfe auch die Aktualität der Webseite, vor allem wenn du nach dem Neuesten zu einem Thema suchst.

18 Sprachenlernen

Verschiedene Sprachen haben zwar unterschiedliche Wörter für die Dinge, aber sie funktioneren manchmal ganz ähnlich. Es kann dir beim Lernen einer Fremdsprache daher helfen, wenn du dir darüber bewusst bist, wie deine Muttersprache funktioniert.

Hier sind ein paar Beispiele:

	Deutsch	Englisch	Italienisch	Russisch	Türkisch
Artikel	3 bestimmte (der, die, das) und 2 unbestimmte (ein, eine)	1 bestimmter (the), zwei unbe-stimmte (a, an)	zwei bestimmte (il, la), drei unbestimmte (una, uno, un)	keine	keine
Satzstellung	Subjekt-Verb-Objekt Fragen: Fragewort an Position 1	Subjekt-Verb-Objekt Fragen: Fragewort an Position 1	Subjekt-Verb-Objekt (Subjekt kann fehlen, wenn es ein Personal-pronomen ist)	freie Satzstellung Fragen: Fragewort an Position 1	Subjekt-Objekt-Verb Fragen: Fragewort an der Position, an der das Erfragte stehen würde
Zeiten: Gegenwart	eine: einfache Form	zwei: einfache (simple) und Verlaufsform (progressive)	eine: einfache Form	eine: einfache Form (das Verb "sein" hat keine Gegenwarts-form)	zwei: einfache und Verlaufsform
Zeiten: Vergangenheit	mehrere	mehrere (simple past, present per-fect, past perfect)	mehrere	eine	zwei
Zeiten: Zukunft	eine	zwei (will-future, going-to-future)	eine	eine	eine
Zählung	145 = einhundert-fünfundvierzig (Einerzahl wird vor Zehnerzahl genannt)	145 = one hundred and forty-five (Reihenfolge wie in der Zahl)	wie im Englischen	wie im Englischen	wie im Englischen

Beispielsätze:

Aussage:

Englisch:	I go to school.
Deutsch:	Ich gehe zur Schule.
Italienisch:	(Io) Vado a scuola.
Russisch:	Я иду в школу.
Türkisch:	(Ben) Okula giderim.

Frage mit Fragewort:

Englisch:	Which languages do you speak?
Deutsch:	Welche Sprachen sprichst du?
Italienisch:	Quale lingue parli?
Russisch:	На каких языках ты говоришь?
Türkisch:	Hangi dileri konuşuyorsun?

Mediation and communication

COMMUNICATION S K I L L S

Sinn entnehmen: Der Schwerpunkt der folgenden Mediation liegt darauf, Originaltexte mit mehr unbekanntem Wortschatz zu verstehen. Achte beim Hören oder Lesen immer darauf, dass du nichts wörtlich übertragen musst und konzentriere dich darauf, dass du dem Gehörten oder Gelesenen einen logischen Sinn geben kannst.

Gezielt hören/lesen: Lies vor dem Hören oder Lesen immer die Aufgabe genau durch. Oft benötigst du nur bestimmte Informationen, auf die du gezielt achten musst.

Zahlen und Internationalismen: Beim Hören musst du dich sehr konzentrieren, um dem normalen Redefluss des Sprechers zu folgen. Je nach Aufgabenstellung helfen dir hier besonders Zahlenangaben und englische oder internationale Wörter, die wir im Deutschen übernommen haben.

Bedeutung ableiten: Dasselbe trifft für das Lesen zu. Außerdem solltest du hier auf Wörter achten, deren Schriftbild dem deutscher Wörter entspricht oder ähnelt und so die Bedeutung eines Wortes ableiten.

Logik: Denke daran: Wenn der Satz keinen Sinn ergibt, hast du irgendwo etwas nicht richtig übertragen.

-29 ## Topic 1

Situation 1

Du machst gerade zusammen mit deinem Cousin ein Praktikum in London. Er hat sich dort ein englisches Handy gekauft und möchte gerne seine Eltern anrufen. Bevor sein Anruf durchgestellt wird, hört er fünf kurze Infotexte seines Telefonanbieters „Blueline". Leider kann dein Cousin nicht alles verstehen und bittet dich um Hilfe.

In der Box findest du Schlüsselwörter, auf die du beim Hören besonders achten solltest. Lies sie vor dem Hören durch und überlege, was sie heißen. Lies sie dir oder deinem/r Nachbarn/in anschließend halblaut vor und versuche, das Lautbild im Ohr zu behalten. Das hilft dir, die Ansagen zu verstehen.

1. Was mache ich, wenn mein Guthaben aufgebraucht ist?	*1. to top up, add credit to your phone*
2. Wie kann ich meinen aktuellen Kontostand abfragen?	*2. your current balance*
3. Zu welchen Dingen bekomme ich Hilfe, wenn ich Taste 3 drücke?	*3. features like e-mail, video and picture messages or Internet access*
4. Mit wem wollen sie mich verbinden?	*4. to put somebody through to*
5. Was muss ich tun, wenn ich mich über die Kosten meines Ferngesprächs informieren möchte?	*5. the cost of a call, text the name*

Situation 2

Du und dein Cousin hört kurz darauf eine Radiowerbung von Blueline.

Erzähle deinem Cousin, worum es geht.

Topic 2

Situation

Deine Klasse hat einen gemeinsamen Kinobesuch geplant. Ihr seid euch noch nicht einig, welchen Film ihr anschauen wollt. Allerdings habt ihr bereits abgesprochen, dass es ein erfolgreicher, spannender und moderner Film sein soll. Ihr konntet euch jedoch noch nicht entscheiden, ob ihr lieber einen Action-Film oder eine Lovestory sehen möchtet.

Du hast von deinem englischen Brieffreund diese Filmkritik geschickt bekommen. Prüfe, ob dieser Film für deine Klasse geeignet ist.

Informiere deine Klasse über …

1. die Handlung,
2 das Besondere des Films,
3. den bisherigen Erfolg des Films.

plot/storyline • successful • dramatic • full of suspense • game show host

Opening: 19 Mar • Directed by: Danny Boyle

Principal actors: Dev Patel, Anil Kapoor, Saurabh Shukla, Freida Pinto, Rajendranath Zutshi

Slumdog Millionaire is an extremely unusual film with scenes which are so awful that you may wish to leave the cinema at once. But if you are strong and tough enough, you will see a fascinating movie which will make you hold your breath.

In the slums of Bombay two little boys have to watch how their mother is killed during religious riots. They make friends with another slum child, Latika, and this friendship will continue throughout their lives.

You can watch how India's technological boom starts. By the time the children grow up, Bombay has become Mumbai. In the slum area where they once lived there are now high-rise flats for richer people. Jamal (Dev Patel) is the younger brother who takes part in the television quiz show "Who Wants To Be a Millionaire?" As the unpleasant Prem Kumar (Anil Kapoor) asks the questions, Jamal remembers situations in his childhood which we see in flashbacks. Mr. Kumar believes that a "slumdog" can only answer his questions by cheating. So he hands Jamal over to the police, hoping that they can discover how he does it. Is Jamal telling the truth? Will he reach the finals and win twenty million rupees? Most importantly, will he finally find the love of his life?

This movie shows how good people triumph over bad ones and the ending is sure to be happy. Jamal is an honest and good boy, his older brother Salim (Madhur Mittal) chooses a life of crime. Latika (Freida Pinto) is beautiful and constant. This impressive movie won the Audience Choice Award at the Chicago International Film Festival and was in the Best Film Category at the British Independent Film Awards in 2008. In 2009 the film won eight Oscars. *(Peggy Richardson)*

Topic 3

,30 **Situation 1**

Du machst mit deiner Familie Urlaub an der Westküste der USA. Als ihr gegen Mittag im Hotelzimmer seid, erhältst du diese Tsunami-Warnung als Telefondurchsage.

Sage deiner Familie was du gehört hast:

1. Was genau ist ein Tsunami?
2. Was wird über die Wellen gesagt?
3. Wovor werden Surfer gewarnt und was müssen die Leute tun, die am Strand oder in der Nähe des Strandes sind?

,31 **Situation 2**

Du bist mit deinem Freund/deiner Freundin in einem Supermarkt in England und ihr hört folgende Werbedurchsage. Dein Freund/deine Freundin kann nicht so gut Englisch. Er/sie möchte wissen, was zu den folgenden Lebensmitteln gesagt wurde.

Informiere deinen Freund/deine Freundin.

bananas • cheese • chicken • apples

,32 **Situation 3**

Wenig später hört ihr noch eine weitere Durchsage.

Informiere deinen Freund/deine Freundin, worum es geht.

Situation 4

Dein englischer Austauschpartner/deine englische Austauschpartnerin interessiert sich für das Produkt auf dem folgenden Werbeplakat.

Beantworte seine/ihre Fragen dazu auf Englisch.

1. Where do the pears come from?
2. What's special about them?
3. What happens on Thursday?

Topic 4

1,33 **Situation 1**

Du und deine Familie fliegen mit einer amerikanischen Fluggesellschaft in den Urlaub. Nach ca. 20 Minuten meldet sich der Pilot mit der folgenden Ansage. Es gibt keine deutsche Übersetzung danach.
Informiere deine Familie darüber, was gesagt wurde.

Situation 2

Deine Freundin ist 17 und hat noch keine richtigen beruflichen Vorstellungen. Sie kann sehr gut auf Menschen zugehen, absolviert gegenwärtig verschiedene Praktika in unterschiedlichen Handelsketten, um Erfahrungen zu sammeln, und verbessert ihr Englisch. Danach möchte sie erst einmal gern irgendwo im Ausland arbeiten. Dafür ist sie schon jetzt ständig auf der Suche nach interessanten Arbeitsmöglichkeiten. Du hast diese Anzeige gefunden.
Erkläre deiner Freundin, warum diese Stelle gut für sie geeignet ist.

"FIT for SPORT", Australia's leading sports shop centres have jobs available for Casual Sales Assistants in the Clothes and Consumer Goods Departments at the Sunshine store in SA.

This is what we'll expect of you:

- no special experience in selling goods as training will be provided. However, experience is an advantage.
- exemplary motivation.
- excellent customer service skills.

The last two points are *musts* for this position.

We offer a great career, extensive training and above average payment.
This is a fantastic opportunity to join a successful, fast growing shopping centre.

Contact: Lucy Capp
LU197, MNO4, South Mall, Sunshine Shopping Centre 50 Park Way
Elizabeth, S Australia 501253
Phone: 18 8252 8011 22

Inhalt

Die Grammatik aus Band 5 findest du online unter ⇨ 547560-0008.

Grammatikbegriffe

Grammatical terms

Lateinisch / Deutsch	Englisch	Englisches Beispiel
Adjektiv / Eigenschaftswort	adjective	quick, small, nice, old
Adverb / Umstandswort	adverb	always, often, quickly, loudly
Aktiv **Ov5**	active voice	The government wrote the Queen's speech.
Bedingungssätze Typ I **Ov7** (If-Sätze + Präsens)	conditional clauses (present)	The Queen can declare war if Parliament tells her to do so.
Bedingungssätze Typ II **Ov7** (If-Sätze + Präteritum)	conditional clauses (past)	There wouldn't be a UK government if the Queen refused to open Parliament.
Demonstrativpronomen/ hinweisendes Fürwort	demonstrative pronoun	this, that, these, those
Gerundium	Gerund	We enjoy going to parties.
Gradadverb **G5**	adverb of degree	very, really, almost
Häufigkeitsadverb	adverb of frequency	always, often, sometimes, never
Hilfsverb **Ov3**	auxiliary	be, have got, do
Indirekte Rede mit Zeitverschiebung **G2**	reported speech (later)	He said he didn't like walking to school.
Indirekte Rede ohne Zeitverschiebung **G1**	reported speech (immediate)	She says that he doesn't like walking to school.

Lateinisch / Deutsch	Englisch	Englisches Beispiel
Infinitiv / Grundform des Verbs	infinitive	to do, to go, to see
modales Hilfsverb / Modalverb Ov 6	modal verb	may, must/n't, need/n't, should/n't, can/'t
Nebensatz	sub-clause	If she arrives late, … .
Objektpronomen Ov 8	object pronoun	me, you, him, her, it, us, them
Passiv in der einfachen Gegenwart Ov 5	passive voice: simple present	These laws are made to protect us.
Passiv in der einfachen Vergangenheit Ov 5	passive voice: simple past	The Queen's speech was actually written by the government.
Perfekt Ov 3, 5	present perfect	Tom has already painted the walls.
Personalpronomen / persönliches Fürwort Ov 8	personal pronoun	I, you, he, she, it, we, you, they
Plural / Mehrzahl	plural	girls, children, babies
Plusquamperfekt / vollendete Vergangenheit G 4	past perfect	It was when a boy had whistled at me on the beach.
Possessivbegleiter / besitzanzeigendes Fürwort Ov 8	possessive pronoun	my, your, his, her, its, our, your, their
Präposition	preposition	in, on, at, about, over
Präsens / einfache Gegenwart Ov 1–3, Ov 5	simple present	I live in Greenwich.
Präteritum / einfache Vergangenheit Ov 1–3, Ov 5	simple past	I watched TV yesterday.
Reflexivpronomen / rückbezügliche Fürwörter G 3	reflexive pronoun	myself, yourself, ourselves, themselves
Relativpronomen	relative pronoun	Sam is the boy who I like.
Relativsatz	relative clause	Everyone who lives here can speak English.
Signalwort Ov 5	signal word	last, ago, yesterday, ever, yet
Singular / Einzahl	singular	a girl, a boy, an apple
Steigerung von Adjektiven	comparison of adjectives	old – older – the oldest, good – better – the best
2. Stammform / 3. Stammform Ov 5	perfect participle / past participle	ate/eaten, did/done, went/gone
Stützwort ‚one' / ‚ones'	prop word 'one' / 'ones'	Which one do you like best?
Substantiv / Hauptwort	noun	book, dog, sandwich
Verb / Tätigkeitswort Ov 1–5	verb	to be, to go, to do, to write
Verlaufsform der Gegenwart Ov 1–2	present progressive	We are having a party.
Verlaufsform der Vergangenheit Ov 4	past progressive	I was walking my dog in the park.
Will-Futur Ov 1–3, Ov 5	'will'-future	I hope it will be warm tomorrow.
Wortstellung im Satz G 6	word order	I like fruit drinks.

Ov1 Vollverben (regelmäßige) in den einzelnen Zeiten

Regular verbs in different tenses

Infinitiv: to live

Aussagen – Kurzformen/Langformen

Pronouns	simple past	present progressive	simple present	will-future
	verb-*ed*	*am/is/are* + verb-*ing*	verb (+s)	*will* + verb
I	I lived	I'm (am) living	I live	I will live
You	You lived	You're (are) living	You live	You will live
He/She/It	He/She/It lived	He's/She's/It's (is) living	He/She/It lives	He/She/It will live
We	We lived	We're (are) living	We live	We will live
You	You lived	You're (are) living	You live	You will live
They	They lived	They're (are) living	They live	They will live

Verneinungen – Kurzformen

Pronouns	simple past	present progressive	simple present	will-future
I	I didn't live	I'm not living	I don't live	I won't live
You	You didn't live	You aren't living	You don't live	You won't live
He/She/It	He/She/It didn't live	He/She/It isn't living	He/She/It doesn't live	He/She/It won't live
We	We didn't live	We aren't living	We don't live	We won't live
You	You didn't live	You aren't living	You don't live	You won't live
They	They didn't live	They aren't living	They don't live	They won't live

Fragen

Pronouns	simple past	present progressive	simple present	will-future
I	Did I live ...?	Am I living ...?	Do I live ...?	Will I live ...?
You	Did you live ...?	Are you living ...?	Do you live ...?	Will you live ...?
He/She/It	Did he/she/it live ...?	Is he/she/it living ...?	Does he/she/it live ...?	Will he/she/it live ...?
We	Did we live ...?	Are we living ...?	Do we live ...?	Will we live ...?
You	Did you live ...?	Are you living ...?	Do you live ...?	Will you live ...?
They	Did they live ...?	Are they living ...?	Do they live ...?	Will they live ...?

Examples:

I **live** in Germany.
I **lived** in England 10 years ago.
When I'm 18, I hope I'**ll live** in my own flat.
Look at this photo. I'**m living** here at the moment with my grandparents.

Ov 2 Vollverben (unregelmäßige) in den einzelnen Zeiten

Irregular verbs in different tenses

Infinitiv: to drive (a car)

Aussagen – Kurzformen/Langformen

Pronouns	simple past	present progressive	simple present	will-future
	2. Form	*am/is/are* + verb-*ing*	verb (+s)	*will* + verb
I	I drove	I'm (am) driving	I drive	I'll (will) drive
You	You drove	You're (are) driving	You drive	You'll (will) drive
He/She/It	He/She/It drove	He's/She's/It's (is) driving	He/She/It drives	He'll/She'll/It'll (will) drive
We	We drove	We're (are) driving	We drive	We'll (will) drive
You	You drove	You're (are) driving	You drive	You'll (will) drive
They	They drove	They're (are) driving	They drive	They'll (will) drive

Verneinungen – Kurzformen

Pronouns	simple past	present progressive	simple present	will-future
I	I didn't drive	I'm not driving	I don't drive	I won't drive
You	You didn't drive	You aren't driving	You don't drive	You won't drive
He/She/It	He/She/It didn't drive	He/She/It isn't driving	He/She/It doesn't drive	He/She/It won't drive
We	We didn't drive	We aren't driving	We don't drive	We won't drive
You	You didn't drive	You aren't driving	You don't drive	You won't drive
They	They didn't drive	They aren't driving	They don't drive	They won't drive

Fragen

Pronouns	simple past	present progressive	simple present	will-future
I	Did I drive …?	Am I driving …?	Do I drive …?	Will I drive …?
You	Did you drive …?	Are you driving …?	Do you drive …?	Will you drive …?
He/She/It	Did he drive …?	Is he driving …?	Does he drive …?	Will he drive …?
We	Did we drive …?	Are we driving …?	Do we drive …?	Will we drive …?
You	Did you drive …?	Are you driving …?	Do you drive …?	Will you drive …?
They	Did they drive …?	Are they driving …?	Do they drive …?	Will they drive …?

Examples:

I **don't drive** to school – I always **go** by bus!
We **drove** to France last September.
I'm sure I'**ll drive** to school in my own car next year.
Where's Dad? – He'**s driving** Mum to the station.

Ov 3 Formen von *be* in den einzelnen Zeiten: Aussagen und Verneinung

The verb 'to be' in different tenses: statements and negations

Aussagen – Langformen/Kurzformen

	past perfect	present perfect	simple past	simple present	will-future
I *Ich*	had been / 'd been *war gewesen*	have been / 've been *bin gewesen*	was *war*	am / 'm *bin*	will be / 'll be *werde sein*
You *Du*	had been / 'd been *warst gewesen*	have been / 've been *bist gewesen*	were *warst*	are / 're *bist*	will be / 'll be *wirst sein*
He/She/It *Er/Sie/Es*	had been / 'd been *war gewesen*	has been / 's been *ist gewesen*	was *war*	is / 's *ist*	will be / 'll be *wird sein*
We *Wir*	had been / 'd been *waren gewesen*	have been / 've been *sind gewesen*	were *waren*	are / 're *sind*	will be / 'll be *werden sein*
You *Ihr*	had been / 'd been *wart gewesen*	have been / 've been *seid gewesen*	were *wart*	are / 're *seid*	will be / 'll be *werdet sein*
They *Sie*	had been / 'd been *waren gewesen*	have been / 've been *sind gewesen*	were *waren*	are / 're *sind*	will be / 'll be *werden sein*

Verneinungen – Kurzformen

	past perfect	present perfect	simple past	simple present	will-future
I	hadn't been	haven't been	wasn't	am not	won't be
You	hadn't been	haven't been	weren't	aren't	won't be
He/She/It	hadn't been	hasn't been	wasn't	isn't	won't be
We	hadn't been	haven't been	weren't	aren't	won't be
You	hadn't been	haven't been	weren't	aren't	won't be
They	hadn't been	haven't been	weren't	aren't	won't be

Beachte!
Nach Personalpronomen verwendet man in der Regel die Kurzformen von *be ('m, 's, 're)*.
Die Langformen *(am, is, are)* benötigst du in der Regel nach Substantiven und bei Fragen und Verneinungen: *Am I …? Is he already …? You aren't … .*

Ov 4 Die Verlaufsform in weiteren Zeiten *The progressive form in different tenses*

Zeit	Bildung	Beispiele
present progressive	*am/are/is* + verb+ *-ing*	I**'m washing** the dishes. *Ich spüle (gerade) ab.* **Is** he **watching** TV? *Schaut er (gerade) fern?*
past progressive	*was/were* + verb + *-ing*	I **was walking** my dog in the park. *Ich habe meinen Hund im Park ausgeführt.* What **were** you **doing**? *Was hast du gemacht?* We **weren't cleaning** the kitchen. *Wir haben die Küche nicht sauber gemacht.*

Beachte!
Die Verlaufsform gibt es auch in anderen Zeiten, z.B.:
I **have been helping** my grandfather for three days. *Ich helfe meinem Großvater schon drei Tage lang.*
We **had been sitting** in our car for 30 minutes when the rain stopped. *Wir hatten 30 Minuten lang in unserem Auto gesessen, als es aufhörte zu regnen.*

Ov 5 Aktiv und Passiv — *Active and passive voice*

	ACTIVE			
Beispiel	The government **wrote** the Queen's speech.	This is the reason why international organisations **have flown out** most of their staff.	Parliament **makes** these laws to protect us and our rights.	Young people **will do** these jobs.
Bildung	**verb-*ed*/ 2. Stammform**	***have*/*has* + verb-*ed*/ 3. Stammform**	**verb** (+s)	***will* + verb**
↑ (Aktiv) Zeitform ↓ (Passiv)	→ **Simple past** • über Vergangenes berichten	→ **Present perfect** • etwas Vergangenes mit Auswirkungen auf die Gegenwart • Ergebnis	→ **Simple present** • regelmäßige Handlungen • Tatsachen • Fakten	→ **Will-future** • Vorhersagen • spontane Entscheidungen • Versprechen, Hilfe
Signalwörter	ago, yesterday, last …, in (year)	just, already, never, for ever, yet, since	always, often, sometimes	in (year), tomorrow, next (*Wochentag*)
Bildung	***was*/*were* + verb-*ed*/ 3. Stammform** (+ by)	***have been*/*has been* + verb-*ed*/ 3. Stammform** (+ by)	***is*/*are* + verb-*ed*/ 3. Stammform** (+ by)	***will be* + verb-*ed*/ 3. Stammform** (+ by)
Beispiel	The Queen's speech **was written** by the government.	This is the reason why most of the staff of international organisations **have been flown out**.	These laws **are made** by Parliament to protect us and our rights.	These jobs **will be done** by young people.
	PASSIVE			

Beachte!

- Ob ein Satz im Aktiv oder Passiv verwendet wird, hängt von der Absicht des Sprechers/der Sprecherin ab.
- Will er/sie ausdrücken, wer etwas tut, getan hat oder tun wird, verwendet er/sie das Aktiv.
- Soll aber mehr betont werden, was mit wem geschieht, verwendet er/sie eine Passivkonstruktion. Hier ist also die Handlung wichtig.
- Falls der/die Handelnde bekannt ist, kann er/sie mit *by* hinzugefügt werden.

Ov 6 Modalverben *Modals*

Mit den Modalverben kann man ausdrücken, was jemand tun kann/darf (***can***), tun sollte (***should***), tun darf (***may***), tun muss (***must***), nicht zu tun braucht (***needn't***) und nicht tun darf (***mustn't***). Mit ihnen kann man Regeln, Empfehlungen und Verbote ausdrücken.
Sie sind für alle Personen gleich und können nur im ***simple present*** verwendet werden. Das Vollverb dahinter steht immer in der Grundform. Bei Fragen setzt man (wie im Deutschen auch) das Modalverb einfach an den Anfang der Frage bzw. hinter das Fragewort.

Aussagen und verneinte Sätze

Beispiel	Übersetzung
You **can have** my new CD. We **should ask** for help. You **mustn't walk** on the grass. I **needn't wash** my clothes. Pauline **must go** to the doctor. Children **shouldn't watch** late night films.	*Du kannst meine neue CD haben.* *Wir sollten um Hilfe bitten.* *Du darfst /Man darf nicht auf dem Gras laufen.* *Ich brauche meine Kleidung nicht zu waschen.* *Pauline muss zum Arzt gehen.* *Kinder sollten keine Spätfilme anschauen.*

Fragen

Beispiel	Übersetzung
May I go out tonight? **Must** we book a table? What **must** students not do?	*Darf ich heute Abend weggehen?* *Müssen wir einen Tisch reservieren?* *Was dürfen Schüler/innen nicht (tun)?*

Beachte!
Die Verneinung von *can, may* und *should* wird einfach durch Anhängen von *not* gebildet:
can't = cannot; may not, should not = shouldn't.
must not (mustn't) heißt **„nicht dürfen“**!
Die Verneinung von *must* ist *need not* (*needn't*) **„nicht müssen“**!

Ov 7 Bedingungssätze Typ I und II — *Conditional clauses type I and II*

Typ 1

Bedingungssätze bestehen aus zwei Teilen: dem Nebensatz mit *if*, der die Bedingung ausdrückt, und dem Hauptsatz, der erklärt, was passiert, wenn diese Bedingung erfüllt wird/nicht erfüllt wird.
Der *if*-Satz steht im *simple present*, im Hauptsatz wird das *will-future* oder *can/may/should/must* … + *verb* oder die Befehlsform verwendet. Der *if*-Satz kann am Anfang oder am Ende des Satzes stehen. Steht der *if*-Satz am Anfang, wird er durch ein Komma abgetrennt.

Aussagen

If YAs **have** a problem, they **must ask** for help.
Wenn YAs ein Problem haben, müssen sie um Hilfe bitten.

Bei der Verneinung wird *will* im Hauptsatz zu *won't*. Im *if*-Satz steht vor der Grundform des Verbs *don't/doesn't*. Verneinungen müssen nicht in beiden Satzteilen gleichzeitig vorkommen.

Verneinte Sätze

If YAs **don't understand** something, they **must ask**.
Wenn YAs etwas nicht verstehen, müssen sie fragen.

Bei Fragen wandert das *will* bzw. das Fragewort und *will* an den Satzanfang.

Fragen

Will anyone **help me** if one of my colleagues **bullies me**?
Wird mir jemand helfen, wenn ich von einem meiner Kollegen belästigt werde?

Typ 2

Bedingungssätze vom Typ 2 drücken eine offene Bedingung aus. Sie beschreiben zum einen Bedingungen, die zwar prinzipiell noch möglich, aber relativ unwahrscheinlich sind. Zum anderen beschreiben sie aber auch Umstände, die nicht mehr anders eintreten können.
Der *if*-Satz steht im *simple past*. Im Hauptsatz steht *would/'d* oder *could* vor dem Verb.

Aussagen

If the Queen **refused** to sign a law, she **could stop** the government's plans.
Wenn sich die Queen weigern würde, ein Gesetz zu unterzeichnen, könnte sie das Vorhaben der Regierung stoppen.

Bei der Verneinung wird *would* im Hauptsatz zu *wouldn't*. Im *if*-Satz steht vor der Grundform des Verbs *didn't*. Verneinungen müssen nicht in beiden Satzteilen gleichzeitig vorkommen.

Verneinte Sätze

If the Queen **refused** to open Parliament, there **wouldn't be** a UK governemnt.
Wenn die Queen sich weigern würde, das Parlament zu eröffnen, gäbe es keine Regierung in Großbritannien.

Bei Fragen wandert das *would* bzw. das Fragewort und *would* an den Satzanfang.

Fragen

Would there **be** a problem if the Queen **refused** to sign a law?
Gäbe es ein Problem, wenn die Queen sich weigern würde, ein Gesetz zu unterzeichnen?

Ov 8 Pronomen *Pronouns*

Personalpronomen *Personal pronouns*	**Objektform** *Object pronouns*	**Possessivpronomen** *Possessive pronouns*
I *ich*	me *mir/mich*	my *mein*
you *du*	you *dir/dich/Ihnen/Sie*	your *dein/Ihr*
he *er*	him *ihm/ihn*	his *sein*
she *sie*	her *ihr/sie*	her *ihr*
it *es*	it *ihm/es*	its *sein*
we *wir*	us *uns*	our *unser*
you *ihr*	you *euch/Ihnen/Sie*	your *euer/Ihr*
they *sie*	them *ihnen/sie*	their *ihr*

Beispiele

I like my cat and my cat loves me. — *Ich liebe meine Katze und meine Katze liebt mich.*

If you help Mr Brown in his garden, he'll give you five pounds. — *Wenn du Mr Brown in seinem Garten hilfst, wird er dir fünf Pfund geben.*

If she hasn't got time, I'll do the shopping for her. — *Wenn sie keine Zeit hat, mache ich den Einkauf für sie.*

She told us that she had won a competition at her school and in the town where she lived. — *Sie erzählte uns, dass sie an ihrer Schule und in der Stadt, wo sie lebt, einen Wettbewerb gewonnen hat.*

Beachte!

Pronomen werden auch FÜRwörter genannt, weil sie für Personen, Tiere oder Gegenstände stehen, um z. B. ein bestimmtes Wort nicht dauernd zu wiederholen. **Personalpronomen** ersetzen das **Subjekt** im Satz (*Emma is from Bristol. – She's from Bristol*). Soll das **Objekt des Satzes** ersetzt werden, verwendest du dafür die **Objektform** der Personalpronomen (*My friends like my pets. – They often feed them*). Possessivpronomen drücken aus, **wem etwas gehört** (*This is my book*).

G1 Indirekte Rede (sofort berichtet) *Reported speech (immediate)*

Rede kann direkt oder indirekt sein. Direkte Rede nennt man die tatsächliche Äußerung einer Person. Von indirekter Rede spricht man, wenn jemand darüber berichtet, was jemand anders gesagt hat. Verben wie *to say, to claim, to think, to explain, to tell someone, to shout, to suggest, to add, to report* mit oder ohne *that* leiten die indirekte Rede ein. Je nachdem, ob direkte Rede sofort oder später erst wiedergegeben wird, verwendet man im Englischen unterschiedliche Zeiten.

Indirekte Rede – sofort berichtet – ohne Zeitverzögerung

Direkte / Wörtliche Rede ***simple present***	**Einleitungssatz** ***simple present***		**Indirekte Rede** ***simple present***
"Most of us have heard of environmental changes."	They write	(that)	most of them have heard of environmental changes.
"I don't like walking to school."	He says	(that)	he doesn't like walking to school.

Setzt man Fragen in die indirekte Rede, braucht man das Wort *if* oder ein Fragewort. *If* wird in diesem Fall mit ‚ob' übersetzt.

"How much hot water do you use to wash your clothes?"	They ask	how	much hot water we use to wash our clothes.
"Are greenhouse gases bad for our world?"	They want to know	if	greenhouse gases are bad for our world.

Übersetzung von Aussagen, verneinten Sätzen und Fragen	
They write that most of them have heard of environmental changes.	*Sie schreiben, dass die meisten von ihnen von Umweltveränderungen gehört haben.*
He says that he doesn't like walking to school.	*Er sagt, dass er nicht gern zur Schule läuft.*
They want to know if greenhouse gases are bad for the world.	*Sie möchten wissen, ob Treibhausgase schlecht für unsere Welt sind.*

Beachte!

Pronomen aus der direkten Rede ändern sich in der indirekten Rede.

I – ich	wird zu	→	he/she – er/sie
we – wir	wird zu	→	they – sie
my – mein	wird zu	→	his/her – sein/ihr
our – unser	wird zu	→	their – ihr (Pl.)

Einige Adverbialbestimmungen der Zeit aus der direkten Rede ändern sich in der indirekten Rede.

this morning	→	that morning
today	→	that day
yesterday	→	the day before
tomorrow	→	the next day
next week	→	the following week

G 2 Indirekte Rede (später berichtet) *Reported speech (later)*

Wird indirekte Rede erst später berichtet, steht das einleitende Verb im *simple past*. Im Folgesatz gibt es dann eine Zeitverschiebung: *simple present* → *simple past*.

Direkte Rede *simple present*	**Einleitungssatz** *simple past*		**Indirekte Rede** *simple past*
"Most of us **know** about the environmental changes in the world."	They **wrote**	(that)	most of them **knew** about the environmental changes in the world.
"I **don't like** walking to school."	He **said**		he **didn't like** walking to school.
"**Are** greenhouse gases bad for our world?"	They **wanted to know**	if	greenhouse gases **were** bad for our world.
"How much hot water **do** you **use** to wash your clothes?"	They **asked**	how much	hot water we **used** to wash our clothes.

Übersetzung von Aussagen, verneinten Sätzen und Fragen	
They wrote that most of them knew about the environmental changes.	*Sie schrieben, dass die meisten von ihnen von Umweltveränderungen wissen/wüssten.*
He said that he didn't like walking to school.	*Er sagte, dass er nicht gern zur Schule läuft/laufe.*
They wanted to know if greenhouse gases were bad for our world.	*Sie wollten wissen, ob Treibhausgase schlecht für unsere Welt seien.*

Beachte!
Manche Verben ändern ihre Form nicht, z.B. *should*:
Dad: "It **should** be OK!" → Dad **told me** that it **should** be OK.

G 3 Reflexivpronomen *Reflexive pronouns*

Mit Reflexivpronomen kannst du ausdrücken, dass jemand etwas selbst oder für sich selbst tut. Somit entspricht es den deutschen Pronomen **mich/mir (selbst), dich/dir (selbst), sich (selbst)** etc. Du kannst es auch benutzen, um zu betonen, dass du etwas selbst gemacht hast.

Bildung

Singular		**Plural**	
I	– myself	we	– ourselves
you	– yourself	you	– yourselves
he	– himself	they	– themselves
she	– herself		
it	– itself		

Beachte!
Verben, die im Deutschen mit ‚sich' gebildet werden, werden nicht automatisch im Englischen von den Reflexivpronomen *-self/-selves* begleitet.
Im Englischen kann „sich waschen" *to wash* oder *to wash yourself* und „sich anziehen" *to dress* oder *to dress yourself* heißen.

Beispielsätze

1. You needn't help me. I can do it **myself.**	*Du brauchst mir nicht zu helfen. Ich kann das allein/selbst tun.*
2. She fell off her bike and hurt **herself.**	*Sie fiel vom Fahrrad und verletzte sich.*
3. Cats always clean **themselves.**	*Katzen putzen sich immer (selbst).*
4. We can see **ourselves** in the mirror.	*Wir können uns im Spiegel sehen.*
5. How much hot water do you use to wash **yourself**?	*Wie viel warmes Wasser brauchst du, um dich zu waschen?*
6. There are a lot of books about how we can train **ourselves** not to overeat.	*Es gibt viele Bücher darüber, wie wir trainieren können, nicht zu viel zu essen/uns nicht zu überfressen.*
7. It's far better for you to do sport **yourself.**	*Es ist viel besser, selbst Sport zu treiben.*

Übersetzung

-self/selves *sich selbst*, *selbst*, *sich*, *Objektform*

G 4 Vollendete Vergangenheit — *Past perfect*

Mit dem *past perfect* kannst du ausdrücken, dass eine **Handlung in der Vergangenheit vor einer anderen** stattgefunden hat. Du erkennst solche Handlungen oft an Signalwörtern wie **nachdem** – *after*, **als** – *when*.
Handlungen im *past perfect* werden oft in Nebensätzen ausgedrückt. Der Hauptsatz drückt die nachfolgende Handlung aus und steht deshalb im *simple past*.

Bildung

Aussagen

had + verb + *-ed*	*had asked*
had + 3. Stammform	*had written*

Verneinung

hadn't + verb + *-ed*	*hadn't asked*
hadn't + 3. Stammform	*hadn't written*

Fragebildung

	Had + …+ verb + *-ed* / 3. Stammform	*Had (he) asked / written …?*
Fragewort +	*had* + … + verb + *-ed* / 3. Stammform	*What had (he) asked / written?*

Beispiele

It was *Das war,*	<u>when</u> a boy **had whistled** at me on the beach. *<u>als</u> am Strand ein Junge hinter mir hergepfiffen hatte.*
	Had he **whistled** at you before? *Hatte er dir schon vorher hinterher gepfiffen?*
'You will get well again,' *Du wirst wieder gesund,*	he **had said** <u>as</u> he ran a finger over a photo. *hatte er gesagt, <u>als</u> er mit dem Finger über das Foto strich.*
	What had he **said** the day before? *Was hatte er am Tag davor gesagt?*

G 5 Gradadverbien — *Adverbs of degree*

Gradadverbien antworten auf die Frage ***How much?*** – Wie viel? / ***How + Adj/Adv?*** – Wie genau …?
Du lernst einige von ihnen als Vokabeln, z. B. *a bit, almost, quite, really, super, very much, …* . Andere können mit *-ly* aus Adjektiven gebildet werden, z. B. *absolutely, extremely, …* . Sie stehen vor dem Wort, das sie näher erklären.

Beispiele

He was **very** sorry because he had forgotten her.	*Es tat ihm* **sehr** *leid, dass er sie vergessen hatte.*
Without his glasses he was **almost** blind.	*Ohne seine Brille war er* **fast** *blind.*
I was **really** glad when he suggested we should walk back home.	*Ich war* **wirklich** *froh, als er vorschlug, nach Hause zu laufen.*

G 6 Die Wortstellung im Satz — *The position of words in a sentence*

Die Wortstellung im Satz ist Subjekt – Hilfsverb/Verb – Objekt. Dabei bilden Verb und Objekt eine feste Einheit, man darf keine anderen Satzteile dazwischenstellen.
Bei der Verneinung wird das Hilfsverb mit *not* verneint, wenn kein Hilfsverb vorhanden ist, wird *do/does + not* vor das Vollverb gestellt.

	Subjekt	**Hilfsverb/Verb**	**Objekt**	
	I	like	fruit drinks.	
	I	don't like	fruit drinks.	
Yesterday	my friend	was		in trouble with her parents.
Yesterday	my friend	wasn't		in trouble with her parents.
	She	has been drinking	alcohol	at parties.
	She	hasn't been drinking	alcohol	at parties.

Bei Fragen wird das Hilfsverb bzw. werden das Fragewort + Hilfsverb an den Satzanfang vor das Subjekt gestellt. Ist kein Hilfsverb vorhanden, wird *do/does* oder *did* eingefügt.

Fragewort	**Hilfsverb**	**Subjekt**	**Verb**	**Objekt**	**Rest des Satzes**
	Does	your teen	recognize	the serious dangers	that go with alcohol and drugs?
	Was	it		Louise?	
How	does	your child	choose	friends?	
What	do	you	think,		Sean?
What	should	I	do?		

Ov 1 – Ov 3 Vollverben (Fragen bilden)

1 On an English exchange

a) *Make a list of the verbs in this text and add their infinitive form.*

A group of young people from Berlin are in South England on a language exchange. During the exchange they live with local families. They learn the language and they also find out about the people and the culture. One afternoon Hussein and his girlfriend, Alina, are at a bus stop. They hear some young British people. Their language sounds like a muddle of Turkish and English. Hussein tells Alina that it's just like back home: He and his mates often mix German and Turkish.
A few days later the same thing happens again. Only this time Alina hears a couple in a shop – and this time the languages are English and Russian. When Alina tells her guest family, they all laugh. "That's pukka English!" explains the daughter, Nasreen. "Mix and match – anything you like!"

b) *Use the verbs below and write full questions on the text. The other words can help you.*

1. to be: who – on an exchange?
2. to live: where – they?
3. to learn: what – they?
4. to find out: what – they also?
5. to be: when – Hussein and Alina – at the bus stop?
6. to sound like: what – language?
7. to be: where – just like that?
8. to mix: what – often?
9. to happen: when – same thing – again?
10. to be: what – languages – this time?
11. to laugh: why – they?
12. to explain: what – Nasreen?

c) *Write five questions where the answer could be 'yes' or 'no'. Use 'do'/'does' or 'is'/'are'.*
Examples: Does the group (do the people) come from England? – No, they don't.
Is Hussein (are Hussein and Alina) from London? – No, they aren't.

d) *Now answer your questions from c).*

Ov 5 Das Passiv im *simple present*

1 News – facts or fiction?

Put the verbs into the right form of the simple present passive and complete the sentences.
Example: Today news and events **are brought** … .

1. Today news and events (*to bring*) to us quicker than ever before.
2. For example, if a bank (*to rob*) in the next town, a video (*to offer*) in minutes on YouTube.
3. Newspapers (*to sell*) and (*to buy*) everywhere, of course.
4. A good thing about the Internet is that news (*to update*) more frequently.
5. But how do you know if the info that (*to give*) there is correct?
6. Some of the news on the Internet (*to invent*) by people who think it's a big joke.
7. Today the world (*to divide*) into two groups – those who want facts and those who want fiction!

Ov 5 Das Passiv im *simple past*

1 TV – Did you know?

a) *Match the sentences and find out about how television was developed.*

1. TV *was invented by*	this because it means ***far sight***?
2. The first televisions *were produced in*	had bigger screens.
3. Did you know that it *was called*	space in the 1960s.
4. Then TV satellites *were launched into*	Zworykin and Farnsworth.
5. More channels *were opened as*	Europe till 1967.
6. Colour TV *wasn't introduced in*	the Internet.
7. Later, models *were developed which*	TV became more popular.
8. In the 1990s TV *was first linked to*	black and white only.

b) *Answer the questions about the first phone. Use the phrases in the box.*

1. **When** was the first phone invented?
2. **Who** was it developed **by**?
3. **Where** was the first call made **from**?
4. **Where** was the first call made **to**?
5. **What** was the first 'mobile' radio phone called?

(from) Boston USA • a 'cave radio' phone (1908) • Alexander Graham Bell and Elisha Gray • (to) Cambridge USA • 1875

Ov 6 Modalverben

1 A holiday flat by the sea

Choose the right modal and complete the sentences.

1. "Joe, the sea looks great! (*must/can*) we drive to the beach before lunch, please?"
2. "Yes, we (*can/must*)! But we (*needn't/can't*) go by car – we (*can't/can*) easily walk there, Sue!"
3. "Good! But I (*mustn't/needn't*) forget my cap and sunglasses! They're in the back of the car."
4. "Well, I guess we (*mustn't/needn't*) take our sweaters with us. It feels very warm now."
5. "No, we (*needn't/can't*). But we (*mustn't/must*) take our anoraks. It (*can/needn't*) get quite windy."
6. "OK. But we really (*must/can*) call Dave and Linda, so they (*must/can*) meet us at the beach bar."
7. "I'll do that now. But Joe, we (*mustn't/can't*) forget to put the cheese in the fridge before we go!"
8. "Don't worry. I (*can/must*) do that, while you call Dave and Linda."
9. "OK, thanks! But please be quick, Joe. I (*must/can't*) wait to see the sea again!"

2 Help the environment

Choose the right beginning and complete the sentences.

☺ You should …	✗ always turn off the lights when you leave a room.
☹ You shouldn't …	✗ go into town by car if you have a lot to carry.
😐 You can (may) …	✗ wash your jeans in cold water if they are very dirty.
😐 You needn't …	✗ walk to school if it isn't too far.
	✗ walk, of course, if you've got a bike. A bike is quicker!
	✗ expect others to save the Earth for you!
	✗ switch off the heating if you are cold. Just turn it down!

Ov 7 Bedingungssätze (*if*-Sätze) Typ I

1 What will they do?

a) *What will the people do in these situations? Use the phrases in the boxes. Start like this:*
1. If Nancy **misses** the train, she'**ll call** her mum. 2. If Tom and Bob **get** …, they'**ll use** … .

1. Nancy / to miss her train / to call her mum

2. Tom and Bob / to get lost / to use their map

3. Karim / to not find his key / to break the chain

4. Diane and Luke / to not get tickets / to watch a DVD

5. Doug / to get a job / to travel to Australia

6. Ina and Gabi / to go to London / to visit Hyde Park

b) *Imagine you can go to Britain, Canada and Australia. Think about one thing you'll do and one that you won't do in each of these countries. The ideas in the box can help you.*
Start like this: If I go to Britain, I'll … /I won't … .

say G'day to everyone • visit Buckingham Palace • go hiking in Scotland • go swimming there in December • take a trip to Montreal • go to a cool concert in Sydney • speak French • build an igloo • take photos of koalas • see Stonehenge • eat kangaroo meat

Ov 7 Bedingungssätze (*if*-Sätze) Typ II

1 If I met the US President, I'd …

a) *What would you do if … Example:* 1. **If I met** the US President, **I'd ask** him about … .

1. … you met the US President? (*ask him about …, take a photo, speak …, …*)
2. … you won a lot of money in a TV quiz show? (*buy/give/save/spend/ …*)
3. … Superman flew through your window? (*be excited/angry/scared/ …, ask him …, …*)
4. … a friend was angry with you? (*ask him/her why, wait for him/her to explain, forget the friend, …*)
5. … your mobile phone got stolen? (*report it to the police, buy/save up for a new one, ask parents, …*)
6. … a firm offered you a job abroad for a year? (*take it/say no, be happy, miss …, worry about …*)
7. … you saw a pickpocket on the job? (*tell the person to stop, call the police, walk away, …*)

b) *What wouldn't you do? Example:* 1. If I met the US President, **I wouldn't speak** German.

Ov 8 Pronomen

1 A film which I really love!

Put in the right pronouns and complete the text about 'Dragon Tears'.

All … friends and … really enjoyed the film Dragon Tears. A kid at … school, called Danny, lent … the DVD and we watched … last weekend. … dad acted in the film! We saw … when … attacked the dragon. The best scene, … all think, is near the end. The heroine, a cool young girl, meets the dragon and becomes … friend. Dragons are really sad creatures and … are very lonely. Lyreena tells this to the people in … village, and they are then safe from harm. Dragons put out … own fire with their tears. The dragon's tears flood the village in the end. This great story was taken from an old Chinese myth. Everyone should try to see … .

we | it | I | its | her | his | my | him | it | our | he | us | their | they

G 1 Indirekte Rede (sofort berichtet)

1 What the experts say

a) *Jane is reading a report on violence in modern life. Read the different expert views:*

1st expert: Some famous old myths and stories <u>are</u> really bloody! So violence <u>is</u> nothing new! We just <u>hear</u> more about it through faster media technology.

2nd expert: It <u>is</u> much worse now. There <u>is</u> more violence on TV – kids just <u>want</u> to copy their heroes.

3rd expert: We <u>don't need</u> violence on TV. But the harm through violent programmes <u>is</u> greatest in kids who <u>don't have</u> a good family background. Kids all <u>need</u> friends and hobbies, too.

4th expert: It <u>isn't</u> just TV – it <u>is</u> all those terrible computer games! The games <u>are</u> violent and many kids <u>do</u> nothing else but <u>play</u> them all day.

b) *Jane calls her friend, Adam, to tell him about what the experts say. Write what she tells him.*
Start like this: Hi, Adam. Hey listen to this! It's a report on violence. The 1st expert says that some famous stories ***are*** really bloody. He or she also ***says*** that violence ***is*** … and that we just ***hear*** … .

G 2 Indirekte Rede (später berichtet)

1 A few days later

a) *Mack had an accident on his skateboard. Read a police officer's questions and Mack's answers.*

What's your name?	– My name is Mack Simpson.
Where do you live?	– I live around the corner, number 51 Green Street.
How old are you?	– I'm 16 years old.
Do your parents know about the accident?	– No, they aren't at home.
Have you got a number to call to let them know?	– I have a number here, in my mobile.

b) *The police officer talks to a colleague a few days later and tells her what Mack said.*
Start like this: The teenager **said** that his name … Mack Simpson, and that he … around the corner. He also **said** that he … 16 years old. He **told** me that his parents … about the accident because they … at home. But he **explained** that he … a number to call them, in his mobile.

2 How the accident happened

a) *In hospital they asked Mack about his accident. Read what he said, write a list of the verbs and add their infinitive form.*

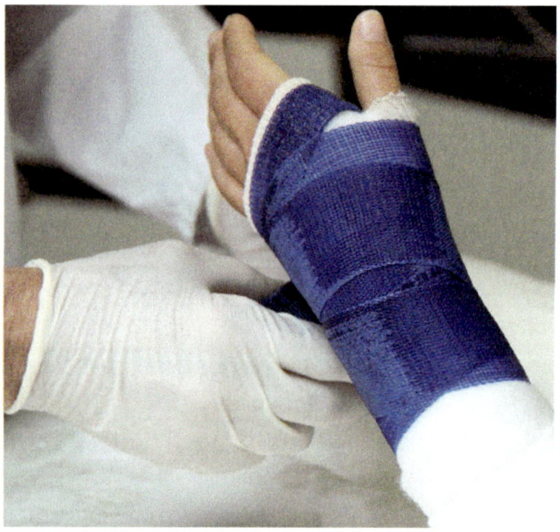

What happened to you?
I hit a streetlamp.

Were you on your bike?
No, I was on my skateboard.

Where were you on the way to?
I wanted to visit my mate.

Why were you in such a hurry?
I needed some snacks for a DVD evening.

Why didn't you see the streetlamp?
A guy shouted my name and I turned my head to look.

Was it someone you knew?
No, I didn't recognize the guy.

b) *Put the sentence parts together and find out what the night nurse told the day nurse about Mack's accident the next morning.*

1. The patient said that he had hit …	+	… his head to look!
2. He explained that he had been …		… the guy.
3. He told me that he had wanted …		… some snacks for a DVD evening.
4. He explained that he had needed …		… his name.
5. He said that a guy had shouted …		… to visit his mate.
6. He added that he had turned …		… on his skateboard.
7. He told me that he hadn't recognized …		… a streetlamp.

G 3 Reflexivpronomen

1 Advertising

Choose the correct word from the box to complete each sentence.

1. This oven is really smart – it cleans … in minutes!
2. Are you learning to drive? – Test … with our 'Drive Alive' DVD before your test!
3. We tested and tasted all the recipes … – 'Fashion Food' is our Book of the Year.
4. I taught … Spanish in five easy steps with 'Steps to Spanish'. BUY IT TODAY!
5. He washed … with 'UltraSoap' and now the girls can't keep away from him!
6. When we let people try a 'Ronny Robot' …, we never get him back!
7. All you kids out there, our Happy Burgers are great! Try for …!
8. Even Clarisse Stilton prepares … for concerts with 'Heart's Breathing Method'!

I – myself
you – yourself
he – himself
she – herself
it – itself
we – ourselves
you – yourselves
they – themselves

2 At summer camp

Choose the correct reflexive pronoun for each sentence.

1. At summer camp you have to do lots of things (*yourself / himself / itself*) every day.
2. But the kids don't have to wake (*yourselves / themselves / himself*) – that's the group leader's job.
3. After they have all washed and dressed (*themselves / ourselves / yourselves*), they make breakfast.
4. But camp is also fun. Last year we all taught (*himself / themselves / ourselves*) to make a safe fire.
5. Of course, our leader Mary-Lou checked them (*yourself / himself / herself*) each time.
6. The best thing was: I taught (*myself / itself / ourselves*) rock climbing!
7. Rock climbing (*herself / themselves / itself*) isn't dangerous but you must follow the safety rules!
8. My rock climbing partner, Jack, hurt (*himself / herself / yourself*) badly because he wasn't careful.
9. But we really enjoyed (*themselves / ourselves / yourselves*) at that camp.
10. So I would like to register (*himself / herself / myself*) for the same camp next year.

G 4 Vollendete Vergangenheit

1 A chain of events

a) *Write five sentences about the things Nick did on Saturday in the order he did them. Start like this:*
1. First he **woke up**. 2. Then he … . 3. Then … . 4. And then … . 5. Finally … .

b) *Write about the five events in a chain. Start like this:*
Nick **woke up** (*simple past*) at … . <u>After</u> **he had woken up** (*past perfect*), he **jogged** (*simple past*) … .

2 Before and after

a) *Look at Tom and Bob's list of things to do. What had they <u>already</u> done <u>before</u> they left on holiday? Write sentences. Start like this:*
Before they left on holiday, they **had <u>already</u> fed** … . Also, they **had <u>already</u> packed** … .

feed the cat ✔ • pack maps ✔ • throw the rubbish in the bins • give their keys to the neighbour ✔ • leave a message on the answerphone ✔ • lock the flat • post letters • take the bottles back to the shop

b) *After they had left, their neighbour did all the things that Tom and Bob had forgotten to do. What did he tell them when they got home? Start like this:*
After I **had thrown** …, I **locked** …! After I **had locked** …, I … . After I **had** …, I … .

G 5 Adverbien (Gradadverbien)

1 Very important words

a) *Find the word (adjective – adverb) pairs. Which two words in the green box are left?*

complete • terrible • extreme
real • special • equal

quite • extremely • especially • very
really • terribly • equally • completely

b) *Choose the right English word from the green box in a) for the German word in each sentence.*

1. The trip up the mountain was (*wirklich*) exciting.
2. The view from the top of the mountain was (*sehr*) beautiful.
3. But the climbers had to be (*ziemlich*) careful when they climbed down again.
4. This was because they were (*sehr*) high up.
5. They were all (*besonders*) proud of the long climb they had just done.
6. But they were all thirsty – and their water bottles were (*komplett/vollständig*) empty!
7. So they were all (*gleich*) happy when they reached their camp.
8. By evening they were (*schrecklich*) tired and (*extrem*) hungry!

G 6 Die Wortstellung im Satz

1 When and where

Choose the right place in the sentences for the words/phrases. Sometimes two answers are correct.

1. last year: (1) There was (2) a trade fair in West London (3).
2. to the fair: (1) On Saturday (2) a group of us went (3) in the afternoon after school (4).
3. at two o'clock: (1) We took (2) the train to London (3).
4. at the station: (1) The train arrived (2) at three o'clock (3).
5. by 3:20 p.m.: (1) We were (2) in Hall 2 (3).
6. in Hall 2: (1) At three o'clock there was (2) a product presentation (3).
7. a moment later: (1) A man walked (2) onto a stage (3) in the middle of the hall (4).
8. suddenly (1) He called out (2) some numbers (3), but I didn't hear them.
9. on the stage: (1) I was more interested (2) in the box (3) but one of my mates checked my ticket.
10. in the end (1) I was (2) surprised (3) to find out that I had won the box!
11. at five o'clock: It was huge! So (1) I rang my dad where he worked (2) in London (3).

2 How often?

Put the words or phrases in the right order and make sensible sentences.

1. **often** – too many products – got – have – shops
2. I – what I need – can – so – find – **never**
3. on the other hand – all OK – I – **sometimes** – three products – which are – see
4. **always** – if that happens – buy – the cheapest product – then I
5. **usually** – they're – expensive – quite – but then

VOCABULARY

SKILLS

Diese Checkliste kann dir helfen, Fehler zu vermeiden und deine Rechtschreibung zu verbessern. Prüfe alle deine Texte damit.

- Schreibung:
  - ☑ ‚gh' wird meist nicht gesprochen. Vergiss es beim Schreiben nicht.
  - ☑ ‚k' kommt vor ‚t' so gut wie nie vor, z.B. action – Aktion, October – Oktober
- Gleiche Aussprache, unterschiedliche Schreibung:
  - ☑ [i:] z.B. teacher, meeting, media, magazine, people, field
  - ☑ [u:] z.B. food, route, to do, swimsuit, supermarket, true, crew
- Gleiche Aussprache, unterschiedliche Schreibung und Bedeutung:
  - ☑ [i:] z.B. see – sehen, sea – Meer; meet – treffen, meat – Fleisch
  - ☑ [u:] z.B. two – zwei, too – auch
- Verdoppelung der Endkonsonanten:
  - ☑ to stop – stopping, stopped
  - ☑ to plan – planning, planned
- ‚y' wird zu ‚ie':
  - ☑ in der 3. Person Singular: z.B. to carry – he carries; to cry – she cries; **aber**: to buy – she buys
  - ☑ im Plural: z.B. city – cities, party – parties; **aber**: boy – boys
  - ☑ bei der Steigerung von Adjektiven: z.B. happy – happier – (the) happiest; easy – easier – (the) easiest
- Ähnlich und doch anders:
  - ☑ Wortendung ‚le':
    z.B. *engl.* simple – *dt.* simpel;
    engl. title – *dt.* Titel;
    engl. middle – *dt.* Mittel
  - ☑ ‚ph' statt ‚f':
    z.B. *engl.* phone – *dt.* Telefon;
    engl. photo – *dt.* Foto
- Großschreibung:
  - ☑ Monatsnamen: z.B. January, July, December
  - ☑ Wochentage: z.B. Monday, Wednesday, Saturday
  - ☑ Eigennamen: z.B. Tom, Lisa, the Brooks, the London Eye, the Thames
  - ☑ geografische Namen: Bristol, Greenwich, Germany, Italy
- Plural:
  - ☑ Der Plural bekommt normalerweise ein -s: z.B. friend – friends, chair – chairs, film – films
  - ☑ Endet ein Wort auf s oder x, wird -es angehängt: z.B. bus – buses, box – boxes
  - ☑ Manche Wörter haben einen unregelmäßigen Plural: z.B. man – men, child – children, shelf – shelves, mouse – mice
- Apostroph:
  - ☑ bei Kurzformen: z.B. she is → she's; they are → they're
  - ☑ beim Genitiv-s: z.B. Sam's bike, Emma's family, the Jacksons' house, the children's games
- Wörterbuch:
  - ☑ Prüfe die Schreibung aller Wörter, bei denen du dir nicht ganz sicher bist, indem du sie im Wörterbuch nachschlägst.

Vocabulary

Auf den folgenden Seiten findest du alle neuen englischen Wörter und Ausdrücke. Sie stehen in der Reihenfolge, wie sie im Buch vorkommen.
Diese Wortliste ist in drei Spalten aufgeteilt:

- Links stehen die englischen Wörter und Sätze.
- In der Mitte werden sie übersetzt.
- Rechts findest du Beispiele, Erklärungen und Tipps, die dir beim Lernen helfen.

Die fett gedruckten Wörter musst du lernen. Normal gedruckte Wörter solltest du wiedererkennen, wenn du sie hörst oder liest.
Gleich nach jedem neuen englischen Wort steht die Lautschrift in eckigen Klammern. Sie zeigt dir, wie das neue Wort ausgesprochen wird. Wie du diese Lautzeichen liest, siehst du unten.

Englische Laute

Mitlaute

[b]	**b**ed	[p]	**p**icture
[d]	**d**ay	[r]	**r**ed
[ð]	**th**e	[s]	**s**ix
[f]	**f**amily	[ʃ]	**sh**e
[g]	**g**o	[t]	**t**en
[ŋ]	morni**ng**	[tʃ]	lun**ch**
[h]	**h**ouse	[v]	**v**ideo
[j]	**y**ou	[w]	**w**e, **o**ne
[k]	**c**an, mil**k**	[z]	ea**s**y
[l]	**l**etter	[ʒ]	revi**s**ion
[m]	**m**an	[dʒ]	pa**ge**
[n]	**n**o	[θ]	**th**ank you

Selbstlaute

[ɑː]	c**ar**
[æ]	**a**pple
[e]	p**e**n
[ə]	**a**gain
[ɜː]	g**ir**l
[ʌ]	b**u**t
[ɪ]	**i**t
[i]	happ**y**
[iː]	t**ea**cher
[ɒ]	d**o**g
[ɔː]	b**a**ll
[ʊ]	b**oo**k
[u]	Jan**u**ary
[uː]	t**oo**, tw**o**

Doppellaute

[aɪ]	**I**, m**y**
[aʊ]	n**ow**, m**ou**se
[eɪ]	n**a**me, th**ey**
[eə]	th**ere**, p**air**
[ɪə]	h**ere**, id**ea**
[əʊ]	hell**o**
[ɔɪ]	b**oy**
[ʊə]	s**ure**

[:] der vorangehende Laut ist lang, z. B. *you* [juː]

['] die folgende Silbe wird betont, z. B. *hello* [hə'ləʊ]

In jeder *Topic* findest du Übungen zum Vokabellernen sowie einen Kasten mit *Useful phrases*, die dir helfen, dich auf Englisch zu verständigen.

Außerdem gibt es zu jeder *Topic* einen Kasten, in dem du Interessantes zur Landeskunde erfährst.

Auf das *Vocabulary* folgt das *Dictionary*, eine alphabetische Wortliste aller englischen Wörter im Buch. Wenn du ein Wort nicht verstehst, kannst du es hier nachschlagen

Abkürzungen und Zeichen

pl	Plural, Mehrzahl
sg	Singular, Einzahl
infml	umgangssprachlich
10	Auf dieser Seite kommen die Wörter vor.

!	Achtung!	! *Information* hat keine Mehrzahl.
↔	ist das Gegenteil von	permanent ↔ temporary
→	ist verwandt mit	drive → driver
=	entspricht	Dear Jenny = Liebe Jenny

Topic 1 A 'global' language

Englisch als Weltsprache

Auf der Welt gibt es insgesamt circa 6500 bis 7000 Sprachen, wobei jedoch über die Hälfte der Bevölkerung auf der Erde eine der zehn meist gesprochenen Sprachen der Welt spricht.
Seit vielen Jahren gilt Englisch als Weltsprache, weil keine andere Sprache so weit verbreitet ist.
Sie wird häufig auch als so genannte *lingua franca* bezeichnet. Unter einer *lingua franca* versteht man im Allgemeinen eine Verkehrssprache, d. h. eine Sprache, die Menschen mit verschiedenen Muttersprachen, z. B. im Handel, zur Verständigung dient.

Englisch wird heute in über 100 Ländern gesprochen, das entspricht ca. der Hälfte aller Länder auf der Erde. 340 Millionen Menschen sprechen Englisch als Muttersprache. Wenn man Englisch hingegen mit anderen Sprachen vergleicht, so steht es nach Hochchinesisch mit 880 Millionen Muttersprachlern und Spanisch mit 360 Millionen Muttersprachlern nur an dritter Stelle.
In vielen Schulen auf der ganzen Welt wird Englisch zudem als erste Fremdsprache unterrichtet. Man nimmt an, dass etwa 750 Millionen Menschen Englisch als Fremdsprache sprechen.
Schätzungen zufolge kommen demnach rund 2 Milliarden Menschen regelmäßig in Kontakt mit der englischen Sprache.

Überlege dir weitere Situationen, in denen Menschen mit unterschiedlichen Muttersprachen Englisch sprechen. Welche Situationen hast du schon erlebt?
In welchen Ländern wird deine Muttersprache gesprochen? Wie viele Menschen sprechen deine Sprache? Recherchiere im Internet.

Check-in

8	**backpacker** ['bækpækə]	Rucksacktourist/ Rucksacktouristin →	backpack+er = *backpacker* A tourist with a bag that you carry on your back.
	Canadian [kə'neɪdiən]	kanadisch; Kanadier/ Kanadierin →	a person who lives in or comes from Canada
	wide [waɪd]	groß, breit, weit →	This table is too *wide*. We can't get it through the door.
	setting ['setɪŋ]	Schauplatz, Rahmen	
	to mention ['menʃn]	erwähnen →	If you *mention* sth, you say sth about it or talk about it for a moment.
	official [ə'fɪʃl]	offiziell	
9	**Prime Minister** (PM) [ˌpraɪm 'mɪnɪstə]	Premierminister/ Premierministerin →	In Britain the *Prime Minister* has more powers than the Queen.
	minister ['mɪnɪstə]	Minister/Ministerin	

Aspects

10	**ever-changing** ['evəˌtʃeɪndʒɪŋ]	sich immer/stetig ändernd →	If sth is *ever-changing*, it is changing all the time.
	perhaps [pə'hæps]	vielleicht →	another word for 'maybe'
	Japanese [ˌdʒæpn'i:z]	japanisch; Japaner/Japanerin	
	tower ['taʊə]	Kontrollturm, Tower	
	phrase [freɪz]	Redewendung, Ausdruck →	I only know a few *phrases* in Japanese.
	pukka *(slang)* ['pʌkə]	echt	
	subtitle ['sʌbˌtaɪtl]	Untertitel	
	mixture ['mɪkstʃə]	Mischung, Gemisch, Mixtur	
	Hinglish ['hɪŋglɪʃ]	Hinglisch *(Mischung aus Hindi und Englisch)*	
	Hindi ['hɪndi]	Hindi →	a language spoken in India
	to **spread, spread, spread** [spred, spred, spred]	(sich) ausbreiten, (sich) verbreiten →	If something *spreads*, it moves to cover a larger and larger area.
	because of [bɪ'kɒz‿əv]	wegen →	We couldn't sleep *because of* the noise.
	Asian ['eɪʃn]	asiatisch; Asiate/Asiatin →	Chinese people and people from India are *Asians*.
	sub-continent [ˌsʌb'kɒntɪnənt]	Subkontinent	
	to **include** [ɪn'klu:d]	einschließen, beinhalten, aufnehmen	
	Spanglish ['spæŋglɪʃ]	Spanglisch *(Mischung aus Spanisch und Englisch)* →	My cousin lives in Spain and speaks *Spanglish*.
	Chinglish ['tʃɪŋlɪʃ]	Chinglisch *(Mischung aus Chinesisch und Englisch)*	

s + z

Im Englischen gibt es Wörter, die man sowohl mit ***s*** als auch mit ***z*** schreiben kann: z. B. ***realise/realize, summarise/summarize*** usw. Früher wurde die Schreibung mit ***s*** eher in Großbritannien verwendet und die Schreibung mit ***z*** eher in den USA. Heutzutage gibt es diese strikte Trennung nicht mehr, weil durch das Fernsehen, das Internet etc. die Grenzen verschwommen sind. Deshalb kommen auch in deinem Schülerbuch beide Schreibweisen vor.
Aber Vorsicht! ***size*** schreibt sich immer mit ***z*** und ***compromise*** immer mit ***s***.

common ['kɒmən]	gemeinsam, gebräuchlich, verbreitet	
sponsor ['spɒnsə]	Sponsor/Sponsorin, Förderer/Förderin →	We need more *sponsors* for the race.
promising ['prɒmɪsɪŋ]	viel versprechend	
to **be able to** (do sth) [bi‿'eɪbl tə]	können, fähig sein (zu) →	They didn't know what to do. They *weren't able to* help him.
fee [fi:]	Gebühr, Abgabe	
to **improve** [ɪm'pru:v]	(sich) verbessern →	to make (or become) better
coaching ['kəʊtʃɪŋ]	Training, Nachhilfe →	special help in a subject or a sports

	coach [kəʊtʃ]	Trainer/Trainerin →	trainer
	former ['fɔːmə]	ehemaliger/ehemalige/ ehemaliges, früherer/ frühere/früheres	
	session ['seʃn]	Einheit, Sitzung, Stunde →	The *session* starts at three and finishes at four o'clock.
	to **assess** [ə'ses]	bewerten, beurteilen, einschätzen	
	trial ['traɪəl]	Prüfung, Test →	The hockey *trials* are next week.
	academy [ə'kædəmi]	Akademie, Hochschule, Lehranstalt	
	trend [trend]	Trend, Entwicklung, Richtung	
	hiking ['haɪkɪŋ]	Wandern, Wander- →	We like *hiking* in the mountains.
11	**Inuktitut** [ɪ'nʊktɪtʊt]	Inuktitut *(Sprache der Inuit)*	
	territory ['terɪtri]	Territorium, Land, Gebiet	
	Aboriginal [ˌæbə'rɪdʒnl]	eingeboren, einheimisch	
	majority [mə'dʒɒrəti]	Mehrheit(en-) →	the majority of us = most of us
	region ['riːdʒn]	Region, Gegend	
	non-official [ˌnɒnə'fɪʃl]	inoffiziell	
	terminal ['tɜːmɪnl]	(Flughafen-)Terminal	
	spot on ['spɒt‿ɒn]	Fokus auf	
	to **cut costs** [kʌt 'kɒsts]	die Kosten senken →	If we want to save the company, we must *cut costs*.
	cost [kɒst]	Preis, Kosten	
	running ['rʌnɪŋ]	laufend	
	call centre ['kɔːl ˌsentə]	Call-Center	
	to **be out of a job** [bi‿ˌaʊt‿əv‿ə 'dʒɒb]	arbeitslos sein	
	podcast ['pɒdkɑːst]	Podcast	
	energetic [ˌenə'dʒetɪk]	energiegeladen, energisch, dynamisch →	energy → *energetic*
	experienced [ɪk'spɪəriənst]	erfahren →	experience → to experience → *experienced*
	according to [ə'kɔːdɪŋ tə]	laut, gemäß →	*According to* the weather forecast, it'll be warm and sunny tomorrow. = The weather forecast says that it'll be warm and sunny tomorrow.

Option 1

12	webzine ['webziːn]	Webmagazin	
	used to *(+ infinitive)* ['juːs‿tə]	früher; pflegte(n) zu →	We *used to* live in Munich. = Wir wohnten früher in München.
	footballer ['fʊtbɔːlə]	Fußballspieler/ Fußballspielerin →	! Das englische Wort *football* kann Fußball oder Football heißen.
	these days ['ðiːz deɪz]	heutzutage →	In the 1980's nobody had a mobile. *These days* you can't imagine life without one.
	sort of ['sɔːt‿əv]	irgendwie	
	bilingual [baɪ'lɪŋgwəl]	zweisprachig, bilingual	

mostly ['məʊstli]	überwiegend, größtenteils, hauptsächlich →	most → *mostly*
hopeless ['həʊpləs]	hoffnungslos →	helpless – homeless – *hopeless*
grandparents *(pl)* ['grænpeərənts]	Großeltern →	mother's and father's parents = *grandparents*

Lerntipp: Neues mit altem Vokabular vernetzen

Tipp 1

Wenn du neue Wörter lernst, ist es gut, wenn du dir überlegst, welche ähnlichen Wörter du bereits kennst.

neu	**bekannt**
unlike	*like*
expression	*expressive*
cultural	*culture*
television	*TV, view*

Tipp 2

Wenn dir sonst etwas einfällt, das dir beim Lernen helfen könnte, dann schreib' es auf.

Man kann aus einem Verb ein Nomen machen, indem man z. B. die Endung ***-ion*** anhängt:
to express → *express**ion***

	amazing [ə'meɪzɪŋ]	erstaunlich	
	mother tongue ['mʌðə ˌtʌŋ]	Muttersprache →	English is my *mother tongue*.
	Zulu ['zu:lu:]	Zulu	
	scholarship ['skɒləʃɪp]	Stipendium →	If you can win a *scholarship* to a school or college, your parents don't have to pay.
	everyone ['evriwʌn]	jeder	
	offside [ˌɒf'saɪd]	im Abseits →	The referee saw that I was *offside*.
	header ['hedə]	Kopfball	
	Cantonese [ˌkantə'ni:z]	kantonesisch; Kantonese/ Kantonesin	
13	**league** [li:g]	Liga, Bund, Bündnis	
	to decide on [dɪ'saɪd‿ɒn]	sich entscheiden für, festlegen	
	trader ['treɪdə]	Händler/Händlerin →	trade → *trader*
	settler ['setlə]	Siedler/Siedlerin →	somebody who goes to a new country and makes their home there
	African ['æfrɪkən]	afrikanisch; Afrikaner/ Afrikanerin →	Mali, Ghana and South Africa are all *African* countries.
	false [fɔ:ls]	falsch →	true ↔ *false*
	memory ['memri]	Memory *(Spiel)*; Erinnerung, Gedächtnis	
	version ['vɜ:ʃn]	Version, Variante →	I enjoyed the Harry Potter book better than the film *version*.

Option 2

14	to **widen** ['waɪdn]	(sich) erweitern, ausweiten →	They *widened* the bridge when they built the new road.
	horizon [hə'raɪzn]	Horizont, Blickfeld	
	colleague ['kɒli:g]	Kollege/Kollegin	

to **give a talk** [ˌɡɪv‿ə 'tɔ:k]	einen Vortrag/eine Rede halten →	He *gave an* interesting *talk* on the English language.
to **develop** [dɪ'veləp]	(sich) entwickeln	
IT [ˌaɪ'ti:]	Informationstechnik, Informatik	
database ['deɪtəbeɪs]	Datenbank	
administrator [əd'mɪnɪstreɪtə]	Administrator/Administratorin, Verwalter/Verwalterin →	He worked as the *administrator* of a database.
trainee [treɪ'ni:]	Trainee, Auszubildender/Auszubildende	
personal ['pɜ:snl]	persönlich →	person → *personal*
bilingual [baɪ'lɪŋɡwəl]	zweisprachig, bilingual	
strength [streŋθ]	Stärke →	strong → *strength*
mobile ['məʊbaɪl]	mobil, beweglich	
creative [kri'eɪtɪv]	kreativ →	In *creative* writing exercises you can use your own ideas.
weakness ['wi:knəs]	Schwäche →	weak → *weakness*
diploma [dɪ'pləʊmə]	Diplom, Abschlusszeugnis →	When you've passed an exam, you're given a *diploma*.
department [dɪ'pɑ:tmənt]	Abteilung, Fachbereich; Branche →	The games *department* is the part of a shop that sells games.
to **get on with** [ɡet‿'ɒn wɪð]	sich verstehen mit, gut auskommen mit	
reliable [rɪ'laɪəbl]	zuverlässig, verlässlich, vertrauenswürdig →	Someone who does what he/she promises is *reliable*.
disabled [dɪ'seɪbld]	behindert →	*Disabled* passengers can ask for help.
advertising *(no pl.)* ['ædvətaɪzɪŋ]	Werbung, Reklame; Werbe-	
basic ['beɪsɪk]	grundlegend, Grund-; einfach →	In the first two years of English you learn a lot of *basic* words and phrases.
salesman, salesmen *(pl)* ['seɪlzmən; 'seɪlzmen]	Vertreter, Verkäufer, Geschäftsmann	
to **communicate** [kə'mju:nɪkeɪt]	kommunizieren, sich verständigen →	The easiest way to *communicate* with people is to speak to them.
chaotic [keɪ'ɒtɪk]	chaotisch, durcheinander →	When everything goes wrong at the same time, it can be *chaotic*.
leather ['leðə]	Leder →	the skin of animals that is used to make shoes, bags, etc.
curly ['kɜ:li]	lockig	
15 to **get upset** [ˌɡet‿ʌp'set]	sich aufregen	
paper work ['peɪpə ˌwɜ:k]	Papierkram	
active ['æktɪv]	aktiv →	action → to act → *active*
uncertain [ʌn'sɜ:tn]	unbestimmt, unsicher	
en route [ɒn 'ru:t]	unterwegs	
hairdressing ['heəˌdresɪŋ]	Frisieren	
floor [flɔ:]	Stockwerk →	I live on the tenth *floor*.
to type [taɪp]	tippen	
to exchange [ɪks'tʃeɪndʒ]	(aus)tauschen	

Words in action

16	explanation [ˌekspləˈneɪʃn]	Erklärung, Erläuterung →	to explain → *explanation*

Check-out

17	**travel agent** [ˈtrævlˌeɪdʒnt]	Reisebürokaufmann/ Reisebürokauffrau →	We got some information from the *travel agent*.
	(job) interview [ˈdʒɒb ˌɪntəvjuː]	Vorstellungsgespräch	
	interviewer [ˈɪntəvjuːə]	Interviewer/Interviewerin →	to interview → interview → *interviewer*

Everyday English: Talking about strengths and weaknesses

Die folgenden *phrases* können dir helfen, wenn du über deine Stärken und Schwächen sprechen möchtest.

I think/I'd say I'm conscientious/reliable/ creative/practical/….	Ich denke/Ich würde sagen, dass ich gewissenhaft/ zuverlässig/kreativ/praktisch veranlagt/ … bin.
I find/don't find it easy to meet people/to learn new skills/….	Es fällt mir leicht/nicht leicht, neue Menschen kennen zu lernen/Ich habe eine schnelle Auffassungsgabe/….
I'm (not so) good with animals/with children/ with my hands/….	Ich bin (nicht so) gut im Umgang mit Tieren/im Umgang mit Kindern/Ich bin (nicht) sehr praktisch veranlagt/….
I like to work alone/outside/with my hands/….	Ich arbeite gerne allein/draußen/mit meinen Händen/….
I don't like computers/offices/working outside in bad weather/….	Ich mag keine Computer/keine Büros/ Bei schlechtem Wetter möchte ich nicht draußen arbeiten/….

Stelle mit einem Partner/einer Partnerin ein Gespräch über deine Stärken/Schwächen nach.

1,34
Sounds: Sentence stress

Wenn du lange Sätze laut liest, ist das manchmal gar nicht so einfach. Hilfreich ist es, die wichtigsten Wörter zu betonen.

a) Hör dir diese Sätze an:

1. You **may** know that **English** is still the most important language in **business**, on the **Internet** and in **technology**.
2. One of our **sponsors** is offering **three free places** to **promising** young **people** who **aren't** able to pay the fees.

Finde Regeln dafür, welche Wörter nicht betont werden.

b) Finde nun die wichtigen Wörter in diesen Sätzen und lies die Sätze laut. Vergleiche dann mit der Aufnahme.

1. English is still an official language in former British colonies like Australia, the US, Canada and India.
2. For example, some international banks and public transport services now have call centres in India.

Topic 2 Living democracy

Das Waffenrecht in den USA

Seit mehr als 200 Jahren ist das Recht, eine Waffe zur Selbstverteidigung zu besitzen und zu tragen, in der amerikanischen Verfassung verankert. Der Umgang mit Waffen wird in über 20000 Waffengesetzen geregelt. Gegner dieses Gesetzes sehen einen Zusammenhang zwischen privatem Waffenbesitz und der hohen Kriminalität in vielen Staaten der USA.
Schätzungsweise jeder dritte Schüler an weiterführenden Schulen in den USA besitzt eine Waffe. Jährlich werden 15000 Menschen in den USA mit Schusswaffen ermordet. Immer wieder wird die Diskussion über die Verschärfung des Waffengesetzes angeregt.

Während der Amtszeit von Bill Clinton wurden die Waffengesetze verschärft. 1994 z. B. wurde ein Gesetz in Kraft gesetzt, das die Überprüfung von Waffenkäufern erlaubte oder eine 5-Tage-Frist zwischen Kauf und Aushändigung der Waffe bestimmte. Auch der Verkauf von Waffen mit mehr als 10 Schuss wurde verboten.
Dieses Gesetz wurde 1997 allerdings vom Obersten Gerichtshof in den USA wieder gelockert.
Im Juni 2008 erklärte der *Supreme Court* ein Gesetz im Stadtbezirk Washington für verfassungswidrig. Es hatte Privatbürgern verboten, Waffen zu besitzen. Der Oberste Gerichtshof entschied, dass jeder Bürger ein Recht darauf hat, zu jagen und sich selbst zu verteidigen. Somit müsse es Bürgern in Washington erlaubt sein, eine Waffe zu besitzen. Allerdings gelte dies nicht für Geistigkranke und verurteilte Verbrecher.

Was hältst du von diesem Gesetz? Glaubst du, dass es richtig ist den Besitz von Waffen zu erlauben? Ist es Privatbürgern in Deutschland auch erlaubt, eine Waffe zu besitzen?

Check-in

26	**democracy** [dɪ'mɒkrəsi]	Demokratie	
	press [pres]	Presse →	newspapers, magazines etc.
	election [ɪ'lekʃn]	Wahl →	to elect → *election*.
	court trial ['kɔ:t traɪəl]	Gerichtsverhandlung	
	court [kɔ:t]	Hof, Gericht(shof) →	Before people can be sent to prison, they have to appear in *court*.
	in public [ɪn 'pʌblɪk]	in der Öffentlichkeit	
27	**journalist** ['dʒɜ:nlɪst]	Journalist/Journalistin →	A *journalist* writes for a newspaper.
	comment ['kɒment]	Kommentar, Bemerkung →	! Achte auf die Betonung: ['–] A *comment* gives your opinion about sth.

Aspects

28	**Middle Ages** [ˌmɪdl‿'eɪdʒɪz]	Mittelalter →	the time in history from 1066 to 1485
	lady ['leɪdi]	Dame, Frau →	another word for a woman
	(not) either of these ['aɪðər‿əv ˌði:z]	(k)eines von beiden	

Democracy

Erstelle ein Cluster zum Thema *Democracy*. Welche Wörter kennst du schon? Welche hast du neu dazu gelernt? Teile die Wörter in verschiedene Gruppen ein (*government, head of state, law* etc.). Finde so viele Wörter wie möglich.

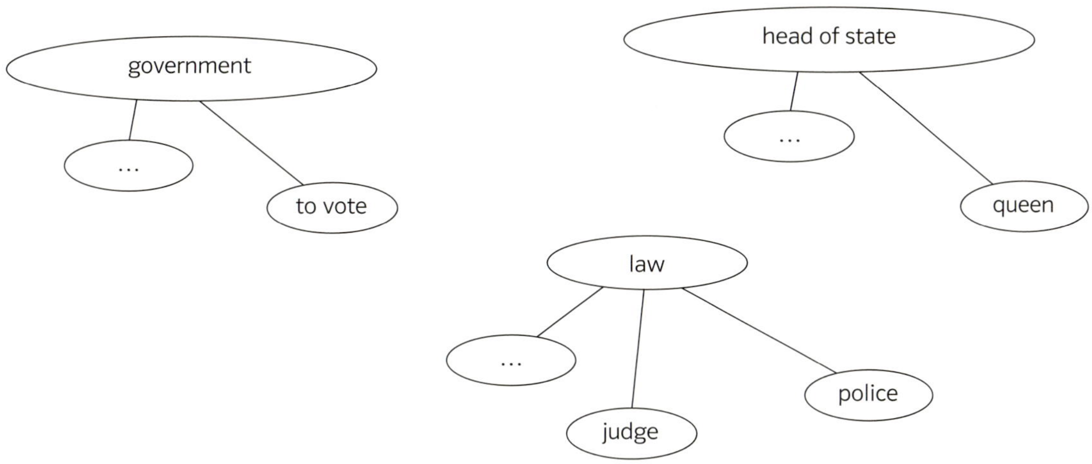

28	**serf** [sɜ:f]	Leibeigener/Leibeigene	
	feudal ['fju:dl]	feudal, Lehns- →	Serfs were lowest in the *feudal* system.
	hut [hʌt]	Hütte	
	social ['səʊʃl]	sozial, gesellschaftlich	
	just [dʒʌst]	direkt	
	soldier ['səʊldʒə]	Soldat/Soldatin →	sb whose job is to fight, usually for his or her country
	freeman, freemen *(pl)* ['fri:mən; 'fri:men]	freier Mann →	free → *freeman*
	baron ['bærn]	Baron	
	bishop ['bɪʃəp]	Bischof →	Barons and *bishops* were very rich.
	loyal ['lɔɪəl]	loyal, treu	
	to **feed, fed, fed** [fi:d, fed, fed]	ernähren, durchfüttern	
	however [haʊ'evə]	jedoch →	The man had lots of money. He wasn't happy, *however*.
	charter ['tʃɑ:tə]	Charta, Satzung, Urkunde	
	to **draw up, drew up, drawn up** [drɔ:‿'ʌp, dru:‿'ʌp, drɔ:n‿'ʌp]	aufsetzen, anfertigen →	They *drew up* rules for the king.
	update ['ʌpdeɪt]	Update, Aktualisierung	
	husband ['hʌzbənd]	Ehemann →	wife ↔ *husband*
	false teeth [fɔ:ls 'ti:θ]	Zahnprothese, Gebiss	
	false [fɔ:ls]	falsch →	true ↔ *false*
	Englishman, Englishmen *(pl)* ['ɪŋglɪʃmən; 'ɪŋglɪʃmen]	Engländer	
	bow [bəʊ]	Bogen	
	arrow ['ærəʊ]	Pfeil	

actually [ˈæktʃuəli]	eigentlich, tatsächlich →	! *actually* ≠ aktuell
to **get rid of** [ɡet ˈrɪd‿əv]	loswerden →	If you've got something you don't like, you'll probably want to *get rid of* it.
blindfolded [ˈblaɪndfəʊldɪd]	mit verbundenen Augen	
pyramid [ˈpɪrəmɪd]	Pyramide	
drawing [drɔːɪŋ]	Zeichnung, Bild →	This is a *drawing* of a car.
29 to **kidnap** [ˈkɪdnæp]	kidnappen, entführen →	When a child is *kidnapped*, the criminals usually want money from the child's parents.
attack [əˈtæk]	Angriff; Anfall	
to **be able to** (do sth) [bi‿ˈeɪbl tə]	können, fähig sein (zu) →	They didn't know what to do. They *weren't able to* help him.
concerned [kənˈsɜːnd]	beunruhigt; betroffen	
safety [ˈseɪfti]	Sicherheit →	safe → *safety*
masked [mɑːskt]	maskiert	
Palestinian [pæləˈstɪniən]	palästinensisch; Palästinenser/Palästinenserin →	A lot of *Palestinians* live in the Gaza Strip.
gunman, gunmen *(pl)* [ˈɡʌnmən; ɡʌnmen]	Schütze, Bewaffneter	
business card [ˈbɪznɪs ˌkɑːd]	Visitenkarte →	Mr Singh has got his own business. It says so on his *business card*.
to **report** [rɪˈpɔːt]	berichten, melden →	a report → *to report*
to **provide** (sb with sth) [prəˈvaɪd]	bereitstellen, besorgen, liefern	
future [ˈfjuːtʃə]	zukünftig →	What are your *future* plans?
kidnapping [ˈkɪdnæpɪŋ]	Kidnapping, Entführung	
common [ˈkɒmən]	gemeinsam; gebräuchlich, verbreitet	
to **fly out** [flaɪ‿ˈaʊt]	ausfliegen, evakuieren →	They *flew* him *out* before the war started.
region [ˈriːdʒn]	Region, Gegend →	The *region* around Loch Ness is very beautiful.
foreigner [ˈfɒrɪnə]	Fremder/Fremde, Ausländer/Ausländerin	
violent [ˈvaɪəlnt]	gewaltsam, gewalttätig, brutal →	violence → *violent*
battle [ˈbætl]	Schlacht, Kampf →	Hundreds were killed in the *battle*.
rival [ˈraɪvl]	rivalisierend; Rivale/Rivalin	
hostage [ˈhɒstɪdʒ]	Geisel	
South American [ˌsaʊθ‿əˈmerɪkən]	südamerikanisch; Südamerikaner/Südamerikanerin →	Lots of *South Americans* speak Spanish.
to **set free** [set‿ˈfriː]	freilassen; freisetzen →	to let go
load [ləʊd]	Ladung, Last, Belastung	
to **increase** [ɪnˈkriːs]	vergrößern; zunehmen, steigen	
to **adapt to** [əˈdæpt tə]	(sich) anpassen an →	Immigrants have to *adapt to* the way of life in their new country.
workplace [ˈwɜːkpleɪs]	Arbeitsplatz, Arbeitsstätte	

to **keep** *(+ -ing)* [ki:p]	etwas weiter/immer wieder tun →	! *Keep **smiling***, and everything will be fine!
to **check out** [tʃek‿'aʊt]	ausstempeln, auschecken →	Don't forget to *check out* when you leave.

Option 1

30 **head of state** [ˌhed‿əv 'steɪt]	Staatsoberhaupt	
duty ['dju:ti]	Pflicht, Aufgabe →	If something is your *duty*, you have to do it.
to **open** ['əʊpn]	eröffnen	
parliament ['pɑ:ləmənt]	Parlament →	! Check the spelling.
Prime Minister (PM) [ˌpraɪm 'mɪnɪstə]	Premierminister/ Premierministerin	
minister ['mɪnɪstə]	Minister/Ministerin →	! Check the stress.

Giving a presentation

Die folgenden Ausdrücke sind nützlich, wenn du eine Präsentation hältst.

Vor der Präsentation	
Today I'd like to talk about ….	Heute werde ich über … sprechen.
I'm going to talk about …, …. and ….	Ich werde über …, … und … sprechen.
First I'll give you information about ….	Zuerst werde ich euch über … informieren.
Then I'll go on with ….	Dann spreche ich über ….
There'll be time for questions at the end of the presentation.	Am Ende der Präsentation können Fragen gestellt werden.
Während der Präsentation	
My first point is ….	Mein erster Punkt ist ….
Secondly, ….	Zweitens ….
Let me add one more point ….	Lasst mich einen weiteren Punkt hinzufügen ….
It's also important to know ….	Es ist auch wichtig zu wissen, dass ….
In my opinion ….	Meiner Meinung nach ….
Many people say/think that ….	Viele Menschen sagen/behaupten ….
The most important point is ….	Der wichtigste Punkt ist ….
Have a look at the chart/picture/etc. ….	Schaut bitte die Tabelle/das Foto/etc. an ….
Nach der Präsentation	
As a result, you can say ….	Als Ergebnis kann man festhalten, dass ….
Have you got any questions?	Gibt es Fragen?

to **elect** [ɪ'lekt]	(aus)wählen →	If you want to be in parliament, you first have to be *elected*.
to **be allowed to** (do sth) [bi:‿ə'laʊd tə]	dürfen →	Children *aren't allowed to* drive cars.
to **refuse** [rɪ'fju:z]	ablehnen, sich weigern →	to say you will not do or accept something
to **pass** [pɑ:s]	verabschieden *(Gesetz)* →	If you *pass* a law, you make a new law.
bill [bɪl]	Gesetz(entwurf)	
treaty ['tri:ti]	(Staats-)Vertrag, Abkommen →	When two countries agree on something, there is an official *treaty*.

nation ['neɪʃn]	Nation	
to **remain** [rɪ'meɪn]	(ver)bleiben →	*to remain* = to stay
neutral ['nju:trl]	neutral →	not pro or con
party ['pɑ:ti]	Partei, Gruppe →	a group of people who are doing something together, or a political group
yet [jet]	dennoch, jedoch	
politics ['pɒlɪtɪks]	Politik →	political → *politics*
to **receive** [rɪ'si:v]	empfangen; erhalten →	reception → *to receive*
ambassador [æm'bæsədə]	Botschafter/Botschafterin	
patron ['peɪtrn]	Schutzherr/Schutzherrin, Patron/Patronin	
present ['preznt]	anwesend →	If you're *present*, you are there.
to **hold**, **held**, **held** [həʊld, held, held]	(ab)halten, festhalten	
to **appoint** [ə'pɔɪnt]	ernennen →	The Queen *appoints* the Prime Minister.
to **discuss** [dɪ'skʌs]	diskutieren	
confidential [ˌkɒnfɪ'denʃl]	vertraulich, geheim	
official [ə'fɪʃl]	offiziell →	The Queen's *official* birthday is in June.
traditional [trə'dɪʃnl]	traditionell	
attraction [ə'trækʃn]	Attraktion, Sehenswürdigkeit →	The Tower of London is a big tourist *attraction*.
similar ['sɪmɪlə]	ähnlich	
to **rule** [ru:l]	herrschen, regieren →	In the past most European countries were *ruled* by kings and queens.
leaflet ['li:flət]	Flugblatt, Prospekt	
to **pass** [pɑ:s]	vorbeifahren	
juicy ['dʒu:si]	saftig; *hier:* schlüpfrig	
gossip ['gɒsɪp]	Tratsch, Klatsch →	I don't want to listen to *gossip*.
monarchy ['mɒnəkɪ]	Monarchie, Königreich	
outdated [ˌaʊt'deɪtɪd]	altmodisch, überholt	
romantic [rə'mæntɪk]	romantisch →	We had a very *romantic* holiday.
31 to **suggest** [sə'dʒest]	vorschlagen →	*to suggest* → suggestion
translation [trænz'leɪʃn]	Übersetzung	
e.g. [i:'dʒi:]	zum Beispiel →	for example
monarch ['mɒnək]	Monarch/Monarchin, Herrscher/Herrscherin	

Option 2

32 **young apprentice** (YA) [jʌŋ‿ə'prentɪs]	minderjähriger Auszubildender/minderjährige Auszubildende →	There are special laws which protect *YAs*.
apprentice [ə'prentɪs]	Auszubildender/Auszubildende	
tricky ['trɪki]	verfahren, kompliziert →	That's a very *tricky* question.
nasty ['nɑ:sti]	garstig, gemein; scheußlich →	nice ↔ *nasty*
comment ['kɒment]	Kommentar, Bemerkung →	! Achte auf die Betonung: ['–] A *comment* gives your opinion about sth.
to **take a joke** [ˌteɪk‿ə 'dʒəʊk]	Spaß verstehen	

colleague ['kɒli:g]	Kollege/Kollegin →	I have some really nice *colleagues*.
protective [prə'tektɪv]	(be)schützend, Schutz-	
clothing ['kləʊðɪŋ]	Kleidung →	clothes → *clothing*
supervisor ['su:pəvaɪzə]	Betreuer/Betreuerin	
opposite ['ɒpəzɪt]	entgegengesetzt, gegenüberliegend	
sex [seks]	Geschlecht; Sexualität, Sex →	If someone is of the opposite *sex* he/she is not the same sex as you.
to **come up behind sb** [ˌkʌm‿ʌp bɪ'haɪnd]	sich jmdm. von hinten nähern	
to **rest** [rest]	*hier:* legen →	He *rested* his hand on my shoulder.
conversation [ˌkɒnvə'seɪʃn]	Unterhaltung, Gespräch	
to **seem** [si:m]	(er)scheinen, wirken →	The dog *seemed* friendly, but it wasn't.
to **develop** [dɪ'veləp]	(sich) entwickeln	
ambitious [æm'bɪʃəs]	ehrgeizig →	An *ambitious* person wants to have success or to be rich and famous.
bad language [bæd 'læŋgwɪdʒ]	Schimpfwörter	
to **read out** [ri:d‿'aʊt]	laut vorlesen →	She *read out* the article to the class.
article ['ɑ:tɪkl]	Artikel	
rude [ru:d]	unhöflich, unverschämt →	Wayne isn't just a bully. He's *rude* to the teachers, too.
sexist ['seksɪst]	sexistisch	
33 duty ['dju:ti]	Pflicht, Aufgabe	
work experience ['wɜ:k‿ɪkˌspɪəriənts]	Praktikum →	I don't want to do *work experience* in an office.
to include [ɪn'klu:d]	einschließen, beinhalten, aufnehmen	
atmosphere ['ætməsfɪə]	Atmosphäre; Stimmung	
to skim [skɪm]	überfliegen	
sheet [ʃi:t]	Blatt →	He gave me a *sheet* of paper and asked me some questions.
to **inform** [ɪn'fɔ:m]	informieren, benachrichtigen	
firmly ['fɜ:mli]	eindeutig, deutlich, fest	
to **treat** [tri:t]	behandeln →	If you don't *treat* your dog right, you'll have trouble with it.
to **bully** ['bʊli]	tyrannisieren	
to **harass** [hə'ræs]	belästigen, drangsalieren	
personal ['pɜ:snl]	persönlich →	person → *personal*
male-dominated ['meɪlˌdɒmɪneɪtɪd]	männlich dominiert	
to **experience** [ɪk'spɪəriənts]	erfahren, erleben →	an experience → *to experience*
sexism ['seksɪsm]	Sexismus	
suitable ['su:təbl]	geeignet, passend →	Food without fish or meat in it is *suitable* for vegetarians.
to **discuss** [dɪ'skʌs]	diskutieren	
use [ju:s]	Verwendung, Nutzung →	I have no *use* for this rubbish.
panel ['pænl]	Expertenrunde, Gremium	

copy ['kɒpi] — Kopie
to distribute [dɪ'strɪbjuːt] — verteilen, austeilen
among [ə'mʌŋ] — unter, zwischen →

! Notice the difference: under ≠ *among*
He stood *among* the trees = in the middle of the forest, but not under a tree.

chairperson ['tʃeəˌpɜːsn] — Vorsitzender/Vorsitzende

Words in action

34 to **check in** [tʃek‿'ɪn] — einstempeln, einchecken

Everyday English: Talking about society

Die folgenden *phrases* können dir helfen, wenn du ein Gespräch zum Thema *society* führst.

I think our government is …	Ich denke, dass unsere Regierung …
I'm glad we don't have … in our country.	Ich bin froh, dass es in unserem Land keine … gibt.
I think it is a good idea to let young people work at it because …	Ich denke, es ist eine gute Idee, junge Leute daran arbeiten zu lassen, denn …
If I was in the government, I would fight for /change/ …	Wenn ich an der Regierung wäre, würde ich für Veränderungen kämpfen/…
I think the main problems in our society today are … and …	Meiner Meinung nach sind die Hauptprobleme in der heutigen Gesellschaft … und …
I think everyone in our society should vote/feel responsible/…	Ich finde, dass jedes Mitglied unserer Gesellschaft zur Wahl gehen sollte/sich verantwortlich für … fühlen sollte/…

Arbeite mit einem Partner/einer Partnerin und denkt euch ein Gespräch zum Thema *society* aus.

1,35 ## Sounds: Word stress

Schreibe die Wörter in die richtige Spalte.

compact purpose capable princess department ice-cream
repeat themselves colony mistake candidate condition

xX	Xx	xXx	Xxx
express	contract	assistant	flexible
…	…	…	…

Topic 3 Our world in our hands

Alternative Energiegewinnung

Unter dem Begriff „Alternative Energie“ versteht man Energie, die im Gegensatz zu fossilen Quellen, wie Kohle oder Erdöl, kontinuierlich und unbegrenzt verfügbar ist z. B. Sonnenenergie, Windkraft, Wasserkraft, Biomasse oder die Erdwärme. Diese Energiegewinnung ist umweltfreundlich, da sie die natürlichen Kreisläufe unserer Erde zur Gewinnung von Energie nutzt. Fossile Energiequellen schaden unserer Umwelt sehr und sind Hauptverursacher des derzeitigen Klimawandels. Bei der Sonnen- oder auch Solarenergie werden die Sonnenstrahlen durch Sonnenkollektoren oder Solarzellen z. B. auf Dächern aufgenommen und in Strom umgewandelt. Bei der Windkraft geschieht diese Umwandlung durch ein vom Wind angetriebenes Windrad. An schnell fließenden Flüssen kann man häufig Turbinen oder Wasserräder sehen, die durch das Wasser in Bewegung gesetzt werden und hierbei elektrische Energie erzeugen. Die Energiegewinnung aus Biomasse erfolgt durch Verbrennen von Sägespänen, Biomüll aus dem Haushalt oder den Ausscheidungen von Tieren, während man bei der Erdwärme durch eine Sonde, die in Hunderte Meter Tiefe reicht, die Wärme der Erdkruste nutzt. Obwohl die Gewinnung fossiler Energie die Umwelt stark schädigt, ist sie immer noch die meist genutzte Energiequelle auf der Welt. Für Großbritannien ist vor allem die Windenergie von Interesse – es gibt Behauptungen, dass alle Haushalte in Großbritannien allein durch die Stromgewinnung aus der Windkraft versorgt werden können. Leider ist der Anteil an erneuerbaren Energien immer noch gering und Großbritannien liegt sogar im europaweiten Vergleich auf den hinteren Plätzen.

Welche Art von alternativer Energiegewinnung hast du schon einmal gesehen oder nutzt du/deine Familie? Wie viel Prozent der Energie wird in Deutschland auf alternativen Wegen gewonnen?

Check-in

40	**organic** [ɔːˈgænɪk]	biologisch angebaut, organisch →	This is an *organic* potato field.
	article [ˈɑːtɪkl]	Artikel	
	leaflet [ˈliːflət]	Flugblatt, Prospekt	
	contrast [ˈkɒntrɑːst]	Kontrast, Gegensatz →	Achte auf die Betonung!
	natural [ˈnætʃrl]	natürlich; Natur-	
	resource [rɪˈzɔːs]	Ressource, Rohstoff; Quelle →	It is important not to waste the world's natural *resources*.
41	**Christmas** [ˈkrɪsməs]	Weihnachten →	We always have a tree at *Christmas*.

Aspects

42	**footprint** [ˈfʊtprɪnt]	Fußabdruck →	foot → footstep → *footprint*
	carbon footprint [ˌkɑːbn ˈfʊtprɪnt]	CO_2 -Bilanz	
	carbon [ˈkɑːbn]	Kohle(nstoff)	
	carbon dioxide (CO_2) [ˌkɑːbn daɪˈɒksaɪd; siː‿əʊ ˈtuː]	Kohlendioxid →	*Carbon dioxide* is a gas.

	total ['təʊtl]	total, gesamt, vollständig →	The *total* number of people living in a country is the whole population.
	amount [ə'maʊnt]	Betrag, Menge, Summe →	! Notice the difference: 1. a large *amount* of water (uncountable) 2. a large number of people (countable)
	to **affect** [ə'fekt]	beeinflussen, beeinträchtigen, betreffen →	Technology *affects* our lives.
	e.g. [iː'dʒiː]	zum Beispiel →	for example
	way [weɪ]	Art, Weise	
	ton [tʌn]	Tonne (*Gewicht*)	
	ourselves [aʊə'selvz]	wir/uns (selbst) →	We looked so funny that we had to laugh at *ourselves*.
	yourself [jɔː'self]	du/dich (selbst)	
	to **heat** [hiːt]	erhitzen, erwärmen; heizen →	We need a lot of energy to *heat* our homes.
	to **raise** [reɪz]	anheben, erhöhen; großziehen *(Kinder)*; aufbringen *(Geld)*	
	to **turn down** [tɜːn 'daʊn]	herunterdrehen	
	thermostat ['θɜːmestæt]	Thermostat, Temperaturregler →	The *thermostat* on our heating is broken.
	standby ['stændbaɪ]	in Bereitschaft, auf Stand-by	
	to **reduce** [rɪ'djuːs]	reduzieren, vermindern	
	to **seem** [siːm]	(er)scheinen, wirken →	The dog *seemed* friendly, but actually it wasn't.
	to **increase** [ɪn'kriːs]	vergrößern; zunehmen, steigen →	to reduce sth ↔ *to increase sth*
	emission [ɪ'mɪʃn]	Ausstoß, Emission	
	packaging ['pækɪdʒɪŋ]	Verpackung, Packmaterial	
	plastic ['plæstɪk]	Plastik(-), Kunststoff(-) →	A material that is light and doesn't break easily.
	to **recycle** [riː'saɪkl]	recyceln, wiederverwerten	
	mark [mɑːk]	Abdruck, Markierung →	to mark → a *mark*
	effect [ɪ'fekt]	Effekt, (Aus-)Wirkung →	a change or event which is the result of sth
	lazy ['leɪzi]	faul, träge	
43	to **go green** [ˌgəʊ 'griːn]	umweltbewusst werden	
	progress ['prəʊgres]	Fortschritt, Entwicklung	
	because of [bɪ'kɒz‿əv]	wegen →	Discrimination *because of* colour is illegal.
	to **report** [rɪ'pɔːt]	berichten, melden →	a report → *to report*
	traditional [trə'dɪʃnl]	traditionell	
	expert ['ekspɜːt]	Experte/Expertin	
	engineer [ˌendʒɪ'nɪə]	Ingenieur/Ingenieurin; Techniker/Technikerin →	somebody whose job is to design, build or repair machines, engines, roads, bridges, etc.
	to **keep up** (with) [kiːp‿'ʌp]	mithalten (mit), Schritt halten (mit)	

trend [trend]	Trend, Entwicklung, Richtung →	We have to keep up with modern *trends*.
textile ['tekstaɪl]	textil, Textil(-)	
builder ['bɪldə]	Baufachmann/Baufachfrau, Baumeister/ Baumeisterin	
to take turns [teɪk 'tɜːnz]	sich abwechseln	
to **go crazy** [gəʊ 'kreɪzi]	ausflippen, durchdrehen →	It's driving me crazy. I'll *go crazy* soon.

Option 1

44 **excuse** [ɪk'skjuːs]	Ausrede, Entschuldigung	
mass [mæs]	Masse →	You can use the word *'mass'* when you talk about a lot of people (e.g. *mass* media).
to **overeat**, **overate**, **overeaten** [ˌəʊvr'iːt, ˌəʊvr'et, ˌəʊvr'iːtn]	zu viel essen, sich überfressen	

Wortbildung I

Aus Verben kannst du Nomen für Menschen bilden, indem du ***-er*** oder ***-r*** anhängst.

*to play → play**er***	*to dream → dream**er***
*to build → build**er***	*to drive → driv**er***
*to work → work**er***	*to rap → rapp**er***
*to write → writ**er***	*to rock → rock**er***
*to sing → sing**er***	*to dance → danc**er***

Aus manchen Verben kannst du zwei Nomen für Menschen bilden: z. B. *employ → employ**er***, employ**ee**.

Finde weitere Beispiele und vervollständige die Liste in deinem Heft.

to **admit** [əd'mɪt]	zugeben →	If you have done something wrong or silly, it is not always easy to *admit* it.
sugar ['ʃʊgə]	Zucker →	You can put it in foods and drinks to make them sweet.
fat [fæt]	Fett →	Butter is a kind of *fat*.
disease [dɪ'ziːz]	Krankheit, Erkrankung →	A lot of *diseases* can be caused by dirty water and bad food.
diabetes [ˌdaɪə'biːtiːz]	Diabetes, Zuckerkrankheit	
Japanese [ˌdʒæpn'iːz]	japanisch; Japaner/ Japanerin →	I know a few words of *Japanese*.
seaweed ['siːwiːd]	Alge, Seetang	
in the long run [ɪn ðə 'lɒŋ rʌn]	langfristig →	I don't think it will matter *in the long run*.
instead of [ɪn'sted‿əv]	statt, anstatt →	They had twelve players *instead of* eleven.
origin ['ɒrɪdʒɪn]	Ursprung, Herkunft, Quelle	
as [æz; əz]	*hier:* genauso	
balance ['bæləns]	Gleichgewicht, Balance	
industrial [ɪn'dʌstriəl]	industriell, Industrie- →	industry → *industrial*

	poison ['pɔɪzn]	Gift	
	soil [sɔɪl]	Erde, Boden →	the (brown) earth that plants grow in
	seed [si:d]	Saat(korn), Samen →	If you put *seeds* in the earth, you will get plants.
	exotic [ɪg'zɒtɪk]	exotisch	
	pretty ['prɪti]	hübsch	
	cocktail ['kɒkteɪl]	Cocktail; Gemisch, Mischung →	A lot of young people like beer and *cocktails*.
	lung [lʌŋ]	Lunge	
	sore [sɔ:]	schmerzhaft, weh, wund →	I have a *sore* stomach and my head hurts.
45	eating ['i:tɪŋ]	Essen	
	to shut, shut, shut [ʃʌt, ʃʌt, ʃʌt]	zumachen, schließen	
	aloud [ə'laʊd]	laut	
	bottled ['bɒtld]	in Flaschen abgefüllt →	I don't drink *bottled* water.
	tap water ['tæp ˌwɔ:tə]	Leitungswasser	
	tap *(BE)* [tæp]	Wasserhahn →	*AE:* faucet
	refreshing [rɪ'freʃɪŋ]	erfrischend	
	handy ['hændi]	praktisch →	! *handy* = praktisch; mobile = Mobiltelefon, Handy
	billion ['bɪljən]	Milliarde *(tausend Millionen)*	
	garbage *(AE)* ['gɑ:bɪdʒ]	Müll, Abfall →	*BE:* rubbish
	filter ['fɪltə]	Filter	
	to **emit** [ɪ'mɪt]	ausstoßen, absondern	
	litre (l) ['li:tə]	Liter →	20 *litres* of water
	to agree on [ə'gri:‿ɒn]	sich einigen auf	
	convincing [kən'vɪntsɪŋ]	überzeugend	
	to split, split, split [splɪt, splɪt, splɪt]	(sich) (auf)teilen, spalten	

Option 2

46	**building** ['bɪldɪŋ]	Bauen	
	building site ['bɪldɪŋ saɪt]	Baustelle	
	to **involve** [ɪn'vɒlv]	involvieren, einbeziehen, beteiligen	
	architect ['ɑ:kɪtekt]	Architekt/Architektin →	An *architect* plans buildings.
	construction [kən'strʌkʃn]	Konstruktion, Aufbau, Bau(-)	
	insulation [ˌɪnsjə'leɪʃn]	Isolierung, Dämmung →	We must put some *insulation* in our roof.
	bricklayer ['brɪkˌleɪə]	Maurer/Maurerin	
	roofer ['ru:fə]	Dachdecker/Dachdeckerin	
	carpenter ['kɑ:pəntə]	Zimmermann, Schreiner/Schreinerin	
	electrician [ˌelɪk'trɪʃn]	Elektriker/Elektrikerin →	The *electrician* checked all our plugs.
	plumber ['plʌmə]	Klempner/Klempnerin; Installateur/Installateurin	

installer [ɪn'stɔ:lə]	Installateur/Installateurin	
gardener ['gɑ:dnə]	Gärtner/Gärtnerin →	garden → *gardener*
kind [kaɪnd]	freundlich, nett →	friendly and good to others
tool [tu:l]	Werkzeug	
field [fi:ld]	(Arbeits-)Gebiet	
glazier ['gleɪziə]	Glaser/Glaserin	
double-glazed [ˌdʌbl'gleɪzd]	doppelt verglast →	The windows in our flat are *double-glazed*.
to **insulate** ['ɪnsjəleɪt]	isolieren, dämmen →	insulation → *to insulate*
to **install** [ɪn'stɔ:l]	einbauen, installieren →	to put in
to **lay, lay, laid** [leɪ, leɪ, leɪd]	(ver)legen	
forest ['fɒrɪst]	Wald	
appliance [ə'plaɪənts]	(Haushalts-)Gerät, Einrichtung →	An oven is an *appliance*.
cell [sel]	Zelle	
supply [sə'plaɪ]	Vorrat, Bestand, Versorgung →	If we use too much oil, we will have problems with our *supplies*.
electrical [ɪ'lektrɪkl]	elektrisch	
turbine ['tɜ:baɪn]	Turbine	
loft [lɒft]	Dachboden, Dachgeschoss →	We have put all our old furniture in the *loft*.
mini ['mɪni]	Mini-	

Gradadverbien

Gradadverbien antworten auf die Frage *How much?* – Wie viele? und *How+Adj/Adv?* – Wie genau …?

a bit *boring*	ein bisschen langweilig	***really*** *funny*	sehr lustig
almost *nothing*	fast nichts	***super*** *cool*	super cool
quite *interesting*	ziemlich interessant	***very*** *important*	sehr wichtig
…			

Finde weitere Beispiele und vervollständige die Liste in deinem Heft.

pump [pʌmp]	(Luft-)Pumpe	
metre ['mi:tə]	Zähler	
cost [kɒst]	Preis, Kosten	
rainwater ['reɪnˌwɔ:tə]	Regenwasser →	There is a *rainwater* tank in the garden.
collector [kə'lektə]	Kollektor, Auffänger; Sammler/Sammlerin	
47 **receptionist** [rɪ'sepʃnɪst]	Empfangsmitarbeiter/ Empfangsmitarbeiterin, Sprechstundenhilfe →	reception → *receptionist*
technician [tek'nɪʃn]	Techniker/Technikerin	
town planner ['taʊn ˌplænə]	Stadtplaner/Stadtplanerin →	to plan → *planner*
painter ['peɪntə]	Maler/Malerin	
digger ['dɪgə]	Erdarbeiter/Erdarbeiterin	
lorry *(BE)* ['lɒri]	Lastwagen →	AE: truck
advertising agent ['ædvətaɪzɪŋ ˌeɪdʒnt]	Anzeigenvertreter/ Anzeigenvertreterin	
politician [ˌpɒlɪ'tɪʃn]	Politiker/Politikerin →	political → *politician*
active ['æktɪv]	aktiv	

to scan [skæn]	scannen, abtasten, nach Details durchsuchen	
loss [lɒs]	Verlust →	to lose → *loss*
plumbing ['plʌmɪŋ]	Rohrleitung; Klempnerarbeit	
renewable [rɪ'nju:əbl]	erneuerbar →	new → *renewable*
natural ['nætʃrl]	natürlich; Natur-	
lighting ['laɪtɪŋ]	Beleuchtung →	We need new *lighting* in our kitchen.
to **cut down on** [kʌt 'daʊn‿ɒn]	einschränken, einsparen, reduzieren	
instead of [ɪn'sted‿əv]	statt, anstatt →	They had twelve players *instead of* eleven.
dryer ['draɪə]	Trockner	
PVC [ˌpi:vi:'si:]	PVC	
atmosphere ['ætməsfɪə]	Atmosphäre; Stimmung; Umgebung →	I like the *atmosphere* in your new flat.
dry [draɪ]	trocken →	*dry* ↔ wet
damp [dæmp]	feucht →	not quite dry, but not really wet
recycling [ri:'saɪklɪŋ]	Recycling, Abfallverwertung	
to act out [ækt‿'aʊt]	vorspielen →	to act → *to act out*

Check-out

49	living ['lɪvɪŋ]	Leben, Existenz
	reflexive pronoun [rɪ'fleksɪv ˌprəʊnaʊn]	Reflexivpronomen

Everyday English: Talking about the media

Diese *phrases* können dir helfen, wenn du dich über das Thema Medien unterhalten willst.

My favourite TV programme(s) is/are …	Meine Lieblingsfernsehsendung(en) ist/ sind …
I think newspapers should give us more facts/are too sensationalist/…	Ich denke, Zeitungen sollten mehr Fakten enthalten/sind zu sensationsgierig/…
I get most of my news from …	Ich informiere mich am häufigsten …
I feel that we don't get enough information about … from TV news programmes.	Ich finde, dass wir nicht genug Informationen zu … in den Fernsehnachrichten erhalten.
I'd like to know more about …	Ich möchte gerne mehr über … erfahren.

Arbeite mit einem Partner/einer Partnerin. Denkt euch einen Dialog zum Thema Medien aus und spielt ihn nach.

1,36 Sounds: One sound makes a difference

The Queen Mary isn't a sheep [i:] → it's a ship [ɪ].

a) Hör genau hin und sage, ob du a. oder b. hörst.

1. a. prize	b. price	4. a. man	b. men
2. a. bad	b. bat	5. a. boat	b. bought
3. a. dog	b. dock		

b) Teste deine/n Partner/in. Wähle a. oder b. und sage die Wörter. Dein/e Partner/in schreibt auf, was er/sie hört. Hat er/sie dich richtig verstanden?

Topic 4 Choices and decisions

Aufbau einer Firma (ein Beispiel)

Executive board Verwaltungs- /Aufsichtsrat
Manager Geschäftsführung

Sales Department Vertrieb	***Purchasing Department*** Einkauf	***Human Resources*** Personalwesen	***Manufacturing*** Produktion	***Finance*** Rechnungswesen
Verkauf von Waren und Dienstleistungen Kommunikation mit den Kunden	Kontrolle des Lagerbestands Lieferantenauswahl Bestellung der benötigten Dinge ….	Stellenausschreibungen Vorstellungsgespräche Personaleinstellung Kündigungen Lohnabrechungen …	Aufbau und Ablauf der Produktion Bedienung der Maschinen …	Planung und Kontrolle der Ausgaben und Einnahmen des Unternehmens …

Welche Firmen (in Deutschland, England oder einem anderen Land) kennst du? Wie sind diese aufgebaut? Handelt es sich um kleine oder große Firmen?

Check-in

56	**decision** [dɪ'sɪʒn]	Entscheidung →	! Achtung Aussprache: to decide [aɪ] → *decision* [ɪ]
	unsure [ʌn'ʃɔː]	unsicher →	sure ↔ *unsure*

Aspects

58	**quite** [kwaɪt]	ziemlich; ganz, völlig →	Andreas only started to learn English last year. He speaks it *quite* well already. I'm *quite* sure. = I'm 100 % sure.
	e.g. [iː'dʒiː]	zum Beispiel →	for example
	responsible [rɪs'pɒnsəbl]	verantwortlich; verantwortungsvoll	
	to **have sex** [ˌhæv 'seks]	Geschlechtsverkehr haben →	My cousin won't *have sex* until she is married.
	sex [seks]	Geschlecht; Sexualität, Sex	
	to **affect** [ə'fekt]	beeinflussen, beeinträchtigen, betreffen	

	table ['teɪbl]	Tabelle	
	employment [ɪm'plɔɪmənt]	Beschäftigung, Anstellung →	the chance of *employment* = the chance of getting work
	marriage ['mærɪdʒ]	Heirat; Ehe →	to marry → *marriage*
	responsibility [rɪsˌpɒnsə'bɪləti]	Verantwortung →	*responsibility* → responsible
	nursery school ['nɜ:sri ˌsku:l]	Kindergarten	
	darling ['dɑ:lɪŋ]	Liebling, Schatz	
	according to [ə'kɔ:dɪŋ tə]	laut, gemäß →	*according to* somebody = in somebody's opinion
	to ring, rang, rung [rɪŋ, ræŋ, rʌŋ]	anrufen	
	limiting ['lɪmɪtɪŋ]	limitierend, einschränkend	
	liberal ['lɪbrl]	frei, liberal →	My parents are very *liberal*.
59	**direction** [dɪ'rekʃn]	(Aus-)Richtung, Anleitung →	direct → *direction*
	schooling ['sku:lɪŋ]	(Schul-)Ausbildung	
	to **stay on** [steɪ‿'ɒn]	dableiben, länger bleiben →	I don't want to *stay on* at school until I'm 19.
	specialist ['speʃlɪst]	Spezialist/Spezialistin; Fach-	
	landscape ['lændskeɪp]	Landschaft →	a view of the country
	gardening ['gɑ:dnɪŋ]	Gärtnern, Gartengestaltung →	garden → *gardening*
	agriculture ['ægrɪkʌltʃə]	Agrikultur, Landwirtschaft	
	special needs [ˌspeʃl 'ni:dz]	besondere Bedürfnisse	
	financial [faɪ'nænʃl]	finanziell →	A lot of young married couples have *financial* problems.
	support [sə'pɔ:t]	Unterstützung, Hilfe	
	specific [spə'sɪfɪk]	spezifisch, speziell, bestimmt →	special → *specific*
	time off [taɪm‿'ɒf]	Freizeit →	She hasn't got a lot of *time off*.
	to **improve** [ɪm'pru:v]	(sich) verbessern →	to make (or become) better
	prospect ['prɒspekt]	Aussicht, Perspektive	
	self-employment [ˌselfɪm'plɔɪmənt]	Selbstständigkeit →	*Self-employment* isn't a good idea for everybody.
	rare [reə]	rar, selten	
	expert ['ekspɜ:t]	Experte/Expertin	
	field [fi:ld]	(Arbeits-)Gebiet	
	to **experience** [ɪk'spɪəriənts]	erfahren, erleben →	When you *experience* something, it happens to you and you find out what it's like.
	inner ['ɪnə]	innerer/innere/inneres, innen	
	to **ignore** [ɪg'nɔ:]	ignorieren →	If you don't look at something and don't listen to it, even if you know it's there, you *ignore* it.
	bitter ['bɪtə]	verbittert, bitter	
	illness ['ɪlnəs]	Krankheit →	ill → *illness*
	to **come true** [kʌm 'tru:]	wahr werden	
	tragic ['trædʒɪk]	tragisch	

critic ['krɪtɪk]	Kritiker/Kritikerin	
novel ['nɒvl]	Roman	

Option 1

60 **automotive** [ˌɔ:tə'məʊtɪv]	Auto-, Fahrzeug-	
internship *(AE)* ['ɪntɜ:nʃɪp]	Praktikum →	*BE:* (work) placement
department [dɪ'pɑ:tmənt]	Abteilung, Fachbereich; Branche →	The games *department* is the part of a shop that sells games.
manufacturing [ˌmænjə'fæktʃrɪŋ]	Herstellung, Fertigung	
human resources [ˌhju:mən rɪ'zɔ:sɪz]	Personalabteilung →	You have to send your application to the *Human Resources* Department.
resource [rɪ'zɔ:s]	Ressource, Rohstoff; Quelle	
development [dɪ'veləpmənt]	Entwicklung →	to develop → *development*
marketing ['mɑ:kɪtɪŋ]	Marketing, Vermarktung, Vertrieb →	using advertisements etc. to try to sell products
sales *(pl)* [seɪlz]	Verkauf, Vertrieb →	to sell → *sales*
IT [ˌaɪ'ti:]	Informationstechnik, Informatik	
safety ['seɪfti]	Sicherheit →	safe → *safety*
finance ['faɪnænts]	Finanzwesen, Finanzen; Finanz-	

Wörter, die in anderen Sprachen ähnlich sind

Manche neuen Wörter kennst du schon aus anderen Sprachen. Das hilft dir, sie dir besser zu merken.

Englisch	Deutsch	Französisch	Türkisch
sport	Sport	sport	spor
university	Universität	université	üniversite
popular	populär	populaire	popüler
automobile	Auto(mobil)	automobile	oto(mobil)

Kennst du noch weitere Wörter oder andere Sprachen? Ergänze die Liste in deinem Heft.

public relations (PR) [ˌpʌblɪk rɪ'leɪʃnz]	Öffentlichkeitsarbeit	
headquarters *(pl)* ['hedˌkwɔ:təz]	Hauptsitz →	The company's *headquarters* are in London.
chief executive officer (CEO) [ˌtʃi:f ɪgˌzekjətɪv 'ɒfɪsə; ˌsi: i:'əʊ]	Generaldirektor/ Generaldirektorin; Geschäftsführer/ Geschäftsführerin →	The *CEO* came to the meeting.
junior ['dʒu:niə]	Junior, der Jüngere	
to **design** [dɪ'zaɪn]	entwerfen, zeichnen →	When you *design* something that you want to build, you make a plan first.
vehicle ['vɪəkl]	Fahrzeug, Vehikel	

vintage car [ˌvɪntɪdʒ 'kɑː]	Oldtimer	
vintage ['vɪntɪdʒ]	alt(modisch)	
to **restore** [rɪ'stɔː]	wiederherstellen, restaurieren →	If you *restore* something to its original state, you make it like it used to be.
great-grandson [ˌgreɪt'grænsʌn]	Urenkel →	I'm the *great-grandson* of my grandfather's father.
electric-powered [ɪ'lektrɪk ˌpaʊəd]	elektrisch betrieben	
extremely [ɪk'striːmli]	extrem, außerordentlich	
manufacturer [ˌmænjə'fæktʃərə]	Hersteller, Produzent, Fabrikant →	someone who makes something in a factory
sector ['sektə]	Sektor, Bereich	
to **develop** [dɪ'veləp]	(sich) entwickeln	
to **manufacture** [ˌmænjə'fæktʃə]	fertigen, herstellen →	to make in a factory
to **include** [ɪn'kluːd]	einschließen, beinhalten, aufnehmen	
rental ['rentl]	Miet-, Verleih- →	We got a car from a *rental* company.
leasing ['liːsɪŋ]	Leasing(-)	
accessories *(pl)* [ək'sesəriz]	Zubehör	
to **finance** ['faɪnænts]	finanzieren	
dealer ['diːlə]	Händler/Händlerin	
salesroom ['seɪlzruːm]	Verkaufsraum →	to sell → sales → *salesroom*
61 **design** [dɪ'zaɪn]	Design, Gestaltung	
super ['suːpə]	super, großartig	
to **assess** [ə'ses]	bewerten, beurteilen, einschätzen	
damage ['dæmɪdʒ]	Schaden, Beschädigung →	The storm caused a lot of *damage*.
body shell ['bɒdi ˌʃel]	Karosserie	
frame [freɪm]	Rahmen, Chassis	
reliable [rɪ'laɪəbl]	zuverlässig, verlässlich, vertrauenswürdig →	Someone you can trust is *reliable*.
flexible ['fleksɪbl]	flexibel, anpassungsfähig	
apart from [ə'pɑːt frəm]	außer, abgesehen von	
basic ['beɪsɪk]	grundlegend, Grund-; einfach →	In the first two years of English you learn a lot of *basic* words and phrases.
to **communicate** [kə'mjuːnɪkeɪt]	kommunizieren, sich verständigen →	The easiest way to *communicate* with people is to speak to them.
to **be able to** (do sth) [bi‿'eɪbl tə]	können, fähig sein (zu) →	They didn't know what to do. They *weren't able to* help him.
to split, split, split [splɪt, splɪt, splɪt]	(sich) (auf)teilen, spalten	
mini ['mɪni]	Mini-	
cover letter ['kʌvə ˌletə]	Begleitbrief, Begleitschreiben	
panel ['pænl]	Expertenrunde, Gremium	

Option 2

62 **extract** ['ekstrækt]	Extrakt, Auszug →	An *extract* from a book is just a small part of the story.
novel ['nɒvl]	Roman	

Wortbildung II

Aus manchen Wörtern kannst du durch Anhängen bestimmter Silben viele neue Wörter bilden.

to drink (trinken)	*drink**er*** *(Trinker)*	*drink**ing*** *(das Trinken)*	***un**drink**able*** (untrinkbar)
to think	…	…	…
to teach	…	…	…

Finde weitere Wörter und vervollständige die Liste in deinem Heft.

context ['kɒntekst]	Kontext, Zusammenhang	
introduction [ˌɪntrə'dʌkʃn]	Einleitung	
to **fight** [faɪt]	bekämpfen	
leukaemia [lju:'ki:miə]	Leukämie, Blutkrebs	
(not) any more [nɒt ˌeni 'mɔ:]	(nicht) mehr →	He finished school last month. He *doesn't* go to school *any more*.
to **fall in love** [fɔ:l‿ɪn 'lʌv]	sich verlieben	
to **stick (over)**, **stuck**, **stuck** [stɪk, stʌk, stʌk]	strecken/stecken (über)	
perhaps [pə'hæps]	vielleicht →	another word for 'maybe'
lazy ['leɪzi]	faul, träge	
to **lift up** [lɪft‿'ʌp]	hochheben, hochziehen	
shoebox ['ʃu:bɒks]	Schuhkarton	
mostly ['məʊstli]	überwiegend, größtenteils, hauptsächlich →	most → *mostly*
to **bring round** [brɪŋ‿'raʊnd]	rüberbringen, vorbeibringen	
to **shrug** (one's shoulders) [ʃrʌg]	mit den Achseln/Schultern zucken →	You can *shrug* your shoulders to show that you don't know or you aren't interested.
to **step** [step]	steigen, treten	
front garden [ˌfrʌnt 'gɑ:dn]	Vorgarten →	a small garden in front of a house
to **hold**, **held**, **held** [həʊld, held, held]	(ab)halten, festhalten	
to **hesitate** ['hezɪteɪt]	zögern →	He *hesitated* before he sat down.
to **chuck sb** [tʃʌk]	jmdn. verlassen, mit jmdm. Schluss machen	
no wonder [nəʊ 'wʌndə]	kein Wunder, dass … →	You say «*No wonder!*» when you are not surprised about something.
to **dump sb** [dʌmp]	mit jmdm. Schluss machen, jmdm. den Laufpass geben →	! Two people can agree to *break it off*. But one person *dumps* the other.
skeleton ['skelɪtn]	Skelett	
bald [bɔ:ld]	kahl, glatzköpfig →	My grandad is *bald* – he has no hair on his head.

	disappointing [ˌdɪsəˈpɔɪntɪŋ]	enttäuschend →	How was the concert? – It was very *disappointing*. The band only played for 45 minutes!
	pile [paɪl]	Stapel, Haufen →	a *pile* of wood
	twig [twɪg]	Zweig	
	hopeful [ˈhəʊpfl]	hoffnungsvoll →	hopeless ↔ *hopeful*
	damp [dæmp]	feucht →	not quite dry, but not really wet
	to **get sth going** [get ˈgəʊɪŋ]	etw. in Gang/Schwung bringen, flottmachen →	Paper can get a fire going.
	to **tip** [tɪp]	(aus)kippen	
	upside down [ˌʌpsaɪd ˈdaʊn]	umgedreht, auf den Kopf gestellt →	Don't hold the bottle *upside down*!
63	to **keep a diary** [ˌkiːp‿ə ˈdaɪəri]	ein Tagebuch/einen Terminkalender führen →	My grandmother *kept a diary* for most of her life.
	bruise [bruːz]	Prellung, Quetschung, Bluterguss	
	spine [spaɪn]	Wirbelsäule	
	official [əˈfɪʃl]	offiziell →	The Queen's *official* birthday is in June.
	pathetic [pəˈθetɪk]	Mitleid erregend, erbärmlich	
	optimism [ˈɒptɪmɪzm]	Optimismus	
	to **flare** [fleə]	lodern, flackern	
	get-well card [ˌget ˈwel ˌkɑːd]	Gute-Besserung-Karte →	Let's send him a *get-well card*.
	to **receive** [rɪˈsiːv]	empfangen, erhalten →	to get
	to **flake** [fleɪk]	zerfallen, zerbröseln, abbröckeln	
	used to *(+ infinitive)* [ˈjuːs‿tə]	früher; pflegte(n) zu →	We *used to* live in Munich. = Wir wohnten früher in München.
	by [baɪ]	neben	
	to **spit, spat, spat** [spɪt, spæt, spæt]	spucken, zischen, fauchen →	Don't *spit*! It's horrible.
	embers *(pl)* [ˈembəz]	Glut, glimmende Asche	

Fire

Erstelle eine Mind map zum Thema *fire*. Welche Wörter kennst du schon? Welche hast du neu dazu gelernt? Finde so viele Wörter wie möglich und vervollständige die Mind map in deinem Heft.

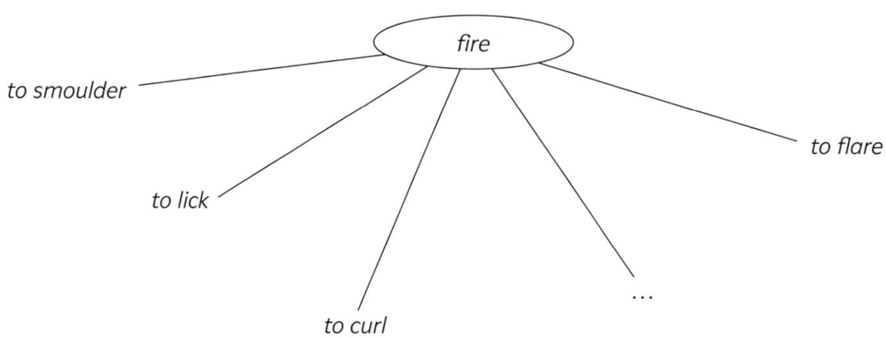

	to **spark** [spɑ:k]	sprühen *(Funken)*; auslösen, entfachen	
	to **unburden** [ʌnˈbɜ:dn]	entlasten, abladen	
	bramble [ˈbræmbl]	Brombeergestrüpp →	I cut my hand on some *brambles*.
	to **run a finger over sth** [rʌn]	mit dem Finger über etw. fahren/streichen	
	thin [θɪn]	dünn →	If you don't eat enough, you'll get too *thin*.
	to **whistle** [ˈwɪsl]	pfeifen	
	whistle [ˈwɪsl]	Pfiff; Trillerpfeife →	The referee blew his *whistle* at three o'clock.
	to **fold** [fəʊld]	falten, knicken, brechen	
	to **squash** [skwɒʃ]	zerdrücken, pressen, quetschen	
	to **melt** [melt]	schmelzen	
	plastic [ˈplæstɪk]	Plastik(-), Kunststoff(-) →	A material that is light and doesn't break easily.
	right [raɪt]	genau, direkt →	She is *right* in front of me.
	matter [ˈmætə]	Materie	
	particle [ˈpɑ:tɪkl]	Teilchen, Partikel	
	solid [ˈsɒlɪd]	fest, solide	
	liquid [ˈlɪkwɪd]	Flüssigkeit; flüssig →	Ice is solid and water is *liquid*.
	grounded [ˈgraʊndɪd]	geerdet, gefestigt	
	bright [braɪt]	hell, leuchtend, strahlend →	In the summer the sun is very *bright*.
	spark [spɑ:k]	Funke(n)	
	gravity [ˈgrævəti]	Schwerkraft, Schwere	
64	to **work out** [ˌwɜ:k‿ˈaʊt]	herausfinden, ausarbeiten →	to work → *to work out*
	tongue [tʌŋ]	Zunge	
	diabetic [ˌdaɪəˈbetɪk]	zuckerkrank; Diabetiker/ Diabetikerin	
	sugar [ˈʃʊgə]	Zucker →	You can put it in foods and drinks to make them sweet.
	can [kæn]	Dose	
	to **hand** [hænd]	(über)geben, aushändigen →	Could you *hand* me the sugar, please?
	to **buzz** [bʌz]	brummen, summen	
	brain(s) [breɪn, breɪnz]	Gehirn; Verstand →	Your *brain* is the part of your head that controls your feelings and how you think and move.
	ghostly [ˈgəʊstli]	geisterhaft	
	ash [æʃ]	Asche	
	ashes *(pl)* [ˈæʃɪz]	Verbrennungsrückstände, Asche	
	moth [mɒθ]	Motte, Falter	
	to **crackle** [ˈkrækl]	knistern, knacken, prasseln	
	dust [dʌst]	Staub →	*Dust* on a road can be very fine earth or sand.
	to **dig**, **dug**, **dug** [dɪg, dʌg, dʌg]	graben, buddeln	
	startled [ˈstɑ:tld]	verblüfft, alarmiert	
	to **frown** [fraʊn]	die Stirn runzeln	

	to **seem** [siːm]	(er)scheinen, wirken →	The dog *seemed* friendly, but it wasn't.
	to **be about to** (do sth) [bi‿əˈbaʊt tə]	im Begriff sein, etw. zu tun	
	instead [ɪnˈsted]	stattdessen, dafür →	If the weather is too cold for swimming, we could go for a walk *instead*.
	patch [pætʃ]	Beet; Fleck, Stelle; Flicken; Augenklappe	
	runner bean [ˈrʌnə ˌbiːn]	Stangenbohne	
	to **wipe** [waɪp]	(ab)wischen, abreiben →	He *wiped* the window with his hand and looked out.
	to **get on** [get‿ˈɒn]	weiterkommen, vorwärtskommen	
	to analyse [ˈænlaɪz]	analysieren	
	setting [ˈsetɪŋ]	Schauplatz, Rahmen	
65	to scan [skæn]	scannen, abtasten, nach Details durchsuchen	
	to react [riˈækt]	reagieren	
	storyline [ˈstɔːrilaɪn]	Handlung →	A story moves along this line.
	optimistic [ˌɒptɪˈmɪstɪk]	optimistisch	
	relationship [rɪˈleɪʃnʃɪp]	Beziehung →	The first *relationship* in life is usually between mother and child.
	to develop [dɪˈveləp]	(sich) entwickeln	
	to act out [ækt‿ˈaʊt]	vorspielen	
	point of view [ˌpɔɪnt‿əv‿ˈvjuː]	Ansicht, Einstellung, Standpunkt →	Your *point of view* is your way of seeing things.
	author [ˈɔːθə]	Autor/Autorin	
	perspective [pəˈspektɪv]	Perspektive, Blickwinkel →	! Achte auf die Aussprache.
	to split, split, split [splɪt, splɪt, splɪt]	(sich) (auf)teilen, spalten	
	mini [ˈmɪni]	Mini-	
	introductory [ˌɪntrəˈdʌktri]	Einleitungs-, einleitend →	introduction → *introductory*
	to **design** [dɪˈzaɪn]	entwerfen, zeichnen	
	character [ˈkærəktə]	Charakter; Figur →	She is a very interesting *character*.

Words in action

66	**adviser** [ədˈvaɪzə]	Berater/Beraterin →	to advise → advice → *adviser*
	writer [ˈraɪtə]	Schriftsteller/Schriftstellerin, Verfasser/Verfasserin →	to write → *writer*

Everyday English: A job interview

Die folgenden *phrases* helfen dir, wenn du ein Vorstellungsgespräch hast.

I'm still at school./left school./did my final exams …	Ich gehe noch zur Schule./Ich habe die Schule abgebrochen./ Ich habe meinen Abschluss gemacht.
I'm interested in the job/placement/… because …	Ich interessiere mich für den Job/das Praktikum /… weil …
I like working outside/with people/with computers/ in a team/…	Ich arbeite gerne im Freien/mit Menschen/mit Computern/in einem Team …
Your website is …	Ihre Website ist …
I'm good at …	Ich bin gut im Umgang mit …
I'm not so good at …	Ich bin nicht so gut im Umgang mit …
My hobbies are …	Meine Hobbys sind …
I think … is important.	Ich denke, es ist wichtig, …
How much will I be paid?	Wie hoch ist mein Lohn/Gehalt?
When will I have to start work in the morning?	Wann beginnt morgens die Arbeit?
Is there a cafeteria?	Gibt es eine Kantine?
I'd like to train to be a/an …	Ich würde mich gerne als … weiterbilden.
I'd like to work with animals/ …	Ich arbeite gerne mit Tieren/…
My 'dream' job would be as a …	Mein Traumberuf wäre …
I don't want to …all my life.	Ich möchte nicht mein Leben lang als … arbeiten.
I'd like to work abroad/ in …	Ich würde gerne im Ausland /in/auf … arbeiten.

Übe mit deinem Partner/deiner Partnerin ein Vorstellungsgespräch ein.

1,37 ## Sounds and spelling

a) Manchmal werden zwei Wörter mit unterschiedlicher Schreibweise und Bedeutung genau gleich ausgesprochen. Hör die die Sätze an und sage, welches die korrekte Schreibung ist.

1. [rəʊd]	a. road	b. rode
2. [feə]	a. fair	b. fare
3. ['weðə]	a. whether	b. weather
4. [breɪk]	a. brake	b. break
5. [bɔ:d]	a. bored	b. board
6. [wi:k]	a. weak	b. week

b) Kannst du zwei Schreibweisen für jeden dieser Laute finden?

1. [si:] 2. [ðeə] 3. [nəʊ] 4. [mi:t] 5. [wʊd]

Dictionary

In dieser alphabetischen Liste ist das Vokabular von *Orange Line 1* bis *6* enthalten. Namen werden in einer gesonderten Liste am Ende des Vokabulars aufgelistet.
Das Zeichen ° bei einem Eintrag weist darauf hin, dass das Wort zum rezeptiven Wortschatz zählt.
Die mit * gekennzeichneten Verben sind unregelmäßig.
Wendungen, die aus mehreren Wörtern bestehen, werden meist unter mehreren Stichwörtern aufgeführt.
So ist z. B. *at home* unter *at* und *home* zu finden.
Die Fundstellen verweisen auf das erstmalige Vorkommen der Wörter, z. B.
about [ə'baʊt] über **I U3,** 40 kommt zum ersten Mal vor in Band I, Unit 3, Seite 40.
dirty ['dɜ:ti] schmutzig **II U1,** 10 kommt zum ersten Mal vor in Band II, Unit 1, Seite 10.
U = Unit, T = Topic, LU = Link-up, FA = Fakultativer Anhang (nur Namen)

A

a, an [ə; ən] ein/eine **I U1,** 10
a bit [ə 'bɪt] ein bisschen **I U2,** 35
a couple of [ə 'kʌpl‿əv] ein paar, einige **V T4,** 65
a few [ə 'fju:] einige, ein paar **II U4,** 52
a lot [ə 'lɒt] viel **II U1,** 15
a lot of [ə 'lɒt‿əv] viel/viele, eine Menge **I U2,** 30
a week [ə 'wi:k] pro Woche, in der Woche **II U4,** 52
*to be **able to (do sth)** [bi‿'eɪbl tə] können, fähig sein (zu) **VI T1,** 10; **VI T2,** 29; **VI T4,** 61
Aboriginal [ˌæbə'rɪdʒnl] eingeboren, einheimisch **VI T1,** 11
Aborigine [ˌæbə'rɪdʒni] Ureinwohner/in Australiens, Aborigine **V T1,** 10
about [ə'baʊt] ungefähr, circa, etwa **III U1,** 11
about [ə'baʊt] über **I U3,** 40
out and about ['aʊt‿nd‿ə'baʊt] unterwegs °**I U4,** 54
to jump about [ˌdʒʌmp‿ə'baʊt] herumspringen **III U4,** 58
What about ...? [wɒt‿ə'baʊt] Was ist mit ...? Wie wäre es mit ...? **I U2,** 30
What's the film about? [wɒts ðə 'fɪlm‿əˌbaʊt] Wovon handelt der Film? °**II U3,** 43
above [ə'bʌv] oben, über, oberhalb **II U5,** 70
abroad [ə'brɔ:d] im/ins Ausland **III U4,** 57
absence ['æbsns] Abwesenheit **IV U2,** 25
academy [ə'kædəmi] Akademie, Hochschule, Lehranstalt **VI T1,** 10
accent ['æksnt] Akzent **II U3,** 36
to **accept** [ək'sept] akzeptieren, hinnehmen; annehmen **V T3,** 44
access ['ækses] Zugang **IV U4,** 65
accessories *(pl)* [ək'sesəriz] Zubehör **VI T4,** 60
accident ['æksɪdnt] Unfall **II U3,** 41
according to [ə'kɔ:dɪŋ tə] laut, gemäß °**VI T1,** 11; °**VI T4,** 58
acre ['eɪkə] Morgen *(Flächenmaß: 40,47 Ar)* **IV U4,** 58
across [ə'krɒs] waagerecht *(im Kreuzworträtsel)* °**II U3,** 42; über, hinüber, quer durch/darüber **III U1,** 10; breit, im Durchmesser **IV U3,** 49
to **act** [ækt] spielen *(Theater)* **I U7,** 90; sich verhalten, handeln, agieren **V T3,** 47
to act out [ækt‿'aʊt] vorspielen °**VI T3,** 47; °**VI T4,** 65
action ['ækʃn] Handlung, Aktion **III U1,** 9
active ['æktɪv] aktiv **VI T1,** 15; °**VI T3,** 47
activity [æk'tɪvəti] Aktivität **III U3,** 47
actor ['æktə] Schauspieler **I U7,** 96
actress ['æktrəs] Schauspielerin **III U2,** 25
actually ['æktʃuəli] eigentlich, tatsächlich **VI T2,** 28
ad [æd] Anzeige; Werbespot **V T1,** 15
to **adapt to** [ə'dæpt tə] (sich) anpassen an **VI T2,** 29
adaptable [ə'dæptəbl] anpassungsfähig **V T3,** 43
adapted [ə'dæptɪd] adaptiert, angepasst °**V T4,** 64
adaptor [ə'dæptə] Adapter **IV U3,** 44
to **add** [æd] hinzufügen, addieren **III U4,** 60
address [ə'dres] Adresse **I U5,** 70
adjective ['ædʒəktɪv] Adjektiv, Eigenschaftswort °**I U1,** 22
administrator [əd'mɪnɪstreɪtə] Administrator/Administratorin, Verwalter/Verwalterin **VI T1,** 14
to **admit** [əd'mɪt] zugeben **VI T3,** 44
adult ['ædʌlt] Erwachsener/Erwachsene **V T2,** 32
advanced [əd'vɑ:nst] fortgeschritten **III U4,** 57
adventure [əd'ventʃə] Abenteuer **II U6,** 80
adverb ['ædvɜ:b] Adverb °**II U7,** 90
adverb of manner [ˌædvɜ:b‿əv 'mænə] Adverb der Art und Weise °**II U7,** 90
advert ['ædvɜ:t] Anzeige, Werbespot **IV U2,** 25
advertising *(no pl.)* ['ædvətaɪzɪŋ] Werbung, Reklame; Werbe- **VI T1,** 14
advertising agent ['ædvətaɪzɪŋ ˌeɪdʒnt] Anzeigenvertreter/ Anzeigenvertreterin **VI T3,** 47
advice [əd'vaɪs] Rat(schlag) **V T1,** 12; **V T2,** 31; **V T3,** 43
careers advice [kə'rɪəz ədˌvaɪs] Berufsberatung **V T3,** 46
to **advise** [əd'vaɪz] raten **III U4,** 59
adviser [əd'vaɪzə] Berater/Beraterin **VI T4,** 66
to **affect** [ə'fekt] beeinflussen, beeinträchtigen, betreffen **VI T3,** 42; **VI T4,** 58
*to be **afraid (of)** [bi:‿ə'freɪd] Angst haben (vor), sich fürchten (vor) **III U4,** 56
African ['æfrɪkən] afrikanisch; Afrikaner/ Afrikanerin **VI T1,** 13
after ['ɑ:ftə] nach *(zeitlich)* **I LUB,** 39
afternoon [ˌɑ:ftə'nu:n] Nachmittag **I U2,** 34

afternoon tea [ˌɑ:ftənu:n 'ti:] Nachmittagstee **I U7,** 94
in the afternoon [ˌɪn ði ˌɑ:ftə'nu:n] nachmittags, am Nachmittag **I U3,** 47
aftershave ['ɑ:ftəʃeɪv] Aftershave, Rasierwasser **III U3,** 46
again [ə'gen] wieder **I U3,** 48
against [ə'genst] gegen **III U1,** 9
age [eɪdʒ] Alter; Zeitalter **III U3,** 40
Middle Ages [ˌmɪdl‿'eɪdʒɪz] Mittelalter **VI T2,** 28
agency ['eɪdʒnsi] Agentur, Behörde **IV U3,** 48
agent ['eɪdʒnt] Agent/Agentin, Vertreter/Vertreterin **IV U3,** 48
advertising agent ['ædvətaɪzɪŋ ˌeɪdʒnt] Anzeigenvertreter/ Anzeigenvertreterin **VI T3,** 47
travel agent ['trævl‿eɪdʒnt] Reisebürokaufmann/ Reisebürokauffrau **VI T1,** 17
ago [ə'gəʊ] vor (*zeitlich*) **II U2,** 26
to **agree** [ə'gri:] zustimmen, einer Meinung sein **V T4,** 60
to agree on [ə'gri:‿ɒn] sich einigen auf °**VI T3,** 45
agriculture ['ægrɪkʌltʃə] Agrikultur, Landwirtschaft **VI T4,** 59
aid [eɪd] Hilfe, Beistand, Förderung **V T3,** 43
air [eə] Luft **II U4,** 55
on the air [ˌɒn ði‿'eə] auf Sendung **II U4,** 55
airline ['eəlaɪn] Fluggesellschaft, Fluglinie **V T4,** 60
airport ['eəpɔ:t] Flughafen **II U7,** 89
alarm [ə'lɑ:m] Alarm **II U7,** 90
alarm clock [ə'lɑ:m ˌklɒk] Wecker **I U5,** 75
album ['ælbəm] Album **IV U5,** 73
alcohol ['ælkəhɒl] Alkohol **IV U2,** 25
A-levels *(pl)* ['eɪlevlz] brit. Abitur **III U4,** 57
alien ['eɪliən] Fremder/Fremde, Außerirdischer/Außerirdische **III U5,** 70; fremd, ausländisch **IV U3,** 48
alive [ə'laɪv] am Leben, lebendig **III U4,** 60
all [ɔ:l] alle/alles; ganz **I U3,** 50
all over [ˌɔ:l‿'əʊvə] überall **IV U1,** 10
all right [ɔ:l 'raɪt] in Ordnung **IV U4,** 64
in all [ɪn‿'ɔ:l] im Ganzen **III U4,** 53
no … at all [ˌnəʊ … ət‿'ɔ:l] überhaupt kein/keine **V T4,** 65
allegiance [ə'li:dʒns] Treue **IV U2,** 23
*to be **allowed to (do sth)** [bi:‿ə'laʊd tə] dürfen **VI T2,** 30
almost ['ɔ:lməʊst] fast, beinahe **III U3,** 39
alone [ə'ləʊn] allein **III U3,** 41
to go it alone [ˌgəʊ‿ɪt‿ə'ləʊn] einen Alleingang starten, es allein schaffen **V T3,** 43
to leave sb alone [ˌli:v‿ə'ləʊn] jmdn. in Ruhe lassen **V T1,** 12
along [ə'lɒŋ] entlang **I U7,** 91
to carry along [ˌkæri‿ə'lɒŋ] mitführen, mitreißen **V T4,** 64
aloud [ə'laʊd] laut °**VI T3,** 45
alphabet ['ælfəbet] Alphabet, Abc **I U1,** 15
alphabetical [ˌælfə'betɪkl] alphabetisch **I U6,** 88
already [ɔ:l'redi] schon **I U2,** 34
also ['ɔ:lsəʊ] auch **I U5,** 68
alternative [ɔ:l'tɜ:nətɪv] Alternative *(Musikrichtung)* **IV U5,** 76; alternativ; Alternative **V T4,** 59
although [ɔ:l'ðəʊ] obwohl **III U3,** 46
always ['ɔ:lweɪz] immer, ständig **I U1,** 16
a.m. [ˌeɪ'em] vormittags (*Uhrzeit*) **III U4,** 57
amazing [ə'meɪzɪŋ] erstaunlich **VI T1,** 12
ambassador [æm'bæsədə] Botschafter/ Botschafterin **VI T2,** 30
ambitious [æm'bɪʃəs] ehrgeizig **VI T2,** 32
ambulance ['æmbjələns] Krankenwagen **III U1,** 9
American [ə'merɪkən] amerikanisch; Amerikaner/Amerikanerin **II U4,** 50
American football [əˌmerɪkən 'fʊtbɔ:l] Football **III U1,** 8
Native American [ˌneɪtɪv‿ə'merɪkən] Ureinwohner/Ureinwohnerin Amerikas, Indianer/Indianerin **IV U1,** 10
South American [ˌsaʊθ‿ə'merɪkən] südamerikanisch; Südamerikaner/ Südamerikanerin **VI T2,** 29
among [ə'mʌŋ] unter, zwischen °**VI T2,** 33
amount [ə'maʊnt] Betrag, Menge, Summe **VI T3,** 42
to **analyse** ['ænlaɪz] analysieren °**VI T4,** 64
ancient ['eɪnʃnt] alt, antik **III U3,** 39
and [ænd] und **I U1,** 11
angry ['æŋgri] verärgert, böse **II U1,** 18
to be angry with [bi: 'æŋgri wɪð] böse sein auf **II U2,** 26
animal ['ænɪml] Tier **I U6,** 82
announcement [ə'naʊntsmənt] Ankündigung; Durchsage **IV U2,** 29
anorak ['ænəræk] Anorak **II U6,** 82
another [ə'nʌðə] noch ein/eine, ein anderer/eine andere/ein anderes **II U3,** 44
answer ['ɑ:ntsə] Antwort **I U4,** 58
to **answer** ['ɑ:ntsə] antworten, beantworten °**I LUA,** 24
answerphone ['ɑ:nsəfəʊn] Anrufbeantworter **III U4,** 59
anti ['æntɪ] gegen-, anti- **V T1,** 12; **V T3,** 41
any ['eni] etwas **II U4,** 54
(not) any more [nɒt ˌeni 'mɔ:] (nicht) mehr **VI T4,** 62
anybody ['eniˌbɒdi] jeder (beliebige) **III U5,** 71
anything ['eniθɪŋ] etwas, irgendetwas **I U5,** 66
anywhere ['eniweə] überall; irgendwo **III U3,** 39
apart from [ə'pɑ:t frəm] außer, abgesehen von **VI T4,** 61
apartment *(AE)* [ə'pɑ:tmənt] Wohnung, Apartment **IV U3,** 42
apple ['æpl] Apfel **I U1,** 14
appliance [ə'plaɪənts] (Haushalts-)Gerät, Einrichtung **VI T3,** 46
applicant ['æplɪkənt] Bewerber/ Bewerberin, Antragsteller/ Antragstellerin **V T1,** 10
application [ˌæplɪ'keɪʃn] Bewerbung, Antrag; Anwendung **V T2,** 29
to **apply (for)** [ə'plaɪ] sich bewerben (um), sich anmelden (zu) **V T1,** 14; **V T2,** 32
to **appoint** [ə'pɔɪnt] ernennen **VI T2,** 30
apprentice [ə'prentɪs] Auszubildender/ Auszubildende **VI T2,** 32
young apprentice (YA) [ˌjʌŋ‿ə'prentɪs] minderjähriger Auszubildender/ minderjährige Auszubildende **VI T2,** 32
apprenticeship [ə'prentɪʃɪp] Lehre, Ausbildung **V T2,** 32
April ['eɪprl] April **I U5,** 70
architect ['ɑ:kɪtekt] Architekt/ Architektin **VI T3,** 46
area ['eəriə] Gebiet; Fläche **II U7,** 94
rest area ['rest ˌeəriə] Rastplatz **IV U4,** 61
arena [ə'ri:nə] Arena, Stadion **II U2,** 22
to **argue** ['ɑ:gju:] streiten, argumentieren **III U2,** 30
to have an **argument** [ˌhæv‿ən‿'ɑ:gjəmənt] sich streiten **III U4,** 52
arm [ɑ:m] Arm **II U3,** 40; Ärmel **IV U2,** 31
around [ə'raʊnd] (um …) herum, umher **II U6,** 78; ungefähr, zirka, etwa **IV U3,** 49
See you around! [ˌsi: jə ə'raʊnd] Bis dann!, Bis … . **IV U2,** 26

to hang around [ˌhæŋ‿ə'raʊnd] rumhängen, herumlungern **VT2,** 28
to **arrest** [ə'rest] festnehmen, verhaften **III U5,** 78
to **arrive** [ə'raɪv] ankommen **I U6,** 86
arrow ['ærəʊ] Pfeil **VI T2,** 28
Art [ɑ:t] Kunst **II U1,** 10
article ['ɑ:tɪkl] Artikel **VI T2,** 32; **VI T3,** 40
artist ['ɑ:tɪst] Künstler/Künstlerin **VT2,** 29
as [æz; əz] als, wie **II U4,** 52; während **IV U3,** 46; genauso **VI T3,** 44
as … as [æz … æz; əz … əz] so … wie … **II U4,** 52
as well as [əz 'wel‿əz] sowohl … als auch **III U4,** 57
ash [æʃ] Asche **VI T4,** 64
ashes *(pl)* ['æʃɪz] Verbrennungsrückstände, Asche **VI T4,** 64
Asian ['eɪʃn] asiatisch; Asiate/Asiatin **VI T1,** 10
to **ask** [ɑ:sk] fragen **I U3,** 44
to ask (for) ['ɑ:sk fə] fragen (nach), bitten (um) **I U4,** 60
*to be **asleep** [ˌbi:‿ə'sli:p] schlafen **II U7,** 94
aspect ['æspekt] Aspekt, Gesichtspunkt, Seite **VT1,** 10; **VT2,** 28; **VT3,** 42; **VT4,** 60
ass *(AE)* [æs] Hintern, Arsch **IV U5,** 80
assembly [ə'sembli] Versammlung, Morgenappell **II U1,** 10
to **assess** [ə'ses] bewerten, beurteilen, einschätzen **VI T1,** 10; **VI T4,** 61
assistant [ə'sɪstnt] Assistent/Assistentin **III U5,** 75
shop assistant ['ʃɒp‿əˌsɪstnt] Verkäufer/Verkäuferin **II U5,** 67
to **assure** [ə'ʃʊə] etw. zusichern, versichern, sicherstellen **VT4,** 66
astronaut ['æstrənɔ:t] Astronaut/Astronautin **IV U3,** 40
at [æt; ət] in, auf, bei, an **I U1,** 10
at any time [æt‿ˌeni 'taɪm] jederzeit **IV U2,** 25
at first [ət 'fɜ:st] zuerst, zunächst **II U6,** 80
at home [ət 'həʊm] zu Hause **I U2,** 26
at last [ət 'lɑ:st] endlich, schließlich **VT3,** 42
at least [ət 'li:st] wenigstens, mindestens **I U6,** 87
at night [ət 'naɪt] nachts **II U3,** 47
at once [ət 'wʌnts] sofort, plötzlich **II U7,** 94
at the back [ət ðə 'bæk] hinten, im hinteren Teil °**II U7,** 96
at the bottom [ət ðə 'bɒtəm] unten, im unteren Teil **III U1,** 14
at the front [ət ðə 'frʌnt] im vorderen Teil, vorne **IV U1,** 9
at the moment [ət ðə 'məʊmənt] im Augenblick, momentan **I U7,** 90
at the top [ət ðə 'tɒp] oben, im oberen Teil **III U1,** 14
atmosphere ['ætməsfɪə] Atmosphäre; Stimmung **VI T2,** 33; Umgebung **VI T3,** 47
attack [ə'tæk] Angriff; Anfall **VI T2,** 29
to **attack** [ə'tæk] angreifen **III U5,** 74
attempt [ə'tempt] Versuch; Anschlag **VT3,** 43
Attention! [ə'tentʃn] Achtung! °**IV U2,** 29
to **attract** [ə'trækt] anziehen **IV U4,** 65
attraction [ə'trækʃn] Attraktion, Sehenswürdigkeit **VI T2,** 30
attractive [ə'træktɪv] attraktiv **IV U2,** 26
audience ['ɔ:diəns] Publikum **III U4,** 53
audition [ɔ:'dɪʃn] Vorsprechen, Vorsingen, Vortanzen **II U5,** 64
August ['ɔ:gəst] August **I U5,** 70
aunt [ɑ:nt] Tante **I U2,** 28
Aussie *(Aus)* ['ɒzi] Australier/Australierin °**VT1,** 12
Australian [ɒs'treɪliən] australisch; Australier/Australierin **II U4,** 50
author ['ɔ:θə] Autor/Autorin °**VI T4,** 65
autograph ['ɔ:təgrɑ:f] Autogramm **I U7,** 96
automotive [ˌɔ:tə'məʊtɪv] Auto-, Fahrzeug- **VI T4,** 60
autumn ['ɔ:təm] Herbst **I U6,** 79
average ['ævrɪdʒ] durchschnittlich **III U5,** 68
award [ə'wɔ:d] Auszeichnung, Preis **IV U5,** 72
away [ə'weɪ] weg **I U3,** 48
to run away [rʌn‿ə'weɪ] wegrennen **I U3,** 48
awesome ['ɔ:səm] toll **IV U2,** 26
awful ['ɔ:fl] schrecklich, furchtbar **III U5,** 72

B

baby, babies *(pl)* ['beɪbi; 'beɪbiz] Baby, Säugling **I U6,** 82
back [bæk] Rücken **II U3,** 41
at the back [ət ðə 'bæk] hinten, im hinteren Teil °**II U7,** 96
like the back of my hand ['bæk‿əv maɪ ˌhænd] wie meine Westentasche **III U2,** 30
back [bæk] Hinter-, rückwärtig **II U4,** 56
back line [ˌbæk 'laɪn] Grundlinie **III U1,** 10
back [bæk] zurück **I U3,** 42
to sit back [ˌsɪt 'bæk] sich zurücklehnen **IV U1,** 16
background ['bækgraʊnd] Hintergrund **IV U1,** 8
backless ['bækləs] rückenfrei **IV U5,** 72
backpacker ['bækpækə] Rucksacktourist/Rucksacktouristin **VI T1,** 8
bacon ['beɪkn] Schinkenspeck **IV U1,** 12
bad [bæd] schlecht **I U5,** 74
bad language [bæd 'læŋgwɪdʒ] Schimpfwörter **VI T2,** 32
bad luck [ˌbæd 'lʌk] Pech **I U4,** 63
badminton ['bædmɪntən] Badminton, Federball **I U3,** 40
bag [bæg] Tasche, Tüte **I U1,** 14
school bag ['sku:l bæg] Schultasche, Schulranzen **I U1,** 14
sleeping bag ['sli:pɪŋ ˌbæg] Schlafsack **I U6,** 84
bagel ['beɪgl] Bagel **IV U1,** 12
baguette [bæg'et] Baguette **VT3,** 47
baker ['beɪkə] Bäcker/Bäckerin **III U2,** 28
balance ['bæləns] Gleichgewicht, Balance **VI T3,** 44
bald [bɔ:ld] kahl, glatzköpfig **VI T4,** 62
ball [bɔ:l] Ball **I U1,** 20
balloon [bə'lu:n] (Heiß-)Luftballon **VT3,** 43
ballroom ['bɔ:lrʊm] Ballsaal **IV U2,** 23
ballroom dancing [ˌbɔ:lrʊm 'dɑ:ntsɪŋ] Gesellschaftstanz **IV U2,** 23
ban [bæn] Verbot, Sperre; Bann **VT3,** 44
to **ban** [bæn] verbieten, ausschließen; (ver)bannen **VT3,** 44
banana [bə'nɑ:nə] Banane **II U1,** 15
to go bananas [ˌgəʊ bə'nɑ:nəz] verrückt werden, durchdrehen **II U5,** 66
band [bænd] Bande; Band, Kapelle **IV U3,** 48
steel band [ˌsti:l 'bænd] Steelband *(Band, deren Instrumente aus leeren Ölfässern bestehen)* **III U4,** 54
to **bang** [bæŋ] fest klopfen **II U7,** 94
bank [bæŋk] Bank **IV U5,** 80
piggy bank ['pɪgi bæŋk] Sparschwein **II U2,** 23
bar [bɑ:] Bar, Kneipe **IV U2,** 30; Tafel, Riegel, Stück; Stange **VT4,** 62
bistro bar [ˌbi:strəʊ 'bɑ:] Bistro **VT3,** 46
burger bar ['bɜ:gə ˌbɑ:] Fastfood-Restaurant **I U5,** 68
snack bar ['snæk ˌbɑ:] Café, Imbissstube **VT3,** 46

barbecue ['bɑ:bɪkju:] Grill(party) **V T1,** 11
bark [bɑ:k] Bellen **III U5,** 78
to **bark** [bɑ:k] bellen **I U3,** 48
barking ['bɑ:kɪŋ] Bellen **IV U4,** 65
barman, barmen *(pl)* ['bɑ:mən, 'bɑ:men] Barmann, Barkeeper **IV U4,** 64
barn [bɑ:n] Scheune **II U7,** 88
barn owl ['bɑ:n‿əʊl] Schleiereule **II U7,** 94
baron ['bærn] Baron **VI T2,** 28
base [beɪs] Base **III U1,** 14; Station, Basis; Fuß **V T4,** 66
baseball ['beɪsbɔ:l] Baseball **III U1,** 9
basement ['beɪsmənt] Kellergeschoss, Untergeschoss **III U3,** 46
basic ['beɪsɪk] grundlegend, Grund-; einfach **VI T1,** 14; **VI T4,** 61
basketball ['bɑ:skɪtbɔ:l] Basketball **I U3,** 40
bass [beɪs] Bass **IV U5,** 76
bat [bæt] Schläger **III U1,** 8
to **bat** [bæt] schlagen **III U1,** 8
bathroom ['bɑ:θrʊm] Bad, Badezimmer **I LUA,** 24
bathtub ['bɑ:θtʌb] Badewanne **IV U3,** 42
batter ['bætə] Schlagmann/Schlagfrau **III U1,** 9
battery ['bætri] Batterie, Akku **II U7,** 95
battle ['bætl] Schlacht, Kampf **VI T2,** 29
BC (= before Christ) [bi:'si:] vor Christus **III U1,** 13
*to **be** [bi:] sein **I U1,** 23
It's a draw. [ˌɪts‿ə 'drɔ:] Es steht unentschieden. **III U1,** 12
to be able to (do sth) [bi‿'eɪbl tə] können, fähig sein (zu) **VI T1,** 10; **VI T2,** 29; **VI T4,** 61
to be about to (do sth) [bi‿ə'baʊt tə] im Begriff sein, etw. zu tun **VI T4,** 64
to be afraid (of) [bi:‿ə'freɪd] Angst haben (vor), sich fürchten (vor) **III U4,** 56
to be allowed to (do sth) [bi:‿ə'laʊd tə] dürfen **VI T2,** 30
to be angry with [bi: 'æŋgri wɪð] böse sein auf **II U2,** 26
to be asleep [ˌbi:‿ə'sli:p] schlafen **II U7,** 94
to be a turn-off ['tɜ:nɒf] abtörnend sein, zum Abgewöhnen sein **V T2,** 28
to be called [bi: 'kɔ:ld] heißen, genannt werden **III U4,** 59
to be cold [bi: 'kəʊld] frieren **II U2,** 24
to be fed up [bi: ˌfed‿'ʌp] die Nase voll haben **I U2,** 34
to be frightened (of) [bi: 'fraɪtnd] Angst haben (vor) **II U6,** 83
to be fun [bi: 'fʌn] Spaß machen **I U3,** 43
to be good with … [bi: 'gʊd wɪð] gut mit … umgehen können **I U2,** 34
to be in a hurry [bi:‿ɪn‿ə 'hʌri] es eilig haben **I U2,** 30
to be into [bi:‿'ɪntə] interessiert sein an **IV U5,** 76
to be lost [bi: 'lɒst] sich verirrt haben **III U3,** 40
to be missing [bi: 'mɪsɪŋ] fehlen **III U1,** 14
to be nuts about [bi: ˌnʌts‿ə'baʊt] verrückt nach … sein **II U1,** 18
to be on [bi:‿'ɒn] an der Reihe sein; im Gange sein, laufen **II U5,** 70; an sein, brennen *(Licht)* **II U7,** 94
to be out of a job [bi‿aʊt‿əv‿ə 'dʒɒb] arbeitslos sein **VI T1,** 11
to be pleased with [bi: 'pli:zd wɪð] zufrieden sein mit **I U6,** 87
to be right [bi: 'raɪt] Recht haben **II U4,** 56
to be sorry [bi: 'sɒri] leidtun **III U3,** 44
to be trapped [bi: 'træpt] in der Falle sitzen **II U6,** 83
to be upset [bi: ʌp'set] aufgeregt sein, bestürzt sein **II U3,** 44
to be welcome to do [bi: 'welkəm] gerne etwas tun können **III U4,** 56
to be worried [bi: 'wʌrid] besorgt sein, beunruhigt sein **I U6,** 87
to be wrong [bi: 'rɒŋ] Unrecht haben **III U3,** 47
beach [bi:tʃ] Strand **III U1,** 10
bean [bi:n] Bohne **II U4,** 54
jelly bean ['dʒeli ˌbi:n] *engl. Süßigkeit* **V T1,** 10
runner bean ['rʌnə ˌbi:n] Stangenbohne **VI T4,** 64
bear [beə] Bär/Bärin **IV U4,** 65
beard [bɪəd] Bart **III U5,** 76
beautiful ['bju:tɪfl] schön, wunderschön **I U6,** 78
because [bɪ'kɒz] weil **I U2,** 30
because of [bɪ'kɒz‿əv] wegen **VI T1,** 10; **VI T3,** 43
*to **become** [bɪ'kʌm] werden **III U2,** 25
bed [bed] Bett **I LUA,** 25
to get out of bed [ˌget‿aʊt‿əv 'bed] aufstehen **II U7,** 94
bedroom ['bedrʊm] Schlafzimmer **I LUA,** 24
before [bɪ'fɔ:] vor; bevor **I LUB,** 39
*to **begin** [bɪ'gɪn] beginnen, anfangen **II U3,** 47
beginning [bɪ'gɪnɪŋ] Anfang, Beginn **IV U1,** 14
behind [bɪ'haɪnd] hinter **I U1,** 18
Belgian ['beldʒən] belgisch; Belgier/Belgierin **IV U1,** 10
to **believe** [bɪ'li:v] glauben **II U1,** 18
bell [bel] Glocke, Klingel **II U2,** 24
The bell rings. [ðə 'bel rɪŋz] Es klingelt. **II U4,** 50
to **belong (to)** [bɪ'lɒŋ] gehören (zu) **V T2,** 28
below [bɪ'ləʊ] unterhalb, unten **IV U1,** 18
beside [bɪ'saɪd] neben, außer **II U1,** 18
best [best] bester/beste/bestes **II U1,** 14; am besten **III U1,** 10
*to **bet** [bet] wetten **II U1,** 14
better ['betə] besser **II U4,** 50
between [bɪ'twi:n] zwischen **I U7,** 90
big [bɪg] groß **I U1,** 12
bike [baɪk] Fahrrad **I LUB,** 38
by bike [baɪ 'baɪk] mit dem Fahrrad **I U4,** 57
bilingual [baɪ'lɪŋgwəl] zweisprachig, bilingual **VI T1,** 12; **VI T1,** 14
bill [bɪl] Rechnung **II U4,** 55; Gesetz(entwurf) **VI T2,** 30
billion ['bɪljən] Milliarde *(tausend Millionen)* **VI T3,** 45
bin [bɪn] Mülleimer, Mülltonne **III U3,** 40
bird [bɜ:d] Vogel **II U4,** 59
birth [bɜ:θ] Geburt **III U1,** 11
birthday ['bɜ:θdeɪ] Geburtstag **I U5,** 68
biscuit ['bɪskɪt] Keks **I U5,** 68
bishop ['bɪʃəp] Bischof **VI T2,** 28
bistro bar [ˌbi:strəʊ 'bɑ:] Bistro **V T3,** 46
bit [bɪt] Stückchen; Auszug, Teil **V T4,** 66
a bit [ə 'bɪt] ein bisschen **I U2,** 35
bite [baɪt] Biss, Stich; Bissen **V T1,** 12
*to **bite** [baɪt] beißen **V T1,** 12
bitter ['bɪtə] verbittert, bitter **VI T4,** 59
black [blæk] schwarz **I LUA,** 24
Black [blæk] Schwarzer/Schwarze **V T3,** 42
blackout *(AE)* ['blækaʊt] Stromausfall **IV U3,** 42
blanket ['blæŋkɪt] (Woll-)Decke **II U6,** 74
wet blanket [wet 'blæŋkɪt] Miesmacher/Miesmacherin **II U6,** 74
blind [blaɪnd] blind **III U3,** 46
blindfolded ['blaɪndfəʊldɪd] mit verbundenen Augen **VI T2,** 28
bling bling *(slang)* [ˌblɪŋ 'blɪŋ] Klunker **IV U5,** 76
bloke [bləʊk] Typ, Kerl **I U7,** 96
blond [blɒnd] blond **II U2,** 28
blond(e)-haired ['blɒnd ˌheəd] blond **III U2,** 25
blood [blʌd] Blut **III U5,** 74
bloody ['blʌdi] blutig; verdammt **III U1,** 12
*to **blow** [bləʊ] blasen **III U2,** 28

to blow up [bləʊ‿ˈʌp] aufblasen °**I U5,** 71
blue [bluː] blau **I LUA,** 24
board [bɔːd] Tafel, Wandtafel **I U1,** 18
notice board [ˈnəʊtɪs bɔːd] schwarzes Brett **III U4,** 57
boat [bəʊt] Boot, Schiff **III U2,** 28
body [ˈbɒdi] Körper **III U5,** 78
body shell [ˈbɒdi ˌʃel] Karosserie **VI T4,** 61
bomb [bɒm] Bombe **IV U3,** 41
boogie [ˈbuːgi] Boogie *(Tanzstil)* °**IV U5,** 80
book [bʊk] Buch **I U1,** 14
exercise book [ˈeksəsaɪz ˌbʊk] Heft, Übungsheft **I U1,** 14
to **book** [bʊk] buchen, reservieren **III U5,** 73
boot [buːt] Stiefel **III U5,** 76
rubber boots *(pl)* [ˌrʌbə ˈbuːts] Gummistiefel **II U6,** 74
rugby boot [ˈrʌgbi buːt] Rugbyschuh, Stollenschuh **III U1,** 8
border [ˈbɔːdə] Grenze **IV U4,** 64
bored [bɔːd] gelangweilt **II U2,** 24
boring [ˈbɔːrɪŋ] langweilig **I U1,** 20
*was/were/is/are **born** [bɔːn] wurde(n)/wird/werden geboren **III U1,** 11
borough [ˈbʌrə] Bezirk, Stadtteil **IV U1,** 9
to **borrow** [ˈbɒrəʊ] borgen, leihen **I U2,** 34
boss [bɒs] Boss, Chef/Chefin **IV U3,** 48
both [bəʊθ] beide **III U3,** 46
It's no **bother.** [ˈbɒðə] Kein Problem. **III U5,** 72
to **bother** [ˈbɒðə] stören, belästigen °**III U3,** 44
bottle [ˈbɒtl] Flasche **I U5,** 68
bottled [ˈbɒtld] in Flaschen abgefüllt **VI T3,** 45
at the **bottom** [ət ðə ˈbɒtəm] unten, im unteren Teil **III U1,** 14
boulevard [ˈbuːləvɑːd] Boulevard, Prachtstraße **IV U5,** 78
bow [bəʊ] Bogen **VI T2,** 28
bowl [bəʊl] Schüssel **II U4,** 50
box, boxes *(pl)* [bɒks; ˈbɒksɪz] Kiste, Schachtel, Kasten **I U5,** 68
fact box [ˈfækt bɒks] Infokasten **III U1,** 8
phone box [ˈfəʊn ˌbɒks] Telefonzelle **III U3,** 44
boy [bɔɪ] Junge **I U1,** 16
boyfriend [ˈbɔɪfrend] Freund *(in einer Paarbeziehung)* **III U4,** 53
brain(s) [breɪn, breɪnz] Gehirn; Verstand **VI T4,** 64
bramble [ˈbræmbl] Brombeergestrüpp **VI T4,** 63
brand [brænd] brand- **IV U2,** 23
brave [breɪv] tapfer, mutig **III U5,** 74
bread [bred] Brot **II U4,** 49
break [breɪk] Pause **II U1,** 12
*to **break** [breɪk] (zer)brechen, kaputtmachen **II U5,** 68
to break out [ˌbreɪk‿ˈaʊt] ausbrechen **V T3,** 44
to **break-dance** [ˈbreɪkdɑːnts] Breakdance tanzen **I LUB,** 38
breakdown [ˈbreɪkdaʊn] Autopanne; Zusammenbruch **IV U4,** 61
breakfast [ˈbrekfəst] Frühstück **I U3,** 44
to have breakfast [hæv ˈbrekfəst] frühstücken **III U2,** 23
bricklayer [ˈbrɪkˌleɪə] Maurer/Maurerin **VI T3,** 46
bridge [brɪdʒ] Brücke **I LUC,** 52
fire **brigade** [ˈfaɪə brɪˌgeɪd] Feuerwehr **III U2,** 28
bright [braɪt] hell, leuchtend, strahlend **VI T4,** 63
brilliant [ˈbrɪljənt] toll, prima; leuchtend **II U5,** 70
*to **bring** [brɪŋ] bringen, mitbringen **I U3,** 43
to bring in [brɪŋ‿ˈɪn] hereinbringen, mitbringen °**I U7,** 93
to bring round [brɪŋ‿ˈraʊnd] rüberbringen, vorbeibringen **VI T4,** 62
British [ˈbrɪtɪʃ] britisch **III U1,** 15
brochure [ˈbrəʊʃə] Broschüre, Prospekt °**III U2,** 27
broke [brəʊk] pleite, abgebrannt **IV U5,** 80
broken [ˈbrəʊkn] kaputt, zerbrochen, gebrochen **I U6,** 84
brother [ˈbrʌðə] Bruder **I LUA,** 25
brown [braʊn] braun **I LUA,** 24
bruise [bruːz] Prellung, Quetschung, Bluterguss **VI T4,** 63
to **brush** [brʌʃ] putzen, bürsten **IV U3,** 46
speech **bubble** [ˈspiːtʃ ˌbʌbl] Sprechblase °**III U3,** 41
buddy *(infml)* [ˈbʌdi] Tauchbegleiter/Tauchbegleiterin; Kumpel, Kamerad/Kameradin **V T4,** 65
*to **build** [bɪld] bauen **III U2,** 22
building [ˈbɪldɪŋ] Bauen **VI T3,** 46
building site [ˈbɪldɪŋ saɪt] Baustelle **VI T3,** 46
builder [ˈbɪldə] Baufachmann/Baufachfrau, Baumeister/Baumeisterin **VI T3,** 43
building [ˈbɪldɪŋ] Gebäude **III U1,** 9
light **bulb** [ˈlaɪt bʌlb] Glühbirne **IV U3,** 44
bully [ˈbʊli] jemand, der andere tyrannisiert **II U3,** 47
to **bully** [ˈbʊli] tyrannisieren **VI T2,** 33
*to go **bump** [gəʊ ˈbʌmp] rumsen °**II U7,** 94
burger [ˈbɜːgə] Hamburger **I U5,** 68
burger bar [ˈbɜːgə ˌbɑː] Fastfood-Restaurant **I U5,** 68
burglar [ˈbɜːglə] Einbrecher/Einbrecherin **II U7,** 90
*to **burn** [bɜːn] (ver)brennen **III U2,** 28
to **bury** [ˈberi] begraben, beerdigen **III U5,** 74
bus, buses *(pl)* [bʌs; ˈbʌsɪz] Bus **I LUC,** 52
bus stop [ˈbʌs ˌstɒp] Bushaltestelle **I LUC,** 52
on the bus [ˌɒn ðə ˈbʌs] im Bus **II U1,** 18
to take a bus tour [ˌteɪk‿ə ˈbʌs tʊə] eine Busfahrt machen **IV U4,** 58
bush [bʊʃ] Busch, Strauch **I U6,** 86
business [ˈbɪznɪs] Geschäft, Branche **IV U1,** 14
business card [ˈbɪznɪs ˌkɑːd] Visitenkarte **VI T2,** 29
businessman, businessmen *(pl)* [ˈbɪznɪsmən; ˈbɪznɪsmen] Geschäftsmann **III U2,** 24
busy [ˈbɪzi] beschäftigt, ausgefüllt **I U2,** 34; belebt **III U2,** 24
but [bʌt] aber **I U2,** 26; außer **IV U5,** 80
butter [ˈbʌtə] Butter **I U7,** 94
button [ˈbʌtn] Auslöser; Knopf **II U7,** 95
*to **buy** [baɪ] kaufen **I U5,** 66
to **buzz** [bʌz] brummen, summen **VI T4,** 64
by [baɪ] bis **II U6,** 78; von **IV U5,** 80; neben **VI T4,** 63
by bike [baɪ ˈbaɪk] mit dem Fahrrad **I U4,** 57
by the way [ˌbaɪ ðə ˈweɪ] übrigens **IV U4,** 61
bye [baɪ] tschüss **I U1,** 16

C

café [ˈkæfeɪ] Café **I U3,** 48
cafeteria [ˌkæfəˈtɪəriə] Cafeteria **I U1,** 20
cage [keɪdʒ] Käfig **V T2,** 32
cake [keɪk] Kuchen **I U5,** 68
calendar [ˈkæləndə] Kalender **I U5,** 71
call [kɔːl] Anruf °**I U6,** 83
call centre [ˈkɔːl ˌsentə] Call-Center **VI T1,** 11
phone call [ˈfəʊn ˌkɔːl] (Telefon-)Anruf °**II U4,** 57

to **call** [kɔ:l] rufen, anrufen, nennen **I U3,** 48
That's what I call .... [ˌðæts wɒt‿'aɪ ˌkɔ:l] Das nenne ich .... **II U1,** 14
to be called [bi: 'kɔ:ld] heißen, genannt werden **III U4,** 59
caller ['kɔ:lə] Anrufer/Anruferin °**III U4,** 59
calm [kɑ:m] ruhig **II U6,** 80
camera ['kæmrə] Kamera, Fotoapparat **II U5,** 62
cameraman, **cameramen** *(pl)* ['kæmrəmæn; 'kæmrəmen] Kameramann **V T2,** 32
camp [kæmp] Camp, Lager **IV U4,** 62
campfire ['kæmpfaɪə] Lagerfeuer **IV U4,** 58
camping ['kæmpɪŋ] Camping, Zelten **I U6,** 84
can [kæn] Dose **VI T4,** 64
*__can__ [kæn] können, dürfen **I U1,** 19
Canadian [kə'neɪdiən] kanadisch; Kanadier/Kanadierin **VI T1,** 8
to **canoe** [kə'nu:] Kanu fahren **III U3,** 40
Cantonese [ˌkɑntə'ni:z] kantonesisch; Kantonese/Kantonesin **VI T1,** 12
canyon ['kænjən] Schlucht, Canyon **IV U4,** 56
cap [kæp] Kappe, Mütze **I U5,** 66
capital city [ˌkæpɪtl 'sɪti] Hauptstadt °**III U2,** 27
capital letter [ˌkæpɪtl 'letə] Großbuchstabe °**II U3,** 37
capsule ['kæpsju:l] Kapsel **III U2,** 22
captain ['kæptɪn] Kapitän **IV U2,** 23
caption ['kæpʃn] Untertitel; Bildunterschrift °**III U2,** 22
car [kɑ:] Auto **I U3,** 49
carbon ['kɑ:bn] Kohle(nstoff) **VI T3,** 42
carbon dioxide (CO_2) [ˌkɑ:bn daɪ'ɒksaɪd; si:‿əʊ 'tu:] Kohlendioxid **VI T3,** 42
carbon footprint [ˌkɑ:bn 'fʊtprɪnt] CO_2 -Bilanz **VI T3,** 42
card [kɑ:d] Karte **I LUB,** 38
business card ['bɪznɪs ˌkɑ:d] Visitenkarte **VI T2,** 29
day travel card [ˌdeɪ 'trævl ˌkɑ:d] Tagesfahrkarte **III U2,** 27
get-well card [ˌget 'wel ˌkɑ:d] Gute-Besserung-Karte **VI T4,** 63
*to take **care** [teɪk 'keə] aufpassen; sich kümmern **IV U2,** 29
to **care** [keə] sich kümmern, sich interessieren, wichtig nehmen **III U4,** 60
I don't care. [aɪ dəʊnt 'keə] Es ist mir egal. **II U4,** 58

career [kə'rɪə] Beruf; Laufbahn, Karriere °**V T1,** 14; **V T3,** 43
careers advice [kə'rɪəz ədˌvaɪs] Berufsberatung **V T3,** 46
careful ['keəfl] vorsichtig; sorgfältig **II U6,** 80
caretaker ['keəteɪkə] Hausmeister/Hausmeisterin **I U1,** 12
carpenter ['kɑ:pəntə] Zimmermann, Schreiner/Schreinerin **VI T3,** 46
carpet ['kɑ:pɪt] Teppichboden **IV U5,** 73
carrot ['kærət] Karotte, Mohrrübe **II U1,** 15
to **carry** ['kæri] tragen **I U6,** 80; befördern **III U2,** 30
to carry along [ˌkæri‿ə'lɒŋ] mitführen, mitreißen **V T4,** 64
cartoon [kɑ:'tu:n] Cartoon, Zeichentrickfilm **III U5,** 68
pencil **case** ['pensl ˌkeɪs] Federmäppchen **I U1,** 14
casino [kə'si:nəʊ] Casino **IV U4,** 57
castle ['kɑ:sl] Schloss, Burg **II U7,** 88
cat [kæt] Katze **I U2,** 26
*to **catch** [kætʃ] fangen, erreichen **III U1,** 8
catcher ['kætʃə] Fänger/Fängerin **III U1,** 14
catering ['keɪtrɪŋ] Gastronomie, Verpflegung, Catering **V T3,** 46
cathedral [kə'θi:drl] Kathedrale, Dom **III U2,** 24
cattle *(pl. only)* ['kætl] (Rind-)Vieh **IV U4,** 58
cattle drive ['kætl ˌdraɪv] Viehtrieb **IV U4,** 58
to **cause** [kɔ:z] verursachen, hervorrufen **V T4,** 60
caution *(no pl)* ['kɔ:ʃn] Vorsicht, Warnung °**V T4,** 60
caviar ['kæviɑ:] Kaviar **IV U5,** 80
CD [ˌsi:'di:] CD **I U5,** 69
CD player [ˌsi:'di: ˌpleɪə] CD-Player **II U4,** 56
cell [sel] Zelle **VI T3,** 46
cell phone *(AE)* ['sel ˌfəʊn] Handy, Mobiltelefon **IV U3,** 42
Celsius (C) ['selsiəs] Celsius **II U6,** 78
cent [sent] Cent *(Währung)* **IV U1,** 13
centimetre (cm) ['sentɪˌmi:tə] Zentimeter **V T4,** 61
centre ['sentə] Zentrum, Mittelpunkt **I LUC,** 52
call centre ['kɔ:l ˌsentə] Call-Center **VI T1,** 11
dive centre ['daɪv ˌsentə] Tauchzentrum **V T1,** 14
information centre [ɪnfə'meɪʃn ˌsentə] Informationszentrum **I LUC,** 52
century ['sentʃri] Jahrhundert **III U1,** 8

ceremony ['serɪməni] Zeremonie **IV U5,** 73
certainly ['sɜ:tnli] sicher, gewiss **III U5,** 72
certificate [sə'tɪfɪkət] Zertifikat, Bescheinigung, Urkunde, Zeugnis **V T1,** 14
Advanced Lifesaving Certificate [ədˌvɑ:nst 'laɪfˌseɪvɪŋ səˌtɪfɪkət] Rettungsschwimmabzeichen °**V T1,** 15
Beginners Diving Certificate [bɪˌgɪnəz 'daɪvɪŋ səˌtɪfɪkət] Grundtauchschein °**V T1,** 15
chain [tʃeɪn] Kette **II U3,** 40
chair [tʃeə] Stuhl **I U1,** 18
chairperson ['tʃeəˌpɜ:sn] Vorsitzender/Vorsitzende °**VI T2,** 33
champagne [ʃæm'peɪn] Champagner **IV U5,** 80
*to take your **chance** [ˌteɪk jɔ: 'tʃɑ:ns] etw. wagen, etw. riskieren **III U3,** 47
change [tʃeɪndʒ] Wechselgeld; Änderung **II U4,** 55
change of place [ˌtʃeɪndʒ‿əv 'pleɪs] Ortswechsel °**III U4,** 55
to **change** [tʃeɪndʒ] (ver)ändern, tauschen, wechseln **II U3,** 42; umsteigen **III U2,** 24
channel ['tʃænl] Kanal; Programm **III U3,** 39
chant [tʃɑ:nt] Sprechgesang °**IV U2,** 29
to **chant** [tʃɑ:nt] rhythmisch rufen; singen **IV U2,** 23
chaos ['keɪɒs] Chaos, Durcheinander **IV U4,** 61
chaotic [keɪ'ɒtɪk] chaotisch, durcheinander **VI T1,** 14
chaperon ['ʃæprəʊn] Begleitperson, Anstandswauwau **IV U5,** 80
character ['kærəktə] Charakter; Figur **VI T4,** 65
charity ['tʃærɪti] Wohltätigkeit, Wohltätigkeitsverein **I U7,** 90
chart [tʃɑ:t] Schaubild, Diagramm °**II U4,** 51
charter ['tʃɑ:tə] Charta, Satzung, Urkunde **VI T2,** 28
charts *(pl)* [tʃɑ:ts] Charts, Hitparade **III U5,** 70
chat [tʃæt] Geplauder, Unterhaltung **I U2,** 33
chat room ['tʃæt rʊm] Chatroom *(Internetforum, wo man sich online unterhalten kann)* **IV U5,** 76
to **chat** [tʃæt] sich unterhalten **I U2,** 33
cheap [tʃi:p] billig **I U5,** 68
check [tʃek] (Über-)Prüfung, Kontrolle **V T2,** 32

to **check** [tʃek] überprüfen **I U6,** 82; untersuchen, kontrollieren **II U3,** 40
to check in [tʃek‿'ɪn] einstempeln, einchecken **VI T2,** 34
to check out [tʃek‿'aʊt] sich etwas ansehen **IV U5,** 76; ausstempeln, auschecken **VI T2,** 29
cheerleader ['tʃɪəˌliːdə] Cheerleader *(Mädchen, das in einer Gruppe eine Sportmannschaft anfeuert)* **IV U2,** 22
cheese [tʃiːz] Käse **I U5,** 68
cream cheese [ˌkriːm 'tʃiːz] Frischkäse **IV U1,** 12
chef [ʃef] Koch/Köchin, Küchenchef/-chefin **V T2,** 32; **V T3,** 46
chemical ['kemɪkl] Chemikalie; chemisch **V T4,** 58
cherry ['tʃeri] Kirsche **IV U1,** 12
chicken ['tʃɪkɪn] Huhn, Hähnchen **II U4,** 49
chief executive officer (CEO) [ˌtʃiːf‿ɪgˌzekjətɪv‿'ɒfɪsə; ˌsiː iː'əʊ] Generaldirektor/Generaldirektorin; Geschäftsführer/Geschäftsführerin **VI T4,** 60
child, children *(pl)* [tʃaɪld; 'tʃɪldrɪn] Kind **I U2,** 26
only child ['əʊnli ˌtʃaɪld] Einzelkind **I U2,** 26
to **chill out** [tʃɪl‿'aʊt] sich entspannen, chillen **IV U5,** 76
Chinese [tʃaɪ'niːz] chinesisch **II U4,** 49
Chinglish ['tʃɪŋlɪʃ] Chinglisch *(Mischung aus Chinesisch und Englisch)* **VI T1,** 10
chip *(AE)* [tʃɪp] Chip °**IV U4,** 63
chips *(pl)* [tʃɪps] Pommes frites **II U1,** 14
chocolate ['tʃɒklət] Schokolade **I U1,** 18
choice [tʃɔɪs] Auswahl, Wahl **IV U3,** 46
to **choke** [tʃəʊk] ersticken, keine Luft bekommen **III U4,** 60
*to **choose** [tʃuːz] (aus)wählen **I U4,** 54
chorus ['kɔːrəs] Refrain **IV U5,** 80
Christmas ['krɪsməs] Weihnachten **VI T3,** 41
to **chuck sb** [tʃʌk] jmdn. verlassen, mit jmdm. Schluss machen **VI T4,** 62
church [tʃɜːtʃ] Kirche **I LUC,** 52
cigarette [ˌsɪgr'et] Zigarette **IV U2,** 25
cinema ['sɪnəmə] Kino **II U1,** 18
circle ['sɜːkl] Kreis **III U3,** 39
citizen ['sɪtɪzn] (Staats-)Bürger/Bürgerin **V T3,** 44
city ['sɪti] Stadt, Großstadt **II U7,** 89
capital city [ˌkæpɪtl 'sɪti] Hauptstadt °**III U2,** 27
civil ['sɪvl] bürgerlich, zivil, Bürger-, Staats- °**V T3,** 45
civil rights *(pl)* [ˌsɪvl 'raɪts] Bürgerrechte °**V T3,** 45
Civil Rights Movement (CRM) [ˌsɪvl 'raɪts ˌmuːvmənt] Bürgerrechtsbewegung **V T3,** 44
to **claim** [kleɪm] beanspruchen, (ein)fordern; behaupten **V T1,** 10
to **clap** [klæp] klatschen **I U1,** 15
class [klɑːs] Schulklasse, Klasse **I U1,** 16; Kurs, Unterricht **II U1,** 18
classic ['klæsɪk] klassisch **V T4,** 62
classroom ['klɑːsrʊm] Klassenzimmer **I U1,** 16
if-**clause** ['ɪfklɔːz] if-Satz °**IV U4,** 59
to **clean** [kliːn] säubern, reinigen **II U3,** 40
cleaning station ['kliːnɪŋ ˌsteɪʃn] Putzerstation **V T4,** 64
clean [kliːn] sauber **III U3,** 40
cleaner ['kliːnə] Raumpfleger/Raumpflegerin, Putzkraft **IV U4,** 63
clear [klɪə] klar **II U7,** 90
to **click** [klɪk] klicken **II U5,** 64
cliff [klɪf] Klippe **II U7,** 93
climate ['klaɪmət] Klima **V T4,** 58
to **climb** ['klaɪm] klettern, steigen, besteigen **II U2,** 30
clock [klɒk] Uhr **I U4,** 54
alarm clock [ə'lɑːm ˌklɒk] Wecker **I U5,** 75
o'clock [ə'klɒk] Uhr *(Zeitangabe)* **I U3,** 40
to **close** [kləʊz] schließen, zumachen **I LUC,** 53
close [kləʊs] nahe **V T2,** 32
closed [kləʊzd] zu, geschlossen °**I U2,** 32
closing ['kləʊzɪŋ] (Ab-)Schluss, Schließung **V T1,** 14
clothes *(pl)* [kləʊðz] Kleider, Kleidung **II U2,** 23
clothing ['kləʊðɪŋ] Kleidung **VI T2,** 32
cloud [klaʊd] Wolke **II U7,** 94
cloudy ['klaʊdi] wolkig **II U6,** 78
club [klʌb] Klub, Verein, Arbeitsgemeinschaft **I LUB,** 39
clue [kluː] Hinweis **II U1,** 13
to have no clue [ˌhæv nəʊ 'kluː] keine Ahnung haben **IV U5,** 80
clumsy ['klʌmzi] ungeschickt, tollpatschig **IV U2,** 31
Hey, clumsy! ['klʌmzi] He, du Tollpatsch! **IV U2,** 31
cluster ['klʌstə] Cluster °**IV U2,** 23
coach [kəʊtʃ] Reisebus **III U2,** 26; Trainer/Trainerin **VI T1,** 10
coaching ['kəʊtʃɪŋ] Training, Nachhilfe **VI T1,** 10
coast [kəʊst] Küste **II U7,** 88
coastline ['kəʊstˌlaɪn] Küstenlinie **III U3,** 38
coat [kəʊt] Mantel **II U7,** 90
cocktail ['kɒkteɪl] Cocktail; Gemisch, Mischung **VI T3,** 44
cocoa ['kəʊkəʊ] Kakao **V T4,** 58
code [kəʊd] Verschlüsselung, Code **IV U3,** 46
coffee ['kɒfiː] Kaffee **III U2,** 26
coke [kəʊk] Cola **II U4,** 49
cold [kəʊld] kalt **I U4,** 62
to be cold [biː 'kəʊld] frieren **II U2,** 24
collage [kɒl'ɑːʒ] Collage °**IV U5,** 81
colleague ['kɒliːg] Kollege/Kollegin **VI T1,** 14; **VI T2,** 32
to **collect** [kə'lekt] sammeln **I LUB,** 38; abholen **II U5,** 71
collector [kə'lektə] Kollektor, Auffänger; Sammler/Sammlerin **VI T3,** 46
college ['kɒlɪdʒ] College; Institut **III U4,** 57
colony ['kɒləni] Kolonie **V T1,** 10
colored *(AE)* ['kʌləd] bunt, farbig; Farbiger/Farbige **V T3,** 44
colorful *(AE)* ['kʌləfl] bunt, farbig **IV U2,** 23
colour ['kʌlə] Farbe **I LUA,** 24
*to **come** [kʌm] kommen **I U2,** 33
Come on. [kʌm‿'ɒn] Komm./Kommt. **I U2,** 35
to come down [kʌm 'daʊn] herunterkommen, sich legen **III U1,** 16
to come in [kʌm‿'ɪn] hereinkommen **I U3,** 48
to come over [kʌm‿'əʊvə] herüberkommen **I U2,** 27
to come true [kʌm 'truː] wahr werden **VI T4,** 59
to come up behind sb [ˌkʌm‿ʌp bɪ'haɪnd] sich jmdm. von hinten nähern **VI T2,** 32
comedy ['kɒmədi] Komödie **III U5,** 68
comfortable ['kʌmpftəbl] komfortabel, bequem **IV U4,** 61
comic ['kɒmɪk] Comic(heft) **I LUB,** 38
comment ['kɒment] Kommentar, Bemerkung **VI T2,** 32
common ['kɒmən] gemeinsam, gebräuchlich, verbreitet **VI T1,** 10; **VI T2,** 29
to **communicate** [kə'mjuːnɪkeɪt] kommunizieren, sich verständigen **VI T1,** 14; **VI T4,** 61
communication [kəˌmjuːnɪ'keɪʃn] Kommunikation, Verständigung **V T4,** 59
community [kə'mjuːnəti] Gemeinde; Gemeinschaft **V T4,** 62

company ['kʌmpəni] Gesellschaft, Firma; Kompanie **III U2,** 30
comparative [kəm'pærətɪv] Komparativ **II U4,** 50
to **compare** [kəm'peə] vergleichen **III U4,** 57
competition [ˌkɒmpə'tɪʃn] Wettbewerb, Turnier **V T2,** 30
to **complete** [kəm'pli:t] ausfüllen, erledigen, fertigstellen, vervollständigen **V T2,** 29
complete [kəm'pli:t] vollständig °**III U1,** 11
comprehensive school [kɒmprɪ'hensɪv ˌsku:l] Gesamtschule **III U4,** 56
compulsory [kəm'pʌlsri] obligatorisch, zwingend **III U4,** 57
computer [ˌkəm'pju:tə] Computer **I LUA,** 25
concerned [kən'sɜ:nd] beunruhigt; betroffen **VI T2,** 29
concert ['kɒnsət] Konzert **II U2,** 23
condition [kən'dɪʃn] Kondition; Bedingung **V T4,** 62
confidential [ˌkɒnfɪ'denʃl] vertraulich, geheim **VI T2,** 30
conqueror ['kɒŋkrə] Eroberer °**III U2,** 28
construction [kən'strʌkʃn] Konstruktion, Aufbau, Bau(-) **VI T3,** 46
contact ['kɒntækt] Kontakt, Verbindung °**V T1,** 14
to **contact** ['kɒntækt] kontaktieren, sich in Verbindung setzen mit **IV U2,** 25
content ['kɒntent] Inhalt **III U4,** 53
context ['kɒntekst] Kontext, Zusammenhang °**VI T4,** 62
continent ['kɒntɪnənt] Kontinent, Erdteil **V T1,** 10
sub-continent [ˌsʌb'kɒntɪnənt] Subkontinent **VI T1,** 10
to **continue** [kən'tɪnju:] fortfahren, andauern, weitergehen, weitermachen **V T4,** 61
contract ['kɒntrækt] Vertrag, Abkommen **V T1,** 14
contrast ['kɒntrɑ:st] Kontrast, Gegensatz °**VI T3,** 40
remote **control** [rɪˌməʊt kən'trəʊl] Fernbedienung, Fernsteuerung **IV U3,** 41
to **control** [kən'trəʊl] kontrollieren, beherrschen **IV U3,** 42
conversation [ˌkɒnvə'seɪʃn] Unterhaltung, Gespräch **VI T2,** 32
convict ['kɒnvɪkt] Sträfling **V T1,** 10
convincing [kən'vɪntsɪŋ] überzeugend °**VI T3,** 45
cook [kʊk] Koch/Köchin **III U5,** 70
to **cook** [kʊk] kochen **IV U3,** 44
cooking ['kʊkɪŋ] Kochen, Koch- **I U3,** 40
cool [ku:l] cool, prima **I U1,** 20; kühl **IV U1,** 16
co-operative [kəʊ'ɒprətɪv] Kooperative **V T4,** 62
cop *(AE)* [kɒp] Polizist/Polizistin **IV U1,** 16
copy ['kɒpi] Kopie °**VI T2,** 33
to **copy** ['kɒpi] abschreiben, kopieren **II U5,** 63
Cor! [kɔ:] Mann! **III U1,** 12
coral ['kɒrəl] Koralle; Korallen- **V T4,** 61
corner ['kɔ:nə] Ecke **III U2,** 26
cornflakes ['kɔ:nfleɪks] Cornflakes **I U5,** 68
Cornish ['kɔ:nɪʃ] kornisch; aus Cornwall **III U3,** 42
to **correct** [kə'rekt] korrigieren, verbessern °**I LUB,** 38
correct [kə'rekt] richtig, korrekt **II U1,** 10
corridor ['kɒrɪdɔ:] Gang, Flur, Korridor **I U7,** 96
cost [kɒst] Preis, Kosten **VI T1,** 11; **VI T3,** 46
to cut costs [kʌt 'kɒsts] die Kosten senken **VI T1,** 11
*to **cost** [kɒst] kosten **IV U3,** 42
cottage ['kɒtɪdʒ] kleines Landhaus, Ferienhaus **III U4,** 54
couch potato ['kaʊtʃ pəˌteɪtəʊ] Fernsehglotzer/Fernsehglotzerin, Couchpotato **III U5,** 75
***could** [kʊd] konnte/konnten **II U4,** 52; könnte/könnten **III U1,** 12
council ['kaʊnsl] Gemeinderat **V T2,** 30
countdown ['kaʊntdaʊn] Countdown **III U5,** 70
country ['kʌntri] Countrymusik **IV U5,** 73
country, countries *(pl)* ['kʌntri; 'kʌntriz] Land **I U2,** 29
in the country [ˌɪn ðə 'kʌntri] auf dem Land **I U6,** 78
couple ['kʌpl] Paar **IV U3,** 48
a couple of [ə 'kʌpl‿əv] ein paar, einige **V T4,** 65
courier ['kʊriə] Kurier **III U2,** 30
course [kɔ:s] Gang *(Menü)* **II U4,** 49; Kurs **V T1,** 14; **V T2,** 32; **V T3,** 46
of course [əv 'kɔ:s] natürlich, selbstverständlich **I U1,** 19
court [kɔ:t] Spielfeld **III U1,** 10; Hof, Gericht(shof) **VI T2,** 26
court trial ['kɔ:t traɪəl] Gerichtsverhandlung **VI T2,** 26
cousin ['kʌzn] Cousin/Cousine **I U2,** 28
cover ['kʌvə] Einband, Titelseite **II U5,** 64
cover letter ['kʌvə ˌletə] Begleitbrief, Begleitschreiben °**VI T4,** 61
cow [kaʊ] Kuh **I U6,** 82
cowboy ['kaʊbɔɪ] Rinderhirte, Cowboy **IV U4,** 57
at the **crack of dawn** [ˌkræk‿əv 'dɔ:n] im Morgengrauen **III U2,** 30
to **crackle** ['krækl] knistern, knacken, prasseln **VI T4,** 64
crash [kræʃ] Unfall, Aufprall; Absturz **V T4,** 64
Crash! [kræʃ] Bumm!, Krach! **III U3,** 47
to **crawl** [krɔ:l] kriechen, krabbeln; schleichen **III U3,** 47
crazy ['kreɪzi] verrückt **I U7,** 96
to drive crazy [draɪv 'kreɪzi] verrückt machen **II U5,** 71
to go crazy [gəʊ 'kreɪzi] ausflippen, durchdrehen **VI T3,** 43
to **creak** [kri:k] knarren, quietschen **II U7,** 94
cream [kri:m] Creme, Sahne **IV U1,** 12
cream cheese [ˌkri:m 'tʃi:z] Frischkäse **IV U1,** 12
ice-cream [aɪs 'kri:m] Eis, Eiscreme **I U7,** 92
creative [kri'eɪtɪv] kreativ **VI T1,** 14
creature ['kri:tʃə] Kreatur, Geschöpf, Lebewesen **V T1,** 10; **V T3,** 47; **V T4,** 65
crew [kru:] Crew, Besatzung, Mannschaft **III U5,** 75
cricket ['krɪkɪt] Kricket **I U7,** 92
crime [kraɪm] Verbrechen; Kriminalität **V T2,** 28
criminal ['krɪmɪnl] Krimineller/Kriminelle, Verbrecher/Verbrecherin; kriminell **V T4,** 60
crisp [krɪsp] Kartoffelchip **I U1,** 18
critic ['krɪtɪk] Kritiker/Kritikerin °**VI T4,** 59
crocodile ['krɒkədaɪl] Krokodil **V T1,** 10
to **cross** [krɒs] überqueren, kreuzen **IV U4,** 64
crossword (puzzle) ['krɒswɜ:d 'pʌzl] Kreuzworträtsel °**I U5,** 71
crowd [kraʊd] Menschenmenge **III U1,** 17
crown [kraʊn] Krone **III U2,** 22
cruise [kru:z] Kreuzfahrt **III U3,** 39
crunchy ['krʌntʃi] knusprig **V T4,** 63
cry [kraɪ] Schrei **III U5,** 74
to **cry** [kraɪ] weinen; schreien, rufen **II U3,** 36
cup [kʌp] Pokal; Tasse, Kelch **III U1,** 13
cupboard ['kʌbəd] Küchenschrank, Schrank **I U1,** 18
cupcake ['kʌpkeɪk] rundes Küchlein **IV U1,** 12
curly ['kɜ:li] lockig **VI T1,** 14
current ['kʌrnt] Strömung; Strom **V T4,** 64

up current ['ʌp ˌkʌrnt] gegen die Strömung **V T4,** 64
curriculum [kə'rɪkjələm] Lehrplan, Stundenplan **IV U2,** 22
curriculum vitae (CV) [kə'rɪkjələm 'vi:taɪ] Lebenslauf **V T1,** 15
curry ['kʌri] Curry *(Gewürz oder Gericht)* **II U4,** 49
curtain ['kɜ:tn] Vorhang **IV U3,** 44
curve [kɜ:v] Kurve **III U4,** 60
customer ['kʌstəmə] Kunde/Kundin **III U2,** 30
customs *(pl)* ['kʌstəmz] Zoll **II U7,** 90
*to **cut** [kʌt] schneiden **V T1,** 10
to cut costs [kʌt 'kɒsts] die Kosten senken **VI T1,** 11
to cut down [kʌt 'daʊn] abholzen, fällen **V T1,** 10
to cut down on [kʌt 'daʊn‿ɒn] einschränken, einsparen, reduzieren **VI T3,** 47
cute [kju:t] niedlich, süß **V T1,** 10

D

dad [dæd] Papa, Vati **I LUA,** 25
daily ['deɪli] täglich **III U5,** 68
dairy ['deəri] Molkerei **III U2,** 30
damage ['dæmɪdʒ] Schaden, Beschädigung **VI T4,** 61
to **damage** ['dæmɪdʒ] beschädigen **V T1,** 10
damn [dæm] verdammt **IV U5,** 80
damp [dæmp] feucht **VI T3,** 47; **VI T4,** 62
dance [dɑ:nts] Tanz **III U4,** 63
dance floor ['dɑ:nts flɔ:] Tanzfläche **IV U2,** 31
square dance ['skweə ˌdɑ:nts] Square Dance **IV U4,** 58
to **dance** [dɑ:nts] tanzen **I U3,** 40
dancehall ['dɑ:ntshɔ:l] Dancehall *(Musikrichtung)* **IV U5,** 73
dancing ['dɑ:ntsɪŋ] Tanzen **IV U2,** 23
ballroom dancing [ˌbɔ:lrʊm 'dɑ:ntsɪŋ] Gesellschaftstanz **IV U2,** 23
danger ['deɪndʒə] Gefahr **V T4,** 64
dangerous ['deɪndʒrəs] gefährlich **II U4,** 56
Danish ['deɪnɪʃ] dänisch; Plundergebäck **IV U1,** 12
to **dare** [deə] wagen, riskieren **IV U2,** 29
dark [dɑ:k] dunkel **I U2,** 34; Dunkelheit, Finsternis **III U3,** 47
darling ['dɑ:lɪŋ] Liebling, Schatz **VI T4,** 58
database ['deɪtəbeɪs] Datenbank **VI T1,** 14
date [deɪt] Datum **I U5,** 70; Verabredung **IV U2,** 26
to **date** [deɪt] sich verabreden **IV U2,** 24
daughter ['dɔ:tə] Tochter **IV U5,** 80
dawn [dɔ:n] Morgendämmerung, Tagesanbruch **III U2,** 30
at the crack of dawn [ˌkræk‿əv 'dɔ:n] im Morgengrauen **III U2,** 30
day [deɪ] Tag **I LUB,** 39
day travel card [ˌdeɪ 'trævl ˌkɑ:d] Tagesfahrkarte **III U2,** 27
Have a nice day. [ˌhæv‿ə naɪs 'deɪ] Einen schönen Tag (noch). **II U4,** 55
one day [wʌn 'deɪ] eines Tages **II U3,** 36
sports day ['spɔ:ts deɪ] Sportfest **I U7,** 90
these days ['ði:z deɪz] heutzutage **VI T1,** 12
to have a day off [ˌhæv‿ə 'deɪ‿ɒf] einen Tag frei haben **V T3,** 46
dead [ded] tot **III U5,** 74; leer **IV U3,** 45
deadly ['dedli] tödlich, tod- **V T1,** 12
deal [di:l] Handel; Abmachung, Übereinkunft **V T4,** 62
dealer ['di:lə] Händler/Händlerin **VI T4,** 60
dear [dɪə] lieb **I U3,** 44; Schatz *(Anrede)* **III U4,** 60
Oh dear! [əʊ 'dɪə] Oje! **III U5,** 73
Dear ... [dɪə] Lieber/Liebe ... *(Anrede in Briefen)* **II U3,** 36
death [deθ] Tod, Todesfall **V T1,** 10; **V T3,** 42; **V T4,** 58
December [dɪ'sembə] Dezember **I U5,** 70
to **decide** [dɪ'saɪd] entscheiden **II U5,** 64
to decide on [dɪ'saɪd‿ɒn] sich entscheiden für, festlegen °**VI T1,** 13
decision [dɪ'sɪʒn] Entscheidung **VI T4,** 56
decompression [ˌdi:kəm'preʃn] Dekompression, Druckverminderung **V T4,** 65
decoration [ˌdek'reɪʃn] Dekoration **IV U1,** 14
deep [di:p] tief **IV U4,** 58
definition [ˌdefɪ'nɪʃn] Definition **II U1,** 20
to **defuse** [ˌdi:'fju:z] entschärfen **IV U3,** 41
degree (°) [dɪ'gri:] Grad **II U6,** 78
delayed [dɪ'leɪd] verspätet, verzögert **IV U4,** 61
to **delete** [dɪ'li:t] löschen *(Text)* **II U5,** 63
deli *(AE)* ['deli] Imbissstube, Deli **IV U1,** 12
to **deliver** [dɪ'lɪvə] (aus)liefern **III U2,** 30
demo ['deməʊ] Demonstration, Demo; Darstellung **V T3,** 42
democracy [dɪ'mɒkrəsi] Demokratie **VI T2,** 26
democratic [ˌdemə'krætɪk] demokratisch **IV U3,** 48
dentist ['dentɪst] Zahnarzt/Zahnärztin **IV U3,** 48
department [dɪ'pɑ:tmənt] Abteilung, Fachbereich; Branche **VI T1,** 14; **VI T4,** 60
department store [dɪ'pɑ:tmənt stɔ:] Kaufhaus **I LUC,** 52
departure [dɪ'pɑ:tʃə] Abflug, Abreise **II U7,** 90
to **describe** [dɪ'skraɪb] beschreiben **IV U4,** 61
description [dɪ'skrɪpʃn] Beschreibung °**III U1,** 15
to **deserve** [dɪ'zɜ:v] verdienen **IV U5,** 80
design [dɪ'zaɪn] Design, Gestaltung **VI T4,** 61
to **design** [dɪ'zaɪn] entwerfen, zeichnen **VI T4,** 60; **VI T4,** 65
designer [dɪ'zaɪnə] Designer/Designerin **IV U5,** 72
desk [desk] Schreibtisch **I U1,** 18; Schalter **II U7,** 90
dessert [dɪ'zɜ:t] Dessert, Nachtisch **II U4,** 49
to **destroy** [dɪ'strɔɪ] zerstören **III U2,** 28
detail ['di:teɪl] Detail, Einzelheit °**V T1,** 14
detective [dɪ'tektɪv] Detektiv/Detektivin **II U2,** 30
detective story [dɪ'tektɪv ˌstɔ:ri] Krimi **III U5,** 68
store detective ['stɔ: dɪˌtektɪv] Kaufhausdetektiv/Kaufhausdetektivin **II U2,** 30
to **develop** [dɪ'veləp] (sich) entwickeln **VI T1,** 14; **VI T2,** 32; **VI T4,** 60
development [dɪ'veləpmənt] Entwicklung **VI T4,** 60
diabetes [ˌdaɪə'bi:ti:z] Diabetes, Zuckerkrankheit **VI T3,** 44
diabetic [ˌdaɪə'betɪk] zuckerkrank; Diabetiker/Diabetikerin **VI T4,** 64
dialogue ['daɪəlɒg] Dialog, Gespräch **III U2,** 29
diamond ['daɪəmənd] Diamant **III U5,** 70
diary ['daɪəri] Tagebuch, Terminkalender °**III U2,** 31
to keep a diary [ˌki:p‿ə 'daɪəri] ein Tagebuch/einen Terminkalender führen **VI T4,** 63
dictionary ['dɪkʃnri] Wörterbuch **III U4,** 63
to **die** [daɪ] sterben **III U5,** 77
diet [daɪət] Diät **II U4,** 52

to go on a diet [ˌgəʊ‿ɒn ə 'daɪət] eine Diät machen **II U4,** 52
difference ['dɪfrns] Unterschied **III U4,** 56
different ['dɪfrnt] anders, verschieden **I U6,** 78
difficult ['dɪfɪklt] schwierig **II U1,** 13
*to **dig** [dɪg] graben, buddeln **VI T4,** 64
to dig up [dɪg‿'ʌp] ausgraben **III U1,** 16
digger ['dɪgə] Erdarbeiter/Erdarbeiterin **VI T3,** 47
digital ['dɪdʒɪtl] digital **II U5,** 62
dime [daɪm] Zehncentstück *(Währung)* **IV U1,** 13
diner *(AE)* ['daɪnə] Imbissstube **IV U4,** 57
dining room ['daɪnɪŋ rʊm] Esszimmer, Speisesaal **I LUA,** 24
dinner ['dɪnə] Abendessen, Mittagessen **IV U4,** 61
carbon **dioxide (CO_2)** [ˌkɑ:bn daɪ'ɒksaɪd; si:‿əʊ 'tu:] Kohlendioxid **VI T3,** 42
diploma [dɪ'pləʊmə] Diplom, Abschlusszeugnis **VI T1,** 14
to **direct** [dɪ'rekt] leiten, anweisen; Regie führen **IV U5,** 74
direct [dɪ'rekt] direkt **III U4,** 53
direction [dɪ'rekʃn] (Aus-)Richtung, Anleitung **VI T4,** 59
director [dɪ'rektə] Direktor/Direktorin, Regisseur/Regisseurin **III U5,** 75
dirt [dɜ:t] Schmutz, Dreck **V T4,** 58
dirty ['dɜ:ti] schmutzig **II U1,** 10
disability [ˌdɪsə'bɪləti] Behinderung; Unfähigkeit **V T1,** 14
disabled [dɪ'seɪbld] behindert **VI T1,** 14
to **disappear** [ˌdɪsə'pɪə] verschwinden **II U6,** 83
disappointed [ˌdɪsə'pɔɪntɪd] enttäuscht **III U4,** 52
disappointing [ˌdɪsə'pɔɪntɪŋ] enttäuschend **VI T4,** 62
disaster [dɪ'zɑ:stə] Desaster, Katastrophe **III U4,** 54
disco ['dɪskəʊ] Disko **I U5,** 74
to **discover** [dɪ'skʌvə] entdecken **IV U4,** 64
discrimination [dɪˌskrɪmɪ'neɪʃn] Diskriminierung; Unterscheidung **V T3,** 41
to **discuss** [dɪ'skʌs] diskutieren **VI T2,** 30; **VI T2,** 33
disease [dɪ'zi:z] Krankheit, Erkrankung **VI T3,** 44
dislikes *(pl)* [dɪ'slaɪks] Abneigungen °**V T2,** 33
to **display** [dɪ'spleɪ] ausstellen, (an)zeigen °**V T1,** 13
disrespect [ˌdɪsrɪ'spekt] Respektlosigkeit, Verachtung **IV U5,** 76
to **diss** *(slang)* [dɪs] beleidigen; schneiden **IV U5,** 76
distance ['dɪstns] Distanz, Entfernung **III U3,** 42
to **distribute** [dɪ'strɪbju:t] verteilen, austeilen °**VI T2,** 33
to **disturb** [dɪ'stɜ:b] stören, belästigen **V T1,** 12
dive [daɪv] Tauch-; Tauchgang **V T4,** 64
dive centre ['daɪv ˌsentə] Tauchzentrum **V T1,** 14
to **dive** [daɪv] tauchen **III U3,** 41
diver ['daɪvə] Taucher/Taucherin **V T1,** 9; **V T4,** 65
divine [dɪ'vaɪn] göttlich °**V T4,** 62
diving ['daɪvɪŋ] Tauch-, Tauchen **V T1,** 14; **V T4,** 64
divorced from [dɪ'vɔ:st frɒm] geschieden von **I U2,** 28
dizzy ['dɪzi] schwindlig **IV U1,** 16
DJ [ˌdi:'dʒeɪ] DJ **I U2,** 33
*to **do** [du:] machen, tun **I U1,** 15
to do sports [du: 'spɔ:ts] Sport treiben **I U7,** 92
doctor ['dɒktə] Arzt/Ärztin **II U3,** 40
to see a doctor [si:‿ə 'dɒktə] zum Arzt gehen **II U4,** 52
docu soap ['dɒkju ˌsəʊp] Dokusoap **III U5,** 68
documentary [ˌdɒkjə'mentri] Dokumentarfilm **III U5,** 68
dog [dɒg] Hund **I U2,** 27
dog-tired [ˌdɒg 'taɪəd] hundemüde **I U3,** 49
to walk the dog [wɔ:k ðə 'dɒg] mit dem Hund spazieren gehen **I U3,** 42
doll [dɒl] Puppe °**IV U3,** 47
dollar ['dɒlə] Dollar *(Währung)* **IV U1,** 12
male-**dominated** ['meɪlˌdɒmɪneɪtɪd] männlich dominiert **VI T2,** 33
domino ['dɒmɪnəʊ] Dominospiel °**II U2,** 26
door [dɔ:] Tür **I U1,** 18
next door [ˌnekst 'dɔ:] nebenan **III U1,** 16
doorbell ['dɔ:bel] Türklingel **II U5,** 66
doorstep ['dɔ:step] Türstufe **III U1,** 16
dope *(slang)* [dəʊp] toll °**IV U5,** 80
dot [dɒt] Punkt, Pünktchen **V T4,** 66
double ['dʌbl] Doppelgänger; das Doppelte **I U7,** 97
double-glazed [ˌdʌbl'gleɪzd] doppelt verglast **VI T3,** 46
down [daʊn] (nach) unten, herunter, hinunter, nieder **II U2,** 30; senkrecht *(im Kreuzworträtsel)* °**II U3,** 42
Down Under [ˌdaʊn‿'ʌndə] Down Under *(Spitzname für Australien)*; in Australien **V T1,** 10
Go down … . ['gəʊ daʊn] Geh … entlang. **I LUC,** 53
to come down [kʌm 'daʊn] herunterkommen, sich legen **III U1,** 16
to go down [gəʊ 'daʊn] hinuntergehen, entlanggehen **II U2,** 30
to lie down [laɪ 'daʊn] (sich) hinlegen, niederlegen **III U3,** 46
to sit down [sɪt 'daʊn] sich (hin)setzen **I U1,** 19
to **download** [ˌdaʊn'ləʊd] herunterladen **II U5,** 63
downstairs [daʊn'steəz] unten, im unteren Stock **I U2,** 27
dragon ['drægn] Drache **IV U1,** 14
drama ['drɑ:mə] Theater, Drama **I U3,** 40
dramatic [drə'mætɪk] dramatisch **III U5,** 68
It's a **draw.** [ˌɪts‿ə 'drɔ:] Es steht unentschieden. **III U1,** 12
*to **draw** [drɔ:] zeichnen **I LUB,** 38
to draw up [drɔ:‿'ʌp] aufsetzen, anfertigen **VI T2,** 28
drawing [drɔ:ɪŋ] Zeichnung, Bild °**VI T2,** 28
dream [dri:m] Traum **I LUA,** 25
to **dream** [dri:m] träumen **IV U5,** 80
dress [dres] Kleid, Kleidung **IV U2,** 23
evening dress ['i:vnɪŋ ˌdres] Abendkleid **IV U5,** 72
to **dress** [dres] sich anziehen **I U3,** 44
drill [drɪl] Bohrer, Bohrmaschine **IV U1,** 17
drink [drɪŋk] Getränk **I U7,** 95
*to **drink** [drɪŋk] trinken **I U5,** 75
to **drip** [drɪp] tropfen (lassen), tröpfeln **IV U3,** 42
cattle **drive** ['kætl ˌdraɪv] Viehtrieb **IV U4,** 58
*to **drive** [draɪv] fahren **I U6,** 86
to drive crazy [draɪv 'kreɪzi] verrückt machen **II U5,** 71
driving licence *(BE)* ['draɪvɪŋ ˌlaɪsnts] Führerschein **V T1,** 14
driver ['draɪvə] Fahrer/Fahrerin **I U4,** 54
driver's license *(AE)* ['draɪvəz ˌlaɪsnts] Führerschein **IV U4,** 64
to **drop** [drɒp] fallen, fallen lassen **II U1,** 18; sinken *(beim Tauchen)* **V T4,** 64
drug [drʌg] Droge; Medikament *(im Amerikanischen)* **IV U2,** 25
drummer ['drʌmə] Schlagzeuger/Schlagzeugerin **IV U5,** 76
drums *(pl)* [drʌmz] Schlagzeug **I U2,** 26

to **dry** [draɪ] trocknen **IV U3,** 42
dry [draɪ] trocken **VI T3,** 47
dryer ['draɪə] Trockner **VI T3,** 47
dump [dʌmp] Dreckloch, Müllkippe **II U7,** 88
to **dump sb** [dʌmp] mit jmdm. Schluss machen, jmdm. den Laufpass geben **VI T4,** 62
to dump sth [dʌmp] abladen, auskippen, verklappen **V T4,** 60
during *(+ noun)* ['djʊərɪŋ] während *(+ Nomen)* **III U1,** 8
dust [dʌst] Staub **VI T4,** 64
dusty ['dʌsti] staubig **IV U4,** 58
Dutch [dʌtʃ] niederländisch; Niederländer/innen **IV U1,** 10
duty ['dju:ti] Pflicht, Aufgabe **VI T2,** 30
DVD [di:vi:'di:] DVD **II U5,** 62
DVD player [ˌdi:vi:'di: ˌpleɪə] DVD-Player **II U5,** 62
to **dye** [daɪ] färben **II U2,** 28

E

each [i:tʃ] jeder/jede/jedes **III U1,** 8; je, jeweils **III U4,** 53
each other [ˌi:tʃ‿'ʌðə] sich gegenseitig **II U1,** 19
ear [ɪə] Ohr **II U3,** 40
early ['ɜ:li] früh **I U3,** 46
to **earn** [ɜ:n] verdienen **V T3,** 46
earth [ɜ:θ] Erde **IV U3,** 40
east [i:st] Osten **I U4,** 54
easy ['i:zi] einfach, leicht **I U1,** 20
*to **eat** [i:t] essen, fressen **I U3,** 44
eating ['i:tɪŋ] Essen **°VI T3,** 45
to **echo** ['ekəʊ] widerhallen **III U5,** 78
eco [i:kəʊ] Öko-, Umwelt- **V T4,** 61
edge [edʒ] Rand, Kante **IV U5,** 78
education [edʒʊ'keɪʃn] Erziehung, Bildung **II U1,** 10
Physical Education (PE) [ˌfɪzɪkl‿edʒʊ'keɪʃn] Sport *(Schulfach)* **II U1,** 10
Religious Education (RE) [rɪˌlɪdʒəs‿edʒʊ'keɪʃn] Religionsunterricht **II U1,** 12
effect [ɪ'fekt] Effekt, (Aus-)Wirkung **VI T3,** 42
e.g. [i:'dʒi:] zum Beispiel **VI T3,** 42; **VI T4,** 58
egg [eg] Ei **I U5,** 68
(not) **either of these** ['aɪðər‿əv ˌði:z] (k)eines von beiden **VI T2,** 28
not … either [ˌnɒt … 'aɪðə] auch nicht **IV U3,** 48
elbow ['elbəʊ] Ellbogen **II U3,** 41

to **elect** [ɪ'lekt] (aus)wählen **VI T2,** 30
election [ɪ'lekʃn] Wahl **VI T2,** 26
electric [ɪ'lektrɪk] elektrisch **IV U1,** 17
electric-powered [ɪ'lektrɪk ˌpaʊəd] elektrisch betrieben **VI T4,** 60
electrical [ɪ'lektrɪkl] elektrisch **VI T3,** 46
electrician [ˌelɪk'trɪʃn] Elektriker/Elektrikerin **VI T3,** 46
electricity [ˌelɪk'trɪsəti] Elektrizität, Strom **IV U3,** 42
elementary school *(AE)* [elɪ'mentri ˌsku:l] Grundschule **IV U2,** 28
elephant ['elɪfənt] Elefant **I U7,** 96
else [els] sonst, noch **I U5,** 66
e-mail ['i:meɪl] E-Mail **I U3,** 44
to **e-mail** ['i:meɪl] E-Mail schreiben **IV U5,** 76; mailen; per E-Mail schicken **V T2,** 29
embarrassing [ɪm'bærəsɪŋ] peinlich **II U2,** 26
embers *(pl)* ['embəz] Glut, glimmende Asche **VI T4,** 63
emergency [ɪ'mɜ:dʒnsi] Notfall, Notlage **III U5,** 70
to **emigrate** ['emɪgreɪt] emigrieren, auswandern **IV U1,** 10
emission [ɪ'mɪʃn] Ausstoß, Emission **VI T3,** 42
to **emit** [ɪ'mɪt] ausstoßen, absondern **VI T3,** 45
employee [ɪm'plɔɪi:] Angestellter/Angestellte, Mitarbeiter/Mitarbeiterin **V T3,** 46
employer [ɪm'plɔɪə] Arbeitgeber/Arbeitgeberin **V T3,** 46
employment [ɪm'plɔɪmənt] Beschäftigung, Anstellung **VI T4,** 58
self-employment [ˌselfɪm'plɔɪmənt] Selbstständigkeit **VI T4,** 59
empty ['empti] leer **II U1,** 18
end [end] Ende, Schluss **II U6,** 84
in the end [ɪn ði:‿'end] schließlich, zum Schluss **II U6,** 80
to **end** [end] enden **I U5,** 76; beenden, abschließen **IV U2,** 26
to end in ['end‿ɪn] enden auf **°II U7,** 90
to end up [ˌend‿'ʌp] enden, landen **IV U4,** 64
ending ['endɪŋ] Ende, Schluss *(einer Geschichte)* **°II U1,** 19
enemy ['enəmi] Feind/Feindin **II U3,** 43
energetic [ˌenə'dʒetɪk] energiegeladen, energisch, dynamisch **VI T1,** 11
energy ['enədʒi] Energie; Kraft **V T4,** 58
engine ['endʒɪn] Motor **IV U1,** 16
engineer [ˌendʒɪ'nɪə] Ingenieur/Ingenieurin; Techniker/Technikerin **VI T3,** 43

English ['ɪŋglɪʃ] englisch **I U1,** 11; Engländer/Engländerinnen **IV U1,** 10
Englishman, Englishmen *(pl)* ['ɪŋglɪʃmən; 'ɪŋglɪʃmen] Engländer **VI T2,** 28
to **enjoy** [ɪn'dʒɔɪ] sich erfreuen, genießen **II U6,** 80
enough [ɪ'nʌf] genug, genügend **III U1,** 14
to **enter** ['entə] sich beteiligen; eintreten, betreten **III U4,** 53
enterprising ['entəpraɪzɪŋ] geschäftstüchtig, unternehmungslustig **V T3,** 43
entry ['entri] Eintrag, Eintragung **V T4,** 66
envelope ['envələʊp] Briefumschlag, Umschlag **II U7,** 90
environment [ɪn'vaɪərnmənt] Umwelt, Umgebung **II U6,** 74
environmental [ɪnˌvaɪərn'mentl] Umwelt-, die Umwelt betreffend, umweltbedingt **V T4,** 60
equal ['i:kwəl] gleich(wertig), Gleich- **V T3,** 40
equipment [ɪ'kwɪpmənt] Ausrüstung, Ausstattung **IV U3,** 41
er [ɜ:] äh **°I U1,** 12
erm [ɜ:m] äh **°II U3,** 38
to **escape** [ɪ'skeɪp] flüchten, entkommen **II U6,** 78
especially [ɪ'speʃli] besonders **III U2,** 30
etc. [ɪt'setrə] usw., et cetera **II U1,** 10
eucalyptus [ˌju:k'lɪptəs] Eukalyptus **V T1,** 10
euro ['jʊərəʊ] Euro *(Währung)* **I U5,** 73
European [ˌjʊərə'pi:ən] europäisch **°II U6,** 85
even ['i:vn] selbst, sogar **I U7,** 90
not even [nɒt‿'i:vn] nicht einmal **III U4,** 54
evening ['i:vnɪŋ] Abend **I U3,** 47
evening dress ['i:vnɪŋ ˌdres] Abendkleid **IV U5,** 72
in the evening [ˌɪn ði: 'i:vnɪŋ] abends, am Abend **I U3,** 47
that evening [ˌdæt‿'i:vnɪŋ] an diesem Abend **II U1,** 19
this evening [ðɪs 'i:vnɪŋ] heute Abend **III U3,** 46
event [ɪ'vent] Veranstaltung, Ereignis **I U7,** 90
ever ['evə] jemals **II U5,** 66
ever-changing ['evəˌtʃeɪndʒɪŋ] sich immer/stetig ändernd **VI T1,** 10
every ['evri] jeder/jede/jedes **I U3,** 40
everybody ['evribɒdi] jeder; alle **IV U2,** 23

everyday ['evrideɪ] alltäglich °**III U1,** 12
everyone ['evriwʌn] jeder **VI T1,** 12
everything ['evriθɪŋ] alles **II U4,** 50
everywhere ['evriweə] überall **II U5,** 71
evidence ['evɪdnts] Beweis °**II U6,** 83
exact [ɪg'zækt] genau, exakt **IV U3,** 46
exam [ɪg'zæm] Examen, Prüfung **III U4,** 57
example [ɪg'zɑ:mpl] Beispiel °**I U1,** 13
for example [fər‿ɪg'zɑ:mpl] zum Beispiel **III U4,** 53
except [ɪk'sept] außer **IV U5,** 76
exchange [ɪks'tʃeɪndʒ] (Aus-)Tausch **I U7,** 94
to **exchange** [ɪks'tʃeɪndʒ] (aus)tauschen °**VI T1,** 15
excited [ɪk'saɪtɪd] aufgeregt **I U5,** 74
exciting [ɪk'saɪtɪŋ] spannend, aufregend **II U4,** 51
excuse [ɪk'skju:s] Ausrede, Entschuldigung **VI T3,** 44
Excuse me! [ɪk'skju:z mi] Entschuldigung! **I U3,** 42
exercise ['eksəsaɪz] Übung, Aufgabe **I U1,** 19
exercise book ['eksəsaɪz ˌbʊk] Heft, Übungsheft **I U1,** 14
to **exercise** ['eksəsaɪz] Sport treiben **II U4,** 52
to **exist** [ɪg'zɪst] existieren **IV U3,** 41
exit ['eksɪt] Ausgang, Abgang, Ausfahrt **IV U4,** 61
exotic [ɪg'zɒtɪk] exotisch **VI T3,** 44
to **expect** [ɪk'spekt] erwarten **III U2,** 30
expensive [ɪk'spensɪv] teuer **I U5,** 68
experience [ɪk'spɪəriənts] Erfahrung, Erlebnis **V T1,** 14; **V T2,** 29; **V T3,** 43; **V T4,** 64
work experience ['wɜ:k‿ɪkˌspɪəriənts] Praktikum **VI T2,** 33
to **experience** [ɪk'spɪəriənts] erfahren, erleben **VI T2,** 33; **VI T4,** 59
experienced [ɪk'spɪəriənst] erfahren **VI T1,** 11
experiment [ɪk'sperɪmənt] Experiment, Versuch **II U1,** 13
expert ['ekspɜ:t] Experte/Expertin **VI T3,** 43; **VI T4,** 59
to **explain** [ɪk'spleɪn] erklären, erläutern **II U5,** 64
explanation [ˌeksplə'neɪʃn] Erklärung, Erläuterung °**VI T1,** 16
to **explore** [ɪk'splɔ:] erkunden, erforschen **IV U3,** 41
export ['ekspɔ:t] Export; Ausfuhr **V T4,** 62
to **export** [ɪk'spɔ:t] exportieren, ausführen **V T4,** 62

extra ['ekstrə] zusätzlich; Zusatz **III U4,** 58
extract ['ekstrækt] Extrakt, Auszug **VI T4,** 62
extremely [ɪk'stri:mli] extrem, außerordentlich **VI T4,** 60
eye [aɪ] Auge **I U2,** 35
eyebrow ['aɪbraʊ] Augenbraue **III U4,** 52

F

fabulous ['fæbjələs] fabelhaft, fantastisch **IV U4,** 57
face [feɪs] Gesicht **I U3,** 48
fact [fækt] Fakt, Tatsache **II U2,** 32
fact box ['fækt bɒks] Infokasten **III U1,** 8
fact file (on) ['fækt faɪl] Ordner mit Informationen (über) **III U2,** 27
in fact [ɪn 'fækt] in der Tat, genau genommen **II U7,** 94
factory ['fæktri] Fabrik, Werk **IV U3,** 48
factual ['fæktʃʊəl] Sach-, sachlich °**IV U1,** 14
Fahrenheit (F) ['færnhaɪt] Fahrenheit **IV U1,** 16
to **faint** [feɪnt] ohnmächtig werden **IV U1,** 17
fair [feə] Messe, Jahrmarkt **I U7,** 90
summer fair ['sʌmə ˌfeə] Sommerfest **I U7,** 90
fair [feə] gerecht, fair **III U1,** 12; blond, hell **III U5,** 68
fall [fɔ:l] Fall, Sturz **V T3,** 40
*to **fall** [fɔ:l] fallen, herunterfallen, hinfallen **II U2,** 26
to fall in love [fɔ:l‿ɪn 'lʌv] sich verlieben **VI T4,** 62
to fall off [fɔ:l‿'ɒf] herunterfallen **II U3,** 40
false [fɔ:ls] falsch **VI T2,** 28
false teeth [fɔ:ls 'ti:θ] Zahnprothese, Gebiss **VI T2,** 28
family ['fæmli] Familie **I LUA,** 25
family tree ['fæmli tri:] Familienstammbaum °**I U2,** 28
famine ['fæmɪn] Hungersnot **IV U1,** 10
famous ['feɪməs] berühmt **I U4,** 54
fan [fæn] Fan **II U5,** 66
fantastic [fæn'tæstɪk] fantastisch, großartig **I U7,** 94
FAQ (frequently asked question) ['fri:kwəntli ˌɑ:skt 'kwestʃən] FAQ (häufig gestellte Frage) °**III U4,** 56
far [fɑ:] weit **II U6,** 78
so far ['səʊ fɑ:] bis jetzt °**III U5,** 77

to go far [gəʊ 'fɑ:] weit kommen, es weit bringen **III U2,** 22
farm [fɑ:m] Bauernhof, Farm **I U6,** 78
farmer ['fɑ:mə] Bauer/Bäuerin, Landwirt/Landwirtin **I U6,** 82
farmhouse ['fɑ:mhaʊs] Bauernhaus **II U7,** 88
fashion ['fæʃn] Mode **II U6,** 82
fast [fɑ:st] schnell **II U4,** 50
fast food [ˌfɑ:st 'fu:d] Schnellimbiss °**II U4,** 50
fat [fæt] Fett **VI T3,** 44
father ['fɑ:ðə] Vater **III U3,** 46
faucet *(AE)* ['fɔ:sɪt] Wasserhahn **IV U3,** 44
favourite ['feɪvrɪt] Lieblings- **I U1,** 12
February ['februəri] Februar **I U5,** 70
fee [fi:] Gebühr, Abgabe **VI T1,** 10
*to **feed** [fi:d] füttern **I U6,** 80; ernähren, durchfüttern **VI T2,** 28
to be fed up [bi: ˌfed‿'ʌp] die Nase voll haben **I U2,** 34
*to **feel** [fi:l] (sich) fühlen **II U3,** 40
to feel for ['fi:l fə] tasten nach **III U3,** 46
to feel homesick [ˌfi:l 'həʊmsɪk] Heimweh haben **IV U4,** 64
to feel sick [fi:l 'sɪk] Übelkeit verspüren **II U3,** 46
to feel sorry for [fi:l 'sɒri] Mitleid haben mit, bedauern **III U1,** 16
feeling ['fi:lɪŋ] Gefühl **III U4,** 54
fence [fens] Zaun **V T3,** 41
ferry ['feri] Fähre **III U3,** 39
festival ['festɪvl] Festival, Fest **IV U1,** 14
fetish ['fetɪʃ] Fetisch °**IV U5,** 80
feudal ['fju:dl] feudal, Lehns- **VI T2,** 28
few [fju:] wenige **II U5,** 71
a few [ə 'fju:] einige, ein paar **II U4,** 52
fiction ['fɪkʃn] Erfindung, Fiktion **III U5,** 68
science fiction [ˌsaɪəns 'fɪkʃn] Sciencefiction **III U5,** 68
field [fi:ld] Feld, Acker **I U6,** 88; (Arbeits-)Gebiet **VI T3,** 46
sports field ['spɔ:ts fi:ld] Sportplatz **I U7,** 92
fierce [fɪəs] bösartig **II U5,** 70
fight [faɪt] Kampf **III U1,** 16
*to **fight** [faɪt] streiten, kämpfen **III U4,** 59; bekämpfen **VI T4,** 62
fighting ['faɪtɪŋ] Kampf(-) **V T3,** 43
figure ['fɪgə] Figur, Gestalt **II U7,** 94; Zahl, Ziffer °**III U1,** 13
fact **file (on)** ['fækt faɪl] Ordner mit Informationen (über) **III U2,** 27
to **fill** [fɪl] füllen **IV U2,** 31

to fill in [fɪl‿'ɪn] ausfüllen, einsetzen **II U5,** 64
film [fɪlm] Film **II U3,** 43
to **film** [fɪlm] filmen **V T2,** 29
filter ['fɪltə] Filter **VI T3,** 45
fin [fɪn] (Schwimm-)Flosse **V T4,** 65
final ['faɪnl] letzter/letzte/letztes **III U5,** 70
finally ['faɪnli] endlich **III U2,** 24
finance ['faɪnænts] Finanzwesen, Finanzen; Finanz- **VI T4,** 60
to **finance** ['faɪnænts] finanzieren **VI T4,** 60
financial [faɪ'næntʃl] finanziell **VI T4,** 59
*to **find** [faɪnd] finden **I U3,** 48
to find out [faɪnd‿'aʊt] herausfinden **I U4,** 62
fine [faɪn] gut, in Ordnung, fein, schön **I U7,** 94; Geldbuße/-strafe **III U2,** 24
finger ['fɪŋgə] Finger **II U3,** 41
to **finish** ['fɪnɪʃ] beenden, erledigen, aufhören **I U2,** 34
fire [faɪə] Feuer, Brand **I U7,** 96; Feuerstelle; Kaminfeuer **III U2,** 28
fire brigade ['faɪə brɪˌgeɪd] Feuerwehr **III U2,** 28
Where's the fire? [ˌweəz ðə 'faɪə] Wo brennt's denn? **I U7,** 96
firestorm ['faɪəstɔ:m] Feuersturm °**III U2,** 28
firework ['faɪəwɜ:k] Feuerwerkskörper, *Plural:* Feuerwerk **IV U1,** 14
firm [fɜ:m] Firma, Unternehmen, Gesellschaft **V T3,** 44
firmly ['fɜ:mli] eindeutig, deutlich, fest **VI T2,** 33
first [fɜ:st] zuerst; erste/erster/erstes **I U4,** 54
at first [ət 'fɜ:st] zuerst, zunächst **II U6,** 80
first of all [ˌfɜ:st‿ɒf‿'ɔ:l] zuerst, zuallererst, zunächst **IV U4,** 62
fish, fish *(pl)* [fɪʃ] Fisch **I U6,** 78
to **fish** [fɪʃ] fischen, angeln **I U6,** 82
fisherman, fishermen *(pl)* ['fɪʃəmən; 'fɪʃəmen] Fischer; Angler **V T4,** 64
fishing ['fɪʃɪŋ] Fischen, Angeln **I U6,** 78
*to have a **fit** [ˌhæv‿ə 'fɪt] einen Anfall bekommen, Zustände kriegen **III U4,** 60
to **fit** [fɪt] passen **II U6,** 76
fit [fɪt] fit **II U4,** 52
to **fix** [fɪks] manipulieren **IV U2,** 31; reparieren; befestigen, anbringen **IV U3,** 41
flag [flæg] Flagge, Fahne **I U2,** 29
to **flake** [fleɪk] zerfallen, zerbröseln, abbröckeln **VI T4,** 63
flame [fleɪm] Flamme **III U2,** 28
flare [fleə] Leuchtfeuer; Lichtschein **IV U3,** 49
to **flare** [fleə] lodern, flackern **VI T4,** 63
flash [flæʃ] Aufblinken, Blitzen **II U7,** 95
flash flood ['flæʃ ˌflʌd] flutartige Überschwemmung, Sintflut **II U6,** 74
to **flash** [flæʃ] blitzen, blinken **IV U1,** 16
flat [flæt] Wohnung **I U2,** 26; flach, platt **IV U1,** 16
flexible ['fleksɪbl] flexibel, anpassungsfähig **VI T4,** 61
flight [flaɪt] Flug **II U2,** 23
flood [flʌd] Überschwemmung, Hochwasser **II U6,** 74
flash flood ['flæʃ ˌflʌd] flutartige Überschwemmung, Sintflut **II U6,** 74
floor [flɔ:] Fußboden **II U5,** 71; Stockwerk **VI T1,** 15
dance floor ['dɑ:nts flɔ:] Tanzfläche **IV U2,** 31
flossy *(slang)* ['flɒsi] aufgemotzt °**IV U5,** 80
flower ['flaʊə] Blume **I U6,** 78
*to **fly** [flaɪ] fliegen **II U7,** 88; wehen **III U3,** 40
to fly out [flaɪ‿'aʊt] ausfliegen, evakuieren **VI T2,** 29
fog [fɒg] Nebel **II U6,** 78
foggy ['fɒgi] neblig **I U6,** 79
to **fold** [fəʊld] falten, knicken, brechen **VI T4,** 63
folder ['fəʊldə] Ordner, Mappe **I U4,** 60
folk [fəʊk] Volksmusik **IV U5,** 73
folks *(Anrede)* [fəʊks] Leute **IV U1,** 16
to **follow** ['fɒləʊ] hinterhergehen, folgen, befolgen **I U7,** 96
following ['fɒləʊɪŋ] folgend/folgender/folgende/folgendes **III U4,** 57
food [fu:d] Essen, Nahrung, Lebensmittel **I U7,** 95
fast food [ˌfɑ:st 'fu:d] Schnellimbiss °**II U4,** 50
foot, feet *(pl)* [fʊt; fi:t] Fuß **I U4,** 54; Fuß *(Längenmaß: 30,48 cm)* **III U1,** 11
on foot [ɒn 'fʊt] zu Fuß **I U4,** 57
football ['fʊtbɔ:l] Fußball **I U1,** 12
American football [əˌmerɪkən 'fʊtbɔ:l] Football **III U1,** 8
footballer ['fʊtbɔ:lə] Fußballspieler/Fußballspielerin **VI T1,** 12
footprint ['fʊtprɪnt] Fußabdruck **VI T3,** 42
carbon footprint [ˌkɑ:bn 'fʊtprɪnt] CO_2 -Bilanz **VI T3,** 42
footstep ['fʊtstep] Schritt **III U3,** 46
for [fɔ:; fə] für **I U1,** 11; seit **II U5,** 69
for example [fər‿ɪg'zɑ:mpl] zum Beispiel **III U4,** 53
for hours [fər‿'aʊəz] stundenlang **II U4,** 52
for miles [fə 'maɪlz] meilenweit **IV U4,** 65
for supper [fə 'sʌpə] zum Abendessen **II U3,** 38
forecast ['fɔ:kɑ:st] Vorhersage *(Wetter)* **II U6,** 78
*to **forecast** ['fɔ:kɑ:st] vorhersagen *(Wetter)* **IV U3,** 41
foreground ['fɔ:graʊnd] Vordergrund **IV U1,** 8
foreign ['fɒrɪn] fremd, ausländisch **II U1,** 10
foreigner ['fɒrɪnə] Fremder/Fremde, Ausländer/Ausländerin **VI T2,** 29
forest ['fɒrɪst] Wald **VI T3,** 46
*to **forget** [fə'get] vergessen **I U4,** 60
fork [fɔ:k] Gabel **II U4,** 50
form [fɔ:m] Form, Formular **II U5,** 64
long form ['lɒŋ fɔ:m] Langform °**I U1,** 16
to **form** [fɔ:m] formen, bilden **IV U5,** 76
formal ['fɔ:ml] formal, formell, förmlich **IV U2,** 23
former ['fɔ:mə] ehemaliger/ehemalige/ehemaliges, früherer/frühere/früheres **VI T1,** 10
forum ['fɔ:rəm] Forum **IV U5,** 76
fossil ['fɒsl] Fossil; fossil, versteinert **V T4,** 61
fossil fuel ['fɒsl ˌfju:əl] fossiler Brennstoff **V T4,** 61
foul [faʊl] Foul **III U1,** 12
to **found** [faʊnd] gründen **IV U1,** 10
frame [freɪm] Rahmen, Chassis **VI T4,** 61
free [fri:] frei **I U3,** 40; kostenlos, umsonst **IV U1,** 12
freedom ['fri:dəm] Freiheit **IV U1,** 9
freeman, freemen *(pl)* ['fri:mən; 'fri:men] freier Mann **VI T2,** 28
to **freestyle** *(slang)* ['fri:staɪl] improvisieren **IV U5,** 76
French [frentʃ] französisch **II U1,** 18
French fries *(AE)* ['frentʃ ˌfraɪz] Pommes frites **IV U1,** 12
frequent ['fri:kwənt] häufig °**III U4,** 56
fresh [freʃ] frisch **II U4,** 54
Friday ['fraɪdeɪ] Freitag **I LUB,** 39
friend [frend] Freund/Freundin **I U1,** 16
to make friends (with) [ˌmeɪk 'frendz] Freundschaft schließen (mit) **IV U4,** 64
friendly ['frendli] freundlich, nett **IV U1,** 14
French **fries** *(AE)* ['frentʃ ˌfraɪz] Pommes frites **IV U1,** 12

to **frighten away** [ˌfraɪtn‿ə'weɪ] abschrecken **II U7,** 88
*to be **frightened** (of) [bi: 'fraɪtnd] Angst haben (vor) **II U6,** 83
frightening ['fraɪtnɪŋ] schrecklich, furchtbar **II U6,** 80
from [frɒm] aus, von **I U1,** 10
divorced from [dɪ'vɔ:st frɒm] geschieden von **I U2,** 28
Where are you from? [ˌweər‿ə jə 'frɒm] Woher kommst du? **I U1,** 11
front [frʌnt] Vorderseite **IV U2,** 31
at the front [ət ðə 'frʌnt] im vorderen Teil, vorne **IV U1,** 9
front garden [ˌfrʌnt 'gɑ:dn] Vorgarten **VI T4,** 62
in front of [ɪn 'frʌnt‿əv] vor **I U3,** 49
to **frown** [fraʊn] die Stirn runzeln **VI T4,** 64
fruit [fru:t] Obst, Frucht **II U1,** 15
frustrated [frʌs'treɪtɪd] frustriert **III U4,** 52
fuel ['fju:əl] Treibstoff; Brennmaterial **V T4,** 61
fossil fuel ['fɒsl ˌfju:əl] fossiler Brennstoff **V T4,** 61
to **fulfill** *(AE)* [fʊl'fɪl] erfüllen, genügen **V T3,** 46
full (of) [fʊl] ganz, voll (von/mit) **III U1,** 11
full-time (F/T) [ˌfʊl'taɪm] Vollzeit- **V T1,** 14; **V T2,** 32
fun [fʌn] Spaß **I U3,** 41
Have fun! [ˌhæv 'fʌn] Viel Spaß! **I U6,** 82
to be fun [bi: 'fʌn] Spaß machen **I U3,** 43
to have fun [ˌhæv 'fʌn] Spaß haben, sich amüsieren **I U6,** 82
funeral ['fju:nrəl] Beerdigung **II U6,** 76
funk [fʌŋk] Funk *(Musikrichtung)* **IV U5,** 76
funny ['fʌni] komisch, lustig **I LUA,** 25
furious ['fjʊəriəs] wütend **III U3,** 47
furniture ['fɜ:nɪtʃə] Möbel **I LUA,** 25
further ['fɜ:ðə] weiter **V T1,** 14
fuse-box ['fju:zbɒks] Sicherungskasten **III U3,** 47
future ['fju:tʃə] Zukunft; Futur **V T4,** 60; zukünftig **VI T2,** 29

G

gallery ['gæləri] Galerie °**V T3,** 45
game [geɪm] Spiel **I U2,** 26
miming game ['maɪmɪŋ geɪm] Pantomime °**I U6,** 81
gang [gæŋ] Gang, Bande **IV U2,** 25
gangster ['gæŋkstə] Gangster/Gangsterin, Verbrecher/Verbrecherin **IV U5,** 76
garbage *(AE)* ['gɑ:bɪdʒ] Müll, Abfall **VI T3,** 45
garden ['gɑ:dn] Garten **I U2,** 26
front garden [ˌfrʌnt 'gɑ:dn] Vorgarten **VI T4,** 62
gardener ['gɑ:dnə] Gärtner/Gärtnerin **VI T3,** 46
gardening ['gɑ:dnɪŋ] Gärtnern, Gartengestaltung **VI T4,** 59
gas [gæs] Gas *(BE)*; Benzin *(AE)* **V T4,** 60
greenhouse gas [ˌgri:nhaʊs 'gæs] Treibhausgas **V T4,** 60
gate [geɪt] Tor, Pforte; Gate **II U7,** 90
GCSE [ˌdʒi:si:es'i:] Prüfung zum Abschluss der Sekundarstufe **III U4,** 57
g'day [gə'deɪ] Tag, hallo *(australische Begrüßung)* °**II U1,** 14
Geography [dʒi'ɒgrəfi] Geografie, Erdkunde **II U1,** 10
German ['dʒɜ:mən] deutsch; Deutscher/Deutsche **I U1,** 17
*to **get** [get] besorgen, kommen, bekommen **I U3,** 44; holen **II U2,** 26; werden **II U6,** 83
get-well card [ˌget 'wel ˌkɑ:d] Gute-Besserung-Karte **VI T4,** 63
to get hungry [get 'hʌŋgri] Hunger bekommen **II U4,** 56
to get interested [get 'ɪntrəstɪd] sich interessieren **III U2,** 31
to get in the way (of) [ˌget‿ɪn‿ðə‿'weɪ] etw. verhindern, im Weg stehen **V T2,** 29
to get into [get‿'ɪntə] einsteigen in *(Auto)* **I U5,** 75
to get into such a state [get‿ˌɪntə sʌtʃ‿ə 'steɪt] durchdrehen, (sich) verrückt machen **III U4,** 60
to get it ['get‿ɪt] etwas verstehen, begreifen **IV U3,** 48
to get lost [get 'lɒst] verloren gehen, sich verirren **I U3,** 48
to get off [get‿'ɒf] aussteigen aus **I U4,** 59
to get on [get‿'ɒn] aufsteigen **III U5,** 74; einsteigen *(in Zug, Bus ...)* **III U2,** 29; weiterkommen, vorwärtskommen **VI T4,** 64
to get onto [get‿'ɒntə] einsteigen *(Bus)* **II U1,** 19
to get on with [get‿'ɒn wɪð] sich verstehen mit, gut auskommen mit **VI T1,** 14
to get out [get‿'aʊt] aussteigen **I U6,** 86; entkommen **III U3,** 47
to get out of bed [ˌget‿aʊt‿əv 'bed] aufstehen **II U7,** 94
to get ready [get 'redi] sich vorbereiten **II U5,** 68
to get rid of [get 'rɪd‿əv] loswerden **VI T2,** 28
to get ... right/wrong [get ... 'raɪt/'rɒŋ] richtig/falsch machen **II U3,** 44
to get sth going [get 'gəʊɪŋ] etw. in Gang/Schwung bringen, flottmachen **VI T4,** 62
to get to ['get tə] kommen zu, kommen nach, erreichen **III U2,** 26
to get up [get‿'ʌp] aufstehen **I U3,** 44
to get upset [ˌget‿ʌp'set] sich aufregen **VI T1,** 15
to get ... wrong [get ... 'rɒŋ] falsch verstehen °**II U3,** 47
ghost [gəʊst] Geist, Gespenst **I U2,** 34
ghostly ['gəʊstli] geisterhaft **VI T4,** 64
girl [gɜ:l] Mädchen **I U1,** 16
girlfriend ['gɜ:lfrend] Freundin *(in einer Paarbeziehung)* **II U3,** 39
*to **give** [gɪv] geben, schenken **I U4,** 60
to give ... a dirty look [ˌgɪv‿ə dɜ:ti 'lʊk] einen vernichtenden Blick zuwerfen **II U1,** 10
to give a talk [ˌgɪv‿ə 'tɔ:k] einen Vortrag/eine Rede halten **VI T1,** 14
to give up [gɪv‿'ʌp] aufgeben **V T3,** 43
glad [glæd] froh **III U4,** 58
glamorous ['glæmrəs] glamourös **IV U5,** 72
glass [glɑ:s] Glas **II U4,** 50
glasses *(pl)* ['glɑ:sɪz] Brille **IV U3,** 48
double-**glazed** [ˌdʌbl'gleɪzd] doppelt verglast **VI T3,** 46
glazier ['gleɪziə] Glaser/Glaserin **VI T3,** 46
glee [gli:] Entzücken **III U4,** 60
global ['gləʊbl] global, Erd- **V T4,** 58
(global) warming [ˌgləʊbl 'wɔ:mɪŋ] (Erd-)Erwärmung **V T4,** 61
globalisation [ˌgləʊblaɪ'zeɪʃn] Globalisierung **V T4,** 60
glove [glʌv] Handschuh **III U1,** 8
to **glow** [gləʊ] leuchten **III U5,** 76
*to **go** [gəʊ] gehen **I U1,** 19
Go down .... ['gəʊ daʊn] Geh ... entlang. **I LUC,** 53
Go left. [gəʊ 'left] Biege nach links ab. **I LUC,** 52
Go right. [gəʊ 'raɪt] Biege nach rechts ab. **I LUC,** 52
to go [tə‿'gəʊ] zum Mitnehmen **IV U1,** 12

to go bananas [ˌgəʊ bəˈnɑːnəz] verrückt werden, durchdrehen **II U5,** 66
to go bump [gəʊ ˈbʌmp] rumsen °**II U7,** 94
to go crazy [gəʊ ˈkreɪzi] ausflippen, durchdrehen **VI T3,** 43
to go down [gəʊ ˈdaʊn] hinuntergehen, entlanggehen **II U2,** 30
to go far [gəʊ ˈfɑː] weit kommen, es weit bringen **III U2,** 22
to go for a walk [ˌgəʊ fər‿ə ˈwɔːk] spazieren gehen **III U5,** 76
to go green [ˌgəʊ ˈgriːn] umweltbewusst werden **VI T3,** 43
to go in [gəʊ‿ˈɪn] hineingehen **II U2,** 26
to go + -ing [gəʊ] … gehen **II U4,** 52
to go it alone [ˌgəʊ‿ɪt‿əˈləʊn] einen Alleingang starten, es allein schaffen **V T3,** 43
to go off [gəʊ‿ˈɒf] losgehen *(Alarm)* **II U7,** 95
to go on [gəʊ‿ˈɒn] andauern; weitermachen **IV U1,** 14
to go on a diet [ˌgəʊ‿ɒn ə ˈdaɪət] eine Diät machen **II U4,** 52
to go out [gəʊ‿ˈaʊt] (hin)ausgehen, erlöschen **II U3,** 38
to go over [gəʊ‿ˈəʊvə] hinübergehen **II U3,** 38
to go places [ˌgəʊ ˈpleɪsɪz] herumreisen **IV U4,** 64
to go red [gəʊ ˈred] rot werden **II U1,** 11
to go up [gəʊ‿ˈʌp] hinaufgehen °**I U4,** 61
to go weak [gəʊ ˈwiːk] schwach werden **III U4,** 60
to go with [ˈgəʊ‿wɪð] passen zu **III U1,** 9
to go without [ˌgəʊ wɪˈðaʊt] ohne … auskommen **II U4,** 52
to go wrong [gəʊ ˈrɒŋ] schief gehen **II U6,** 85
goal [gəʊl] Tor, Ziel **I U1,** 12
winning goal [ˈwɪnɪŋ gəʊl] Siegtreffer **III U4,** 58
goalkeeper [ˈgəʊlˌkiːpə] Torwart **III U1,** 10
goblin [ˈgɒblɪn] Kobold **II U7,** 90
My **God!** [maɪ ˈgɒd] Mein Gott! **II U6,** 82
gold [gəʊld] Gold **II U7,** 90
good [gʊd] gut **I U1,** 16
Good grief! [gʊd ˈgriːf] Du liebe Zeit! **II U2,** 28
Good luck! [ˌgʊd ˈlʌk] Viel Glück! **I U4,** 63
Good morning! [ˈgʊd ˈmɔːnɪŋ] Guten Morgen! **I U1,** 16
I'm good at … [aɪm ˈgʊd‿ət] ich bin gut in … **I U1,** 20
to be good with … [biː ˈgʊd wɪð] gut mit … umgehen können **I U2,** 34
to have a good time [ˌhæv‿ə gʊd ˈtaɪm] sich amüsieren **I U5,** 75
goodbye [gʊdˈbaɪ] auf Wiedersehen **I U1,** 19
goods *(pl)* [gʊdz] Güter, Waren **IV U4,** 57
gossip [ˈgɒsɪp] Tratsch, Klatsch **VI T2,** 30
government [ˈgʌvnmənt] Regierung **V T1,** 14; **V T3,** 44; **V T4,** 60
to **grab** [græb] greifen, schnappen **III U3,** 47
grade *(AE)* [greɪd] Klasse, Note **IV U2,** 22
to **graduate** [ˈgrædjueɪt] den Schulabschluss machen **IV U2,** 28
grammar [ˈgræmə] Grammatik °**II U1,** 16
grammar school [ˈgræmə ˌskuːl] Gymnasium **III U4,** 57
gramme [græm] Gramm **III U1,** 11
grandad [ˈgrændæd] Opa **I LUA,** 25
grandma [ˈgrændmɑː] Oma **I LUA,** 25
grandparents *(pl)* [ˈgrænpeərənts] Großeltern **VI T1,** 12
great-**grandson** [ˌgreɪtˈgrænsʌn] Urenkel **VI T4,** 60
grass [grɑːs] Gras, Rasen **III U1,** 8
grave [greɪv] Grab **III U5,** 69
gravestone [ˈgreɪvstəʊn] Grabstein **III U5,** 74
gravity [ˈgrævəti] Schwerkraft, Schwere **VI T4,** 63
great [greɪt] großartig, toll **I U2,** 26; groß **III U2,** 22
great-grandson [ˌgreɪtˈgrænsʌn] Urenkel **VI T4,** 60
Greek [griːk] griechisch; Grieche/Griechin **I U2,** 29
green [griːn] grün **I LUA,** 24
greenhouse [ˈgriːnhaʊs] Gewächshaus **II U6,** 81
greenhouse gas [ˌgriːnhaʊs ˈgæs] Treibhausgas **V T4,** 60
greeting [ˈgriːtɪŋ] Gruß, Begrüßung °**V T2,** 28
grey [greɪ] grau **III U5,** 77
grid [grɪd] Gitter, Tabelle **III U4,** 57
Good **grief!** [gʊd ˈgriːf] Du liebe Zeit! **II U2,** 28
ground [graʊnd] Boden **II U2,** 26
grounded [ˈgraʊndɪd] geerdet, gefestigt **VI T4,** 63
group [gruːp] Gruppe **I U4,** 54
*to **grow** [grəʊ] wachsen (lassen); anbauen; zunehmen **V T4,** 63
to **guarantee** [ˌgærnˈtiː] garantieren, sicherstellen, bürgen **V T4,** 62
national **guard** [ˌnæʃnl ˈgɑːd] Nationalgarde °**V T3,** 44
to **guard** [gɑːd] bewachen **II U7,** 90
to **guess** [ges] raten, vermuten **III U4,** 57
guest [gest] Gast **III U5,** 72
guide [gaɪd] Führer/Führerin; Handbuch °**V T1,** 11
guitar [gɪˈtɑː] Gitarre **IV U5,** 76
gun [gʌn] Schusswaffe **III U5,** 78
gunman, gunmen *(pl)* [ˈgʌnmən; gʌnmen] Schütze, Bewaffneter **VI T2,** 29
gunshot [ˈgʌnʃɒt] Schuss **III U5,** 78
guy [gaɪ] Typ, Kerl; *Plural:* Leute **IV U5,** 79
gym [dʒɪm] Turnhalle **I U3,** 40

H

Ha! [hɑː] Ha! **III U4,** 58
hair [heə] Haar, Haare **II U2,** 28
hairdresser [ˈheəˌdresə] Friseur/Friseurin **II U2,** 28
hairdressing [ˈheəˌdresɪŋ] Frisieren **VI T1,** 15
hairdryer [ˈheəˌdraɪə] Föhn **IV U3,** 44
half [hɑːf] halb **II U6,** 83; Hälfte **IV U4,** 62
half an hour [ˌhɑːf‿ən‿ˈaʊə] eine halbe Stunde **II U2,** 26
half past (two) [ˈhɑːf pɑːst] halb (drei) **I U3,** 40
half-price [ˌhɑːfˈpraɪs] zum halben Preis **III U1,** 12
half-sister [ˈhɑːfˌsɪstə] Halbschwester **I U2,** 26
hall [hɔːl] Halle, Saal, Flur **I U3,** 40
ham [hæm] Schinken **II U4,** 49
hand [hænd] Hand **II U3,** 41
Hands off! [hændz‿ˈɒf] Hände weg! **II U4,** 50
to **hand** [hænd] (über)geben, aushändigen **VI T4,** 64
handbag [ˈhænbæg] Handtasche **III U2,** 24
handy [ˈhændi] praktisch **VI T3,** 45
*to **hang around** [ˌhæŋ‿əˈraʊnd] rumhängen, herumlungern **V T2,** 28
to hang out [hæŋ‿ˈaʊt] sich herumtreiben **III U4,** 54
to hang up [hæŋ‿ˈʌp] aufhängen °**V T1,** 15
Hang on! [ˈhæŋ‿ɒn] Moment mal! Warte mal! **I U6,** 82
to **happen** [ˈhæpn] geschehen, passieren **I U6,** 86
happy [ˈhæpi] glücklich, froh **I U2,** 33

to **harass** [hə'ræs] belästigen, drangsalieren **VI T2,** 33
harbor *(AE)* ['hɑ:bə] Hafen **IV U1,** 9
hard [hɑ:d] hart; schwierig, stark **II U6,** 82
harm [hɑ:m] Schaden, Verletzung **III U4,** 60
hat [hæt] Hut **II U2,** 26
hate [heɪt] Hass **II U1,** 10
to **hate** [heɪt] hassen **II U1,** 10
*to **have** [hæv] haben **I U5,** 68
Have a nice day. [ˌhæv‿ə naɪs 'deɪ] Einen schönen Tag (noch). **II U4,** 55
Have fun! [ˌhæv 'fʌn] Viel Spaß! **I U6,** 82
to have a day off [ˌhæv‿ə 'deɪ‿ɒf] einen Tag frei haben **V T3,** 46
to have a fit [ˌhæv‿ə 'fɪt] einen Anfall bekommen, Zustände kriegen **III U4,** 60
to have a good time [ˌhæv‿ə gʊd 'taɪm] sich amüsieren **I U5,** 75
to have a look [ˌhæv‿ə 'lʊk] (an)schauen, nachschauen **III U5,** 72
to have an argument [ˌhæv‿ən‿'ɑ:gjəmənt] sich streiten **III U4,** 52
to have a party [ˌhæv‿ə 'pɑ:ti] eine Party feiern **I U5,** 68
to have breakfast [hæv 'brekfəst] frühstücken **III U2,** 23
to have fun [ˌhæv 'fʌn] Spaß haben, sich amüsieren **I U6,** 82
to have got [hæv 'gɒt] besitzen, haben **I U2,** 30
to have no clue [ˌhæv nəʊ 'klu:] keine Ahnung haben **IV U5,** 80
to have sex [ˌhæv 'seks] Geschlechtsverkehr haben **VI T4,** 58
to have supper [hæv 'sʌpə] zu Abend essen **I U3,** 44
to have to ['hæv tə] müssen **II U5,** 64
he [hi:] er **I U1,** 12
head [hed] Kopf **II U3,** 36
head of state [ˌhed‿əv 'steɪt] Staatsoberhaupt **VI T2,** 30
header ['hedə] Kopfball **VI T1,** 12
heading ['hedɪŋ] Überschrift °**IV U2,** 32
headline ['hedlaɪn] Überschrift, Schlagzeile °**V T4,** 58
headphones *(pl)* ['hedfəʊnz] Kopfhörer **II U4,** 56
headquarters *(pl)* ['hedˌkwɔ:təz] Hauptsitz **VI T4,** 60
health [helθ] Gesundheit **V T2,** 32
healthy ['helθi] gesund **II U4,** 50
*to **hear** [hɪə] hören **I U6,** 78
heart [hɑ:t] Herz **V T4,** 66
heat [hi:t] Hitze **IV U1,** 17
to **heat** [hi:t] erhitzen, erwärmen; heizen **VI T3,** 42
heating ['hi:tɪŋ] Heizung **II U6,** 78
heavy ['hevi] schwer **II U4,** 51
heavy metal [ˌhevi 'metl] Heavy Metal **IV U5,** 76
height [haɪt] Höhe, Größe **III U1,** 11
helicopter ['helɪˌkɒptə] Helikopter, Hubschrauber **II U6,** 83
hell [hel] Hölle **IV U5,** 80
Hello! [he'ləʊ] Hallo! **I U1,** 10
helmet ['helmət] Helm **III U1,** 8
help [help] Hilfe **I U2,** 34
to **help** [help] helfen **I U2,** 34
helper ['helpə] Helfer/Helferin **V T1,** 14
helpful ['helpfəl] hilfreich **II U5,** 71
helpless ['helpləs] hilflos **III U3,** 46
helpline ['helplaɪn] telefonischer Beratungsdienst, Notruf °**III U4,** 59
her [hɜ:] ihr/ihre; sie **I U2,** 26
Her Majesty [hə 'mædʒəsti] Ihre Majestät °**III U5,** 78
here [hɪə] hier **I U1,** 12
Here you are! ['hɪə ju:‿ɑ:] Bitte schön! **I U1,** 20
hero, heroes *(pl)* ['hɪərəʊ; 'hɪərəʊz] Held **II U3,** 43
heroine ['herəʊɪn] Heldin **III U5,** 68
herself [hɜ:'self] sie/sich (selbst) **VI T3,** 42
to **hesitate** ['hezɪteɪt] zögern **VI T4,** 62
Hi! [haɪ] Hi! **I U1,** 10
Hi, there! ['haɪ ðeə] Hallo! **IV U2,** 26
*to **hide** [haɪd] (sich) verstecken **I U6,** 86
high [haɪ] hoch, groß **II U2,** 30
high-tech [ˌhaɪ'tek] high-tech **IV U3,** 42
high school *(AE)* ['haɪ ˌsku:l] High School *(weiterführende Schule in den USA, Oberstufe)* **IV U2,** 22
to **highlight** ['haɪlaɪt] hervorheben, markieren °**IV U2,** 28
highway *(AE)* ['haɪweɪ] Bundesstraße, Highway **IV U4,** 57
hiking ['haɪkɪŋ] Wandern, Wander- **VI T1,** 10
hill [hɪl] Berg, Hügel **IV U4,** 58
him [hɪm] ihn, ihm **I U4,** 60
himself [hɪm'self] er/sich (selbst) **III U1,** 17
Hindi ['hɪndi] Hindi **VI T1,** 10
Hinglish ['hɪŋglɪʃ] Hinglisch *(Mischung aus Hindi und Englisch)* **VI T1,** 10
hip hop ['hɪp hɒp] Hip-Hop **III U4,** 53
his [hɪz] sein/seine **I LUA,** 25
Hispanic [hɪ'spænɪk] hispanisch, lateinamerikanisch; Hispano-Amerikaner/-Amerikanerin **IV U4,** 64
historical [hɪ'stɒrɪkl] geschichtlich, historisch **V T1,** 14
History ['hɪstəri] Geschichte **II U1,** 10
hit [hɪt] Hit **III U5,** 70
*to **hit** [hɪt] schlagen, treffen **II U3,** 36
hobby, hobbies *(pl)* ['hɒbi; 'hɒbiz] Hobby **I LUB,** 38
hockey ['hɒki] Hockey **II U1,** 16
ice hockey ['aɪs ˌhɒki] Eishockey **II U2,** 23
*to **hold** [həʊld] (ab)halten, festhalten **VI T2,** 30; **VI T4,** 62
holiday ['hɒlədeɪ] Feiertag **IV U4,** 60
holiday(s) ['hɒlədeɪ(z)] Urlaub, Ferien **II U7,** 88
home [həʊm] Zuhause, Heim; nach Hause **I U1,** 11; Heimat(-) **III U1,** 8
at home [ət 'həʊm] zu Hause **I U2,** 26
home plate ['həʊm ˌpleɪt] Home Plate **III U1,** 14
to take home [ˌteɪk 'həʊm] nach Hause bringen **I U2,** 35
homecoming ['həʊmkʌmɪŋ] Homecoming *(Schulfest an amerikanischen High Schools)* **IV U2,** 22
homecoming queen [ˌhəʊmkʌmɪŋ 'kwi:n] Ballkönigin **IV U2,** 23
*to feel **homesick** [ˌfi:l 'həʊmsɪk] Heimweh haben **IV U4,** 64
homework ['həʊmwɜ:k] Hausaufgabe(n) **I U1,** 19
homie *(slang)* ['həʊmi] Kumpel **IV U5,** 76
honest ['ɒnɪst] ehrlich **IV U2,** 31
to **hoot** [hu:t] schreien, rufen *(Eule)* **II U7,** 94
to **hope** [həʊp] hoffen **I U5,** 72
hopeful ['həʊpfl] hoffnungsvoll **VI T4,** 62
hopeless ['həʊpləs] hoffnungslos **VI T1,** 12
horizon [hə'raɪzn] Horizont, Blickfeld **VI T1,** 14
horoscope ['hɒrəskəʊp] Horoskop **II U6,** 80
horrible ['hɒrəbl] schrecklich, furchtbar **II U2,** 24
horse [hɔ:s] Pferd **I LUB,** 38
hospital ['hɒspɪtl] Krankenhaus **II U3,** 36
host [həʊst] Gastgeber; Talkmaster **III U5,** 70
hostage ['hɒstɪdʒ] Geisel **VI T2,** 29
hot [hɒt] heiß **I U6,** 79; toll; scharf **IV U2,** 26
hotel [həʊ'tel] Hotel **III U2,** 27
hotel suite [həʊ'tel ˌswi:t] Hotelsuite **III U2,** 27
hotline ['hɒtlaɪn] Hotline **IV U4,** 61

English – German

hound [haʊnd] Jagdhund **III U5,** 70
hour ['aʊə] Stunde **I U2,** 34
hours *(pl)* ['aʊəz] Öffnungszeiten **I U4,** 62
for hours [fər‿'aʊəz] stundenlang **II U4,** 52
half an hour [ˌhɑ:f‿ən‿'aʊə] eine halbe Stunde **II U2,** 26
house [haʊs] Haus **I LUA,** 25
house-sitter [ˌhaʊs'sɪtə] Haussitter/Haussitterin °**IV U1,** 15
how [haʊ] wie **I U1,** 11
How are you? [ˌhaʊ‿'ɑ: ju:] Wie geht es dir/Ihnen/euch? **I U6,** 83
how many [haʊ 'meni] wie viele **I U5,** 68
How much are ... ? [ˌhaʊ 'mʌtʃ‿ɑ:] Wie viel kosten ... ? **I U5,** 66
How much is ... ? [ˌhaʊ 'mʌtʃ‿ɪz] Wie viel kostet ... ? **I U5,** 66
How old are you? [haʊ‿'əʊld‿ɑ: ju:] Wie alt bist du? **I U1,** 11
how to ... ['haʊ tə] wie man ... °**II U3,** 37
however [haʊ'evə] jedoch **VI T2,** 28
huge [hju:dʒ] riesig, gewaltig **IV U1,** 14
human ['hju:mən] Mensch; menschlich **IV U3,** 41
human resources [ˌhju:mən rɪ'zɔ:sɪz] Personalabteilung **VI T4,** 60
hundred ['hʌndrəd] hundert **II U2,** 23
hungry ['hʌŋgri] hungrig **II U1,** 14
to get hungry [get 'hʌŋgri] Hunger bekommen **II U4,** 56
hunting ['hʌntɪŋ] Jagen **III U5,** 74
*to be in a **hurry** [bi:‿ɪn‿ə 'hʌri] es eilig haben **I U2,** 30
Hurry up! [ˌhʌri‿'ʌp] Beeil dich! **I U2,** 30
*to **hurt** [hɜ:t] verletzen, weh tun **II U3,** 40
hurt [hɜ:t] verletzt **III U5,** 74
hurtful ['hɜ:tfl] verletzend °**IV U2,** 27
husband ['hʌzbənd] Ehemann **VI T2,** 28
hut [hʌt] Hütte **VI T2,** 28
hyphen ['haɪfn] Bindestrich °**V T2,** 34

I

I [aɪ] ich **I U1,** 10
I'd like to [ˌaɪd 'laɪk tə] ich würde gern **II U2,** 22
I don't care. [aɪ dəʊnt 'keə] Es ist mir egal. **II U4,** 58
I'd rather [aɪd 'rɑ:ðə] ich würde lieber **II U2,** 22
I'm having .... [aɪm 'hævɪŋ] Ich nehme .... **II U1,** 14
I'm scared. [aɪm 'skeəd] Ich habe Angst. **II U3,** 44
I want my ... pierced. [aɪ 'wɒnt maɪ ... 'pɪəst] Ich möchte mein/e ... piercen lassen. **III U4,** 52
ice [aɪs] Eis **II U2,** 23
ice-cream [aɪs 'kri:m] Eiscreme **I U7,** 92
ice hockey ['aɪs ˌhɒki] Eishockey **II U2,** 23
ice rink ['aɪs rɪŋk] Eis-/Schlittschuhbahn **II U2,** 23
icon ['aɪkɒn] Ikone **III U3,** 47
idea [aɪ'dɪə] Idee, Einfall **I LUB,** 38
no idea [ˌnəʊ‿aɪ'dɪə] keine Ahnung **III U3,** 46
idiot ['ɪdɪət] Idiot, Dummkopf **I U1,** 21
if [ɪf] wenn, falls; ob **II U7,** 90
if-clause ['ɪfklɔ:z] if-Satz °**IV U4,** 59
to **ignore** [ɪg'nɔ:] ignorieren **VI T4,** 59
ill [ɪl] krank; schlecht **IV U2,** 25
illegal [ɪ'li:gl] illegal, unrechtmäßig, rechtswidrig **IV U3,** 48
illness ['ɪlnəs] Krankheit **VI T4,** 59
image ['ɪmɪdʒ] Bild, Image, Abbild, Vorstellung °**IV U4,** 57
to **imagine** [ɪ'mædʒɪn] sich (etwas) vorstellen **III U4,** 57
immigrant ['ɪmɪgrənt] Immigrant/Immigrantin, Einwanderer/Einwanderin **IV U1,** 9
to **immigrate** ['ɪmɪgreɪt] immigrieren, einwandern **IV U1,** 10
immigration [ˌɪmɪ'greɪʃn] Immigration, Einwanderung **IV U1,** 10
importance [ɪm'pɔ:tnts] Bedeutung, Wichtigkeit °**V T3,** 47
important [ɪm'pɔ:tnt] wichtig; einflussreich **II U6,** 74
impression [ɪm'preʃn] Eindruck °**II U4,** 57
to **improve** [ɪm'pru:v] (sich) verbessern **VI T1,** 10; **VI T4,** 59
in [ɪn] in; herein **I U1,** 10; von, aus **V T2,** 28
in all [ɪn‿'ɔ:l] im Ganzen **III U4,** 53
in fact [ɪn 'fækt] in der Tat, genau genommen **II U7,** 94
in front of [ɪn 'frʌnt‿əv] vor **I U3,** 49
in public [ɪn 'pʌblɪk] in der Öffentlichkeit **VI T2,** 26
in the end [ɪn ði:‿'end] schließlich, zum Schluss **II U6,** 80
in the long-run [ɪn ðə 'lɒŋrʌn] langfristig **VI T3,** 44
in turn [ɪn 'tɜ:n] abwechselnd, der Reihe nach °**V T3,** 45
inch [ɪnʃ] Zoll *(Längenmaß: 2,54cm)* **III U1,** 11
to **include** [ɪn'klu:d] einschließen, beinhalten, aufnehmen **VI T1,** 10; **VI T4,** 60
including [ɪn'klu:dɪŋ] einschließlich, inklusive **V T3,** 43
to **increase** [ɪn'kri:s] vergrößern; zunehmen, steigen **VI T2,** 29; **VI T3,** 42
independent [ˌɪndɪ'pendənt] unabhängig **III U3,** 46; Independent *(Musikrichtung)* **IV U5,** 76
Indian ['ɪndiən] indisch **II U4,** 49
indie ['ɪndi] Indie *(Musikrichtung)* **IV U5,** 76
industrial [ɪn'dʌstriəl] industriell, Industrie- **VI T3,** 44
industry ['ɪndəstri] Industrie **III U5,** 68
info ['ɪnfəʊ] Info °**III U4,** 58
to **inform** [ɪn'fɔ:m] informieren, benachrichtigen **VI T2,** 33
information [ˌɪnfə'meɪʃn] Information/Informationen **I LUC,** 52
information centre [ɪnfə'meɪʃn ˌsentə] Informationszentrum **I LUC,** 52
inheritor [ɪn'herɪtə] Erbe/Erbin **III U5,** 76
inner ['ɪnə] innerer/innere/inneres, innen **VI T4,** 59
inside [ɪn'saɪd] innen, drin, nach drinnen **I U5,** 75
to **install** [ɪn'stɔ:l] einbauen, installieren **VI T3,** 46
installer [ɪn'stɔ:lə] Installateur/Installateurin **VI T3,** 46
instead [ɪn'sted] stattdessen, dafür **VI T4,** 64
instead of [ɪn'sted‿əv] statt, anstatt **VI T3,** 44; **VI T3,** 47
instruction [ɪn'strʌkʃn] Instruktion, Anweisung °**II U4,** 59
instructor [ɪn'strʌktə] Lehrer/Lehrerin, Ausbilder/Ausbilderin **V T1,** 14; **V T4,** 64
to **insulate** ['ɪnsjəleɪt] isolieren, dämmen **VI T3,** 46
insulation [ˌɪnsjə'leɪʃn] Isolierung, Dämmung **VI T3,** 46
insurance [ɪn'ʃʊərns] Versicherung **V T1,** 14
intelligent [ɪn'telɪdʒnt] intelligent, klug; vernünftig **IV U3,** 42
inter-cultural [ˌɪntə'kʌltʃrl] interkulturell **V T4,** 58
interest ['ɪntrəst] Interesse **IV U3,** 46
interested ['ɪntrəstɪd] interessiert **II U1,** 18
to get interested [get 'ɪntrəstɪd] sich interessieren **III U2,** 31
interesting ['ɪntrəstɪŋ] interessant **II U4,** 51

international [ˌɪntəˈnæʃnl] international **III U3,** 39
Internet [ˈɪntənet] Internet **II U1,** 14
to surf the Internet [ˌsɜːf ði‿ˈɪntənet] im Internet surfen **II U1,** 14
internship *(AE)* [ˈɪntɜːnʃɪp] Praktikum **VI T4,** 60
Interstate *(AE)* [ˌɪntəˈsteɪt] Autobahn **IV U4,** 57
interview [ˈɪntəvjuː] Interview **II U1,** 17; Vorstellungsgespräch °**VI T1,** 17
to **interview** [ˈɪntəvjuː] interviewen **II U1,** 17
interviewer [ˈɪntəvjuːə] Interviewer/Interviewerin °**VI T1,** 17
into [ˈɪntə] in; in … hinein **I U3,** 44
to get into [get‿ˈɪntə] einsteigen in *(Auto)* **I U5,** 75
to run into [rʌn‿ˈɪntə] laufen gegen, stoßen gegen **III U1,** 17
introduction [ˌɪntrəˈdʌkʃn] Einleitung **VI T4,** 62
introductory [ˌɪntrəˈdʌktri] Einleitungs-, einleitend **VI T4,** 65
Inuktitut [ɪˈnʊktɪtʊt] Inuktitut *(Sprache der Inuit)* **VI T1,** 11
to **invent** [ɪnˈvent] erfinden **III U4,** 53
invention [ɪnˈventʃn] Erfindung **IV U3,** 41
inventor [ɪnˈventə] Erfinder/Erfinderin **IV U5,** 74
invitation [ˌɪnvɪˈteɪʃn] Einladung **I U5,** 70
to **invite** [ɪnˈvaɪt] einladen **I U5,** 68
to **involve** [ɪnˈvɒlv] involvieren, einbeziehen, beteiligen **VI T3,** 46
IQ [ˌaɪˈkjuː] IQ *(Intelligenzquotient)* **IV U3,** 43
Irish [ˈaɪrɪʃ] irisch **II U7,** 90; Iren/Irinnen **IV U1,** 10
to **iron** [aɪən] bügeln **II U7,** 90
irregular [ɪˈregjələ] unregelmäßig °**II U2,** 26
island [ˈaɪlənd] Insel **II U6,** 82
islander [ˈaɪləndə] Inselbewohner/Inselbewohnerin **V T4,** 64
it [ɪt] es **I U1,** 12
It said … . [ɪt ˈsed] Es lautete … . **II U2,** 30
IT [ˌaɪˈtiː] Informationstechnik, Informatik **VI T1,** 14; **VI T4,** 60
Italian [ɪˈtæliən] italienisch; Italiener/Italienerin **I U2,** 29
to **itch** [ɪtʃ] jucken **V T4,** 66
item [ˈaɪtəm] Punkt, Gegenstand, Thema °**IV U1,** 17
its [ɪts] sein/seine; ihr/ihre **III U1,** 8
itself [ɪtˈself] es/sich (selbst) **VI T3,** 42

J

jacket [ˈdʒækɪt] Jacke **I U6,** 86
jail [dʒeɪl] Gefängnis **V T1,** 10
jam [dʒæm] Marmelade **I U7,** 94
traffic jam [ˈtræfɪk ˌdʒæm] Stau **III U2,** 22
January [ˈdʒænjuəri] Januar **I U5,** 70
Japanese [ˌdʒæpnˈiːz] japanisch; Japaner/Japanerin **VI T1,** 10; **VI T3,** 44
jazz [dʒæz] Jazz **II U3,** 45
jealous (of) [ˈdʒeləs] eifersüchtig, neidisch (auf) **II U3,** 45
jeans *(pl)* [dʒiːnz] Jeans **IV U2,** 23
jelly bean [ˈdʒeli ˌbiːn] *engl. Süßigkeit* **V T1,** 10
jellyfish, jellyfish *(pl)* [ˈdʒelifɪʃ] Qualle **V T1,** 12
jerk *(slang)* [dʒɜːk] Trottel **IV U2,** 26
jewel [ˈdʒuːəl] Juwel **III U2,** 22
jewellery [ˈdʒuːəlri] Schmuck **III U5,** 70
job [dʒɒb] Arbeitsstelle, Job **II U6,** 80
job interview [ˈdʒɒb ˌɪntəvjuː] Vorstellungsgespräch °**VI T1,** 17
on the job [ˌɒn ðə ˈdʒɒb] bei der Arbeit **III U5,** 70
to be out of a job [bi‿aʊt‿əv‿ə ˈdʒɒb] arbeitslos sein **VI T1,** 11
to **jog** [dʒɒg] joggen **II U4,** 52
jogger [dʒɒgə] Jogger/Joggerin **IV U1,** 9
to **join** [dʒɔɪn] beitreten, sich anschließen; verbinden **IV U4,** 58
joke [dʒəʊk] Witz **I U1,** 20
to take a joke [ˌteɪk‿ə ˈdʒəʊk] Spaß verstehen **VI T2,** 32
to **joke** [dʒəʊk] scherzen, Witze machen **I U6,** 82
journalist [ˈdʒɜːnlɪst] Journalist/Journalistin **VI T2,** 27
journey [ˈdʒɜːni] Reise, Fahrt **II U7,** 90
judge [dʒʌdʒ] Kampfrichter **II U5,** 70
juice [dʒuːs] Saft **IV U2,** 30
juicy [ˈdʒuːsi] saftig; schlüpfrig **VI T2,** 30
July [dʒʊˈlaɪ] Juli **I U5,** 70
long **jump** [ˈlɒŋ ˌdʒʌmp] Weitsprung **I U7,** 90
to **jump** [dʒʌmp] springen **II U2,** 30
to jump about [ˌdʒʌmp‿əˈbaʊt] herumspringen **III U4,** 58
to jump up [dʒʌmp‿ˈʌp] hochspringen, aufspringen **II U6,** 82
June [dʒuːn] Juni **I U5,** 70
junior [ˈdʒuːniə] Junior, der Jüngere **VI T4,** 60
just [dʒʌst] nur, gerade, einfach **I U2,** 30; direkt **VI T2,** 28

K

kangaroo [ˌkæŋgrˈuː] Känguru **V T1,** 9
*to **keep** [kiːp] (be)halten **II U4,** 55; aufbewahren **IV U3,** 44
to keep *(+ -ing)* [kiːp] etwas weiter/immer wieder tun **VI T2,** 29
Keep out! [kiːp‿ˈaʊt] Eintritt verboten! **I U2,** 26
to keep a diary [ˌkiːp‿ə ˈdaɪəri] ein Tagebuch/einen Terminkalender führen **VI T4,** 63
to keep away [kiːp‿əˈweɪ] sich fernhalten, wegbleiben **V T1,** 12
to keep up (with) [kiːp‿ˈʌp] mithalten (mit), Schritt halten (mit) **VI T3,** 43
keeper [ˈkiːpə] Wärter/Wärterin, Aufseher/Aufseherin; Inhaber/Inhaberin **V T2,** 32
key [kiː] Schlüssel **II U5,** 67
to **kick** [kɪk] treten **I U5,** 74
kickboard [ˈkɪkbɔːd] Kickboard, Roller **IV U1,** 9
kid [kɪd] Kind **I U3,** 44
to **kidnap** [ˈkɪdnæp] kidnappen, entführen **VI T2,** 29
kidnapping [ˈkɪdnæpɪŋ] Kidnapping, Entführung **VI T2,** 29
to **kill** [kɪl] töten; tot machen *(Volleyball)* **III U1,** 10
killer [ˈkɪlə] Mörder/Mörderin **V T3,** 42
kilo (kg) [ˈkɪləʊ] Kilo(gramm) **II U4,** 54
kilometre (km) [ˈkɪləʊˌmiːtə; kɪˈlɒmɪtə] Kilometer **III U2,** 27
kind [kaɪnd] Art, Sorte **III U2,** 30; freundlich, nett **VI T3,** 46
Kinetoscope [kɪˈnetəskəʊp] Kinetoskop °**IV U5,** 74
king [kɪŋ] König **III U2,** 22
kiss [kɪs] Kuss **IV U2,** 26
to **kiss** [kɪs] küssen **III U5,** 68
PE **kit** [ˌpiː‿ˈiː kɪt] Sportzeug **II U1,** 10
kitchen [ˈkɪtʃɪn] Küche **I LUA,** 24
knee [niː] Knie **II U3,** 41
knife, knives *(pl)* [naɪf; naɪvz] Messer **II U4,** 50
knight [naɪt] Ritter **II U2,** 22
knock [nɒk] Klopfen, Schlag **I U2,** 34
to **knock** [nɒk] klopfen; stoßen, schlagen **III U5,** 78
to knock out [nɒk‿ˈaʊt] k.o. schlagen, umhauen **III U1,** 17
*to **know** [nəʊ] wissen, kennen **I U4,** 58
koala [kəʊˈɑːlə] Koala **V T1,** 10

English – German

L

lab(oratory) [læb; lə'bɒrətri] Labor **II U2,** 23
label ['leɪbl] Etikett; Beschriftung; Siegel **V T4,** 62
to **label** ['leɪbl] beschriften, benennen, etikettieren **V T4,** 62
lad [læd] Junge **III U1,** 12
lady ['leɪdi] Dame, Frau **VI T2,** 28
lake [leɪk] See **III U3,** 42
lamb [læm] Lamm, Lammfleisch **II U4,** 49
lamp [læmp] Lampe, Leuchte **IV U3,** 44
land [lænd] Land **I LUB,** 38
to **land** [lænd] landen **III U3,** 39
landscape ['lændskeɪp] Landschaft **VI T4,** 59
lane [leɪn] Fahrspur, Gasse **IV U5,** 80
language ['læŋgwɪdʒ] Sprache **I U2,** 29
bad language [bæd 'læŋgwɪdʒ] Schimpfwörter **VI T2,** 32
lantern ['læntən] Laterne **I U7,** 90
laptop ['læptɒp] Laptop **I U2,** 34
large [lɑ:dʒ] groß, riesig **I U5,** 66
lassi ['lasɪ] Lassi *(Jogurtgetränk)* **II U4,** 49
to **last** [lɑ:st] dauern, anhalten **IV U4,** 64
last [lɑ:st] letzter/letzte/letztes **I U7,** 90
at last [ət 'lɑ:st] endlich, schließlich **V T3,** 42
last night [lɑ:st 'naɪt] gestern Abend/Nacht **II U3,** 37
late [leɪt] (zu) spät, verspätet **I U1,** 16
Latino [lə'ti:nəʊ] Latinomusik; Latino **IV U5,** 73
to **laugh** [lɑ:f] lachen **I U5,** 74
to laugh at ['lɑ:f‿ət] auslachen, sich lustig machen über **II U3,** 36
launch [lɔ:nʃ] Einführung, Start; Abschuss **V T4,** 61
to **launch** [lɔ:nʃ] einführen, herausbringen; starten, abschießen **V T4,** 61
law [lɔ:] Gesetz(gebung), Recht **V T1,** 10; **V T3,** 44
*to **lay** [leɪ] (ver)legen **VI T3,** 46
lazy ['leɪzi] faul, träge **VI T4,** 62
lead [led] Blei **IV U2,** 31
leader ['li:də] Führer/Führerin, Anführer/Anführerin **II U6,** 80
leaf, leaves *(pl)* [li:f; li:vz] Blatt **III U4,** 60
leaflet ['li:flət] Flugblatt, Prospekt **VI T2,** 30; **VI T3,** 40
league [li:g] Liga, Bund, Bündnis **VI T1,** 13
to **lean out** [li:n‿'aʊt] (sich) hinauslehnen **II U7,** 94
*to **learn** [lɜ:n] lernen **I U3,** 40; erfahren **III U1,** 8
leasing ['li:sɪŋ] Leasing(-) **VI T4,** 60
least [li:st] am wenigsten **IV U5,** 76
at least [ət 'li:st] wenigstens, mindestens **I U6,** 87
leather ['leðə] Leder **VI T1,** 14
*to **leave** [li:v] lassen, verlassen, abfahren **I U3,** 43; (weg)gehen **II U1,** 18
to leave sb alone [ˌli:v‿ə'ləʊn] jmdn. in Ruhe lassen **V T1,** 12
left [left] linker/linke/linkes; links **I U4,** 55
Go left. [gəʊ 'left] Biege nach links ab. **I LUC,** 52
on the left [ɒn ðə 'left] links **I U2,** 28
to turn left [tɜ:n 'left] links abbiegen **II U7,** 97
left [left] übrig **II U4,** 54
leg [leg] Bein **II U3,** 41
legal ['li:gl] legal, rechtlich, Rechts- **IV U3,** 48
lemonade [ˌlemə'neɪd] Limonade **I U5,** 68
*to **lend** [lend] leihen **II U7,** 90
leprechaun ['leprəkɔ:n] Gnom, Kobold °**II U7,** 90
less [les] weniger **IV U2,** 29
lesson ['lesn] Unterrichtsstunde **I U1,** 15
*to **let** [let] lassen **III U4,** 52
Let's .... [lets] Lasst uns .... **I U1,** 10
to let sb down [let 'daʊn] jmdn. im Stich lassen, jmdn. enttäuschen **V T2,** 30
letter ['letə] Buchstabe; Brief **I U1,** 15
capital letter [ˌkæpɪtl 'letə] Großbuchstabe °**II U3,** 37
cover letter ['kʌvə ˌletə] Begleitbrief, Begleitschreiben °**VI T4,** 61
lettuce ['letɪs] Kopfsalat **II U4,** 54; Geld *(Slang)* °**IV U5,** 80
leukaemia [lju:'ki:miə] Leukämie, Blutkrebs **VI T4,** 62
level ['levl] Ebene, Niveau **III U4,** 57
liberal ['lɪbrl] frei, liberal **VI T4,** 58
library ['laɪbri] Bibliothek, Bücherei **III U4,** 56
driving **licence** *(BE)* ['draɪvɪŋ ˌlaɪsnts] Führerschein **V T1,** 14
driver's **license** *(AE)* ['draɪvəz ˌlaɪsnts] Führerschein **IV U4,** 64
to **lie** [laɪ] lügen **IV U2,** 31
*to **lie** [laɪ] liegen **III U3,** 46
to lie down [laɪ 'daʊn] (sich) hinlegen, niederlegen **III U3,** 46
life, lives *(pl)* [laɪf; laɪvz] Leben **II U3,** 42
lifeguard ['laɪfgɑ:d] Rettungsschwimmer/Rettungsschwimmerin **III U3,** 40
lifestyle ['laɪfstaɪl] Lebensart **IV U5,** 80
to **lift up** [lɪft‿'ʌp] hochheben, hochziehen **VI T4,** 62
light [laɪt] Licht **II U7,** 94
light bulb ['laɪt bʌlb] Glühbirne **IV U3,** 44
light [laɪt] leicht; hell **V T4,** 61
lighting ['laɪtɪŋ] Beleuchtung **VI T3,** 47
to **like** [laɪk] mögen, gern haben **I U3,** 44
I'd like to [ˌaɪd 'laɪk tə] ich würde gern **II U2,** 22
would like [wʊd 'laɪk] hätte(n) gern, möchte(n) gern **II U4,** 52
like [laɪk] wie *(Vergleich)* **I U6,** 86
like the back of my hand ['bæk‿əv maɪ ˌhænd] wie meine Westentasche **III U2,** 30
likes *(pl)* [laɪks] Vorlieben °**V T2,** 33
limit ['lɪmɪt] Limit, Grenze, Beschränkung **V T3,** 47
limiting ['lɪmɪtɪŋ] limitierend, einschränkend **VI T4,** 58
limousine [ˌlɪmə'zi:n] Limousine **IV U5,** 80
line [laɪn] Zeile, Text, Linie **I U3,** 43
back line [ˌbæk 'laɪn] Grundlinie **III U1,** 10
ocean **liner** ['əʊʃn ˌlaɪnə] Ozeandampfer **III U3,** 39
link [lɪŋk] Verbindung, Bindeglied **III U5,** 70; Link; Verknüpfung **V T1,** 14
to **link** [lɪŋk] verbinden, verknüpfen **V T1,** 14
lion ['laɪən] Löwe **II U5,** 68
sea lion ['si: ˌlaɪən] Seelöwe **V T2,** 32
lip balm ['lɪp bɑ:m] Lippenpflegestift **II U6,** 82
liquid ['lɪkwɪd] Flüssigkeit; flüssig **VI T4,** 63
list [lɪst] Liste **I U5,** 68
to **listen** ['lɪsn] zuhören, anhören **I U1,** 11
litre (l) ['li:tə] Liter **VI T3,** 45
little ['lɪtl] klein **I U6,** 82; wenig **IV U3,** 48
to **live** [lɪv] wohnen, leben **I U3,** 45
live [laɪv] live **III U4,** 53
living ['lɪvɪŋ] Leben, Existenz °**VI T3,** 49
living room ['lɪvɪŋ rʊm] Wohnzimmer **I LUA,** 24
load [ləʊd] Ladung, Last, Belastung **VI T2,** 29
loan [ləʊn] Darlehen, Kredit **V T3,** 46
to **loan** [ləʊn] ausleihen, verleihen **V T3,** 46
local ['ləʊkl] lokal, örtlich **III U2,** 24; einheimisch, ortsansässig **V T4,** 64
to **lock** [lɒk] abschließen **III U3,** 47

locker [ˈlɒkə] Schließfach **II U1,** 10
loft [lɒft] Dachboden, Dachgeschoss **VI T3,** 46
logbook [ˈlɒgbʊk] Logbuch **V T4,** 66
logo [ˈləʊgəʊ] Logo; Firmenzeichen **V T4,** 62
lonely [ˈləʊnli] einsam **III U1,** 16
long [lɒŋ] lang **I U3,** 44
as long as [əz ˈlɒŋ‿əz] solange wie **I U7,** 94
in the long-run [ɪn ðə ˈlɒŋrʌn] langfristig **VI T3,** 44
long form [ˈlɒŋ fɔ:m] Langform °**I U1,** 16
long jump [ˈlɒŋ ˌdʒʌmp] Weitsprung **I U7,** 90
look [lʊk] Blick, Aussehen **II U1,** 10
to give … a dirty look [ˌgɪv‿ə dɜ:ti ˈlʊk] einen vernichtenden Blick zuwerfen **II U1,** 10
to have a look [ˌhæv‿ə ˈlʊk] (an)schauen, nachschauen **III U5,** 72
to **look** [lʊk] sehen, schauen, aussehen **I U1,** 12
to look after [lʊk‿ˈɑ:ftə] sich kümmern um, aufpassen auf **II U1,** 14
to look at [ˈlʊk‿ət] (sich) ansehen **I U6,** 82
to look for [ˈlʊk fə] suchen nach **I U6,** 81
to look round [lʊk ˈraʊnd] sich umsehen **II U1,** 18
to look up [lʊk‿ˈʌp] (hin)aufschauen; nachschlagen **II U2,** 30
lorry *(BE)* [ˈlɒri] Lastwagen **VI T3,** 47
*to **lose** [lu:z] verlieren **II U4,** 52
Lost and Found [ˈlɒst ˌənd ˈfaʊnd] Fundbüro **III U4,** 56
to be lost [bi: ˈlɒst] sich verirrt haben **III U3,** 40
to get lost [get ˈlɒst] verloren gehen, sich verirren **I U3,** 48
loss [lɒs] Verlust **VI T3,** 47
a **lot** [ə ˈlɒt] viel **II U1,** 15
a lot of [ə ˈlɒt‿əv] viel/viele, eine Menge **I U2,** 30
lots (of) [ˈlɒts‿əv] viel/viele **II U7,** 88
lots of love [ˌlɒts‿əv ˈlʌv] viele Grüße *(am Briefende)* **III U4,** 58
loud [laʊd] laut **II U7,** 91
love [lʌv] Liebe; Herzliche Grüße (*am Briefende*) **I U6,** 78
lots of love [ˌlɒts‿əv ˈlʌv] viele Grüße *(am Briefende)* **III U4,** 58
to fall in love [fɔ:l‿ɪn ˈlʌv] sich verlieben **VI T4,** 62
to **love** [lʌv] lieben, gern mögen **I U3,** 44

low [ləʊ] niedrig, tief **V T4,** 67
low-cut [ˈləʊkʌt] tief ausgeschnitten **IV U5,** 72
loyal [ˈlɔɪəl] loyal, treu **VI T2,** 28
luck [lʌk] Glück **I U4,** 63
bad luck [ˌbæd ˈlʌk] Pech **I U4,** 63
Good luck! [ˌgʊd ˈlʌk] Viel Glück! **I U4,** 63
lucky [ˈlʌki] glücklich **I U1,** 16
you're lucky [ˌjʊə ˈlʌki] du hast Glück **I U1,** 16
luckily [ˈlʌkɪli] glücklicherweise **IV U2,** 24
luggage [ˈlʌgɪdʒ] Gepäck **II U7,** 90
lunch [lʌntʃ] Mittagessen **I U1,** 18
lunchtime [ˈlʌntʃtaɪm] Mittag, Mittagszeit **I U1,** 19
lung [lʌŋ] Lunge **VI T3,** 44
lyrics [ˈlɪrɪks] Liedtext **IV U5,** 81

M

machine [məˈʃi:n] Maschine, Apparat **IV U5,** 80
mad [mæd] verrückt; wütend **II U1,** 18
magazine [mægəˈzi:n] Zeitschrift, Magazin **I U2,** 33
main [meɪn] Haupt- **II U4,** 49
Her **Majesty** [hə ˈmædʒəsti] Ihre Majestät °**III U5,** 78
majority [məˈdʒɒrəti] Mehrheit(en-) **VI T1,** 11
*to **make** [meɪk] machen, tun **I U1,** 11
to make friends (with) [ˌmeɪk ˈfrendz] Freundschaft schließen (mit) **IV U4,** 64
to make it [ˈmeɪk‿ɪt] es schaffen **III U4,** 58
to make sb do sth [meɪk] jmdn. veranlassen, etw. zu tun; jmdn. dafür gewinnen, etw. zu tun **V T3,** 45
to make sure [meɪk ˈʃʊə] sichergehen **II U6,** 82
to make up [meɪk‿ˈʌp] erfinden, sich ausdenken **I U4,** 62
make-up [ˈmeɪkʌp] Make-up, Schminke **I U7,** 90
male-dominated [ˈmeɪlˌdɒmɪneɪtɪd] männlich dominiert **VI T2,** 33
man, men *(pl)* [mæn; men] Mann **I U4,** 62
manager [ˈmænɪdʒə] Manager/Managerin **I U2,** 26
adverb of **manner** [ˌædvɜ:b‿əv ˈmænə] Adverb der Art und Weise °**II U7,** 90
mansion [ˈmænʃn] Villa °**IV U1,** 15
manta ray [ˈmænta ˌreɪ] Mantarochen **V T4,** 64

to **manufacture** [ˌmænjəˈfæktʃə] fertigen, herstellen **VI T4,** 60
manufacturer [ˌmænjəˈfæktʃərə] Hersteller, Produzent, Fabrikant **VI T4,** 60
manufacturing [ˌmænjəˈfæktʃrɪŋ] Herstellung, Fertigung **VI T4,** 60
many [ˈmeni] viele, etliche **I U5,** 68
how many [haʊ ˈmeni] wie viele **I U5,** 68
map [mæp] Stadtplan, Landkarte **I LUC,** 52
mind map [ˈmaɪnd mæp] Wörternetz (*eine Art Schaubild*) °**III U1,** 19
maple [ˈmeɪpl] Ahorn **IV U1,** 12
march [mɑ:tʃ] Marsch **V T3,** 44
to **march** [mɑ:tʃ] marschieren **V T3,** 44
March [mɑ:tʃ] März **I U5,** 70
mark [mɑ:k] Fleck **I U2,** 30; Note *(in der Schule)* **II U3,** 44; Abdruck, Markierung **VI T3,** 42
to **mark** [mɑ:k] markieren **IV U1,** 14
market [ˈmɑ:kɪt] Markt **II U2,** 22
marketing [ˈmɑ:kɪtɪŋ] Marketing, Vermarktung, Vertrieb **VI T4,** 60
marriage [ˈmærɪdʒ] Heirat; Ehe **VI T4,** 58
married to [ˈmærid tə] verheiratet mit **I U2,** 28
to **marry** [ˈmæri] heiraten **III U2,** 32
masked [mɑ:skt] maskiert **VI T2,** 29
mass [mæs] Masse **VI T3,** 44
match [mætʃ] Spiel, Wettkampf **II U2,** 24
to **match** [mætʃ] passen zu; zuordnen, zusammenfügen **IV U2,** 30
to match up [ˈmætʃ‿ʌp] zusammenfügen °**II U4,** 52
mate [meɪt] Kamerad/Kameradin, Kumpel **III U4,** 60
material [məˈtɪəriəl] Material; Stoff **IV U2,** 24
Maths [mæθs] Mathematik **II U1,** 10
matter [ˈmætə] Angelegenheit, Frage **IV U5,** 76; Materie **VI T4,** 63
no matter [nəʊ ˈmætə] egal **IV U5,** 80
What's the matter? [ˌwɒts ðə ˈmætə] Was ist los? **III U5,** 76
to **matter** [ˈmætə] von Bedeutung sein, ausmachen **IV U5,** 76
***may** [meɪ] kann/könnte(n) vielleicht **II U4,** 55; dürfen **IV U2,** 28
May [meɪ] Mai **I U5,** 70
maybe [ˈmeɪbi] vielleicht **I U7,** 96
me [mi:] mich, mir **I LUB,** 38
meal [mi:l] Mahlzeit **II U4,** 52
*to **mean** [mi:n] bedeuten, meinen **I U4,** 55
mean [mi:n] gemein **IV U2,** 31
meaning [ˈmi:nɪŋ] Bedeutung °**I U7,** 98

measurement ['meʒəmənt] Maßeinheit, Maß °**III U3,** 43
meat [mi:t] Fleisch **III U3,** 44
mechanic [mə'kænɪk] Mechaniker/Mechanikerin **IV U4,** 64
media *(pl)* ['mi:diə] Medien **V T3,** 42
mediation [ˌmi:di'eɪʃn] Sprachmittlung °**III U1,** 13
medium ['mi:diəm] mittel **I U5,** 66
*to **meet** [mi:t] (sich) treffen **I U3,** 45
meeting ['mi:tɪŋ] Treffen, Besprechung **II U1,** 12
to **melt** [melt] schmelzen **VI T4,** 63
member ['membə] Mitglied **V T2,** 28
memory ['memri] Erinnerung, Gedächtnis; Memory *(Spiel)* °**VI T1,** 13
to **mention** ['menʃn] erwähnen °**VI T1,** 8
menu ['menju:] Speisekarte, Menü **II U1,** 14
Meow! [mi:'aʊ] Miau! °**I U2,** 35
mess [mes] Durcheinander, Unordnung **III U2,** 31
to **mess around** [ˌmes‿ə'raʊnd] herumalbern **V T2,** 26
message ['mesɪdʒ] Nachricht **II U3,** 38
text message ['tekst ˌmesɪdʒ] SMS **I U6,** 80
messy ['mesi] unordentlich, chaotisch, durcheinander **V T4,** 67
metal ['metl] Metal *(Musikrichtung)*; Metall **IV U5,** 76
heavy metal [ˌhevi 'metl] Heavy Metal **IV U5,** 76
metre ['mi:tə] Meter **III U2,** 27; Zähler **VI T3,** 46
Mexican ['meksɪkən] mexikanisch; Mexikaner/Mexikanerin **IV U4,** 64
mice *(pl)* [maɪs] Mäuse **I U3,** 45
microphone ['maɪkrəfəʊn] Mikrofon **II U5,** 71
microwave ['maɪkrəʊweɪv] Mikrowelle **IV U3,** 44
middle ['mɪdl] Mitte; Mittel- **IV U4,** 65
Middle Ages [ˌmɪdl‿'eɪdʒɪz] Mittelalter **VI T2,** 28
middle school *(AE)* ['mɪdl ˌsku:l] Mittelschule *(weiterführende Schule in den USA, Mittelstufe)* **IV U2,** 28
midnight ['mɪdnaɪt] Mitternacht **II U6,** 78
***might** [maɪt] könnte/könnten **IV U4,** 64
mile [maɪl] Meile *(brit. Längenmaß)* **II U6,** 74
for miles [fə‿'maɪlz] meilenweit **IV U4,** 65
milestone ['maɪlstəʊn] Meilenstein **V T3,** 44
milk [mɪlk] Milch **I U5,** 68
milkman, milkmen *(pl)* ['mɪlkmən; 'mɪlkmen] Milchmann **III U2,** 30
milkshake ['mɪlkʃeɪk] Milchshake **IV U1,** 12
milky ['mɪlki] milchig **V T4,** 63
million ['mɪlɪən] Million **II U2,** 23
to **mime** [maɪm] pantomimisch darstellen °**I U6,** 81
miming game ['maɪmɪŋ geɪm] Pantomime °**I U6,** 81
mind [maɪnd] Geist, Verstand **III U5,** 71
He had something on his mind. [maɪnd] Ihn beschäftigte etwas. **III U5,** 71
mind map ['maɪnd mæp] Wörternetz *(eine Art Schaubild)* °**III U1,** 19
Would you **mind ... ?** [ˌwʊd jə 'maɪnd] Hätten Sie/Hättest du etwas dagegen ... ? **III U4,** 56
mineral ['mɪnərəl] Mineral- **II U4,** 49
mini ['mɪni] Mini- **VI T3,** 46; °**VI T4,** 61; °**VI T4,** 65
minister ['mɪnɪstə] Minister/Ministerin **VI T1,** 9; **VI T2,** 30
Prime Minister (PM) [ˌpraɪm 'mɪnɪstə] Premierminister/in **VI T1,** 9; **VI T2,** 30
minute ['mɪnɪt] Minute **I U4,** 64
to **miss** [mɪs] vermissen, fehlen; verpassen **II U6,** 76; verfehlen **III U4,** 56
to miss a turn [mɪs ə 'tɜ:n] einmal aussetzen °**II U6,** 79
Miss [mɪs] Frau *(Anrede)* **I U7,** 94
missing ['mɪsɪŋ] fehlend °**I U4,** 64
to be missing [bi: 'mɪsɪŋ] fehlen **III U1,** 14
mission ['mɪʃn] Mission, Auftrag, Aufgabe **V T4,** 62
mistake [mɪ'steɪk] Fehler **IV U2,** 26
mister ['mɪstə] Sie *(Anrede)* **IV U1,** 17
to **mix** [mɪks] mixen, mischen **V T3,** 44
mixture ['mɪkstʃə] Mischung, Gemisch, Mixtur **VI T1,** 10
to **moan** [məʊn] (sich) (be)klagen, stöhnen **III U1,** 16
mobile ['məʊbaɪl] Handy, Mobiltelefon **I U1,** 11
mobile ['məʊbaɪl] mobil, beweglich **VI T1,** 14
model ['mɒdl] Model; Modell **III U2,** 25
modern ['mɒdn] modern **IV U3,** 41
moment ['məʊmənt] Moment, Augenblick **I U7,** 90
at the moment [ət ðə 'məʊmənt] im Augenblick, momentan **I U7,** 90
monarch ['mɒnək] Monarch/Monarchin, Herrscher/Herrscherin °**VI T2,** 31
monarchy ['mɒnəkɪ] Monarchie, Königreich **VI T2,** 30
Monday ['mʌndeɪ] Montag **I LUB,** 39
on Mondays [ɒn 'mʌndeɪz] montags **I LUB,** 39
money ['mʌni] Geld **I U5,** 67
pocket money ['pɒkɪt ˌmʌni] Taschengeld **II U2,** 22
to **monitor** ['mɒnɪtə] überwachen **IV U3,** 41
monster ['mɒnstə] Monster **IV U1,** 12
month [mʌnθ] Monat **I U5,** 70
mood [mu:d] Stimmung, Laune **V T3,** 46
moon [mu:n] Mond **II U7,** 94
moor [mɔ:] Hochmoor **II U6,** 74
more [mɔ:] mehr **I U2,** 29
morning ['mɔ:nɪŋ] Morgen, Vormittag **I U1,** 16
Good morning! ['gʊd 'mɔ:nɪŋ] Guten Morgen! **I U1,** 16
in the morning [ˌɪn ðə 'mɔ:nɪŋ] morgens, am Morgen, vormittags **I U3,** 47
(the) next morning [ˌnekst 'mɔ:nɪŋ] am nächsten Morgen **II U1,** 18
most [məʊst] das meiste, die meisten **I U3,** 44
mostly ['məʊstli] überwiegend, größtenteils, hauptsächlich **VI T1,** 12; **VI T4,** 62
motel [məʊ'tel] Motel **IV U3,** 44
moth [mɒθ] Motte, Falter **VI T4,** 64
mother ['mʌðə] Mutter **III U3,** 46
mother tongue ['mʌðə ˌtʌŋ] Muttersprache **VI T1,** 12
motion ['məʊʃn] Bewegung **IV U5,** 74
motor ['məʊtə] Motor **IV U5,** 74
motorbike ['məʊtəbaɪk] Motorrad **IV U4,** 57
mountain ['maʊntɪn] Berg **IV U3,** 48
mouse, mice *(pl)* [maʊs; maɪs] Maus **I U1,** 10
mouth [maʊθ] Mund **II U3,** 41
move [mu:v] Schritt, Bewegung **IV U2,** 27
to **move** [mu:v] (sich) bewegen; umziehen **II U6,** 78
movement ['mu:vmənt] Bewegung **V T3,** 44
Civil Rights Movement (CRM) [ˌsɪvl 'raɪts ˌmu:vmənt] Bürgerrechtsbewegung **V T3,** 44
movie *(AE)* ['mu:vi] Film **IV U2,** 26
silent movie [ˌsaɪlənt 'mu:vi] Stummfilm **IV U5,** 74
movies *(AE)* ['mu:viz] Kino **IV U2,** 26
MP3 [empi:'θri:] MP3 **II U5,** 62
MP3 player [empi:'θri: ˌpleɪə] MP3-Player **II U5,** 62

Mr ['mɪstə] Herr *(Anrede)* **I U1,** 12
Mrs ['mɪsɪz] Frau *(Anrede)* **I U1,** 12
much [mʌtʃ] viel **I U5,** 66
How much are ... ? [ˌhaʊ 'mʌtʃ‿ɑ:] Wie viel kosten ... ? **I U5,** 66
How much is ... ? [ˌhaʊ 'mʌtʃ‿ɪz] Wie viel kostet ... ? **I U5,** 66
muddle ['mʌdl] Durcheinander °**III U3,** 42
mule [mju:l] Maultier **IV U4,** 58
multinational [ˌmʌlti'næʃnl] multinational **V T4,** 60
mum [mʌm] Mama, Mutti **I LUA,** 25
mural ['mjʊərl] Graffiti, Wandmalerei **V T2,** 29
murder ['mɜ:də] Mord, Ermordung **V T3,** 42
museum [mju:'zi:əm] Museum **I LUC,** 52
music ['mju:zɪk] Musik **I U2,** 34
musical ['mju:zɪkl] Musical **III U5,** 68
musician [mju:'zɪʃn] Musiker/Musikerin **IV U5,** 76
***must** [mʌst] müssen **I U7,** 94
my [maɪ] mein/meine **I U1,** 10
My God! [maɪ 'gɒd] Mein Gott! **II U6,** 82
My name is .... [maɪ 'neɪm‿ɪz] Ich heiße .... **I U1,** 10
myself [maɪ'self] ich/mich (selbst) **III U5,** 78
mystery ['mɪstəri] Geheimnis, Rätsel **III U5,** 76
myth [mɪθ] Mythos **III U5,** 69

N

name [neɪm] Name **I U1,** 10
My name is .... [maɪ 'neɪm‿ɪz] Ich heiße .... **I U1,** 10
What's your name? [ˌwɒts jə 'neɪm] Wie heißt du? **I U1,** 11
to **name** [neɪm] (be)nennen **IV U1,** 10
nasty ['nɑ:sti] garstig, gemein; scheußlich **VI T2,** 32
nation ['neɪʃn] Nation **VI T2,** 30
national ['næʃnl] national **II U6,** 82; National-, landesweit **III U1,** 10
national guard [ˌnæʃnl 'gɑ:d] Nationalgarde °**V T3,** 44
national park [ˌnæʃnl 'pɑ:k] Nationalpark **IV U4,** 56
native ['neɪtɪv] eingeboren, einheimisch, gebürtig **IV U1,** 10
Native American [ˌneɪtɪv‿ə'merɪkən] Ureinwohner/Ureinwohnerin Amerikas, Indianer/Indianerin **IV U1,** 10

natural ['nætʃrl] natürlich; Natur- **VI T3,** 47
near [nɪə] in der Nähe von, nahe **I LUC,** 53
nearly ['nɪəli] fast, annähernd **III U1,** 16
need [ni:d] Bedürfnis, Bedarf; Erfordernis **V T2,** 28
special needs [ˌspeʃl 'ni:dz] besondere Bedürfnisse **VI T4,** 59
to **need** [ni:d] brauchen, benötigen, müssen **II U1,** 21
negative ['negətɪv] Verneinung °**III U5,** 71; negativ, verneint °**IV U5,** 83
neighborhood *(AE)* ['neɪbəhʊd] Viertel; Nachbarschaft **IV U1,** 9
neighbour ['neɪbə] Nachbar/Nachbarin **II U7,** 90
neon ['ni:ɒn] neonfarben **IV U1,** 9
nephew ['nefju:] Neffe **III U5,** 76
nervous ['nɜ:vəs] nervös, aufgeregt **II U5,** 71
net [net] Netz **III U1,** 10
neutral ['nju:trl] neutral **VI T2,** 30
never ['nevə] niemals **I U3,** 44
new [nju:] neu **I U1,** 10
news *(sg.)* [nju:z] Nachricht(en), Neuigkeit(en) **III U4,** 58
breaking news [ˌbreɪkɪŋ 'nju:z] neueste Nachrichten **IV U2,** 22
newsagent ['nju:sˌeɪdʒənt] Zeitschriftenhändler/ Zeitschriftenhändlerin **I LUC,** 52
newspaper ['nju:sˌpeɪpə] Zeitung **III U2,** 24
next [nekst] nächster/nächste/nächstes **I U5,** 69; als Nächstes °**II U1,** 19
next door [ˌnekst 'dɔ:] nebenan **III U1,** 16
(the) next morning [ˌnekst 'mɔ:nɪŋ] am nächsten Morgen **II U1,** 18
next to ['nekst tə] neben **I U2,** 28
nice [naɪs] nett **I U1,** 12; schön **II U4,** 54
nickel ['nɪkl] Nickel *(Währung)* **IV U1,** 13
nickname ['nɪkneɪm] Spitzname **IV U5,** 73
night [naɪt] Nacht, Abend **I U3,** 44
at night [ət 'naɪt] nachts **II U3,** 47
last night [lɑ:st 'naɪt] gestern Abend/ Nacht **II U3,** 37
night nurse ['naɪt nɜ:s] Nachtschwester **I U3,** 47
nightmare ['naɪtmeə] Albtraum **V T4,** 61
no [nəʊ] nein, nicht; kein/keine **I U1,** 12
no ... at all [ˌnəʊ ... ət‿'ɔ:l] überhaupt kein/keine **V T4,** 65
no idea [ˌnəʊ‿aɪ'dɪə] keine Ahnung **III U3,** 46
no one ['nəʊwʌn] niemand **II U2,** 30

no wonder [nəʊ 'wʌndə] kein Wunder, dass ... **VI T4,** 62
No. ['nʌmbə] Nummer **V T1,** 10
nobody ['nəʊbədi] niemand **V T3,** 44
noise [nɔɪz] Geräusch, Lärm **I U2,** 35
none [nʌn] keiner/keine **II U7,** 88
non-official [ˌnɒnə'fɪʃl] inoffiziell **VI T1,** 11
non-stop [ˌnɒn'stɒp] non-stop, durchgehend, ohne Unterbrechung **V T3,** 43
non-violent [ˌnɒn'vaɪəlnt] gewaltfrei **V T3,** 44
normal ['nɔ:ml] normal **I U3,** 44
north [nɔ:θ] Norden **I U4,** 55
nose [nəʊz] Nase **II U3,** 41
not [nɒt] nicht **I U1,** 16
(not) any more [nɒt ˌeni 'mɔ:] (nicht) mehr **VI T4,** 62
not ... either [ˌnɒt ... 'aɪðə] auch nicht **IV U3,** 48
not even [nɒt‿'i:vn] nicht einmal **III U4,** 54
not ... yet [jet] noch nicht **II U5,** 66
note [nəʊt] Notiz, Anmerkung **II U1,** 11
sick note ['sɪk ˌnəʊt] Krankmeldung **II U2,** 28
to take notes [teɪk 'nəʊts] sich Notizen machen °**II U4,** 55
nothing ['nʌθɪŋ] nichts **II U4,** 50
notice ['nəʊtɪs] Anschlag, Notiz **III U4,** 57
notice board ['nəʊtɪs bɔ:d] schwarzes Brett **III U4,** 57
to **notice** ['nəʊtɪs] bemerken **III U3,** 46
noun [naʊn] Nomen °**III U1,** 19
novel ['nɒvl] Roman **VI T4,** 62
November [nəʊ'vembə] November **I U5,** 70
now [naʊ] jetzt, nun **I U1,** 20
right now [ˌraɪt 'naʊ] jetzt gleich, in diesem Augenblick **I U7,** 92
nowhere ['nəʊweə] nirgendwo(hin) **IV U4,** 65
number ['nʌmbə] Nummer, Zahl **I U1,** 11
phone number ['fəʊn ˌnʌmbə] Telefonnummer **I U1,** 11
nurse [nɜ:s] Krankenschwester, Krankenpfleger **I U3,** 47
night nurse ['naɪt nɜ:s] Nachtschwester **I U3,** 47
nursery school ['nɜ:sri ˌsku:l] Kindergarten **VI T4,** 58
nutrition [nju:'trɪʃn] Ernährung(slehre) **V T2,** 32
*to be **nuts about** [bi: ˌnʌts‿ə'baʊt] verrückt nach ... sein **II U1,** 18
nutty ['nʌti] nussig; schmackhaft **V T4,** 63

English – German

O

object [ˈɒbdʒɪkt] Objekt, Gegenstand °**IV U3,** 44
observatory [əbˈzɜːvətri] Observatorium, Sternwarte **I U5,** 73
ocean [ˈəʊʃn] Ozean **III U3,** 39
ocean liner [ˈəʊʃn ˌlaɪnə] Ozeandampfer **III U3,** 39
October [ɒkˈtəʊbə] Oktober **I U5,** 70
octopus [ˈɒktəpəs] Oktopus, Krake **V T1,** 12
Blue Ring Octopus [ˌbluː rɪŋ ˈɒktəpəs] blaugeringelter Krake °**V T1,** 12
odd one out [ɒd wʌn‿ˈaʊt] das nicht dazu passende (Wort) **II U5,** 72
odour [ˈəʊdə] Geruch, Duft **V T2,** 28
of [ɒv; əv] von **I U2,** 26
of course [əv ˈkɔːs] natürlich, selbstverständlich **I U1,** 19
off [ɒf] herunter, ab, weg von **II U3,** 36
to get off [get‿ˈɒf] aussteigen aus **I U4,** 59
to have a day off [ˌhæv‿ə ˈdeɪ‿ɒf] einen Tag frei haben **V T3,** 46
to send off [send‿ˈɒf] vom Platz verweisen **III U1,** 12
to switch off [ˌswɪtʃ‿ˈɒf] ausschalten **IV U1,** 17
to take off [ˌteɪk‿ˈɒf] abheben, starten, abfliegen **IV U1,** 16
offer [ˈɒfə] Angebot **IV U5,** 77
to **offer** [ˈɒfə] anbieten **V T4,** 60
office [ˈɒfɪs] Büro **II U2,** 31
post office [ˈpəʊst‿ɒfɪs] Postamt **III U2,** 26
officer [ˈɒfɪsə] Beamter/Beamtin **III U3,** 39
chief executive officer (CEO) [ˌtʃiːf‿ɪgˌzekjətɪv‿ˈɒfɪsə; ˌsiː iːˈəʊ] Generaldirektor/Generaldirektorin; Geschäftsführer/Geschäftsführerin **VI T4,** 60
official [əˈfɪʃl] Beamter/Beamtin **IV U1,** 10; offiziell **VI T1,** 8; **VI T2,** 30; **VI T4,** 63
offside [ˌɒfˈsaɪd] im Abseits **VI T1,** 12
often [ˈɒfn] oft **I U3,** 44
oh [əʊ] oh °**I U1,** 12
Oh dear! [əʊ ˈdɪə] Oje! **III U5,** 73
oil [ɔɪl] Öl **V T4,** 58
Oink-oink! [ɔɪŋk‿ɔɪŋk] Grunz! °**I U6,** 82
OK [əʊˈkeɪ] o.k. **I U1,** 12
is OK with us [ɪz‿əʊˈkeɪ wɪð‿ʌs] ist uns recht **I U6,** 78
We're OK. [ˌwɪər‿əʊˈkeɪ] Es geht uns gut. **I U6,** 83
old [əʊld] alt **I U1,** 11
How old are you? [haʊ‿ˈəʊld‿ɑː juː] Wie alt bist du? **I U1,** 11
on [ɒn] auf, an **I U1,** 14
to … on [ɒn] weiter- **IV U3,** 48
on foot [ɒn ˈfʊt] zu Fuß **I U4,** 57
on Mondays [ɒn ˈmʌndeɪz] montags **I LUB,** 39
on one's own [ɒn wʌnz‿ˈəʊn] (ganz) allein **V T3,** 40
on record [ɒn ˈrekɔːd] verzeichnet, dokumentiert **III U3,** 40
on the air [ˌɒn ði‿ˈeə] auf Sendung **II U4,** 55
on the bus [ˌɒn ðə ˈbʌs] im Bus **II U1,** 18
on the job [ˌɒn ðə ˈdʒɒb] bei der Arbeit **III U5,** 70
on the left [ɒn ðə ˈleft] links **I U2,** 28
on the right [ɒn ðə ˈraɪt] rechts **I U2,** 28
on time [ɒn ˈtaɪm] pünktlich **IV U3,** 46
to be on [biː‿ˈɒn] an der Reihe sein; im Gange sein, laufen **II U5,** 70; an sein, brennen *(Licht)* **II U7,** 94
once [wʌnts] einmal, einst **II U3,** 36
at once [ət ˈwʌnts] sofort, plötzlich **II U7,** 94
one day [wʌn ˈdeɪ] eines Tages **II U3,** 36
one(s) [wʌn(z)] *(Platzhalter für ein Nomen)* **III U2,** 25
online [ˌɒnˈlaɪn] online, im Internet **V T1,** 14
only [ˈəʊnli] nur, bloß, erst **I U2,** 26; einziger/einzige/einziges **III U5,** 76
only child [ˈəʊnli ˌtʃaɪld] Einzelkind **I U2,** 26
onto [ˈɒntuː; ˈɒntə] (auf …) hinauf, auf **II U1,** 19
Oops! [uːps] Hoppla! Huch! °**I U1,** 20
to **open** [ˈəʊpn] öffnen, aufmachen **I U1,** 19; sich öffnen, aufgehen **III U5,** 74 ; eröffnen **VI T2,** 30
open [ˈəʊpn] offen, geöffnet **II U2,** 23
opera [ˈɒprə] Oper **V T1,** 9
to **operate** [ˈɒpəreɪt] bedienen; operieren **IV U3,** 41
opinion [əˈpɪnjən] Meinung **V T3,** 42
opportunity [ˌɒpəˈtjuːnəti] Gelegenheit; Möglichkeit **V T4,** 58
opposite [ˈɒpəzɪt] gegenüber °**II U4,** 49; Gegenteil °**IV U1,** 18; entgegengesetzt, gegenüberliegend **VI T2,** 32
oppression [əˈpreʃn] Unterdrückung **IV U1,** 10
optimism [ˈɒptɪmɪzm] Optimismus **VI T4,** 63
optimistic [ˌɒptɪˈmɪstɪk] optimistisch **VI T4,** 65
option [ˈɒpʃn] Auswahlmöglichkeit, Option **V T1,** 10; **V T2,** 28; **V T3,** 42; **V T4,** 60
or [ɔː] oder **I U1,** 11
orange [ˈɒrɪndʒ] Orange; orange **II U4,** 54
order [ˈɔːdə] Reihenfolge, Ordnung **IV U3,** 46; Befehl, Anweisung **V T3,** 47
to **order** [ˈɔːdə] bestellen **II U4,** 49
organic [ɔːˈgænɪk] biologisch angebaut, organisch **VI T3,** 40
organisation [ˌɔːgnaɪˈzeɪʃn] Organisation, Unternehmen **V T4,** 62
to **organize** [ˈɔːgənaɪz] organisieren **I U7,** 90
organizer [ˈɔːgənaɪzə] Organisator/Organisatorin, Veranstalter/Veranstalterin **III U4,** 53
origin [ˈɒrɪdʒɪn] Ursprung, Herkunft, Quelle **VI T3,** 44
other [ˈʌðə] anderer/andere/anderes **I U7,** 91
each other [ˌiːtʃ‿ˈʌðə] sich gegenseitig **II U1,** 19
our [ˈaʊə] unser/unsere **I U2,** 26
ourselves [aʊəˈselvz] wir/uns (selbst) **VI T3,** 42
out [aʊt] heraus, hinaus, draußen, außerhalb **I U3,** 42
Keep out! [kiːp‿ˈaʊt] Eintritt verboten! **I U2,** 26
out and about [ˈaʊt‿nd‿əˈbaʊt] unterwegs °**I U4,** 54
out of [ˈaʊt‿əv] aus … heraus **I U3,** 49
to get out [get‿ˈaʊt] aussteigen **I U6,** 86
to knock out [nɒk‿ˈaʊt] k.o. schlagen, umhauen **III U1,** 17
to sort out [sɔːt‿ˈaʊt] klären, regeln *(ein Problem)* **I U2,** 30
to take out [teɪk‿ˈaʊt] herausnehmen **I U3,** 42
to work out [ˌwɜːk‿ˈaʊt] herausfinden; ausarbeiten °**III U3,** 43
the **Outback** [ˈaʊtbæk] das Outback *(australisches Hinterland)* **V T1,** 9
outdated [ˌaʊtˈdeɪtɪd] altmodisch, überholt **VI T2,** 30
outer space [ˌaʊtə ˈspeɪs] Weltraum, Weltall **VI T4,** 59
outgoing [ˈaʊtgəʊɪŋ] aufgeschlossen, kontaktfreudig **V T3,** 47
outrageous [aʊtˈreɪdʒəs] gewagt; empörend **IV U5,** 72
outside [aʊtˈsaɪd] außerhalb, draußen, nach draußen **I U2,** 30
oven [ˈʌvn] Backofen **I U3,** 42

over ['əʊvə] über **I U2,** 26; vorbei, vorüber **II U5,** 70
all over [ˌɔ:l‿'əʊvə] überall **IV U1,** 10
over easy [ˌəʊvər‿'i:zi] beidseitig gebraten *(Ei)* **IV U4,** 61
over there [ˌəʊvə 'ðeə] da drüben **I U5,** 66
to come over [kʌm‿'əʊvə] herüberkommen **I U2,** 27
to run over [rʌn‿'əʊvə] hinüberrennen **IV U1,** 17
*to **overdo** [ˌəʊvə'du:] übertreiben **IV U2,** 26
*to **overeat** [ˌəʊvr'i:t] zu viel essen, sich überfressen **VI T3,** 44
overheard [ˌəʊvə'hɜ:d] zufällig mitgehört °**III U1,** 14
to **owe** [əʊ] verdanken, schulden **V T3,** 43
barn **owl** ['bɑ:n‿əʊl] Schleiereule **II U7,** 94
to **own** [əʊn] besitzen **IV U4,** 58
own [əʊn] eigener/eigene/eigenes **II U6,** 76
on one's own [ɒn wʌnz‿'əʊn] (ganz) allein **V T3,** 40
owner ['əʊnə] Besitzer/Besitzerin **II U5,** 71

P

pacemaker ['peɪsˌmeɪkə] Herzschrittmacher **IV U3,** 41
to **pack** [pæk] packen **I U6,** 80
packaging ['pækɪdʒɪŋ] Verpackung, Packmaterial **VI T3,** 42
packet ['pækɪt] Päckchen, Paket **I U5,** 68
page [peɪdʒ] Seite **I U1,** 19
pain [peɪn] Schmerz **IV U3,** 48
paint [peɪnt] Farbe **II U3,** 40
to **paint** [peɪnt] (an)malen, (an)streichen **I U7,** 90
painter ['peɪntə] Maler/Malerin **VI T3,** 47
pair [peə] Paar °**I U1,** 22
palace ['pælɪs] Palast **III U2,** 22
Palestinian [pælə'stɪniən] palästinensisch; Palästinenser/ Palästinenserin **VI T2,** 29
pancake ['pænkeɪk] Pfannkuchen **IV U1,** 12
panel ['pænl] Tafel, Platte; Element **V T4,** 59; Expertenrunde, Gremium °**VI T2,** 33; °**VI T4,** 61
solar panel [ˌsəʊlə 'pænl] Sonnenkollektor **V T4,** 59
to **panic** ['pænɪk] sich aufregen, in Panik geraten **II U5,** 70

panther ['pæntθə] Panter **II U2,** 25
paper ['peɪpə] Papier; Zeitung; Dokument **IV U1,** 14
paper work ['peɪpə ˌwɜ:k] Papierkram **VI T1,** 15
parachuting ['pærəˌʃu:tɪŋ] Fallschirmspringen **V T3,** 40
parade [pə'reɪd] Parade, Umzug **IV U1,** 14
paradise ['pærəˌdaɪs] Paradies **III U3,** 40
paragliding ['pærəˌglaɪdɪŋ] Paragliding, Gleitschirmfliegen **V T3,** 40
parents *(pl)* ['peərənts] Eltern **I U2,** 26
park [pɑ:k] Park **I U3,** 40
national park [ˌnæʃnl 'pɑ:k] Nationalpark **IV U4,** 56
(park) ranger [ˌpɑ:k 'reɪndʒə] Parkaufseher/Parkaufseherin, Ranger **IV U4,** 58
theme park ['θi:m ˌpɑ:k] Freizeitpark **IV U2,** 22
parliament ['pɑ:ləmənt] Parlament **VI T2,** 30
part [pɑ:t] Teil **II U3,** 47; Rolle **II U5,** 70
to take part in [teɪk 'pɑ:t‿ɪn] teilnehmen an **III U4,** 53
particle ['pɑ:tɪkl] Teilchen, Partikel **VI T4,** 63
partner ['pɑ:tnə] Partner/Partnerin **I U1,** 15
part-time (P/T) [ˌpɑ:t'taɪm] Teilzeit- **V T1,** 14; **V T2,** 32
party ['pɑ:ti] Party, Feier **I U5,** 68; Partei, Gruppe **VI T2,** 30
to have a party [ˌhæv‿ə 'pɑ:ti] eine Party feiern **I U5,** 68
to **pass** [pɑ:s] weitergeben, herüberreichen **II U1,** 18; bestehen **IV U2,** 28; vorübergehen **IV U3,** 48; vorbeifahren **VI T2,** 30; verabschieden *(Gesetz)* **VI T2,** 30
passenger ['pæsndʒə] Passagier/ Passagierin, Beifahrer/Beifahrerin **III U3,** 39
passport ['pɑ:spɔ:t] (Reise-)Pass **III U3,** 44
passports *(pl)* ['pɑ:spɔ:ts] Passkontrolle **III U3,** 44
past [pɑ:st] vorbei, vorüber **I U7,** 97; nach *(Uhrzeit)* **II U1,** 12; Vergangenheit **II U1,** 13
half past (two) ['hɑ:f pɑ:st] halb (drei) **I U3,** 40
pastrami [pəs'trɑ:mi] Pastrami **IV U1,** 12
patch [pætʃ] Beet; Fleck, Stelle; Flicken; Augenklappe **VI T4,** 64
path [pɑ:θ] Pfad, Weg **II U4,** 56

pathetic [pə'θetɪk] Mitleid erregend, erbärmlich **VI T4,** 63
patient ['peɪʃnt] Patient/Patientin **III U5,** 70
patron ['peɪtrn] Schutzherr/Schutzherrin, Patron/Patronin **VI T2,** 30
pause [pɔ:z] Pause °**III U5,** 74
pay [peɪ] Lohn, Gehalt, Bezahlung **V T1,** 14; **V T3,** 44; **V T4,** 62
*to **pay (for)** [peɪ] (be)zahlen **IV U2,** 30
PC [ˌpi:'si:] PC **II U5,** 63; Polizeibeamter/ Polizeibeamtin °**III U5,** 71
pea [pi:] Erbse **II U4,** 54
peace [pi:s] Friede **II U7,** 88
peaceful ['pi:sfl] friedlich **V T3,** 45
pear [peə] Birne **II U4,** 54
peer [pɪə] Gleichaltriger/Gleichaltrige **V T2,** 28
pen [pen] Füller **I U1,** 14
pence *(pl)* [pents] Pence *(Währung)* **I U5,** 67
pencil ['pensl] Bleistift **I U1,** 14
pencil case ['pensl ˌkeɪs] Federmäppchen **I U1,** 14
penknife, penknives *(pl)* ['pennaɪf; 'pennaɪvz] Taschenmesser **I U6,** 84
people ['pi:pl] Leute, Menschen **I U2,** 29
per [pɜ:] pro **III U2,** 27
per cent (%) [pə 'sent] Prozent **IV U1,** 10
perfect ['pɜ:fɪkt] perfekt, vollkommen **V T2,** 32
to **perform** [pə'fɔ:m] aufführen, auftreten **III U4,** 53
performance [pə'fɔ:məns] Aufführung, Vorstellung **III U4,** 53
perhaps [pə'hæps] vielleicht **VI T1,** 10; **VI T4,** 62
period *(AE)* ['pɪəriəd] Unterrichtsstunde; Periode, Zeitabschnitt **IV U2,** 29
permanent ['pɜ:mnənt] permanent, dauerhaft **V T1,** 14
permission [pə'mɪʃn] Erlaubnis **IV U2,** 25
person ['pɜ:sn] Person **II U3,** 42
personal ['pɜ:snl] persönlich **VI T1,** 14; **VI T2,** 33
perspective [pə'spektɪv] Perspektive, Blickwinkel °**VI T4,** 65
pet [pet] Haustier, Liebling **III U5,** 70
phone [fəʊn] Telefon **I U1,** 11
cell phone *(AE)* ['sel ˌfəʊn] Handy, Mobiltelefon **IV U3,** 42
phone box ['fəʊn ˌbɒks] Telefonzelle **III U3,** 44
phone call ['fəʊn ˌkɔ:l] (Telefon-)Anruf °**II U4,** 57
phone number ['fəʊn ˌnʌmbə] Telefonnummer **I U1,** 11

English – German

to **phone** [fəʊn] anrufen, telefonieren **I U2,** 33
phonetic [fə'netɪk] phonetisch °**III U5,** 75
photo ['fəʊtəʊ] Foto, Fotografie **II U5,** 64
photographer [fə'tɒgrəfə] Fotograf/Fotografin **IV U5,** 73
photography [fə'tɒgrəfi] Fotografie **V T2,** 32
phrase [freɪz] Redewendung, Ausdruck **VI T1,** 10
physical ['fɪzɪkl] physisch, körperlich **II U1,** 10
Physical Education (PE) [ˌfɪzɪkl‿edʒʊ'keɪʃn] Sport *(Schulfach)* **II U1,** 10
to **pick** [pɪk] pflücken; auswählen **I U6,** 78
to pick up [pɪk‿'ʌp] aufheben, abholen **II U1,** 18
picker ['pɪkə] Pflücker/Pflückerin **IV U4,** 64
pickpocket ['pɪkˌpɒkɪt] Taschendieb/Taschendiebin **III U2,** 24
picture ['pɪktʃə] Bild **I U1,** 14; Film **IV U5,** 73
to take pictures [teɪk 'pɪktʃəz] fotografieren, Fotos machen **II U5,** 62
piece [pi:s] Stück **IV U3,** 48
pier [pɪə] Pier, Landungssteg **III U2,** 26
I want my … **pierced.** [aɪ 'wɒnt maɪ … 'pɪəst] Ich möchte mein/e … piercen lassen. **III U4,** 52
pig [pɪg] Schwein **I U6,** 82
piggy bank ['pɪgi bæŋk] Sparschwein **II U2,** 23
pile [paɪl] Stapel, Haufen **VI T4,** 62
pilot ['paɪlət] Pilot/Pilotin **IV U1,** 16
pink [pɪŋk] pink, rosa **I LUA,** 24
pioneer [ˌpaɪə'nɪə] Pionier/Pionierin, Wegbereiter/Wegbereiterin **V T3,** 43
pipe [paɪp] Pfeife **III U5,** 72
pitch [pɪtʃ] Spielfeld **III U1,** 10
pitcher ['pɪtʃə] Pitcher/Pitcherin **III U1,** 14
pizza ['pi:tsə] Pizza **I U5,** 68
place [pleɪs] Platz, Stelle, Ort **I U2,** 26
change of place [ˌtʃeɪndʒ‿əv 'pleɪs] Ortswechsel °**III U4,** 55
to go places [ˌgəʊ 'pleɪsɪz] herumreisen **IV U4,** 64
to take place [teɪk 'pleɪs] stattfinden **III U4,** 53
plan [plæn] Plan **II U5,** 66
to **plan** [plæn] planen **II U4,** 52
plane [pleɪn] Flugzeug **II U2,** 23
planet ['plænɪt] Planet **IV U3,** 41
town **planner** ['taʊn ˌplænə] Stadtplaner/Stadtplanerin **VI T3,** 47
plant [plɑ:nt] Pflanze **II U6,** 74
plastic ['plæstɪk] Plastik(-), Kunststoff(-) **VI T3,** 42; **VI T4,** 63
plate [pleɪt] Teller **II U4,** 50
home plate ['həʊm ˌpleɪt] Home Plate **III U1,** 14
platform ['plætfɔ:m] Plattform, Tribüne, Bahnsteig **IV U4,** 56
play [pleɪ] Theaterstück, Spiel **I U7,** 90
to **play** [pleɪ] spielen **I U1,** 14
player ['pleɪə] Spieler/Spielerin, Mitspieler/Mitspielerin **III U1,** 8
CD player [ˌsi:'di: ˌpleɪə] CD-Player **II U4,** 56
DVD player [ˌdi:vi:'di: ˌpleɪə] DVD-Player **II U5,** 62
playground ['pleɪgraʊnd] Schulhof, Spielplatz **I U1,** 18
please [pli:z] bitte **I U1,** 19
*to be **pleased with** [bi: 'pli:zd wɪð] zufrieden sein mit **I U6,** 87
to **pledge** [pledʒ] geloben **IV U2,** 23
to **plough** [plaʊ] pflügen **IV U3,** 41
plug [plʌg] Stecker, Stöpsel **IV U3,** 44
plumber ['plʌmə] Klempner/Klempnerin; Installateur/Installateurin **VI T3,** 46
plumbing ['plʌmɪŋ] Rohrleitung; Klempnerarbeit **VI T3,** 47
plural ['plʊrəl] Plural, Mehrzahl **I U6,** 88
plus [plʌs] plus, zuzüglich **IV U3,** 46
p.m. [ˌpi:'em] nachmittags *(Uhrzeit)* **III U3,** 41
pocket ['pɒkɪt] Hosen-/Jackentasche **II U2,** 22
pocket money ['pɒkɪt ˌmʌni] Taschengeld **II U2,** 22
podcast ['pɒdkɑ:st] Podcast **VI T1,** 11
poem ['pəʊɪm] Gedicht **III U4,** 53
poet ['pəʊɪt] Dichter/Dichterin, Poet/Poetin **III U4,** 53
poetry ['pəʊətri] Lyrik **III U4,** 53
poetry slam ['pəʊətri ˌslæm] Poetry Slam *(Gedichtwettbewerb)* **III U4,** 53
point [pɔɪnt] Punkt **II U4,** 53
point of view [ˌpɔɪnt‿əv‿'vju:] Ansicht, Einstellung, Standpunkt °**VI T4,** 65
to **point** [pɔɪnt] zeigen °**I U1,** 18
to point (to) [pɔɪnt] zeigen (auf), deuten (auf) **IV U1,** 16
poison ['pɔɪzn] Gift **VI T3,** 44
police [pə'li:s] Polizei **I U6,** 87
policeman, policemen *(pl)* [pə'li:smən; pə'li:smen] Polizist **II U2,** 31
policy ['pɒlɪsi] Politik, politische Linie; Grundsatz **V T3,** 44
Polish ['pəʊlɪʃ] polnisch **I U2,** 29
polite [pə'laɪt] höflich **II U3,** 39
political [pə'lɪtɪkl] politisch **IV U3,** 48
politician [ˌpɒlɪ'tɪʃn] Politiker/Politikerin **VI T3,** 47
politics ['pɒlɪtɪks] Politik **VI T2,** 30
pollution [pə'lu:ʃn] (Umwelt-)Verschmutzung **III U2,** 30
pompom ['pɒmpɒm] Pompon *(bunte Quaste der Cheerleader)* **IV U2,** 23
pony ['pəʊni] Pony **II U6,** 74
swimming **pool** ['swɪmɪŋ ˌpu:l] Schwimmbecken; Schwimmbad **III U3,** 40
poor [pɔ:; pʊə] arm **III U5,** 76
pop [pɒp] Popmusik **IV U5,** 73
to **pop** [pɒp] knallen (lassen) **IV U5,** 80
popular ['pɒpjələ] populär, beliebt **II U2,** 23
population [ˌpɒpjə'leɪʃn] Bevölkerung **III U2,** 27
pork [pɔ:k] Schweinefleisch **II U4,** 49
port [pɔ:t] Hafen **III U3,** 39
to **pose** [pəʊz] posieren; (sich) darstellen **IV U5,** 73
position [pə'zɪʃn] Position **V T3,** 44
positive ['pɒzətɪv] positiv, bejaht °**IV U5,** 83
possible ['pɒsəbl] möglich **III U4,** 57
post [pəʊst] Pfosten, Mast **III U1,** 13
post office ['pəʊst‿ɒfɪs] Postamt **III U2,** 26
to **post** [pəʊst] aufgeben *(einen Brief)*, abschicken, posten *(im Internetforum)* **IV U5,** 76
postcard ['pəʊstkɑ:d] Postkarte **I U6,** 78
poster ['pəʊstə] Poster, Plakat **I U1,** 11
pot [pɒt] Topf **II U7,** 90
potato, potatoes *(pl)* [pə'teɪtəʊ; pə'teɪtəʊz] Kartoffel **II U4,** 54
couch potato ['kaʊtʃ pəˌteɪtəʊ] Fernsehglotzer/Fernsehglotzerin, Couchpotato **III U5,** 75
pound (£) [paʊnd] Pfund *(Währung)* **I U5,** 66
pound (lb) [paʊnd] Pfund *(Gewicht)* **II U4,** 52
poverty ['pɒvəti] Armut **IV U1,** 11
powder ['paʊdə] Puder, Pulver **III U5,** 77
power ['paʊə] Kraft, Stärke, Macht **II U6,** 74
practice ['præktɪs] Training **III U1,** 16
to **practise** ['præktɪs] üben, proben, praktizieren **II U5,** 66
to **prepare** [prɪ'peə] vorbereiten, zubereiten **V T2,** 32
present ['preznt] Geschenk **I U5,** 69; Gegenwart, Präsens °**II U2,** 26

to **present** [prɪ'zent] präsentieren; verleihen **IV U5,** 73
present ['preznt] anwesend **VI T2,** 30
presentation [ˌprezn'teɪʃn] Präsentation °**III U1,** 14
president ['prezɪdnt] Präsident/ Präsidentin °**II U3,** 42
press [pres] Presse **VI T2,** 26
to **press** [pres] drücken, pressen **II U7,** 95
to **pretend** [prɪ'tend] vorgeben, tun als ob °**V T2,** 26
pretty ['prɪti] ziemlich **IV U1,** 17; hübsch **VI T3,** 44
price [praɪs] Preis **I U7,** 95
half-price [ˌhɑ:f'praɪs] zum halben Preis **III U1,** 12
pride [praɪd] Stolz; Hochmut **V T3,** 42
primary school ['praɪməri ˌsku:l] Grundschule **III U4,** 57
Prime Minister (PM) [ˌpraɪm 'mɪnɪstə] Premierminister/Premierministerin **VI T1,** 9; **VI T2,** 30
prince [prɪns] Prinz **III U2,** 25
to **print** [prɪnt] drucken **II U5,** 64
pristine ['prɪsti:n] makellos, rein **IV U5,** 80
private ['praɪvɪt] privat **III U4,** 57
prize [praɪz] Preis **IV U2,** 22
pros and cons [ˌprəʊz‿ənd 'kɒnz] Für und Wider, Pro und Kontra, Vor- und Nachteile **V T4,** 60
probably ['prɒbəbli] wahrscheinlich **II U7,** 88
problem ['prɒbləm] Problem, Schwierigkeit **I U1,** 20
to **produce** [prə'dju:s] herstellen, produzieren **IV U5,** 74
producer [prə'dju:sə] Produzent/ Produzentin, Erzeuger/Erzeugerin **V T4,** 62
product ['prɒdʌkt] Produkt, Artikel, Ware **V T4,** 60
production [prə'dʌkʃn] Herstellung, Produktion **IV U5,** 73
professional [prə'feʃnl] professionell, beruflich, Berufs- **V T1,** 14
profile ['prəʊfaɪl] Profil; Porträt; Steckbrief **V T3,** 43
programme ['prəʊgræm] Programm, Sendung *(TV, Radio)* **III U5,** 68
progress ['prəʊgres] Fortschritt, Entwicklung **VI T3,** 43
project ['prɒdʒekt] Projekt **I U2,** 34
promise ['prɒmɪs] Versprechen °**II U6,** 77
to **promise** ['prɒmɪs] versprechen **II U6,** 77
promising ['prɒmɪsɪŋ] viel versprechend **VI T1,** 10
reflexive **pronoun** [rɪ'fleksɪv ˌprəʊnaʊn] Reflexivpronomen °**VI T3,** 49
prospect ['prɒspekt] Aussicht, Perspektive **VI T4,** 59
to **protect** [prə'tekt] (be)schützen **V T1,** 10
protective [prə'tektɪv] (be)schützend, Schutz- **VI T2,** 32
protest ['prəʊtest] Protest **V T3,** 41
to **protest** [prə'test] protestieren **V T3,** 40
protester [prə'testə] Protestierender/ Protestierende, Demonstrant/ Demonstrantin **V T3,** 44
proud of ['praʊd‿əv] stolz auf **III U4,** 58
to **provide** (sb with sth) [prə'vaɪd] bereitstellen, besorgen, liefern **VI T2,** 29
provider [prə'vaɪdə] Anbieter/ Anbieterin, Lieferant/Lieferantin; Provider °**V T1,** 14
public ['pʌblɪk] öffentlich **IV U1,** 9
in public [ɪn 'pʌblɪk] in der Öffentlichkeit **VI T2,** 26
public relations (PR) [ˌpʌblɪk rɪ'leɪʃnz] Öffentlichkeitsarbeit **VI T4,** 60
public school [ˌpʌblɪk 'sku:l] staatliche Schule (USA), Privatschule (GB) **IV U2,** 28
pudding ['pʊdɪŋ] Pudding; Nachtisch **II U4,** 49
pukka *(slang)* ['pʌkə] echt **VI T1,** 10
to **pull** [pʊl] ziehen **II U4,** 57
pump [pʌmp] (Luft-)Pumpe **VI T3,** 46
punk [pʌŋk] Punk **III U2,** 31; Punkmusik **IV U5,** 76
pupil ['pju:pl] Schüler/Schülerin **I U1,** 10
purple ['pɜ:pl] lila, violett **I LUA,** 24
to **push** [pʊʃ] stoßen, schieben, drücken **II U3,** 36
*to **put** [pʊt] setzen, stellen, legen **I U3,** 42
to put down [pʊt 'daʊn] auflegen *(Telefon)*; hinlegen, hinstellen °**II U7,** 89
to put in [pʊt‿'ɪn] einsetzen **II U7,** 95; einschieben **III U4,** 58; hinzufügen **IV U1,** 12
to put on [pʊt‿'ɒn] aufsetzen; anziehen **I U6,** 81; auftragen *(Make-up)* **II U5,** 71
to put out [pʊt‿'aʊt] ausmachen; löschen **III U2,** 28; hinausstellen **III U4,** 55
to put up [pʊt‿'ʌp] aufstellen, aufbauen **I U6,** 84
puzzle ['pʌzl] Rätsel, Puzzle **III U4,** 62
crossword puzzle ['krɒswɜ:d 'pʌzl] Kreuzworträtsel °**I U5,** 71
PVC [ˌpi:vi:'si:] PVC **VI T3,** 47
pyramid ['pɪrəmɪd] Pyramide °**VI T2,** 28

Q

qualification [ˌkwɒlɪfɪ'keɪʃn] Qualifikation, Befähigung **V T2,** 32
quality ['kwɒləti] Qualität; Eigenschaft °**V T2,** 31
quarter ['kwɔ:tə] Viertel **III U3,** 42; Vierteldollar *(Währung)* **IV U1,** 13
quarter past ['kwɔ:tə pɑ:st] Viertel nach **I U3,** 42
quarter to ['kwɔ:tə tə] Viertel vor **I U3,** 42
queen [kwi:n] Königin **II U5,** 62
homecoming queen [ˌhəʊmkʌmɪŋ 'kwi:n] Ballkönigin **IV U2,** 23
question ['kwestʃn] Frage **I U2,** 31
question mark ['kwestʃən ˌmɑ:k] Fragezeichen °**IV U1,** 17
questionnaire [ˌkwestʃə'neə] Fragebogen °**II U4,** 53
queue [kju:] Warteschlange **III U2,** 22
quick [kwɪk] schnell **I U6,** 86
quiet ['kwaɪət] ruhig, still, leise **I U6,** 78; Ruhe, Stille **II U7,** 88
*to **quit** [kwɪt] aufgeben, mit etw. aufhören; kündigen **V T3,** 46
quite [kwaɪt] ziemlich; ganz, völlig **VI T4,** 58
quiz [kwɪz] Quiz, Rätsel °**I U1,** 13
quota ['kwəʊtə] Quote **IV U1,** 10

R

race [reɪs] Wettlauf, Rennen **I U7,** 92; Rasse **V T3,** 44
to run a race [ˌrʌn‿ə 'reɪs] einen Wettlauf machen **I U7,** 92
racial ['reɪʃl] Rassen- **V T3,** 41
radio ['reɪdiəʊ] Radio **I U2,** 33
radio show ['reɪdiəʊ ˌʃəʊ] Radiosendung **I U2,** 33
raid [reɪd] Razzia; Angriff **IV U4,** 65
rain [reɪn] Regen **II U6,** 78
to **rain** [reɪn] regnen **I U4,** 62
rainwater ['reɪnˌwɔ:tə] Regenwasser **VI T3,** 46
rainy ['reɪni] regnerisch, verregnet **I U6,** 79
to **raise** [reɪz] anheben, erhöhen; großziehen *(Kinder)*; aufbringen *(Geld)* **VI T3,** 42

rally ['ræli] Jugendtreffen, Versammlung; Rallye **IV U2,** 22
ranch [ræntʃ] Ranch **IV U4,** 57
(park) **ranger** [ˌpɑ:k 'reɪndʒə] Parkaufseher/Parkaufseherin, Ranger **IV U4,** 58
rap [ræp] Rap **I U1,** 15
to **rap** [ræp] rappen **I U3,** 40
rapper ['ræpə] Rapper/Rapperin **IV U5,** 76
rare [reə] rar, selten **VI T4,** 59
I'd **rather** [aɪd 'rɑ:ðə] ich würde lieber **II U2,** 22
raw [rɔ:] grob, roh **IV U5,** 80
R&B [ˌɑ:r‿n'bi:] R&B **IV U5,** 73
to **reach** [ri:tʃ] erreichen **II U6,** 78
to **react** [ri'ækt] reagieren °**VI T4,** 65
reaction [ri'ækʃn] Reaktion, Resonanz °**V T3,** 42
*to **read** [ri:d] lesen **I LUB,** 38
to read out [ri:d‿'aʊt] laut vorlesen **VI T2,** 32
reader ['ri:də] Leser/Leserin **V T3,** 46; Lesebuch, Leseheft, Lektüre °**V T4,** 66
reading ['ri:dɪŋ] Lesen °**III U5,** 74; Lesung; Lektüre °**V T2,** 31
ready ['redi] fertig, bereit **II U4,** 50
to get ready [get 'redi] sich vorbereiten **II U5,** 68
real [rɪəl] echt, richtig, wirklich **II U3,** 38
to **realise** ['rɪəlaɪz] erkennen, sich klar werden **V T2,** 33; **V T4,** 62
reality [ri'æləti] Realität, Wirklichkeit **IV U3,** 41
reality show [ri'æləti ˌʃəʊ] Realityshow **III U5,** 68
really ['rɪəli] wirklich **I U2,** 34
reason ['ri:zn] Grund **V T3,** 46
to **receive** [rɪ'si:v] empfangen, erhalten **VI T2,** 30; **VI T4,** 63
reception [rɪ'sepʃn] Rezeption, Empfang **III U5,** 72
receptionist [rɪ'sepʃnɪst] Empfangsmitarbeiter/Empfangsmitarbeiterin, Sprechstundenhilfe **VI T3,** 47
recipe ['resɪpi:] Rezept **I U7,** 94
to **recognise** ['rekəgnaɪz] erkennen °**V T3,** 49
record ['rekɔ:d] (Schall-)Platte **IV U3,** 43; Aufnahme, Aufzeichnung; Beleg; Akte **V T3,** 47
on record [ɒn 'rekɔ:d] verzeichnet, dokumentiert **III U3,** 40
to **record** [rɪ'kɔ:d] aufnehmen, aufzeichnen **II U5,** 63
recording [rɪ'kɔ:dɪŋ] Aufnahme **IV U3,** 46
to **recycle** [ri:'saɪkl] recyceln, wieder verwerten **VI T3,** 42
recycling [ri:'saɪklɪŋ] Recycling, Abfallverwertung **VI T3,** 47
red [red] rot **I LUA,** 24
to go red [gəʊ 'red] rot werden **II U1,** 11
to **reduce** [rɪ'dju:s] reduzieren, vermindern **VI T3,** 42
reef [ri:f] Riff **V T1,** 10; **V T4,** 61
ref(eree) [ˌrefr'i:] Schiedsrichter/Schiedsrichterin **III U1,** 12; Referenz *(Person)* **V T1,** 15
reference ['refrns] Referenz; Bezug, Verweis **V T1,** 14
reflexive pronoun [rɪ'fleksɪv ˌprəʊnaʊn] Reflexivpronomen °**VI T3,** 49
refrain [rɪ'freɪn] Refrain **IV U5,** 78
refreshing [rɪ'freʃɪŋ] erfrischend **VI T3,** 45
refrigerator [rɪ'frɪdʒreɪtə] Kühlschrank **IV U3,** 42
to **refuse** [rɪ'fju:z] ablehnen, sich weigern **VI T2,** 30
reggae ['regeɪ] Reggae **IV U5,** 73
region ['ri:dʒn] Region, Gegend **VI T1,** 11; **VI T2,** 29
to **register** ['redʒɪstə] (sich) registrieren, (sich) anmelden **IV U5,** 76
registration [ˌredʒɪ'streɪʃn] Registrierung, Erfassung **II U1,** 10
regular ['regjələ] Stammkunde/Stammkundin **III U2,** 31; regelmäßig, regulär **V T3,** 46
to **rehearse** [rɪ'hɜ:s] proben *(ein Theaterstück)* **I U7,** 90
public **relations** (PR) [ˌpʌblɪk rɪ'leɪʃnz] Öffentlichkeitsarbeit **VI T4,** 60
relationship [rɪ'leɪʃnʃɪp] Beziehung **VI T4,** 65
reliable [rɪ'laɪəbl] zuverlässig, verlässlich, vertrauenswürdig **VI T1,** 14; **VI T4,** 61
religion [rɪ'lɪdʒn] Religion **V T3,** 42
religious [rɪ'lɪdʒəs] religiös **II U1,** 12
Religious Education (RE) [rɪˌlɪdʒəs‿edʒʊ'keɪʃn] Religionsunterricht **II U1,** 12
to **relive** [ˌri:'lɪv] noch einmal erleben **III U2,** 22
to **remain** [rɪ'meɪn] (ver)bleiben **VI T2,** 30
to **remember** [rɪ'membə] sich erinnern (an), sich merken **I U3,** 49
to **reminisce** [ˌremɪ'nɪs] zurückdenken, in Erinnerungen schwelgen **IV U5,** 80
remixed ['ri:mɪkst] neu gemischt °**V T2,** 31
remote [rɪ'məʊt] fern, abgelegen **V T1,** 12
remote control [rɪˌməʊt kən'trəʊl] Fernbedienung, Fernsteuerung **IV U3,** 41
renewable [rɪ'nju:əbl] erneuerbar **VI T3,** 47
rent [rent] Miete, Pacht **V T3,** 46
to **rent** [rent] mieten, pachten **V T3,** 46
rental ['rentl] Miet-, Verleih- **VI T4,** 60
to **repair** [rɪ'peə] reparieren **IV U1,** 17
to **repeat** [rɪ'pi:t] wiederholen °**III U5,** 75
to **replace** [rɪ'pleɪs] ersetzen °**V T1,** 16
report [rɪ'pɔ:t] Bericht, Meldung; Zeugnis **IV U3,** 40
to **report** [rɪ'pɔ:t] berichten, melden **VI T2,** 29; **VI T3,** 43
reporter [rɪ'pɔ:tə] Reporter/Reporterin **I U7,** 92
to **require** [rɪ'kwaɪə] benötigen, brauchen; anfordern **V T1,** 15
rescue ['reskju:] Rettung **III U5,** 70
to **rescue** ['reskju:] retten **II U6,** 83
research [rɪ'sɜ:tʃ] Recherche, Forschung, Untersuchung **IV U3,** 41
reservation [ˌrezə'veɪʃn] Reservat; Reservierung **IV U4,** 56
resource [rɪ'zɔ:s] Ressource, Rohstoff; Quelle **VI T4,** 60
human resources [ˌhju:mən rɪ'zɔ:sɪz] Personalabteilung **VI T4,** 60
respect [rɪ'spekt] Respekt **III U4,** 53
response [rɪ'spɒns] Reaktion, Antwort **III U4,** 53
responsibility [rɪsˌpɒnsə'bɪləti] Verantwortung **VI T4,** 58
responsible [rɪs'pɒnsəbl] verantwortlich; verantwortungsvoll **VI T4,** 58
rest [rest] Rest **III U1,** 17; Rast, Ruhe **V T3,** 42
rest area ['rest ˌeəriə] Rastplatz **IV U4,** 61
to **rest** [rest] sich ausruhen, sich entspannen **III U3,** 46; rasten, ausruhen; liegen **V T3,** 42; legen **VI T2,** 32
restaurant ['restrənt] Restaurant **II U4,** 55
to **restore** [rɪ'stɔ:] wiederherstellen, restaurieren **VI T4,** 60
result [rɪ'zʌlt] Ergebnis, Resultat **IV U4,** 62
*to **retell** [ri:'tel] nacherzählen, nochmals erzählen °**V T4,** 67
review [rɪ'vju:] Kritik **III U5,** 73
revision [rɪ'vɪʒn] Wiederholung °**I U2,** 32
*to **rewrite** [ˌri:'raɪt] noch einmal schreiben °**II U4,** 58
rhyme [raɪm] Reim °**I LUA,** 25

rhyming ['raɪmɪŋ] (sich) reimend °**II U4,** 58
rice [raɪs] Reis **II U4,** 49
rich [rɪtʃ] reich **III U2,** 25
ride [raɪd] Ritt, Fahrt; Mitfahrgelegenheit **IV U4,** 65
*to **ride** [raɪd] fahren, reiten **I LUB,** 38
riding ['raɪdɪŋ] Reiten **IV U4,** 58
horseback riding ['hɔ:sbæk ˌraɪdɪŋ] Reiten **IV U4,** 58
right [raɪt] Recht **V T3,** 42
civil rights *(pl)* [ˌsɪvl 'raɪts] Bürgerrechte °**V T3,** 45
Civil Rights Movement (CRM) [ˌsɪvl 'raɪts ˌmu:vmənt] Bürgerrechtsbewegung **V T3,** 44
right [raɪt] richtig, korrekt **I U1,** 13; rechter/rechte/rechtes; rechts **I U4,** 55; genau, direkt **VI T4,** 63
all right [ɔ:l 'raɪt] in Ordnung **IV U4,** 64
Go right. [gəʊ 'raɪt] Biege nach rechts ab. **I LUC,** 52
on the right [ɒn ðə 'raɪt] rechts **I U2,** 28
right away [raɪt‿ə'weɪ] sofort, gleich **II U4,** 57
right now [ˌraɪt 'naʊ] jetzt gleich, in diesem Augenblick **I U7,** 92
to be right [bi: 'raɪt] Recht haben **II U4,** 56
to get … right [get … 'raɪt] richtig machen **II U3,** 44
to turn right [tɜ:n 'raɪt] rechts abbiegen **II U7,** 97
ring [rɪŋ] Ring **III U3,** 41
rubber ring [ˌrʌbə 'rɪŋ] Schwimmreifen **III U3,** 41
*to **ring** [rɪŋ] klingeln **I U5,** 75; anrufen °**VI T4,** 58
The bell rings. [ðə 'bel rɪŋz] Es klingelt. **II U4,** 50
to ring out [ˌrɪŋ‿'aʊt] erklingen, ertönen **V T3,** 42
ice **rink** ['aɪs rɪŋk] Eis-/Schlittschuhbahn **II U2,** 23
riot [raɪət] Aufruhr, Ausschreitung, Unruhe **V T3,** 44
rise [raɪz] Aufstieg, Anstieg **IV U5,** 74
*to **rise** [raɪz] steigen, wachsen, zunehmen **II U6,** 78
rival ['raɪvl] Rivale/Rivalin, Konkurrent/Konkurrentin **IV U2,** 31
rival ['raɪvl] rivalisierend; Rivale/Rivalin **VI T2,** 29
river ['rɪvə] Fluss **I LUC,** 52
road [rəʊd] Straße, Landstraße **I LUC,** 52
to **roar** [rɔ:] dröhnen **IV U1,** 16

to **rob** [rɒb] rauben, ausrauben **III U2,** 24
robber ['rɒbə] Räuber/Räuberin **IV U3,** 48
robot ['rəʊbɒt] Roboter **IV U3,** 41
rock [rɒk] Rockmusik; Stein, Felsen **IV U5,** 73
to **rock** [rɒk] rocken; schaukeln **IV U5,** 80
rodeo [rəʊ'deɪəʊ; 'rəʊdiəʊ] Rodeo **IV U4,** 57
role [rəʊl] Rolle **II U1,** 10
romantic [rə'mæntɪk] romantisch **VI T2,** 30
roof [ru:f] Dach **I U2,** 26
roofer ['ru:fə] Dachdecker/Dachdeckerin **VI T3,** 46
room [ru:m; rʊm] Zimmer, Raum, Platz **I U1,** 16
chat room ['tʃæt rʊm] Chatroom *(Internetforum, wo man sich online unterhalten kann)* **IV U5,** 76
dining room ['daɪnɪŋ rʊm] Esszimmer, Speisesaal **I LUA,** 24
living room ['lɪvɪŋ rʊm] Wohnzimmer **I LUA,** 24
roping ['rəʊpɪŋ] Einfangen der Rinder mit dem Lasso **IV U4,** 58
round [raʊnd] Runde **III U4,** 53; (um …) herum **IV U1,** 17
route [ru:t; raʊt] Route °**III U2,** 24
en route [ɒn 'ru:t] unterwegs °**VI T1,** 15
row [rəʊ] Reihe **III U1,** 15
royal ['rɔɪəl] königlich **III U2,** 22
RSVP [ˌɑ:r‿es vi: 'pi:] um Antwort wird gebeten °**I U5,** 70
rubber ['rʌbə] Radiergummi **I U1,** 14; Gummi; Kautschuk **III U3,** 41
rubber boots *(pl)* [ˌrʌbə 'bu:ts] Gummistiefel **II U6,** 74
rubber ring [ˌrʌbə 'rɪŋ] Schwimmreifen **III U3,** 41
rubbish ['rʌbɪʃ] Abfall, Abfälle, Müll **I U6,** 84; Unsinn **II U7,** 94
rucksack ['rʌksæk] Rucksack **III U2,** 24
rude [ru:d] unhöflich, unverschämt **VI T2,** 32
rugby ['rʌgbi] Rugby **III U1,** 8
rugby boot ['rʌgbi bu:t] Rugbyschuh, Stollenschuh **III U1,** 8
rule [ru:l] Regel, Vorschrift **I U3,** 43
to **rule** [ru:l] herrschen, regieren **VI T2,** 30
ruler ['ru:lə] Lineal **I U1,** 14; Herrscher/Herrscherin **V T3,** 46
run [rʌn] Lauf **II U4,** 57; Runde **III U1,** 9
*to **run** [rʌn] rennen, laufen **I U3,** 48
to run a finger over sth [rʌn] mit dem Finger über etw. fahren/streichen **VI T4,** 63

to run a race [ˌrʌn‿ə 'reɪs] einen Wettlauf machen **I U7,** 92
to run away [rʌn‿ə'weɪ] wegrennen **I U3,** 48
to run into [rʌn‿'ɪntə] laufen gegen, stoßen gegen **III U1,** 17
to run on ['rʌn‿ɒn] laufen mit *(Auto)* **V T4,** 61
to run out [rʌn‿'aʊt] ausgehen *(Zeit)*, ablaufen *(Zeit)* **IV U1,** 10
to run over [rʌn‿'əʊvə] hinüberrennen **IV U1,** 17
to run upstairs [ˌrʌn‿ʌp'steəz] die Treppe hinaufrennen **III U3,** 47
runaway ['rʌnəˌweɪ] Ausreißer/Ausreißerin **III U5,** 71
runner ['rʌnə] Läufer/Läuferin **I U7,** 92
runner bean ['rʌnə ˌbi:n] Stangenbohne **VI T4,** 64
running ['rʌnɪŋ] laufend **VI T1,** 11
Russian ['rʌʃn] russisch; Russe/Russin **I U2,** 29

S

sacred ['seɪkrɪd] heilig **IV U4,** 56
sad [sæd] traurig, bedauerlich **II U1,** 19
safe [seɪf] sicher **III U3,** 40
safety ['seɪfti] Sicherheit **VI T2,** 29; **VI T4,** 60
to **sail** [seɪl] segeln, fahren *(Schiff)* **III U3,** 39
salad ['sæləd] Salat **II U4,** 49
sales *(pl)* [seɪlz] Verkauf, Vertrieb **VI T4,** 60
sales talk ['seɪlz tɔ:k] Verkaufsgespräch °**V T4,** 63
salesman, salesmen *(pl)* ['seɪlzmən; 'seɪlzmen] Vertreter, Verkäufer, Geschäftsmann **VI T1,** 14
salesroom ['seɪlzru:m] Verkaufsraum **VI T4,** 60
salt [sɔ:lt] Salz **V T1,** 12
saltie *(Aus)* ['sɔ:lti] Salzwasserkrokodil °**V T1,** 12
saltwater ['sɔ:ltˌwɔ:tə] Salzwasser **V T1,** 12
the **same** [seɪm] derselbe/dieselbe/dasselbe; gleich **III U1,** 19
sand [sænd] Sand **III U1,** 10
sandwich ['sænwɪdʒ] Sandwich, belegtes Brot **I U1,** 14
sandy ['sændi] sandig **III U3,** 40
satellite ['sætlaɪt] Satellit **IV U3,** 41
Saturday ['sætədeɪ] Samstag **I U2,** 34
sausage ['sɒsɪdʒ] Wurst, Würstchen **II U4,** 49

English – German

to **save** [seɪv] retten; sparen **II U6,** 80
*to **say** [seɪ] sagen, sprechen **I U1,** 11
It said .... [ɪt 'sed] Es lautete ....
II U2, 30
What does it say? [ˌwɒt dʌz‿ɪt 'seɪ]
Was steht da? **II U3,** 44
to **scan** [skæn] scannen, abtasten, nach Details durchsuchen °**VI T3,** 47; °**VI T4,** 65
to **scare** ['skeə] Angst machen **IV U3,** 49
scared [skeəd] verängstigt **I U2,** 35
I'm scared. [aɪm 'skeəd] Ich habe Angst. **II U3,** 44
scary ['skeəri] unheimlich, gruselig **II U7,** 95
scene [si:n] Szene, Schauplatz **IV U5,** 80
scenery ['si:nri] Landschaft **IV U4,** 56
scholarship ['skɒləʃɪp] Stipendium **VI T1,** 12
school [sku:l] Schule **I U1,** 10
comprehensive school [kɒmprɪ'hensɪv ˌsku:l] Gesamtschule **III U4,** 56
elementary school *(AE)* [elɪ'mentri ˌsku:l] Grundschule **IV U2,** 28
grammar school ['græmə ˌsku:l] Gymnasium **III U4,** 57
high school *(AE)* ['haɪ ˌsku:l] High School *(weiterführende Schule in den USA, Oberstufe)* **IV U2,** 22
middle school *(AE)* ['mɪdl ˌsku:l] Mittelschule *(weiterführende Schule in den USA, Mittelstufe)* **IV U2,** 28
nursery school ['nɜ:sri ˌsku:l] Kindergarten **VI T4,** 58
primary school ['praɪməri ˌsku:l] Grundschule **III U4,** 57
public school [ˌpʌblɪk 'sku:l] staatliche Schule (USA), Privatschule (GB) **IV U2,** 28
school bag ['sku:l bæg] Schultasche, Schulranzen **I U1,** 14
School of the Air [ˌsku:l‿əv ði 'eə] School of the Air *(Fernunterricht per Internet)* **VT1,** 11
schooling ['sku:lɪŋ] (Schul-)Ausbildung **VI T4,** 59
Science ['saɪəns] Wissenschaft, Naturwissenschaft **II U1,** 10
science fiction [ˌsaɪəns 'fɪkʃn] Sciencefiction **III U5,** 68
scientist ['saɪəntɪst] Wissenschaftler/Wissenschaftlerin **III U5,** 77
scone [skɒn] Scone *(Gebäck)* **I U7,** 94
score [skɔ:] Punktestand, Spielstand **III U1,** 12
to **score** [skɔ:] punkten, ein Tor schießen **III U1,** 9
Scottish ['skɒtɪʃ] schottisch **II U3,** 36
screen [skri:n] Bildschirm, Leinwand **III U5,** 68
screen shot ['skri:n ˌʃɒt] Screenshot **III U5,** 68
script [skrɪpt] Drehbuch **III U5,** 69
sea [si:] Meer **II U7,** 88
sea lion ['si: ˌlaɪən] Seelöwe **VT2,** 32
sea wasp ['si: ˌwɒsp] Seewespe **VT1,** 12
seal [si:l] Seehund, Robbe **VT1,** 12
search [sɜ:tʃ] Suche; Such- °**IV U5,** 73
to **search** [sɜ:tʃ] (durch)suchen °**IV U3,** 46
seasick ['si:sɪk] seekrank **IV U1,** 11
seaside ['si:saɪd] Küste, Meeresküste **III U5,** 70
season ['si:zn] Jahreszeit, Saison **I U6,** 79
seat [si:t] Sitz, Sitzplatz **II U2,** 23
seaweed ['si:wi:d] Alge, Seetang **VI T3,** 44
second ['seknd] Sekunde **I U2,** 30
secondly ['sekndli] zweitens **IV U4,** 62
secret ['si:krət] geheim, heimlich **IV U3,** 48
secretary ['sekrətri] Sekretär/Sekretärin **III U4,** 56
sector ['sektə] Sektor, Bereich **VI T4,** 60
*to **see** [si:] sehen **I U2,** 33; besuchen **II U1,** 19
See you! ['si: jə] Bis dann!, Bis .... **I U5,** 70
See you around! [ˌsi: jə ə'raʊnd] Bis dann!, Bis .... **IV U2,** 26
to see a doctor [si:‿ə 'dɒktə] zum Arzt gehen **II U4,** 52
seed [si:d] Saat(korn), Samen **VI T3,** 44
seeker ['si:kə] Suchender/Suchende °**VT1,** 14
to **seem** [si:m] (er)scheinen, wirken **VI T2,** 32; **VI T3,** 42; **VI T4,** 64
segregation *(no pl)* [ˌsegrɪ'geɪʃn] (Rassen-)Trennung **VT3,** 44
seldom ['seldəm] selten **III U5,** 68
self-employment [ˌselfɪm'plɔɪmənt] Selbstständigkeit **VI T4,** 59
*to **sell** [sel] verkaufen **I U7,** 90
*to **send** [send] schicken **I U6,** 80
to send in [send‿'ɪn] einschicken **II U5,** 64
to send off [send‿'ɒf] vom Platz verweisen **III U1,** 12
sense [sens] Sinn, Bedeutung **VT3,** 47
sensible ['sensɪbl] vernünftig **III U3,** 40
sentence ['sentəns] Satz °**I U1,** 13; Verurteilung, Urteil, Strafe **VT1,** 10
September [sep'tembə] September **I U5,** 70
serf [sɜ:f] Leibeigener/Leibeigene **VI T2,** 28
series, series *(pl)* ['sɪəri:z] Serie **III U5,** 70
servant ['sɜ:vnt] Diener/Dienerin **III U5,** 76
service ['sɜ:vɪs] Service, Dienst **II U6,** 83
session ['seʃn] Veranstaltung **III U4,** 57; Einheit, Sitzung, Stunde **VI T1,** 10
*to **set** [set] stellen, einstellen **II U7,** 90
to set free [set‿'fri:] freilassen; freisetzen **VI T2,** 29
to set off [set‿'ɒf] auslösen *(Alarm)* **II U7,** 95; aufbrechen, sich auf den Weg machen **IV U4,** 64
to set the table [ˌset ðə 'teɪbl] den Tisch decken **II U4,** 50
to set up [set‿'ʌp] einrichten, aufbauen, gründen **IV U5,** 74
setting ['setɪŋ] Schauplatz, Rahmen **VI T4,** 64
settler ['setlə] Siedler/Siedlerin **VI T1,** 13
several ['sevrl] mehrere, verschiedene **VT3,** 43
sex [seks] Geschlecht; Sexualität, Sex **VI T2,** 32; **VI T4,** 58
to have sex [ˌhæv 'seks] Geschlechtsverkehr haben **VI T4,** 58
sexism ['seksɪsm] Sexismus **VI T2,** 33
sexist ['seksɪst] sexistisch **VI T2,** 32
shade [ʃeɪd] Schatten, Schattierung **VT4,** 66
shadow ['ʃædəʊ] Schatten **IV U5,** 78
*to **shake** [ʃeɪk] schütteln, zittern **III U4,** 60
Shall we ... ? ['ʃæl‿wi:] Wollen wir ... ? **III U4,** 59
shape [ʃeɪp] Form **IV U5,** 72
to **share** [ʃeə] teilen **III U5,** 78
shark [ʃɑ:k] Hai **VT1,** 12
Great White Shark [ˌgreɪt waɪt 'ʃɑ:k] Weißer Hai °**VT1,** 12
she [ʃi:] sie **I U1,** 12
shed [ʃed] Schuppen **I U2,** 26
sheep, sheep *(pl)* [ʃi:p] Schaf **I U6,** 78
sheet [ʃi:t] Blatt **VI T2,** 33
shelf, shelves *(pl)* [ʃelf; ʃelvz] Regal, Regalbrett **I U2,** 30
body **shell** ['bɒdi ˌʃel] Karosserie **VI T4,** 61
ship [ʃɪp] Schiff **I U4,** 54
shipping ['ʃɪpɪŋ] Schifffahrt, Verschiffung **VT4,** 60
shirt [ʃɜ:t] Hemd **I U3,** 44
shocked [ʃɒkt] geschockt, schockiert **III U5,** 74
shoe [ʃu:] Schuh **I U1,** 12
shoebox ['ʃu:bɒks] Schuhkarton **VI T4,** 62
*to **shoot** [ʃu:t] (ab)schießen, erschießen **VT3,** 44

shop [ʃɒp] Laden, Geschäft **I U2,** 26
shop assistant ['ʃɒp‿əˌsɪstnt] Verkäufer/Verkäuferin **II U5,** 67
sports shop ['spɔ:ts ʃɒp] Sportgeschäft **I U5,** 66
to **shop** [ʃɒp] einkaufen **V T2,** 34
shopping ['ʃɒpɪŋ] Einkauf(en) **I U5,** 66
short [ʃɔ:t] kurz **I U4,** 55
shorts *(pl)* [ʃɔ:ts] Shorts, kurze Hose **II U1,** 10
shot [ʃɒt] Schuss, Schlag **III U5,** 68; Aufnahme, Foto; Einstellung **V T4,** 65
screen shot ['skri:n ˌʃɒt] Screenshot **III U5,** 68
***should** [ʃʊd] sollte/sollten **II U4,** 52
shoulder ['ʃəʊldə] Schulter **IV U2,** 31
to **shout** [ʃaʊt] schreien, rufen **I U1,** 15
show [ʃəʊ] Show, Sendung, Schau **I U2,** 33
radio show ['reɪdiəʊ ˌʃəʊ] Radiosendung **I U2,** 33
reality show [ri'æləti ˌʃəʊ] Realityshow **III U5,** 68
talk show ['tɔ:k ˌʃəʊ] Talkshow **III U5,** 68
*to **show** [ʃəʊ] zeigen **I U4,** 65
shower ['ʃaʊə] Regenguss; Dusche **II U6,** 74
to **shrug (one's shoulders)** [ʃrʌg] mit den Achseln/Schultern zucken **VI T4,** 62
to **shuffle** ['ʃʌfl] mischen °**II U6,** 79
*to **shut** [ʃʌt] zumachen, schließen °**VI T3,** 45
shutter ['ʃʌtə] Verschluss, Klappe, Blende **IV U5,** 74
shuttle ['ʃʌtl] Raumfähre **IV U3,** 41
shy [ʃaɪ] schüchtern **III U4,** 57
sick [sɪk] krank **II U3,** 46
sick note ['sɪk ˌnəʊt] Krankmeldung **II U2,** 28
to feel sick [fi:l 'sɪk] Übelkeit verspüren **II U3,** 46
side [saɪd] Seite **III U2,** 26
sunny side up [ˌsʌni saɪd‿'ʌp] Spiegelei **IV U4,** 61
sidewalk *(AE)* ['saɪdwɔ:k] Gehweg °**IV U1,** 15
sight [saɪt] Sehenswürdigkeit; Sicht, Anblick **IV U4,** 57
sign [saɪn] Schild, Zeichen **I U2,** 26
vital signs *(pl)* [ˌvaɪtl 'saɪnz] Lebenszeichen **IV U5,** 78
to **sign** [saɪn] unterschreiben **II U5,** 66
signal ['sɪgnl] Signal **II U2,** 26; Zeichen **III U1,** 10
silent ['saɪlənt] still, leise **IV U5,** 74
silent movie [ˌsaɪlənt 'mu:vi] Stummfilm **IV U5,** 74
silly ['sɪli] dumm; Dummkopf **II U1,** 11
similar ['sɪmɪlə] ähnlich **VI T2,** 30
since [sɪnts] seit, seitdem **III U2,** 30
*to **sing** [sɪŋ] singen **I U2,** 33
singer ['sɪŋə] Sänger/Sängerin **II U1,** 14
sink [sɪŋk] Waschbecken *(im Amerikanischen),* Spülbecken **IV U3,** 44
to **sip** [sɪp] schluckweise trinken **IV U5,** 80
sir [s3:] mein Herr (*Anrede*) **III U5,** 72
Sir [s3:] Sir *(Anrede für einen Ritter)* °**III U5,** 75
sister ['sɪstə] Schwester **I LUA,** 25
half-sister ['hɑ:fˌsɪstə] Halbschwester **I U2,** 26
*to **sit** [sɪt] sitzen **I U3,** 48
to sit back [ˌsɪt 'bæk] sich zurücklehnen **IV U1,** 16
to sit down [sɪt 'daʊn] sich (hin)setzen **I U1,** 19
to sit with ['sɪt wɪθ] sich setzen zu **I U5,** 74
sitcom ['sɪtkɒm] Situationskomödie **III U5,** 70
building **site** ['bɪldɪŋ saɪt] Baustelle **VI T3,** 46
situation [ˌsɪtju'eɪʃn] Situation **V T4,** 60
six-pack ['sɪkspæk] Waschbrettbauch **V T2,** 28
to **skate** [skeɪt] Inlineskates fahren, skaten **I LUB,** 38
skateboard ['skeɪtbɔ:d] Skateboard **I U4,** 54
skates *(pl)* [skeɪts] Inlineskates **I U4,** 54
skeleton ['skelɪtn] Skelett **VI T4,** 62
skiing ['ski:ɪŋ] Skifahren **IV U4,** 62
skill [skɪl] Fertigkeit, Geschick **IV U4,** 58
to **skim** [skɪm] überfliegen °**VI T2,** 33
skimming ['skɪmɪŋ] Überfliegen °**III U2,** 28
skirt [sk3:t] Rock **II U1,** 10
sky [skaɪ] Himmel **II U7,** 94
skyscraper ['skaɪˌskreɪpə] Wolkenkratzer **IV U1,** 9
poetry **slam** ['pəʊətri ˌslæm] Poetry Slam *(Gedichtwettbewerb)* **III U4,** 53
slamster ['slæmstə] Teilnehmer/ Teilnehmerin an einem Poetry Slam **III U4,** 53
slang [slæŋ] Slang °**IV U5,** 76
slave [sleɪv] Sklave/Sklavin **V T3,** 44; **V T4,** 60
slavery ['sleɪvri] Sklaverei **V T3,** 44
sleep [sli:p] Schlaf **IV U3,** 46
*to **sleep** [sli:p] schlafen **I U3,** 46
sleeping bag ['sli:pɪŋ ˌbæg] Schlafsack **I U6,** 84
sleepy ['sli:pi] schläfrig, verschlafen **II U7,** 94
slice [slaɪs] Scheibe **IV U1,** 12
slip [slɪp] Beleg, Schein **IV U2,** 25
slow [sləʊ] langsam **I U2,** 34
slug [slʌg] Nacktschnecke **V T3,** 47
small [smɔ:l] klein **I U2,** 26
smart [smɑ:t] schlau, klug **IV U3,** 40
smell [smel] Geruch, Gestank **III U3,** 46
*to **smell** [smel] riechen **III U2,** 28
to **smile** [smaɪl] lächeln **I U3,** 43
smoke [sməʊk] Rauch **III U2,** 28
to **smoke** [sməʊk] rauchen **III U5,** 72
smooth [smu:θ] weich, geschmeidig, glatt **V T4,** 63
smuggler ['smʌglə] Schmuggler/ Schmugglerin **III U3,** 39
snack [snæk] Imbiss, Snack **II U4,** 55
snack bar ['snæk ˌbɑ:] Café, Imbissstube **V T3,** 46
snake [sneɪk] Schlange **V T1,** 10
Brown Snake [ˌbraʊn 'sneɪk] Braunschlange, Braunotter °**V T1,** 12
snapshot ['snæpʃɒt] Schnappschuss **IV U1,** 16
to **sniff** [snɪf] schnüffeln, schnuppern **III U5,** 78
snow [snəʊ] Schnee **II U6,** 79
to **snow** [snəʊ] schneien **II U6,** 79
snowboarding ['snəʊbɔ:dɪŋ] Snowboarden **V T3,** 41
snowy ['snəʊi] verschneit **I U6,** 79
so [səʊ] so, also, deshalb **I U2,** 26
so far ['səʊ fɑ:] bis jetzt °**III U5,** 77
soap [səʊp] Seife; Seifenoper **I U7,** 97
docu soap ['dɒkju ˌsəʊp] Dokusoap **III U5,** 68
soccer *(AE)* ['sɒkə] Fußball **IV U2,** 29
social ['səʊʃl] sozial, gesellschaftlich **VI T2,** 28
society [sə'saɪəti] Gesellschaft; Verein **V T3,** 44
socket ['sɒkɪt] Steckdose **IV U3,** 44
sofa ['səʊfə] Sofa, Couch **I LUA,** 25
soft [sɒft] leise; weich, sanft **II U7,** 94
soil [sɔɪl] Erde, Boden **VI T3,** 44
solar ['səʊlə] Sonnen-, Solar-, solar **IV U3,** 49
solar panel [ˌsəʊlə 'pænl] Sonnenkollektor **V T4,** 59
solar system ['səʊlə ˌsɪstəm] Sonnensystem **IV U3,** 49
soldier ['səʊldʒə] Soldat/Soldatin **VI T2,** 28
solid ['sɒlɪd] fest, solide **VI T4,** 63
solo ['səʊləʊ] allein, Allein-, solo, Solo- **V T3,** 43
to **solve** [sɒlv] lösen, aufklären **III U5,** 76
some [sʌm] einige; etwas **II U1,** 13
somebody ['sʌmbədi] jemand **III U5,** 71

somehow ['sʌmhaʊ] irgendwie **IV U4,** 65
someone ['sʌmwʌn] jemand **II U5,** 70
something ['sʌmθɪŋ] etwas **II U4,** 56
sometimes ['sʌmtaɪmz] manchmal **I U3,** 44
somewhere ['sʌmweə] irgendwo **II U4,** 57
son [sʌn] Sohn **III U5,** 74
song [sɒŋ] Lied **I U2,** 33
soon [su:n] bald **I U6,** 78
sore [sɔ:] schmerzhaft, weh, wund **VI T3,** 44
sorry ['sɒri] Tut mir leid., Entschuldigung. **I U1,** 12
I'm sorry about .... [aɪm 'sɒri‿ə,baʊt] Es tut mir leid wegen .... °**II U3,** 39
to be sorry [bi: 'sɒri] leidtun **III U3,** 44
to feel sorry for [fi:l 'sɒri] Mitleid haben mit, bedauern **III U1,** 16
sort [sɔ:t] Art, Sorte °**III U4,** 58
sort of ['sɔ:t‿əv] irgendwie **VI T1,** 12
to **sort** [sɔ:t] sortieren °**I U1,** 21
to sort out [sɔ:t‿'aʊt] klären, regeln *(ein Problem)* **I U2,** 30
soul [səʊl] Soulmusik; Seele **IV U5,** 73
sound [saʊnd] Ton, Geräusch, Klang **I U6,** 85
to **sound** [saʊnd] klingen, sich anhören **III U5,** 76
soup [su:p] Suppe **II U1,** 15
sour ['saʊə] sauer **II U4,** 49
source [sɔ:s] Quelle; Grund °**V T4,** 62
south [saʊθ] Süden **I U4,** 55
South American [,saʊθ‿ə'merɪkən] südamerikanisch; Südamerikaner/Südamerikanerin **VI T2,** 29
southwest [,saʊθ'west] Südwesten **II U6,** 78
souvenir [,su:və'nɪə] Souvenir, Andenken **III U2,** 25
spa [spɑ:] Wellness-Center, Spa **V T4,** 64
space [speɪs] Raum, Platz; Weltraum **IV U3,** 40
outer space [,aʊtə 'speɪs] Weltraum, Weltall **IV U3,** 40
space station ['speɪs ,steɪʃn] Weltraumstation **IV U3,** 40
spaceship ['speɪsʃɪp] Raumschiff **IV U3,** 49
spaghetti [spə'geti] Spaghetti **II U1,** 13
Spanglish ['spæŋglɪʃ] Spanglisch *(Mischung aus Spanisch und Englisch)* **VI T1,** 10
Spanish ['spænɪʃ] spanisch, Spanisch **IV U4,** 64
spark [spɑ:k] Funke(n) **VI T4,** 63
to **spark** [spɑ:k] sprühen *(Funken)*; auslösen, entfachen **VI T4,** 63
*to **speak** [spi:k] sprechen **I U4,** 62
speaking ['spi:kɪŋ] am Apparat **III U4,** 59
speaker ['spi:kə] Sprecher/Sprecherin **III U3,** 39
special ['speʃl] besonders, speziell **III U4,** 53; Spezialität **IV U1,** 12
special needs [,speʃl 'ni:dz] besondere Bedürfnisse **VI T4,** 59
specialist ['speʃlɪst] Spezialist/Spezialistin; Fach- **VI T4,** 59
specific [spə'sɪfɪk] spezifisch, speziell, bestimmt **VI T4,** 59
spectacular [spek'tækjələ] spektakulär **III U2,** 22
speech [spi:tʃ] (An-)Sprache, Rede; Sprechen **V T3,** 44
speech bubble ['spi:tʃ ,bʌbl] Sprechblase °**III U3,** 41
*to **spell** [spel] buchstabieren **I U4,** 60
spelling ['spelɪŋ] Orthographie, Rechtschreibung °**II U3,** 43
*to **spend** [spend] verbringen; ausgeben **I U6,** 83
spicy ['spaɪsi] würzig, pikant **II U4,** 49
spider ['spaɪdə] Spinne **V T1,** 12
Sydney Funnel Web Spider ['sɪdni ,fʌnl web 'spaɪdə] australische Trichternetzspinne °**V T1,** 12
spin-off ['spɪn‿ɒf] Nebenprodukt **IV U3,** 41
spine [spaɪn] Wirbelsäule **VI T4,** 63
spirit ['spɪrɪt] Geist; Stimmung **V T3,** 43
*to **spit** [spɪt] spucken, zischen, fauchen **VI T4,** 63
*to **split** [splɪt] (sich) (auf)teilen, spalten °**VI T3,** 45; °**VI T4,** 61; °**VI T4,** 65
sponge [spʌndʒ] Schwamm **I U7,** 90
sponsor ['spɒnsə] Sponsor/Sponsorin, Förderer/Förderin **VI T1,** 10
spooky ['spu:ki] unheimlich **I U2,** 35
spoon [spu:n] Löffel **II U4,** 50
sport [spɔ:t] Sport **I U1,** 12
sports day ['spɔ:ts deɪ] Sportfest **I U7,** 90
sports field ['spɔ:ts fi:ld] Sportplatz **I U7,** 92
sports shop ['spɔ:ts ʃɒp] Sportgeschäft **I U5,** 66
to do sports [du: 'spɔ:ts] Sport treiben **I U7,** 92
sporty ['spɔ:ti] sportlich **III U2,** 25
spot on ['spɒt‿ɒn] Fokus auf **VI T1,** 11
to **spray** [spreɪ] (be)sprühen, lackieren **IV U4,** 64
*to **spread** [spred] (sich) ausbreiten, (sich) verbreiten **VI T1,** 10
spring [sprɪŋ] Frühling **I U6,** 78
square dance ['skweə ,dɑ:nts] Square Dance **IV U4,** 58
to **squash** [skwɒʃ] zerdrücken, pressen, quetschen **VI T4,** 63
stadium ['steɪdiəm] Stadion **III U1,** 8
staff [stɑ:f] Personal; Kollegium **III U4,** 56
stage [steɪdʒ] Bühne **IV U5,** 74
stairs *(pl)* [steəz] Treppe **III U3,** 46
stall [stɔ:l] Stand, Bude **I U7,** 90
stall holder ['stɔ:l ,həʊldə] Standbesitzer/Standbesitzerin **II U4,** 54
white elephant stall [,waɪt 'elɪfənt stɔ:l] Trödelstand **I U7,** 96
stamp [stæmp] Briefmarke **III U3,** 41
stand [stænd] Tribüne **III U1,** 9; (Messe-)Stand **V T4,** 63
*to **stand** [stænd] stehen **III U3,** 46
standby ['stændbaɪ] in Bereitschaft, auf Stand-by **VI T3,** 42
star [stɑ:] Star; Stern **III U5,** 70
word star ['wɜ:d stɑ:] Wortstern °**I U1,** 22
start [stɑ:t] Anfang, Beginn, Start **II U1,** 10
to **start** [stɑ:t] anfangen, starten **I U3,** 44
starter ['stɑ:tə] Vorspeise **II U4,** 49
startled ['stɑ:tld] verblüfft, alarmiert **VI T4,** 64
state [steɪt] Staat, Land; staatlich **III U4,** 57
head of state [,hed‿əv 'steɪt] Staatsoberhaupt **VI T2,** 30
statement ['steɪtmənt] Aussage, Behauptung °**III U5,** 71
station ['steɪʃn] Wache, Station, Bahnhof **I U6,** 87
cleaning station ['kli:nɪŋ ,steɪʃn] Putzerstation **V T4,** 64
space station ['speɪs ,steɪʃn] Weltraumstation **IV U3,** 40
statistics *(pl)* [stə'tɪstɪks] Statistik °**IV U4,** 62
statue ['stætʃu:] Statue, Standbild **IV U5,** 73
to **stay** [steɪ] bleiben **I U4,** 60
to stay on [steɪ‿'ɒn] dableiben, länger bleiben **VI T4,** 59
to stay out [steɪ‿'aʊt] wegbleiben **III U4,** 59
to stay with ['steɪ wɪð] wohnen bei **I U6,** 78
*to **steal** [sti:l] stehlen **II U4,** 57

steel band [ˌsti:l 'bænd] Steelband *(Band, deren Instrumente aus leeren Ölfässern bestehen)* **III U4,** 54
steelworker ['sti:lˌwɜ:kə] Stahlarbeiter/Stahlarbeiterin °**IV U1,** 15
step [step] Stufe, Schritt **IV U1,** 9
to **step** [step] steigen, treten **VI T4,** 62
stepdad ['stepdæd] Stiefvater **I U2,** 26
stick [stɪk] Stock **II U2,** 26
*to **stick (over)** [stɪk] strecken/stecken (über) **VI T4,** 62
still (picture) ['stɪl ˌpɪktʃə] Standfoto **IV U5,** 74
still [stɪl] noch, immer noch **II U1,** 21; dennoch **IV U2,** 26
*to **sting** [stɪŋ] stechen, beißen **V T1,** 12
stinger suit [ˌstɪŋə 'su:t] Quallen-Schutzanzug **V T1,** 12
*to **stink** [stɪŋk] stinken **V T2,** 32
stomach ['stʌmək] Magen, Bauch **II U3,** 41
stone [stəʊn] Stein **II U6,** 82; *brit. Gewichtseinheit* (= 6,35kg) **III U3,** 43
stop [stɒp] Halt, Haltestelle **I LUC,** 52
bus stop ['bʌs ˌstɒp] Bushaltestelle **I LUC,** 52
to **stop** [stɒp] aufhören (mit), (an)halten **I U3,** 42
to stop + -ing [stɒp] aufhören etw. zu tun **II U4,** 52
store [stɔ:] Kaufhaus, Geschäft, Laden **II U2,** 30
department store [dɪ'pɑ:tmənt stɔ:] Kaufhaus **I LUC,** 52
store detective ['stɔ: dɪˌtektɪv] Kaufhausdetektiv/Kaufhausdetektivin **II U2,** 30
storm [stɔ:m] Sturm **II U6,** 81
stormy ['stɔ:mi] stürmisch **II U6,** 78
story ['stɔ:ri] Geschichte, Erzählung **I U1,** 21
detective story [dɪ'tektɪv ˌstɔ:ri] Krimi **III U5,** 68
storyline ['stɔ:rilaɪn] Handlung **VI T4,** 65
stranded ['strændɪd] gestrandet **IV U4,** 61
strange [streɪndʒ] merkwürdig, seltsam **I U2,** 35
stranger ['streɪndʒə] Fremder/Fremde **III U3,** 41
strawberry ['strɔ:bri] Erdbeere **IV U1,** 12
stream [stri:m] Bach **II U6,** 82
street [stri:t] Straße **I LUC,** 52
strength [streŋθ] Stärke **VI T1,** 14
stress [stres] Stress; Betonung **IV U3,** 46
strict [strɪkt] streng, strikt **III U4,** 52
string [strɪŋ] Schnur, Kordel, Bindfaden **IV U5,** 74

strong [strɒŋ] stark **III U5,** 74
student ['stju:dnt] Student/Studentin, Schüler/Schülerin **IV U2,** 22
studies *(pl)* ['stʌdiz] Studium; Lernen **V T2,** 32
studio ['stju:diəʊ] Studio **I U2,** 33
to **study** ['stʌdi] studieren; lernen **II U6,** 74
stuff [stʌf] Zeug, Sachen **IV U4,** 64
stupid ['stju:pɪd] dumm, blöd **I U2,** 35
style [staɪl] Stil; Frisur **III U2,** 31
sub-continent [ˌsʌb'kɒntɪnənt] Subkontinent **VI T1,** 10
subject ['sʌbdʒɪkt] Schulfach; Thema **II U1,** 13
to **substitute** ['sʌbstɪtju:t] auswechseln, ersetzen **III U1,** 17
subtitle ['sʌbˌtaɪtl] Untertitel **VI T1,** 10
suburb ['sʌbɜ:b] Vorort **IV U5,** 76
success [sək'ses] Erfolg **V T3,** 43
successful [sək'sesfl] erfolgreich **V T1,** 14; **V T3,** 43; **V T4,** 62
such [sʌtʃ] solch **V T3,** 44
That **sucks!** [ðæt 'sʌks] Das ist ätzend! **V T2,** 30
suddenly ['sʌdnli] plötzlich, auf einmal **I U2,** 35
sugar ['ʃʊgə] Zucker **VI T3,** 44; **VI T4,** 64
to **suggest** [sə'dʒest] vorschlagen **VI T2,** 31
suggestion [sə'dʒestʃn] Vorschlag, Anregung °**II U4,** 53
suit [su:t] Anzug **IV U2,** 31
stinger suit [ˌstɪŋə 'su:t] Quallen-Schutzanzug **V T1,** 12
to **suit** [su:t] passen (zu) °**V T2,** 33
suitable ['su:təbl] geeignet, passend **VI T2,** 33
hotel **suite** [həʊ'tel ˌswi:t] Hotelsuite **III U2,** 27
to **sum up** [ˌsʌm‿'ʌp] zusammenfassen °**V T4,** 67
summary ['sʌmri] Zusammenfassung °**III U3,** 47
summer ['sʌmə] Sommer **I U6,** 79
summer fair ['sʌmə ˌfeə] Sommerfest **I U7,** 90
sun [sʌn] Sonne **III U3,** 40
Sunday ['sʌndeɪ] Sonntag **I LUB,** 39
sunny ['sʌni] sonnig **I U6,** 79
suntan ['sʌntæn] Sonnenbräune **II U1,** 14
super ['su:pə] super, großartig **VI T4,** 61
superlative [su:'pɜ:lətɪv] Superlativ **II U4,** 50
supermarket ['su:pəˌmɑ:kɪt] Supermarkt **I LUC,** 52
supervisor ['su:pəvaɪzə] Betreuer/Betreuerin **VI T2,** 32

supper ['sʌpə] Abendessen **I U3,** 44
for supper [fə 'sʌpə] zum Abendessen **II U3,** 38
to have supper [hæv 'sʌpə] zu Abend essen **I U3,** 44
supply [sə'plaɪ] Vorrat, Bestand, Versorgung **VI T3,** 46
support [sə'pɔ:t] Unterstützung, Hilfe **VI T4,** 59
to **support** [sə'pɔ:t] unterstützen **IV U5,** 80
supporter [sə'pɔ:tə] Anhänger/Anhängerin **IV U2,** 23
supreme [su:'pri:m] höchster/höchste/höchstes, oberster/oberste/oberstes **V T3,** 46
sure [ʃʊə] sicher **I U1,** 16
to make sure [meɪk 'ʃʊə] sichergehen **II U6,** 82
to **surf** [sɜ:f] (wind)surfen **II U1,** 14
to surf the Internet [ˌsɜ:f ði‿'ɪntənet] im Internet surfen **II U1,** 14
surfboard ['sɜ:fbɔ:d] Surfbrett **V T1,** 14
surfer ['sɜ:fə] Surfer/Surferin **V T1,** 12
surfing ['sɜ:fɪŋ] Wellenreiten, Surfen **II U1,** 14
surprised [sə'praɪzd] überrascht, erstaunt **II U1,** 18
surprising [sə'praɪzɪŋ] überraschend **II U7,** 96
survey ['sɜ:veɪ] Umfrage **I U4,** 56
survival [sə'vaɪvl] Überleben **IV U2,** 26
to **survive** [sə'vaɪv] überleben, bestehen, durchstehen **V T1,** 12
suspense [sə'spents] Spannung **IV U3,** 48
swap [swɒp] Tausch **II U7,** 88
to **swap** [swɒp] tauschen **I LUB,** 38
sweatshirt ['swetʃɜ:t] Sweatshirt **II U1,** 10
sweet [swi:t] süß **I LUA,** 24; Bonbon, Süßigkeit **II U4,** 53
to **swerve** [swɜ:v] ausweichen, ausscheren **III U4,** 60
*to **swim** [swɪm] schwimmen **I LUB,** 38
swimmer ['swɪmə] Schwimmer/Schwimmerin **III U3,** 39
swimming pool ['swɪmɪŋ ˌpu:l] Schwimmbecken; Schwimmbad **III U3,** 40
swimsuit ['swɪmsu:t] Badeanzug **III U3,** 40
switch [swɪtʃ] Schalter **IV U3,** 44
to **switch off** [ˌswɪtʃ‿'ɒf] ausschalten **IV U1,** 17
to switch on [swɪtʃ‿'ɒn] einschalten, anmachen **IV U3,** 42
symbol ['sɪmbl] Symbol, Sinnbild, Zeichen **IV U1,** 9
synonym ['sɪnənɪm] Synonym °**IV U5,** 83

syrup ['sɪrəp] Sirup **IV U1,** 12
system ['sɪstəm] System **III U4,** 57
solar system ['səʊlə ˌsɪstəm] Sonnensystem **IV U3,** 49

T

table ['teɪbl] Tisch **I U1,** 18; Tabelle **VI T4,** 58
table-tennis ['teɪblˌtenɪs] Tischtennis **II U7,** 88
to set the table [ˌset ðə 'teɪbl] den Tisch decken **II U4,** 50
*to **take** [teɪk] nehmen, mitnehmen, wegnehmen, bringen **I U3,** 42; dauern, *(Zeit)* brauchen **III U3,** 39
to take a bus tour [ˌteɪk‿ə 'bʌs tʊə] eine Busfahrt machen **IV U4,** 58
to take a joke [ˌteɪk‿ə 'dʒəʊk] Spaß verstehen **VI T2,** 32
to take care [teɪk 'keə] aufpassen; sich kümmern **IV U2,** 29
to take home [ˌteɪk 'həʊm] nach Hause bringen **I U2,** 35
to take notes [teɪk 'nəʊts] sich Notizen machen °**II U4,** 55
to take off [ˌteɪk‿'ɒf] ausziehen, abnehmen **III U3,** 46; abheben, starten, abfliegen **IV U1,** 16
to take out [teɪk‿'aʊt] herausnehmen **I U3,** 42
to take part in [teɪk 'pɑ:t‿ɪn] teilnehmen an **III U4,** 53
to take pictures [teɪk 'pɪktʃəz] fotografieren, Fotos machen **II U5,** 62
to take place [teɪk 'pleɪs] stattfinden **III U4,** 53
to take turns [teɪk 'tɜ:nz] sich abwechseln °**VI T3,** 43
to take your chance [ˌteɪk jɔ: 'tʃɑ:ns] etw. wagen, etw. riskieren **III U3,** 47
takeaway ['teɪkəweɪ] Restaurant mit Straßenverkauf; Essen zum Mitnehmen **II U4,** 48
talent ['tælənt] Talent **V T2,** 32
talk [tɔ:k] Vortrag; Rede, Gespräch **V T4,** 60
sales talk ['seɪlz tɔ:k] Verkaufsgespräch °**V T4,** 63
talk show ['tɔ:k ˌʃəʊ] Talkshow **III U5,** 68
to give a talk [ˌgɪv‿ə 'tɔ:k] einen Vortrag/eine Rede halten **VI T1,** 14
to **talk** [tɔ:k] sprechen, reden **I U1,** 10
to talk to ['tɔ:k tə] sprechen mit, reden mit **II U2,** 28
talkie ['tɔ:ki] Tonfilm **IV U5,** 74
tall [tɔ:l] groß, hoch **II U3,** 36
tap *(BE)* [tæp] Wasserhahn **VI T3,** 45
tap water ['tæp ˌwɔ:tə] Leitungswasser **VI T3,** 45
task [tɑ:sk] Aufgabe, Auftrag **IV U3,** 46
to **taste** [teɪst] schmecken **I U7,** 94
tasty ['teɪsti] schmackhaft **II U4,** 50
Pizza is tastier. ['pi:tsə ɪz ˌteɪstɪə] Pizza schmeckt besser. **II U4,** 50
tattoo [tæt'u:] Tätowierung **III U4,** 52
taxi ['tæksi] Taxi **III U2,** 30
tea [ti:] Tee, Abendessen **I U7,** 94
afternoon tea [ˌɑ:ftənu:n 'ti:] Nachmittagstee **I U7,** 94
*to **teach** [ti:tʃ] lehren **I LUB,** 38
teacher ['ti:tʃə] Lehrer/Lehrerin **I U1,** 12
team [ti:m] Mannschaft, Team **II U2,** 23
tear [tɪə] Träne **V T4,** 66
technical ['teknɪkl] technisch; handwerklich, fachlich **V T2,** 32
technician [tek'nɪʃn] Techniker/Technikerin **VI T3,** 47
Technology [tek'nɒlədʒi] Technik **II U1,** 10
teen [ti:n] Jugendliche/Jugendlicher **II U6,** 80
teenage ['ti:neɪdʒ] jugendlich **III U4,** 53
teenager ['ti:nˌeɪdʒə] Teenager, Jugendliche/Jugendlicher **III U2,** 24
telephone ['telɪfəʊn] Telefon °**V T2,** 29
*to **tell** [tel] erzählen, sagen **I U3,** 49
temperature ['temprətʃə] Temperatur **II U6,** 78
temporary ['temprəri] vorübergehend, temporär, befristet **V T1,** 14; **V T3,** 47
tenant ['tenənt] Mieter/Mieterin °**V T3,** 41
tennis ['tenɪs] Tennis **III U1,** 15
table-tennis ['teɪblˌtenɪs] Tischtennis **II U7,** 88
tent [tent] Zelt **I U6,** 84
term [tɜ:m] Trimester *(Einteilung des englischen Schuljahrs)* °**II U1,** 10
terminal ['tɜ:mɪnl] (Flughafen-)Terminal °**VI T1,** 11
terrible ['terəbl] schrecklich, furchtbar **I U2,** 35
territory ['terɪtri] Territorium, Land, Gebiet **VI T1,** 11
test [test] Test, Klassenarbeit **II U3,** 44
to **test** [test] testen, prüfen **V T4,** 61
text [tekst] Text °**I U2,** 27
text message ['tekst ˌmesɪdʒ] SMS **I U6,** 80
to **text** [tekst] Textnachricht (SMS) schicken, simsen **III U4,** 54
textile ['tekstaɪl] textil, Textil(-) **VI T3,** 43
than [ðən] als **I U4,** 55
to **thank** [θæŋk] danken **I U4,** 60
thank you ['θæŋk‿ju:] danke **I U1,** 12
thanks [θæŋks] danke **II U2,** 26
thanks to ['θæŋks tə] dank (dir/ihnen), wegen **III U2,** 24
that [ðæt] das, jenes **I U1,** 12
that (bad) ['ðæt bæd] so (schlimm) **II U2,** 24
that evening [ˌdæt‿'i:vnɪŋ] an diesem Abend **II U1,** 19
That's what I call .... [ˌðæts wɒt‿'aɪ ˌkɔ:l] Das nenne ich .... **II U1,** 14
that's why ['ðæts ˌwaɪ] deshalb **II U1,** 18
the [ðə; ði] der/die/das **I U1,** 11
theater *(AE)* ['θɪətə] Theater; Kino **IV U1,** 9
their [ðeə] ihr/ihre **I U2,** 30
them [ðem] sie, ihnen **I U4,** 60
theme park ['θi:m ˌpɑ:k] Freizeitpark **IV U2,** 22
themselves [ðəm'selvz] sie/sich (selbst) **VI T3,** 42
then [ðen] dann **I LUB,** 38
there [ðeə] dort, da **I U2,** 26
over there [ˌəʊvə 'ðeə] da drüben **I U5,** 66
there are [ðer‿'ɑ:] da sind, es gibt **I U2,** 32
there is [ðer‿'ɪz] da ist, es gibt **I U2,** 32
thermostat ['θɜ:mestæt] Thermostat, Temperaturregler **VI T3,** 42
these [ði:z] diese, diese hier **I U6,** 84
these days ['ði:z deɪz] heutzutage **VI T1,** 12
they [ðeɪ] sie *(Mehrzahl)* **I U1,** 16; man **III U1,** 10
thick [θɪk] dick *(nicht für Personen)*; dumm **III U1,** 16
thin [θɪn] dünn **VI T4,** 63
thing [θɪŋ] Sache, Ding **I U3,** 40
*to **think** [θɪŋk] denken **I U3,** 49; glauben **II U4,** 50
to think about ['θɪŋk‿əˌbaʊt] nachdenken über, denken an °**II U7,** 95
to think of ['θɪŋk‿əv] denken an °**II U3,** 39
third [θɜ:d] dritter/dritte/drittes **I U5,** 70; Drittel **V T3,** 46
this [ðɪs] dies; dieser/diese/dieses **I U1,** 12
this evening [ðɪs 'i:vnɪŋ] heute Abend **III U3,** 46
those [ðəʊz] diese dort, jene **I U6,** 84
though [ðəʊ] trotzdem, dennoch **IV U5,** 80
thoughtful ['θɔ:tfl] aufmerksam, fürsorglich **IV U2,** 26
thousand ['θaʊznd] tausend **II U2,** 23

to **threaten** ['θretn] (be)drohen **V T1,** 10
thriller ['θrɪlə] Thriller **III U5,** 68
through [θru:] durch **II U4,** 57
*to **throw** [θrəʊ] werfen **I U3,** 49
Thursday ['θɜ:zdeɪ] Donnerstag **I LUB,** 39
to **tick** [tɪk] abhaken °**II U5,** 65
ticket ['tɪkɪt] Ticket, Fahrschein, Eintrittskarte **I U7,** 90
tiger ['taɪgə] Tiger **I U2,** 26
tights *(pl)* [taɪts] Strumpfhose **V T1,** 12
till [tɪl] bis **IV U4,** 64
time [taɪm] Zeit **I U2,** 30; Mal **II U1,** 18
at any time [æt‿eni 'taɪm] jederzeit **IV U2,** 25
on time [ɒn 'taɪm] pünktlich **IV U3,** 46
time off [taɪm‿'ɒf] Freizeit **VI T4,** 59
to have a good time [ˌhæv‿ə gʊd 'taɪm] sich amüsieren **I U5,** 75
What's the time, please? [ˌwɒts ðə 'taɪm ˌpli:z] Wie viel Uhr ist es, bitte?; Wie spät ist es, bitte? **I U3,** 42
What time ... ? [wɒt 'taɪm] (Um) wie viel Uhr ... ? **III U1,** 12
to **time** [taɪm] stoppen, die Zeit nehmen **I U7,** 92
timeline ['taɪmlaɪn] Zeitleiste °**I U4,** 63
timetable ['taɪmteɪbl] Stundenplan, Fahrplan **II U1,** 12
tin [tɪn] Büchse **III U2,** 30
tiny ['taɪni] winzig **I LUA,** 25
tip [tɪp] Tipp **II U4,** 52; Trinkgeld **IV U1,** 12
to **tip** [tɪp] (aus)kippen **VI T4,** 62
tired ['taɪəd] müde **II U3,** 38
dog-tired [ˌdɒg 'taɪəd] hundemüde **I U3,** 49
title ['taɪtl] Titel, Überschrift **II U3,** 42; Bezeichnung **V T1,** 15
to [tʊ; tə] zu, nach, bis **I U1,** 19
toast [təʊst] Toast **IV U1,** 12
tobacco [tə'bækəʊ] Tabak **IV U2,** 25
today [tə'deɪ] heute **I U2,** 29
toe [təʊ] Zeh **II U3,** 41
together [tə'geðə] zusammen, miteinander **I LUB,** 38
toilet ['tɔɪlɪt] Toilette **I U1,** 19
tomato, tomatoes *(pl)* [tə'mɑ:təʊ; tə'mɑ:təʊz] Tomate **I U5,** 68
tomorrow [tə'mɒrəʊ] morgen **II U1,** 18
ton [tʌn] Tonne *(Gewicht)* **VI T3,** 42
tongue [tʌŋ] Zunge **VI T4,** 64
mother tongue ['mʌðə ˌtʌŋ] Muttersprache **VI T1,** 12
tongue twister ['tʌŋ ˌtwɪstə] Zungenbrecher °**II U4,** 55
tonight [tə'naɪt] heute Abend, heute Nacht **I U6,** 84
too [tu:] auch **I U1,** 10; zu **I U5,** 66
tool [tu:l] Werkzeug **VI T3,** 46
tooth, teeth *(pl)* [tu:θ; ti:θ] Zahn **III U5,** 74
false teeth [fɔ:ls 'ti:θ] Zahnprothese, Gebiss **VI T2,** 28
toothache ['tu:θeɪk] Zahnschmerzen **IV U3,** 48
top [tɒp] Spitze, oberer Teil **IV U1,** 8
at the top [ət ðə 'tɒp] oben, im oberen Teil **III U1,** 14
topic ['tɒpɪk] Thema **I U2,** 33
torch, torches *(pl)* [tɔ:tʃ; 'tɔ:tʃɪz] Taschenlampe, Fackel **I U6,** 84
torn [tɔ:n] hin- und hergerissen, zerrissen **V T2,** 30
total ['təʊtl] total, gesamt, vollständig **VI T3,** 42
to **touch** [tʌtʃ] berühren; antippen **III U3,** 47
tough [tʌf] hart, rau, zäh **III U5,** 68
tour [tʊə] Tour, Fahrt, Reise **IV U1,** 16
tourist ['tʊərɪst] Tourist/Touristin **III U2,** 24
towards [tə'wɔ:dz] in Richtung, auf ... zu, darauf zu **III U5,** 78
tower ['taʊə] Turm **III U2,** 22; Kontrollturm, Tower **VI T1,** 10
town [taʊn] Stadt **I U3,** 41
town planner ['taʊn ˌplænə] Stadtplaner/Stadtplanerin **VI T3,** 47
toy [tɔɪ] Spielzeug **III U2,** 24
tractor ['træktə] Traktor **IV U3,** 41
trade [treɪd] Handel **V T4,** 58
trader ['treɪdə] Händler/Händlerin **VI T1,** 13
tradition [trə'dɪʃn] Tradition **III U2,** 30
traditional [trə'dɪʃnl] traditionell **VI T2,** 30; **VI T3,** 43
traffic ['træfɪk] Verkehr **III U2,** 22
traffic jam ['træfɪk ˌdʒæm] Stau **III U2,** 22
tragic ['trædʒɪk] tragisch **VI T4,** 59
train [treɪn] Zug **I U4,** 54
to **train** [treɪn] eine Ausbildung machen **V T2,** 32; ausbilden, lernen; trainieren **V T3,** 47
trainee [treɪ'ni:] Trainee, Auszubildender/Auszubildende **VI T1,** 14
trainers *(pl)* ['treɪnəz] Turnschuhe **III U4,** 56
training ['treɪnɪŋ] Training, Ausbildung **III U4,** 58
translation [trænz'leɪʃn] Übersetzung °**VI T2,** 31
transport ['trænspɔ:t] Transport **I U4,** 57
transport *(no pl)* ['trænspɔ:t] Verkehrsmittel, Beförderung **III U2,** 27
to **transport** [træn'spɔ:t] transportieren **IV U4,** 57
*to be **trapped** [bi: 'træpt] in der Falle sitzen **II U6,** 83
travel ['trævl] Reise **III U5,** 70
day travel card [ˌdeɪ 'trævl ˌkɑ:d] Tagesfahrkarte **III U2,** 27
travel agent ['trævl‿eɪdʒnt] Reisebürokaufmann/Reisebürokauffrau **VI T1,** 17
to **travel** ['trævl] reisen **III U3,** 38
to **treat** [tri:t] behandeln **VI T2,** 33
treatment ['tri:tmənt] Behandlung **V T3,** 45
treaty ['tri:ti] (Staats-)Vertrag, Abkommen **VI T2,** 30
tree [tri:] Baum **I U1,** 20
family tree ['fæmli tri:] Familienstammbaum °**I U2,** 28
trend [trend] Trend, Entwicklung, Richtung **VI T3,** 43
trendy ['trendi] modisch **III U2,** 22
trial ['traɪəl] Prüfung, Test **VI T1,** 10
court trial ['kɔ:t traɪəl] Gerichtsverhandlung **VI T2,** 26
tribe [traɪb] (Volks-)Stamm **IV U4,** 56
trick [trɪk] Trick, Streich **I U3,** 40
tricky ['trɪki] verfahren, kompliziert **VI T2,** 32
trip [trɪp] Ausflug, Reise **I U6,** 80
trolley ['trɒli] Gepäckwagen, Einkaufswagen, Handkarren **III U3,** 44
trouble ['trʌbl] Schwierigkeiten, Ärger **I U2,** 30
trousers *(pl)* ['traʊzəz] Hose **II U1,** 10
truck *(AE)* [trʌk] Lastwagen, Truck **IV U4,** 57
trucker *(AE)* ['trʌkə] Lastwagenfahrer/Lastwagenfahrerin, Trucker **IV U4,** 57
true [tru:] wahr **II U1,** 18
to come true [kʌm 'tru:] wahr werden **VI T4,** 59
to **trust** [trʌst] vertrauen **III U3,** 46
to **try** [traɪ] versuchen, probieren **II U1,** 10
tryout *(AE)* ['traɪaʊt] Auswahlverfahren *(im Sport)* **IV U2,** 22
T-shirt ['ti:ʃɜ:t] T-Shirt **I U2,** 30
tucker ['tʌkə] Essen *(australischer Ausdruck)* °**II U1,** 14
Tuesday ['tju:zdeɪ] Dienstag **I LUB,** 39
tug [tʌg] Ziehen, Zupfen **III U3,** 46
tunnel ['tʌnl] Tunnel, Unterführung **I U4,** 54
turbine ['tɜ:baɪn] Turbine **VI T3,** 46
turkey ['tɜ:ki] Truthahn, Pute **IV U1,** 12
Turkish ['tɜ:kɪʃ] türkisch **I U2,** 29

in **turn** [ɪn 'tɜ:n] abwechselnd, der Reihe nach °**V T3,** 45
It's your turn. [ɪts jɔ: 'tɜ:n] Du bist dran. **II U1,** 13
to take turns [teɪk 'tɜ:nz] sich abwechseln °**VI T3,** 43
to **turn** [tɜ:n] drehen, sich umdrehen **III U5,** 74; werden **V T4,** 64
to turn back [tɜ:n 'bæk] umkehren, zurückgehen **II U1,** 19
to turn down [tɜ:n 'daʊn] herunterdrehen **VI T3,** 42
to turn left/right [tɜ:n 'left/'raɪt] links/rechts abbiegen **II U7,** 97
to turn off [tɜ:n‿'ɒf] abschalten, ausschalten **I U5,** 75
to turn on [ˌtɜ:n‿'ɒn] einschalten, anmachen **IV U3,** 44
to turn over [ˌtɜ:n‿'əʊvə] (sich) umdrehen **II U7,** 94
to turn round [tɜ:n 'raʊnd] (sich) umdrehen **II U1,** 18
to be a **turn-off** ['tɜ:nɒf] abtörnend sein, zum Abgewöhnen sein **V T2,** 28
turnover ['tɜ:nˌəʊvə] Umsatz, Absatz **V T4,** 62
TV [ˌti:'vi:] Fernsehen, Fernseher **I LUA,** 25
twice [twaɪs] zweimal **III U5,** 68
twig [twɪg] Zweig **VI T4,** 62
type [taɪp] Typ, Art, Sorte **IV U4,** 62
to **type** [taɪp] tippen °**VI T1,** 15
typical ['tɪpɪkl] typisch, kennzeichnend **V T1,** 16

U

umbrella [ʌm'brelə] Regenschirm **II U6,** 81
to **unburden** [ʌn'bɜ:dn] entlasten, abladen **VI T4,** 63
uncertain ['ʌnsɜ:tn] unbestimmt, unsicher **VI T1,** 15
uncle ['ʌŋkl] Onkel **I U2,** 28
under ['ʌndə] unter **I U1,** 18
underground ['ʌndəgraʊnd] U-Bahn **III U2,** 23
to **underline** [ˌʌndə'laɪn] unterstreichen **II U1,** 18
underlined [ˌʌndə'laɪnd] unterstrichen °**I U7,** 98
*to **understand** [ˌʌndə'stænd] verstehen **III U5,** 74
underwater [ˌʌndə'wɔ:tə] Unterwasser- **V T4,** 64
unfair [ʌn'feə] ungerecht, unfair **V T3,** 45
unfriendly [ʌn'frendli] unfreundlich **IV U5,** 79
unhappy [ʌn'hæpi] unglücklich **I U2,** 33
unhealthy [ʌn'helθi] ungesund **II U4,** 53
uniform ['ju:nɪfɔ:m] Uniform **I U3,** 44
union ['ju:njən] Liga; Vereinigung, Union **III U1,** 11
unit ['ju:nɪt] Kapitel, Einheit °**IV U1,** 8
universe ['ju:nɪvɜ:s] Universum, Weltraum **V T3,** 46
university [ˌju:nɪ'vɜ:səti] Universität **IV U2,** 28
unless [ən'les] es sei denn, (dass) … **V T1,** 12
unsure [ʌn'ʃɔ:] unsicher **VI T4,** 56
until [ʌn'tɪl; n'tɪl] bis **II U4,** 56
up [ʌp] auf, hinauf, oben **II U2,** 30
Hurry up! [ˌhʌri‿'ʌp] Beeil dich! **I U2,** 30
to dig up [dɪg‿'ʌp] ausgraben **III U1,** 16
to get up [get‿'ʌp] aufstehen **I U3,** 44
to go up [gəʊ‿'ʌp] hinaufgehen °**I U4,** 61
to wake up [weɪk‿'ʌp] aufwecken; aufwachen **I U3,** 48
to walk up to [wɔ:k‿'ʌp tə] hingehen, zugehen auf **III U5,** 75
up current ['ʌp ˌkʌrnt] gegen die Strömung **V T4,** 64
up to ['ʌp tə] bis zu **III U4,** 53
What's up? [ˌwɒts‿'ʌp] Was ist los? **I U1,** 16
update ['ʌpdeɪt] Update, Aktualisierung **VI T2,** 28
to **update** [ʌp'deɪt] aktualisieren °**II U5,** 62
upper ['ʌpə] oberer/obere/oberes **IV U2,** 28
*to be **upset** [bi: ʌp'set] aufgeregt sein, bestürzt sein **II U3,** 44
to get upset [ˌget ʌp'set] sich aufregen **VI T1,** 15
upside down [ˌʌpsaɪd 'daʊn] umgedreht, auf den Kopf gestellt **VI T4,** 62
upstairs [ʌp'steəz] oben, im oberen Stock **I U2,** 27
to run upstairs [ˌrʌn‿ʌp'steəz] die Treppe hinaufrennen **III U3,** 47
urgent ['ɜ:dʒnt] dringend **V T1,** 10
us [ʌs] uns **I U4,** 60
use [ju:s] Verwendung, Nutzung **VI T2,** 33
to **use** [ju:z] benutzen, verwenden **I U4,** 54
used to (+ infinitive) ['ju:s‿tə] früher; pflegte(n) zu **VI T1,** 12; **VI T4,** 63
useful ['ju:sfl] nützlich **IV U3,** 45
useless ['ju:sləs] nutzlos **III U4,** 54
usually ['ju:ʒli] normalerweise, gewöhnlich **II U4,** 53

V

vacancy ['veɪknsi] Stellenangebot, offene Stelle; freies Zimmer **V T1,** 14
vacation *(AE)* [və'keɪʃn] Ferien, Urlaub **IV U1,** 12
valid ['vælɪd] gültig, zulässig **V T1,** 14
valuable ['væljuəbl] wertvoll **III U2,** 22
van [væn] Lieferwagen **I U6,** 86
vegetable ['vedʒtəbl] Gemüse **II U1,** 15
vehicle ['vɪəkl] Fahrzeug, Vehikel **VI T4,** 60
venom ['venəm] Gift *(z. B. von Schlangen und Insekten)*; Bosheit **V T1,** 12
verb [vɜ:b] Verb °**II U1,** 20
verse [vɜ:s] Vers, Strophe **IV U5,** 78
version ['vɜ:ʃn] Version, Variante °**VI T1,** 13
very ['veri] sehr **I U1,** 20; aller- **IV U1,** 16
video ['vɪdiəʊ] Video **I LUB,** 38
view [vju:] Aussicht, Sicht **III U2,** 22
point of view [ˌpɔɪnt‿əv‿'vju:] Ansicht, Einstellung, Standpunkt °**VI T4,** 65
to **view** [vju:] anschauen, betrachten **IV U5,** 76
viewer ['vju:ə] Zuschauer/Zuschauerin **III U5,** 68
village ['vɪlɪdʒ] Dorf **III U4,** 54
vinegar ['vɪnɪgə] Essig **V T1,** 12
vintage ['vɪntɪdʒ] alt(modisch) **VI T4,** 60
vintage car [ˌvɪntɪdʒ 'kɑ:] Oldtimer **VI T4,** 60
violence ['vaɪəlnts] Gewalt(tätigkeit) **V T3,** 42
violent ['vaɪəlnt] gewaltsam, gewalttätig, brutal **VI T2,** 29
virtual ['vɜ:tʃuəl] virtuell **IV U3,** 41
working visa ['wɜ:kɪŋ ˌvi:zə] Arbeitserlaubnis **V T1,** 14
visit ['vɪzɪt] Besuch **I U7,** 94
to **visit** ['vɪzɪt] besuchen, besichtigen **I U4,** 54
visitor ['vɪzɪtə] Besucher/Besucherin **I U4,** 55
vital ['vaɪtl] lebenswichtig, unerlässlich; Lebens- **IV U5,** 78
vital signs *(pl)* [ˌvaɪtl 'saɪnz] Lebenszeichen **IV U5,** 78
vocabulary [vəʊ'kæbjəlri] Wortschatz, Vokabular °**II U1,** 20
voice [vɔɪs] Stimme **II U2,** 31
volleyball ['vɒlibɔ:l] Volleyball **I U3,** 40
voluntary ['vɒləntri] freiwillig; ehrenamtlich **V T2,** 32
volunteer [ˌvɒlən'tɪə] Freiwilliger/Freiwillige; freiwillig **V T2,** 29
vote [vəʊt] Abstimmung, Stimme **IV U2,** 31

to vote [vəʊt] abstimmen, wählen **IV U2,** 31
V-shaped ['vi:ˌʃeɪpt] V-förmig °**IV U3,** 49

W

to **wait** [weɪt] warten **I U5,** 69
to wait for ['weɪt fɔ:] warten auf **I U6,** 86
waiter ['weɪtə] Kellner, Bedienung **II U4,** 55
*to **wake** [weɪk] (auf)wecken **II U7,** 94
to wake up [weɪk‿'ʌp] aufwecken; aufwachen **I U3,** 48
walk [wɔ:k] Spaziergang **III U5,** 76
to go for a walk [ˌgəʊ fər‿ə 'wɔ:k] spazieren gehen **III U5,** 76
to **walk** [wɔ:k] gehen, laufen **I U4,** 54
to walk the dog [wɔ:k ðə 'dɒg] mit dem Hund spazieren gehen **I U3,** 42
to walk up to [wɔ:k‿'ʌp tə] hingehen, zugehen auf **III U5,** 75
wall [wɔ:l] Wand, Mauer **I U1,** 18
wallet ['wɒlɪt] Brieftasche, Geldbeutel **II U4,** 56
to **want (to)** ['wɒnt tə] wollen, mögen **I U4,** 54
to want sb to do sth [wɒnt] wollen, dass jemand etwas tut **III U4,** 52
war [wɔ:] Krieg **IV U1,** 10
wardrobe ['wɔ:drəʊb] Kleiderschrank, Garderobe **I U2,** 30
warm [wɔ:m] warm **II U2,** 25
(global) **warming** [ˌgləʊbl 'wɔ:mɪŋ] (Erd-)Erwärmung **V T4,** 61
to **warn** [wɔ:n] warnen, ermahnen **V T4,** 61
warning ['wɔ:nɪŋ] Warn-; Warnung **IV U3,** 46
to **wash** [wɒʃ] (sich) waschen **I U3,** 44
waste [weɪst] Verschwendung; Abfall **V T2,** 30
to **waste** [weɪst] verschwenden **V T2,** 30
to **watch** [wɒtʃ] ansehen, beobachten **I LUB,** 38; achten auf **II U2,** 31
Watch out! [wɒtʃ‿'aʊt] Achtung!, Pass(t) auf! °**IV U2,** 31
water ['wɔ:tə] Wasser **I U5,** 68
tap water ['tæp ˌwɔ:tə] Leitungswasser **VI T3,** 45
wave [weɪv] Welle **III U4,** 60
to **wave** [weɪv] winken, schwenken **II U6,** 83
way [weɪ] Weg **I U3,** 42; Art, Weise **VI T3,** 42
by the way [ˌbaɪ ðə 'weɪ] übrigens **IV U4,** 61
He is on his way to .... [ˌhi:‿ɪz‿ɒn hɪz 'weɪ tə] Er ist auf dem Weg zu .... **I U3,** 42
to get in the way (of) [ˌget‿ɪn‿ðə‿'weɪ] etw. verhindern, im Weg stehen **V T2,** 29
Which way ... ? [wɪtʃ 'weɪ] Auf welche Art ... ?, Auf welchem Weg ... ? °**III U3,** 39
we [wi:] wir **I U1,** 16
weak [wi:k] schwach **III U4,** 60
to go weak [gəʊ 'wi:k] schwach werden **III U4,** 60
weakness ['wi:knəs] Schwäche **VI T1,** 14
weapon ['wepən] Waffe **V T3,** 44
*to **wear** [weə] anhaben, tragen **I U3,** 45
weather ['weðə] Wetter **II U1,** 14
weatherman, weathermen *(pl)* ['weðəmən; 'weðəmen] Meteorologe °**II U6,** 78
webcam ['webkæm] Webcam °**II U5,** 63
website ['websaɪt] Website, Internetauftritt **II U5,** 64
webzine ['webzi:n] Webmagazin °**VI T1,** 12
Wednesday ['wenzdeɪ] Mittwoch **I LUB,** 39
week [wi:k] Woche **I LUB,** 39
a week [ə 'wi:k] pro Woche, in der Woche **II U4,** 52
weekday ['wi:kdeɪ] Wochentag, Werktag **V T1,** 14
weekend [ˌwi:k'end] Wochenende **I U3,** 45
weight [weɪt] Gewicht **III U1,** 11
to **welcome** ['welkəm] willkommen heißen **I U7,** 90
*to be **welcome to do** [bi: 'welkəm] gerne etwas tun können **III U4,** 56
Welcome (to) ... ['welkəm tə] Willkommen (in) ... **III U4,** 57
You're welcome. [jʊə 'welkəm] Bitte sehr!, Gern geschehen! **I U1,** 19
as **well as** [əz 'wel‿əz] sowohl ... als auch **III U4,** 57
well [wel] also, na ja, nun gut **I U2,** 29
Welsh [welʃ] walisisch; Waliser/ Waliserin **III U3,** 42
west [west] Westen **I U4,** 54
western ['westən] Western-, Western; westlich **IV U4,** 58
wet [wet] nass **II U6,** 74
wet blanket [wet 'blæŋkɪt] Miesmacher/Miesmacherin **II U6,** 74
wetsuit ['wetsu:t] Taucheranzug, Neoprenanzug **V T4,** 64
what [wɒt] welcher/welche/welches **I LUA,** 25; was **I U1,** 11
What about ... ? [wɒt‿ə'baʊt] Was ist mit ...? Wie wäre es mit ...? **I U2,** 30
What a laugh! [ˌwɒt‿ə 'lɑ:f] Wie lustig! **III U1,** 17
What a week! [ˌwɒt‿ə 'wi:k] Was für eine Woche! **II U2,** 22
What does it say? [ˌwɒt dʌz‿ɪt 'seɪ] Was steht da? **II U3,** 44
What's the film about? [wɒts ðə 'fɪlm‿əˌbaʊt] Wovon handelt der Film? °**II U3,** 43
What's the matter? [ˌwɒts ðə 'mætə] Was ist los? **III U5,** 76
What's the time, please? [ˌwɔts ðə 'taɪm ˌpli:z] Wie viel Uhr ist es, bitte?; Wie spät ist es, bitte? **I U3,** 42
What's up? [ˌwɒts‿'ʌp] Was ist los? **I U1,** 16
What's your name? [ˌwɒts jə 'neɪm] Wie heißt du? **I U1,** 11
What time ... ? [wɒt 'taɪm] (Um) wie viel Uhr ... ? **III U1,** 12
whatever [wɒt'evə] was auch immer; egal welche **IV U4,** 58
when [wen] wenn, als; wann **I U2,** 33
where [weə] wo, wohin **I U1,** 11
Where are you from? [ˌweər‿ə jə 'frɒm] Woher kommst du? **I U1,** 11
Where's the fire? [ˌweəz ðə 'faɪə] Wo brennt's denn? **I U7,** 96
which [wɪtʃ] welcher/welche/welches **II U1,** 14; der/dem/den/die/das *(Relativpronomen)* **II U3,** 42
Which way ... ? [wɪtʃ 'weɪ] Auf welche Art ... ?, Auf welchem Weg ... ? °**III U3,** 39
while [waɪl] während **IV U4,** 61
to **whisper** ['wɪspə] flüstern, zuflüstern **II U1,** 18
whistle ['wɪsl] Pfiff; Trillerpfeife **VI T4,** 63
to **whistle** ['wɪsl] pfeifen **VI T4,** 63
white [waɪt] weiß **I LUA,** 24
white elephant stall [ˌwaɪt 'elɪfənt stɔ:l] Trödelstand **I U7,** 96
who [hu:] wer, wem, wen **I U5,** 70; der/ dem/den/die *(Relativpronomen)* **II U3,** 42
whole [həʊl] ganz **IV U1,** 11
whom [hu:m] dem/der *(Relativpronomen)* **III U3,** 46
whose [hu:z] wessen **II U5,** 68; dessen/ deren *(Relativpronomen)* **III U3,** 47
why [waɪ] warum **I U5,** 70
wicked ['wɪkɪd] großartig **II U5,** 70
wide [waɪd] groß, breit, weit **VI T1,** 8
to **widen** ['waɪdn] (sich) erweitern, ausweiten **VI T1,** 14

wife, wives *(pl)* [waɪf; waɪvz] Ehefrau **III U5,** 74
wig [wɪg] Perücke **II U2,** 28
wild [waɪld] wild **III U5,** 76
*__will ('ll), won't__ [wɪl; wəʊnt] werden, werden nicht *(futurisch)* **II U6,** 76
*to **win** [wɪn] gewinnen, siegen **II U7,** 91
wind [wɪnd] Wind **I U2,** 35
windmill ['wɪnmɪl] Windmühle; Windrad, Windkraftanlage **V T4,** 59
window ['wɪndəʊ] Fenster **I U1,** 18
to **windsurf** ['wɪnsɜ:f] windsurfen **III U3,** 40
windy ['wɪndi] windig **I U6,** 79
wing [wɪŋ] Flügel **V T4,** 65
winner ['wɪnə] Gewinner/Gewinnerin, Sieger/Siegerin **III U4,** 53
winter ['wɪntə] Winter **I U6,** 79
to **wipe** [waɪp] (ab)wischen, abreiben **VI T4,** 64
wish [wɪʃ] Wunsch **III U4,** 53
to **wish** [wɪʃ] wünschen **III U4,** 58
I wish I had … [wɪʃ] Ich wünschte, ich hätte … **III U4,** 58
with [wɪð] mit **I U1,** 14; bei **II U1,** 11
within [wɪ'ðɪn] innerhalb **III U2,** 24
without [wɪ'ðaʊt] ohne **I U4,** 54
to go without [ˌgəʊ wɪ'ðaʊt] ohne … auskommen **II U4,** 52
wizard ['wɪzəd] Zauberer **II U5,** 69
wolf, wolves *(pl)* [wʊlf; wʊlvz] Wolf **III U5,** 74
woman, women *(pl)* ['wʊmən; 'wɪmɪn] Frau **I U4,** 62
no **wonder** [nəʊ 'wʌndə] kein Wunder, dass … **VI T4,** 62
wood [wʊd] Holz **III U3,** 41
Woof! [wʊf] Wau! °**I U2,** 27
word [wɜ:d] Wort **I U1,** 15
word star ['wɜ:d stɑ:] Wortstern °**I U1,** 22
work [wɜ:k] Arbeit **I U3,** 47
paper work ['peɪpə ˌwɜ:k] Papierkram **VI T1,** 15
work experience ['wɜ:k‿ɪkˌspɪəriənts] Praktikum **VI T2,** 33
to **work** [wɜ:k] arbeiten, funktionieren **I U3,** 48
to work out [ˌwɜ:k‿'aʊt] herausfinden, ausarbeiten **VI T4,** 64
worker ['wɜ:kə] Arbeiter/Arbeiterin, Angestellter/Angestellte **IV U3,** 48
workman, workmen *(pl)* ['wɜ:kmən; 'wɜ:kmen] Handwerker **IV U1,** 17
workplace ['wɜ:kpleɪs] Arbeitsplatz, Arbeitsstätte **VI T2,** 29
worksheet ['wɜ:kʃi:t] Arbeitsblatt **I U4,** 58
workshop ['wɜ:kʃɒp] Workshop; Werkstatt **III U4,** 53
world [wɜ:ld] Erde, Welt **III U1,** 13
worldwide [ˌwɜ:ld'waɪd] weltweit **V T4,** 60
*to be **worried** [bi: 'wʌrid] besorgt sein, beunruhigt sein **I U6,** 87
worry ['wʌri] Sorge °**III U4,** 54
to **worry** ['wʌri] sich Sorgen machen **I U6,** 82; ängstigen, beunruhigen **II U3,** 45
worse [wɜ:s] schlimmer, schlechter **II U4,** 50
worst [wɜ:st] schlimmster/schlimmste/schlimmstes, schlechtester/schlechteste/schlechtestes **II U4,** 50
*__would__ [wʊd] würde/würden **III U3,** 47
would like [wʊd 'laɪk] hätte(n) gern, möchte(n) gern **II U4,** 52
Would you mind … ? [ˌwʊd jə 'maɪnd] Hätten Sie/Hättest du etwas dagegen … ? **III U4,** 56
wow [waʊ] toll, wow °**I U1,** 12
*to **write** [raɪt] schreiben **I U3,** 43
to write down ['raɪt ˌdaʊn] aufschreiben °**I LUB,** 38
writer ['raɪtə] Schriftsteller/Schriftstellerin, Verfasser/Verfasserin **VI T4,** 66
wrong [rɒŋ] falsch **I U1,** 16
to be wrong [bi: 'rɒŋ] Unrecht haben **III U3,** 47
to get … wrong [get … 'rɒŋ] falsch machen **II U3,** 44; falsch verstehen °**II U3,** 47
to go wrong [gəʊ 'rɒŋ] schief gehen **II U6,** 85

Y

yard [jɑ:d] Elle *(Längenmaß: 0,914 m)* **III U3,** 43
yeah *(slang)* [jeə] ja **IV U1,** 16
year [jɪə] Jahr, Jahrgangsstufe **I U1,** 10
yearbook ['jɪəbʊk] Jahrbuch **IV U2,** 22
year-old [ˌjɪər‿'əʊld] -jährig; -Jähriger/-Jährige **III U4,** 53
yellow ['jeləʊ] gelb **I LUA,** 24
yes [jes] ja **I U1,** 12
yesterday ['jestədeɪ] gestern **II U2,** 26
yet [jet] dennoch, jedoch **VI T2,** 30
not … yet [jet] noch nicht **II U5,** 66
you [ju:; jə] du, ihr **I U1,** 11; dich, dir, Sie, Ihnen, euch **I LUB,** 38; man **III U1,** 8
Here you are! ['hɪə ju:‿ɑ:] Bitte schön! **I U1,** 20
thank you ['θæŋk‿ju:] danke **I U1,** 12
you're lucky [ˌjʊə 'lʌki] du hast Glück **I U1,** 16
You're welcome. [jʊə 'welkəm] Bitte sehr!, Gern geschehen! **I U1,** 19
young [jʌŋ] jung **I U3,** 45
young apprentice (YA) [jʌŋ‿ə'prentɪs] minderjähriger Auszubildender/minderjährige Auszubildende **VI T2,** 32
your [jɔ:] dein/deine, euer/eure, Ihr/Ihre **I U1,** 11
Yours [jɔ:z] Dein …/Deine …/Euer …/Eure … *(in Briefen)* **II U3,** 36
yourself [jɔ:'self] du/dich (selbst) **VI T3,** 42
yourselves [jɔ:'selvz] ihr/euch/Sie/sich (selbst) **VI T3,** 42
youth [ju:θ] Jugend **II U3,** 38
yukky ['jʌki] ekelhaft **III U4,** 57
yummy ['jʌmi] lecker **V T4,** 63

Z

zone [zəʊn] Zone °**IV U4,** 60
zoo [zu:] Zoo, Tierpark **II U2,** 22
zookeeper ['zu:ki:pə] Tierpfleger/Tierpflegerin, Wärter/Wärterin **II U2,** 26
Zulu ['zu:lu:] Zulu **VI T1,** 12

Boys' names

Abdur ['æbdə] **VI T4,** 61
Abu ['ɑ:bu:] **V T4,** 64
Adam ['ædəm] **VI T4,** 62
Aidan ['eɪdn] **V T2,** 29
Alan ['ælən] **VI T2,** 29
Ali ['ɑ:li] **VI T1,** 14
Angus ['æŋgəs] **II FA,** 103
Arthur ['ɑ:θə] **III FA,** 84
Ben [ben] **I U2,** 27
Bob [bɒb] **I U6,** 78
Bobby ['bɒbi] **VI T1,** 10
Brad [bræd] **IV U2,** 24
Bradley ['brædli] **IV U3,** 42
Brandon ['brændən] **IV U1,** 16
Bruce [bru:s] **IV U4,** 59
Burt [bɜ:t] **II U4,** 55
Cal [kæl] **IV U2,** 30
Carly ['kɑ:li] **IV U5,** 76
Cavendish ['kævndɪʃ] **VI T4,** 60
Chandler ['tʃændlə] **II U3,** 37
Charles [ˌtʃɑ:lz] **III U5,** 76
Charlie ['tʃɑ:li] **I U2,** 33
Daniel ['dænjəl] **II U4,** 51
Dave [deɪv] **III U1,** 9
David ['deɪvɪd] **I U2,** 28

Davy ['deɪvi] **VT1,** 14
Derek ['derɪk] **II U4,** 51
Dicken ['dɪkn] **II FA,** 110
Diego [di'eɪgəʊ] **IV U1,** 12
Donny ['dɒni] **IV U4,** 64
Douglas ['dʌgləs] **II FA,** 102
Ector ['ektə] **III FA,** 84
Ellroy ['elrɔi] **IV U2,** 24
Emilio [ɪ'mɪliəʊ] **VT3,** 46
Eric ['erɪk] **I FA,** 102
Frank [fræŋk] **IV U1,** 16
Fred [fred] **III U3,** 41
Gelert ['gelət] **III U5,** 69
Hassan [hə'sɑ:n] **VI T1,** 14
Henry ['henri] **II FA,** 114
Homer ['həʊmə] **VI T4,** 60
Ian ['i:ən] **III U5,** 75
Jack [dʒæk] **I FA,** 102
Jake [dʒeɪk] **II U1,** 14
Jakob ['dʒeɪkb] **VI T1,** 12
James [dʒeɪmz] **I U2,** 28
Jay [dʒeɪ] **III U5,** 73
Jim [dʒɪm] **I U5,** 73
Jo [dʒəʊ] **I FA,** 105
Joel ['dʒəʊəl] **VT4,** 64
Joey ['dʒəʊi] **II U3,** 37
John [dʒɒn] **I U4,** 57
José [heʊ'zeɪ] **IV U1,** 12
Judd [dʒʌd] **VT2,** 28
Jude [dʒu:d] **VI T3,** 44
Jules [dʒu:lz] **VT2,** 31
Karim [kə'rɪm] **IV U1,** 15
Kay [keɪ] **III FA,** 84
Kingsley ['kɪŋzli] **III U2,** 34
Kofi ['kəʊfi] **VT4,** 60
Leo ['lɪ:eʊ] **III U1,** 16
Leon ['lɪɒn] **III U1,** 11
Leroy ['li:rɔɪ] **IV U2,** 33
Llywelyn [lə'welɪn] **III U5,** 74
Marc [mɑ:k] **III U4,** 53
Mark [mɑ:k] **I U4,** 61
Mat [mæt] **VT1,** 17
Matt [mæt] **II U2,** 31
Miguel [mɪ'gel] **VT2,** 30
Mike [maɪk] **III U4,** 62
Miles [maɪlz] **IV U2,** 30
Nelson ['nelsn] **I U1,** 13
Pablo ['pɑ:bləʊ] **IV U4,** 63
Patrick ['pætrɪk] **II U7,** 88
Paul [pɔ:l] **I U6,** 85
Pete [pi:t] **II U1,** 11
Peter ['pi:tə] **I U4,** 61
Phil [fɪl] **I U2,** 28
Ray [reɪ] **III U4,** 58
Reg [redʒ] **III U2,** 30
Richard ['rɪtʃəd] **I U2,** 27
Rick [rɪk] **IV U4,** 68
Rob [rɒb] **I U2,** 26
Robert ['rɒbət] **II U4,** 51
Rodger ['rɒdʒə] **III U5,** 77
Roger ['rɒdʒə] **II U3,** 36
Ross [rɒs] **II U3,** 37
Sam [sæm] **I U1,** 16
Steve [sti:v] **I U1,** 23
Ted [ted] **I U2,** 26
Terry ['teri] **I U1,** 10
Thomas ['tɒməs] **I LUA,** 25
Tim [tɪm] **I LUA,** 25
Todd [tɒd] **II U3,** 36
Tom [tɒm] **I U1,** 10
Tony ['təʊni] **I LUA,** 25
Tyler ['taɪlə] **IV U2,** 27
Uther ['ju:θə] **III FA,** 84
Vince [vɪns] **VI T1,** 11
William ['wɪljəm] **VT1,** 11
Zach [zæk] **VT2,** 30; **VT4,** 64

Girls' names

Alison ['ælɪsən] **II U5,** 67
Alysha [ə'lɪʃə] **IV U2,** 30
Amanda [ə'mændə] **III U5,** 75
Amber ['æmbə] **VT4,** 64
Andrea ['ændriə] **VI T1,** 12
Anna ['ænə] **I U3,** 47
Brenda ['brendə] **IV U2,** 33
Carrie ['kæri] **III U4,** 54
Chloé ['kləʊi] **VT2,** 30
Connie ['kɒni] **VT1,** 14
Cora ['kɔ:rə] **VT1,** 17
Daisy ['deɪzi] **III U4,** 54
Debbie ['debi] **II U3,** 36
Dinah ['daɪnə] **IV U4,** 61
Donna ['dɒnə] **IV U2,** 30
Dorothy ['dɒrəθi] **II U5,** 68
Elena ['elɪnə] **I U2,** 28
Em [em] **II FA,** 114
Emma ['emə] **I U1,** 12
Farah ['fɑ:rə] **I U2,** 26
Faye [feɪ] **VI T1,** 12
Fiona [fi'əʊnə] **I U1,** 23
Glinda ['glɪndə] **II FA,** 114
Grace [greɪs] **I U2,** 26
Helen ['helən] **II U7,** 88
Igraine [ɪ'greɪn] **III FA,** 84
Ina ['i:nə] **VI T1,** 12
Jade [dʒeɪd] **I U2,** 27
Jaden ['dʒeɪdn] **VT2,** 30
Jane [dʒeɪn] **III U2,** 29
Jenna ['dʒenə] **III U4,** 59
Jenny ['dʒeni] **I U4,** 57
Jo [dʒəʊ] **VT3,** 46
Julie ['dʒu:li] **III U4,** 62
Kate [keɪt] **I U4,** 57
Kath [kæθ] **I U6,** 78
Kim [kɪm] **IV U1,** 16
Laura ['lɔ:rə] **II U1,** 11
Lauren ['lɔ:rən] **III U4,** 54
Laurie ['lɒri] **IV U1,** 15
Lisa ['li:sə] **I U1,** 10
Louise [lu'i:z] **VI T4,** 63
Margaret ['mɑ:grət] **VT1,** 11
Maria [mə'ri:ə] **I U2,** 28
Marita [mə'ri:tə] **IV U4,** 64
Mariya [mə'ri:ə] **IV U2,** 33
Mary ['meəri] **I U4,** 57
Mel [mel] **VI T4,** 61
Mia ['mi:ə] **VI T1,** 14
Monika ['mɒnɪkə] **II U3,** 37
Nadine [neɪ'di:n] **I U1,** 13
Nancy ['nænsi] **III U1,** 9
Nasreen [nʌs'ri:n] **I U2,** 26
Nicola ['nɪklə] **I FA,** 100
Nicole [nɪ'kəʊl] **II U3,** 36
Nina ['ni:nə] **IV U2,** 27
Nyla ['naɪlə] **III U4,** 54
Olivia [ɒ'lɪviə] **VT2,** 32
Pat [pæt] **II U1,** 16
Paula ['pɔ:lə] **III U1,** 11
Paula-Jo [ˌpɔ:lə 'dʒəʊ] **IV U2,** 27
Phoebe ['fi:bi] **II U3,** 37
Pru [pru:] **III U2,** 31
Rachel ['reɪtʃl] **II U3,** 37
Sally ['sæli] **I U6,** 85
Sandy ['sændi] **IV U2,** 23
Sarah ['seərə] **I U2,** 28
Sharleen [ʃə'li:n] **IV U2,** 30
Sharon ['ʃærən] **VT1,** 17
Stella ['stelə] **II FA,** 104
Sue [su:] **I U2,** 27
Susan ['su:zn] **I U2,** 28
Suzanne [su:'zæn] **I U1,** 11
Tamara [tə'mɑ:rə] **I LUA,** 25
Tammy ['tæmi] **IV U2,** 24
Terri ['teri] **IV U2,** 27
Tess [tes] **I U6,** 85
Tessa ['tesə] **VI T4,** 59
Tilly ['tɪli] **I LUA,** 25
Tina ['ti:nə] **I LUA,** 25
Toni Ann [ˌtəʊni 'æn] **III U2,** 34
Tracy ['treɪsi] **I U2,** 28
Trina ['tri:nə] **III U1,** 15
Virginia [və'dʒɪnjə] **III FA,** 96
Yolanda [jə'lændə] **VI T2,** 30
Zahra ['zɑ:rə] **VT4,** 64
Zameera [zə'mi:rə] **VT4,** 60

Surnames

Akodu [ə'kəʊdʊ] **III U4,** 58
Barnes ['bɑ:nz] **III U1,** 16
Barrymore ['bærimɔ:] **III U5,** 76

Baskerville ['bæskəvɪl] **III U5,** 70
Bell [bel] **II U4,** 52
Berry [beri] **III U1,** 9
Black [blæk] **II U1,** 11
Bland [blænd] **II FA,** 108
Brook [brʊk] **I U1,** 12
Brown [braʊn] **II U1,** 11
Buah ['bʊə] **V T4,** 63
Burns [bɜːnz] **III U5,** 71
Cage [keɪdʒ] **III U1,** 9
Canterville ['kæntəvɪl] **III FA,** 94
Carter ['kɑːtə] **I U1,** 12
Cartwright ['kɑːtraɪt] **III U2,** 30
Clarke [klɑːk] **III U3,** 46
Conte ['kɒnteɪ] **V T3,** 46
Dawson ['dɔːsn] **V T1,** 11
Delaney [də'leɪni] **V T3,** 46
Dhlomo ['dləʊmə] **VI T1,** 12
Downham ['daʊnəm] **VI T4,** 62
Forster ['fɔːstə] **IV U3,** 42
Fox [fɒks] **IV U3,** 50
George [dʒɔːdʒ] **III U1,** 11
Gibbs [gɪbz] **III U4,** 56
Gruntle ['grʌntl] **II FA,** 108
Gulch [gʌltʃ] **II FA,** 114
Gusman ['gʌzmən] **IV U4,** 63
Hall [hɔːl] **III U5,** 75
Healthiman ['helθɪmæn] **VI T3,** 44
Howard [haʊəd] **II U1,** 14
Hunter [hʌntə] **I U6,** 82
Jackson ['dʒæksn] **I U1,** 10
Jiayi [ˌdʒɪ'aɪ] **VI T1,** 12
Johnston ['dʒɒntstn] **VI T2,** 29
Jones [dʒəʊnz] **III U4,** 60
Keenan ['kiːnən] **VI T3,** 44
Lean [liːn] **I FA,** 104
Longbow ['lɒŋbəʊ] **VI T4,** 60
MacDonald [mək'dɒnld] **IV U2,** 23
Mahal [mə'hæl] **VI T1,** 10
Marco ['mɑːkəʊ] **II U1,** 11
Martin ['mɑːtɪn] **I FA,** 106
McArthur [mək'ɑːθə] **II FA,** 102
Monte ['mɒnteɪ] **I U2,** 28
Morley ['mɔːli] **III U4,** 54
Muir [mjʊə] **II FA,** 103
Newman ['njuːmən] **I U1,** 12
O'Brien [əʊ'braɪən] **II U7,** 88
Otis ['əʊtɪs] **III FA,** 94
Pilch [pɪltʃ] **I U2,** 28
Prynn [prɪn] **III U4,** 60
Reece [riːs] **III U4,** 59
Richards ['rɪtʃədz] **II U3,** 45
Richstone ['rɪtʃsteʊn] **III U5,** 72
Robbins ['rɒbɪnz] **III U3,** 45
Rose [rəʊz] **I U4,** 60
Simpson ['sɪmpsən] **III U5,** 70
Smith [smɪθ] **III U4,** 53
Spencer ['spentsə] **I U2,** 28
Stapleton ['steɪpltən] **III U5,** 77
Stavros ['stʌvrəs] **I U2,** 28
Taylor ['teɪlə] **I U1,** 10
Tiny ['taɪni] **I LUA,** 25
Wang [wæŋ] **VI T1,** 14
Watson ['wɒtsn] **III U5,** 69
White [waɪt] **III U2,** 29
Wilkins ['wɪlkɪnz] **III U4,** 60
Willis ['wɪlɪs] **III U5,** 75
Ziebarth ['tsiːbət] **VI T1,** 12

Place names

Abergavenny [ˌæbəgə'veni] **III U1,** 11
Atlanta [ət'læntə] **IV U5,** 76
Austin ['ɒstɪn] **IV U5,** 76
Avondale ['eɪvndeɪl] **III U5,** 69
Ayers Rock [ˌeəz 'rɒk] **V T1,** 9
Baker Street ['beɪkə ˌstriːt] **III U5,** 76
Barcelona [ˌbɑːsl'əʊnə] **III U1,** 13
Bath [bɑːθ] **I U6,** 79
Bondi Beach [ˌbɒndaɪ 'biːtʃ] **V T1,** 8
Boston ['bɒstn] **III U1,** 15
Boulder Way ['bəʊldə ˌweɪ] **VI T4,** 60
Brighton ['braɪtn] **III U3,** 38
Brisbane ['brɪzbən] **V T1,** 14
Bristol ['brɪstl] **I U1,** 12
Bronx [brɒŋks] **IV U1,** 9
Brooklyn ['brʊklɪn] **IV U1,** 9
Cairns [keənz] **V T1,** 14
Camden ['kæmdən] **II U2,** 22
Canary Wharf [kən'eəri ˌwɔːf] **III U2,** 27
Cape Town ['keɪp taʊn] **VI T1,** 12
Castle Garden [ˌkɑːsl 'gɑːdn] **IV U1,** 10
Central Park [ˌsentrl 'pɑːk] **IV U1,** 8
the **Channel** [ðə 'tʃænl] **III U3,** 39
Chicago [ʃɪ'kɑːgəʊ] **III U1,** 9
Chinatown ['tʃaɪnətaʊn] **IV U1,** 9
Chunnel ['tʃʌnl] Tunnel durch den Ärmelkanal **III U3,** 39
Colorado [ˌkɒlr'ɑːdəʊ] **IV U4,** 61
Cornwall ['kɔːnwɔːl] **II U6,** 78
Covent Garden [ˌkɒvnt 'gɑːdn] **III U2,** 24
Cutty Sark Gardens [kʌti ˌsɑːk 'gɑːdnz] **I U4,** 54
Dartmoor ['dɑːtmɔː] **III U5,** 76
Darwin ['dɑːwɪn] **V T1,** 16
Detroit [də'trɔɪt] **VI T4,** 60
Devon ['devn] **II U6,** 78
Dover ['dəʊvə] **III U3,** 38
Dublin ['dʌblɪn] **II U7,** 88
Eastbourne ['iːstbɔːn] **III U3,** 38
Ellis Island [ˌelɪs 'aɪlənd] **IV U1,** 9
Exmoor ['eksmɔː] **II ZI,** 8
Falmouth ['fælməθ] **III U3,** 42
Folkestone ['fəʊkstən] **III U3,** 38
Franklin ['fræŋklɪn] **V T1,** 14
Gaza City [ˌgɑːzə 'sɪti] **VI T2,** 29
Glasgow ['glæzgəʊ] **II FA,** 102
Goldcoast ['gəʊldˌkəʊst] **V T1,** 14
Grand Canyon [ˌgrænd 'kænjən] **IV U4,** 56
Great Barrier Reef Marine Park [ˌgreɪt ˌbæriə 'riːf mə'riːn ˌpɑːk] **V T1,** 10
Great Tower Street [ˌgreɪt 'taʊə ˌstriːt] **III U2,** 26
Greenwich ['grenɪdʒ] **I U1,** 10
Greenwich Village [ˌgrenɪdʒ 'vɪlɪdʒ] **IV U1,** 16
Hamburg ['hæmbɜːg] **VI T1,** 12
Hastings ['heɪstɪŋz] **III U3,** 38
Heathrow [ˌhiːθ'rəʊ] **III U3,** 39
Hollyoaks ['hɒliəʊks] **III U5,** 70
Hollywood ['hɒliwʊd] **III U5,** 68
Hong Kong [ˌhɒŋ 'kɒŋ] **VI T1,** 12
Houses of Parliament [ˌhaʊzɪz‿əv 'pɑːləmənt] **I FA,** 114
Istanbul [ˌɪstæn'bʊl] **I U1,** 13
Kilkenny [kɪl'keni] **II U7,** 93
Las Vegas [ˌlæs 'veɪgəs] **IV U4,** 57
Limerick ['lɪmrɪk] **II ZI,** 8
Liverpool ['lɪvəpuːl] **V T1,** 11
Loch Ness [ˌlɒx 'nes] **II ZI,** 8
London ['lʌndən] **I U1,** 10
London Bridge [ˌlʌndən 'brɪdʒ] **III U2,** 29
Los Angeles (LA) [lɒs‿'ændʒɪliːz] **IV U4,** 60
Madrid [mə'drɪd] **I U1,** 13
Manhattan [mæn'hætn] **IV U1,** 8
Marble Arch ['mɑːbl ˌɑːtʃ] **III U2,** 24
Mark Lane ['mɑːk ˌleɪn] **III U2,** 26
Melbourne ['melbən] **V T1,** 16
Memphis ['memfɪs] **V T3,** 42
Mexico City [ˌmeksɪkəʊ 'sɪti] **IV U4,** 65
Miami [maɪ'æmi] **IV U4,** 60
Moher ['məʊhə] **II U7,** 93
Montgomery [mən'gʌmri] **V T3,** 44
Moscow ['mɒskəʊ] Moskau **III U3,** 46
Nairobi [naɪ'rəʊbi] **I U1,** 13
Neston ['nestn] **I U6,** 78
New Amsterdam [ˌnjuː 'æmstədæm] **IV U1,** 10
New York [ˌnjuː 'jɔːk] **I U4,** 55
New York City (NYC) [ˌnjuː jɔːk 'sɪti] **IV U1,** 8
New York Harbor [ˌnjuː jɔːk 'hɑːbə] **IV U1,** 9
Nottingham ['nɒtɪŋəm] **II U2,** 25
Paris ['pærɪs] **I U1,** 13
Perth [pɜːθ] **II ZI,** 8
Philadelphia [ˌfɪlə'delfiə] **V T2,** 29
Phoenix ['fiːnɪks] **IV U3,** 49
Piccadilly Circus [ˌpɪkədɪli 'sɜːkəs] **III U2,** 24
Prescott ['preskət] **IV U3,** 49

Queens [kwi:nz] **IV U1,** 9
Reno ['ri:nəʊ] **IV U4,** 58
Rome [rəʊm] **IV U1,** 18
Round Rock [ˌraʊnd 'rɒk] **IV U5,** 76
Salisbury ['sɔ:lzbri] **III U3,** 38
Seattle [si'ætl] **IV U4,** 60
Shannon ['ʃænən] **II U7,** 93
Sherwood Forest [ˌʃɜ:wʊd 'fɒrɪst] **II-FA,** 110
Shoreditch [ʃɔ:'dɪtʃ] **III U2,** 31
Southampton [saʊ'θæmtən] **III U3,** 38
Staten Island [ˌstætn 'aɪlənd] **IV U1,** 9
Stonehenge [stəʊn'hendʒ] **III U3,** 39
Sydney ['sɪdni] **V T1,** 8
Sydney Cove [ˌsɪdni 'kəʊv] **V T1,** 10
Taronga Zoo [təˌrɒŋgə 'zu:] **V T1,** 11
Tokyo ['təʊkiəʊ] **I U1,** 13
Tower Hill [ˌtaʊə 'hɪl] **III U2,** 26
Townsville ['taʊnzvɪl] **V T1,** 10
Twickenham ['twikənəm] **III U1,** 8
Uluru [u:'lu:ru:] Uluru = Ayers Rock *(heiliger Berg der Aborigines)* **V T1,** 9
Urquhart Castle [ˌɜ:kət 'kɑ:sl] **II FA,** 102
Vancouver [væn'ku:və] **VI T1,** 11
Washington DC [ˌwɒʃɪŋtən di:'si:] **V T3,** 44
Wembley Stadium ['wembli 'steɪdiəm] **III U1,** 13
Westminster ['wesmɪnstə] **VI T2,** 30
Wildcroft ['waɪldkrɒft] **I FA,** 100
Wiltshire ['wɪltʃə] **I U6,** 78
Wimbledon ['wɪmbldn] **III U1,** 15
Winnipeg ['wɪnɪpeg] **VI T1,** 11
Wordsworth Way [ˌwɜ:dzwəθ 'weɪ] **V T1,** 11

Geographical names

Africa ['æfrɪkə] **V T4,** 60
Alabama [ˌælə'bæmə] **V T3,** 44
America [ə'merɪkə] **II U3,** 36
Arizona [ˌærɪ'zəʊnə] **IV U3,** 49
Asia ['eɪʒə] Asien **IV U1,** 10
Atlantic [ət'læntɪk] **IV U1,** 11
Australia [ɒs'treɪliə] Australien **II ZI,** 8
Belgium ['beldʒəm] Belgien **IV U1,** 10
Britain ['brɪtn] **II FA,** 102
British Isles [ˌbrɪtɪʃ 'aɪlz] Britische Inseln **II ZI,** 8
California [ˌkælɪ'fɔ:niə] **IV U3,** 42
Canada ['kænədə] Kanada **III U5,** 76
China ['tʃaɪnə] **III U1,** 13
East Africa [ˌi:st_'æfrɪkə] Ostafrika **VI T3,** 41
Eastern Europe [ˌi:stn 'jʊərəp] Osteuropa **IV U1,** 10
England ['ɪŋglənd] England **I U2,** 29
Ethiopia [i:θi'əʊpiə] Äthiopien **VI T3,** 41
Europe ['jʊərəp] Europa **IV U1,** 10
France [frɑ:nts] **III U3,** 39
Gaza ['gɑ:zə] **VI T2,** 29
Gaza Strip [ˌgɑ:zə 'strɪp] Gazastreifen **VI T2,** 29
Germany ['dʒɜ:məni] Deutschland **I U2,** 29
Ghana ['gɑ:nə] **V T4,** 59
Great Barrier Reef [ˌgreɪt ˌbæriə 'ri:f] **V T1,** 9
Great Blasket Island [ˌgreɪt ˌblɑ:skɪt 'aɪlənd] **III U3,** 42
Greece [gri:s] Griechenland **I U2,** 29
Hawaii [hə'waɪ] **IV U4,** 62
India ['ɪndiə] Indien **IV U1,** 10
Ireland ['aɪələnd] Irland **II U6,** 85
Irish Sea [ˌaɪrɪʃ 'si:] **III U3,** 38
Isle of Dogs [ˌaɪl_əv 'dɒgz] **I U4,** 54
Isle of Wight [ˌaɪl_əv 'waɪt] **III U3,** 38
Israel ['izreɪl] Israel **VI T2,** 27
Italy ['ɪtəli] Italien **I U2,** 29
Kansas ['kænzəs] **II FA,** 114
Lebanon ['lebənən] Libanon **VI T2,** 27
Little Oyster Island [ˌlɪtl_ɔɪstə 'aɪlənd] **IV U1,** 10
Maldives ['mɔ:ldi:vz] die Malediven **V T4,** 60
Manitoba [ˌmænɪ'təʊbə] **VI T1,** 11
Mexico ['meksɪkəʊ] Mexiko **IV U1,** 10
Michigan ['mɪʃɪgən] **VI T4,** 60
Mongolia [mɒŋ'gəʊliə] die Mongolei **V T4,** 59
Nevada [nə'vɑ:də] Nevada **IV U4,** 58
New Mexico [ˌnju: 'meksɪkəʊ] **IV U4,** 61
New Zealand [ˌnju: 'zi:lənd] Neuseeland **VI T3,** 44
North America [ˌnɔ:θ_ə'merɪkə] Nordamerika **VI T1,** 11
Northern Europe [ˌnɔ:ðən 'jʊərəp] Nordeuropa **IV U1,** 10
Northern Ireland [ˌnɔ:ðn_'aɪələnd] Nordirland **II U7,** 89
North Sea [ˌnɔ:θ 'si:] Nordsee **III U3,** 38
Northwest Territories [ˌnɔ:θwest 'teritriz] Nordwestterritorien **VI T1,** 11
Norway ['nɔ:weɪ] Norwegen **IV U1,** 10
Nunavut ['nu:nəvət] Nunavut *(Region in Kanada)* **VI T1,** 11
Oz [ɒz] Oz *(Spitzname für Australien)* **V T1,** 8
Philippines ['fɪlɪpi:nz] Philippinen **IV U1,** 10
Poland ['pəʊlənd] Polen **I U2,** 29
Quebec [kwɪ'bek] **VI T1,** 11
Republic of Ireland [rɪˌpʌblɪk_əv_'aɪələnd] Republik Irland **II U7,** 88
Rockies (Rocky Mountains) ['rɒkiz] **V T3,** 41
Russia ['rʌʃə] Russland **I U2,** 29
Scilly Isles ['sɪli ˌaɪlz] **II U6,** 78
Scotland ['skɒtlənd] Schottland **II ZI,** 8
South Africa [ˌsaʊθ_'æfrɪkə] Südafrika **VI T1,** 9; **VI T2,** 27
South America [ˌsaʊθ_ə'merɪkə] Südamerika **VI T1,** 17
South England [ˌsaʊθ 'ɪŋglənd] **III U3,** 39
Spain [speɪn] Spanien **III U3,** 40
Tasmania [tæz'meɪniə] **V T1,** 14
Tennessee [ˌtenə'si:] **V T3,** 44
Texas ['teksəs] **IV U1,** 16
the Thames [temz] **I U4,** 54
Turkey ['tɜ:ki] Türkei **I U2,** 29
United Kingdom (UK) [ju:ˌnaɪtɪd 'kɪŋdəm] Vereinigtes Königreich von Großbritannien und Nordirland **III U3,** 38
US [ju:'es] USA **IV U1,** 9
Vermont [və'mɒnt] **VI T2,** 28
Wales [weɪlz] Wales **II ZI,** 8
Western Australia [ˌwestən ɒs'treɪliə] **II U1,** 14

Other names

Academy Award [əˌkædəmi ə'wɔ:d] **IV U5,** 73
Alpha Centauri [ˌælfə sen'tɔ:ri] **IV U3,** 49
Apache Lake [əˌpætʃi 'leɪk] **IV U4,** 64
Aquarius [ə'kweəriəs] Wassermann **II U6,** 80
Arsenal ['ɑ:snl] **III U1,** 16
Bakerloo Line [ˌbeɪkəlu: 'laɪn] **III U2,** 24
Baskerville Hall ['bæskəvɪl ˌhɔ:l] **III U5,** 76
Batman ['bætmæn] **III U5,** 75
BBC [ˌbi:bi:'si:] BBC *(britische Rundfunkanstalt)* **VI T2,** 29
Bell Tower ['bel ˌtaʊə] **III U2,** 29
Big Ben [ˌbɪg 'ben] **III U2,** 22
Birdie Seed [ˌbɜ:di 'si:d] **VI T3,** 44
Blue Eagles [ˌblu: 'i:glz] **IV U2,** 22
Bollywood ['bɒliwʊd] **III U5,** 68
Bono ['bəʊnəʊ] **V T3,** 42
Boxing Day ['bɒksɪŋ ˌdeɪ] **I FA,** 114
Brooklyn Bridge [ˌbrʊklɪn 'brɪdʒ] **IV U1,** 9
Brushstroke Gang ['brʌʃstrəʊk ˌgæŋ] **V T2,** 30
BTec [bi:'tek] **VI T1,** 14
Buckingham Palace [ˌbʌkɪŋəm 'pælɪs] **III U2,** 22
Cadillac ['kædɪlæk] **IV U4,** 64
Chicago Cubs [ˌʃɪ'kɑ:gəʊ 'kʌbz] **III U1,** 9
Cincinnati Reds [ˌsɪnsɪnæti 'redz] **III U1,** 9

Circle Line ['sɜ:kl ˌlaɪn] **III U2,** 24
Cutty Sark [ˌkʌti 'sɑ:k] **I U4,** 54
DLR [ˌdi:‿el‿'ɑ:] **I U4,** 55
Docklands Light Railway ['dɒkləndz ˌlaɪt 'reɪlweɪ] **I U4,** 55
Dynamo Moscow ['daɪnəməʊ 'mɒskəʊ] **III U1,** 16
Eagle ['i:gl] **VI T4,** 60
Embankment [ɪm'bæŋkmənt] **III U2,** 24
Empire State Building [ˌempaɪə 'steɪt ˌbɪldɪŋ] **IV U1,** 8
Eurofoot ['jʊərəʊˌfʊt] **VI T1,** 10
FA Cup [ˌef‿eɪ 'kʌp] **III U1,** 13
Fairtrade [ˌfeə'treɪd] Fairer Handel **V T4,** 62
Friar Tuck [ˌfraɪə 'tʌk] **II FA,** 110
General Motors (GM) [ˌdʒenrl 'məʊtəz] **VI T4,** 60
GMT ['dʒi:em'ti:] **I U4,** 55
GPS [ˌdʒi:pi:'es] **IV U3,** 41
Grammy Award [ˌgræmi ə'wɔ:d] **IV U5,** 73
Green Corps ['gri:n ˌkɔ:] **V T1,** 14
Greenroad ['gri:nrəʊd] **VI T4,** 60
Greenwich Mean Time [ˌgrenɪdʒ 'mi:n taɪm] **I U4,** 55
Harbour Bridge ['hɑ:bə ˌbrɪdʒ] **V T1,** 9
Harrods ['hærədz] **II U2,** 23
Harry Potter [ˌhæri 'pɒtə] **II U1,** 11
House of Commons [ˌhaʊs‿əv 'kɒmənz] *(britisches Unterhaus)* **VI T2,** 30
House of Lords [ˌhaʊs‿əv 'lɔ:dz] *(britisches Oberhaus)* **VI T2,** 30
Hualapai [ˌhʊələ'peɪ] **IV U4,** 56
IBM [ˌaɪbi:'em] **V T3,** 43
James Bond [ˌdʒeɪmz 'bɒnd] **I FA,** 104
Little John [ˌlɪtl 'dʒɒn] **II FA,** 110
Little Rock Nine [ˌlɪtl ˌrɒk 'naɪn] **V T3,** 44
London Dungeon [ˌlʌndən 'dʌndʒn] **III U2,** 22
London Eye [ˌlʌndən‿'aɪ] **III U2,** 22
London Knights [ˌlʌndən 'naɪts] **II U2,** 22
London Underground [ˌlʌndən 'ʌndəgraʊnd] **III U2,** 23
Madonna [mə'dɒnə] **III U2,** 25
Magna Carta [ˌmægnə 'kɑ:tə] **VI T2,** 28
Maid Marian [ˌmeɪd 'mæriən] **II FA,** 110
Man U ['mæn ju:] **III U5,** 70
Mars [mɑ:z] **VI T1,** 14
Meridian Line [mə'rɪdiən 'laɪn] **I U4,** 54
Merlin ['mɜ:lɪn] **III FA,** 84
Mohawk ['məʊhɔ:k] **IV U1,** 15
Monument ['mɒnjəmənt] **III U2,** 24
MTV [ˌemti:'vi:] **I U6,** 82
Mustang ['mʌstæŋ] **IV U5,** 80
Napoleon [nə'pəʊliən] **II U5,** 62
NASA ['næsə] NASA *(US-Weltraumbehörde)* **IV U3,** 41
Nobel Peace Prize [nəʊˌbel 'pi:s ˌpraɪz] **V T3,** 44
NVQ (National Vocational Qualification) [ˌenvi:'kju:] Berufsqualifikation in England °**V T2,** 32
the **Olympics** *(Olympic Games)* [əʊ'lɪmpɪks; əʊˌlɪmpɪk 'geɪmz] Olympiade, Olympische Spiele **V T1,** 11
Oscar ['ɒskə] **IV U5,** 73
Palace of Westminster [ˌpælɪs əv 'wesmɪnstə] **III U2,** 22
PowerPoint ['paʊəpɔɪnt] **V T2,** 33
Robin Hood [ˌrɒbɪn 'hʊd] **II FA,** 110
Route 66 [ru:t] **IV U4,** 64
Royal Family ['rɔɪəl 'fæmli] königliche Familie **III U2,** 22
Royal Observatory [ˌrɔɪəl əb'zɜ:vətri] **I U4,** 55
Sherlock Holmes [ˌʃɜ:lɒk 'həʊmz] **III U5,** 70
Shrove Tuesday [ˌʃrəʊv 'tju:zdeɪ] **I FA,** 115
Skywalk ['skaɪwɔ:k] **IV U4,** 56
Solitaire [ˌsɒlɪ'teə] **VI T2,** 32
Speaker's Corner [ˌspi:kəz 'kɔ:nə] **VI T2,** 27
Statue of Liberty [ˌstætʃu:‿əv 'lɪbəti] **IV U1,** 9
St James's Park [snt ˌdʒeɪmzɪz 'pɑ:k] **III U2,** 24
St Paul's Cathedral [snt ˌpɔ:lz kə'θi:drl] **III U2,** 24
Swallow ['swɒləʊ] **VI T4,** 60
Taco Bell [ˌtɑ:kəʊ 'bel] **IV U5,** 80
Taj Mahal [ˌtɑ:dʒ mə'hɑ:l] **II U4,** 48
Thanksgiving [ˌθæŋks'gɪvɪŋ] **IV U4,** 60
Thomas Tallis School [ˌtɒməs tælɪs 'sku:l] **I U1,** 10
Times Square [ˌtaɪmz 'skweə] **IV U1,** 9
Titanic [taɪ'tænɪk] **III U3,** 39
Tower of London [ˌtaʊər‿əv 'lʌndən] **III U2,** 22
Tube [tju:b] Londoner U-Bahn **III U2,** 22
UFO *(Unidentified Flying Object)* ['ju:ef'əʊ] **IV U3,** 49
Valentine ['væləntaɪn] **II U6,** 85
Video Music Award [ˌvɪdiəʊ 'mu:zɪk əˌwɔ:d] **IV U5,** 73
White House ['waɪt ˌhaʊs] **II U3,** 43
William the Conqueror [ˌwɪljəm ðə 'kɒŋkrə] **III U2,** 28
Will Scarlet [ˌwɪl 'skɑ:lət] **II FA,** 110
Wizard of Oz [ˌwɪzəd əv‿'ɒz] **II U5,** 64
Wrigley Field Stadium [ˌrɪgli fi:ld 'steɪdiəm] **III U1,** 9
YouTube ['ju:tju:b] **V T2,** 32

Famous names

Angelina Jolie [ændʒˌli:nə 'dʒəʊli] **III U2,** 25
Annie Moore [ˌæni 'mɔ:] **IV U1,** 10
Arthur Conan Doyle [ˌɑ:θə ˌkəʊnən 'dɔɪl] **III U5,** 75
Beyoncé [bɪ'jɒnseɪ] **IV U5,** 73
Black Eyed Peas [ˌblæk‿aɪd 'pi:z] **IV U5,** 77
B Section ['bi: ˌsekʃn] **IV U5,** 80
50 Cent [ˌfɪfti 'sent] **VI T1,** 9
Champion Jack Dupree [ˌtʃæmpiən ˌdʒæk dʊ'preɪ] **V T3,** 42
Charlie Chaplin [ˌtʃɑ:li 'tʃæplɪn] **III U4,** 62
David Beckham [ˌdeɪvɪd 'bekəm] **III U2,** 25
Derrek Lee [ˌderɪk 'li:] **III U1,** 9
Eadweard Muybridge [ˌedwəd 'maɪbrɪdʒ] **IV U5,** 74
Edwin Porter [ˌedwɪn 'pɔ:tə] **IV U5,** 74
Fergie ['fɜ:gi] **IV U5,** 80
Green Day ['gri:n ˌdeɪ] **IV U5,** 73
James Cook [ˌdʒeɪmz 'kʊk] **V T1,** 10
Jennifer Hudson [ˌdʒenɪfə 'hʌdsn] **IV U5,** 72
Led Zeppelin [ˌled 'zeplɪn] **IV U5,** 76
Lil Jon [ˌlɪl 'dʒɒn] **IV U5,** 76
Ludacris ['lu:dəkrɪs] **IV U5,** 73
Martin Luther King [ˌmɑ:tɪn ˌlu:θə 'kɪŋ] **V T3,** 42
Naomi Campbell [ˌneɪəmi: 'kæmbl] **III U2,** 25
Nelly Furtado [ˌneli fə'tɑ:dəʊ] **IV U5,** 73
Nicole Kidman [nɪˌkəʊl 'kɪdmən] **IV U5,** 72
Pink [pɪŋk] **IV U5,** 73
Queen Elizabeth [ˌkwi:n‿ɪ'lɪzəbəθ] **I U5,** 73
Robbie Williams [ˌrɒbi 'wɪljəmz] **II U1,** 14
Robin Leach [ˌrɒbɪn 'li:tʃ] **IV U5,** 80
Rosa Parks [ˌrəʊzə 'pɑ:ks] **V T3,** 44
Samuel Ellis [ˌsæmjʊəl‿'elɪs] **IV U1,** 10
Sean Paul [ˌʃɔ:n 'pɔ:l] **IV U5,** 73
Shakespeare ['ʃeɪkspɪə] **II U5,** 62
Steve Fossett [sti:v 'fɒsət] **V T3,** 43
Thomas Edison [ˌtɒməs‿'edɪsn] **IV U5,** 74
U2 [ju'tu:] **V T3,** 42
Zandra Rhodes [ˌzændrə 'rəʊdz] **IV U5,** 72
Zeng Peiyan [ˌzeŋ 'pejæn] **VI T1,** 9

A

ab off [ɒf]
abbröckeln to flake [fleɪk]
Abc alphabet ['ælfəbet]
Abdruck mark [mɑ:k]
Abend evening ['i:vnɪŋ]; night [naɪt]
am Abend in the evening [ˌɪn ði: 'i:vnɪŋ]
an diesem Abend that evening [ˌdæt‿'i:vnɪŋ]
heute Abend this evening [ðɪs 'i:vnɪŋ]; tonight [tə'naɪt]
zu Abend essen to have supper [hæv 'sʌpə]
Abendessen dinner ['dɪnə]; supper ['sʌpə]; tea [ti:]
zum Abendessen for supper [fə 'sʌpə]
Abendkleid evening dress ['i:vnɪŋ ˌdres]
abends in the evening [ˌɪn ði: 'i:vnɪŋ]
Abenteuer adventure [əd'ventʃə]
aber but [bʌt]
abfahren to leave [li:v]
Abfall garbage *(AE)* ['gɑ:bɪdʒ]; rubbish ['rʌbɪʃ]; waste [weɪst]
Abfälle rubbish ['rʌbɪʃ]
Abfallverwertung recycling [ri:'saɪklɪŋ]
abfliegen to take off [ˌteɪk‿'ɒf]
Abflug departure [dɪ'pɑ:tʃə]
Abgabe fee [fi:]
Abgang exit ['eksɪt]
abgebrannt broke [brəʊk]
in Flaschen **abgefüllt** bottled ['bɒtld]
abgelegen remote [rɪ'məʊt]
abgesehen von apart from [ə'pɑ:t frəm]
zum **Abgewöhnen sein** to be a turn-off ['tɜ:nɒf]
abhalten to hold [həʊld]
abheben to take off [ˌteɪk‿'ɒf]
abholen to collect [kə'lekt]; to pick up [pɪk‿'ʌp]
abholzen to cut down [kʌt 'daʊn]
Abitur A-levels *(pl)* ['eɪlevlz]
Abkommen contract ['kɒntrækt]; treaty ['tri:ti]
abladen to dump sth [dʌmp]; to unburden [ʌn'bɜ:dn]
ablaufen *(Zeit)* to run out [rʌn‿'aʊt]
ablehnen to refuse [rɪ'fju:z]
Abmachung deal [di:l]
abnehmen *(Hut)* to take off [ˌteɪk‿'ɒf]
Aborigine Aborigine [ˌæbə'rɪdʒni]
abreiben to wipe [waɪp]
Abreise departure [dɪ'pɑ:tʃə]
Absatz turnover ['tɜ:nˌəʊvə]
abschalten to turn off [tɜ:n‿'ɒf]
abschicken *(einen Brief)* to post [pəʊst]
abschießen to shoot [ʃu:t]
abschließen to lock [lɒk]
Abschluss closing ['kləʊzɪŋ]
Abschlusszeugnis diploma [dɪ'pləʊmə]
abschrecken to frighten away [ˌfraɪtn‿ə'weɪ]
abschreiben to copy ['kɒpi]
Abschuss launch [lɔ:nʃ]
im **Abseits** offside [ˌɒf'saɪd]
absondern to emit [ɪ'mɪt]
abstimmen to vote [vəʊt]
Abstimmung vote [vəʊt]
Absturz crash [kræʃ]
Abteilung department [dɪ'pɑ:tmənt]
abtörnend sein to be a turn-off ['tɜ:nɒf]
Abwesenheit absence ['æbsns]
abwischen to wipe [waɪp]
achten auf to watch [wɒtʃ]
Acker field [fi:ld]
Adapter adaptor [ə'dæptə]
addieren to add [æd]
Administrator/Administratorin administrator [ə'dmɪnɪstreɪtə]
Adresse address [ə'dres]
Afrikaner/Afrikanerin African ['æfrɪkən]
afrikanisch African ['æfrɪkən]
Aftershave aftershave ['ɑ:ftəʃeɪv]
Agent/Agentin agent ['eɪdʒnt]
Agentur agency ['eɪdʒnsi]
agieren to act [ækt]
Agrikultur agriculture ['ægrɪkʌltʃə]
ähnlich similar ['sɪmɪlə]
Ahorn maple ['meɪpl]
Akademie academy [ə'kædəmi]
Akku battery ['bætri]
Akte record ['rekɔ:d]
Aktion action ['ækʃn]
aktiv active ['æktɪv]
Aktivität activity [æk'tɪvəti]
Aktualisierung update ['ʌpdeɪt]
Akzent accent ['æksnt]
akzeptieren to accept [ək'sept]
Alarm alarm [ə'lɑ:m]
alarmiert startled ['stɑ:tld]
Albtraum nightmare ['naɪtmeə]
Album album ['ælbəm]
Alge seaweed ['si:wi:d]
Alkohol alcohol ['ælkəhɒl]
alle everybody ['evribɒdi]
alle/alles all [ɔ:l]
aller- very ['veri]
allein alone [ə'ləʊn]; solo ['səʊləʊ]
(ganz) allein on one's own [ɒn wʌnz‿'əʊn]
Allein- solo ['səʊləʊ]
einen **Alleingang starten** to go it alone [ˌgəʊ‿ɪt‿ə'ləʊn]
alles everything ['evriθɪŋ]
alles klar all right [ɔ:l 'raɪt]
Alphabet alphabet ['ælfəbet]
alphabetisch alphabetical [ˌælfə'betɪkl]
als as [æz; əz]
als *(Vergleich)* than [ðən]
als *(zeitlich)* when [wen]
also so [səʊ]; well [wel]
alt ancient ['eɪnʃnt]; old [əʊld]; vintage ['vɪntɪdʒ]
Alter age [eɪdʒ]
alternativ alternative [ɔ:l'tɜ:nətɪv]
Alternative alternative [ɔ:l'tɜ:nətɪv]
altmodisch outdated [ˌaʊt'deɪtɪd]; vintage ['vɪntɪdʒ]
Amerikaner American [ə'merɪkən]
Hispano-Amerikaner/-Amerikanerin Hispanic [hɪ'spænɪk]
amerikanisch American [ə'merɪkən]
sich **amüsieren** to have a good time [ˌhæv‿ə gʊd 'taɪm]; to have fun [ˌhæv 'fʌn]
an at [æt; ət]; on [ɒn]
an sein to be on [bi:‿'ɒn]
anbauen to grow [grəʊ]
anbieten to offer ['ɒfə]
Anblick sight [saɪt]
anbringen to fix [fɪks]
andauern to continue [kən'tɪnju:]; to go on [gəʊ‿'ɒn]
Andenken souvenir [ˌsu:və'nɪə]
anderer/andere/anderes other ['ʌðə]
ein anderer/eine andere/ein anderes another [ə'nʌðə]
ändern to change [tʃeɪndʒ]
sich immer/stetig **ändernd** ever-changing ['evəˌtʃeɪndʒɪŋ]
anders different ['dɪfrnt]
Änderung change [tʃeɪndʒ]
Anfall attack [ə'tæk]
Anfang beginning [bɪ'gɪnɪŋ]; start [stɑ:t]
anfangen to begin [bɪ'gɪn]; to start [stɑ:t]
anfordern to require [rɪ'kwaɪə]
Anführer/Anführerin leader ['li:də]
Angebot offer ['ɒfə]
Angelegenheit matter ['mætə]
angeln to fish [fɪʃ]
Angeln fishing ['fɪʃɪŋ]
Angestellter/Angestellte employee [ɪm'plɔɪi:]; worker ['wɜ:kə]
Angler fisherman, fishermen *(pl)* ['fɪʃəmən; 'fɪʃəmen]
angreifen to attack [ə'tæk]
Angriff attack [ə'tæk]; raid [reɪd]
Angst haben (vor) to be afraid (of) [bi:‿ə'freɪd]; to be frightened (of) [bi: 'fraɪtnd]
Angst machen to scare [skeə]
Ich habe Angst. I'm scared. [aɪm 'skeəd]
ängstigen to worry ['wʌri]

anhaben to wear [weə]
anhalten to stop [stɒp]
Anhänger/Anhängerin supporter [sə'pɔ:tə]
anheben to raise [reɪz]
anhören to listen ['lɪsn]
sich anhören to sound [saʊnd]
fest **anklopfen** to bang [bæŋ]
ankommen to arrive [ə'raɪv]
Ankündigung announcement [ə'naʊntsmənt]
Anleitung direction [dɪ'rekʃn]
anmachen to switch on [swɪtʃ‿'ɒn]; to turn on [ˌtɜ:n‿'ɒn]
anmalen to paint [peɪnt]
anmelden to register ['redʒɪstə]
sich anmelden (zu) to apply (for) [ə'plaɪ]
sich anmelden to register ['redʒɪstə]
Anmerkung note [nəʊt]
annähernd nearly ['nɪəli]
annehmen to accept [ək'sept]
Anorak anorak ['ænəræk]
anpassen an to adapt to [ə'dæpt tə]
sich anpassen an to adapt to [ə'dæpt tə]
anpassungsfähig adaptable [ə'dæptəbl]; flexible ['fleksɪbl]
Anrufbeantworter answerphone ['ɑ:nsəfəʊn]
anrufen to call [kɔ:l]; to phone [fəʊn]
anschauen to have a look [ˌhæv‿ə 'lʊk]; to view [vju:]
Anschlag attempt [ə'tempt]; notice ['nəʊtɪs]
sich **anschließen** to join [dʒɔɪn]
ansehen to look at ['lʊk‿ət]; to watch [wɒtʃ]
sich ansehen to look at ['lʊk‿ət]
sich etwas ansehen to check out [tʃek‿'aʊt]
Ansprache speech [spi:tʃ]
Anstandswauwau chaperon ['ʃæprəʊn]
anstatt instead of [ɪn'sted‿əv]
Anstellung employment [ɪm'plɔɪmənt]
Anstieg rise [raɪz]
anstreichen to paint [peɪnt]
anti- anti ['æntɪ]
antik ancient ['eɪnʃnt]
antippen to touch [tʌtʃ]
Antrag application [ˌæplɪ'keɪʃn]
Antragsteller/Antragstellerin applicant ['æplɪkənt]
Antwort answer ['ɑ:ntsə]; response [rɪ'spɒns]
anweisen to direct [dɪ'rekt]
Anweisung order ['ɔ:də]
Anwendung application [ˌæplɪ'keɪʃn]
anwesend present ['preznt]
Anzeige ad [æd]; advert ['ædvɜ:t]
Anzeigenvertreter/Anzeigenvertreterin advertising agent ['ædvətaɪzɪŋ ˌeɪdʒnt]
anziehen to attract [ə'trækt]; to put on [pʊt‿'ɒn]
sich anziehen to dress [dres]
Anzug suit [su:t]
Apartment apartment *(AE)* [ə'pɑ:tmənt]
Apfel apple ['æpl]
Apparat machine [mə'ʃi:n]
am Apparat speaking ['spi:kɪŋ]
April April ['eɪprl]
Arbeit work [wɜ:k]
arbeiten to work [wɜ:k]
Arbeiter/Arbeiterin worker ['wɜ:kə]
Arbeitgeber/Arbeitgeberin employer [ɪm'plɔɪə]
Arbeitsblatt worksheet ['wɜ:kʃi:t]
Arbeitserlaubnis working visa ['wɜ:kɪŋ ˌvi:zə]
Arbeitsgebiet field [fi:ld]
Arbeitsgemeinschaft club [klʌb]
arbeitslos sein to be out of a job [bi‿aʊt‿əv‿ə 'dʒɒb]
Arbeitsplatz workplace ['wɜ:kpleɪs]
Arbeitsstätte workplace ['wɜ:kpleɪs]
Arbeitsstelle job [dʒɒb]
Architekt/Architektin architect ['ɑ:kɪtekt]
Arena arena [ə'ri:nə]
Ärger trouble ['trʌbl]
argumentieren to argue ['ɑ:gju:]
arm poor [pɔ:; pʊə]
Arm arm [ɑ:m]
Ärmel arm [ɑ:m]
Armut poverty ['pɒvəti]
Arsch ass *(AE)* [æs]
Art kind [kaɪnd]; type [taɪp]; way [weɪ]
Artikel article ['ɑ:tɪkl]
Arzt/Ärztin doctor ['dɒktə]
zum Arzt gehen to see a doctor [si:‿ə 'dɒktə]
Asche ash [æʃ]; ashes *(pl)* ['æʃɪz]
glimmende Asche embers *(pl)* ['embəz]
Asiate/Asiatin Asian ['eɪʃn]
asiatisch Asian ['eɪʃn]
Aspekt aspect ['æspekt]
Assistent/Assistentin assistant [ə'sɪstnt]
Astronaut/Astronautin astronaut ['æstrənɔ:t]
Atmosphäre atmosphere ['ætməsfɪə]
Attraktion attraction [ə'trækʃn]
attraktiv attractive [ə'træktɪv]
auch also ['ɔ:lsəʊ]; too [tu:]
sowohl … als auch as well as [əz 'wel‿əz]
auf at [æt; ət]; on [ɒn]; onto ['ɒntu:; 'ɒntə]; up [ʌp]
auf … zu towards [tə'wɔ:dz]
auf dem Land in the country [ˌɪn ðə 'kʌntri]
auf einmal suddenly ['sʌdnli]
auf Sendung on the air [ˌɒn ði‿'eə]
auf Wiedersehen goodbye [gʊd'baɪ]
Aufbau construction [kən'strʌkʃn]
aufbauen to put up [pʊt‿'ʌp]; to set up [set‿'ʌp]
aufbewahren to keep [ki:p]
Aufblinken flash [flæʃ]
aufbrechen to set off [set‿'ɒf]
aufbringen *(Geld)* to raise [reɪz]
Auffänger collector [kə'lektə]
aufführen to perform [pə'fɔ:m]
Aufführung performance [pə'fɔ:məns]
Aufgabe duty ['dju:ti]; exercise ['eksəsaɪz]; mission ['mɪʃn]; task [tɑ:sk]
aufgeben to give up [gɪv‿'ʌp]; to quit [kwɪt]; *(einen Brief)* to post [pəʊst]
aufgehen to open ['əʊpn]
aufgeregt excited [ɪk'saɪtɪd]; nervous ['nɜ:vəs]; upset [ʌp'set]
aufgeschlossen outgoing ['aʊtgəʊɪŋ]
aufheben to pick up [pɪk‿'ʌp]
aufhören to finish ['fɪnɪʃ]; to stop [stɒp]
aufhören etw. zu tun to stop + -ing [stɒp]
aufhören mit to stop [stɒp]; to quit [kwɪt]
aufklären to solve [sɒlv]
aufmachen to open ['əʊpn]
aufmerksam thoughtful ['θɔ:tfl]
Aufnahme record ['rekɔ:d]; recording [rɪ'kɔ:dɪŋ]; shot [ʃɒt]
aufnehmen to include [ɪn'klu:d]; to record [rɪ'kɔ:d]
aufpassen to take care [teɪk 'keə]
aufpassen auf to look after [lʊk‿'ɑ:ftə]
Aufprall crash [kræʃ]
sich **aufregen** to get upset [ˌget‿ʌp'set]; to panic ['pænɪk]
aufregend exciting [ɪk'saɪtɪŋ]
Aufruhr riot [raɪət]
aufschauen to look up [lʊk‿'ʌp]
Aufseher/Aufseherin keeper ['ki:pə]
aufsetzen to draw up [drɔ:‿'ʌp]; to put on [pʊt‿'ɒn]
aufspringen to jump up [dʒʌmp‿'ʌp]
aufstehen to get out of bed [ˌget‿aʊt‿əv 'bed]; to get up [get‿'ʌp]
aufsteigen to get on [get‿'ɒn]
aufstellen to put up [pʊt‿'ʌp]
Aufstieg rise [raɪz]
Auftrag mission ['mɪʃn]; task [tɑ:sk]
auftragen *(Make-up)* to put on [pʊt‿'ɒn]
auftreten to perform [pə'fɔ:m]

aufwachen to wake up [weɪk‿'ʌp]
aufwecken to wake [weɪk]; to wake up [weɪk‿'ʌp]
aufzeichnen to record [rɪ'kɔ:d]
Aufzeichnung record ['rekɔ:d]
Auge eye [aɪ]
Augenblick moment ['məʊmənt]
im Augenblick at the moment [ət ðə 'məʊmənt]
in diesem Augenblick right now [ˌraɪt 'naʊ]
Augenbraue eyebrow ['aɪbraʊ]
Augenklappe patch [pætʃ]
August August ['ɔ:gəst]
aus from [frɒm]; in [ɪn]
aus … heraus out of ['aʊt‿əv]
ausarbeiten to work out [ˌwɜ:k‿'aʊt]
ausbilden to train [treɪn]
Ausbilder/Ausbilderin instructor [ɪn'strʌktə]
Ausbildung apprenticeship [ə'prentɪʃɪp]; schooling ['sku:lɪŋ]; training ['treɪnɪŋ]
eine Ausbildung machen to train [treɪn]
ausbrechen to break out [ˌbreɪk‿'aʊt]
ausbreiten to spread [spred]
sich ausbreiten to spread [spred]
auschecken to check out [tʃek‿'aʊt]
sich **ausdenken** to make up [meɪk‿'ʌp]
Ausdruck phrase [freɪz]
Ausfahrt exit ['eksɪt]
ausfliegen to fly out [flaɪ‿'aʊt]
ausflippen to go crazy [gəʊ 'kreɪzi]
Ausflug trip [trɪp]
Ausfuhr export ['ekspɔ:t]
ausführen to export [ɪk'spɔ:t]
ausfüllen to complete [kəm'pli:t]; to fill in [fɪl‿'ɪn]
Ausgang exit ['eksɪt]
ausgeben to spend [spend]
ausgehen to go out [gəʊ‿'aʊt]; *(Zeit)* to run out [rʌn‿'aʊt]
ausgraben to dig up [dɪg‿'ʌp]
aushändigen to hand [hænd]
auskippen to dump sth [dʌmp]; to tip [tɪp]
gut **auskommen mit** to get on with [get‿'ɒn wɪð]
ohne … **auskommen** to go without [ˌgəʊ wɪ'ðaʊt]
auslachen to laugh at ['lɑ:f‿ət]
im **Ausland** abroad [ə'brɔ:d]
ins Ausland abroad [ə'brɔ:d]
Ausländer/Ausländerin foreigner ['fɒrɪnə]
ausländisch alien ['eɪliən]; foreign ['fɒrɪn]
ausleihen to loan [ləʊn]

ausliefern to deliver [dɪ'lɪvə]
auslösen *(Alarm)* to set off [set‿'ɒf]
Auslöser button ['bʌtn]
ausmachen to matter ['mætə]; to put out [pʊt‿'aʊt]
ausrauben to rob [rɒb]
Ausrede excuse [ɪk'skju:s]
Ausreißer/Ausreißerin runaway ['rʌnəˌweɪ]
Ausrichtung direction [dɪ'rekʃn]
ausruhen to rest [rest]
sich ausruhen to rest [rest]
Ausrüstung equipment [ɪ'kwɪpmənt]
ausschalten to switch off [ˌswɪtʃ‿'ɒf]; to turn off [tɜ:n‿'ɒf]
ausscheren to swerve [swɜ:v]
ausschließen to ban [bæn]
Ausschreitung riot [raɪət]
aussehen to look [lʊk]
Aussehen look [lʊk]
außer apart from [ə'pɑ:t frəm]; beside [bɪ'saɪd]; but [bʌt]; except [ɪk'sept]
außerhalb outside [aʊt'saɪd]
Außerirdischer/Außerirdische alien ['eɪliən]
außerordentlich extremely [ɪk'stri:mli]
Aussicht prospect ['prɒspekt]; view [vju:]
Ausstattung equipment [ɪ'kwɪpmənt]
aussteigen to get out [get‿'aʊt]
aussteigen aus to get off [get‿'ɒf]
ausstempeln to check out [tʃek‿'aʊt]
Ausstoß emission [ɪ'mɪʃn]
ausstoßen to emit [ɪ'mɪt]
Austausch exchange [ɪks'tʃeɪndʒ]
Australier Australian [ɒs'treɪliən]
australisch Australian [ɒs'treɪliən]
Auswahl choice [tʃɔɪs]
auswählen to choose [tʃu:z]; to elect [ɪ'lekt]
Auswahlmöglichkeit option ['ɒpʃn]
Auswahlverfahren *(im Sport)* tryout *(AE)* ['traɪaʊt]
auswandern to emigrate ['emɪgreɪt]
auswechseln to substitute ['sʌbstɪtju:t]
ausweichen to swerve [swɜ:v]
ausweiten to widen ['waɪdn]
Auswirkung effect [ɪ'fekt]
Auszeichnung award [ə'wɔ:d]
ausziehen to take off [ˌteɪk‿'ɒf]
Auszubildender/Auszubildende apprentice [ə'prentɪs]; trainee [treɪ'ni:]
minderjähriger Auszubildender/ minderjährige Auszubildende young apprentice (YA) [jʌŋ‿ə'prentɪs]
Auszug bit [bɪt]; extract ['ekstrækt]
Auto car [kɑ:]
Auto- automotive [ˌɔ:tə'məʊtɪv]

Autobahn Interstate *(AE)* [ˌɪntə'steɪt]
Autogramm autograph ['ɔ:təgrɑ:f]
Autopanne breakdown ['breɪkdaʊn]

B

Baby baby, babies *(pl)* ['beɪbi; 'beɪbiz]
Bach stream [stri:m]
Bäcker/Bäckerin baker ['beɪkə]
Backofen oven ['ʌvn]
Badeanzug swimsuit ['swɪmsu:t]
Badewanne bathtub ['bɑ:θtʌb]
Badezimmer bathroom ['bɑ:θrʊm]
Badminton badminton ['bædmɪntən]
Bagel bagel ['beɪgl]
Baguette baguette [bæg'et]
Bahnhof station ['steɪʃn]
Bahnsteig platform ['plætfɔ:m]
Balance balance ['bæləns]
bald soon [su:n]
Ball ball [bɔ:l]
Ballkönigin homecoming queen [ˌhəʊmkʌmɪŋ 'kwi:n]
Ballsaal ballroom ['bɔ:lrʊm]
Banane banana [bə'nɑ:nə]
Band band [bænd]
Bande band [bænd]; gang [gæŋ]
Bank bank [bæŋk]
Bann ban [bæn]
bannen to ban [bæn]
Bar bar [bɑ:]
Bär/Bärin bear [beə]
Barkeeper barman, barmen *(pl)* ['bɑ:mən, 'bɑ:men]
Barmann barman, barmen *(pl)* ['bɑ:mən, 'bɑ:men]
Baron baron ['bærn]
Bart beard [bɪəd]
Base base [beɪs]
Baseball baseball ['beɪsbɔ:l]
Basis base [beɪs]
Basketball basketball ['bɑ:skɪtbɔ:l]
Bass bass [beɪs]
Batterie battery ['bætri]
Bau(-) construction [kən'strʌkʃn]
Bauch stomach ['stʌmək]
bauen to build [bɪld]
Bauen building ['bɪldɪŋ]
Bauer/Bäuerin farmer ['fɑ:mə]
Bauernhaus farmhouse ['fɑ:mhaʊs]
Bauernhof farm [fɑ:m]
Baufachmann/Baufachfrau builder ['bɪldə]
Baum tree [tri:]
Baumeister/Baumeisterin builder ['bɪldə]
Baustelle building site ['bɪldɪŋ saɪt]
Beamter/Beamtin officer ['ɒfɪsə]; official [ə'fɪʃl]

beanspruchen to claim [kleɪm]
Bedarf need [niːd]
bedauerlich sad [sæd]
bedeuten to mean [miːn]
Bedeutung sense [sens]
von Bedeutung sein to matter ['mætə]
bedienen to operate ['ɒpəreɪt]
Bedienung waiter ['weɪtə]
Bedingung condition [kən'dɪʃn]
bedrohen to threaten ['θretn]
Bedürfnis need [niːd]
besondere Bedürfnisse special needs [ˌspeʃl 'niːdz]
Beeil dich! Hurry up! [ˌhʌri‿'ʌp]
beeinflussen to affect [ə'fekt]
beeinträchtigen to affect [ə'fekt]
beenden to end [end]; to finish ['fɪnɪʃ]
beerdigen to bury ['beri]
Beerdigung funeral ['fjuːnrəl]
Beet patch [pætʃ]
Befähigung qualification [ˌkwɒlɪfɪ'keɪʃn]
Befehl order ['ɔːdə]
befestigen to fix [fɪks]
befolgen to follow ['fɒləʊ]
befördern to carry ['kæri]
Beförderung transport *(no pl.)* ['trænspɔːt]
befristet temporary ['temprəri]
Beginn beginning [bɪ'gɪnɪŋ]; start [stɑːt]
beginnen to begin [bɪ'gɪn]; to start [stɑːt]
Begleitperson chaperon ['ʃæprəʊn]
begraben to bury ['beri]
begreifen to get it ['get‿ɪt]
behalten to keep [kiːp]
behandeln to treat [triːt]
Behandlung treatment ['triːtmənt]
behaupten to claim [kleɪm]
beherrschen to control [kən'trəʊl]
behindert disabled [dɪ'seɪbld]
Behinderung disability [ˌdɪsə'bɪləti]
Behörde agency ['eɪdʒnsi]
bei at [æt; ət]; with [wɪð]
beide both [bəʊθ]
Beifahrer/Beifahrerin passenger ['pæsndʒə]
Bein leg [leg]
beinahe almost ['ɔːlməʊst]
beinhalten to include [ɪn'kluːd]
zum **Beispiel** e.g. [iː'dʒiː]; for example [fər‿ɪg'zɑːmpl]
beißen to bite [baɪt]; to sting [stɪŋ]
Beistand aid [eɪd]
beitreten to join [dʒɔɪn]
bekämpfen to fight [faɪt]
sich **beklagen** to moan [məʊn]
bekommen to get [get]
belästigen to disturb [dɪ'stɜːb]; to harass [hə'ræs]
Belastung load [ləʊd]
belebt busy ['bɪzi]
Beleg record ['rekɔːd]; slip [slɪp]
beleidigen to diss *(slang)* [dɪs]
Beleuchtung lighting ['laɪtɪŋ]
Belgier/Belgierin Belgian ['beldʒən]
belgisch Belgian ['beldʒən]
beliebt popular ['pɒpjələ]
bellen to bark [bɑːk]
Bellen bark [bɑːk]; barking ['bɑːkɪŋ]
bemerken to notice ['nəʊtɪs]
Bemerkung comment ['kɒment]
benachrichtigen to inform [ɪn'fɔːm]
benennen to label ['leɪbl]; to name [neɪm]
benötigen to need [niːd]; to require [rɪ'kwaɪə]
benutzen to use [juːz]
Benzin *(AE)* gas [gæs]
beobachten to watch [wɒtʃ]
bequem comfortable ['kʌmpftəbl]
Berater/Beraterin adviser [əd'vaɪzə]
Bereich sector ['sektə]
bereit ready ['redi]
in **Bereitschaft** standby ['stændbaɪ]
bereitstellen to provide (sb with sth) [prə'vaɪd]
Berg hill [hɪl]; mountain ['maʊntɪn]
Bericht report [rɪ'pɔːt]
berichten to report [rɪ'pɔːt]
Beruf career [kə'rɪə]
beruflich professional [prə'feʃnl]
Berufs- professional [prə'feʃnl]
Berufsberatung careers advice [kə'rɪəz əd̩ˌvaɪs]
berühmt famous ['feɪməs]
berühren to touch [tʌtʃ]
Besatzung crew [kruː]
beschädigen to damage ['dæmɪdʒ]
Beschädigung damage ['dæmɪdʒ]
beschäftigt busy ['bɪzi]
Beschäftigung employment [ɪm'plɔɪmənt]
Bescheinigung certificate [sə'tɪfɪkət]
Beschränkung limit ['lɪmɪt]
beschreiben to describe [dɪ'skraɪb]
beschriften to label ['leɪbl]
Beschriftung label ['leɪbl]
beschützen to protect [prə'tekt]
beschützend protective [prə'tektɪv]
besichtigen to visit ['vɪzɪt]
besitzen to have got [hæv 'gɒt]; to own [əʊn]
Besitzer/Besitzerin owner ['əʊnə]
besonders special ['speʃl]; especially [ɪ'speʃli]
besondere Bedürfnisse special needs [ˌspeʃl 'niːdz]
besorgen to get [get]; to provide (sb with sth) [prə'vaɪd]
besorgt sein to be worried [biː 'wʌrid]
Besprechung meeting ['miːtɪŋ]
besprühen to spray [spreɪ]
besser better ['betə]
Bestand supply [sə'plaɪ]
bestehen to pass [pɑːs]; to survive [sə'vaɪv]
besteigen to climb ['klaɪm]
bestellen to order ['ɔːdə]
bester/beste/bestes best [best]
am besten best [best]
bestimmt specific [spə'sɪfɪk]
bestürzt sein to be upset [biː ʌp'set]
Besuch visit ['vɪzɪt]
besuchen to see [siː]; to visit ['vɪzɪt]
Besucher/Besucherin visitor ['vɪzɪtə]
beteiligen to involve [ɪn'vɒlv]
sich beteiligen to enter ['entə]
Betonung stress [stres]
betrachten to view [vjuː]
Betrag amount [ə'maʊnt]
betreffen to affect [ə'fekt]
betreten to enter ['entə]
Betreuer/Betreuerin supervisor ['suːpəvaɪzə]
betroffen concerned [kən'sɜːnd]
Bett bed [bed]
beunruhigen to worry ['wʌri]
beunruhigt concerned [kən'sɜːnd]
beunruhigt sein to be worried [biː 'wʌrid]
beurteilen to assess [ə'ses]
Bevölkerung population [ˌpɒpjə'leɪʃn]
bevor before [bɪ'fɔː]
bewachen to guard [gɑːd]
Bewaffneter gunman, gunmen *(pl)* ['gʌnmən; gʌnmen]
bewegen to move [muːv]
sich bewegen to move [muːv]
beweglich mobile ['məʊbaɪl]
Bewegung motion ['məʊʃn]; move [muːv]; movement ['muːvmənt]
sich **bewerben (um)** to apply (for) [ə'plaɪ]
Bewerber/Bewerberin applicant ['æplɪkənt]
Bewerbung application [ˌæplɪ'keɪʃn]
bewerten to assess [ə'ses]
bezahlen to pay (for) [peɪ]
Bezahlung pay [peɪ]
Bezeichnung title ['taɪtl]
Beziehung relationship [rɪ'leɪʃnʃɪp]
Bezirk borough ['bʌrə]
Bezug reference ['refrns]
Bibliothek library ['laɪbri]
Bild picture ['pɪktʃə]
bilden to form [fɔːm]
Bildschirm screen [skriːn]
Bildung education [edʒʊ'keɪʃn]

bilingual bilingual [baɪ'lɪŋgwəl]
billig cheap [tʃi:p]
Bindeglied link [lɪŋk]
Bindfaden string [strɪŋ]
biologisch angebaut organic [ɔ:'gænɪk]
Birne pear [peə]
bis till [tɪl]; to [tʊ; tə]; until [ʌn'tɪl; n'tɪl]
Bis .... See you! ['si: jə]; See you around! [ˌsi: jə ə'raʊnd]
Bis dann! See you! ['si: jə]; See you around! [ˌsi: jə ə'raʊnd]
bis zu up to ['ʌp tə]
Bischof bishop ['bɪʃəp]
Biss bite [baɪt]
ein **bisschen** a bit [ə 'bɪt]
Bissen bite [baɪt]
Bistro bistro bar [ˌbi:strəʊ 'bɑ:]
bitte please [pli:z]
Bitte schön! Here you are! ['hɪə ju:‿ɑ:]
Bitte sehr! You're welcome. [jʊə 'welkəm]
bitten (um) to ask (for) ['ɑ:sk fə]
bitter bitter ['bɪtə]
blasen to blow [bləʊ]
Blatt leaf, leaves *(pl)* [li:f; li:vz]; sheet [ʃi:t]
blau blue [blu:]
Blei lead [led]
bleiben to remain [rɪ'meɪn]; to stay [steɪ]
länger bleiben to stay on [steɪ‿'ɒn]
Bleistift pencil ['pensl]
Blende shutter ['ʃʌtə]
Blick look [lʊk]
einen vernichtenden Blick zuwerfen to give ... a dirty look [ˌgɪv‿ə dɜ:ti 'lʊk]
Blickfeld horizon [hə'raɪzn]
blind blind [blaɪnd]
blinken to flash [flæʃ]
blitzen to flash [flæʃ]
Blitzen flash [flæʃ]
blöd stupid ['stju:pɪd]
blond blond [blɒnd]; blond(e)-haired ['blɒnd ˌheəd]; fair [feə]
bloß only ['əʊnli]
Blume flower ['flaʊə]
Blut blood [blʌd]
Bluterguss bruise [bru:z]
blutig bloody ['blʌdi]
Blutkrebs leukaemia [lju:'ki:miə]
Boden ground [graʊnd]; soil [sɔɪl]
Bogen bow [bəʊ]
Bohne bean [bi:n]
Bohrer drill [drɪl]
Bohrmaschine drill [drɪl]
Bombe bomb [bɒm]
Bonbon sweet [swi:t]
Boot boat [bəʊt]
borgen to borrow ['bɒrəʊ]
bösartig fierce [fɪəs]
böse angry ['æŋgri]
böse sein auf to be angry with [bi: 'æŋgri wɪð]
Bosheit venom ['venəm]
Boss boss [bɒs]
Botschafter/Botschafterin ambassador [æm'bæsədə]
Boulevard boulevard ['bu:ləvɑ:d]
Branche business ['bɪznɪs]; department [dɪ'pɑ:tmənt]
brand- brand [brænd]
Brand fire [faɪə]
brauchen to need [ni:d]; to require [rɪ'kwaɪə]; *(Zeit)* to take [teɪk]
braun brown [braʊn]
Breakdance tanzen to break-dance ['breɪkdɑ:nts]
brechen to break [breɪk]; to fold [fəʊld]
breit across [ə'krɒs]; wide [waɪd]
brennen to burn [bɜ:n]; *(Licht)* to be on [bi:‿'ɒn]
Brennmaterial fuel ['fju:əl]
fossiler **Brennstoff** fossil fuel ['fɒsl ˌfju:əl]
schwarzes **Brett** notice board ['nəʊtɪs bɔ:d]
Brief letter ['letə]
Briefmarke stamp [stæmp]
Brieftasche wallet ['wɒlɪt]
Briefumschlag envelope ['envələʊp]
Brille glasses *(pl)* ['glɑ:sɪz]
bringen to bring [brɪŋ]; to take [teɪk]
es weit bringen to go far [gəʊ 'fɑ:]
nach Hause bringen to take home [ˌteɪk 'həʊm]
britisch British ['brɪtɪʃ]
Brombeergestrüpp bramble ['bræmbl]
Brot bread [bred]
belegtes Brot sandwich ['sænwɪdʒ]
Brücke bridge [brɪdʒ]
Bruder brother ['brʌðə]
brummen to buzz [bʌz]
brutal violent ['vaɪəlnt]
Buch book [bʊk]
buchen to book [bʊk]
Bücherei library ['laɪbri]
Büchse tin [tɪn]
Buchstabe letter ['letə]
buchstabieren to spell [spel]
buddeln to dig [dɪg]
Bude stall [stɔ:l]
bügeln to iron [aɪən]
Bühne stage [steɪdʒ]
Bumm! Crash! [kræʃ]
Bund league [li:g]
Bundesstraße highway *(AE)* ['haɪweɪ]
Bündnis league [li:g]
bunt colored *(AE)* ['kʌləd]; colorful *(AE)* ['kʌləfl]
Burg castle ['kɑ:sl]
bürgen to guarantee [ˌgærn'ti:]
Bürger/Bürgerin citizen ['sɪtɪzn]
Bürgerrechtsbewegung Civil Rights Movement (CRM) [ˌsɪvl 'raɪts ˌmu:vmənt]
Büro office ['ɒfɪs]
bürsten to brush [brʌʃ]
Bus bus, buses *(pl)* [bʌs; 'bʌsɪz]
im Bus on the bus [ˌɒn ðə 'bʌs]
Busch bush [bʊʃ]
eine **Busfahrt machen** to take a bus tour [ˌteɪk‿ə 'bʌs tʊə]
Bushaltestelle bus stop ['bʌs ˌstɒp]
Butter butter ['bʌtə]

C

Café café ['kæfeɪ]; snack bar ['snæk ˌbɑ:]
Cafeteria cafeteria [ˌkæfə'tɪəriə]
Call-Center call centre ['kɔ:l ˌsentə]
Camp camp [kæmp]
Camping camping ['kæmpɪŋ]
Canyon canyon ['kænjən]
Cartoon cartoon [kɑ:'tu:n]
Casino casino [kə'si:nəʊ]
Catering catering ['keɪtrɪŋ]
CD CD [ˌsi:'di:]
CD-Player CD player [ˌsi:'di: ˌpleɪə]
Celsius Celsius (C) ['selsiəs]
Cent *(Währung)* cent [sent]
Champagner champagne [ʃæm'peɪn]
Chaos chaos ['keɪɒs]
chaotisch chaotic [keɪ'ɒtɪk]; messy ['mesi]
Charakter character ['kærəktə]
Charta charter ['tʃɑ:tə]
Charts charts *(pl)* [tʃɑ:ts]
Chassis frame [freɪm]
Chatroom *(Internetforum, wo man sich online unterhalten kann)* chat room ['tʃæt rʊm]
Cheerleader *(Mädchen, das in einer Gruppe eine Sportmannschaft anfeuert)* cheerleader ['tʃɪəˌli:də]
Chef/Chefin boss [bɒs]
Chemikalie chemical ['kemɪkl]
chemisch chemical ['kemɪkl]
chillen to chill out [tʃɪl‿'aʊt]
chinesisch Chinese [tʃaɪ'ni:z]
Chinglish *(Mischung aus Chinesisch und Englisch)* Chinglish ['tʃɪŋlɪʃ]
circa about [ə'baʊt]
CO_2-Bilanz carbon footprint [ˌkɑ:bn 'fʊtprɪnt]

Cocktail cocktail ['kɒkteɪl]
Code code [kəʊd]
Cola coke [kəʊk]
College college ['kɒlɪdʒ]
Comic comic ['kɒmɪk]
Comicheft comic ['kɒmɪk]
Computer computer [ˌkəm'pju:tə]
cool cool [ku:l]
Cornflakes cornflakes ['kɔ:nfleɪks]
aus **Cornwall** Cornish ['kɔ:nɪʃ]
Couch sofa ['səʊfə]
Couchpotato couch potato ['kaʊtʃ pəˌteɪtəʊ]
Countdown countdown ['kaʊntdaʊn]
Countrymusik country ['kʌntri]
Cousin/Cousine cousin ['kʌzn]
Cowboy cowboy ['kaʊbɔɪ]
Creme cream [kri:m]
Crew crew [kru:]
Curry *(Gewürz oder Gericht)* curry ['kʌri]

D

da there [ðeə]
da drüben over there [ˌəʊvə 'ðeə]
da ist there is [ðer‿'ɪz]
da sind there are [ðer‿'ɑ:]
dableiben to stay on [steɪ‿'ɒn]
Dach roof [ru:f]
Dachboden loft [lɒft]
Dachdecker/Dachdeckerin roofer ['ru:fə]
Dachgeschoss loft [lɒft]
dafür instead [ɪn'sted]
Dame lady ['leɪdi]
dämmen to insulate ['ɪnsjəleɪt]
Dämmung insulation [ˌɪnsjə'leɪʃn]
Dancehall *(Musikrichtung)* dancehall ['dɑ:ntshɔ:l]
dänisch Danish ['deɪnɪʃ]
dank thanks to ['θæŋks tə]
danke thanks [θæŋks]; thank you ['θæŋk‿ju:]
danken to thank [θæŋk]
dann then [ðen]
darauf zu towards [tə'wɔ:dz]
Darlehen loan [ləʊn]
darstellen to pose [pəʊz]
sich darstellen to pose [pəʊz]
Darstellung demo ['deməʊ]
quer **darüber** across [ə'krɒs]
das the [ðə; ði]; that [ðæt]
Datenbank database ['deɪtəbeɪs]
Datum date [deɪt]
dauerhaft permanent ['pɜ:mnənt]
dauern to last [lɑ:st]; to take [teɪk]
Decke blanket ['blæŋkɪt]
dein/deine your [jɔ:]
Dein … *(in Briefen)* Yours [jɔ:z]
Deine … *(in Briefen)* Yours [jɔ:z]
Dekompression decompression [ˌdi:kəm'preʃn]
Dekoration decoration [ˌdek'reɪʃn]
Deli deli *(AE)* ['deli]
dem whom [hu:m]
Demo demo ['deməʊ]
Demokratie democracy [dɪ'mɒkrəsi]
demokratisch democratic [ˌdemə'krætɪk]
Demonstrant/Demonstrantin protester [prə'testə]
Demonstration demo ['deməʊ]
denken to think [θɪŋk]
dennoch yet [jet]; still [stɪl]; though [ðəʊ]
der the [ðə; ði]; whom [hu:m]
der/dem/den/die *(Relativpronomen)* who [hu:]
der/dem/den/die/das *(Relativpronomen)* which [wɪtʃ]
deren whose [hu:z]
derselbe/dieselbe/dasselbe the same [seɪm]
Desaster disaster [dɪ'zɑ:stə]
deshalb that's why ['ðæts ˌwaɪ]
Design design [dɪ'zaɪn]
Designer/Designerin designer [dɪ'zaɪnə]
dessen whose [hu:z]
Dessert dessert [dɪ'zɜ:t]
Detektiv/Detektivin detective [dɪ'tektɪv]
deuten (auf) to point (to) [pɔɪnt]
deutlich firmly ['fɜ:mli]
deutsch German ['dʒɜ:mən]
Deutscher/Deutsche German ['dʒɜ:mən]
Dezember December [dɪ'sembə]
Diabetes diabetes [ˌdaɪə'bi:ti:z]
Diabetiker/Diabetikerin diabetic [ˌdaɪə'betɪk]
Dialog dialogue ['daɪəlɒg]
Diamant diamond ['daɪəmənd]
Diät diet [daɪət]
eine Diät machen to go on a diet [ˌgəʊ‿ɒn ə 'daɪət]
dich you [ju:; jə]
dich selbst yourself [jɔ:'self]
Dichter/Dichterin poet ['pəʊɪt]
dick thick [θɪk]
die the [ðə; ði]
Diener/Dienerin servant ['sɜ:vnt]
Dienst service ['sɜ:vɪs]
Dienstag Tuesday ['tju:zdeɪ]
dies this [ðɪs]
diese these [ði:z]
an diesem Abend that evening [ˌðæt‿'i:vnɪŋ]
diese dort those [ðəʊz]
diese hier these [ði:z]
dieser/diese/dieses this [ðɪs]
digital digital ['dɪdʒɪtl]
Ding thing [θɪŋ]
Diplom diploma [dɪ'pləʊmə]
dir you [ju:; jə]
direkt direct [dɪ'rekt]; right [raɪt]; just [dʒʌst]
Direktor/Direktorin director [dɪ'rektə]
Disko disco ['dɪskəʊ]
Diskriminierung discrimination [dɪˌskrɪmɪ'neɪʃn]
diskutieren to discuss [dɪ'skʌs]
Distanz distance ['dɪstns]
DJ DJ [ˌdi:'dʒeɪ]
Dokument paper ['peɪpə]
Dokumentarfilm documentary [ˌdɒkjə'mentri]
dokumentiert on record [ɒn 'rekɔ:d]
Dokusoap docu soap ['dɒkju ˌsəʊp]
Dollar *(Währung)* dollar ['dɒlə]
Dom cathedral [kə'θi:drl]
Donnerstag Thursday ['θɜ:zdeɪ]
Doppelgänger double ['dʌbl]
doppelt verglast double-glazed [ˌdʌbl'gleɪzd]
das **Doppelte** double ['dʌbl]
Dorf village ['vɪlɪdʒ]
dort there [ðeə]
Dose can [kæn]; tin [tɪn]
Down Under *(Spitzname für Australien)* Down Under [ˌdaʊn‿'ʌndə]
Drache dragon ['drægn]
Drama drama ['drɑ:mə]
dramatisch dramatic [drə'mætɪk]
drangsalieren to harass [hə'ræs]
draußen outside [aʊt'saɪd]
Dreck dirt [dɜ:t]
Drehbuch script [skrɪpt]
drehen to turn [tɜ:n]
drin inside [ɪn'saɪd]
dringend urgent ['ɜ:dʒnt]
Drittel third [θɜ:d]
dritter/dritte/drittes third [θɜ:d]
Droge drug [drʌg]
drohen to threaten ['θretn]
dröhnen to roar [rɔ:]
drücken to press [pres]; to push [pʊʃ]
drucken to print [prɪnt]
Druckverminderung decompression [ˌdi:kəm'preʃn]
du you [ju:; jə]
du selbst yourself [jɔ:'self]
Du bist dran. It's your turn. [ɪts jɔ: 'tɜ:n]
Duft odour ['əʊdə]
dumm silly ['sɪli]; stupid ['stju:pɪd]; thick [θɪk]
Dummkopf idiot ['ɪdiət]; silly ['sɪli]
dunkel dark [dɑ:k]
Dunkelheit dark ['dɑ:k]
dünn thin [θɪn]

durch through [θru:]
quer durch across [ə'krɒs]
durchdrehen to go bananas [ˌgəʊ bə'nɑ:nəz]; to go crazy [gəʊ 'kreɪzi]
durcheinander chaotic [keɪ'ɒtɪk]; messy ['mesi]
Durcheinander chaos ['keɪɒs]; mess [mes]
durchfüttern to feed [fi:d]
durchgehend non-stop [ˌnɒn'stɒp]
im **Durchmesser** across [ə'krɒs]
Durchsage announcement [ə'naʊntsmənt]
durchschnittlich average ['ævrɪdʒ]
durchstehen to survive [sə'vaɪv]
dürfen can [kæn]; may [meɪ]; to be allowed to (do sth) [bi:‿ə'laʊd tə]
nicht dürfen mustn't ['mʌsnt]
Dusche shower ['ʃaʊə]
DVD DVD [di:vi:'di:]
DVD-Player DVD player [ˌdi:vi:'di: ˌpleɪə]
dynamisch energetic [ˌenə'dʒetɪk]

E

Ebene level ['levl]
echt real [rɪəl]
Ecke corner ['kɔ:nə]
Effekt effect [ɪ'fekt]
egal welche whatever [wɒt'evə]
Es ist mir egal. I don't care. [aɪ dəʊnt 'keə]
Ehe marriage ['mærɪdʒ]
Ehefrau wife, wives *(pl)* [waɪf; waɪvz]
ehemaliger/ehemalige/ehemaliges former ['fɔ:mə]
Ehemann husband ['hʌzbənd]
ehrenamtlich voluntary ['vɒləntri]
ehrgeizig ambitious [æm'bɪʃəs]
ehrlich honest ['ɒnɪst]
Ei egg [eg]
eifersüchtig (auf) jealous (of) ['dʒeləs]
eigener/eigene/eigenes own [əʊn]
eigentlich actually ['æktʃuəli]
es **eilig haben** to be in a hurry [bi:‿ɪn‿ə 'hʌri]
ein/eine a, an [ə; ən]
ein paar a few [ə 'fju:]
eines von beiden either of these ['aɪðər‿əv ˌði:z]
einander each other [ˌi:tʃ‿'ʌðə]
Einband cover ['kʌvə]
einbauen to install [ɪn'stɔ:l]
einbeziehen to involve [ɪn'vɒlv]
Einbrecher/Einbrecherin burglar ['bɜ:glə]
einchecken to check in [tʃek‿'ɪn]
eindeutig firmly ['fɜ:mli]
einfach basic ['beɪsɪk]; easy ['i:zi]
Einfall idea [aɪ'dɪə]
Einfangen der Rinder mit dem Lasso roping ['rəʊpɪŋ]
einflussreich important [ɪm'pɔ:tnt]
einfordern to claim [kleɪm]
einführen to launch [lɔ:nʃ]
Einführung launch [lɔ:nʃ]
eingeboren Aboriginal [ˌæbə'rɪdʒnl]; native ['neɪtɪv]
einheimisch Aboriginal [ˌæbə'rɪdʒnl]; local ['ləʊkl]; native ['neɪtɪv]
Einheit session ['seʃn]
einige a few [ə 'fju:]; any ['eni]; some [sʌm]; a couple of [ə 'kʌpl‿əv]
Einkauf shopping ['ʃɒpɪŋ]
einkaufen to shop [ʃɒp]
Einkaufen shopping ['ʃɒpɪŋ]
Einkaufswagen trolley ['trɒli]
einladen to invite [ɪn'vaɪt]
Einladung invitation [ˌɪnvɪ'teɪʃn]
einleitend introductory [ˌɪntrə'dʌktri]
Einleitung introduction [ˌɪntrə'dʌkʃn]
Einleitungs- introductory [ˌɪntrə'dʌktri]
einmal once [wʌnts]
einrichten to set up [set‿'ʌp]
Einrichtung appliance [ə'plaɪənts]
einsam lonely ['ləʊnli]
einschalten to switch on [swɪtʃ‿'ɒn]; to turn on [ˌtɜ:n‿'ɒn]
einschätzen to assess [ə'ses]
einschicken to send in [send‿'ɪn]
einschieben to put in [pʊt‿'ɪn]
einschließen to include [ɪn'klu:d]
einschließlich including [ɪn'klu:dɪŋ]
einschränken to cut down on [kʌt 'daʊn‿ɒn]
einschränkend limiting ['lɪmɪtɪŋ]
einsetzen to fill in [fɪl‿'ɪn]; to put in [pʊt‿'ɪn]
einsparen to cut down on [kʌt 'daʊn‿ɒn]
einst once [wʌnts]
einsteigen *(in Zug, Bus …)* to get on [get‿'ɒn]; *(Bus)* to get onto [get‿'ɒntə]; *(Auto)* to get into [get‿'ɪntə]
einstellen to set [set]
Einstellung shot [ʃɒt]
einstempeln to check in [tʃek‿'ɪn]
Eintrag entry ['entri]
Eintragung entry ['entri]
eintreten to enter ['entə]
Eintritt verboten! Keep out! [ki:p‿'aʊt]
Eintrittskarte ticket ['tɪkɪt]
Einwanderer/Einwanderin immigrant ['ɪmɪgrənt]
einwandern to immigrate ['ɪmɪgreɪt]
Einwanderung immigration [ˌɪmɪ'greɪʃn]
Einzelkind only child ['əʊnli ˌtʃaɪld]
einziger/einzige/einziges only ['əʊnli]
Eis ice [aɪs]; ice-cream [aɪs 'kri:m]
Eisbahn ice rink ['aɪs rɪŋk]
Eiscreme ice-cream [aɪs 'kri:m]
Eishockey ice hockey ['aɪs ˌhɒki]
ekelhaft yukky ['jʌki]
Elefant elephant ['elɪfənt]
Elektriker/Elektrikerin electrician [ˌelɪk'trɪʃn]
elektrisch electric [ɪ'lektrɪk]; electrical [ɪ'lektrɪkl]
elektrisch betrieben electric-powered [ɪ'lektrɪk ˌpaʊəd]
Elektrizität electricity [ˌelɪk'trɪsəti]
Element panel ['pænl]
Ellbogen elbow ['elbəʊ]
Elle *(Längenmaß: 0,914 m)* yard [jɑ:d]
Eltern parents *(pl)* ['peərənts]
E-Mail e-mail ['i:meɪl]
E-Mail schreiben to e-mail ['i:meɪl]
per E-Mail schicken to e-mail ['i:meɪl]
emigrieren to emigrate ['emɪgreɪt]
Emission emission [ɪ'mɪʃn]
Empfang reception [rɪ'sepʃn]
empfangen to receive [rɪ'si:v]
Empfangsmitarbeiter/Empfangsmitarbeiterin receptionist [rɪ'sepʃnɪst]
empörend outrageous [aʊt'reɪdʒəs]
Ende end [end]
enden to end [end]; to end up [ˌend‿'ʌp]
endlich at last [ət 'lɑ:st]; finally ['faɪnli]
Energie energy ['enədʒi]
energiegeladen energetic [ˌenə'dʒetɪk]
energisch energetic [ˌenə'dʒetɪk]
Engländer Englishman, Englishmen *(pl)* ['ɪŋglɪʃmən; 'ɪŋglɪʃmen]
Engländer/Engländerinnen English ['ɪŋglɪʃ]
englisch English ['ɪŋglɪʃ]
entdecken to discover [dɪ'skʌvə]
entfachen to spark [spɑ:k]
Entfernung distance ['dɪstns]
entführen to kidnap ['kɪdnæp]
Entführung kidnapping ['kɪdnæpɪŋ]
entgegengesetzt opposite ['ɒpəzɪt]
entkommen to escape [ɪ'skeɪp]; to get out [get‿'aʊt]
entlang along [ə'lɒŋ]
entlanggehen to go down [gəʊ 'daʊn]
entlasten to unburden [ʌn'bɜ:dn]
entschärfen to defuse [ˌdi:'fju:z]
entscheiden to decide [dɪ'saɪd]
Entscheidung decision [dɪ'sɪʒn]
Entschuldigung excuse [ɪk'skju:s]
Entschuldigung! Excuse me! [ɪk'skju:z mi]
sich **entspannen** to chill out [tʃɪl‿'aʊt]; to rest [rest]
jmdn. **enttäuschen** to let sb down [let 'daʊn]

German – English

enttäuschend disappointing [ˌdɪsəˈpɔɪntɪŋ]
enttäuscht disappointed [ˌdɪsəˈpɔɪntɪd]
entwerfen to design [dɪˈzaɪn]
entwickeln to develop [dɪˈveləp]
sich entwickeln to develop [dɪˈveləp]
Entwicklung development [dɪˈveləpmənt]; progress [ˈprəʊgres]; trend [trend]
Entzücken glee [gliː]
er he [hiː]
er selbst himself [hɪmˈself]
erbärmlich pathetic [pəˈθetɪk]
Erbe/Erbin inheritor [ɪnˈherɪtə]
Erbse pea [piː]
Erd- global [ˈgləʊbl]
Erdarbeiter/Erdarbeiterin digger [ˈdɪgə]
Erdbeere strawberry [ˈstrɔːbri]
Erde earth [ɜːθ]; soil [sɔɪl]; world [wɜːld]
Erderwärmung (global) warming [ˌgləʊbl ˈwɔːmɪŋ]
Erdkunde Geography [dʒiˈɒgrəfi]
Erdteil continent [ˈkɒntɪnənt]
Ereignis event [ɪˈvent]
erfahren to experience [ɪkˈspɪəriənts]; to learn [lɜːn]
erfahren experienced [ɪkˈspɪəriənst]
Erfahrung experience [ɪkˈspɪəriənts]
Erfassung registration [ˌredʒɪˈstreɪʃn]
erfinden to invent [ɪnˈvent]; to make up [meɪk‿ˈʌp]
Erfinder/Erfinderin inventor [ɪnˈventə]
Erfindung fiction [ˈfɪkʃn]; invention [ɪnˈventʃn]
Erfolg success [səkˈses]
erfolgreich successful [səkˈsesfl]
Erfordernis need [niːd]
erforschen to explore [ɪkˈsplɔː]
sich **erfreuen** to enjoy [ɪnˈdʒɔɪ]
erfrischend refreshing [rɪˈfreʃɪŋ]
erfüllen to fulfill *(AE)* [fʊlˈfɪl]
Ergebnis result [rɪˈzʌlt]
erhalten to receive [rɪˈsiːv]
erhitzen to heat [hiːt]
erhöhen to raise [reɪz]
sich **erinnern (an)** to remember [rɪˈmembə]
in **Erinnerungen schwelgen** to reminisce [ˌremɪˈnɪs]
erkennen to realise [ˈrɪəlaɪz]
erklären to explain [ɪkˈspleɪn]
erklingen to ring out [ˌrɪŋ‿ˈaʊt]
Erkrankung disease [dɪˈziːz]
erkunden to explore [ɪkˈsplɔː]
Erlaubnis permission [pəˈmɪʃn]
erläutern to explain [ɪkˈspleɪn]
erleben to experience [ɪkˈspɪəriənts]
Erlebnis experience [ɪkˈspɪəriənts]
erledigen to complete [kəmˈpliːt]; to finish [ˈfɪnɪʃ]
erlöschen to go out [gəʊ‿ˈaʊt]
ermahnen to warn [wɔːn]
Ermordung murder [ˈmɜːdə]
ernähren to feed [fiːd]
Ernährung nutrition [njuːˈtrɪʃn]
Ernährungslehre nutrition [njuːˈtrɪʃn]
ernennen to appoint [əˈpɔɪnt]
erneuerbar renewable [rɪˈnjuːəbl]
eröffnen to open [ˈəʊpn]
erreichen to catch [kætʃ]; to get to [ˈget tə]; to reach [riːtʃ]
erscheinen to seem [siːm]
erschießen to shoot [ʃuːt]
erschrecken to scare [ˈskeə]
ersetzen to substitute [ˈsʌbstɪtjuːt]
erst only [ˈəʊnli]
erstaunlich amazing [əˈmeɪzɪŋ]
erstaunt surprised [səˈpraɪzd]
erste/erster/erstes first [fɜːst]
ersticken to choke [tʃəʊk]
ertönen to ring out [ˌrɪŋ‿ˈaʊt]
Erwachsener/Erwachsene adult [ˈædʌlt]
erwärmen to heat [hiːt]
Erwärmung (global) warming [ˌgləʊbl ˈwɔːmɪŋ]
erwarten to expect [ɪkˈspekt]
erweitern to widen [ˈwaɪdn]
sich erweitern to widen [ˈwaɪdn]
erzählen to tell [tel]
Erzählung story [ˈstɔːri]
Erzeuger/Erzeugerin producer [prəˈdjuːsə]
Erziehung education [edʒʊˈkeɪʃn]
es it [ɪt]
es selbst itself [ɪtˈself]
es gibt there are [ðer‿ˈɑː]; there is [ðer‿ˈɪz]
Es lautete .... It said .... [ɪt ˈsed]
es sei denn, (dass) ... unless [ənˈles]
essen to eat [iːt]
zu viel essen to overeat [ˌəʊvrˈiːt]
Essen food [fuːd]
Essen zum Mitnehmen takeaway [ˈteɪkəweɪ]
Essig vinegar [ˈvɪnɪgə]
Esszimmer dining room [ˈdaɪnɪŋ rʊm]
et cetera etc. [ɪtˈsetrə]
Etikett label [ˈleɪbl]
etikettieren to label [ˈleɪbl]
etliche many [ˈmeni]
etwa about [əˈbaʊt]; around [əˈraʊnd]
etwas any [ˈeni]; anything [ˈeniθɪŋ]; some [sʌm]; something [ˈsʌmθɪŋ]
euch you [juː; jə]
euch selbst yourselves [jɔːˈselvz]
euer/eure your [jɔː]
Euer ... *(in Briefen)* Yours [jɔːz]
Eure ... *(in Briefen)* Yours [jɔːz]
Eukalyptus eucalyptus [ˌjuːkˈlɪptəs]
Euro *(Währung)* euro [ˈjʊərəʊ]
evakuieren to fly out [flaɪ‿ˈaʊt]
exakt exact [ɪgˈzækt]
Examen exam [ɪgˈzæm]
existieren to exist [ɪgˈzɪst]
exotisch exotic [ɪgˈzɒtɪk]
Experiment experiment [ɪkˈsperɪmənt]
Experte/Expertin expert [ˈekspɜːt]
Export export [ˈekspɔːt]
exportieren to export [ɪkˈspɔːt]
Extrakt extract [ˈekstrækt]
extrem extremely [ɪkˈstriːmli]

F

fabelhaft fabulous [ˈfæbjələs]
Fabrik factory [ˈfæktri]
Fabrikant manufacturer [ˌmænjəˈfæktʃərə]
Fach- specialist [ˈspeʃlɪst]
Fachbereich department [dɪˈpɑːtmənt]
fachlich technical [ˈteknɪkl]
Fackel torch, torches *(pl)* [tɔːtʃ; ˈtɔːtʃɪz]
fähig sein (zu) to be able to (do sth) [bi‿ˈeɪbl tə]
Fahne flag [flæg]
Fähre ferry [ˈferi]
fahren to drive [draɪv]; to ride [raɪd]; *(Schiff)* to sail [seɪl]
mit dem Finger über etw. fahren to run a finger over sth [rʌn]
Fahrenheit Fahrenheit (F) [ˈfærnhaɪt]
Fahrer/Fahrerin driver [ˈdraɪvə]
Fahrplan timetable [ˈtaɪmteɪbl]
Fahrrad bike [baɪk]
mit dem Fahrrad by bike [baɪ ˈbaɪk]
Fahrschein ticket [ˈtɪkɪt]
Fahrspur lane [leɪn]
Fahrt journey [ˈdʒɜːni]; ride [raɪd]; tour [tʊə]
Fahrzeug vehicle [ˈvɪəkl]
Fahrzeug- automotive [ˌɔːtəˈməʊtɪv]
fair fair [feə]
Fakt fact [fækt]
Fall fall [fɔːl]
in der **Falle sitzen** to be trapped [biː ˈtræpt]
fällen to cut down [kʌt ˈdaʊn]
fallen to drop [drɒp]; to fall [fɔːl]
fallen lassen to drop [drɒp]
falls if [ɪf]
Fallschirmspringen parachuting [ˈpærəˌʃuːtɪŋ]
falsch false [fɔːls]; wrong [rɒŋ]
falsch machen to get ... wrong [get ... ˈrɒŋ]

falten to fold [fəʊld]
Falter moth [mɒθ]
Familie family ['fæmli]
Fan fan [fæn]
fangen to catch [kætʃ]
Fänger/Fängerin catcher ['kætʃə]
fantastisch fabulous ['fæbjələs]; fantastic [fæn'tæstɪk]
Farbe colour ['kʌlə]; paint [peɪnt]
färben to dye [daɪ]
farbig colored *(AE)* ['kʌləd]; colorful *(AE)* ['kʌləfl]
Farbiger/Farbige colored *(AE)* ['kʌləd]
Farm farm [fɑ:m]
fast almost ['ɔ:lməʊst]; nearly ['nɪəli]
Fastfood-Restaurant burger bar ['bɜ:gə ˌbɑ:]
fauchen to spit [spɪt]
faul lazy ['leɪzi]
Februar February ['februəri]
Federball badminton ['bædmɪntən]
Federmäppchen pencil case ['pensl ˌkeɪs]
fehlen to be missing [bi: 'mɪsɪŋ]; to miss [mɪs]
Fehler mistake [mɪ'steɪk]
Feier party ['pɑ:ti]
eine Party **feiern** to have a party [ˌhæv‿ə 'pɑ:ti]
Feiertag holiday ['hɒlədeɪ]
fein fine [faɪn]
Feind/Feindin enemy ['enəmi]
Feld field [fi:ld]
Felsen rock [rɒk]
Fenster window ['wɪndəʊ]
Ferien holiday(s) ['hɒlədeɪ(z)]; vacation *(AE)* [və'keɪʃn]
Ferienhaus cottage ['kɒtɪdʒ]
fern remote [rɪ'məʊt]
Fernbedienung remote control [rɪˌməʊt kən'trəʊl]
sich **fernhalten** to keep away [ki:p‿ə'weɪ]
Fernsehen TV [ˌti:'vi:]
Fernseher TV [ˌti:'vi:]
Fernsehglotzer/Fernsehglotzerin couch potato ['kaʊtʃ pəˌteɪtəʊ]
Fernsteuerung remote control [rɪˌməʊt kən'trəʊl]
fertig ready ['redi]
fertigen to manufacture [ˌmænjə'fæktʃə]
Fertigkeit skill [skɪl]
fertigstellen to complete [kəm'pli:t]
Fertigung manufacturing [ˌmænjə'fæktʃrɪŋ]
fest firmly ['fɜ:mli]; solid ['sɒlɪd]
Fest festival ['festɪvl]
festhalten to hold [həʊld]
Festival festival ['festɪvl]
festnehmen to arrest [ə'rest]
Fett fat [fæt]
feucht damp [dæmp]
feudal feudal ['fju:dl]
Feuer fire [faɪə]
Feuerstelle fire [faɪə]
Feuerwehr fire brigade ['faɪə brɪˌgeɪd]
Feuerwerk fireworks *(pl)* ['faɪəwɜ:ks]
Feuerwerkskörper firework ['faɪəwɜ:k]
Figur character ['kærəktə]; figure ['fɪgə]
Fiktion fiction ['fɪkʃn]
Film film [fɪlm]; movie *(AE)* ['mu:vi]; picture ['pɪktʃə]
filmen to film [fɪlm]
Filter filter ['fɪltə]
Finanz- finance ['faɪnænts]
Finanzen finance ['faɪnænts]
finanziell financial [faɪ'næntʃl]
finanzieren to finance ['faɪnænts]
Finanzwesen finance ['faɪnænts]
finden to find [faɪnd]
Finger finger ['fɪŋgə]
Finsternis dark ['dɑ:k]
Firma company ['kʌmpəni]; firm [fɜ:m]
Firmenzeichen logo ['ləʊgəʊ]
Fisch fish, fish *(pl)* [fɪʃ]
fischen to fish [fɪʃ]
Fischen fishing ['fɪʃɪŋ]
Fischer fisherman, fishermen *(pl)* ['fɪʃəmən; 'fɪʃəmen]
fit fit [fɪt]
flach flat [flæt]
Fläche area ['eəriə]
flackern to flare [fleə]
Flagge flag [flæg]
Flamme flame [fleɪm]
Flasche bottle ['bɒtl]
in Flaschen abgefüllt bottled ['bɒtld]
Fleck mark [mɑ:k]; patch [pætʃ]
Fleisch meat [mi:t]
flexibel flexible ['fleksɪbl]
Flicken patch [pætʃ]
fliegen to fly [flaɪ]
Flosse fin [fɪn]
flottmachen to get sth going [get 'gəʊɪŋ]
Flüche bad language [bæd 'læŋgwɪdʒ]
flüchten to escape [ɪ'skeɪp]
Flug flight [flaɪt]
Flugblatt leaflet ['li:flət]
Flügel wing [wɪŋ]
Fluggesellschaft airline ['eəlaɪn]
Flughafen airport ['eəpɔ:t]
Fluglinie airline ['eəlaɪn]
Flugzeug plane [pleɪn]
Flur corridor ['kɒrɪdɔ:]; hall [hɔ:l]
Fluss river ['rɪvə]
flüssig liquid ['lɪkwɪd]
Flüssigkeit liquid ['lɪkwɪd]
flüstern to whisper ['wɪspə]
flutartige Überschwemmung flash flood ['flæʃ ˌflʌd]
folgen to follow ['fɒləʊ]
folgend/folgender/folgende/folgendes following ['fɒləʊɪŋ]
Föhn hairdryer ['heəˌdraɪə]
Football American football [əˌmerɪkən 'fʊtbɔ:l]
Förderer/Förderin sponsor ['spɒnsə]
fordern to claim [kleɪm]
Förderung aid [eɪd]
Form form [fɔ:m]; shape [ʃeɪp]
formal formal ['fɔ:ml]
formell formal ['fɔ:ml]
formen to form [fɔ:m]
förmlich formal ['fɔ:ml]
Formular form [fɔ:m]
Forschung research [rɪ'sɜ:tʃ]
fortfahren to continue [kən'tɪnju:]
fortgeschritten advanced [əd'vɑ:nst]
Fortschritt progress ['prəʊgres]
Forum forum ['fɔ:rəm]
fossil fossil ['fɒsl]
fossiler Brennstoff fossil fuel ['fɒsl ˌfju:əl]
Fossil fossil ['fɒsl]
Foto photo ['fəʊtəʊ]; shot [ʃɒt]
Fotos machen to take pictures [teɪk 'pɪktʃəz]
Fotoapparat camera ['kæmrə]
Fotograf/Fotografin photographer [fə'tɒgrəfə]
Fotografie photo ['fəʊtəʊ]; photography [fə'tɒgrəfi]
fotografieren to take pictures [teɪk 'pɪktʃəz]
Foul foul [faʊl]
Frage matter ['mætə]; question ['kwestʃn]
fragen to ask [ɑ:sk]
fragen nach to ask (for) ['ɑ:sk fə]
französisch French [frentʃ]
Frau lady ['leɪdi]; woman, women *(pl)* ['wʊmən; 'wɪmɪn]
Frau *(Anrede)* Miss [mɪs]; Mrs ['mɪsɪz]
frei free [fri:]; liberal ['lɪbrl]
freier Mann freeman, freemen *(pl)* ['fri:mən; 'fri:men]
Freiheit freedom ['fri:dəm]
freilassen to set free [set‿'fri:]
freisetzen to set free [set‿'fri:]
Freitag Friday [fraɪdeɪ]
freiwillig voluntary ['vɒləntri]; volunteer [ˌvɒlən'tɪə]
Freiwilliger/Freiwillige volunteer [ˌvɒlən'tɪə]
Freizeit time off [taɪm‿'ɒf]
Freizeitpark theme park ['θi:m ˌpɑ:k]

German – English

fremd alien ['eɪliən]; foreign ['fɒrɪn]
Fremder/Fremde alien ['eɪliən]; foreigner ['fɒrɪnə]; stranger ['streɪndʒə]
fressen to eat [iːt]
Freund/Freundin friend [frend]
Freund *(in einer Paarbeziehung)* boyfriend ['bɔɪfrend]
Freundin *(in einer Paarbeziehung)* girlfriend ['gɜːlfrend]
freundlich friendly ['frendli]; kind [kaɪnd]
Freundschaft schließen (mit) to make friends (with) [ˌmeɪk 'frendz]
Friede peace [piːs]
friedlich peaceful ['piːsfl]
frieren to be cold [biː 'kəʊld]
frisch fresh [freʃ]
Frischkäse cream cheese [ˌkriːm 'tʃiːz]
Friseur/Friseurin hairdresser ['heəˌdresə]
Frisieren hairdressing ['heəˌdresɪŋ]
Frisur style [staɪl]
froh glad [glæd]; happy ['hæpi]
Frucht fruit [fruːt]
früh early ['ɜːli]
früherer/frühere/früheres former ['fɔːmə]
Frühling spring [sprɪŋ]
Frühstück breakfast ['brekfəst]
frühstücken to have breakfast [hæv 'brekfəst]
frustriert frustrated [frʌs'treɪtɪd]
fühlen to feel [fiːl]
sich fühlen to feel [fiːl]
Führer/Führerin leader ['liːdə]
Führerschein driver's license *(AE)* ['draɪvəz ˌlaɪsnts]; driving licence *(BE)* ['draɪvɪŋ ˌlaɪsnts]
füllen to fill [fɪl]
Füller pen [pen]
Fundbüro Lost and Found ['lɒst ˌənd 'faʊnd]
Funk *(Musikrichtung)* funk [fʌŋk]
Funke spark [spɑːk]
Funken spark [spɑːk]
funktionieren to work [wɜːk]
für for [fɔː; fə]
Für und Wider pros and cons [ˌprəʊz‿ənd 'kɒnz]
furchtbar awful ['ɔːfl]; frightening ['fraɪtnɪŋ]; horrible ['hɒrəbl]; terrible ['terəbl]
sich **fürchten (vor)** to be afraid (of) [biː‿ə'freɪd]
fürsorglich thoughtful ['θɔːtfl]
Fuß foot, feet *(pl)* [fʊt; fiːt]
Fuß *(Längenmaß: 30,48 cm)* foot, feet *(pl)* [fʊt; fiːt]
zu Fuß on foot [ɒn 'fʊt]
Fußabdruck footprint ['fʊtprɪnt]
Fußball football ['fʊtbɔːl]; soccer *(AE)* ['sɒkə]
Fußballspieler/Fußballspielerin footballer ['fʊtbɔːlə]
Fußboden floor [flɔː]
füttern to feed [fiːd]
Futur future ['fjuːtʃə]

G

Gabel fork [fɔːk]
Gang corridor ['kɒrɪdɔː]; *(Menü)* course [kɔːs]; gang [gæŋ]
etw. in Gang bringen to get sth going [get 'gəʊɪŋ]
im Gange sein to be on [biː‿'ɒn]
Gangster/Gangsterin gangster ['gæŋkstə]
ganz all [ɔːl]; full (of) [fʊl]; quite [kwaɪt]; whole [həʊl]
ganz schön pretty ['prɪti]
im Ganzen in all [ɪn‿'ɔːl]
garantieren to guarantee [ˌgærn'tiː]
Garderobe wardrobe ['wɔːdrəʊb]
garstig nasty ['nɑːsti]
Garten garden ['gɑːdn]
Gartengestaltung gardening ['gɑːdnɪŋ]
Gärtner/Gärtnerin gardener ['gɑːdnə]
Gärtnern gardening ['gɑːdnɪŋ]
Gas *(BE)* gas [gæs]
Gasse lane [leɪn]
Gast guest [gest]
Gastgeber host [həʊst]
Gastronomie catering ['keɪtrɪŋ]
Gate gate [geɪt]
Gebäude building ['bɪldɪŋ]
geben to hand [hænd]; to give [gɪv]
Gebiet area ['eəriə]; field [fiːld]; territory ['terɪtri]
Gebiss false teeth [fɔːls 'tiːθ]
gebräuchlich common ['kɒmən]
gebrochen broken ['brəʊkn]
Gebühr fee [fiː]
Geburt birth [bɜːθ]
gebürtig native ['neɪtɪv]
Geburtstag birthday ['bɜːθdeɪ]
Gedicht poem ['pəʊɪm]
geeignet suitable ['suːtəbl]
geerdet grounded ['graʊndɪd]
Gefahr danger ['deɪndʒə]
gefährlich dangerous ['deɪndʒrəs]
Gefängnis jail [dʒeɪl]
gefestigt grounded ['graʊndɪd]
Gefühl feeling ['fiːlɪŋ]
gegen- anti ['æntɪ]
gegen against [ə'genst]
Gegend region ['riːdʒn]
sich **gegenseitig** each other [ˌiːtʃ‿'ʌðə]
gegenüberliegend opposite ['ɒpəzɪt]
Gehalt pay [peɪ]
geheim confidential [ˌkɒnfɪ'denʃl]; secret ['siːkrət]
Geheimnis mystery ['mɪstəri]
gehen to go [gəʊ]; to leave [liːv]; to walk [wɔːk]
Gehirn brain(s) [breɪn, breɪnz]
gehören (zu) to belong (to) [bɪ'lɒŋ]
Geisel hostage ['hɒstɪdʒ]
Geist ghost [gəʊst]; mind [maɪnd]; spirit ['spɪrɪt]
geisterhaft ghostly ['gəʊstli]
gelangweilt bored [bɔːd]
gelb yellow ['jeləʊ]
Geld money ['mʌni]
Geldbeutel wallet ['wɒlɪt]
Geldbuße fine [faɪn]
Geldstrafe fine [faɪn]
Gelegenheit opportunity [ˌɒpə'tjuːnəti]
geloben to pledge [pledʒ]
gemein mean [miːn]; nasty ['nɑːsti]
Gemeinde community [kə'mjuːnəti]
Gemeinderat council ['kaʊnsl]
gemeinsam common ['kɒmən]
Gemeinschaft community [kə'mjuːnəti]
Gemisch cocktail ['kɒkteɪl]; mixture ['mɪkstʃə]
Gemüse vegetable ['vedʒtəbl]
genannt werden to be called [biː 'kɔːld]
genau exact [ɪg'zækt]; right [raɪt]
genau genommen in fact [ɪn 'fækt]
genauso as [æz; əz]
Generaldirektor/Generaldirektorin chief executive officer (CEO) [ˌtʃiːf‿ɪgˌzekjətɪv‿'ɒfɪsə; ˌsiː iː'əʊ]
genießen to enjoy [ɪn'dʒɔɪ]
genug enough [ɪ'nʌf]
genügen to fulfill *(AE)* [fʊl'fɪl]
genügend enough [ɪ'nʌf]
geöffnet open ['əʊpn]
Geografie Geography [dʒi'ɒgrəfi]
Gepäck luggage ['lʌgɪdʒ]
Gepäckwagen trolley ['trɒli]
Geplauder chat [tʃæt]
Gerät appliance [ə'plaɪənts]
Geräusch noise [nɔɪz]; sound [saʊnd]
gerecht fair [feə]
Gericht court [kɔːt]
Gerichtshof court [kɔːt]
Gerichtsverhandlung court trial ['kɔːt traɪəl]
Gern geschehen! You're welcome. [jʊə 'welkəm]
gern haben to like [laɪk]
gern mögen to love [lʌv]
Geruch odour ['əʊdə]; smell [smel]

gesamt total ['təʊtl]
Gesamtschule comprehensive school [kɒmprɪ'hensɪv ˌsku:l]
Geschäft business ['bɪznɪs]; shop [ʃɒp]; store [stɔ:]
Geschäftsführer/Geschäftsführerin chief executive officer *(CEO)* [ˌtʃi:f‿ɪgˌzekjətɪv‿'ɒfɪsə; ˌsi: i:'əʊ]
Geschäftsmann businessman, businessmen *(pl)* ['bɪznɪsmən; 'bɪznɪsmen]; salesman, salesmen *(pl)* ['seɪlzmən; 'seɪlzmen]
geschäftstüchtig enterprising ['entəpraɪzɪŋ]
geschehen to happen ['hæpn]
Geschenk present ['preznt]
Geschichte History ['hɪstəri]; story ['stɔ:ri]
geschichtlich historical [hɪ'stɒrɪkl]
Geschick skill [skɪl]
geschieden von divorced from [dɪ'vɔ:st frɒm]
Geschlecht sex [seks]
Geschlechtsverkehr haben to have sex [ˌhæv 'seks]
geschmeidig smooth [smu:θ]
geschockt shocked [ʃɒkt]
Geschöpf creature ['kri:tʃə]
Gesellschaft company ['kʌmpəni]; firm [fɜ:m]; society [sə'saɪəti]
gesellschaftlich social ['səʊʃl]
Gesellschaftstanz ballroom dancing [ˌbɔ:lrʊm 'dɑ:ntsɪŋ]
Gesetz bill [bɪl]; law [lɔ:]
Gesetzentwurf bill [bɪl]
Gesetzgebung law [lɔ:]
Gesicht face [feɪs]
Gesichtspunkt aspect ['æspekt]
Gespenst ghost [gəʊst]
Gespräch conversation [ˌkɒnvə'seɪʃn]; dialogue ['daɪəlɒg]; talk [tɔ:k]
Gestalt figure ['fɪgə]
Gestaltung design [dɪ'zaɪn]
Gestank smell [smel]
gestern yesterday ['jestədeɪ]
gestern Abend last night [lɑ:st 'naɪt]
gestern Nacht last night [lɑ:st 'naɪt]
gestrandet stranded ['strændɪd]
gesund healthy ['helθi]
Gesundheit health [helθ]
Getränk drink [drɪŋk]
Gewächshaus greenhouse ['gri:nhaʊs]
gewagt outrageous [aʊt'reɪdʒəs]
Gewalt violence ['vaɪələnts]
gewaltfrei non-violent [ˌnɒn'vaɪələnt]
gewaltig huge [hju:dʒ]
gewaltsam violent ['vaɪələnt]
gewalttätig violent ['vaɪələnt]
Gewalttätigkeit violence ['vaɪələnts]
Gewicht weight [weɪt]
gewinnen to win [wɪn]
jmdn. dafür gewinnen, etw. zu tun to make sb do sth [meɪk]
Gewinner/Gewinnerin winner ['wɪnə]
gewiss certainly ['sɜ:tnli]
gewöhnlich usually ['ju:ʒli]
Gift poison ['pɔɪzn]; *(von Schlangen und Insekten)* venom ['venəm]
Gitarre guitar [gɪ'tɑ:]
Gitter grid [grɪd]
glamourös glamorous ['glæmrəs]
Glas glass [glɑ:s]
Glaser/Glaserin glazier ['gleɪziə]
glatt smooth [smu:θ]
glatzköpfig bald [bɔ:ld]
glauben to believe [bɪ'li:v]; to think [θɪŋk]
gleich equal ['i:kwəl]; the same [seɪm]
gleich right away [raɪt‿ə'weɪ]
Gleich- equal ['i:kwəl]
Gleichaltriger/Gleichaltrige peer [pɪə]
Gleichgewicht balance ['bæləns]
gleichwertig equal ['i:kwəl]
Gleitschirmfliegen paragliding ['pærəˌglaɪdɪŋ]
global global ['gləʊbl]
Globalisierung globalisation [ˌgləʊblaɪ'zeɪʃn]
Glocke bell [bel]
Glück luck [lʌk]
du hast Glück you're lucky [ˌjʊə 'lʌki]
Viel Glück! Good luck! [ˌgʊd 'lʌk]
glücklich happy ['hæpi]; lucky ['lʌki]
glücklicherweise luckily ['lʌkɪli]
Glühbirne light bulb ['laɪt bʌlb]
Glut embers *(pl)* ['embəz]
Gold gold [gəʊld]
Mein **Gott!** My God! [maɪ 'gɒd]
Grab grave [greɪv]
graben to dig [dɪg]
Grabstein gravestone ['greɪvstəʊn]
Grad degree (°) [dɪ'gri:]
Graffiti mural ['mjʊərl]
Gramm gramme (g) [græm]
Gras grass [grɑ:s]
grau grey [greɪ]
greifen to grab [græb]
Grenze border ['bɔ:də]; limit ['lɪmɪt]
Grieche/Griechin Greek [gri:k]
griechisch Greek [gri:k]
Grill barbecue ['bɑ:bɪkju:]
Grillparty barbecue ['bɑ:bɪkju:]
grob raw [rɔ:]
groß big [bɪg]; great [greɪt]; large [lɑ:dʒ]; tall [tɔ:l]; wide [waɪd]
großartig fantastic [fæn'tæstɪk]; great [greɪt]; super ['su:pə]; wicked ['wɪkɪd]
Größe height [haɪt]
Großeltern grandparents *(pl)* ['grænpeərənts]
Großstadt city ['sɪti]
größtenteils mostly ['məʊstli]
großziehen *(Kinder)* to raise [reɪz]
grün green [gri:n]
Grund reason ['ri:zn]
Grund- basic ['beɪsɪk]
gründen to found [faʊnd]; to set up [set‿'ʌp]
grundlegend basic ['beɪsɪk]
Grundlinie back line [ˌbæk 'laɪn]
Grundsatz policy ['pɒlɪsi]
Grundschule elementary school *(AE)* [elɪ'mentri ˌsku:l]; primary school ['praɪməri ˌsku:l]
Gruppe group [gru:p]; party ['pɑ:ti]
gruselig scary ['skeəri]
gültig valid ['vælɪd]
Gummi rubber ['rʌbə]
Gummistiefel rubber boots *(pl)* [ˌrʌbə 'bu:ts]
gut all right [ɔ:l 'raɪt]; fine [faɪn]; good [gʊd]
Gute-Besserung-Karte get-well card [ˌget 'wel ˌkɑ:d]
Es geht uns gut. We're OK. [ˌwɪər‿əʊ'keɪ]
Guten Morgen! Good morning! ['gʊd 'mɔ:nɪŋ]
gut mit … umgehen können to be good with … [bi: 'gʊd wɪð]
ich bin gut in … I'm good at … [aɪm 'gʊd‿ət]
Güter goods *(pl)* [gʊdz]
Gymnasium grammar school ['græmə ˌsku:l]

H

Ha! Ha! [hɑ:]
Haar, Haare hair [heə]
haben to have [hæv]; to have got [hæv 'gɒt]
keine Ahnung haben to have no clue [ˌhæv nəʊ 'klu:]
Hafen harbor *(AE)* ['hɑ:bə]; port [pɔ:t]
Hähnchen chicken ['tʃɪkɪn]
Hai shark [ʃɑ:k]
halb half [hɑ:f]
halb (drei) half past (two) ['hɑ:f pɑ:st]
eine halbe Stunde half an hour [ˌhɑ:f‿ən‿'aʊə]
zum halben Preis half-price [ˌhɑ:f'praɪs]
Halbschwester half-sister ['hɑ:fˌsɪstə]
Hälfte half [hɑ:f]
Halle hall [hɔ:l]

German – English

Hallo! Hello! [he'ləʊ]; Hi, there! ['haɪ ðeə]
halten to hold [həʊld]; to keep [ki:p]; to stop [stɒp]
Haltestelle stop [stɒp]
Hand hand [hænd]
Hände weg! Hands off! [hændz͜'ɒf]
Handel deal [di:l]; trade [treɪd]
handeln to act [ækt]
Handkarren trolley ['trɒli]
Händler/Händlerin dealer ['di:lə]; trader ['treɪdə]
Handlung action ['ækʃn]; storyline ['stɔ:rilaɪn]
Handschuh glove [glʌv]
Handtasche handbag ['hænbæg]
Handwerker workman, workmen *(pl)* ['wɜ:kmən; 'wɜ:kmen]
handwerklich technical ['teknɪkl]
Handy cell phone *(AE)* ['sel ˌfəʊn]; mobile ['məʊbaɪl]
hart hard [hɑ:d]; tough [tʌf]
Hass hate [heɪt]
hassen to hate [heɪt]
hätte(n) gern would like [wʊd 'laɪk]
Haufen pile [paɪl]
Haupt- main [meɪn]
hauptsächlich mostly ['məʊstli]
Hauptsitz headquarters *(pl)* ['hedˌkwɔ:təz]
Haus house [haʊs]
zu Hause at home [ət 'həʊm]
Hausaufgabe(n) homework ['həʊmwɜ:k]
Haushaltsgerät appliance [ə'plaɪənts]
Hausmeister/Hausmeisterin caretaker ['keəteɪkə]
Haustier pet [pet]
Heavy Metal heavy metal [ˌhevi 'metl]
Heft exercise book ['eksəsaɪz ˌbʊk]
heilig sacred ['seɪkrɪd]
Heim home [həʊm]
Heimat(-) home [həʊm]
heimlich secret ['si:krət]
Heimweh haben to feel homesick [ˌfi:l 'həʊmsɪk]
Heirat marriage ['mærɪdʒ]
heiraten to marry ['mæri]
heiß hot [hɒt]
heißen to be called [bi: 'kɔ:ld]
Ich heiße .... My name is .... [maɪ 'neɪm͜ɪz]
Heißluftballon balloon [bə'lu:n]
heizen to heat [hi:t]
Heizung heating ['hi:tɪŋ]
Held hero, heroes *(pl)* ['hɪərəʊ; 'hɪərəʊz]
Heldin heroine ['herəʊɪn]
helfen to help [help]
Helfer/Helferin helper ['helpə]
Helikopter helicopter ['helɪˌkɒptə]
hell bright [braɪt]; fair [feə]; light [laɪt]
Helm helmet ['helmət]
Hemd shirt [ʃɜ:t]
heraus out [aʊt]
herausbringen to launch [lɔ:nʃ]
herausfinden to find out [faɪnd͜'aʊt]; to work out [ˌwɜ:k͜'aʊt]
herausnehmen to take out [teɪk͜'aʊt]
Herbst autumn ['ɔ:təm]
herein in [ɪn]
hereinkommen to come in [kʌm͜'ɪn]
Herkunft origin ['ɒrɪdʒɪn]
Herr *(Anrede)* Mr ['mɪstə]
herrschen to rule [ru:l]
Herrscher/Herrscherin ruler ['ru:lə]
herstellen to manufacture [ˌmænjə'fæktʃə]; to produce [prə'dju:s]
Hersteller manufacturer [ˌmænjə'fæktʃərə]
Herstellung manufacturing [ˌmænjə'fæktʃrɪŋ]; production [prə'dʌkʃn]
herüberkommen to come over [kʌm͜'əʊvə]
herüberreichen to pass [pɑ:s]
(um ...) **herum** around [ə'raʊnd]; round [raʊnd]
herumalbern to mess around [ˌmes͜ə'raʊnd]
herumlungern to hang around [ˌhæŋ͜ə'raʊnd]
herumreisen to go places [ˌgəʊ 'pleɪsɪz]
herumspringen to jump about [ˌdʒʌmp͜ə'baʊt]
sich **herumtreiben** to hang out [hæŋ͜'aʊt]
herunter down [daʊn]; off [ɒf]
herunterdrehen to turn down [tɜ:n 'daʊn]
herunterfallen to fall [fɔ:l]; to fall off [fɔ:l͜'ɒf]
herunterkommen to come down [kʌm 'daʊn]
herunterladen to download [ˌdaʊn'ləʊd]
hervorrufen to cause [kɔ:z]
Herz heart [hɑ:t]
Herzliche Grüße love [lʌv]
Herzschrittmacher pacemaker ['peɪsˌmeɪkə]
heute today [tə'deɪ]
heute Abend tonight [tə'naɪt]
heute Nacht tonight [tə'naɪt]
heutzutage these days ['ði:z deɪz]
Hi! Hi! [haɪ]
hier here [hɪə]
High School high school *(AE)* ['haɪ ˌsku:l]
high-tech high-tech [ˌhaɪ'tek]
Highway highway *(AE)* ['haɪweɪ]
Hilfe aid [eɪd]; help [help]; support [sə'pɔ:t]
hilflos helpless ['helpləs]
hilfreich helpful ['helpfəl]
Himmel sky [skaɪ]
hinauf up [ʌp]
(auf ...) hinauf onto ['ɒntu:; 'ɒntə]
die Treppe **hinaufrennen** to run upstairs [ˌrʌn͜ʌp'steəz]
hinaufschauen to look up [lʊk͜'ʌp]
hinaus out [aʊt]
hinausgehen to go out [gəʊ͜'aʊt]
hinauslehnen to lean out [li:n͜'aʊt]
sich hinauslehnen to lean out [li:n͜'aʊt]
hinausstellen to put out [pʊt͜'aʊt]
Hindi Hindi ['hɪndi]
hineingehen to go in [gəʊ͜'ɪn]
hinfallen to fall [fɔ:l]
hingehen to walk up to [wɔ:k͜'ʌp tə]
Hinglisch *(Mischung aus Hindi und Englisch)* Hinglish ['hɪŋglɪʃ]
hinlegen to lie down [laɪ 'daʊn]
sich hinlegen to lie down [laɪ 'daʊn]
hinnehmen to accept [ək'sept]
sich **hinsetzen** to sit down [sɪt 'daʊn]
hinter behind [bɪ'haɪnd]
Hinter- back [bæk]
Hintergrund background ['bækgraʊnd]
hinterhergehen to follow ['fɒləʊ]
Hintern ass *(AE)* [æs]
hinüber across [ə'krɒs]
hinübergehen to go over [gəʊ͜'əʊvə]
hinüberrennen to run over [rʌn͜'əʊvə]
hin- und hergerissen torn [tɔ:n]
hinunter down [daʊn]
hinuntergehen to go down [gəʊ 'daʊn]
Hinweis clue [klu:]
hinzufügen to add [æd]; to put in [pʊt͜'ɪn]
Hip-Hop hip hop ['hɪp hɒp]
hispanisch Hispanic [hɪ'spænɪk]
historisch historical [hɪ'stɒrɪkl]
Hit hit [hɪt]
Hitparade charts *(pl)* [tʃɑ:ts]
Hitze heat [hi:t]
Hobby hobby, hobbies *(pl)* ['hɒbi; 'hɒbiz]
hoch high [haɪ]; tall [tɔ:l]
hochheben to lift up [lɪft͜'ʌp]
Hochmoor moor [mɔ:]
Hochmut pride [praɪd]
Hochschule academy [ə'kædəmi]
hochspringen to jump up [dʒʌmp͜'ʌp]
höchster/höchste/höchstes supreme [su:'pri:m]
Hochwasser flood [flʌd]
hochziehen to lift up [lɪft͜'ʌp]
Hockey hockey ['hɒki]
Hof court [kɔ:t]

hoffen to hope [həʊp]
hoffnungslos hopeless ['həʊpləs]
hoffnungsvoll hopeful ['həʊpfl]
höflich polite [pə'laɪt]
Höhe height [haɪt]
holen to get [get]
Hölle hell [hel]
Holz wood [wʊd]
Homecoming *(Schulfest an amerikanischen High Schools)* homecoming ['həʊmkʌmɪŋ]
hören to hear [hɪə]
Horizont horizon [hə'raɪzn]
Horoskop horoscope ['hɒrəskəʊp]
Hose trousers *(pl)* ['traʊzəz]
kurze Hose shorts *(pl)* [ʃɔːts]
Hosentasche pocket ['pɒkɪt]
Hotel hotel [həʊ'tel]
Hotelsuite hotel suite [həʊ'tel ˌswiːt]
Hotline hotline ['hɒtlaɪn]
hübsch pretty ['prɪti]
Hubschrauber helicopter ['helɪˌkɒptə]
Hügel hill [hɪl]
Huhn chicken ['tʃɪkɪn]
Hund dog [dɒg]
mit dem Hund spazieren gehen to walk the dog [wɔːk ðə 'dɒg]
hundemüde dog-tired [ˌdɒg 'taɪəd]
hundert hundred ['hʌndrəd]
Hunger bekommen to get hungry [get 'hʌŋgri]
Hungersnot famine ['fæmɪn]
hungrig hungry ['hʌŋgri]
Hut hat [hæt]
Hütte hut [hʌt]

I

ich I [aɪ]
ich selbst myself [maɪ'self]
Ich heiße .... My name is .... [maɪ 'neɪm‿ɪz]
Ich nehme .... I'm having .... [aɪm 'hævɪŋ]
ich würde gern I'd like to [ˌaɪd 'laɪk tə]
ich würde lieber I'd rather [aɪd 'rɑːðə]
Idee idea [aɪ'dɪə]
Idiot idiot ['ɪdɪət]
ignorieren to ignore [ɪg'nɔː]
ihm him [hɪm]
ihn him [hɪm]
ihnen them [ðem]
Ihnen you [juː; jə]
ihr you [juː; jə]; its [ɪts]
ihr selbst yourselves [jɔː'selvz]
ihr/ihre her [hɜː]; their [ðeə]
Ihr/Ihre your [jɔː]
Ikone icon ['aɪkɒn]
illegal illegal [ɪ'liːgl]
im Begriff sein, etw. zu tun to be about to (do sth) [bi‿ə'baʊt tə]
im Gange sein to be on [biː‿'ɒn]
im Ganzen in all [ɪn‿'ɔːl]
im unteren Teil at the bottom [ət ðə 'bɒtəm]
im vorderen Teil at the front [ət ðə 'frʌnt]
Imbiss snack [snæk]
Imbissstube deli *(AE)* ['deli]; diner *(AE)* ['daɪnə]; snack bar ['snæk ˌbɑː]
immer always ['ɔːlweɪz]
immer wieder tun to keep *(+ -ing)* [kiːp]
immer noch still [stɪl]
Immigrant/Immigrantin immigrant ['ɪmɪgrənt]
Immigration immigration [ˌɪmɪ'greɪʃn]
immigrieren to immigrate ['ɪmɪgreɪt]
improvisieren to freestyle *(slang)* ['friːstaɪl]
in at [æt; ət]; in [ɪn]; into ['ɪntə]
in Australien Down Under [ˌdaʊn‿'ʌndə]
in ... hinein into ['ɪntə]
Independent *(Musikrichtung)* independent [ˌɪndɪ'pendənt]
Indianer/Indianerin Native American [ˌneɪtɪv‿ə'merɪkən]
Indie *(Musikrichtung)* indie ['ɪndi]
indisch Indian ['ɪndiən]
Industrie industry ['ɪndəstri]
Industrie- industrial [ɪn'dʌstriəl]
industriell industrial [ɪn'dʌstriəl]
Infokasten fact box ['fækt bɒks]
Informatik IT [ˌaɪ'tiː]
Information/Informationen information [ˌɪnfə'meɪʃn]
Informationstechnik IT [ˌaɪ'tiː]
Informationszentrum information centre [ɪnfə'meɪʃn ˌsentə]
informieren to inform [ɪn'fɔːm]
Ingenieur/Ingenieurin engineer [ˌendʒɪ'nɪə]
Inhaber/Inhaberin keeper ['kiːpə]
Inhalt content ['kɒntent]
inklusive including [ɪn'kluːdɪŋ]
Inlineskates skates *(pl)* [skeɪts]
Inlineskates fahren to skate [skeɪt]
innen inner ['ɪnə]; inside [ɪn'saɪd]
innerer/innere/inneres inner ['ɪnə]
innerhalb within [wɪ'ðɪn]
inoffiziell non-official [ˌnɒnə'fɪʃl]
Insel island ['aɪlənd]
Inselbewohner/Inselbewohnerin islander ['aɪləndə]
insgesamt in all [ɪn‿'ɔːl]
Installateur/Installateurin installer [ɪn'stɔːlə]; plumber ['plʌmə]
installieren to install [ɪn'stɔːl]
Institut college ['kɒlɪdʒ]
intelligent intelligent [ɪn'telɪdʒnt]
interessant interesting ['ɪntrəstɪŋ]
Interesse interest ['ɪntrəst]
sich **interessieren** to get interested [get 'ɪntrəstɪd]
interessiert interested ['ɪntrəstɪd]
interessiert sein an to be into [biː‿'ɪntə]
interkulturell inter-cultural [ˌɪntə'kʌltʃrl]
international international [ˌɪntə'næʃnl]
Internet Internet ['ɪntənet]
im Internet online [ˌɒn'laɪn]
im Internet surfen to surf the Internet [ˌsɜːf ði‿'ɪntənet]
Internetauftritt website ['websaɪt]
Interview interview ['ɪntəvjuː]
interviewen to interview ['ɪntəvjuː]
Inuktitut *(Sprache der Inuit)* Inuktitut [ɪ'nʊktɪtʊt]
involvieren to involve [ɪn'vɒlv]
IQ *(Intelligenzquotient)* IQ [ˌaɪ'kjuː]
Iren/Irinnen Irish ['aɪrɪʃ]
irgendetwas anything ['eniθɪŋ]
irgendjemand anybody ['eniˌbɒdi]
irgendwie somehow ['sʌmhaʊ]; sort of ['sɔːt‿əv]
irgendwo anywhere ['eniweə]; somewhere ['sʌmweə]
irisch Irish ['aɪrɪʃ]
isolieren to insulate ['ɪnsjəleɪt]
Isolierung insulation [ˌɪnsjə'leɪʃn]
Italiener/Italienerin Italian [ɪ'tæliən]
italienisch Italian [ɪ'tæliən]

J

ja yes [jes]; yeah *(slang)* [jeə]
Jacke jacket ['dʒækɪt]
Jackentasche pocket ['pɒkɪt]
Jagdhund hound [haʊnd]
Jagen hunting ['hʌntɪŋ]
Jahr year [jɪə]
Jahrbuch yearbook ['jɪəbʊk]
Jahreszeit season ['siːzn]
Jahrgangsstufe year [jɪə]
Jahrhundert century ['sentʃri]
-jährig year-old [ˌjɪər‿'əʊld]
-Jähriger/-Jährige year-old [ˌjɪər‿'əʊld]
Jahrmarkt fair [feə]
Januar January ['dʒænjuəri]
Japaner/Japanerin Japanese [ˌdʒæpn'iːz]
japanisch Japanese [ˌdʒæp'niːz]
Jazz jazz [dʒæz]
je each [iːtʃ]

Jeans jeans *(pl)* [dʒi:nz]
jeder/jede/jedes each [i:tʃ]; every ['evri]
jeder everybody ['evribɒdi]; everyone ['evriwʌn]
jeder (beliebige) anybody ['eni,bɒdi]
jederzeit at any time [æt‿eni 'taɪm]
jedoch yet [jet]; however [haʊ'evə]
jemals ever ['evə]
jemand somebody ['sʌmbədi]; someone ['sʌmwʌn]
jene those [ðəʊz]
jenes that [ðæt]
jetzt now [naʊ]
jetzt gleich right now [,raɪt 'naʊ]
jeweils each [i:tʃ]
Job job [dʒɒb]
joggen to jog [dʒɒg]
Jogger/Joggerin jogger [dʒɒgə]
Journalist/Journalistin journalist ['dʒɜ:nlɪst]
jucken to itch [ɪtʃ]
Jugend youth [ju:θ]
jugendlich teenage ['ti:neɪdʒ]
Jugendliche/Jugendlicher teenager ['ti:n,eɪdʒə]; teen [ti:n]
Jugendtreffen rally ['ræli]
Juli July [dʒʊ'laɪ]
jung young [jʌŋ]
Junge boy [bɔɪ]; lad [læd]
der **Jüngere** junior ['dʒu:niə]
Juni June [dʒu:n]
Junior junior ['dʒu:niə]
Juwel jewel ['dʒu:əl]

K

Kaffee coffee ['kɒfi:]
Käfig cage [keɪdʒ]
kahl bald [bɔ:ld]
Kakao cocoa ['kəʊkəʊ]
Kalender calendar ['kæləndə]
kalt cold [kəʊld]
Kamera camera ['kæmrə]
Kamerad/Kameradin buddy *(infml)* ['bʌdi]; mate [meɪt]
Kameramann cameraman, cameramen *(pl)* ['kæmrəmæn; 'kæmrəmen]
Kaminfeuer fire [faɪə]
Kampf battle ['bætl]; fight [faɪt]; fighting ['faɪtɪŋ]
Kampf- fighting ['faɪtɪŋ]
kämpfen to fight [faɪt]
Kampfrichter judge [dʒʌdʒ]
Kanadier/Kanadierin Canadian [kə'neɪdiən]
kanadisch Canadian [kə'neɪdiən]
Kanal channel ['tʃænl]
Känguru kangaroo [,kæŋgr'u:]
Kante edge [edʒ]
Kantonese Cantonese [,kɑntə'ni:z]
kantonesisch Cantonese [,kɑntə'ni:z]
Kanu fahren to canoe [kə'nu:]
Kanzler/Kanzlerin chancellor ['tʃɑ:ntsələ]
Kapelle band [bænd]
Kapitän captain ['kæptɪn]
Kappe cap [kæp]
Kapsel capsule ['kæpsju:l]
kaputt broken ['brəʊkn]
kaputtmachen to break [breɪk]
Karosserie body shell ['bɒdi ,ʃel]
Karotte carrot ['kærət]
Karriere career [kə'rɪə]
Karte card [kɑ:d]
Kartoffel potato, potatoes *(pl)* [pə'teɪtəʊ; pə'teɪtəʊz]
Kartoffelchip crisp [krɪsp]
Käse cheese [tʃi:z]
Kasten box, boxes *(pl)* [bɒks; 'bɒksɪz]
Katastrophe disaster [dɪ'zɑ:stə]
Kathedrale cathedral [kə'θi:drl]
Katze cat [kæt]
kaufen to buy [baɪ]
Kaufhaus department store [dɪ'pɑ:tmənt stɔ:]; store [stɔ:]
Kaufhausdetektiv/Kaufhausdetektivin store detective ['stɔ: dɪ,tektɪv]
Kautschuk rubber ['rʌbə]
Kaviar caviar ['kæviɑ:]
kein/keine no [nəʊ]
keine Ahnung no idea [,nəʊ‿aɪ'dɪə]
keines von beidem not either of these [nɒt 'aɪðər‿əv ,ði:z]
überhaupt kein/keine no … at all [,nəʊ … ət‿'ɔ:l]
keiner/keine none [nʌn]
Keks biscuit ['bɪskɪt]
Kelch cup [kʌp]
Kellergeschoss basement ['beɪsmənt]
Kellner waiter ['weɪtə]
kennen to know [nəʊ]
kennzeichnend typical ['tɪpɪkl]
Kerl bloke [bləʊk]; guy [gaɪ]
Kette chain [tʃeɪn]
Kickboard kickboard ['kɪkbɔ:d]
kicken to kick [kɪk]
kidnappen to kidnap ['kɪdnæp]
Kidnapping kidnapping ['kɪdnæpɪŋ]
Kilo(gramm) kilo (kg) ['ki:ləʊ]
Kilometer kilometre ['kɪləʊ,mi:tə; kɪ'lɒmɪtə]
Kind child, children *(pl)* [tʃaɪld; 'tʃɪldrɪn]; kid [kɪd]
Kindergarten nursery school ['nɜ:sri ,sku:l]
Kino cinema ['sɪnəmə]; movies *(AE)* ['mu:viz]; theater *(AE)* ['θɪətə]
kippen to tip [tɪp]
Kirche church [tʃɜ:tʃ]
Kirsche cherry ['tʃeri]
Kiste box, boxes *(pl)* [bɒks; 'bɒksɪz]
klagen to moan [məʊn]
Klang sound [saʊnd]
Klappe shutter ['ʃʌtə]
klar clear [klɪə]
sich klar werden to realise ['rɪəlaɪz]
klären *(ein Problem)* to sort out [sɔ:t‿'aʊt]
Klasse class [klɑ:s]; grade *(AE)* [greɪd]
Klassenarbeit test [test]
Klassenzimmer classroom ['klɑ:srʊm]
klassisch classic ['klæsɪk]
Klatsch gossip ['gɒsɪp]
klatschen to clap [klæp]
Kleid dress [dres]
Kleider clothes *(pl)* [kləʊðz]
Kleiderschrank wardrobe ['wɔ:drəʊb]
Kleidung clothes *(pl)* [kləʊðz]; clothing ['kləʊðɪŋ]; dress [dres]
klein little ['lɪtl]; small [smɔ:l]
Klempner/Klempnerin plumber ['plʌmə]
Klempnerarbeit plumbing ['plʌmɪŋ]
klettern to climb ['klaɪm]
klicken to click [klɪk]
Klima climate ['klaɪmət]
Klingel bell [bel]
klingeln to ring [rɪŋ]
Es klingelt. The bell rings. [ðə 'bel rɪŋz]
klingen to sound [saʊnd]
Klippe cliff [klɪf]
klopfen to knock [nɒk]
fest klopfen to bang [bæŋ]
Klopfen knock [nɒk]
Klub club [klʌb]
klug intelligent [ɪn'telɪdʒnt]; smart [smɑ:t]
Klunker bling bling *(slang)* [,blɪŋ 'blɪŋ]
knacken to crackle ['krækl]
knallen to pop [pɒp]
knallen lassen to pop [pɒp]
knarren to creak [kri:k]
Kneipe bar [bɑ:]
knicken to fold [fəʊld]
Knie knee [ni:]
knistern to crackle ['krækl]
Knopf button ['bʌtn]
knusprig crunchy ['krʌntʃi]
Koala koala [kəʊ'ɑ:lə]
Kobold goblin ['gɒblɪn]
Koch/Köchin chef [ʃef]; cook [kʊk]
kochen to cook [kʊk]
Kochen cooking ['kʊkɪŋ]
Kohle carbon ['kɑ:bn]
Kohlendioxid carbon dioxide (CO_2) [,kɑ:bn daɪ'ɒksaɪd; si:‿əʊ 'tu:]

Kohlenstoff carbon ['kɑ:bn]
Kollege/Kollegin colleague ['kɒli:g]
Kollegium staff [stɑ:f]
Kollektor collector [kə'lektə]
Kolonie colony ['kɒləni]
komfortabel comfortable ['kʌmpftəbl]
komisch funny ['fʌni]
kommen to come [kʌm]; to get [get]
Komm./Kommt. Come on. [kʌm‿'ɒn]
kommen nach to get to ['get tə]
kommen zu to get to ['get tə]
Kommentar comment ['kɒment]
Kommunikation communication [kəˌmju:nɪ'keɪʃn]
kommunizieren to communicate [kə'mju:nɪkeɪt]
Komödie comedy ['kɒmədi]
Kompanie company ['kʌmpəni]
Komparativ comparative [kəm'pærətɪv]
kompliziert tricky ['trɪki]
Kondition condition [kən'dɪʃn]
König king [kɪŋ]
Königin queen [kwi:n]
königlich royal ['rɔɪəl]
Königreich monarchy ['mɒnəkɪ]
Konkurrent/Konkurentin rival ['raɪvl]
können can [kæn]; to be able to (do sth) [bi‿'eɪbl tə]
konnte/konnten could [kʊd]
könnte/könnten could [kʊd]; might [maɪt]
kann/könnte(n) vielleicht may [meɪ]
Konstruktion construction [kən'strʌkʃn]
kontaktfreudig outgoing ['aʊtgəʊɪŋ]
kontaktieren to contact ['kɒntækt]
Kontinent continent ['kɒntɪnənt]
Kontrolle check [tʃek]
kontrollieren to check [tʃek]; to control [kən'trəʊl]
Kontrollturm tower ['taʊə]
Konzert concert ['kɒnsət]
Kooperative co-operative [kəʊ'ɒprətɪv]
Kopf head [hed]
Kopfball header ['hedə]
Kopfhörer headphones *(pl)* ['hedfəʊnz]
Kopfsalat lettuce ['letɪs]
kopieren to copy ['kɒpi]
Koralle coral ['kɒrəl]
Korallen- coral ['kɒrəl]
Kordel string [strɪŋ]
kornisch Cornish ['kɔ:nɪʃ]
Körper body ['bɒdi]
körperlich physical ['fɪzɪkl]
korrekt correct [kə'rekt]; right [raɪt]
Korridor corridor ['kɒrɪdɔ:]
kosten to cost [kɒst]
Kosten cost [kɒst]
die Kosten senken to cut costs [kʌt 'kɒsts]

kostenlos free [fri:]
krabbeln to crawl [krɔ:l]
Krach! Crash! [kræʃ]
Kraft energy ['enədʒi]; power ['paʊə]
Krake octopus ['ɒktəpəs]
krank ill [ɪl]; sick [sɪk]
Krankenhaus hospital ['hɒspɪtl]
Krankenpfleger nurse [nɜ:s]
Krankenschwester nurse [nɜ:s]
Krankenwagen ambulance ['æmbjələns]
Krankheit disease [dɪ'zi:z]; illness ['ɪlnəs]
Krankmeldung sick note ['sɪk ˌnəʊt]
kreativ creative [kri'eɪtɪv]
Kreatur creature ['kri:tʃə]
Kredit loan [ləʊn]
Kreis circle ['sɜ:kl]
kreuzen to cross [krɒs]
Kreuzfahrt cruise [kru:z]
Kricket cricket ['krɪkɪt]
kriechen to crawl [krɔ:l]
Krieg war [wɔ:]
Krimi detective story [dɪ'tektɪv ˌstɔ:ri]
Kriminalität crime [kraɪm]
kriminell criminal ['krɪmɪnl]
Krimineller/Kriminelle criminal ['krɪmɪnl]
Kritik review [rɪ'vju:]
Krokodil crocodile ['krɒkədaɪl]
Krone crown [kraʊn]
Küche kitchen ['kɪtʃɪn]
Kuchen cake [keɪk]
Küchenchef/-chefin chef [ʃef]
Küchenschrank cupboard ['kʌbəd]
Kuh cow [kaʊ]
kühl cool [ku:l]
Kühlschrank refrigerator [rɪ'frɪdʒreɪtə]
sich **kümmern** to care [keə]; to take care [teɪk 'keə]
sich kümmern um to look after [lʊk‿'ɑ:ftə]
Kumpel buddy *(infml)* ['bʌdi]; homie *(slang)* ['həʊmi]; mate [meɪt]
Kunde/Kundin customer ['kʌstəmə]
kündigen to quit [kwɪt]
Kunst Art [ɑ:t]
Künstler/Künstlerin artist ['ɑ:tɪst]
Kunststoff(-) plastic ['plæstɪk]
Kurier courier ['kʊriə]
Kurs class [klɑ:s]; course [kɔ:s]
Kurve curve [kɜ:v]
kurz short [ʃɔ:t]
Kuss kiss [kɪs]
küssen to kiss [kɪs]
Küste coast [kəʊst]; seaside ['si:saɪd]
Küstenlinie coastline ['kəʊstˌlaɪn]

L

Labor lab(oratory) [læb; lə'bɒrətri]
lächeln to smile [smaɪl]
lachen to laugh [lɑ:f]
lackieren to spray [spreɪ]
Laden shop [ʃɒp]; store [stɔ:]
Ladung load [ləʊd]
Lager camp [kæmp]
Lagerfeuer campfire ['kæmpfaɪə]
Lamm lamb [læm]
Lammfleisch lamb [læm]
Lampe lamp [læmp]
Land country, countries *(pl)* ['kʌntri; 'kʌntriz]; land [lænd]; state [steɪt]; territory ['terɪtri]
landen to land [lænd]; to end up [ˌend‿'ʌp]
landesweit national ['næʃnl]
Landkarte map [mæp]
Landschaft landscape ['lændskeɪp]; scenery ['si:nri]
Landstraße road [rəʊd]
Landungssteg pier [pɪə]
Landwirt/Landwirtin farmer ['fɑ:mə]
Landwirtschaft agriculture ['ægrɪkʌltʃə]
lang long [lɒŋ]
langfristig in the long-run [ɪn ðə 'lɒŋrʌn]
langsam slow [sləʊ]
langweilig boring ['bɔ:rɪŋ]
Laptop laptop ['læptɒp]
Lärm noise [nɔɪz]
lassen to leave [li:v]; to let [let]
jmdn. im Stich lassen to let sb down [let 'daʊn]
Lasst uns .... Let's .... [lets]
Lassi *(Jogurtgetränk)* lassi ['lasɪ]
Last load [ləʊd]
Lastwagen lorry *(BE)* ['lɒri]; truck *(AE)* [trʌk]
Lastwagenfahrer/Lastwagenfahrerin trucker *(AE)* ['trʌkə]
lateinamerikanisch Hispanic [hɪ'spænɪk]
Laterne lantern ['læntən]
Latino Latino [lə'ti:nəʊ]
Latinomusik Latino [lə'ti:nəʊ]
Lauf run [rʌn]
Laufbahn career [kə'rɪə]
laufen to run [rʌn]; to walk [wɔ:k]; to be on [bi:‿'ɒn]
laufen gegen to run into [rʌn‿'ɪntə]
laufen mit *(Auto)* to run on ['rʌn‿ɒn]
laufend running ['rʌnɪŋ]
Läufer/Läuferin runner ['rʌnə]
jmdm. den **Laufpass geben** to dump sb [dʌmp]
Laune mood [mu:d]
laut loud [laʊd]

Es **lautete ....** It said .... [ɪt 'sed]
Leasing(-) leasing ['li:sɪŋ]
leben to live [lɪv]
Leben life, lives *(pl)* [laɪf; laɪvz]
am Leben alive [ə'laɪv]
lebendig alive [ə'laɪv]
Lebens- vital ['vaɪtl]
Lebensart lifestyle ['laɪfstaɪl]
Lebenslauf curriculum vitae (CV) [kə'rɪkjələm 'vi:taɪ]
Lebensmittel food [fu:d]
lebenswichtig vital ['vaɪtl]
Lebenszeichen vital signs *(pl)* [ˌvaɪtl 'saɪnz]
Lebewesen creature ['kri:tʃə]
lecker yummy ['jʌmi]
Leder leather ['leðə]
leer empty ['empti]; dead [ded]
legal legal ['li:gl]
legen to lay [leɪ]; to put [pʊt]; to rest [rest]
sich legen to come down [kʌm 'daʊn]
Lehns- feudal ['fju:dl]
Lehranstalt academy [ə'kædəmi]
Lehre apprenticeship [ə'prentɪʃɪp]
lehren to teach [ti:tʃ]
Lehrer/Lehrerin instructor [ɪn'strʌktə]; teacher ['ti:tʃə]
Lehrplan curriculum [kə'rɪkjələm]
Leibeigener/Leibeigene serf [sɜ:f]
leicht easy ['i:zi]; light [laɪt]
leidtun to be sorry [bi: 'sɒri]
Tut mir leid. sorry ['sɒri]
leihen to borrow ['bɒrəʊ]; to lend [lend]
Leinwand screen [skri:n]
leise quiet ['kwaɪət]; silent ['saɪlənt]; soft [sɒft]
leiten to direct [dɪ'rekt]
Leitungswasser tap water ['tæp ˌwɔ:tə]
lernen to learn [lɜ:n]; to study ['stʌdi]; to train [treɪn]
Lernen studies *(pl)* ['stʌdiz]
lesen to read [ri:d]
Leser/Leserin reader ['ri:də]
letzter/letzte/letztes final ['faɪnl]; last [lɑ:st]
Leuchte lamp [læmp]
leuchten to glow [gləʊ]
leuchtend bright [braɪt]; brilliant ['brɪljənt]
Leuchtfeuer flare [fleə]
Leukämie leukaemia [lju:'ki:miə]
Leute folks *(Anrede)* [fəʊks]; people ['pi:pl]
liberal liberal ['lɪbrl]
Licht light [laɪt]
Lichtschein flare [fleə]
lieb dear [dɪə]
Liebe ... *(Anrede in Briefen)* Dear ... [dɪə]
Lieber ... *(Anrede in Briefen)* Dear ... [dɪə]
Liebe love [lʌv]
lieben to love [lʌv]
ich würde **lieber** I'd rather [aɪd 'rɑ:ðə]
Liebling darling ['dɑ:lɪŋ]; pet [pet]
Lieblings- favourite ['feɪvrɪt]
Lied song [sɒŋ]
Liedtext lyrics ['lɪrɪks]
liefern to deliver [dɪ'lɪvə]; to provide (sb with sth) [prə'vaɪd]
Lieferwagen van [væn]
liegen to lie [laɪ]; to rest [rest]
Liga league [li:g]; union ['ju:njən]
lila purple ['pɜ:pl]
Limit limit ['lɪmɪt]
limitierend limiting ['lɪmɪtɪŋ]
Limonade lemonade [ˌlemə'neɪd]
Limousine limousine [ˌlɪmə'zi:n]
Lineal ruler ['ru:lə]
Linie line [laɪn]
Link link [lɪŋk]
linker/linke/linkes left [left]
links left [left]; on the left [ɒn ðə 'left]
links abbiegen to turn left [tɜ:n 'left]
Lippenpflegestift lip balm ['lɪp bɑ:m]
Liste list [lɪst]
Liter litre (l) ['li:tə]
live live [laɪv]
Loch dump [dʌmp]
lockig curly ['kɜ:li]
lodern to flare [fleə]
Löffel spoon [spu:n]
Logbuch logbook ['lɒgbʊk]
Logo logo ['ləʊgəʊ]
Lohn pay [peɪ]
lokal local ['ləʊkl]
löschen to put out [pʊt‿'aʊt]; *(Text)* to delete [dɪ'li:t]
lösen to solve [sɒlv]
losgehen *(Alarm)* to go off [gəʊ‿'ɒf]
loswerden to get rid of [get 'rɪd‿əv]
Löwe lion ['laɪən]
loyal loyal ['lɔɪəl]
Luft air [eə]
keine Luft bekommen to choke [tʃəʊk]
Luftballon balloon [bə'lu:n]
Luftpumpe pump [pʌmp]
lügen to lie [laɪ]
Lunge lung [lʌŋ]
lustig funny ['fʌni]
sich lustig machen über to laugh at ['lɑ:f‿ət]
Lyrik poetry ['pəʊətri]

M

machen to do [du:]; to make [meɪk]
eine Diät machen to go on a diet [ˌgəʊ‿ɒn ə 'daɪət]
sich lustig machen über to laugh at ['lɑ:f‿ət]
Spaß machen to be fun [bi: 'fʌn]
Macht power ['paʊə]
Mädchen girl [gɜ:l]
Magazin magazine [mægə'zi:n]
Magen stomach ['stʌmək]
Mahlzeit meal [mi:l]
Mai May [meɪ]
mailen to e-mail ['i:meɪl]
makellos pristine ['prɪsti:n]
Make-up make-up ['meɪkʌp]
Mal *(zeitlich)* time [taɪm]
malen to paint [peɪnt]
Maler/Malerin painter ['peɪntə]
Mama mum [mʌm]
man you [ju:; jə]; they [ðeɪ]
Manager/Managerin manager ['mænɪdʒə]
manchmal sometimes ['sʌmtaɪmz]
manipulieren to fix [fɪks]
Mann man, men *(pl)* [mæn; men]
männlich dominiert male-dominated ['meɪlˌdɒmɪneɪtɪd]
Mannschaft crew [kru:]; team [ti:m]
Mantarochen manta ray ['mænta ˌreɪ]
Mantel coat [kəʊt]
Mappe folder ['fəʊldə]
Marketing marketing ['mɑ:kɪtɪŋ]
markieren to mark [mɑ:k]
Markierung mark [mɑ:k]
Markt market ['mɑ:kɪt]
Marmelade jam [dʒæm]
Marsch march [mɑ:tʃ]
marschieren to march [mɑ:tʃ]
März March [mɑ:tʃ]
Maschine machine [mə'ʃi:n]
maskiert masked [mɑ:skt]
Masse mass [mæs]
Mast post [pəʊst]
Material material [mə'tɪəriəl]
Materie matter ['mætə]
Mathematik Maths [mæθs]
Mauer wall [wɔ:l]
Maultier mule [mju:l]
Maurer/Maurerin bricklayer ['brɪkˌleɪə]
Maus mouse, mice *(pl)* [maʊs; maɪs]
Mechaniker/Mechanikerin mechanic [mə'kænɪk]
Medien media *(pl)* ['mi:diə]
Medikament drug [drʌg]
Meer sea [si:]
Meeresküste seaside ['si:saɪd]
mehr more [mɔ:]

mehrere several ['sevrl]
Mehrheit majority [mə'dʒɒrəti]
Mehrheiten- majority [mə'dʒɒrəti]
Mehrzahl plural ['plʊərəl]
Meile *(brit. Längenmaß)* mile [maɪl]
Meilenstein milestone ['maɪlstəʊn]
meilenweit for miles [fə‿'maɪlz]
mein/meine my [maɪ]
  Mein Gott! My God! [maɪ 'gɒd]
  mein Herr (Anrede) sir [sɜ:]
Meinung opinion [ə'pɪnjən]
  einer Meinung sein to agree [ə'gri:]
das **meiste** most [məʊst]
  die meisten most [məʊst]
melden to report [rɪ'pɔ:t]
Meldung report [rɪ'pɔ:t]
Menge amount [ə'maʊnt]
  eine Menge a lot of [ə 'lɒt‿əv]
Mensch human ['hju:mən]
Menschen people ['pi:pl]
Menschenmenge crowd [kraʊd]
menschlich human ['hju:mən]
Menü menu ['menju:]
sich **merken** to remember [rɪ'membə]
merkwürdig strange [streɪndʒ]
Messe fair [feə]
Messer knife, knives *(pl)* [naɪf; naɪvz]
Messestand stand [stænd]
Metal *(Musikrichtung)* metal ['metl]
Metall metal ['metl]
Meter metre ['mi:tə]
Mexikaner/Mexikanerin Mexican ['meksɪkən]
mexikanisch Mexican ['meksɪkən]
mich me [mi:]
  mich (selbst) myself [maɪ'self]
Miesmacher/Miesmacherin wet blanket [wet 'blæŋkɪt]
Miet- rental ['rentl]
Miete rent [rent]
mieten to rent [rent]
Mikrofon microphone ['maɪkrəfəʊn]
Mikrowelle microwave ['maɪkrəʊweɪv]
Milch milk [mɪlk]
milchig milky ['mɪlki]
Milchmann milkman, milkmen *(pl)* ['mɪlkmən; 'mɪlkmen]
Milchshake milkshake ['mɪlkʃeɪk]
Milliarde *(tausend Millionen)* billion ['bɪljən]
Million million ['mɪlɪən]
mindestens at least [ət 'li:st]
Mineral- mineral ['mɪnərəl]
Minestrone minestrone [ˌmɪnɪ'strəʊni]
Mini- mini ['mɪni]
Minister/Ministerin minister ['mɪnɪstə]
Minute minute ['mɪnɪt]
mir me [mi:]
mischen to mix [mɪks]
Mischung cocktail ['kɒkteɪl]; mixture ['mɪkstʃə]
Mission mission ['mɪʃn]
mit with [wɪð]
Mitarbeiter/Mitarbeiterin employee [ɪm'plɔɪi:]
mitbringen to bring [brɪŋ]
miteinander together [tə'geðə]
Mitfahrgelegenheit ride [raɪd]
mitführen to carry along [ˌkæri‿ə'lɒŋ]
Mitglied member ['membə]
mithalten (mit) to keep up (with) [ki:p‿'ʌp]
Mitleid erregend pathetic [pə'θetɪk]
mitnehmen to take [teɪk]
zum **Mitnehmen** to go [tə‿'gəʊ]
mitreißen to carry along [ˌkæri‿ə'lɒŋ]
Mitspieler/Mitspielerin player ['pleɪə]
Mittagessen dinner ['dɪnə]; lunch [lʌntʃ]
Mittagszeit lunchtime ['lʌntʃtaɪm]
Mitte middle ['mɪdl]
mittel medium ['mi:diəm]
Mittel- middle ['mɪdl]
Mittelalter Middle Ages [ˌmɪdl‿'eɪdʒɪz]
Mittelpunkt centre ['sentə]
Mittelschule *(weiterführende Schule in den USA, Mittelstufe)* middle school *(AE)* ['mɪdl ˌsku:l]
Mitternacht midnight ['mɪdnaɪt]
Mittwoch Wednesday ['wenzdeɪ]
mixen to mix [mɪks]
Mixtur mixture ['mɪkstʃə]
Möbel furniture ['fɜ:nɪtʃə]
mobil mobile ['məʊbaɪl]
Mobiltelefon cell phone *(AE)* ['sel ˌfəʊn]; mobile ['məʊbaɪl]
möchte(n) gern would like [wʊd 'laɪk]
Mode fashion ['fæʃn]
Model model ['mɒdl]
Modell model ['mɒdl]
modern modern ['mɒdn]
modisch trendy ['trendi]
mögen to like [laɪk]
  gern mögen to love [lʌv]
möglich possible ['pɒsəbl]
Möglichkeit opportunity [ˌɒpə'tju:nəti]
Mohrrübe carrot ['kærət]
Molkerei dairy ['deəri]
Moment moment ['məʊmənt]
  Moment mal! Hang on! ['hæŋ‿ɒn]
momentan at the moment [ət ðə 'məʊmənt]
Monarchie monarchy ['mɒnəkɪ]
Monat month [mʌnθ]
Mond moon [mu:n]
Monster monster ['mɒnstə]
Montag Monday ['mʌndeɪ]
montags on Mondays [ɒn 'mʌndeɪz]
Mord murder ['mɜ:də]
Mörder/Mörderin killer ['kɪlə]
morgen tomorrow [tə'mɒrəʊ]
Morgen morning ['mɔ:nɪŋ]; *(Flächenmaß: 40,47 Ar)* acre ['eɪkə];
  am Morgen in the morning [ˌɪn ðə 'mɔ:nɪŋ]
  am nächsten Morgen the next morning [ˌnekst 'mɔ:nɪŋ]
  Guten Morgen! Good morning! ['gʊd 'mɔ:nɪŋ]
Morgenappell assembly [ə'sembli]
Morgendämmerung dawn [dɔ:n]
morgens in the morning [ˌɪn ðə 'mɔ:nɪŋ]
Motel motel [məʊ'tel]
Motor engine ['endʒɪn]; motor ['məʊtə]
Motorrad motorbike ['məʊtəbaɪk]
Motte moth [mɒθ]
MP3 MP3 [empi:'θri:]
  MP3-Player MP3 player [empi:'θri: ˌpleɪə]
müde tired ['taɪəd]
Müll garbage *(AE)* ['gɑ:bɪdʒ]; rubbish ['rʌbɪʃ]
Mülleimer bin [bɪn]
Müllkippe dump [dʌmp]
Mülltonne bin [bɪn]
multinational multinational [ˌmʌlti'næʃnl]
Mund mouth [maʊθ]
Museum museum [mju:'zi:əm]
Musical musical ['mju:zɪkl]
Musik music ['mju:zɪk]
Musiker/Musikerin musician [mju:'zɪʃn]
müssen must [mʌst]; to have to ['hæv tə]; to need [ni:d]
mutig brave [breɪv]
Mutter mother ['mʌðə]
Muttersprache mother tongue ['mʌðə ˌtʌŋ]
Mutti mum [mʌm]
Mütze cap [kæp]
Mythos myth [mɪθ]

N

nach to [tʊ; tə]; *(zeitlich)* after ['ɑ:ftə]; *(Uhrzeit)* past [pɑ:st]
  nach draußen outside [aʊt'saɪd]
  nach drinnen inside [ɪn'saɪd]
  nach Hause home [həʊm]
  nach Hause bringen to take home [ˌteɪk 'həʊm]
Nachbar/Nachbarin neighbour ['neɪbə]
Nachbarschaft neighborhood *(AE)* ['neɪbəhʊd]
Nachhilfe coaching ['kəʊtʃɪŋ]
Nachmittag afternoon [ˌɑ:ftə'nu:n]
  am Nachmittag in the afternoon [ˌɪn ði ˌɑ:ftə'nu:n]

nachmittags in the afternoon [ˌɪn ði ˌɑ:ftə'nu:n]
Nachmittagstee afternoon tea [ˌɑ:ftənu:n 'ti:]
Nachricht message ['mesɪdʒ]
Nachricht(en) news *(sg.)* [nju:z]
neueste Nachrichten breaking news [ˌbreɪkɪŋ 'nju:z]
nachschauen to have a look [ˌhæv‿ə 'lʊk]
nachschlagen to look up [lʊk‿'ʌp]
nächster/nächste/nächstes next [nekst]
am nächsten Morgen the next morning [ˌnekst 'mɔ:nɪŋ]
Nacht night [naɪt]
heute Nacht tonight [tə'naɪt]
nachts at night [ət 'naɪt]
Nachtisch dessert [dɪ'zɜ:t]; pudding ['pʊdɪŋ]
Nachtschwester night nurse ['naɪt nɜ:s]
Nacktschnecke slug [slʌg]
nahe close [kləʊs]; near [nɪə]
in der **Nähe von** near [nɪə]
sich jmdm. von hinten **nähern** to come up behind sb [ˌkʌm‿ʌp bɪ'haɪnd]
Nahrung food [fu:d]
Name name [neɪm]
Nase nose [nəʊz]
die Nase voll haben to be fed up [bi: ˌfed‿'ʌp]
nass wet [wet]
Nation nation ['neɪʃn]
national national ['næʃnl]
National- national ['næʃnl]
Nationalpark national park [ˌnæʃnl 'pɑ:k]
Natur- natural ['nætʃrl]
natürlich natural ['nætʃrl]
natürlich of course [əv 'kɔ:s]
Naturwissenschaft Science ['saɪəns]
Nebel fog [fɒg]
neben beside [bɪ'saɪd]; by [baɪ]; next to ['nekst tə]
nebenan next door [ˌnekst 'dɔ:]
Nebenprodukt spin-off ['spɪn‿ɒf]
neblig foggy ['fɒgi]
Neffe nephew ['nefju:]
nehmen to take [teɪk]
Ich nehme .... I'm having .... [aɪm 'hævɪŋ]
neidisch (auf) jealous (of) ['dʒeləs]
nein no [nəʊ]
nennen to call [kɔ:l]; to name [neɪm]
neonfarben neon ['ni:ɒn]
Neoprenanzug wetsuit ['wetsu:t]
nervös nervous ['nɜ:vəs]
nett friendly ['frendli]; kind [kaɪnd]; nice [naɪs]
Netz net [net]
neu new [nju:]
Neuigkeit(en) news *(sg.)* [nju:z]
neutral neutral ['nju:trl]
nicht no [nəʊ]; not [nɒt]
auch nicht not ... either [ˌnɒt ... 'aɪðə]
nicht einmal not even [nɒt‿'i:vn]
(nicht) mehr (not) any more [nɒt ˌeni 'mɔ:]
noch nicht not ... yet [jet]
nichts nothing ['nʌθɪŋ]
Nickel *(Währung)* nickel ['nɪkl]
nie never ['nevə]
nieder down [daʊn]
Niederländer/Niederländerinnen Dutch [dʌtʃ]
niederländisch Dutch [dʌtʃ]
niederlegen to lie down [laɪ 'daʊn]
niedlich cute [kju:t]
niedrig low [ləʊ]
niemals never ['nevə]
niemand nobody ['nəʊbədi]; no one ['nəʊwʌn]
nirgendwo nowhere ['nəʊweə]
nirgendwohin nowhere ['nəʊweə]
Niveau level ['levl]
noch else [els]; still [stɪl]
noch ein/noch eine another [ə'nʌðə]
noch nicht not ... yet [jet]
non-stop non-stop [ˌnɒn'stɒp]
Norden north [nɔ:θ]
normal normal ['nɔ:ml]
normalerweise usually ['ju:ʒli]
Note grade *(AE)* [greɪd]; mark [mɑ:k]
Notfall emergency [ɪ'mɜ:dʒnsi]
Notiz note [nəʊt]; notice ['nəʊtɪs]
Notlage emergency [ɪ'mɜ:dʒnsi]
November November [nəʊ'vembə]
Nummer number ['nʌmbə]
nun now [naʊ]
nur only ['əʊnli]
nussig nutty ['nʌti]
nützlich useful ['ju:sfl]
nutzlos useless ['ju:sləs]
Nutzung use [ju:s]

O

ob if [ɪf]
oben above [ə'bʌv]; at the top [ət ðə 'tɒp]; up [ʌp]; upstairs [ʌp'steəz]
oberer/obere/oberes upper ['ʌpə]
oberer Teil top [tɒp]
oberhalb above [ə'bʌv]
oberster/oberste/oberstes supreme [su:'pri:m]
obligatorisch compulsory [kəm'pʌlsri]
Observatorium observatory [əb'zɜ:vətri]
Obst fruit [fru:t]
obwohl although [ɔ:l'ðəʊ]
oder or [ɔ:]
offen open ['əʊpn]
öffentlich public ['pʌblɪk]
in der **Öffentlichkeit** in public [ɪn 'pʌblɪk]
Öffentlichkeitsarbeit public relations (PR) [ˌpʌblɪk rɪ'leɪʃnz]
offiziell official [ə'fɪʃl]; officially [ə'fɪʃli]
öffnen to open ['əʊpn]
sich öffnen to open ['əʊpn]
Öffnungszeiten hours *(pl)* ['aʊəz]
oft often ['ɒfn]
ohne without [wɪ'ðaʊt]
ohne ... auskommen to go without [ˌgəʊ wɪ'ðaʊt]
ohnmächtig werden to faint [feɪnt]
Ohr ear [ɪə]
Oje! Oh dear! [əʊ 'dɪə]
o.k. OK [əʊ'keɪ]
Öko- eco [i:kəʊ]
Oktober October [ɒk'təʊbə]
Oktopus octopus ['ɒktəpəs]
Öl oil [ɔɪl]
Oldtimer vintage car [ˌvɪntɪdʒ 'kɑ:]
Oma grandma ['grændmɑ:]
Onkel uncle ['ʌŋkl]
online online [ˌɒn'laɪn]
Opa grandad ['grændæd]
Oper opera ['ɒprə]
operieren to operate ['ɒpəreɪt]
Optimismus optimism ['ɒptɪmɪzm]
optimistisch optimistic [ˌɒptɪ'mɪstɪk]
Option option ['ɒpʃn]
Orange orange ['ɒrɪndʒ]
Ordner folder ['fəʊldə]
Ordner mit Informationen (über) fact file (on) ['fækt faɪl]
Ordnung order ['ɔ:də]
in Ordnung all right [ɔ:l 'raɪt]
Organisation organisation [ˌɔ:gnaɪ'zeɪʃn]
Organisator/Organisatorin organizer ['ɔ:gənaɪzə]
organisch organic [ɔ:'gænɪk]
organisieren to organize ['ɔ:gənaɪz]
Ort place [pleɪs]
örtlich local ['ləʊkl]
ortsansässig local ['ləʊkl]
Osten east [i:st]
das **Outback** the Outback ['aʊtbæk]
Ozean ocean ['əʊʃn]
Ozeandampfer ocean liner ['əʊʃn ˌlaɪnə]

P

ein **paar** a couple of [ə 'kʌpl‿əv]; a few [ə 'fju:]

Paar couple ['kʌpl]
Pacht rent [rent]
pachten to rent [rent]
Päckchen packet ['pækɪt]
packen to pack [pæk]
Packmaterial packaging ['pækɪdʒɪŋ]
Paket packet ['pækɪt]
Palast palace ['pælɪs]
Palästinenser/Palästinenserin Palestinian [pælə'stɪniən]
palästinensisch Palestinian [pælə'stɪniən]
in **Panik geraten** to panic ['pænɪk]
Panter panther ['pænθə]
Papa dad [dæd]
Papier paper ['peɪpə]
Papierkram paper work ['peɪpə ˌwɜ:k]
Parade parade [pə'reɪd]
Paradies paradise ['pærəˌdaɪs]
Paragliding paragliding ['pærəˌglaɪdɪŋ]
Park park [pɑ:k]
Parkaufseher/Parkaufseherin (park) ranger [ˌpɑ:k 'reɪndʒə]
Parlament parliament ['pɑ:ləmənt]
Partei party ['pɑ:ti]
Partikel particle ['pɑ:tɪkl]
Partner/Partnerin partner ['pɑ:tnə]
Party party ['pɑ:ti]
eine Party feiern to have a party [ˌhæv‿ə 'pɑ:ti]
Pass passport ['pɑ:spɔ:t]
Passagier/Passagierin passenger ['pæsndʒə]
passen to fit [fɪt]
passen zu to go with ['gəʊ‿wɪð]; to match [mætʃ]
passend suitable ['su:təbl]
das nicht dazu passende odd one out [ɒd wʌn‿'aʊt]
Passkontrolle passports *(pl)* ['pɑ:spɔ:ts]
Patient/Patientin patient ['peɪʃnt]
Patron/Patronin patron ['peɪtrn]
Pause break [breɪk]
PC PC [ˌpi:'si:]
Pech bad luck [ˌbæd 'lʌk]
peinlich embarrassing [ɪm'bærəsɪŋ]
Pence *(Währung)* pence *(pl)* [pents]
perfekt perfect ['pɜ:fɪkt]
Periode period ['pɪəriəd]
permanent permanent ['pɜ:mnənt]
Person person ['pɜ:sn]
Personal staff [stɑ:f]
Personalabteilung human resources [ˌhju:mən rɪ'zɔ:sɪz]
persönlich personal ['pɜ:snl]
Perspektive prospect ['prɒspekt]
Perücke wig [wɪg]
Pfad path [pɑ:θ]
Pfannkuchen pancake ['pænkeɪk]
Pfeife pipe [paɪp]
pfeifen to whistle ['wɪsl]
Pfeil arrow ['ærəʊ]
Pferd horse [hɔ:s]
Pfiff whistle ['wɪsl]
Pflanze plant [plɑ:nt]
pflegte(n) zu used to *(+ infinitive)* ['ju:s‿tə]
Pflicht duty ['dju:ti]
pflücken to pick [pɪk]
Pflücker/Pflückerin picker ['pɪkə]
pflügen to plough [plaʊ]
Pforte gate [geɪt]
Pfosten post [pəʊst]
Pfund *(Währung)* pound (£) [paʊnd]
Pfund *(Gewicht)* pound (lb) [paʊnd]
physisch physical ['fɪzɪkl]
Pier pier [pɪə]
pikant spicy ['spaɪsi]
Pilot/Pilotin pilot ['paɪlət]
pink pink [pɪŋk]
Pionier/Pionierin pioneer [ˌpaɪə'nɪə]
Pitcher/Pitcherin pitcher ['pɪtʃə]
Pizza pizza ['pi:tsə]
Plakat poster ['pəʊstə]
Plan plan [plæn]
planen to plan [plæn]
Planet planet ['plænɪt]
Plastik(-) plastic ['plæstɪk]
platt flat [flæt]
Platte panel ['pænl]; record ['rekɔ:d]
Plattform platform ['plætfɔ:m]
Platz place [pleɪs]; room [ru:m; rʊm]; space [speɪs]
pleite broke [brəʊk]
plötzlich at once [ət 'wʌnts]; suddenly ['sʌdnli]
Plundergebäck Danish ['deɪnɪʃ]
Plural plural ['plʊərəl]
plus plus [plʌs]
Podcast podcast ['pɒdkɑ:st]
Poet/Poetin poet ['pəʊɪt]
Poetry Slam *(Gedichtwettbewerb)* poetry slam ['pəʊətri ˌslæm]
Pokal cup [kʌp]
Politik policy ['pɒlɪsi]; politics ['pɒlɪtɪks]
Politiker/Politikerin politician [ˌpɒlɪ'tɪʃn]
politisch political [pə'lɪtɪkl]
politische Linie policy ['pɒlɪsi]
Polizei police [pə'li:s]
Polizist policeman, policemen *(pl)* [pə'li:smən; pə'li:smen]
Polizist/Polizistin cop *(AE)* [kɒp]
polnisch Polish ['pəʊlɪʃ]
Pommes frites French fries *(AE)* ['frentʃ ˌfraɪz]; chips *(pl)* [tʃɪps]
Pompon *(bunte Quaste der Cheerleader)* pompom ['pɒmpɒm]
Pony pony ['pəʊni]
Popmusik pop [pɒp]
populär popular ['pɒpjələ]
Porträt profile ['prəʊfaɪl]
posieren to pose [pəʊz]
Position position [pə'zɪʃn]
Postamt post office ['pəʊst‿ˌɒfɪs]
posten *(im Internetforum)* to post [pəʊst]
Poster poster ['pəʊstə]
Postkarte postcard ['pəʊstkɑ:d]
Prachtstraße boulevard ['bu:ləvɑ:d]
Praktikum internship *(AE)* ['ɪntɜ:nʃɪp]; work experience ['wɜ:k‿ɪkˌspɪəriənts]
praktisch handy ['hændi]
praktizieren to practise ['præktɪs]
präsentieren to present [prɪ'zent]
prasseln to crackle ['krækl]
Preis award [ə'wɔ:d]; cost [kɒst]; price [praɪs]; prize [praɪz]
zum halben Preis half-price [ˌhɑ:f'praɪs]
Prellung bruise [bru:z]
Premierminister/Premierministerin Prime Minister (PM) [ˌpraɪm 'mɪnɪstə]
Presse press [pres]
pressen to press [pres]; to squash [skwɒʃ]
prima brilliant ['brɪljənt]; cool [ku:l]
Prinz prince [prɪns]
privat private ['praɪvɪt]
Privatschule (GB) public school [ˌpʌblɪk 'sku:l]
pro per [pɜ:]
Pro und Kontra pros and cons [ˌprəʊz‿ənd 'kɒnz]
proben to practise ['præktɪs]; *(ein Theaterstück)* to rehearse [rɪ'hɜ:s]
probieren to try [traɪ]
Problem problem ['prɒbləm]
Produkt product ['prɒdʌkt]
Produktion production [prə'dʌkʃn]
Produzent manufacturer [ˌmænjə'fæktʃərə]
Produzent/Produzentin producer [prə'dju:sə]
produzieren to produce [prə'dju:s]
professionell professional [prə'feʃnl]
Profil profile ['prəʊfaɪl]
Programm channel ['tʃænl]; programme ['prəʊgræm]
Projekt project ['prɒdʒekt]
Prospekt leaflet ['li:flət]
Protest protest ['prəʊtest]
protestieren to protest [prə'test]
Protestierender/Protestierende protester [prə'testə]
Prozent per cent (%) [pə 'sent]
prüfen to test [test]

Prüfung check [tʃek]; exam [ɪɡ'zæm]; trial ['traɪəl]
Publikum audience ['ɔ:diəns]
Pudding pudding ['pʊdɪŋ]
Puder powder ['paʊdə]
Pulver powder ['paʊdə]
Pumpe pump [pʌmp]
Punk punk [pʌŋk]
Punkmusik punk [pʌŋk]
Punkt dot [dɒt]; point [pɔɪnt]
Pünktchen dot [dɒt]
punkten to score [skɔ:]
Punktestand score [skɔ:]
pünktlich on time [ɒn 'taɪm]
Pute turkey ['tɜ:ki]
putzen to brush [brʌʃ]
Putzerstation cleaning station ['kli:nɪŋ ˌsteɪʃn]
Putzkraft cleaner ['kli:nə]
Puzzle puzzle ['pʌzl]
PVC PVC [ˌpi:vi:'si:]

Q

Qualifikation qualification [ˌkwɒlɪfɪ'keɪʃn]
Qualle jellyfish, jellyfish *(pl)* ['dʒelifɪʃ]
Quallen-Schutzanzug stinger suit [ˌstɪŋə 'su:t]
Quelle origin ['ɒrɪdʒɪn]; resource [rɪ'zɔ:s]
quetschen to squash [skwɒʃ]
Quetschung bruise [bru:z]
quietschen to creak [kri:k]
Quote quota ['kwəʊtə]

R

Radiergummi rubber ['rʌbə]
Radio radio ['reɪdiəʊ]
Radiosendung radio show ['reɪdiəʊ ˌʃəʊ]
Rahmen frame [freɪm]; setting ['setɪŋ]
Rallye rally ['ræli]
Ranch ranch [ræntʃ]
Rand edge [edʒ]
Ranger (park) ranger [ˌpɑ:k 'reɪndʒə]
Rap rap [ræp]
rappen to rap [ræp]
Rapper/Rapperin rapper ['ræpə]
rar rare [reə]
Rasen grass [ɡrɑ:s]
Rasierwasser aftershave ['ɑ:ftəʃeɪv]
Rasse race [reɪs]
Rassen- racial ['reɪʃl]
Rassentrennung segregation *(no pl)* [ˌseɡrɪ'ɡeɪʃn]
Rast rest [rest]
rasten to rest [rest]
Rastplatz rest area ['rest ˌeəriə]
Rat advice [əd'vaɪs]
raten to advise [əd'vaɪz]; to guess [ɡes]
Ratschlag advice [əd'vaɪs]
Rätsel mystery ['mɪstəri]; puzzle ['pʌzl]
rau tough [tʌf]
rauben to rob [rɒb]
Räuber/Räuberin robber ['rɒbə]
Rauch smoke [sməʊk]
rauchen to smoke [sməʊk]
Raum room [ru:m; rʊm]; space [speɪs]
Raumfähre shuttle ['ʃʌtl]
Raumpfleger/Raumpflegerin cleaner ['kli:nə]
Raumschiff spaceship ['speɪsʃɪp]
Razzia raid [reɪd]
R&B R&B [ˌɑ:r‿n'bi:]
Reaktion response [rɪ'spɒns]
Realität reality [ri'æləti]
Realityshow reality show [ri'æləti ˌʃəʊ]
Recherche research [rɪ'sɜ:tʃ]
Rechnung bill [bɪl]
Recht law [lɔ:]; right [raɪt]
Recht haben to be right [bi: 'raɪt]
rechter/rechte/rechtes right [raɪt]
rechtlich legal ['li:ɡl]
rechts right [raɪt]; on the right [ɒn ðə 'raɪt]
rechts abbiegen to turn right [tɜ:n 'raɪt]
Rechts- legal ['li:ɡl]
rechtswidrig illegal [ɪ'li:ɡl]
recyceln to recycle [ri:'saɪkl]
Recycling recycling [ri:'saɪklɪŋ]
Rede speech [spi:tʃ]; talk [tɔ:k]
eine Rede halten to give a talk [ˌɡɪv‿ə 'tɔ:k]
reden to talk [tɔ:k]
reden mit to talk to ['tɔ:k tə]
Redewendung phrase [freɪz]
reduzieren to cut down on [kʌt 'daʊn‿ɒn]; to reduce [rɪ'dju:s]
Referenz reference ['refrns]; *(Person)* referee [ˌrefr'i:]
Refrain chorus ['kɔ:rəs]; refrain [rɪ'freɪn]
Regal shelf, shelves *(pl)* [ʃelf; ʃelvz]
Regalbrett shelf, shelves *(pl)* [ʃelf; ʃelvz]
Regel rule [ru:l]
regelmäßig regular ['reɡjələ]
regeln *(ein Problem)* to sort out [sɔ:t‿'aʊt]
Regen rain [reɪn]
Regenguss shower ['ʃaʊə]
Regenschirm umbrella [ʌm'brelə]
Regenwasser rainwater ['reɪnˌwɔ:tə]
Reggae reggae ['reɡeɪ]
Regie führen to direct [dɪ'rekt]
regieren to rule [ru:l]
Regierung government ['ɡʌvnmənt]
Region region ['ri:dʒn]
Regisseur/Regisseurin director [dɪ'rektə]
registrieren to register ['redʒɪstə]
sich registrieren to register ['redʒɪstə]
Registrierung registration [ˌredʒɪ'streɪʃn]
regnen to rain [reɪn]
regnerisch rainy ['reɪni]
regulär regular ['reɡjələ]
reich rich [rɪtʃ]
Reihe row [rəʊ]
Reihenfolge order ['ɔ:də]
rein pristine ['prɪsti:n]
reinigen to clean [kli:n]
Reis rice [raɪs]
Reise journey ['dʒɜ:ni]; tour [tʊə]; trip [trɪp]; travel ['trævl]
Reisebürokaufmann/Reisebürokauffrau travel agent ['trævl‿ˌeɪdʒnt]
Reisebus coach [kəʊtʃ]
reisen to travel ['trævl]
Reisepass passport ['pɑ:spɔ:t]
reiten to ride [raɪd]
Reiten horseback riding ['hɔ:sbæk ˌraɪdɪŋ]; riding ['raɪdɪŋ]
Reklame advertising *(no pl.)* ['ædvətaɪzɪŋ]
Religion religion [rɪ'lɪdʒn]
Religionsunterricht Religious Education (RE) [rɪˌlɪdʒəs‿edʒʊ'keɪʃn]
religiös religious [rɪ'lɪdʒəs]
rennen to run [rʌn]
Rennen race [reɪs]
reparieren to fix [fɪks]; to repair [rɪ'peə]
Reporter/Reporterin reporter [rɪ'pɔ:tə]
Reservat reservation [ˌrezə'veɪʃn]
reservieren to book [bʊk]
Reservierung reservation [ˌrezə'veɪʃn]
Respekt respect [rɪ'spekt]
Respektlosigkeit disrespect [ˌdɪsrɪ'spekt]
Ressource resource [rɪ'zɔ:s]
Rest rest [rest]
Restaurant restaurant ['restrɒnt]
Restaurant mit Straßenverkauf takeaway ['teɪkəweɪ]
restaurieren to restore [rɪ'stɔ:]
Resultat result [rɪ'zʌlt]
retten to rescue ['reskju:]; to save [seɪv]
Rettung rescue ['reskju:]
Rettungsschwimmer/Rettungsschwimmerin lifeguard ['laɪfɡɑ:d]
Rezept recipe ['resɪpi:]
Rezeption reception [rɪ'sepʃn]
Richter judge [dʒʌdʒ]
richtig correct [kə'rekt]; right [raɪt]

richtig machen to get ... right [get ... 'raɪt]
Richtung direction [dɪ'rekʃn]; trend [trend]
in Richtung towards [tə'wɔ:dz]
riechen to smell [smel]
Riegel bar [bɑ:]
riesig huge [hju:dʒ]; large [lɑ:dʒ]
Riff reef [ri:f]
Rinderhirte cowboy ['kaʊbɔɪ]
Rindvieh cattle *(pl. only)* ['kætl]
Ring ring [rɪŋ]
riskieren to dare [deə]
etw. riskieren to take your chance [ˌteɪk jɔ: 'tʃɑ:ns]
Ritt ride [raɪd]
Ritter knight [naɪt]
Rivale/Rivalin rival ['raɪvl]
rivalisierend rival ['raɪvl]
Robbe seal [si:l]
Roboter robot ['rəʊbɒt]
Rock skirt [skɜ:t]
rocken to rock [rɒk]
Rockmusik rock [rɒk]
Rodeo rodeo [rəʊ'deɪəʊ; 'rəʊdiəʊ]
roh raw [rɔ:]
Rohrleitung plumbing ['plʌmɪŋ]
Rohstoff resource [rɪ'zɔ:s]
Rolle part [pɑ:t]; role [rəʊl]
Roller kickboard ['kɪkbɔ:d]
Roman novel ['nɒvl]
romantisch romantic [rə'mæntɪk]
rosa pink [pɪŋk]
rot red [red]
rot werden to go red [gəʊ 'red]
rüberbringen to bring round [brɪŋ‿'raʊnd]
Rücken back [bæk]
rückenfrei backless ['bækləs]
Rucksack rucksack ['rʌksæk]
Rucksacktourist/Rucksacktouristin backpacker ['bækpækə]
rückwärtig back [bæk]
rufen to call [kɔ:l]; to cry [kraɪ]; to shout [ʃaʊt]; *(Eule)* to hoot [hu:t]
rhythmisch rufen to chant [tʃɑ:nt]
Rugby rugby ['rʌgbi]
Rugbyschuh rugby boot ['rʌgbi bu:t]
Ruhe quiet ['kwaɪət]; rest [rest]
jmdn. in Ruhe lassen to leave sb alone [ˌli:v‿ə'ləʊn]
ruhig calm [kɑ:m]; quiet ['kwaɪət]
rumhängen to hang around [ˌhæŋ‿ə'raʊnd]
Runde round [raʊnd]; run [rʌn]
Russe/Russin Russian ['rʌʃn]
russisch Russian ['rʌʃn]

S

Saal hall [hɔ:l]
Saat seed [si:d]
Saatkorn seed [si:d]
Sache thing [θɪŋ]
Saft juice [dʒu:s]
saftig juicy ['dʒu:si]
sagen to say [seɪ]; to tell [tel]
Sahne cream [kri:m]
Saison season ['si:zn]
Salat salad ['sæləd]
Salz salt [sɔ:lt]
Salzwasser saltwater ['sɔ:ltˌwɔ:tə]
Samen seed [si:d]
sammeln to collect [kə'lekt]
Sammler/Sammlerin collector [kə'lektə]
Samstag Saturday ['sætədeɪ]
Sand sand [sænd]
sandig sandy ['sændi]
Sandwich sandwich ['sænwɪdʒ]
sanft soft [sɒft]
Sänger/Sängerin singer ['sɪŋə]
Satellit satellite ['sætlaɪt]
Satzung charter ['tʃɑ:tə]
sauber clean [kli:n]
säubern to clean [kli:n]
sauer sour ['saʊə]
Säugling baby, babies *(pl)* ['beɪbi; 'beɪbiz]
Schachtel box, boxes *(pl)* [bɒks; 'bɒksɪz]
Schaden damage ['dæmɪdʒ]; harm [hɑ:m]
Schaf sheep, sheep *(pl)* [ʃi:p]
es **schaffen** to make it ['meɪk‿ɪt]
es allein schaffen to go it alone [ˌgəʊ‿ɪt‿ə'ləʊn]
Schallplatte record ['rekɔ:d]
Schalter desk [desk]; switch [swɪtʃ]
scharf hot [hɒt]
Schatten shade [ʃeɪd]; shadow ['ʃædəʊ]
Schattierung shade [ʃeɪd]
Schatz darling ['dɑ:lɪŋ]; *(Anrede)* dear [dɪə]
Schau show [ʃəʊ]
schauen to have a look [ˌhæv‿ə 'lʊk]; to look [lʊk]
schaukeln to rock [rɒk]
Schauplatz scene [si:n]; setting ['setɪŋ]
Schauspieler actor ['æktə]
Schauspielerin actress ['æktrəs]
Scheibe slice [slaɪs]
Schein slip [slɪp]
scheinen to seem [si:m]
schenken to give [gɪv]
scherzen to joke [dʒəʊk]
Scheune barn [bɑ:n]
scheußlich nasty ['nɑ:sti]
schicken to send [send]
per E-Mail schicken to e-mail ['i:meɪl]
schieben to push [pʊʃ]
Schiedsrichter/Schiedsrichterin ref(eree) [ˌrefr'i:]
schief gehen to go wrong [gəʊ 'rɒŋ]
schießen to shoot [ʃu:t]
Schiff boat [bəʊt]
Schifffahrt shipping ['ʃɪpɪŋ]
Schild sign [saɪn]
Schimpfwörter bad language [bæd 'læŋgwɪdʒ]
Schinken ham [hæm]
Schinkenspeck bacon ['beɪkn]
Schlacht battle ['bætl]
Schlaf sleep [sli:p]
schlafen to be asleep [ˌbi:‿ə'sli:p]; to sleep [sli:p]
schläfrig sleepy ['sli:pi]
Schlafsack sleeping bag ['sli:pɪŋ ˌbæg]
Schlafzimmer bedroom ['bedrʊm]
Schlag knock [nɒk]; shot [ʃɒt]
schlagen to bang [bæŋ]; to bat [bæt]; to hit [hɪt]; to knock [nɒk]
k.o. schlagen to knock out [nɒk‿'aʊt]
Schläger bat [bæt]
Schlagmann/Schlagfrau batter ['bætə]
Schlagzeug drums *(pl)* [drʌmz]
Schlagzeuger/Schlagzeugerin drummer ['drʌmə]
Schlange queue [kju:]; snake [sneɪk]
schlau smart [smɑ:t]
schlecht bad [bæd]; ill [ɪl]
schlechter worse [wɜ:s]
schlechtester/schlechteste/schlechtestes worst [wɜ:st]
schleichen to crawl [krɔ:l]
Schleiereule barn owl ['bɑ:n‿əʊl]
schließen to close [kləʊz]
Schließfach locker ['lɒkə]
schließlich at last [ət 'lɑ:st]; in the end [ɪn ði:‿'end]
Schließung closing ['kləʊzɪŋ]
schlimmer worse [wɜ:s]
schlimmster/schlimmste/schlimmstes worst [wɜ:st]
Schlittschuhbahn ice rink ['aɪs rɪŋk]
Schloss castle ['kɑ:sl]
Schlucht canyon ['kænjən]
schlüpfrig juicy ['dʒu:si]
schlürfen to sip [sɪp]
Schluss end [end]
mit jmdm. Schluss machen to chuck sb [tʃʌk]; to dump sb [dʌmp]
zum Schluss in the end [ɪn ði:‿'end]
Schlüssel key [ki:]
schmackhaft nutty ['nʌti]; tasty ['teɪsti]
schmecken to taste [teɪst]
Pizza schmeckt besser. Pizza is tastier. ['pi:tsə ɪz ˌteɪstɪə]

schmelzen to melt [melt]
Schmerz pain [peɪn]
schmerzhaft sore [sɔ:]
Schminke make-up ['meɪkʌp]
Schmuck jewellery ['dʒu:əlri]
Schmuggler/Schmugglerin smuggler ['smʌglə]
Schmutz dirt [dɜ:t]
schmutzig dirty ['dɜ:ti]
schnappen to grab [græb]
Schnappschuss snapshot ['snæpʃɒt]
Schnee snow [snəʊ]
schneiden to cut [kʌt]
schneien to snow [snəʊ]
schnell fast [fɑ:st]; quick [kwɪk]
schnüffeln to sniff [snɪf]
schnuppern to sniff [snɪf]
Schnur string [strɪŋ]
schockiert shocked [ʃɒkt]
Schokolade chocolate ['tʃɒklət]
schön beautiful ['bju:tɪfl]; fine [faɪn]; nice [naɪs]
schon already [ɔ:l'redi]
schottisch Scottish ['skɒtɪʃ]
Schrank cupboard ['kʌbəd]
einen **Schrecken einjagen** to scare ['skeə]
schrecklich awful ['ɔ:fl]; frightening ['fraɪtnɪŋ]; horrible ['hɒrəbl]; terrible ['terəbl]
Schrei cry [kraɪ]
schreiben to write [raɪt]
  E-Mail schreiben to e-mail ['i:meɪl]
Schreibtisch desk [desk]
schreien to cry [kraɪ]; to shout [ʃaʊt]; *(Eule)* to hoot [hu:t]
Schreiner/Schreinerin carpenter ['kɑ:pəntə]
Schriftsteller/Schriftstellerin writer ['raɪtə]
Schritt footstep ['fʊtstep]; move [mu:v]; step [step]
  Schritt halten (mit) to keep up (with) [ki:p‿'ʌp]
schüchtern shy [ʃaɪ]
Schuh shoe [ʃu:]
Schuhkarton shoebox ['ʃu:bɒks]
den **Schulabschluss machen** to graduate ['grædjueɪt]
Schulausbildung schooling ['sku:lɪŋ]
schulden to owe [əʊ]
Schule school [sku:l]
Schüler/Schülerin pupil ['pju:pl]; student ['stju:dnt]
Schulfach subject ['sʌbdʒɪkt]
Schulhof playground ['pleɪgraʊnd]
Schulklasse class [klɑ:s]
Schulranzen school bag ['sku:l bæg]
Schultasche school bag ['sku:l bæg]
Schulter shoulder ['ʃəʊldə]
  mit den Schultern zucken to shrug (one's shoulders) [ʃrʌg]
Schuppen shed [ʃed]
Schuss gunshot ['gʌnʃɒt]; shot [ʃɒt]
Schüssel bowl [bəʊl]
Schusswaffe gun [gʌn]
schütteln to shake [ʃeɪk]
Schutz- protective [prə'tektɪv]
Quallen-**Schutzanzug** stinger suit [ˌstɪŋə 'su:t]
Schütze gunman, gunmen *(pl)* ['gʌnmən; gʌnmen]
schützen to protect [prə'tekt]
schützend protective [prə'tektɪv]
Schutzherr/Schutzherrin patron ['peɪtrn]
schwach weak [wi:k]
  schwach werden to go weak [gəʊ 'wi:k]
Schwäche weakness ['wi:knəs]
Schwamm sponge [spʌndʒ]
schwarz black [blæk]
Schwarzer/Schwarze Black [blæk]
Schwein pig [pɪg]
Schweinefleisch pork [pɔ:k]
schwenken to wave [weɪv]
schwer heavy ['hevi]
Schwere gravity ['grævəti]
Schwerkraft gravity ['grævəti]
Schwester sister ['sɪstə]
schwierig difficult ['dɪfɪklt]; hard [hɑ:d]
Schwierigkeit problem ['prɒbləm]
Schwimmbad swimming pool ['swɪmɪŋ ˌpu:l]
Schwimmbecken swimming pool ['swɪmɪŋ ˌpu:l]
schwimmen to swim [swɪm]
Schwimmer/Schwimmerin swimmer ['swɪmə]
Schwimmflosse fin [fɪn]
Schwimmreifen rubber ring [ˌrʌbə 'rɪŋ]
schwindlig dizzy ['dɪzi]
etw. in **Schwung bringen** to get sth going [get 'gəʊɪŋ]
Sciencefiction science fiction [ˌsaɪəns 'fɪkʃn]
Scone *(Gebäck)* scone [skɒn]
Screenshot screen shot ['skri:n ˌʃɒt]
See lake [leɪk]
Seehund seal [si:l]
seekrank seasick ['si:sɪk]
Seele soul [səʊl]
Seelöwe sea lion ['si: ˌlaɪən]
Seetang seaweed ['si:wi:d]
Seewespe sea wasp ['si: ˌwɒsp]
segeln to sail [seɪl]
sehen to see [si:]; to look [lʊk]
Sehenswürdigkeit attraction [ə'trækʃn]; sight [saɪt]
sehr very ['veri]
Seife soap [səʊp]
Seifenoper soap [səʊp]
sein to be [bi:]
  an der Reihe sein to be on [bi:‿'ɒn]
  an sein to be on [bi:‿'ɒn]
sein his [hɪz]; its [ɪts]
seit for [fɔ:]; since [sɪnts]
seitdem since [sɪnts]
Seite page [peɪdʒ]; side [saɪd]
Sekretär/Sekretärin secretary ['sekrətri]
Sektor sector ['sektə]
Sekunde second ['seknd]
Selbstständigkeit self-employment [ˌselfɪm'plɔɪmənt]
selbstverständlich of course [əv 'kɔ:s]
selten rare [reə]; seldom ['seldəm]
seltsam strange [streɪndʒ]
Sendung programme ['prəʊgræm]; show [ʃəʊ]
  auf Sendung on the air [ˌɒn ði‿'eə]
September September [sep'tembə]
Serie series, series *(pl)* ['sɪəri:z]
Service service ['sɜ:vɪs]
sich **setzen** to sit down [sɪt 'daʊn]
  sich setzen zu to sit with ['sɪt wɪθ]
Sex sex [seks]
Sexismus sexism ['seksɪsm]
sexistisch sexist ['seksɪst]
Sexualität sex [seks]
Shorts shorts *(pl)* [ʃɔ:ts]
Show show [ʃəʊ]
sicher safe [seɪf]; sure [ʃʊə]; certainly ['sɜ:tnli]
sichergehen to make sure [meɪk 'ʃʊə]
Sicherheit safety ['seɪfti]
sicherstellen to assure [ə'ʃʊə]; to guarantee [ˌgærn'ti:]
Sicherungskasten fuse-box ['fju:zbɒks]
Sicht sight [saɪt]; view [vju:]
sie she [ʃi:]; her [hɜ:]
  sie *(Mehrzahl)* they [ðeɪ]; them [ðem]
  sie (selbst) herself [hɜ:'self]; themselves [ðəm'selvz]
Sie *(Anrede)* mister ['mɪstə]
  Sie (selbst) yourselves [jɔ:'selvz]
Siedler/Siedlerin settler ['setlə]
Siegel label ['leɪbl]
siegen to win [wɪn]
Sieger/Siegerin winner ['wɪnə]
Siegtreffer winning goal ['wɪnɪŋ gəʊl]
Signal signal ['sɪgnl]
simsen to text [tekst]
singen to sing [sɪŋ]; to chant [tʃɑ:nt]
sinken *(beim Tauchen)* to drop [drɒp]
Sinn sense [sens]
Sinnbild symbol ['sɪmbl]
Sintflut flash flood ['flæʃ ˌflʌd]
Sirup syrup ['sɪrəp]

Situation situation [ˌsɪtju'eɪʃn]
Situationskomödie sitcom ['sɪtkɒm]
Sitz seat [si:t]
sitzen to sit [sɪt]
in der Falle sitzen to be trapped [bi: 'træpt]
Sitzplatz seat [si:t]
Sitzung session ['seʃn]
Skateboard skateboard ['skeɪtbɔ:d]
skaten to skate [skeɪt]
Skelett skeleton ['skelɪtn]
Skifahren skiing ['ski:ɪŋ]
Sklave/Sklavin slave [sleɪv]
Sklaverei slavery ['sleɪvri]
SMS text message ['tekst ˌmesɪdʒ]
Snack snack [snæk]
Snowboarden snowboarding ['snəʊbɔ:dɪŋ]
so so [səʊ]
so (schlimm) that (bad) ['ðæt bæd]
so … wie … as … as [æz … æz; əz … əz]
Sofa sofa ['səʊfə]
sofort at once [ət 'wʌnts]; right away [raɪt‿ə'weɪ]
sogar even ['i:vn]
Sohn son [sʌn]
solange wie as long as [əz 'lɒŋ‿əz]
solar solar ['səʊlə]
Solar- solar ['səʊlə]
solch such [sʌtʃ]
Soldat/Soldatin soldier ['səʊldʒə]
solide solid ['sɒlɪd]
sollte/sollten should [ʃʊd]
solo solo ['səʊləʊ]
Solo- solo ['səʊləʊ]
Sommer summer ['sʌmə]
Sommerfest summer fair ['sʌmə ˌfeə]
Sonne sun [sʌn]
Sonnen- solar ['səʊlə]
Sonnenbräune suntan ['sʌntæn]
Sonnenkollektor solar panel [ˌsəʊlə 'pænl]
Sonnensystem solar system ['səʊlə ˌsɪstəm]
sonnig sunny ['sʌni]
Sonntag Sunday ['sʌndeɪ]
sonst else [els]
sich **Sorgen machen** to worry ['wʌri]
sorgfältig careful ['keəfl]
Sorte kind [kaɪnd]; type [taɪp]
Soulmusik soul [səʊl]
Souvenir souvenir [ˌsu:və'nɪə]
sozial social ['səʊʃl]
Spa spa [spɑ:]
Spaghetti spaghetti [spə'geti]
Spanglisch *(Mischung aus Spanisch und Englisch)* Spanglish ['spæŋglɪʃ]
spanisch Spanish ['spænɪʃ]
Spanisch Spanish ['spænɪʃ]
spannend exciting [ɪk'saɪtɪŋ]
Spannung suspense [sə'spents]
sparen to save [seɪv]
Sparschwein piggy bank ['pɪgi bæŋk]
Spaß fun [fʌn]
Spaß verstehen to take a joke [ˌteɪk‿ə 'dʒəʊk]
Spaß haben to have fun [ˌhæv 'fʌn]
Spaß machen to be fun [bi: 'fʌn]
Viel Spaß! Have fun! [ˌhæv 'fʌn]
spät late [leɪt]
zu spät late [leɪt]
spazieren gehen to go for a walk [ˌgəʊ fər‿ə 'wɔ:k]
Spaziergang walk [wɔ:k]
Speisekarte menu ['menju:]
Speisesaal dining room ['daɪnɪŋ rʊm]
spektakulär spectacular [spek'tækjələ]
Sperre ban [bæn]
Spezialist/Spezialistin specialist ['speʃlɪst]
Spezialität special ['speʃl]
speziell special ['speʃl]; specific [spə'sɪfɪk]
spezifisch specific [spə'sɪfɪk]
Spiegelei sunny side up [ˌsʌni saɪd‿'ʌp]
Spiel game [geɪm]; match [mætʃ]; play [pleɪ]
spielen to play [pleɪ]; *(Theater)* to act [ækt]
Spieler/Spielerin player ['pleɪə]
Spielfeld court [kɔ:t]; pitch [pɪtʃ]
Spielplatz playground ['pleɪgraʊnd]
Spielstand score [skɔ:]
Spielzeug toy [tɔɪ]
Spinne spider ['spaɪdə]
Spitze top [tɒp]
Spitzname nickname ['nɪkneɪm]
Sponsor/Sponsorin sponsor ['spɒnsə]
Sport sport [spɔ:t]; *(Schulfach)* Physical Education (PE) [ˌfɪzɪkl‿edʒʊ'keɪʃn]
Sport treiben to do sports [du: 'spɔ:ts]; to exercise ['eksəsaɪz]
Sportfest sports day ['spɔ:ts deɪ]
Sportgeschäft sports shop ['spɔ:ts ʃɒp]
sportlich sporty ['spɔ:ti]
Sportplatz sports field ['spɔ:ts fi:ld]
Sportzeug PE kit [ˌpi:‿'i: kɪt]
Sprache language ['læŋgwɪdʒ]; speech [spi:tʃ]
sprechen to say [seɪ]; to speak [spi:k]; to talk [tɔ:k]
sprechen mit to talk to ['tɔ:k tə]
Sprechen speech [spi:tʃ]
Sprecher/Sprecherin speaker ['spi:kə]
Sprechstundenhilfe receptionist [rɪ'sepʃnɪst]
springen to jump [dʒʌmp]
sprühen to spray [spreɪ]; *(Funken)* to spark [spɑ:k]
spucken to spit [spɪt]
Spülbecken sink [sɪŋk]
Square Dance square dance ['skweə ˌdɑ:nts]
Staat state [steɪt]
staatlich state [steɪt]
staatliche Schule (USA) public school [ˌpʌblɪk 'sku:l]
Staatsbürger/Staatsbürgerin citizen ['sɪtɪzn]
Staatsoberhaupt head of state [ˌhed‿əv 'steɪt]
Staatsvertrag treaty ['tri:ti]
Stadion arena [ə'ri:nə]; stadium ['steɪdiəm]
Stadt city ['sɪti]; town [taʊn]
Stadtplan map [mæp]
Stadtplaner/Stadtplanerin town planner ['taʊn ˌplænə]
Stadtteil borough ['bʌrə]
Stamm tribe [traɪb]
Stammkunde/Stammkundin regular ['regjələ]
Stand stall [stɔ:l]; stand [stænd]
Standbesitzer/Standbesitzerin stall holder ['stɔ:l ˌhəʊldə]
Standbild statue ['stætʃu:]
auf **Stand-by** standby ['stændbaɪ]
Standfoto still (picture) ['stɪl ˌpɪktʃə]
ständig always ['ɔ:lweɪz]
Stange bar [bɑ:]
Stangenbohne runner bean ['rʌnə ˌbi:n]
Stapel pile [paɪl]
Star star [stɑ:]
stark hard [hɑ:d]; strong [strɒŋ]
Stärke power ['paʊə]; strength [streŋθ]
Start launch [lɔ:nʃ]; start [stɑ:t]
starten to launch [lɔ:nʃ]; to start [stɑ:t]; to take off [ˌteɪk‿'ɒf]
Station base [beɪs]; station ['steɪʃn]
statt instead of [ɪn'sted‿əv]
stattdessen instead [ɪn'sted]
stattfinden to take place [teɪk 'pleɪs]
Statue statue ['stætʃu:]
Stau traffic jam ['træfɪk ˌdʒæm]
Staub dust [dʌst]
staubig dusty ['dʌsti]
stechen to sting [stɪŋ]
Steckbrief profile ['prəʊfaɪl]
Steckdose socket ['sɒkɪt]
stecken (über) to stick (over) [stɪk]
Stecker plug [plʌg]
Steelband *(Band, deren Instrumente aus leeren Ölfässern bestehen)* steel band [ˌsti:l 'bænd]
stehen to stand [stænd]

im Weg stehen to get in the way (of) [ˌget‿ɪn‿ðə ˈweɪ]
stehlen to steal [stiːl]
steigen to climb [ˈklaɪm]; to increase [ɪnˈkriːs]; to rise [raɪz]; to step [step]
Stein rock [rɒk]; stone [stəʊn]
Stelle patch [pætʃ]; place [pleɪs]
stellen to put [pʊt]; *(Uhr)* to set [set]
auf den Kopf gestellt upside down [ˌʌpsaɪd ˈdaʊn]
Stellenangebot vacancy [ˈveɪknsi]
sterben to die [daɪ]
Stern star [stɑː]
Sternwarte observatory [əbˈzɜːvətri]
Stich bite [baɪt]
Stiefel boot [buːt]
Stiefvater stepdad [ˈstepdæd]
Stil style [staɪl]
still quiet [ˈkwaɪət]; silent [ˈsaɪlənt]
Stille quiet [ˈkwaɪət]
Stimme voice [vɔɪs]
Stimmung atmosphere [ˈætməsfɪə]; mood [muːd]; spirit [ˈspɪrɪt]
stinken to stink [stɪŋk]
Stipendium scholarship [ˈskɒləʃɪp]
die **Stirn runzeln** to frown [fraʊn]
Stock stick [stɪk]
im oberen Stock upstairs [ʌpˈsteəz]
im unteren Stock downstairs [daʊnˈsteəz]
Stockwerk floor [flɔː]
Stoff material [məˈtɪəriəl]
stöhnen to moan [məʊn]
Stollenschuh rugby boot [ˈrʌgbi buːt]
stolz auf proud of [ˈpraʊd‿əv]
Stolz pride [praɪd]
Stöpsel plug [plʌg]
stören to disturb [dɪˈstɜːb]
stoßen to knock [nɒk]; to push [pʊʃ]
stoßen gegen to run into [rʌn‿ˈɪntə]
Strafe sentence [ˈsentəns]
Sträfling convict [ˈkɒnvɪkt]
strahlend bright [braɪt]
Strand beach [biːtʃ]
Straße road [rəʊd]; street [striːt]
Strauch bush [bʊʃ]
strecken (über) to stick (over) [stɪk]
Streich trick [trɪk]
streichen to paint [peɪnt]
mit dem Finger über etw. streichen to run a finger over sth [rʌn]
streiten to argue [ˈɑːgjuː]; to fight [faɪt]
sich streiten to have an argument [ˌhæv‿ən‿ˈɑːgjəmənt]
streng strict [strɪkt]
Stress stress [stres]
strikt strict [strɪkt]
Strom current [ˈkʌrnt]; electricity [ˌelɪkˈtrɪsəti]
Stromausfall blackout *(AE)* [ˈblækaʊt]
Strömung current [ˈkʌrnt]
gegen die Strömung up current [ˈʌp ˌkʌrnt]
Strophe verse [vɜːs]
Strumpfhose tights *(pl)* [taɪts]
Stück bar [bɑː]; piece [piːs]
Stückchen bit [bɪt]
Student/Studentin student [ˈstjuːdnt]
studieren to study [ˈstʌdi]
Studio studio [ˈstjuːdiəʊ]
Studium studies *(pl)* [ˈstʌdiz]
Stufe step [step]
Stuhl chair [tʃeə]
Stummfilm silent movie [ˌsaɪlənt ˈmuːvi]
Stunde hour [ˈaʊə]; session [ˈseʃn]
eine halbe Stunde half an hour [ˌhɑːf‿ən‿ˈaʊə]
stundenlang for hours [fər‿ˈaʊəz]
Stundenplan curriculum [kəˈrɪkjələm]; timetable [ˈtaɪmteɪbl]
Sturm storm [stɔːm]
stürmisch stormy [ˈstɔːmi]
Sturz fall [fɔːl]
Subkontinent sub-continent [ˌsʌbˈkɒntɪnənt]
suchen nach to look for [ˈlʊk fə]
Südamerikaner/Südamerikanerin South American [ˌsaʊθ‿əˈmerɪkən]
südamerikanisch South American [ˌsaʊθ‿əˈmerɪkən]
Süden south [saʊθ]
Südwesten southwest [ˌsaʊθˈwest]
Summe amount [əˈmaʊnt]
summen to buzz [bʌz]
super super [ˈsuːpə]
Superlativ superlative [suːˈpɜːlətɪv]
Supermarkt supermarket [ˈsuːpəˌmɑːkɪt]
Suppe soup [suːp]
Surfbrett surfboard [ˈsɜːfbɔːd]
surfen to surf [sɜːf]
im Internet surfen to surf the Internet [ˌsɜːf ði‿ˈɪntənet]
Surfen surfing [ˈsɜːfɪŋ]
Surfer/Surferin surfer [ˈsɜːfə]
süß cute [kjuːt]; sweet [swiːt]
Süßigkeit sweet [swiːt]
Sweatshirt sweatshirt [ˈswetʃɜːt]
Symbol symbol [ˈsɪmbl]
System system [ˈsɪstəm]
Szene scene [siːn]

T

Tabak tobacco [təˈbækəʊ]
Tabelle grid [grɪd]; table [ˈteɪbl]
Tafel bar [bɑː]; board [bɔːd]; panel [ˈpænl]
Tag day [deɪ]
Einen schönen Tag (noch). Have a nice day. [ˌhæv‿ə naɪs ˈdeɪ]
eines Tages one day [wʌn ˈdeɪ]
ein **Tagebuch führen** to keep a diary [ˌkiːp‿ə ˈdaɪəri]
Tagesanbruch dawn [dɔːn]
Tagesfahrkarte day travel card [ˌdeɪ ˈtrævl ˌkɑːd]
täglich daily [ˈdeɪli]
Talent talent [ˈtælənt]
Talkmaster host [həʊst]
Talkshow talk show [ˈtɔːk ˌʃəʊ]
Tante aunt [ɑːnt]
Tanz dance [dɑːnts]
tanzen to dance [dɑːnts]
Breakdance tanzen to break-dance [ˈbreɪkdɑːnts]
Tanzen dancing [ˈdɑːntsɪŋ]
Tanzfläche dance floor [ˈdɑːnts flɔː]
tapfer brave [breɪv]
Tasche bag [bæg]
Taschendieb/Taschendiebin pickpocket [ˈpɪkˌpɒkɪt]
Taschengeld pocket money [ˈpɒkɪt ˌmʌni]
Taschenlampe torch, torches *(pl)* [tɔːtʃ; ˈtɔːtʃɪz]
Taschenmesser penknife, penknives *(pl)* [ˈpennaɪf; ˈpennaɪvz]
Tasse cup [kʌp]
tasten nach to feel for [ˈfiːl fə]
in der **Tat** in fact [ɪn ˈfækt]
Tätowierung tattoo [tætˈuː]
Tatsache fact [fækt]
tatsächlich actually [ˈæktʃuəli]
Tauch- dive [daɪv]; diving [ˈdaɪvɪŋ]
Tauchbegleiter/Tauchbegleiterin buddy *(infml)* [ˈbʌdi]
tauchen to dive [daɪv]
Tauchen diving [ˈdaɪvɪŋ]
Taucher/Taucherin diver [ˈdaɪvə]
Taucheranzug wetsuit [ˈwetsuːt]
Tauchgang dive [daɪv]
Tauchzentrum dive centre [ˈdaɪv ˌsentə]
Tausch exchange [ɪksˈtʃeɪndʒ]; swap [swɒp]
tauschen to change [tʃeɪndʒ]; to swap [swɒp]
tausend thousand [ˈθaʊznd]
Taxi taxi [ˈtæksi]
Team team [tiːm]
Technik Technology [tekˈnɒlədʒi]
Techniker/Technikerin engineer [ˌendʒɪˈnɪə]; technician [tekˈnɪʃn]
technisch technical [ˈteknɪkl]
Tee tea [tiː]
Teenager teenager [ˈtiːnˌeɪdʒə]
Teil bit [bɪt]; part [pɑːt]

Teilchen particle ['pɑ:tɪkl]
teilen to share [ʃeə]
teilnehmen an to take part in [teɪk 'pɑ:t‿ɪn]
Teilzeit- part-time (P/T) [ˌpɑ:t'taɪm]
Telefon phone [fəʊn]
telefonieren to phone [fəʊn]
Telefonnummer phone number ['fəʊn ˌnʌmbə]
Telefonzelle phone box ['fəʊn ˌbɒks]
Teller plate [pleɪt]
Temperatur temperature ['temprətʃə]
Temperaturregler thermostat ['θɜ:mestæt]
temporär temporary ['temprəri]
Tennis tennis ['tenɪs]
Teppichboden carpet ['kɑ:pɪt]
einen **Terminkalender führen** to keep a diary [ˌki:p‿ə 'daɪəri]
Territorium territory ['terɪtri]
Test test [test]; trial ['traɪəl]
testen to test [test]
teuer expensive [ɪk'spensɪv]
textil textile ['tekstaɪl]
Textil(-) textile ['tekstaɪl]
Textnachricht (SMS) schicken to text [tekst]
Theater theater *(AE)* ['θɪətə]
Theaterstück play [pleɪ]
Thema subject ['sʌbdʒɪkt]; topic ['tɒpɪk]
Thermostat thermostat ['θɜ:mestæt]
Thriller thriller ['θrɪlə]
Ticket ticket ['tɪkɪt]
tief deep [di:p]; low [ləʊ]
Tier animal ['ænɪml]
Tierpark zoo [zu:]
Tierpfleger/Tierpflegerin zookeeper ['zu:ki:pə]
Tiger tiger ['taɪgə]
Tipp tip [tɪp]
Tisch table ['teɪbl]
den Tisch decken to set the table [ˌset ðə 'teɪbl]
Tischtennis table-tennis ['teɪblˌtenɪs]
Titel title ['taɪtl]
Titelseite cover ['kʌvə]
Toast toast [təʊst]
Tochter daughter ['dɔ:tə]
tod- deadly ['dedli]
Tod death [deθ]
Todesfall death [deθ]
tödlich deadly ['dedli]
Toilette toilet ['tɔɪlɪt]
toll awesome ['ɔ:səm]; brilliant ['brɪljənt]; great [greɪt]; hot [hɒt]
tollpatschig clumsy ['klʌmzi]
Tomate tomato, tomatoes *(pl)* [tə'mɑ:təʊ; tə'mɑ:təʊz]
Ton sound [saʊnd]
Tonfilm talkie ['tɔ:ki]
Tonne *(Gewicht)* ton [tʌn]
Topf pot [pɒt]
Tor gate [geɪt]; goal [gəʊl]
ein Tor schießen to score [skɔ:]
Torwart goalkeeper ['gəʊlˌki:pə]
tot dead [ded]
total total ['təʊtl]
töten to kill [kɪl]
Tour tour [tʊə]
Tourist/Touristin tourist ['tʊərɪst]
Tower tower ['taʊə]
Tradition tradition [trə'dɪʃn]
traditionell traditional [trə'dɪʃnl]
träge lazy ['leɪzi]
tragen to carry ['kæri]
tragisch tragic ['trædʒɪk]
Trainee trainee [treɪ'ni:]
Trainer/Trainerin coach [kəʊtʃ]
trainieren to train [treɪn]
Training practice ['præktɪs]; training ['treɪnɪŋ]; coaching ['kəʊtʃɪŋ]
Traktor tractor ['træktə]
Träne tear [tɪə]
Transport transport ['trænspɔ:t]
transportieren to transport [træn'spɔ:t]
Tratsch gossip ['gɒsɪp]
Traum dream [dri:m]
träumen to dream [dri:m]
traurig sad [sæd]
treffen to hit [hɪt]; to meet [mi:t]
sich treffen to meet [mi:t]
Treffen meeting ['mi:tɪŋ]
Treibhausgas greenhouse gas [ˌgri:nhaʊs 'gæs]
Treibstoff fuel ['fju:əl]
Trend trend [trend]
Treppe stairs *(pl)* [steəz]
die Treppe hinaufrennen to run upstairs [ˌrʌn‿ʌp'steəz]
treten to kick [kɪk]; to step [step]
treu loyal ['lɔɪəl]
Treue allegiance [ə'li:dʒns]
Tribüne platform ['plætfɔ:m]; stand [stænd]
Trick trick [trɪk]
Trillerpfeife whistle ['wɪsl]
trinken to drink [drɪŋk]
schluckweise trinken to sip [sɪp]
Trinkgeld tip [tɪp]
trocken dry [draɪ]
trocknen to dry [draɪ]
Trockner dryer ['draɪə]
Trödelstand white elephant stall [ˌwaɪt 'elɪfənt stɔ:l]
tröpfeln to drip [drɪp]
tropfen (lassen) to drip [drɪp]
Trottel jerk *(slang)* [dʒɜ:k]
trotzdem though [ðəʊ]
Truck truck *(AE)* [trʌk]
Trucker trucker *(AE)* ['trʌkə]
Truthahn turkey ['tɜ:ki]
tschüss bye [baɪ]
T-Shirt T-shirt ['ti:ʃɜ:t]
tun to do [du:]; to make [meɪk]
Tunnel tunnel ['tʌnl]
Tür door [dɔ:]
Turbine turbine ['tɜ:baɪn]
türkisch Turkish ['tɜ:kɪʃ]
Türklingel doorbell ['dɔ:bel]
Turm tower ['taʊə]
Turnhalle gym [dʒɪm]
Turnier competition [ˌkɒmpə'tɪʃn]
Turnschuhe trainers ['treɪnəz]
Türstufe doorstep ['dɔ:step]
Tüte bag [bæg]
Typ bloke [bləʊk]; guy [gaɪ]; type [taɪp]
typisch typical ['tɪpɪkl]
tyrannisieren to bully ['bʊli]

U

U-Bahn underground ['ʌndəgraʊnd]
Übelkeit verspüren to feel sick [fi:l 'sɪk]
üben to exercise ['eksəsaɪz]; to practise ['præktɪs]
über above [ə'bʌv]; across [ə'krɒs]; over ['əʊvə]; about [ə'baʊt]
überall all over [ˌɔ:l‿'əʊvə]; anywhere ['eniweə]; everywhere ['evriweə]
Übereinkunft deal [di:l]
sich **überfressen** to overeat [ˌəʊvr'i:t]
übergeben to hand [hænd]
überholt outdated [ˌaʊt'deɪtɪd]
überleben to survive [sə'vaɪv]
Überleben survival [sə'vaɪvl]
überprüfen to check [tʃek]
Überprüfung check [tʃek]
überqueren to cross [krɒs]
überraschend surprising [sə'praɪzɪŋ]
überrascht surprised [sə'praɪzd]
Überschrift title ['taɪtl]
Überschwemmung flood [flʌd]
flutartige Überschwemmung flash flood ['flæʃ ˌflʌd]
übertreiben to overdo [ˌəʊvə'du:]
überwachen to monitor ['mɒnɪtə]
überwiegend mostly ['məʊstli]
übrig left [left]
übrigens by the way [ˌbaɪ ðə 'weɪ]
Übung exercise ['eksəsaɪz]
Übungsheft exercise book ['eksəsaɪz ˌbʊk]
Uhr clock [klɒk]; *(Zeitangabe)* o'clock [ə'klɒk]
Um wie viel Uhr …? What time … ? [wɒt 'taɪm]

Wie viel Uhr ist es, bitte? What's the time, please? [ˌwɒts ðə ˈtaɪm ˌpliːz]
umdrehen to turn over [ˌtɜːn‿ˈəʊvə]; to turn round [tɜːn ˈraʊnd]
sich umdrehen to turn [tɜːn]; to turn over [ˌtɜːn‿ˈəʊvə]; to turn round [tɜːn ˈraʊnd]
Umfrage survey [ˈsɜːveɪ]
Umgebung atmosphere [ˈætməsfɪə]; environment [ɪnˈvaɪərnmənt]
umgedreht upside down [ˌʌpsaɪd ˈdaʊn]
umhauen to knock out [nɒk‿ˈaʊt]
umher around [əˈraʊnd]
umkehren to turn back [tɜːn ˈbæk]
Umsatz turnover [ˈtɜːnˌəʊvə]
Umschlag envelope [ˈenvələʊp]
sich **umsehen** to look round [lʊk ˈraʊnd]
umsonst free [friː]
umsteigen to change [tʃeɪndʒ]
Umwelt environment [ɪnˈvaɪərnmənt]
die Umwelt betreffend environmental [ɪnˌvaɪərnˈmentl]
Umwelt- eco [iːkəʊ]; environmental [ɪnˌvaɪərnˈmentl]
umweltbedingt environmental [ɪnˌvaɪərnˈmentl]
umweltbewusst werden to go green [ˌgəʊ ˈgriːn]
Umweltverschmutzung pollution [pəˈluːʃn]
umziehen to move [muːv]
Umzug parade [pəˈreɪd]
unabhängig independent [ˌɪndɪˈpendənt]
unbestimmt uncertain [ˈʌnsɜːtn]
und and [ænd]
unerlässlich vital [ˈvaɪtl]
Unfähigkeit disability [ˌdɪsəˈbɪləti]
Unfall accident [ˈæksɪdnt]; crash [kræʃ]
unfreundlich unfriendly [ʌnˈfrendli]
ungefähr about [əˈbaʊt]; around [əˈraʊnd]
ungeschickt clumsy [ˈklʌmzi]
ungesund unhealthy [ʌnˈhelθi]
unglücklich unhappy [ʌnˈhæpi]
unheimlich scary [ˈskeəri]; spooky [ˈspuːki]
unhöflich rude [ruːd]
Uniform uniform [ˈjuːnɪfɔːm]
Union union [ˈjuːnjən]
Universität university [ˌjuːnɪˈvɜːsəti]
Universum universe [ˈjuːnɪvɜːs]
unordentlich messy [ˈmesi]
Unordnung mess [mes]
Unrecht haben to be wrong [biː ˈrɒŋ]
unrechtmäßig illegal [ɪˈliːgl]
Unruhe riot [raɪət]
uns us [ʌs]
uns selbst ourselves [aʊəˈselvz]
unser/unsere our [ˈaʊə]
unsicher uncertain [ˈʌnsɜːtn]; unsure [ʌnˈʃɔː]
Unsinn rubbish [ˈrʌbɪʃ]
unten at the bottom [ət ðə ˈbɒtəm]; below [bɪˈləʊ]; down [daʊn]; downstairs [daʊnˈsteəz]
nach unten down [daʊn]
unter under [ˈʌndə]
ohne **Unterbrechung** non-stop [ˌnɒnˈstɒp]
Unterdrückung oppression [əˈpreʃn]
Unterführung tunnel [ˈtʌnl]
Untergeschoss basement [ˈbeɪsmənt]
unterhalb below [bɪˈləʊ]
sich **unterhalten** to chat [tʃæt]
Unterhaltung chat [tʃæt]; conversation [ˌkɒnvəˈseɪʃn]
Unternehmen firm [fɜːm]; organisation [ˌɔːgnaɪˈzeɪʃn]
unternehmungslustig enterprising [ˈentəpraɪzɪŋ]
Unterricht class [klɑːs]
unterrichten to teach [tiːtʃ]
Unterrichtsstunde period *(AE)* [ˈpɪəriəd]; lesson [ˈlesn]
Unterschied difference [ˈdɪfrns]
unterschreiben to sign [saɪn]
unterstreichen to underline [ˌʌndəˈlaɪn]
unterstützen to support [səˈpɔːt]
Unterstützung support [səˈpɔːt]
untersuchen to check [tʃek]
Untersuchung research [rɪˈsɜːtʃ]
Untertitel subtitle [ˈsʌbˌtaɪtl]
Unterwasser- underwater [ˌʌndəˈwɔːtə]
unverschämt rude [ruːd]
Update update [ˈʌpdeɪt]
Ureinwohner/Ureinwohnerin Amerikas Native American [ˌneɪtɪv‿əˈmerɪkən]
Ureinwohner/Ureinwohnerin Australiens Aborigine [ˌæbəˈrɪdʒni]
Urenkel great-grandson [ˌgreɪtˈgrænsʌn]
Urkunde certificate [səˈtɪfɪkət]; charter [ˈtʃɑːtə]
Urlaub holiday(s) [ˈhɒlədeɪ(z)]; vacation *(AE)* [vəˈkeɪʃn]
Ursprung origin [ˈɒrɪdʒɪn]
Urteil sentence [ˈsentəns]
usw. etc. [ɪtˈsetrə]

V

Vater father [ˈfɑːðə]
Vati dad [dæd]
Vehikel vehicle [ˈvɪəkl]
sich **verabreden** to date [deɪt]
Verabredung date [deɪt]
verabschieden *(Gesetz)* to pass [pɑːs]
Verachtung disrespect [ˌdɪsrɪˈspekt]
verändern to change [tʃeɪndʒ]
verängstigt scared [skeəd]
jmdn. **veranlassen, etw. zu tun** to make sb do sth [meɪk]
veranstalten to hold [həʊld]
Veranstalter/Veranstalterin organizer [ˈɔːgənaɪzə]
Veranstaltung event [ɪˈvent]; session [ˈseʃn]
verantwortlich responsible [rɪsˈpɒnsəbl]
Verantwortung responsibility [rɪsˌpɒnsəˈbɪləti]
verantwortungsvoll responsible [rɪsˈpɒnsəbl]
verärgert angry [ˈæŋgri]
verbannen to ban [bæn]
verbessern to improve [ɪmˈpruːv]
sich verbessern to improve [ɪmˈpruːv]
verbieten to ban [bæn]
verbinden to join [dʒɔɪn]; to link [lɪŋk]
Verbindung link [lɪŋk]
sich in Verbindung setzen mit to contact [ˈkɒntækt]
verbittert bitter [ˈbɪtə]
verbleiben to remain [rɪˈmeɪn]
verblüfft startled [ˈstɑːtld]
Verbot ban [bæn]
Verbrechen crime [kraɪm]
Verbrecher/Verbrecherin criminal [ˈkrɪmɪnl]; gangster [ˈgæŋkstə]
verbreiten to spread [spred]
sich verbreiten to spread [spred]
verbreitet common [ˈkɒmən]
verbrennen to burn [bɜːn]
Verbrennungsrückstände ashes *(pl)* [ˈæʃɪz]
verbringen to spend [spend]
mit **verbundenen Augen** blindfolded [ˈblaɪndfəʊldɪd]
verdammt bloody [ˈblʌdi]; damn [dæm]
verdanken to owe [əʊ]
verdienen to deserve [dɪˈzɜːv]; to earn [ɜːn]
Verein club [klʌb]; society [səˈsaɪəti]
Vereinigung union [ˈjuːnjən]
verfahren tricky [ˈtrɪki]
Verfasser/Verfasserin writer [ˈraɪtə]
verfehlen to miss [mɪs]
Vergangenheit past [pɑːst]
vergessen to forget [fəˈget]
doppelt **verglast** double-glazed [ˌdʌblˈgleɪzd]
vergleichen to compare [kəmˈpeə]
vergrößern to increase [ɪnˈkriːs]
verhaften to arrest [əˈrest]
sich **verhalten** to act [ækt]
verheiratet mit married to [ˈmærid tə]

etw. **verhindern** to get in the way (of) [ˌget‿ɪn‿ðə‿ˈweɪ]
sich **verirren** to get lost [get ˈlɒst]
sich verirrt haben to be lost [biː ˈlɒst]
Verkauf sales *(pl)* [seɪlz]
verkaufen to sell [sel]
Verkäufer salesman, salesmen *(pl)* [ˈseɪlzmən; ˈseɪlzmen]
Verkäufer/Verkäuferin shop assistant [ˈʃɒp‿əˌsɪstnt]
Verkaufsraum salesroom [ˈseɪlzruːm]
Verkehr traffic [ˈtræfɪk]
Verkehrsmittel transport *(no pl.)* [ˈtrænspɔːt]
verklappen to dump sth [dʌmp]
verknüpfen to link [lɪŋk]
Verknüpfung link [lɪŋk]
verlassen to leave [liːv]
jmdn. verlassen to chuck sb [tʃʌk]
verlässlich reliable [rɪˈlaɪəbl]
verlegen to lay [leɪ]
Verleih- rental [ˈrentl]
verleihen to loan [ləʊn]; to present [prɪˈzent]
verletzen to hurt [hɜːt]
verletzt hurt [hɜːt]
Verletzung harm [hɑːm]
sich **verlieben** to fall in love [fɔːl‿ɪn ˈlʌv]
verlieren to lose [luːz]
verloren gehen to get lost [get ˈlɒst]
Verlust loss [lɒs]
Vermarktung marketing [ˈmɑːkɪtɪŋ]
vermindern to reduce [rɪˈdjuːs]
vermissen to miss [mɪs]
vermuten to guess [ges]
vernünftig intelligent [ɪnˈtelɪdʒnt]; sensible [ˈsensɪbl]
Verpackung packaging [ˈpækɪdʒɪŋ]
verpassen to miss [mɪs]
Verpflegung catering [ˈkeɪtrɪŋ]
verregnet rainy [ˈreɪni]
verrückt crazy [ˈkreɪzi]; mad [mæd]
verrückt machen to drive crazy [draɪv ˈkreɪzi]
verrückt nach … sein to be nuts about [biː ˌnʌts‿əˈbaʊt]
verrückt werden to go bananas [ˌgəʊ bəˈnɑːnəz]
Vers verse [vɜːs]
Versammlung assembly [əˈsembli]; rally [ˈræli]
verschieden different [ˈdɪfrnt]
verschiedene several [ˈsevrl]
Verschiffung shipping [ˈʃɪpɪŋ]
verschlafen sleepy [ˈsliːpi]
Verschluss shutter [ˈʃʌtə]
Verschlüsselung code [kəʊd]
Verschmutzung pollution [pəˈluːʃn]
verschneit snowy [ˈsnəʊi]
verschwenden to waste [weɪst]
Verschwendung waste [weɪst]
verschwinden to disappear [ˌdɪsəˈpɪə]
versichern to assure [əˈʃʊə]
Versicherung insurance [ɪnˈʃʊərns]
Versorgung supply [səˈplaɪ]
verspätet delayed [dɪˈleɪd]; late [leɪt]
versprechen to promise [ˈprɒmɪs]
Verstand brain(s) [breɪn, breɪnz]; mind [maɪnd]
sich **verständigen** to communicate [kəˈmjuːnɪkeɪt]
Verständigung communication [kəˌmjuːnɪˈkeɪʃn]
verstecken to hide [haɪd]
sich verstecken to hide [haɪd]
verstehen to understand [ˌʌndəˈstænd]
etwas verstehen to get it [ˈget‿ɪt]
sich verstehen mit to get on with [get‿ˈɒn wɪð]
versteinert fossil [ˈfɒsl]
Versuch attempt [əˈtempt]; experiment [ɪkˈsperɪmənt]
versuchen to try [traɪ]
Vertrag contract [ˈkɒntrækt]; treaty [ˈtriːti]
vertrauen to trust [trʌst]
vertrauenswürdig reliable [rɪˈlaɪəbl]
vertraulich confidential [ˌkɒnfɪˈdenʃl]
Vertreter salesman, salesmen *(pl)* [ˈseɪlzmən; ˈseɪlzmen]
Vertreter/Vertreterin agent [ˈeɪdʒnt]
Vertrieb marketing [ˈmɑːkɪtɪŋ]; sales *(pl)* [seɪlz]
verursachen to cause [kɔːz]
Verurteilung sentence [ˈsentəns]
vervollständigen to complete [kəmˈpliːt]
Verwalter/Verwalterin administrator [ədˈmɪnɪstreɪtə]
Verweis reference [ˈrefrns]
verwenden to use [juːz]
Verwendung use [juːs]
verzeichnet on record [ɒn ˈrekɔːd]
verzögert delayed [dɪˈleɪd]
Video video [ˈvɪdiəʊ]
Vieh cattle *(pl. only)* [ˈkætl]
Viehtrieb cattle drive [ˈkætl ˌdraɪv]
viel a lot [ə ˈlɒt]; much [mʌtʃ]
viel versprechend promising [ˈprɒmɪsɪŋ]
viel/viele a lot of [ə ˈlɒt‿əv]; lots (of) [ˈlɒts‿əv]
Viel Glück! Good luck! [ˌgʊd ˈlʌk]
viele many [ˈmeni]
vielleicht perhaps [pəˈhæps]; maybe [ˈmeɪbi]
Viertel neighborhood *(AE)* [ˈneɪbəhʊd]; quarter [ˈkwɔːtə]
Viertel nach quarter past [ˈkwɔːtə pɑːst]
Viertel vor quarter to [ˈkwɔːtə tə]
Vierteldollar *(Währung)* quarter [ˈkwɔːtə]
violett purple [ˈpɜːpl]
virtuell virtual [ˈvɜːtʃuəl]
Visitenkarte business card [ˈbɪznɪs ˌkɑːd]
Vogel bird [bɜːd]
Volksmusik folk [fəʊk]
Volksstamm tribe [traɪb]
voll (von) full (of) [fʊl]
voll ausgebildet fully-qualified [ˌfʊliˈkwɒlɪfaɪd]
voll qualifiziert fully-qualified [ˌfʊliˈkwɒlɪfaɪd]
Volleyball volleyball [ˈvɒlibɔːl]
völlig quite [kwaɪt]
vollkommen perfect [ˈpɜːfɪkt]
vollständig total [ˈtəʊtl]
Vollzeit- full-time (F/T) [ˌfʊlˈtaɪm]
von by [baɪ]; from [frɒm]; in [ɪn]; of [ɒv; əv]
vor before [bɪˈfɔː]; in front of [ɪn ˈfrʌnt‿əv]; *(zeitlich)* ago [əˈgəʊ]
vorbei over [ˈəʊvə]; past [pɑːst]
vorbeibringen to bring round [brɪŋ‿ˈraʊnd]
vorbeifahren to pass [pɑːs]
vorbereiten to prepare [prɪˈpeə]
sich vorbereiten to get ready [get ˈredi]
Vordergrund foreground [ˈfɔːgraʊnd]
Vorderseite front [frʌnt]
Vorgarten front garden [ˌfrʌnt ˈgɑːdn]
Vorhang curtain [ˈkɜːtn]
Vorhersage *(Wetter)* forecast [ˈfɔːkɑːst]
vorhersagen *(Wetter)* to forecast [ˈfɔːkɑːst]
laut **vorlesen** to read out [riːd‿ˈaʊt]
Vormittag morning [ˈmɔːnɪŋ]
vormittags in the morning [ˌɪn ðə ˈmɔːnɪŋ]; *(Uhrzeit)* a.m. [ˌeɪˈem]
vorne at the front [ət ðə ˈfrʌnt]
Vorort suburb [ˈsʌbɜːb]
Vorrat supply [səˈplaɪ]
vorschlagen to suggest [səˈdʒest]
Vorschrift rule [ruːl]
vorsichtig careful [ˈkeəfl]
Vorsingen audition [ɔːˈdɪʃn]
Vorspeise starter [ˈstɑːtə]
Vorsprechen audition [ɔːˈdɪʃn]
sich (etwas) **vorstellen** to imagine [ɪˈmædʒɪn]
Vorstellung performance [pəˈfɔːməns]
Vortanzen audition [ɔːˈdɪʃn]
Vor- und Nachteile pros and cons [ˌprəʊz‿ənd ˈkɒnz]
Vortrag talk [tɔːk]

einen Vortrag halten to give a talk [ˌgɪv‿ə 'tɔ:k]
vorüber over ['əʊvə]; past [pɑ:st]
vorübergehen to pass [pɑ:s]
vorübergehend temporary ['temprəri]
vorwärtskommen to get on [get‿'ɒn]

W

wachsen to grow [grəʊ]; to rise [raɪz]
wachsen lassen to grow [grəʊ]
Waffe weapon ['wepən]
wagen to dare [deə]
etw. wagen to take your chance [ˌteɪk jɔ: 'tʃɑ:ns]
Wahl choice [tʃɔɪs]; election [ɪ'lekʃn]
wählen to choose [tʃu:z]; to elect [ɪ'lekt]; to vote [vəʊt]
wahr true [tru:]
wahr werden to come true [kʌm 'tru:]
während *(+ Nomen)* during *(+ noun)* ['djʊərɪŋ]
während as [æz; əz]; while [waɪl]
wahrscheinlich probably ['prɒbəbli]
Wald forest ['fɒrɪst]
Waliser/Waliserin Welsh [welʃ]
walisisch Welsh [welʃ]
Wand wall [wɔ:l]
Wander- hiking ['haɪkɪŋ]
Wandern hiking ['haɪkɪŋ]
Wandmalerei mural ['mjʊərl]
Wandtafel board [bɔ:d]
wann when [wen]
Ware product ['prɒdʌkt]
Waren goods *(pl)* [gʊdz]
warm warm [wɔ:m]
Warn- warning ['wɔ:nɪŋ]
warnen to warn [wɔ:n]
Warnung warning ['wɔ:nɪŋ]
warten to wait [weɪt]
Warte mal! Hang on! ['hæŋ‿ɒn]
warten auf to wait for ['weɪt fɔ:]
Wärter/Wärterin keeper ['ki:pə]; zookeeper ['zu:ki:pə]
Warteschlange queue [kju:]
warum why [waɪ]
was what [wɒt]
was auch immer whatever [wɒt'evə]
Was ist los? What's up? [ˌwɒts‿'ʌp]
Was ist mit …? What about … ? [wɒt‿ə'baʊt]
Waschbecken *(im Amerikanischen)* sink [sɪŋk]
Waschbrettbauch six-pack ['sɪkspæk]
(sich) **waschen** to wash [wɒʃ]
Wasser water ['wɔ:tə]
Wasserhahn faucet *(AE)* ['fɔ:sɪt]; tap *(BE)* [tæp]

Website website ['websaɪt]
Wechselgeld change [tʃeɪndʒ]
wechseln to change [tʃeɪndʒ]
wecken to wake [weɪk]
Wecker alarm clock [ə'lɑ:m ˌklɒk]
weg away [ə'weɪ]
Weg path [pɑ:θ]; way [weɪ]
Er ist auf dem Weg zu …. He is on his way to …. [ˌhi:‿ɪz‿ɒn hɪz 'weɪ tə]
sich auf den Weg machen to set off [set‿'ɒf]
Wegbereiter/Wegbereiterin pioneer [ˌpaɪə'nɪə]
wegbleiben to keep away [ki:p‿ə'weɪ]; to stay out [steɪ‿'aʊt]
wegen because of [bɪ'kɒz‿əv]
weggehen to leave [li:v]
wegnehmen to take [teɪk]
wegrennen to run away [rʌn‿ə'weɪ]
weh sore [sɔ:]
weh tun to hurt [hɜ:t]
wehen to fly [flaɪ]
weich smooth [smu:θ]; soft [sɒft]
sich **weigern** to refuse [rɪ'fju:z]
Weihnachten Christmas ['krɪsməs]
weil because [bɪ'kɒz]
weinen to cry [kraɪ]
Weise way [weɪ]
weit far [fɑ:]; wide [waɪd]
weiter further ['fɜ:ðə]
es weit bringen to go far [gəʊ 'fɑ:]
weit kommen to go far [gəʊ 'fɑ:]
weiter- to … on [ɒn]
weiter tun to keep *(+ -ing)* [ki:p]
weitergeben to pass [pɑ:s]
weitergehen to continue [kən'tɪnju:]
weiterkommen to get on [get‿'ɒn]
weitermachen to continue [kən'tɪnju:]; to go on [gəʊ‿'ɒn]
Weitsprung long jump ['lɒŋ ˌdʒʌmp]
welcher/welche/welches what [wɒt]; which [wɪtʃ]
Welle wave [weɪv]
Wellenreiten surfing ['sɜ:fɪŋ]
Wellness-Center spa [spɑ:]
Welt world [wɜ:ld]
Weltall outer space [ˌaʊtə 'speɪs]
Weltraum outer space [ˌaʊtə 'speɪs]; space [speɪs]; universe ['ju:nɪvɜ:s]
Weltraumstation space station ['speɪs ˌsteɪʃn]
weltweit worldwide [ˌwɜ:ld'waɪd]
wem who [hu:]
wen who [hu:]
wenig little ['lɪtl]
weniger less [les]
am wenigsten least [li:st]
wenige few [fju:]
wenigstens at least [ət 'li:st]

wenn if [ɪf]; when [wen]
wenn nicht unless [ən'les]
wer who [hu:]
Werbe- advertising *(no pl.)* ['ædvətaɪzɪŋ]
Werbespot ad [æd]; advert ['ædvɜ:t]
Werbung advertising *(no pl.)* ['ædvətaɪzɪŋ]
werden to become [bɪ'kʌm]; to get [get]; *(futurisch)* will ('ll) [wɪl]
werfen to throw [θrəʊ]
Werk factory ['fæktri]
Werkstatt workshop ['wɜ:kʃɒp]
Werktag weekday ['wi:kdeɪ]
Werkzeug tool [tu:l]
wertvoll valuable ['væljuəbl]
wessen whose [hu:z]
Westen west [west]
Western(-) western ['westən]
westlich western ['westən]
Wettbewerb competition [ˌkɒmpə'tɪʃn]
wetten to bet [bet]
Wetter weather ['weðə]
Wettkampf match [mætʃ]
Wettlauf race [reɪs]
einen Wettlauf machen to run a race [ˌrʌn‿ə 'reɪs]
wichtig important [ɪm'pɔ:tnt]
widerhallen to echo ['ekəʊ]
wie as [æz; əz]; *(Vergleich)* like [laɪk]
wie how [haʊ]
Wie alt bist du? How old are you? [haʊ‿'əʊld‿ɑ: ju:]
Wie geht es dir/Ihnen/euch? How are you? [ˌhaʊ‿'ɑ: ju:]
Wie heißt du? What's your name? [ˌwɒts jə 'neɪm]
Wie spät ist es, bitte? What's the time, please? [ˌwɒts ðə 'taɪm ˌpli:z]
wie viele how many [haʊ 'meni]
Wie viel kosten … ? How much are …? [ˌhaʊ 'mʌtʃ‿ɑ:]
Wie viel kostet … ? How much is …? [ˌhaʊ 'mʌtʃ‿ɪz]
Wie viel Uhr … ? What time … ? [wɒt 'taɪm]
Wie viel Uhr ist es, bitte? What's the time, please? [ˌwɒts ðə 'taɪm ˌpli:z]
Wie wäre es mit …? What about … ? [wɒt‿ə'baʊt]
wieder again [ə'gen]
wieder verwerten to recycle [ri:'saɪkl]
wiederherstellen to restore [rɪ'stɔ:]
auf **Wiedersehen** goodbye [gʊd'baɪ]
wild wild [waɪld]
Willkommen (in) … Welcome (to) … ['welkəm tə]
willkommen heißen to welcome ['welkəm]
Wind wind [wɪnd]

windig windy ['wɪndi]
Windkraftanlage windmill ['wɪnmɪl]
Windmühle windmill ['wɪnmɪl]
Windrad windmill ['wɪnmɪl]
windsurfen to surf [sɜːf]; to windsurf ['wɪnsɜːf]
winken to wave [weɪv]
Winter winter ['wɪntə]
winzig tiny ['taɪni]
wir we [wiː]
wir selbst ourselves [aʊə'selvz]
Wirbelsäule spine [spaɪn]
wirken to seem [siːm]
wirklich real [rɪəl]; really ['rɪəli]
Wirklichkeit reality [ri'æləti]
Wirkung effect [ɪ'fekt]
wischen to wipe [waɪp]
wissen to know [nəʊ]
Wissenschaft Science ['saɪəns]
Wissenschaftler/Wissenschaftlerin scientist ['saɪəntɪst]
Witz joke [dʒəʊk]
Witze machen to joke [dʒəʊk]
wo where [weə]
Woche week [wiːk]
in der Woche a week [ə 'wiːk]
pro Woche a week [ə 'wiːk]
Wochenende weekend [ˌwiːk'end]
Wochentag weekday ['wiːkdeɪ]
Woher kommst du? Where are you from? [ˌwear‿ə jə 'frɒm]
wohin where [weə]
Wohltätigkeit charity ['tʃærɪti]
Wohltätigkeitsverein charity ['tʃærɪti]
wohnen to live [lɪv]
wohnen bei to stay with ['steɪ wɪð]
Wohnung apartment *(AE)* [ə'pɑːtmənt]; flat [flæt]
Wohnzimmer living room ['lɪvɪŋ rʊm]
Wolf wolf, wolves *(pl)* [wʊlf; wʊlvz]
Wolke cloud [klaʊd]
Wolkenkratzer skyscraper ['skaɪˌskreɪpə]
wolkig cloudy ['klaʊdi]
Wolldecke blanket ['blæŋkɪt]
wollen to want (to) ['wɒnt tə]
Workshop workshop ['wɜːkʃɒp]
Wort word [wɜːd]
Wörterbuch dictionary ['dɪkʃnri]
wund sore [sɔː]
kein **Wunder, dass ...** no wonder [nəʊ 'wʌndə]
wunderschön beautiful ['bjuːtɪfl]
Wunsch wish [wɪʃ]
wünschen to wish [wɪʃ]
würde/würden would [wʊd]
Wurst sausage ['sɒsɪdʒ]
Würstchen sausage ['sɒsɪdʒ]
würzig spicy ['spaɪsi]
wütend furious ['fjʊəriəs]; mad [mæd]

Z

zäh tough [tʌf]
Zahl number ['nʌmbə]
zahlen to pay (for) [peɪ]
Zähler metre ['miːtə]
Zahn tooth, teeth *(pl)* [tuːθ; tiːθ]
Zahnarzt/Zahnärztin dentist ['dentɪst]
Zahnprothese false teeth [fɔːls 'tiːθ]
Zahnschmerzen toothache ['tuːθeɪk]
Zauberer wizard ['wɪzəd]
Zaun fence [fens]
Zeh toe [təʊ]
Zehncentstück *(Währung)* dime [daɪm]
Zeichen sign [saɪn]; signal ['sɪgnl]; symbol ['sɪmbl]
Zeichentrickfilm cartoon [kɑː'tuːn]
zeichnen to design [dɪ'zaɪn]; to draw [drɔː]
zeigen to show [ʃəʊ]
zeigen (auf) to point (to) [pɔɪnt]
Zeile line [laɪn]
Zeit time [taɪm]
Du liebe Zeit! Good grief! [gʊd 'griːf]
Zeitabschnitt period *(AE)* ['pɪəriəd]
Zeitalter age [eɪdʒ]
Zeitschrift magazine [mægə'ziːn]
Zeitschriftenhändler/Zeitschriftenhändlerin newsagent ['njuːsˌeɪdʒənt]
Zeitung newspaper ['njuːsˌpeɪpə]; paper ['peɪpə]
Zelle cell [sel]
Zelt tent [tent]
Zelten camping ['kæmpɪŋ]
Zentimeter centimetre (cm) ['sentɪˌmiːtə]
Zentrum centre ['sentə]
zerbrechen to break [breɪk]
zerbrochen broken ['brəʊkn]
zerbröseln to flake [fleɪk]
zerdrücken to squash [skwɒʃ]
Zeremonie ceremony ['serɪməni]
zerfallen to flake [fleɪk]
zerrissen torn [tɔːn]
zerstören to destroy [dɪ'strɔɪ]
Zertifikat certificate [sə'tɪfɪkət]
Zeug stuff [stʌf]
Zeugnis certificate [sə'tɪfɪkət]; report [rɪ'pɔːt]
ziehen to pull [pʊl]
Ziehen tug [tʌg]
Ziel goal [gəʊl]
ziemlich pretty ['prɪti]; quite [kwaɪt]
Zigarette cigarette [ˌsɪgr'et]
Zimmer room [ruːm; rʊm]
freies Zimmer vacancy ['veɪknsi]
Zimmermann carpenter ['kɑːpəntə]
zirka around [ə'raʊnd]

zischen to spit [spɪt]
zittern to shake [ʃeɪk]
zögern to hesitate ['hezɪteɪt]
Zoll customs *(pl)* ['kʌstəmz]
Zoll *(Längenmaß: 2,54 cm)* inch [ɪnʃ]
Zoo zoo [zuː]
zu to [tʊ; tə]
zuallererst first of all [ˌfɜːst‿ɒf‿'ɔːl]
Zubehör accessories *(pl)* [ək'sesəriz]
zubereiten to prepare [prɪ'peə]
mit den Achseln **zucken** to shrug (one's shoulders) [ʃrʌg]
Zucker sugar ['ʃʊgə]
zuckerkrank diabetic [ˌdaɪə'betɪk]
Zuckerkrankheit diabetes [ˌdaɪə'biːtiːz]
zuerst at first [ət 'fɜːst]; first [fɜːst]; first of all [ˌfɜːst‿ɒf‿'ɔːl]
zuflüstern to whisper ['wɪspə]
zufrieden sein mit to be pleased with [biː 'pliːzd wɪð]
Zug train [treɪn]
Zugang access ['ækses]
zugeben to admit [əd'mɪt]
zugehen auf to walk up to [wɔːk‿'ʌp tə]
Zuhause home [həʊm]
zuhören to listen ['lɪsn]
Zukunft future ['fjuːtʃə]
zukünftig future ['fjuːtʃə]
zulässig valid ['vælɪd]
Zulu Zulu ['zuːluː]
zumachen to close [kləʊz]
zunächst at first [ət 'fɜːst]; first of all [ˌfɜːst‿ɒf‿'ɔːl]
zunehmen to grow [grəʊ]; to increase [ɪn'kriːs]; to rise [raɪz]
Zunge tongue [tʌŋ]
zuordnen to match [mætʃ]
Zupfen tug [tʌg]
zurück back [bæk]
zurückdenken to reminisce [ˌremɪ'nɪs]
zurückgehen to turn back [tɜːn 'bæk]
sich **zurücklehnen** to sit back [ˌsɪt 'bæk]
zusammen together [tə'geðə]
Zusammenbruch breakdown ['breɪkdaʊn]
zusammenfügen to match [mætʃ]
Zusatz extra ['ekstrə]
zusätzlich extra ['ekstrə]
Zuschauer/Zuschauerin viewer ['vjuːə]
etw. **zusichern** to assure [ə'ʃʊə]
zustimmen to agree [ə'griː]
zuverlässig reliable [rɪ'laɪəbl]
zuzüglich plus [plʌs]
Zweig twig [twɪg]
zweimal twice [twaɪs]
zweisprachig bilingual [baɪ'lɪŋgwəl]
zweitens secondly ['sekndli]
zwingend compulsory [kəm'pʌlsri]
zwischen between [bɪ'twiːn]

In the classroom

What you can say ...

... if you meet people or say 'goodbye':

I'm very pleased to meet you.	Freut mich sehr, Sie kennen zu lernen.
Nice to meet you!	Schön dich kennen zu lernen.
Goodbye./Bye. See you tomorrow/next	Auf Wiedersehen./Tschüss. Bis morgen/nächste/-n/-s ... .

... if you need help:

Can you give me a hand, please?	Kannst du/Können Sie mir bitte helfen?
I don't understand this.	Ich verstehe das nicht.
What's that in English/German?	Was heißt das auf Englisch/Deutsch?
Can I say: ...?/What does ... mean?	Kann ich ... sagen?/Was bedeutet ...?
How do you do/change/ ... this?	Wie macht/ändert/ ... man das?
Is this right? I'm not sure.	Ist das richtig? Ich bin mir nicht sicher.
Could you write it down, please?	Könntest du/Könnten Sie das bitte aufschreiben?
Could I ask you a question, please?	Könnte ich dir/Ihnen bitte eine Frage stellen?
Pardon?	Wie bitte?
Could you repeat that, please?	Könntest du/Könnten Sie das bitte wiederholen?
Could you show me that again, please?	Könntest du/Könnten Sie mir das bitte nochmal zeigen?
I'm sorry (to bother you), but could I please borrow your mobile/...?	Entschuldige, (dass ich dich störe,) aber kann ich bitte dein Handy/... ausleihen?

... if you have a discussion:

In my opinion/I think/	Meiner Meinung nach/ich denke/ ... .
You are absolutely right/wrong.	Du hast/Sie haben völlig Recht/Unrecht/nicht Recht.
On the one hand ... , on the other hand	Einerseits ..., andererseits ... .
I think we should read newspapers/watch .../... .	Ich denke, wir sollten Zeitungen lesen/... schauen/... .
The best news reports/... are in .../on	Die besten Nachrichten/... findet man in .../auf ... .
The biggest problem we have today is	Unser größtes Problem heutzutage ist ... .
I have the feeling/impression that	Ich habe das Gefühl/den Eindruck, dass ... .
What we really need to do is	Wir müssen unbedingt ... .
I'm really interested in working abroad/	Ich möchte am liebsten im Ausland arbeiten ... .
The most important thing in a job is money/	Das Wichtigste bei einem Job ist Geld/ ... .
I'd like a job where I can meet people/	Ich möchte einen Job, in dem ich Menschen treffe/ ... .

... if you give a talk/presentation:

Today I'd like to/I am going to talk about/ give a (PowerPoint) presentation on	Heute möchte ich über ... reden/eine (PowerPoint-) Präsentation zum Thema ... halten.
The title of the talk/presentation is	Der Titel des Referats/der Präsentation lautet ... .
It will last about ... minutes.	Es/Sie wird etwa ... Minuten dauern.
It would be good if you kept any questions until the end.	Es wäre gut, wenn ihr eure/Sie Ihre Fragen erst am Schluss stellen könntet/könnten.
I shall be happy to answer them after the	Ich beantworte sie gerne nach der/dem ... .
Here/on the left/right you can see	Hier/auf der linken/rechten Seite seht ihr/sehen Sie ... .
I hope you liked my talk/... .	Ich hoffe, euch/Ihnen hat mein Referat/... gefallen.

... if you want to talk about stories/poems/songs:

I think this story/... is good/funny/brilliant/	Ich finde diese Geschichte/... gut/witzig/toll/ ....
I think it's sad/a bit boring/ ... because	Ich finde sie/es traurig/etwas langweilig/..., weil ... .
I've read/heard/... better ones.	Ich habe schon bessere gelesen/gehört/... .
In my opinion ...was better because	Meiner Meinung nach war ... besser, weil ... .
I think the ending/... is right/wrong/too	Ich denke, dass das Ende/... richtig/falsch/zu ... ist.

... if you work with a partner:	
Whose turn is it?	Wer ist dran?
What are we going to do first?	Was machen wir zuerst?
Let's write down our ideas.	Lasst uns unsere Ideen aufschreiben.
Let's act the story/play a game.	Lasst uns die Geschichte vorspielen/ein Spiel spielen.
You can be ... and I'll be	Du kannst ... spielen und ich spiele ... ..
I don't understand what you mean.	Ich verstehe nicht, was du meinst.
What did you find on the Internet?	Was hast du im Internet gefunden?
I really like your idea.	Mir gefällt deine Idee sehr gut.
What do you suggest?	Was schlägst du vor?
Where shall we start?	Wo sollen wir anfangen?
I think we need	Ich denke, wir brauchen ... .

... if you want to present results:	
We did a survey on .../to find out/because we wanted to know	Wir haben eine Umfrage zu ... gemacht/um herauszufinden/weil wir wissen wollten ... .
We asked all the girls/boys in our group/class/ in class	Wir haben alle Mädchen/Jungen in unserer Gruppe/ Klasse/in Klasse ... gefragt ... .
There were ... girls/boys. The total number was	Es gab ... Mädchen/Jungen. Die Gesamtzahl war ... .
We'd like to explain/show you some figures.	Wir möchten euch/Ihnen einige Zahlen erläutern/zeigen.
The grid/flow chart/ ... shows	Die Tabelle/das Flussdiagramm/ ... zeigt ... .
A key to the symbols is at the side/	Ein Schlüssel zu den Symbolen ist an der Seite/ ... .
The red/ ... bar/the scale represents	Die rote/ ... Säule/die Skala stellt ... dar.
You can see that most/more than .../no pupils	Klar ist, dass die meisten/mehr als .../keine Schüler ... .
If we compare ... with ..., we can see that	Wenn wir ... mit ... vergleichen, sehen wir, dass ... .
We were surprised/disappointed/ ... to find that	Wir waren überrascht/enttäuscht/ ..., dass ... .
Thank you for listening.	Wir bedanken uns für eure/Ihre Aufmerksamkeit.
Are there any questions?/Does anyone have a question?	Gibt es Fragen?

What the teacher might say to you ...

... if he/she has a question:	
What's the problem?/What's wrong?	Was ist das Problem?/Was ist los?
Describe what you can see/the people/ what's happening.	Beschreibe was du siehst/ihr seht/die Menschen/was passiert.
What do you think of ...?	Was haltet ihr von ...?
Have you got any other ideas/comments/...?	Habt ihr andere/sonstige Ideen/Anmerkungen/...?
What could be the message/the meaning of ...?	Was könnte die Aussage/Bedeutung von ... sein?
... if he/she gives you instructions:	
Be careful with the word order/... .	Achtet auf die Satzstellung/... .
Make a grid/poster/... (like this).	Macht eine Tabelle/ein Poster/... (wie diese/s).
Match the questions/pictures with the answers/ sentences.	Ordnet den Fragen/Bildern die Antworten/Sätze zu.
Define these jobs/... .	Erklärt diese Berufe/... .
Present your topic/poster/... to the class.	Präsentiert der Klasse euer Topic/Poster/ ... .

List of irregular verbs

to **be** [bi:]	**was/were** [wɒz/wɜ:]	**been** [bi:n]	sein
to **beat** [bi:t]	**beat** [bi:t]	**beaten** [bi:tn]	besiegen, schlagen
to **become** [bɪ'kʌm]	**became** [bɪ'keɪm]	**become** [bɪ'kʌm]	werden
to **begin** [bɪ'gɪn]	**began** [bɪ'gæn]	**begun** [bɪ'gʌn]	beginnen, anfangen
to **bet** [bet]	**bet** [bet]	**bet** [bet]	wetten
to **build** [bɪld]	**built** [bɪlt]	**built** [bɪlt]	bauen
to **blow** [bləʊ]	**blew** [blu:]	**blown** [bləʊn]	blasen
to **break** [breɪk]	**broke** [brəʊk]	**broken** ['brəʊkn]	(zer)brechen; kaputtmachen
to **bring** [brɪŋ]	**brought** [brɔ:t]	**brought** [brɔ:t]	bringen, mitbringen
to **burn** [bɜ:n]	**burnt** [bɜ:nt]	**burnt** [bɜ:nt]	(ver)brennen
to **buy** [baɪ]	**bought** [bɔ:t]	**bought** [bɔ:t]	kaufen
to **catch** [kætʃ]	**caught** [kɔ:t]	**caught** [kɔ:t]	fangen
to **choose** [tʃu:z]	**chose** [tʃəʊz]	**chosen** ['tʃəʊzn]	wählen, auswählen
to **come** [kʌm]	**came** [keɪm]	**come** [kʌm]	kommen
to **cut** [kʌt]	**cut** [kʌt]	**cut** [kʌt]	schneiden
to **dig up** [dɪg‿'ʌp]	**dug up** [dʌg‿'ʌp]	**dug up** [dʌg‿'ʌp]	ausgraben
to **do** [du:]	**did** [dɪd]	**done** [dʌn]	machen, tun
to **draw** [drɔ:]	**drew** [dru:]	**drawn** [drɔ:n]	zeichnen
to **drink** [drɪŋk]	**drank** [dræŋk]	**drunk** [drʌŋk]	trinken
to **drive** [draɪv]	**drove** [drəʊv]	**driven** ['drɪvn]	fahren
to **eat** [i:t]	**ate** [et/eɪt]	**eaten** ['i:tn]	essen, fressen
to **fall** [fɔ:l]	**fell** [fel]	**fallen** ['fɔ:ln]	fallen, herunterfallen, hinfallen
to **feed** [fi:d]	**fed** [fed]	**fed** [fed]	füttern
to **feel** [fi:l]	**felt** [felt]	**felt** [felt]	fühlen, sich fühlen
to **fight** [faɪt]	**fought** [fɔ:t]	**fought** [fɔ:t]	kämpfen
to **find** [faɪnd]	**found** [faʊnd]	**found** [faʊnd]	finden
to **fly** [flaɪ]	**flew** [flu:]	**flown** [fləʊn]	fliegen
to **forecast** ['fɔ:kɑ:st]	**forecast** ['fɔ:kɑ:st]	**forecast** ['fɔ:kɑ:st]	vorhersagen *(Wetter)*
to **forget** [fə'get]	**forgot** [fə'gɒt]	**forgotten** [fə'gɒtn]	vergessen
to **get** [get]	**got** [gɒt]	**got** [gɒt]	kommen, bekommen; werden
to **give** [gɪv]	**gave** [geɪv]	**given** ['gɪvn]	geben, schenken
to **go** [gəʊ]	**went** [went]	**gone** [gɒn]	gehen
to **hang out** [hæŋ‿'aʊt]	**hung out** [hʌŋ‿'aʊt]	**hung out** [hʌŋ‿'aʊt]	sich herumtreiben
to **have** [hæv]	**had** [hæd]	**had** [hæd]	haben
to **hear** [hɪə]	**heard** [hɜ:d]	**heard** [hɜ:d]	hören
to **hide** [haɪd]	**hid** [hɪd]	**hidden** ['hɪdn]	verstecken, sich verstecken
to **hit** [hɪt]	**hit** [hɪt]	**hit** [hɪt]	schlagen, treffen
to **hold** [həʊld]	**held** [held]	**held** [held]	halten
to **hurt** [hɜ:t]	**hurt** [hɜ:t]	**hurt** [hɜ:t]	verletzen, weh tun
to **keep** [ki:p]	**kept** [kept]	**kept** [kept]	(be)halten
to **know** [nəʊ]	**knew** [nju:]	**known** [nəʊn]	wissen, kennen
to **lay** [leɪ]	**laid** [leɪd]	**lain** [leɪn]	legen
to **lead** [li:d]	**led** [led]	**led** [led]	führen
to **lean** [li:n]	**leant** [lent]	**leant** [lent]	(sich)lehnen
to **learn** [lɜ:n]	**learnt** [lɜ:nt]	**learnt** [lɜ:nt]	lernen
to **leave** [li:v]	**left** [left]	**left** [left]	lassen, verlassen, abfahren
to **lend** [lend]	**lent** [lent]	**lent** [lent]	leihen

to **let** [let]	**let** [let]	**let** [let]	lassen
to **lie** [laɪ]	**lay** [leɪ]	**lain** [leɪn]	liegen
to **lose** [lu:z]	**lost** [lɒst]	**lost** [lɒst]	verlieren
to **make** [meɪk]	**made** [meɪd]	**made** [meɪd]	machen
to **mean** [mi:n]	**meant** [ment]	**meant** [ment]	bedeuten, meinen
to **meet** [mi:t]	**met** [met]	**met** [met]	treffen, sich treffen
to **overdo** [ˌəʊvə'du:]	**overdid** [ˌəʊvə'dɪd]	**overdone** [ˌəʊvə'dʌn]	übertreiben
to **pay** [peɪ]	**paid** [peɪd]	**paid** [peɪd]	(be)zahlen
to **put** [pʊt]	**put** [pʊt]	**put** [pʊt]	setzen, stellen, legen
to **read** [ri:d]	**read** [red]	**read** [red]	lesen
to **rebuild** [ˌri:'bɪld]	**rebuilt** [ˌri:'bɪlt]	**rebuilt** [ˌri:'bɪlt]	wieder aufbauen, wiederherstellen
to **ride** [raɪd]	**rode** [rəʊd]	**ridden** ['rɪdn]	fahren, reiten
to **ring** [rɪŋ]	**rang** [ræŋ]	**rung** [rʌŋ]	klingeln; anrufen
to **rise** [raɪz]	**rose** [rəʊz]	**risen** ['rɪzn]	steigen, wachsen, zunehmen
to **run** [rʌn]	**ran** [ræn]	**run** [rʌn]	rennen, laufen
to **say** [seɪ]	**said** [sed]	**said** [sed]	sagen, sprechen
to **see** [si:]	**saw** [sɔ:]	**seen** [si:n]	sehen; besuchen
to **sell** [sel]	**sold** [səʊld]	**sold** [səʊld]	verkaufen
to **send** [send]	**sent** [sent]	**sent** [sent]	schicken
to **set** [set]	**set** [set]	**set** [set]	stellen, einstellen
to **shake** [ʃeɪk]	**shook** [ʃʊk]	**shaken** ['ʃeɪkn]	schütteln, zittern
to **show** [ʃəʊ]	**showed** [ʃəʊd]	**shown** [ʃəʊn]	zeigen
to **sing** [sɪŋ]	**sang** [sæŋ]	**sung** [sʌŋ]	singen
to **sit** [sɪt]	**sat** [sæt]	**sat** [sæt]	sitzen
to **sleep** [sli:p]	**slept** [slept]	**slept** [slept]	schlafen
to **smell** [smel]	**smelt** [smelt]	**smelt** [smelt]	riechen
to **speak** [spi:k]	**spoke** [spəʊk]	**spoken** ['spəʊkn]	sprechen
to **spell** [spel]	**spelt** [spelt]	**spelt** [spelt]	buchstabieren
to **spend** [spend]	**spent** [spent]	**spent** [spent]	verbringen, ausgeben
to **spread** [spred]	**spread** [spred]	**spread** [spred]	(sich) ausbreiten, verbreiten
to **stand** [stænd]	**stood** [stʊd]	**stood** [stʊd]	stehen
to **steal** [sti:l]	**stole** [stəʊl]	**stolen** ['stəʊln]	stehlen
to **stick** [stɪk]	**stuck** [stʌk]	**stuck** [stʌk]	kleben, stecken
to **swim** [swɪm]	**swam** [swæm]	**swum** [swʌm]	schwimmen
to **take** [teɪk]	**took** [tʊk]	**taken** ['teɪkn]	nehmen, mitnehmen, bringen
to **teach** [ti:tʃ]	**taught** [tɔ:t]	**taught** [tɔ:t]	lehren
to **tell** [tel]	**told** [təʊld]	**told** [təʊld]	erzählen, sagen
to **think** [θɪŋk]	**thought** [θɔ:t]	**thought** [θɔ:t]	denken, glauben
to **throw** [θrəʊ]	**threw** [θru:]	**thrown** [θrəʊn]	werfen
to **understand** [ˌʌndə'stænd]	**understood** [ˌʌndə'stʊd]	**understood** [ˌʌndə'stʊd]	verstehen
to **unwind** [ʌn'waɪnd]	**unwound** [ʌn'waʊnd]	**unwound** [ʌn'waʊnd]	sich abwickeln
to **upset** [ʌp'set]	**upset** [ʌp'set]	**upset** [ʌp'set]	erschrecken, durcheinander bringen, umstoßen
to **wake** [weɪk]	**woke** [wəʊk]	**woken** ['wəʊkn]	(auf)wecken
to **wear** [weə]	**wore** [wɔ:]	**worn** [wɔ:n]	anhaben, tragen
to **win** [wɪn]	**won** [wɒn]	**won** [wɒn]	gewinnen, siegen
to **write** [raɪt]	**wrote** [rəʊt]	**written** ['rɪtn]	schreiben

Lösungen/Lösungsvorschläge Check-out

Topic 1, page 17

Option 1

1 Talk about the role of English in the world.

a) mother tongue – a person's main language
official language – language of a country (e.g. used by government)
bilingual person – speaker of two languages
foreign language – language of a different country
world language – international language

b) – helping a foreign person at the airport
– making a phone call
– writing a letter/application

2 Present facts and figures about the English language.

a) 1. Over 700 **million** people speak English as a foreign language.
2. It was spread by traders and **settlers**.
3. It's the official language in **more than 55** countries.
4. It's an official language in the **US**, **Australia**, Canada and India.
5. South **Africa** has 11 official languages.
6. English is used by **pilots** internationally.

b) United Kingdom, Canada, USA, India

Option 2

1 Talk about strenghts and weaknesses.

a) 1. helpful
2. reliable
3. enterprising
4. strong

b) 1. If a doctor is unfriendly or clumsy, it could be dangerous!
2. If a fireman is nervous, it can cause problems.
3. If a teacher is unreliable/not reliable, that can be dangerous or cause problems.
4. If a builder isn't careful/is careless, it can cause problems or even be dangerous.

c) I don't think I could be a doctor because I faint at the sight of blood/when I see blood.
I could work as a teacher because I'm friendly and I don't get angry easily.
I don't think that I would be a good fireman because I'm nervous and afraid of fire.
I think that working as a builder is not the right thing for me because it's physically very hard work (and I'm not that strong).

2 Decide why English could be important in certain jobs.

important: emergency helper, person at a tourist information desk, secretary in a big company, international coach, (bank manager, policeman)
useful: newsagent, film director, diving instructor, travel agent

3 Prepare yourself for a job interview.

a) *Lösungsvorschlag*
1. I left school in 2010.
2. Geography and English
3. Yes, I've had some practical experience in a company/ … which lasted two weeks.
4. I've worked in a … ./I've delivered newspapers./I've done some voluntary work in an environmental/charity organisation/… . I looked after my neighbour's pets all summer./…

b) *Lösungsvorschlag*
I think I should get the job because I'm enterprising/ reliable/ … . I like working with people/I did a work placement at … and it went very well./My English is quite good./I'm very good at … .

Topic 2, page 35

Option 1

1 Recognise important people/groups of people in politics in the US/UK.

a)

US	UK
president	king/queen (monarch) Prime Minister monarchy
citizens government political parties	

b) – A monarchy is ruled by a king or a queen.
– The government rules a country and makes laws.
– The citizens are the people who live in a country.

c) The president, the Prime Minister, the government and political parties are elected.

d) The citizens can take part in elections/vote for a person/ party.

2 Describe the Queen's role as Head of State.

- goes to important social events
- signs treaties
- meets foreign ambassadors
- meets the Prime Minister once a week
- reads the Queen's Speech

3 Talk about the Queen's power/activities and what she isn't allowed to do.

1. right
2. The Queen can't write new laws.
3. The Queen is not allowed to enter the House of Commons.
4. She has to open Parliament each year.
5. right
6. right
7. She can appoint a Prime Minister.
8. right

4 Explain who your Head of State and head of government are. What do they do in their positions?
Individuelle Schülerlösung

Option 2

1 Give advice on problems at work.

1. If a colleague got too close, I'd tell him/her not to stand so close to me and if he/she didn't stop, I would tell my supervisor.
2. If some colleagues took off their protective clothing, I'd speak to my supervisor about it.
3. If someone made nasty comments about my religion, I'd inform my supervisor.
4. If my supervisor gave other YAs more interesting projects than me, I'd try to talk with him/her about this problem.
5. If a lot of my colleagues told sexist and rude jokes, I'd try to ignore them. If they continued, I'd tell them they're not funny. If they still didn't stop, I'd tell my supervisor.
6. If a colleague said I should watch a video clip on the Internet during work, I'd say no because it's not right to do free-time activities at work.
7. If I didn't understand how to use a piece of equipment, I'd ask a colleague, my supervisor or my teacher for help.

2 Talk about rights and duties at work.

a) – equal opportunities for all YAs
– be treated fairly/with respect/get suitable work to do
– not to be discriminated against
– to work in a place free of sexism
– to have safe working conditions

b) – to wear protective clothing if it is needed
– to work as well as you can (and not watch videos or surf the Internet at work)
– to report sexist jokes/nasty comments/problems/bad treatment

Topic 3, page 49

Option 1

1 Discuss healthy living.

a) – do some sport like swimming
– eat lots of vegetables and fruit
– try to stay calm even if you have a lot of stress

b) – After I have eaten food that isn't so healthy, I try to eat extremely healthy food the next day.
– Healthy food doesn't taste so good and it's too expensive.

2 Talk about yourself, your friends and the environment.
My mum always makes *herself* sandwiches to take to work and she tells me I should at least eat some fruit. But I never make *myself* breakfast. I often buy *myself* a bagel on the way to school. I think it's OK for you to buy *yourself* chocolate – my friends and I do that sometimes. But we keep *ourselves* fit with sport and enjoy *ourselves* at the same time! One of my friends, Tom, doesn't do much to keep *himself* fit. He and his mate get *themselves* computer games and they play them all weekend. But at least he rides his bike to school like us. It's important for us all to teach *ourselves* about what's healthy for the environment, too.

Option 2

1 Report on eco jobs.

a) – shop assistant
– mechanic in a car production
– cook, chef in a hotel
– ranger in a national park

b) 1. = picture 3
2. = picture 2
3. = picture 4
4. = picture 1

c) The chef in the hotel said that all the kitchen appliances ran on solar cells and that they recycled waste.
The mechanic said that people still needed cars and that they needed to design low energy cars that don't pollute the air.
The ranger said that people didn't think and that they disturbed plants and animals even in protected areas like that one.
The worker in the grocer's shop said that they only sold healthy products which came from local farms.

2 Describe your 'dream' job.
I think it's important to have a friendly boss who pays you well and gives you some space to be creative. Also it is good to work in a nice team where everybody tries to work together to get great results.

Topic 4, page 67

Option 1

1 Talk about choices in the UK at 16.

a) continue schooling or go for training/start working

b)
schooling:	– go to specialist college
	– stay at own school
training/work:	– do an apprenticeship
	– find a job with training where the employer organises the training

2 Decide about an internship.

a) I think the company sounds *pretty* good. My dad says that they're *really* modern. Also, they make cars that go *extremely* fast. And as you know, *really* fast cars are my big hobby!
For this internship it's *especially* important to have *quite* good marks in Math(s). So that's OK for me. The advert also says that they're looking for *very* reliable young people who are also *really* flexible. Well, maybe I should apply. What do you think?

b) No, I would not do an internship in an automotive company because I'm not interested in cars at all and I'm not good at Math(s)!

Option 2

1 Understand how some ill people feel.

a) *Individuelle Schülerlösung*
b) I'd advise other people not to watch the ill person and act normally so that they don't feel worse/that they are not normal/that something is wrong with them. Maybe you could offer help if someone needs help or you could visit him/her.

2 Decide what is really important to you in life.

Lösungsvorschlag:
The most important thing to me is to get a driving licence. (I need to get a summer job and save money and maybe my parents will help me). I'd love to travel abroad and see the world. (When I'm 18, I can 'work and travel' – the Internet can help me to find jobs abroad.) Another important thing is to live with my best friends. (When I start training or go abroad, I can then look for a flat with friends.) But this is the least important thing.

3 Analyse an extract from a novel.

a) Picture 3 is a scene from the extract. It shows 16-year-old Tessa and Adam in Adam's garden. Tessa had fainted and Adam had given her a coke.
b) *Lösungsvorschlag:*
Hi Nelly,
I've just finished the novel 'Before I die'. I really think the book is great because we see the world through Tessa's eyes. We know how she feels and what she thinks but it's still not too dramatic. The book is sad, of course, because she dies in the end. But you learn a lot about real life and it makes you think about your own life.
Yours, Paul

Lösungen/Lösungsvorschläge Test yourself!

Test yourself! 1, page 18–21

A Reading

1 The capital of Nunavut is Iqaluit. The region is about 2 million km².
2 a. 2 Nunavut is in the north of Canada.; b. 1 The school is in Iqaluit.; c. 3 The city's name means 'place of many fish'.; d. 1 The region was founded in 1999.; e. 3 At school there kids learn Inuktitut.; f. 2 Sleds are important for carrying tools.; g. 1 Iqaluit kids would be lost without a youth club.
3 One of Mike and Tom's hobbies is *igloo building*. They are worried about *the big alcohol problem*. Valerie likes to go *skidooing* in winter but she is worried about the thin ice which is caused by *global warming*. Amber is interested in playing *computer games*. She is worried about *how expensive food* is.

B Language

a. 2 opinions, b. 1 areas of land, c. 3 stay alive

C Listening

1 picture C
2 b.
3 a. That's wrong. It is mostly a hobby for girls. b. That's wrong. The sounds may be like echoing, or like a bird calling, like the blowing of the wind or the noise of breaking ice. c. That's right. d. That's right. e. That's wrong. The performers mix traditional with more modern music. f. Lucie Idlout won the Canadian Aboriginal Awards in 2003.

D Speaking

1 Describing

1 In the first picture you can see someone who is racing on his dog sled.
2 The second picture shows a person who is skidooing. He/She is jumping and doing some tricks with the skidoo.
3 Two boys are sitting in front of two computers. They are in a youth club/at school/in an Internet café. They are playing computer games/looking for information on the Internet/hanging out.
4 You can see two people who are building an igloo. They are standing inside the igloo and trying to fix/finish the roof with the last few blocks of ice.

I would prefer to take part in a dog race/driving with the skidoo/playing computer games/building an igloo … because … .

2 Discussing

Yes, I would like to live in the Arctic region because … ./No, I wouldn't like to live there because … .

Pros: winter sports (during) the whole year, a lot of snow and wide open spaces – live close to nature. Modern technology: skidoos; Internet, distance learning make people's lives easier; … .
Cons: too cold, no summer activities like swimming in a pool outside/in a lake, you can't wear summer clothes; may have to travel far to go to the cinema/a youth club etc.; lots of foods and goods are expensive as they are flown in to the region … .

3 Role play

You: My name is … . And I'm from … . I also spend a lot of time in our local youth club. I'm calling to find out more about activities you're offering for young people.
Doug: …
You: Well, I go to the youth club to meet my friends. And I like going to the movie/film nights there.
Doug: …
You: We don't have a summer camp. But we've got other summer events, for example a big live music festival with many cool bands or different workshops.
Doug: …
You: What kind of event is it? How long does it last?

Doug: …
You: That sounds really interesting! Is it difficult to build an igloo?
Doug: …
You: Snowmobile racing? Wow!/Really? Have you got any/Are there any pictures of the snowmobile race?
Doug: …

E Mediation and communication

a. Die *'Build the best igloo' Competition* ist ein Wettbewerb, bei welchem es darum geht, das beste Iglu zu bauen.
b. Der Veranstalter versucht damit den Menschen zu zeigen, wie wichtig Konstruktion und Technik im Alltag sind und wie sie helfen können, praktische Probleme zu lösen.
c. Ja, es gibt besondere Regeln. Man darf nur traditionelle und umweltfreundliche Werkzeuge, wie z.B. Schneeschaufeln und Sägen für den Iglubau verwenden.
d. Die Preisrichter überprüfen mit dem Reifen die Stabilität des Iglus.
e. „Bonus points" (Sonderpunkte/Zusatzpunkte) erhalten die Teams, wenn sie eine Nacht in ihrem Iglu verbringen.
f. Jedes Mitglied des Gewinner-Teams erhält einen tollen Iglu-Pokal aus Glas, in welchen sein Name eingraviert wurde.

F Writing

1 *Lösungsvorschlag*:
- activities: race along the river, big concert on the market square, 'Miss and Mister Town' competition
- sponsors: city council, local shops, local newspaper or radio station
- activities to make money: make cakes or pancakes and sell them, pack people's shopping bags in the supermarket

2 *Lösungsvorschlag*: Our youth club in … is planning a two-day Spring Festival. The festival is called 'Spring to Life' because we want to get young people active. We would like to offer many different activities like a charity race along the river and a big concert on the market square. We've even found some good musicians who are interested but we don't have enough sponsors. We would be very happy to have your support.

Test yourself! 2, page 36-39

A Reading

1 a. – 6; b. – 3; c. – 5; d. – 8; e. – 2; f. – 4; g. – 7; h. – 1

2

Early days	Changes	Goals today
h. The idea started in the 19th century.	i. The Commonwealth was only multiracial after India joined.	c. Now the Commonwealth is a lot of different countries that organize activities together.
d. The British Empire got richer and used slavery.	e. The British Commonwealth then became just the 'Commonwealth'.	a. Democracy and human rights are now important for the Commonwealth countries.
g. The first colonies to be independent were 'white'.	b. The Commonwealth's first African-ruled state was Ghana.	f. Today they want to fight poverty and intolerance.

B Language

1 a. equal/the same, b. at first, c. dropped, d. together
2 a. independent; b. nation, state; c. population; d. poverty

C Listening

1 a. She's from India.
b. Life was really hard at that time.
c. Member states now try to build bridges between countries.
d. Today they try to give people a better quality of life (1.) and look after the planet (2.).
e. CYP is short for the **C**ommonwealth **Y**outh **P**rogramme. It offers training in many areas, for example in youth development.

2 a. The people on the Commonwealth Youth Programme are between **15 and 29**.
b. There are courses at all levels: You can train to become a **youth worker**.
c. Vasanti wants to do a course in **Youth** Development.
d. Volunteers in Chandigarh do street plays or **concerts** in villages.

3 a. – 3, b. – 2, c. – 4, d. – 1

D Speaking

1 Describing

a.
1 The woman in the photo is in a field or a garden. She's digging to grow plants, trees, vegetables or cereals. She needs to be fit and strong and she needs to know about growing vegetables or cereals.
2 The volunteer could be in a primary school or in a children's home. He is looking after the children there, teaching or helping them with their homework. He needs to speak a language the children understand and needs to know how to teach a subject or subjects. He also needs to know how to work with children and has to be really patient.

b. *Individuelle Schülerlösung:*
I would like to work in/at …
As a volunteer, I'd like to help to …
I'm good at … ./I have a lot of experience with …

2 Role play

EVS: …

You: Hello. This is … . I'm interested in working as a volunteer in a project abroad.

Sandy: …

You: I'd like to work on/in a building project. But I'm not sure what country I'd like to go to.

Sandy: …

You: I've already worked on/in a building project and I'm really good at working with wood.

Sandy: …

You: Oh my God! What happened (to the old village)?

Sandy: …

You: I'll help where the organisers need me./I'll help with any job the organisers ask/need me to do.

Sandy: …

You: Could you please send me the forms and information by e-mail?

Sandy: …

You: I'll go to the doctor right away. I'll try to do everything as soon as possible. Thank you very much for your help. I'm really looking forward to taking part in your project. Goodbye!

E Mediation and communication

a. Die Sportveranstaltung ist eine Eröffnungsfeier für die 2010 in Indien stattfindenden „Commonwealth Games".
b. Teilnehmen können die 85 Mitgliedsländer des Commonwealth.
c. Zu den angebotenen Sportarten gehören Leichtathletik, Boxen, Badminton, Rad fahren, Turnen, Hockey, Tischtennis, Gewichtheben, Schießen, Bowling, Rugby und Korbball.
d. Die erste Veranstaltung dieser Art fand 1930 in Kanada statt.
e. Das letzte Event war in Melbourne, Australien.
f. Die Spiele werden Green Games genannt, da die Veranstalter verdeutlichen wollen, dass die Umwelt durch die Spiele nicht gefährdet oder zerstört wird.

F Writing

1 *Lösungsvorschlag:*

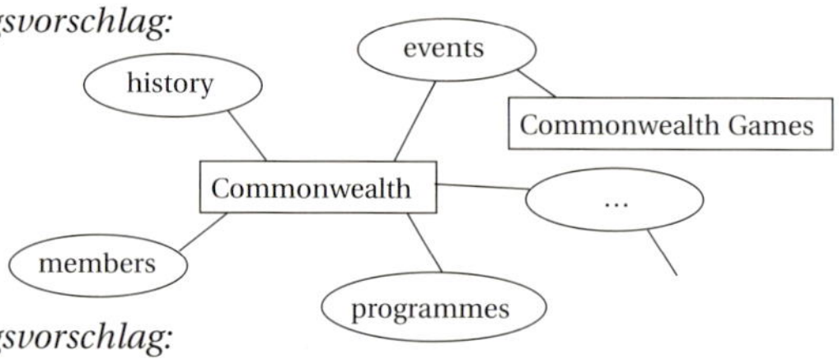

2 *Lösungsvorschlag:*

There are 53 states in the Commonwealth today. Many of these countries were once British colonies. The Commonwealth became multiracial when India joined in 1947. Today the member states organize lots of activities together because they want to fight poverty and intolerance and fight for democracy and human rights all around the world. There is also a Commonwealth Youth Programme for young people who want to do training and voluntary work in their countries.

Test Yourself! 3, page 50 – 53

A Reading

1 bacteria – Bakterien; filter – Filter; method – Methode; disinfection – Desinfektion; transparent – transparent, durchsichtig; plastic – Plastik; factor – Faktor; contaminated – kontaminiert, verschmutzt

2 a. filter, b. contaminated, c. bacteria, d. factor, e. method, f. transparent, g. plastic, h. disinfection

3 a. The flyer is about a campaign informing people about the importance of water and ways to make it safe to drink.

4 a. A special straw is a recent technology in water purification.
b. But this method is too expensive to use in poorer countries.
c. An advantage of SODIS is that it's a cheap way of getting clean household water supplies.
d. An important factor for this method is the type of bottles used.

B Language

a. alternatives, b. (clean) water, c. disaster

C Listening

1 a. 1. Canada, b. 2. Ghana, c. 1. three weeks, d. 1. 800 wells, e. 3. $7,000.

2 the weather is too hot; has to drink bottled water; has to work with very old equipment

D Speaking

1 **Describing**

a. *Lösungsvorschlag:*

Similar	Different
both pictures are about water	girl/woman, black/white
the girl and the woman are both looking at you	the girl is wearing traditional clothes; the woman is wearing nearly nothing; the way they are looking at you is very different: the girl looks unhappy, the woman is smiling happily
both are holding 'water' in their hand	the girl has a gun full of water (water gun) in her hand/the woman has got a bottle of water
…	the woman is an actress/a celebrity (Jennifer Aniston)/ the girl is probably just any child

The first poster is from UNICEF and it is campaigning against water pollution or water shortage. The second poster is an advert for mineral water which you can buy in bottles.

b. *Lösungsvorschlag:*
I think the caption "A shot of contaminated water" matches poster A best because at first you think the gun is dangerous like a real gun. But then you see that it's a toy but it's the water inside which is dangerous.

c. *Lösungsvorschlag:*
I would support the UNICEF campaign because a little money from each of us, or volunteers from here can make a big difference and save many lives. We all know that children need help most and they can't choose where or how they live. You feel shocked that dirty water can kill so many people.

2 **Role play**

You: Excuse me, which organisation are you collecting money for?
Man: …
You: Thank you. Yes, I think I've heard the name already. I'd like to know more about it.
Man: …
You: Do you send bottled water there/to thos countries/to the people there?
Man: …
You: But aren't there some areas/regions/places where people only have very little water? What does WaterAid do in such regions?
Man: …
You: Thank you very much for the information. Sorry, I can't give you any money now – I need to think about it/read more about it./ I'd like to give some money to your organisation because I think it's very important to support the people who live in poorer countries. Here you are. Goodbye.

E Mediation and communication

a. SODIS uses UV light from the sun for disinfection.
b. If you use it the wrong way, SODIS won't kill all the bacteria. Then the water will still be contaminated and dangerous to drink.
c. The disinfection normally takes at least six hours. But if it is cloudy, it could take two days or more.
d. The bottles in the pictures are made of special plastic or glass.
e. Yes. You shouldn't use dirty or damaged bottles.

F Writing

1 *Lösungsvorschlag:*

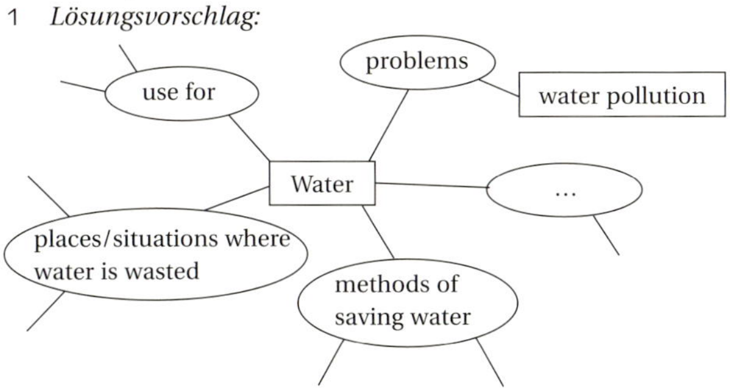

2 *Lösungsvorschlag:*
Our campaign: Water means life! Water is very valuable so don't waste it.
More children die from contaminated water than through war. And millions of people in poor countries don't have clean drinking water. And here we just let the water run when we brush our teeth, take showers for hours and buy expensive water in bottles! So it's time to save water and spend money: Give what you can to the charities that help to supply people with clean water! Please check our website if you'd like to know more about how to support our campaign.

Test Yourself! 4, page 68–71

A Reading

1 a. 3 … the message which clothes give.
b. 2 rules of how to dress

2 elegant – elegant; romantic – romantisch; shocking – schockierend, version – Version; personality – Persönlichkeit

3 (check answers)

4 a. You can choose a style to give the impression which you want to give.
b. But people may get a different impression from the impression that you intend.
c. This is because the colour or clothes that you wear may give their own message.
d. Even in jobs without written dress codes you should think about what you wear.
e. A good tip for a job interview is to dress better than you would as an employee.

5 *Lösungsvorschlag*:
I would probably wear black trousers and something white or not too dark on top. I wouldn't wear a strong red or orange because I think people notice you too much: It catches the eye – like a big stop sign!

B Language

a. suit, b. contrasting, c. helmet, d. chance

C Listening

1 1 c. sales department, 2 e. TV company, 3 a. transport company

2 if they have a dress code

3 a. thinks jackets are fine.
b. says clothes rules are OK.
c. thinks a tie may be good at interviews.

D Speaking

1 **Describing**
Lösungsvorschläge.

a. 1: woman, blond, white shirt, black trousers, hands in pockets
2: man, white cap, white T-shirt with big '25', hip-hop style, cool
3: man, brown hair, smart, jacket, white shirt, colourful tie

4: girl, blond hair, sun glasses, laughing, black top, blue skirt, jewellery, pink tights

b. 1: sales, marketing, a secretary's office
   2: DJ, basketball payer
   3: sales, marketing, a secretary's office, technical assistant
   4: shop assistant in a fashion shop, model

c. *Individuelle Schülerlösung*

2 **Role Play**

Interviewer:	...
You:	I've always been interested in travelling.
Interviewer:	...
You:	Last summer, I had a summer job at a travel agency. I had the following tasks: looking for lights, answering the phone, connecting people ...
Interviewer:	...
You:	I really like to travel. I speak English and Turkish.
Interviewer:	...
You:	I think clothes are important in this job because you work with people.
Interviewer:	...
You:	I agree with your dress code, of course.
Interviewer:	...
You:	When would I start working?
Interviewer:	...
You:	That's no problem. Thank you very much for the interview. Goodbye.

E Mediation and communication

Lösungsvorschlag:

a. Das ist die Sängerin Susan Boyle.

b. Sie ist 47 Jahre alt und singt gerade in der britischen Talentshow „Britain's Got Talent".

c. Sie fanden sie fantastisch.

d. Sie wurden gefragt, ob sie zustimmen, dass das Aussehen nicht wichtig ist, wenn die Stimme bzw. der Charakter stimmt.

e. Nein, einer sagt ja, der andere nein.

f. 1: Im Showbusiness ist Aussehen wichtig, weil wir Leute sehen wollen, die sehr attraktiv sind. Susan Boyle ist das komplette Gegenteil davon und deswegen wird sie auch nie ein Star werden. Der Verfasser kann sie sich nicht in einem Musical vorstellen.
   2: Die Stimme von Susan Boyle ist paradiesisch, deswegen ist alles andere egal. Die Verfasserin sieht sie als Vorbild für alle „normalen" Menschen, die sich niemals getraut haben, nach den Sternen zu greifen.

F Writing

1

It is important to me that he or she smiles in a nice way/has a friendly face/...
I look at the way he or she acts – if he or she is polite/impolite/friendly/...
I think that the colour of his/her clothes is important/gives a message about the character of the person.
It's (not) important to me that a person's clothes match his/her job.

2

Dos and Don'ts at a job interview/Checklist for your job interview

1. **Dress code**: The clothes you wear should match the job that you apply for. If you are not sure if body jewellery or tattoos are allowed, cover them before the interview.
2. **Look neat**: Make sure that your clothes, hair and shoes look clean and sensible. Try always to look a bit better than you would as an employee.
3. **Check your colours**: Try to wear blue or green. Avoid red.
4. **Less is more**: Don't overdo your make-up.
5. **Full attention**: Turn off your mobile and your MP3 player before the interview.
6. **Hat free/No hats**: Hats, headscarves or caps are not suitable at a job interview.

Lösungen/Lösungsvorschläge Grammatik

Grammatikübungen (Grammar practice)

Ov 1–3 Vollverben (Fragen bilden)

1 On an English exchange

a)

are – to be live – to live learn – to learn find out – to find out are – to be hear – to hear sounds – to sound tells – to tell 's (is) – to be	mix – to mix happens – to happen hears – to hear are – to be tells – to tell laugh – to laugh 's (is) – to be explains – to explain mix – to mix match – to match like – to like

b) 1. Who is on an exchange?
2. Where do they live?
3. What do they learn?
4. What do they also find out?
5. When are Hussein and Alina at a bus stop?
6. What language does it sound like?
7. Where is it just like that?
8. What do they often mix?
9. When does the same thing happen again?
10. What languages are they this time?
11. Why do they laugh?
12. What does Nasreen explain?

c) 1. Are Alina and Hussein at a bus stop one afternoon?
2. Is Alina Hussein's sister?
3. Does Alina tell anybody about the couple in the shop?
4. Do the members of her guest family laugh?
5. Do Hussein and his mates often mix English and Turkish?

d) 1. Yes, they are. 2. No, she isn't. 3. Yes, she does.
4. Yes, they do. 5. No, they don't.

Ov 5 Das Passiv im *simple present*

1 News – facts or fiction?

1. Today news and events *are brought* to us quicker than ever before.
2. For example, if a bank *is robbed* in the next town, a video *is offered* in minutes on YouTube.
3. Newspapers *are sold* and *bought* everywhere, of course.
4. A good thing about the Internet is that news *is updated* more frequently.
5. But how do you know if the info that *is given* there is correct?
6. Some of the news on the Internet *is invented* by people who think it's a big joke.
7. Today the world *is divided* into two groups – those who want facts and those who want fiction!

Ov 5 Das Passiv im *simple past*

1 TV – Did you know?

a) 1. TV was invented by Zworykin and Farnsworth.
2. The first televisions were produced in black and white only.
3. Did you know that it was called this because it means *far sight*?
4. Then TV satellites were launched into space in the 1960s.
5. More channels were opened as TV became more popular.
6. Colour TV wasn't introduced in Europe till 1967.
7. Later, models were developed which had bigger screens.
8. In the 1990s TV was first linked to the Internet.

b) 1. The first phone was invented in 1875.
2. It was developed by Alexander Graham Bell and Elisha Gray.
3. The first call was made from Boston in the USA.
4. The first call was made to Cambridge, USA.
5. The first 'mobile' radio phone was called a 'cave radio' phone (1908).

Ov 6 Modalverben

1 A holiday flat by the sea

1. "Joe, the sea looks great! **Can** we drive to the beach before lunch, please?"
2. "Yes, we **can**! But we **needn't** go by car – we **can** easily walk there, Sue!"
3. "Good! But I **mustn't** forget my cap and sunglasses! They're in the back of the car."
4. "Well, I guess we **needn't** take our sweaters with us. It feels very warm now."
5. "No, we **needn't**. But we **must** take our anoraks. It **can** get quite windy."
6. "OK. But we really **must** call Dave and Linda, so they **can** meet us at the beach bar."
7. "I'll do that now. But Joe, we **mustn't** forget to put the cheese in the fridge before we go!"
8. "Don't worry. I **can** do that while you call Dave and Linda."
9. "OK, thanks! But please be quick, Joe. I **can't** wait to see the sea again!"

2 Help the environment

You should always turn off the lights when you leave a room.
You can/may go into town by car if you have a lot to carry.
You shouldn't wash your jeans in cold water if they are very dirty.
You should walk to school if it isn't too far.
You needn't walk, of course, if you've got a bike. A bike is quicker!
You shouldn't expect others to save the Earth for you!
You needn't switch off the heating if you are cold. Just turn it down!

Ov 7 Bedingungssätze (*if*-Sätze) Typ I

1 What will they do?

a) 1. If Nancy misses the train, she'll call her mum.
2. If Tom and Bob get lost, they'll use their map.
3. If Karim doesn't find his key, he'll break the chain.
4. If Diane and Luke don't get tickets, they'll watch a DVD.
5. If Doug gets a job, he'll travel to Australia.
6. If Ina and Gabi go to London, they'll visit Hyde Park.

b) If I go to Britain, I'll visit Buckingham Palace./I won't go hiking in Scotland.
If I go to Canada, I'll build an igloo./I won't speak French.
If I go to Australia, I'll take photos of koalas./I won't eat kangaroo meat.

Ov 7 Bedingungssätze (*if*-Sätze) Typ II

1 If I met the US President, I'd ...

a) 1. If I met the US President, I'd ask him about his hobbies.
2. If I won a lot of money in a TV quiz show, I'd spend it on a holiday in Australia.
3. If Superman flew through my window, I'd be very excited.
4. If a friend was angry with me, I'd ask him why.
5. If my mobile phone got stolen, I'd report it to the police.
6. If a firm offered me a job abroad for a year, I'd be happy.
7. If I saw a pickpocket on the job, I'd call the police.

b) 2. If I won a lot of money in a TV quiz show, I wouldn't buy a big car.
3. If Superman flew through my window, I wouldn't be scared.
4. If a friend was angry with me, I wouldn't forget the friend.
5. If my mobile phone got stolen, I wouldn't ask my parents for money.
6. If a firm offered me a job abroad for a year, I wouldn't say no to the firm.
7. If I saw a pickpocket on the job, I wouldn't walk away.

Ov 8 Pronomen

1 A film which I really love!

All my friends and **I** really enjoyed the film Dragon Tears. A kid at *our* school, called Danny, lent us the DVD and we watched *it* last weekend. *His* Dad acted in the film! We saw *him* when *he* attacked the dragon. The best scene, *we* all think, is near the end. The heroine, a cool young girl, meets the dragon and becomes *its* friend. Dragons are really sad creature and *they* are very lonely. Lyreena tells this to the people in *her* village, and they are then safe from harm. Dragons put out *their* own fire with their tears. The dragon's tears flood the village in the end. This great story was taken from an old Chinese myth. Everyone should try to see *it*.

G 1 Indirekte Rede (sofort berichtet)

1 What the experts say

b) Hi, Adam. Hey listen to this! It's a report on violence. The 1st expert says that some famous old myths and stories are really bloody. He or she also says that violence is nothing new and that we just hear more about it through faster media technology.
But the 2nd expert thinks that it's much worse now and that there is more violence on TV. The kids just want to copy their heroes. And the 3rd one says that we don't need violence on TV. He thinks that the harm through violent programmes is greatest in kids who don't have a good family background. And he says that kids all need friends and hobbies, too. The last expert believes that it isn't just TV, it is all those terrible computer games. They are violent and many kids do nothing else but play them all day.

G 2 Indirekte Rede (später berichtet)

1 A few days later

b) The teenager said that his name was Mack Simpson, and that he lived around the corner. He also said that he was 16 years old. He told me that his parents didn't know about the accident because they weren't at home. But he explained that he had a number to call them, in his mobile.

2 How the accident happened

a) hit – to hit
was – to be
wanted – to want
needed – to need
shouted – to shout
turned – to turn
didn't recognize – not/to recognize

b) 1. The patient said that he had hit a streetlamp.
2. He explained that he had been on his skateboard.
3. He told me that he had wanted to visit his mate.
4. He explained that he had needed some snacks for a DVD evening.
5. He said that a guy had shouted his name.
6. He added that he had turned his head to look.
7. He told me that he hadn't recognized the guy.

G 3 Reflexivpronomen

1 Advertising

1. This oven is really smart – it cleans **itself** in minutes!
2. Are you learning to drive? – Test **yourself** with our 'Drive Alive' DVD before your test!
3. We tested and tasted all the recipes **ourselves** – 'Fashion Food' is our Book of the Year.
4. I taught **myself** Spanish in five easy steps with 'Steps to Spanish'. BUY IT TODAY!
5. He washed **himself** with 'UltraSoap' and now the girls can't keep away from him!
6. When we let people try a 'Ronny Robot' **themselves**, we never get him back!

7. All you kids out there, our Happy Burgers are great! Try for **yourselves**!
8. Even Clarisse Stilton prepares **herself** for concerts with 'Heart's Breathing Method'!

2 At summer camp

1. At summer camp you have to do lots of things *yourself* every day.
2. But the kids don't have to wake *themselves* – that's the group leader's job.
3. After they have all washed and dressed *themselves*, they make breakfast.
4. But camp is also fun. Last year we all taught *ourselves* to make a safe fire.
5. Of course, our leader Mary-Lou checked them *herself* each time.
6. The best thing was: I taught *myself* rock climbing!
7. Rock climbing *itself* isn't dangerous but you must follow the safety rules!
8. My rock climbing partner, Jack, hurt *himself* badly because he wasn't careful.
9. But we really enjoyed *ourselves* at that camp.
10. So I would like to register *myself* for the same camp next year.

G 4 Vollendete Vergangenheit

1 A chain of events

a) 1. First he woke up.
2. Then he jogged for three hours.
3. Then he had a shower.
4. And then he cooked a surprise meal.
5. Finally he called his girlfriend.

b) 1. Nick woke up at 8:20.
2. After he had woken up, he jogged for one hour.
3. After he had jogged, he had a shower.
4. After he had had a shower, he cooked a smeal.
5. And after he had cooked a meal, he called his girlfriend.

2 Before and after

a) Before they left on holiday, they had already fed the cat. Also, they had already packed the maps in their backpacks. They had already given their keys to the neighbour. And they had already left a message on the answerphone.

b) After I had thrown the rubbish in the bins, I locked the flat! After I had locked the flat, I posted the letters. After I had posted the letters, I took the bottles back to the shop.

G 5 Adverbien (Gradadverbien)

1 Very important words

a) complete – completely
terrible – terribly
extreme – extremely
real – really
special – especially
equal – equally
Left: quite, very

b) 1. The trip up the mountain was *really* exciting.
2. The view from the top of the mountain was *very* beautiful.
3. But the climbers had to be *quite* careful when they climbed down again.
4. This was because they were *very* high up.
5. They were all *especially* proud of the long climb they had just done.
6. But they were all thirsty – and their water bottles were *completely* empty!
7. So they were all *equally* happy when they reached their camp.
8. By evening they were *terribly* tired and *extremely* hungry!

G 6 Die Wortstellung im Satz

1 When and where

1. last year: (1)/(3)
2. to the fair: (3)
3. at two o'clock: (1)/(3)
4. at the station (2)
5. by 3:20 p.m.: (3)
6. in Hall 2: (3)
7. a moment later: (1)/(4)
8. suddenly: (1)/(3)
9. on the stage: (3)
10. in the end: (1)/(3)
11. at five o'clock: (1)/(3)

2 How often?

1. Shops have often got too many products.
2. So I can never find what I need.
3. On the other hand I sometimes see three products which are all OK.
4. If that happens, then I always buy the cheapest product.
5. But then they're usually quite expensive.

	GB 	IRELAND 
15th century	**1455–1485:** The 'Battle of the Roses' is fought and Henry VII becomes king.	**1494:** The Irish parliament meets with permission of the English King.
16th century	**1534:** Henry VIII becomes head of the Church of England. **1542:** Mary Stuart becomes Queen of Scotland. **1558–1603:** Under Elisabeth I England becomes a great power in Europe.	**1569–1583:** The rebellion against Elisabeth I fails. **1595:** A new rebellion starts.
17th century	**1642–1646:** There is civil war between soldiers of the king and soldiers of Parliament. **1649:** King Charles I is executed. The monarchy is abolished and a republic called the "Commonwealth" is created under Cromwell. **1660:** Charles II becomes king.	**1649–1650:** England sends Oliver Cromwell to end rebellions in Ireland. He defeats the Irish with 120,000 soldiers. During this time nearly half of the Irish population dies.
18th century	**1775:** Great Britain wants their American colonies to pay taxes. **1783:** Britain accepts the United States of America as an independent country. **1793:** The war between France and Great Britain starts.	**1703:** Catholics are oppressed and many emigrate to the USA. **1720:** The British parliament declares its right to rule Ireland. **1798:** Rebellion of United Irishmen.
19th century	**1801:** Great Britain and Ireland become the United Kingdom. **1805:** At Trafalgar the British defeat Napoleon. **1815:** At Waterloo England defeats the French again and the war is over. **1877:** Queen Victoria becomes Empress of India.	**1823:** Daniel O'Connell starts a movement to fight for freedom from Britain. **1843:** The first railway in Ireland is built. **1846–1851:** During the "Great Famine" over 1.5 million Irish die and over 1 million emigrate.
20th century	**1914–1918:** World War I **1939–1945:** World War II **1947:** India becomes independent. The British empire begins to break up. **1968:** Britain sends troops to Northern Ireland. **1994:** The Channel Tunnel opens.	**1916:** The Easter Rising: Irish republicans try to end British rule in Ireland. **1921:** The Irish Free State is created. **1955:** Ireland joins the United Nations. **1956:** The IRA (Irish Republican Army) starts its attacks in Northern Ireland.
21st century	**2001:** Britain supports the plans of US president Bush to attack Iraq. **2005:** London's Underground and buses are attacked by Islamic terrorists. **2009:** The last British soldiers leave Iraq.	**2001:** The IRA agrees to lay down their weapons and apologizes for the murder of hundreds of civilians. **2005:** The EU recognises Irish as a working language.

USA 	Australia 	
1492: The American continent is discovered by Christopher Columbus.		15th century
1565: The first colony is founded by the Spanish in St. Augustine.		16th century
1620: The Mayflower arrives in Massachusetts. **1626:** The Dutch buy Manhattan from a Native American tribe.	**1606:** On February 26th a Dutchman, Willem Janszoon, landed on Australian soil in what is now called Queensland. **1642:** Abel Tasman made a map of the coast of North Australia.	17th century
1775: The war against Britain starts. **July 4, 1776:** Declaration of Independence **1789:** George Washington becomes the first president. **1791:** The Bill of Rights is passed.	**1770:** Captain James Cook discovered Australia and claimed the land for England. **1788:** On January 26th first convicts arrived at Sydney Cove. Many had escaped the death sentence in England. This day later became Australia Day.	18th century
1854: First struggles against slavery **1861:** The Civil War begins. **1865:** The war ends and slaves are freed. **1890:** A massacre at Wounded Knee ends the war against Native Americans.	**1842:** The city of Sydney was founded at the Sydney Cove Colony. **1851:** Gold was found in Victoria and the Australian Gold Rush began. **1869:** Aboriginal children were first taken away from their families by government officials. **1879:** The Royal National Park (2nd in the world) was opened south of Sydney.	19th century
1917–1918: About 116,000 US soldiers die in World War I. **1920–1933:** Prohibition: Alcohol is forbidden all over the US. **1931:** The Empire State Building is completed. **1941:** Japan attacks Pearl Harbour and Germany declares war on the US. **1963:** Martin Luther King gives his famous speech "I have a dream". **1968:** King is shot in Memphis.	**1908:** The capital, Canberra, was founded. **1915–1918:** Australia sent many thousands of soldiers to Europe to fight for Britain. Over 60,000 died and more than 160,000 were wounded. **1919:** Australia became independent of Britain. **1942:** The first modern road train was used. **1948–1975:** Two million immigrants arrived in Australia. **1951:** The School of the Air started. **1970:** Aboriginal children were removed from their families for the last time. **1975:** The Great Barrier Reef Marine Park opened.	20th century
2001: On September 11th the Pentagon and the World Trade Center in New York are attacked. 3000 people die. **2003:** The US starts a war against Iraq. **2009:** Barack Obama becomes the first Black president.	**2000:** The Summer Olympics took place. **2008:** On February 13th the Australian Prime Minister apologised to Aborigines for the 'Stolen Generations'.	21st century

The British system = A parliamentary democracy

The United Kingdom has two branches of government. Parliament controls the Monarchy.

The Monarchy (King or queen)
hereditary

Duties
- open and close Parliament
- sign laws + treaties made by parliament
- declare war if parliament decides it
- must follow the wishes of Parliament
- cannot enter the House of Commons

Rights
- cannot be put in prison
- doesn't need a driving licence

Parliament

elected by people

Parties[5]= *Labour, Conservative, Liberal, Democrats, …*

House of Commons (646 members)

House of Lords (about 740 members)

hereditary or appointed by government

Duties
- debate policy, laws and treaties

Rights
- can make or reject laws and treaties
- can decide to go to war
- can reject PM

Head of State
hereditary

Duties
- represent[1] the state
- appoint the PM, Cabinet Ministers[2] and other officials (e.g. judges, officers in the army[3], …)
- must follow instructions from PM / government

Rights
- must be informed about Cabinet decisions[4]

Government

elected by majority[6] party

Head of Government Prime Minister

Duties
- choose Cabinet Ministers
- lead the Cabinet (PM + Ministers) meetings
- control the Civil Service[7]
- inform and instruct the Queen

Rights
- can dismiss Cabinet ministers

Cabinet Ministers
appointed by PM

Duties
- make policy
- draw up treaties and bills
- control ministries[8]

The American system = A constitutional democracy

The United States of America has three branches of government. Each controls the other two.

Congress

Senate (100 Senators: 2 from each state)

House of Representatives (435 Congressmen/women)

- can impeach[9] and remove the President.
- may ignore[10] the President's veto.
- The Senate approves the appointment[11] of members of Supreme Court.
- The Senate approves treaties made by President.

The President
- controls foreign policy and makes treaties.
- may veto laws made by Congress.
- can recommend laws.
- appoints members of the Supreme Court.

The Supreme Court
- watches over the Constitution and interprets the laws.
- can call laws made by Congress unconstitutional.
- can call the President's decisions unconstitutional.

The people
- elect a President for four years.
- elect Senators for six years.
- elect one third of Representatives every two years.

Do you agree with these statements? Give reasons for your answer.

1. *All British people love the Queen.*
2. *The American President is the most powerful man in the world.*

[1]to represent [ˌreprɪ'zent] – *repräsentieren,* [2]Minister ['mɪnɪstər] – *Minster/-in,* [3]army ['ɑːmi] – *Armee,* [4]decision [dɪ'sɪʒən] – *Entscheidung,* [5]party [pɑːti] – *Partei,* [6]majority [mə'dʒɒrəti] – *Mehrheit,* [7]Civil Service ['sɪvəl'sɜːvɪs] – *Staatsdienst,* [8]ministry ['mɪnɪstri] – *Ministerium,* [9]to impeach so. [ɪm'piːtʃ] – *jdn. seines Amtes entheben,* [10]to ignore [ɪg'nɔːr] – *ignorieren,* [11]to approve the appointment [ə'pruːv ˌðiː ə'pɔɪntmənt] – *eine Ernennung anerkennen*

Bildquellennachweis

Cover.1 Getty Images (fotonika/Berg), München; **4.1** Fotosearch Stock Photography (Stockbyte), Waukesha, WI; **4.2** Imago, Berlin; **4.3** iStockphoto (Huchen Lu), Calgary, Alberta; **4.4** Alamy Images (WoodyStock), Abingdon, Oxon; **4.5** Das Fotoarchiv, Essen; **4.6** iStockphoto (Sven Klaschik), Calgary, Alberta; **4.7** iStockphoto (Geoffrey Stradling), Calgary, Alberta; **4.8** Alamy Images (Eddie Gerald), Abingdon, Oxon; **5.1** iStockphoto (Wide Angle), Calgary, Alberta; **5.9** iStockphoto (Andreas Reh), Calgary, Alberta; **5.10** Alamy Images (Chad Ehlers/Alamy), Abingdon, Oxon; **5.12** Corbis (Inspirestock/Corbis), Düsseldorf; **5.13** Vestergaard Frandsen SA, Lausanne; **5.13** iStockphoto (Biliana), Calgary, Alberta; **5.15** iStockphoto (Anna Bryukhanova), Calgary, Alberta; **5.16** iStockphoto (Eyecrave LLC), Calgary, Alberta; **8.1** Getty Images, München; **9.1** Das Fotoarchiv, Essen; **9.2** Getty Images (Gallo Images/Getty Images), München; **9.3** Alamy Images (Martin Berry/Alamy), Abingdon, Oxon; **9.4** Imago, Berlin; **10.1** Harper Collins Publishers (2006, B K Mahal), New York, N. Y. 10022-5299; **10.2** Fotosearch Stock Photography (Stockbyte), Waukesha, WI; **10.3** Corbis (Stephanie Weiler/zefa), Düsseldorf; **11.1** Corbis (Christopher Morris), Düsseldorf; **11.2** laif (B.&C. Alexander/Arcticphoto), Köln; **11.3** Klett-Archiv (Hamida Aziz), Stuttgart; **11.4** www.cartoonstock.com (Fran), Bath; **12.1** iStockphoto (Alexander Hafemann), Calgary, Alberta; **12.2** iStockphoto (Jane norton), Calgary, Alberta; **12.3** iStockphoto (Lise Gagne), Calgary, Alberta; **12.4** iStockphoto (Huchen Lu), Calgary, Alberta; **13; 13.3** Dream Maker Software (RF), Colorado; **13.2** Geoatlas, Hendaye; **13.4** Klett-Archiv (Klett-Archiv, Stuttgart), Stuttgart; **14.1** iStockphoto (Huchen Lu), Calgary, Alberta; **14.2; 14.3** JupiterImages photos.com, Tucson, AZ; **15.1** iStockphoto (Brent Bossom), Calgary, Alberta; **16.1** iStockphoto (Huchen Lu), Calgary, Alberta; **16.2** iStockphoto (Brent Bossom), Calgary, Alberta; **16.3** JupiterImages photos.com, Tucson, AZ; **17.1** iStockphoto (Jacob Wackerhausen), Calgary, Alberta; **17.2** iStockphoto (Jeffrey Smith), Calgary, Alberta; **17.3** shutterstock (WizData, inc.), New York, NY; **17.4** iStockphoto (Sean Locke), Calgary, Alberta; **18.1; 18.2** Alamy Images (Bryan & Cherry Alexander Photography), Abingdon, Oxon; **18.3** iStockphoto (Thomas Gordon), Calgary, Alberta; **19.1** iStockphoto (Sergei Butorin), Calgary, Alberta; **19.2** Alamy Images (GM Photo Images), Abingdon, Oxon; **19.3** Alamy Images (Visual&Written SL), Abingdon, Oxon; **20.1** shutterstock (Marcel Jancovic), New York, NY; **20.2** iStockphoto (Wsmahar), Calgary, Alberta; **20.3** Alamy Images (Bryan & Cherry Alexander Photography), Abingdon, Oxon; **20.4** Alamy Images (WoodyStock), Abingdon, Oxon; **21.1** Alamy Images (Royal Geographical Society), Abingdon, Oxon; **22.1** shutterstock (Radoslav Stoilov), New York, NY; **22.2** shutterstock (Katrina Leigh), New York, NY; **23.1** Imago, Berlin; **24.1** shutterstock (Andy Z.), New York, NY; **26.1** Corbis (Les Stone/Sygma/Corbis), Düsseldorf; **27.1** Alamy Images (Eddie Gerald), Abingdon, Oxon; **27.3** Das Fotoarchiv, Essen; **27.3** Alamy Images (TNT Magazine/Alamy), Abingdon, Oxon; **27.4** Picture-Alliance, Frankfurt; **28.1** Bridgeman Art Library Ltd. (Roy 2 B VII f.78 Reaping corn harvest in August, from the Queen Mary Psalter, c.1310-20 (vellum) by English School (14th century) British Library, London, UK/© British Library Board. All Rights Reserved), Berlin; **29.1** www.cartoonstock.com (Mike Baldwin/Cornered), Bath; **29.2** www.cartoonstock.com (Jerry King), Bath; **29.3** Getty Images (BBC via Getty Images), München; **30.1** Corbis (Reuters), Düsseldorf; **30.2; 30.3** Corbis (Pool Photograph), Düsseldorf; **30.4** Picture Press (David Secombe/Camera Press), Hamburg; **30.5** Ullstein Bild GmbH (iT), Berlin; **30.6** Alamy Images (brianengland), Abingdon, Oxon; **34.1** Corbis (Brooks Kraft), Düsseldorf; **34.2** iStockphoto (Geoffrey Stradling), Calgary, Alberta; **34.4** iStockphoto (David Joyner), Calgary, Alberta; **34.5** shutterstock (Mikhail Levit), New York, NY; **34.6** iStockphoto (Sven Klaschik), Calgary, Alberta; **36** Alamy Images (Blend Images), Abingdon, Oxon; **38** Alamy Images (Steve Skjold), Abingdon, Oxon; **38.1** iStockphoto (Julee Wyld), Calgary, Alberta; **39.1** Logo, Stuttgart; **40.1** Corbis (Inspirestock/Corbis), Düsseldorf; **40.2** Alamy Images (Ashley Cooper), Abingdon, Oxon; **41.1** Alamy Images (Janine Wiedel), Abingdon, Oxon; **41.2** iStockphoto (Klaas Lingbeek-van Kranen), Calgary, Alberta; **41.3** Alamy Images (Chad Ehlers/Alamy), Abingdon, Oxon; **41.4** Alamy Images (Keith Morris), Abingdon, Oxon; **42.1** iStockphoto (MHJ), Calgary, Alberta; **43.1** iStockphoto (Andreas Reh), Calgary, Alberta; **43.2** iStockphoto (Jeanell Norvell), Calgary, Alberta; **44.1** iStockphoto (Andrea Skjold), Calgary, Alberta; **44.1** iStockphoto (Monolinea), Calgary, Alberta; **44.2** iStockphoto (Ivanmateev), Calgary, Alberta; **44.2** iStockphoto (kemie), Calgary, Alberta; **45.1** iStockphoto (Roman Chmiel), Calgary, Alberta; **45.2** iStockphoto (Redmal), Calgary, Alberta; **46.1** iStockphoto (konkrete), Calgary, Alberta; **46.2** Alamy Images (Matthew Lambley), Abingdon, Oxon; **46.3** iStockphoto (Vladimir Mucibabic), Calgary, Alberta; **46.4** shutterstock (Lisa F. Young), New York, NY; **46.5** iStockphoto (Gene Chutka), Calgary, Alberta; **46.6** iStockphoto (Robert Nystrom), Calgary, Alberta; **48.1** JupiterImages photos.com, Tucson, AZ; **48.2** iStockphoto (Jon Schulte), Calgary, Alberta; **49.1** iStockphoto (morganl), Calgary, Alberta; **49.2** Corbis (Image Source), Düsseldorf; **49.3** MEV Verlag GmbH, Augsburg; **49.4** Alamy Images (Arco Images/Delpho, M.), Abingdon, Oxon; **50.1** Vestergaard Frandsen SA, Lausanne; **50.2** Eawag Water and Sanitation in Developing Countries, Dübendorf; **52.1** Unicef/Jung von Matt, Schweden; **52.2** SmartWater Technology Limited (Mario Testino), Shropshire; **53.1** Eawag Water and Sanitation in Developing Countries, Dübendorf; **55.1** Alamy Images (Janine Wiedel Photolibrary), Abingdon, Oxon; **55.2** Fotosearch Stock Photography (Image Source RF), Waukesha, WI; **55.3** MEV Verlag GmbH, Augsburg; **56.1** Corbis (Walter Lockwood/Corbis), Düsseldorf; **57.1** Getty Images (Punchstock), München; **57.2** Alamy Images (UK Stock Images Ltd), Abingdon, Oxon; **57.4** Corbis, Düsseldorf; **57.4** Alamy Images (Janine Wiedel), Abingdon, Oxon; **58.1** iStockphoto (Nikada), Calgary, Alberta; **58.2** www.cartoonstock.com (Grizelda), Bath; **59.1** iStockphoto (Resonants), Calgary, Alberta; **59.2** The Random House Group Limited, London; **60.1** iStockphoto (Wide Angle), Calgary, Alberta; **60.2** iStockphoto (Claylib), Calgary, Alberta; **60.3** iStockphoto (EasyBuy4u), Calgary, Alberta; **62.1** iStockphoto (Biliana), Calgary, Alberta; **62.2** iStockphoto (Eyecrave LLC), Calgary, Alberta; **62.3** iStockphoto (Linda & Colin McKie), Calgary, Alberta; **63.1** iStockphoto (Zande Basenjis), Calgary, Alberta; **63.2** iStockphoto (Fluxfoto), Calgary, Alberta; **64.1** iStockphoto (Pailoolom), Calgary, Alberta; **64.2** Reinhard-Tierfoto, Heiligkreuzsteinach; **66.1** iStockphoto (Kati Molin), Calgary, Alberta; **68.1** iStockphoto (Sharon Dominick), Calgary, Alberta; **68.2** iStockphoto (Anna Bryukhanova), Calgary, Alberta; **68.3** iStockphoto (paresh khot), Calgary, Alberta; **68.4** iStockphoto (aldra), Calgary, Alberta; **68.5** Corbis (Tracy Kahn), Düsseldorf; **68.6** Ullstein Bild GmbH (Reuters), Berlin; **68.7** iStockphoto (TommL), Calgary, Alberta; **68.8** Corbis (Corbis Yellow), Düsseldorf; **70.1** Alamy Images (imagebroker/Alamy), Abingdon, Oxon; **70.2** iStockphoto (Nikita Buida), Calgary, Alberta; **70.3** shutterstock (Serg Zastavkin), New York, NY; **70.4** shutterstock (Serhiy Kyrychenko), New York, NY; **71.1** Corbis (Reuters), Düsseldorf; **72.1** Corbis RF (Corbis), Düsseldorf; **72.2** Corbis (Richard Cummins/CORBIS), Düsseldorf; **72.3** iStockphoto (Bryan Faust Photography), Calgary, Alberta; **72.4** Alamy Images (Pictures Colour Library), Abingdon, Oxon; **73.1** Photographic service of the Council of the EU © Eu, Bruxelles; **73.2** Photographic service of the Council of the EU © European Communities; **88.2** Alamy Images (Archives du 7eme Art), Abingdon, Oxon; **89.1** Alamy Images (Buzzshotz), Abingdon, Oxon; **89.2** iStockphoto (RF/Caswell), Calgary, Alberta; **103.1** iStockphoto (Tony Campbell), Calgary, Alberta; **107.1** shutterstock (Galina Barskaya), New York, NY; **108.1** iStockphoto (-art-siberia-), Calgary, Alberta; **109.1** Corbis (zefa), Düsseldorf; **109.2** Corbis (Image Source), Düsseldorf; **109.3** shutterstock (s74), New York, NY; **109.4** Argum (Einberger), München; **109.5** iStockphoto (David Claassen), Calgary, Alberta; **109.6** shutterstock (Stephen Finn), New York, NY; **110.1** shutterstock (Jason Stitt), New York, NY; **110.3** shutterstock (Vladimir Daragan), New York, NY; **110.4** iStockphoto (Birgitte Magnus), Calgary, Alberta; **110.5** iStockphoto (tomazl.sopca.com), Calgary, Alberta; **111** JupiterImages photos.com, Tucson, AZ; **111.1** iStockphoto (Jacus), Calgary, Alberta; **112.1** iStockphoto (Videowok), Calgary, Alberta; **230.1; 230.2; 231.1; 231.2** Dream Maker Software (RF), Colorado; **232.1** Fotosearch Stock Photography (Brand X Pictures), Waukesha, WI; **232.2; 232.3** MEV Verlag GmbH, Augsburg; **232.4** Getty Images RF (Photodisc), München; **118.1** shutterstock (Robert F. Balazik), New York, NY; **124.1** Ingram Publishing, Tattenhall Chester; **131.1** Avenue Images GmbH RF (image100), Hamburg; **137.1** Fotolia LLC (RF/Yuri Arcurs), New York; **Vorsatz hinten** Perthes World Atlas, 2nd Printing 2009, Revised, p. 78–79, Gotha 2006

Sollte es in einem Einzelfall nicht gelungen sein, den korrekten Rechteinhaber ausfindig zu machen, so werden berechtigte Ansprüche selbstverständlich im Rahmen der üblichen Regelungen abgegolten.

Canada: Political